CW00968957

A DICTIONARY OF INTERMEDIATE JAPANESE GRAMMAR

A DICTIONARY OF INTERMEDIATE JAPANESE GRAMMAR

日本語文法辞典【中級編】

Seiichi Makino
and
Michio Tsutsui

the japan times PUBLISHING

A Dictionary of Intermediate Japanese Grammar
日本語文法辞典【中級編】
1995年6月20日　初版発行
2022年3月20日　第53刷発行
著　者　牧野成一・筒井通雄
発行者　伊藤秀樹
発行所　株式会社 ジャパンタイムズ出版
〒102-0082 東京都千代田区一番町2-2 一番町第二TGビル2F
電話　050-3646-9500［出版営業部］
ISBN978-4-7890-0775-7

First edition: June 1995
53rd printing: March 2022

Editorial assistance: OPTIMA Corp.
Cover art: Akihiro Kurata.

Published by The Japan Times Publishing, Ltd.
2F Ichibancho Daini TG Bldg., 2-2 Ichibancho, Chiyoda-ku,
Tokyo 102-0082, Japan
Phone: 050-3646-9500
https://jtpublishing.co.jp/

ISBN978-4-7890-0775-7

Printed in Japan

Preface

This is a dictionary of intermediate Japanese grammar, a companion volume to *A Dictionary of Basic Japanese Grammar* published in 1986 by the same authors. While *DBJG* was designed primarily for students and teachers of beginning-level Japanese, this volume is designed for students and teachers of intermediate-level Japanese. After examining relevant textbooks, some references on sentence patterns, and authentic sources used in intermediate and advanced Japanese courses, we have chosen approximately 200 entries which we believe to be the most important grammatical items for intermediate Japanese learners.

The format of this dictionary is the same as that of *A Dictionary of Basic Japanese Grammar*. For the convenience of readers who have not used *DBJG*, we have repeated from that text the sections To the Reader and Grammatical Terms. In this volume, however, we have modified To the Reader slightly and have added some entries to Grammatical Terms. Along with the Japanese index, there is an English index that lists the English equivalents for each entry. One difference between the two volumes is that no romanization has been provided for example sentences in *A Dictionary of Intermediate Japanese Grammar*. Instead, *furigana* (hiragana over kanji) is used.

Needless to say we owe a great deal to our predecessors, whose works are listed in the references. Without their linguistic insights we could never have written this dictionary. We would like to thank our colleagues, friends, and spouses, who have kindly answered our persistent questions and shared their language intuition. However, for fear of omission, we would rather not attempt a comprehensive listing of names. Even so, we want to mention three individuals who made this publication possible, first, Ms. Chiaki Sekido from the Japan Times, who edited our manuscript most conscientiously and effectively, and helped us invaluably with her comments and suggestions. Also, our thanks go to Ms. Carmel Dowd and Ms. Sharon Tsutsui, who edited our English to make it more readable.

We sincerely hope that this dictionary will be useful in furthering our readers' understanding of Japanese.

Spring of 1995

Seiichi Makino
Michio Tsutsui

TABLE OF CONTENTS

To the Reader

This dictionary consists of the following parts:

A. *Grammatical Terms* contains brief explanations or informal definitions of the grammatical terms used in this book. If readers find that they are not familiar with these terms, it is suggested that they read this section carefully.

B. *Special Topics in Intermediate Japanese Grammar* discusses selected topics: Japanese discourse grammar, newspaper grammar, conversational strategies, and sentence structure analysis for reading comprehension. The section introduces readers to a number of important concepts with which they should be familiar in order to improve their reading and conversational skills.

C. *Main Entries* constitutes the core of this volume. Each entry is organized as follows:

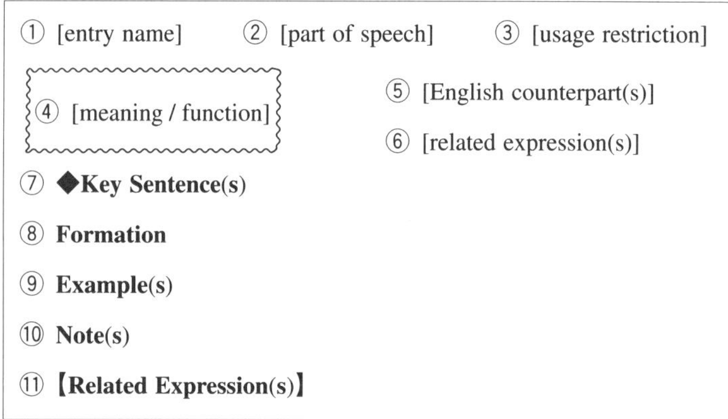

① [entry name]: Each entry is given in romanized spelling followed by its *hiragana* version. Entries are alphabetically ordered based on their romanized spellings.

② [part of speech]: Each entry is followed by its part of speech.

③ [usage restriction]: <s> or <w> is provided when the entry item is used only in spoken Japanese or only in written Japanese and formal speeches, respectively.

④ [meaning / function]: The general meaning or function of the entry item is given in the box below the entry name.

⑤ [English counterpart(s)]: English expressions equivalent to the entry item are given to the right of the box.

⑥ [related expression(s)]: Items which are semantically related to the entry item are listed as [REL. *aaa*, ***bbb***, *ccc*]. Expressions in plain type like *aaa* are explained in the entry under **【Related Expression(s)】** (⑪). Expressions in bold type like ***bbb*** contain comparisons to the entry item under **【Related Expression(s)】** for ***bbb***.

⑦ **◆Key Sentence(s):** Key sentences present typical sentence patterns in frames according to sentence structure. The recurrent elements are printed in red. and the elements which commonly occur with them are in bold.

⑧ **Formation:** The word formation rules / connection forms for each item are provided with examples. The recurrent elements are printed in red.

⑨ **Example(s):** Example sentences are provided for each entry.

⑩ **Note(s):** Notes contain important points concerning the use of the item.

⑪ **【Related Expression(s)】**: Expressions which are semantically close to the entry item are compared and their differences are explained.

(⇨ ***aaa*** (DBJG: 000–000)) in Formation, Notes, and 【Related Expression(s)】 indicates that the item which was referred to (i.e., ***aaa***) is explained on pp. 000–000 of the companion volume: *A Dictionary of Basic Japanese Grammar.*

D. *Appendixes* contains information such as *katakana* word transcription rules, compound verbs, compound particles, conjunctions, prefixes and suffixes, counters, cooccurrence, and functional expressions and grammar patterns.

E. *Indexes* provides both a Japanese index and an English index. The Japanese index includes the main entries, the items explained in 【Related Expression(s)】, and the items covered in *A Dictionary of Basic Japanese Grammar.* The English index includes English counterparts of the main entry items.

List of Abbreviations

Adj(*i*) = *i*-type adjective (e.g. *takai*, *yasui*)
Adj(*na*) = *na*-type adjective (e.g. *genkida*, *shizukada*)
Adv. = adverb
AdvP = adverb phrase
Aff. = affirmative
Ant. = antonym
AP = adjective phrase
Aux. = auxiliary
Comp. prt. = compound particle
Conj. = conjunction
Cop. = copula (e.g. *da*, *desu*)
DBJG = *A Dictionary of Basic Japanese Grammar*
Dem. adj. = demonstrative adjective (e.g. *kono*, *sonna*)
D.O. = direct object
Fml. = formal
Gr. = Group
Inf. = informal
Int. = interjection
Irr. = irregular
KS = Key Sentence
LSV = Location + Subject + Verb
N = noun
Neg. = negative
Nom. = nominalizer (e.g. *no*, *koto*)
NP = noun phrase
Phr. = phrase
Pl. = plural
Pot. = potential
Pref. = prefix (e.g. *o*-, *go*-)
Pro. = pronoun
Prt. = particle

REL. = Related Expression
S = sentence
<s> = used in conversation only
Sconc = concessive clause (i.e. a clause which ends with *-temo* or *-demo*)
Scond = conditional clause (i.e. a clause which ends with *-ba* and *-tara*)
Sinf = sentence that ends with an informal predicate
SLV = Subject + Location + Verb
S.o. = someone
S.t. = something
SOV = Subject + Object + Verb
SV = Subject + Verb
Str. = structure
Suf. = suffix (e.g. *-sa*, *-ya*)
V = verb
Vcond = conditional stem of Gr. 1 Verb (e.g. *hanase* of *hanaseba*)
Vinf = informal form of Verb (e.g. *hanasu*, *hanashita*)
V*masu* = *masu*-stem of Verb (e.g. *hanashi* of *hanashimasu*, *tabe* of *tabemasu*)
VN = Chinese-origin compound noun which forms a verb by affixing *suru* (e.g. *benkyō*, *yakusoku*)
Vneg = informal negative stem of Verb (e.g. *hanasa* of *hanasanai*, *tabe* of *tabenai*)
VP = verb phrase
Vpot = verb potential form (e.g. *yomeru*, *taberareru*)
Vstem = stem of Gr. 2 Verb (e.g. *tabe* of *taberu*)
V*te* = *te*-form of Verb (e.g. *hanashite*, *tabete*)
Vvol = volitional form of Verb (e.g. *hanasō*, *tabeyō*)
<w> = used in writing and formal speech only
Wh-word = an interrogative word (e.g. *nani*, *doko*)

List of Symbols

⇨ = Refer to.

? = The degree of unacceptability is indicated by the number of question marks, three being the highest.

* = ungrammatical or unacceptable (in other words, no native speaker would accept the asterisked sentence.)

{A / B} C = AC or BC (e.g. {V / Adj(*i*)}inf = Vinf or Adj(*i*)inf)

ø = zero (in other words, nothing should be used at a place where ø occurs. Thus, Adj(*na*) {ø / *datta*} *kamoshirenai* is either Adj(*na*) *kamoshirenai* or Adj(*na*) *datta kamoshirenai*.)

Grammatical Terms

The following are brief explanations of some grammatical terms used in this dictionary.

Active Sentence A sentence which describes an action from the agent's point of view. (cf. Passive Sentence) In active sentences, the subject is the agent. Sentences (a) and (b) below are an active and a passive sentence, respectively.

(a) 先生はジョンをしかった。
(The teacher scolded John.)

(b) ジョンは先生にしかられた。
(John was scolded by the teacher.)

Agent One who initiates and / or completes an action or an event. The agent is not always in the subject position. Compare the positions of the agent *Bill* in (a) and (b).

(a) **ビル**はマーサをぶった。
(Bill hit Martha.)

(b) マーサは**ビル**にぶたれた。
(Martha was hit by Bill.)

Appositive Clause (Construction) A clause which modifies a noun (or noun phrase) and explains *what* the modified noun is. In (a), *Meari ga Tomu ni atta* 'Mary met Tom' is an appositive clause, and is what *jijitsu* 'the fact' refers to.

(a) 私はメアリーがトムに会った**事実**を知っている。
(I know the fact that Mary met Tom.)

Auxiliary Adjective A dependent adjective that is preceded by and attached to a verb or another adjective. The bold-printed parts of the following sentences are typical auxiliary adjectives.

(a) 私はジョンに行って**ほしい**。
(I want John to go there.)

(b) この辞書は使い**やすい**。
(This dictionary is easy to use.)

(c) 私はすしが食べ**たい**。
(I want to eat sushi.)

(d) ベスは大学を出た**らしい**。
(Beth seems to have graduated from college.)

(e) 花子は寂しい**ようだ**。
(Hanako looks lonely.)

(f) このお菓子はおいし**そうだ**。
(This cake looks delicious.)

Auxiliary Verb A verb which is used in conjunction with a preceding verb or adjective. The bold-faced words of the following sentences are typical auxiliary verbs.

(a) ビルは今手紙を書いて**いる**。
(Bill is writing a letter now.)

(b) 窓が開けて**ある**。
(The window has been opened.) (= The window is open.)

(c) 僕は宿題をして**しまった**。
(I have done my homework.)

(d) 私は友達にお金を貸して**あげた**。
(I loaned money to my friend.)

(e) このコンピューターは高**すぎる**。
(This computer is too expensive.)

(f) ジョージはスポーツカーを欲し**がっている**。
(lit. George is showing signs of wanting a sports car. (= George

wants a sports car.))

(g) あっ！　雨が降って**来た**！
(Gee! It's started to rain!)

Causative Sentence　A sentence in which someone / something makes or lets someone / something do s.t. as in (a) and (b).

(a) 先生は学生に漢字を覚えさせた。
(The teacher made his students memorize kanji.)

(b) それは私にさせて下さい。
(Let me do it.)

(c) 僕はハンカチをしめらせた。
(I dampened my handkerchief.)

Compound Particle　A particle which consists of more than one word but functions like a single particle. For example, the compound particle *to shite wa* consists of the particle *to*, the *te*-form of *suru* and the particle *wa*, but it is used like a single particle to mean 'for.'　(cf. Double Particle)

Compound Sentence　A sentence which consists of clauses combined by coordinate conjunctions such as *ga* meaning 'but' or by continuative forms of verbs, adjectives or the copula such as V*te*, Adj. *te* and Cop. *te* meaning '~ and.'

(a) 僕は泳いだ**が**スミスさんは泳がなかった。
(I swam but Mr. Smith didn't.)

(b) 吉田さんは東京に行っ**て**鈴木さんに会った。
(Mr. Yoshida went to Tokyo and met Mr. Suzuki.)

Conditional　A word, phrase, or clause which expresses a condition, as in (a), (b) and (c).

(a) **翻訳の仕事なら**やります。
(I will take it on if it's a translation job.)

(b) **安ければ**買うかも知れない。
(I might buy it if it is cheap.)

(c) **山田さんから電話があったら**知らせて下さい。
(If Mr. Yamada calls me, please let me know.)

Continual Verb A verb which represents a continual action, as in (a).

(a) 待つ (to wait); 食べる (to eat); 踊る (to dance); 教える (to teach)

With the auxiliary verb *iru*, a continual verb expresses an action in progress, as in (b).

(b) ジョンはメアリーを**待っている**。
(John is waiting for Mary.)

Contrastive Marker A particle which marks contrast. For example, when X is contrasted with Y, it is typically marked by the particle *wa*. X and Y usually appear in S_1 and S_2, respectively in S_1 *ga* S_2, as shown in (a).

(a) ジョン**は**来たが，ビル**は**来なかった。
(John came here, but Bill didn't.)

Coordinate Conjunction A conjunction that combines two sentences without subordinating one to the other. A typical coordinate conjunction is *ga* 'but.'

Example:

(a) 走っていますが，ちっともやせません。
(I'm running, but I haven't lost any weight at all.)

Demonstrative A pronoun or adjective which specifies someone or something by pointing it out, as in (a) and (b).

(a) {**これ** / **それ** / **あれ**} は何ですか。
(What is {this / that / that over there}?)

(b) {**この**本 / **その**本 / **あの**本} は私のです。
({This book / That book / That book over there} is mine.)

The interrogative words which correspond to demonstrative pronouns and demonstrative adjectives are *dore* and *dono*, respectively.

Dependent Noun A noun which must be preceded by a modifier, as in (a) and (b).

(a) A: 明日田中先生に会う**つもり**ですか。
(Are you going to meet Prof. Tanaka tomorrow?)

B: はい，その**つもり**です。
(Yes, I am.)

(b) サンドラはトムを知っている**はず**だ。
(I expect that Sandra knows Tom.)

Direct Object The direct object of a verb is the direct recipient of an action represented by the verb. It can be animate or inanimate. An animate direct object is the direct experiencer of some action (as in (a) and (b) below). An inanimate direct object is typically something which is created, exchanged or worked on, in short, the recipient of the action of the verb (as in (c), (d) and (e) below).

(a) 山口先生は**学生**をよくほめる。
(Prof. Yamaguchi often praises his students.)

(b) かおりは**一郎**をだました。
(Kaori deceived Ichiro.)

(c) 僕は**本**を書いた。
(I wrote a book.)

(d) 一郎はみどりに**スカーフ**をやった。
(Ichiro gave a scarf to Midori.)

(e) 私は**ドア**を開けておいた。
(I kept the door open.)

Although direct objects are marked by the particle *o*, nouns or noun phrases marked by *o* are not always direct objects, as shown in (f) and (g).

(⇨ ***o***[2] (DBJG: 349–51); ***o***[4] (DBJG: 352–54)

(f) 花子は一郎の大学入学**を**喜んだ。
(Hanako was glad that Ichiro entered college.)

(g) トムはその時公園**を**歩いていた。
(At that time Tom was walking in the park.)

Double Particle A sequence of two particles. The first particle is usually a case particle and the second is an adverbial particle such as *wa* 'topic / contrast marker,' *mo* 'also, even,' and *shika* 'only' or the possessive particle *no*.

(a) 東京**からは**田中さんが来た。
(lit. From Tokyo Mr. Tanaka came.)

(b) 私はミラーさん**とも**話した。
(I talked with Mr. Miller, too.)

(c) これは父**からの**手紙だ。
(This is a letter from my father.)

Embedded Sentence A sentence within another sentence is an embedded sentence. The bold-faced part of each sentence below is the embedded sentence. An embedded sentence is marked by a subordinate conjunction such as *kara* 'because,' *keredomo* 'although,' *node* 'because,' *noni* 'although,' *to* 'if,' the quote marker *to* 'that,' a nominalizer (*no* or *koto*) or the head noun of a relative clause.

(a) 山田は**頭が痛**いと言った。
(Yamada said that he had a headache.)

(b) 山田は**頭が痛い**ので学校を休んだ。
(Yamada didn't go to school, because he had a headache.)

(c) 山田は**外国に行く**のが大好きだ。
(Yamada loves to go to a foreign country.)

(d) 山田は**空手を習った**ことがある。
(Yamada has learned *karate* before.)

Experiencer A person who experiences s.t. that is beyond human control such as ability, desire, need, fondness, and emotion. A human passive subject can also be regarded as an experiencer. The bold-faced parts of the following examples are all experiencers.

(a) **私**は日本語が少し分かります。
(I can understand Japanese a little.)

(b) **僕**はスポーツカーが欲しい。
(I want a sports car.)

(c) **うちの息子**は数学が嫌いだ。
(Our son hates math.)

(d) **母**は犬が怖いんです。
(My mother is scared of dogs, you know.)

(e) **友達**は電車の中で財布をすられた。
(My friend got his purse stolen on the train.)

Formal / Informal Forms Verb / adjective(*i* / *na*) / copula forms that are used in formal and informal situations are formal forms and informal forms, respectively. A formal situation is a situation in which relationship between the speaker and the hearer(s) is formal, and an informal situation is a situation in which the human relationship is informal. The formal and informal forms of verbs / adjectives(*i* / *na*) and copula can be exemplified by the following chart:

Formal Forms	Informal Forms
行きます	行く
大きいです	大きい
元気です	元気だ
学生です	学生だ

Informal forms are required by some grammatical structures.
(⇨Appendix 4 (DBJG: 589–99))

Gr. 1 / Gr. 2 Verbs Gr. 1 and Gr. 2 Verbs are Japanese verb groups: If a verb's informal, negative, nonpast form has the [*a*] sound before *nai* as in (a), the verb belongs to Group 1, and if not, as in (b), it belongs to Group

2. There are only two irregular verbs (i.e., *kuru* 'come' and *suru* 'do') that belong to neither the Gr. 1 nor to the Gr. 2.

(a) Gr. 1 Verbs: 切らない [kir*a* - *nai*]
読まない，書かない，待たない，死なない，会わない，話さない

(b) Gr. 2 Verbs: 着ない [k*i* - *nai*], 食べない [tabe - *nai*]
いない，寝ない，起きない，出来ない

Hearer The person who receives a spoken or written message. In this dictionary the term "hearer" is used in a broader sense to mean the person to whom the speaker or the writer communicates.

Imperative Form A conjugated verb form that indicates a command, as in *Hanase!* 'Talk!,' '*Tabero!* 'Eat it!,' *Shiro!* 'Do it!' or *Koi!* 'Come!'

Indefinite Pronoun A pronoun which does not refer to something specifically. *No* in B's sentence in (a) is an indefinite pronoun. Here, *no* is used for *jisho* 'dictionary,' but does not refer to a specific dictionary.

(a) A: どんな辞書が欲しいんですか。
(What kind of dictionary do you want?)

B: 小さい**の**が欲しいんです。
(I want a small one.)

Indirect Object The indirect object of a verb is the recipient of the direct object of the main verb, and is marked by the particle *ni*. In (a), for example, the indirect object is *Midori*, a recipient of a *scarf*, which is the direct object of the verb *yatta*. It can be inanimate, as in (b). The main verbs which involve the indirect object are typically donative verbs (as in (a) and (b)).

(a) 一郎は**みどり**にスカーフをやった。
(Ichiro gave a scarf to Midori.)

(b) 台風は**九州地方**に多大の被害を与えた。
(The typhoon brought great damage to the Kyushu area.)

Informal Form (⇨Formal / Informal Forms)

Intransitive Verb A verb which does not require a direct object. The action or state identified by the intransitive verb is related only to the subject of the sentence. For example, the verb *hashitta* 'ran' in (a) is an intransitive verb because the action of running is related only to the subject.

(cf. Transitive Verb)

(a) 鈴木さんは**走った**。
(Mr. Suzuki ran.)

Intransitive verbs typically indicate *movement* (such as *iku* 'go,' *kuru* 'come,' *aruku* 'walk,' *tobu* 'fly,' *noru* 'get onto'), *spontaneous change* (such as *naru* 'become,' *kawaru* 'change,' *tokeru* 'melt,' *fukuramu* 'swell,' *hajimaru* 'begin'), *human emotion* (such as *yorokobu* 'rejoice,' *kanashimu* 'feel sad,' *omou* 'feel'), and *birth / death* (such as *umareru* 'be born,' *shinu* 'die').

(⇨ Appendix 3 (DBJG: 585–88)

***I*-type Adjective** An adjective whose nonpast prenominal form ends with *i*. Examples of *i*-type adjectives are *takai* 'high, expensive' and *tsuyoi* 'strong,' as seen in (a). (cf. *Na*-type Adjective)

(a) 高**い**本
(an expensive book)
強**い**人
(a strong person)

I-type adjectives are further subdivided into two types: *i*-type adjectives which end with *shi-i* and those with non-*shi-i* endings. Most adjectives with *shi-i* endings express human emotion (such as *ureshii* 'happy,' *kanashii* 'sad,' *sabishii* 'lonely,' *kurushii* 'painful'); the non-*shi-i* adjectives are used for objective descriptions (such as *kuroi* 'black,' *shiroi* 'white,' *hiroi* 'spacious,' *takai* 'high, expensive').

Main Clause When a sentence consists of two clauses, one marked by a subordinate conjunction (such as *kara*, *keredo*, *node*, and *noni*) and the other not marked by a subordinate conjunction, the latter is called a main clause. The bold-faced parts of (a) and (b) are main clauses.

(a) **山田は**頭が痛いのに**学校に行った**。

(*Yamada went to school*, although he had a headache.)

(b) **和子は**夫が優しいから**幸福だ。**
(*Kazuko is happy*, because her husband is kind.)

When a sentence has a relative clause, the non-relative clause part is also referred to as a main clause as in (c).

(c) **私はきのう,** 友達から借りた**ビデオを家で見た。**
(*Yesterday I watched a video* which I borrowed from my friend.)

***Na*-type Adjective** An adjective whose nonpast prenominal form ends with *na*. For example, *shizukada* 'quiet' and *genkida* 'healthy' are *na*-type adjectives, as in (a). (cf. *I*-type Adjective)

(a) 静か**な**家
(a quiet house)
元気**な**人
(a healthy person)

Na-type adjectives are very similar to nouns. Some *na*-type adjectives can be used as real nouns as shown in (b). All *na*-type adjectives behave as nouns when they are used before the copula *da*, as shown in (c).

(b) **健康**は大事ですよ。
(Health is important, you know.)

cf. 健康**な**人
(a healthy person)

ご**親切**は忘れません。
(I'll never forget your kindness.)

cf. 親切**な**人
(a kind person)

(c) この人は**元気** / **学生** {だ / です / だった / でした / じゃない / じゃありません / じゃなかった / じゃありませんでした}。
(This person {is / was / isn't / wasn't} healthy / a student.)

Nominalizer A nominalizer is a particle that makes a sentence into a noun phrase or clause. There are two nominalizers *no* and *koto*: the former represents the speaker's empathetic feeling towards an event / state expressed in the nominalized noun phrase / clause; the latter represents the speaker's relatively anti-empathetic feeling towards an event / state.

(⇨ ***no***[3] (DBJG: 318–22); ***koto***[2] (DBJG: 193–96)

Noun Phrase / Clause		Particle	Predicate
Sentence	Nominalizer		
日本語を読む	**の / こと**	は	難しい。
(Reading Japanese is difficult.)			

The nominalized sentence can be used in any position where an ordinary noun or a noun phrase / clause can be used.

Participial Construction The construction which expresses an action accompanying situation expressed in the main clause. The participial construction often involves *te*-form, as in (a) and (b).

(a) 私はコートを脱い**で**ハンガーにかけた。
(Taking off my coat, I hung it on a hanger.)

(b) ソファーに座っ**て**新聞を読んだ。
(Sitting on the sofa I read newspaper.)

Passive Sentence A sentence which describes an action by someone from the viewpoint of someone else who is affected by that action. (cf. Active Sentence) (a) and (b) are passive sentences.

(a) 私はビルにぶたれた。
(I was beaten by Bill.)

(b) 太郎は秋子に泣かれた。
(lit. Taro was annoyed by the fact that Akiko cried. (= Taro was annoyed by Akiko's crying.))

Potential Form A verb form that expresses competence in the sense of 'can do s.t.' The formation is as follows:

Gr. 1 Verbs Vcond + る e.g. 話せる (can talk)

Gr. 2 Verbs Vstem + られる e.g. 食べられる (can eat)

Vstem + れる e.g. 食べれる (can eat)

Irr. Verbs 来る 来られる, 来れる (can come)

する 出来る (can do)

Predicate The part of a sentence which makes a statement about the subject. The core of the predicate consists either of a verb, an adjective, or a noun followed by a form of the copula *da*. Optionally, objects and other adjectival and / or adverbial modifiers may be present. In (a), (b) and (c) the predicates are printed in bold type.

(a) 松本さんは**よく映画を見る**。
(Mr. Matsumoto sees movies often.)

(b) 私の家は**スミスさんのより新しい**。
(My house is newer than Mr. Smith's.)

(c) ジョンは**日本語の学生です**。
(John is a student of Japanese language.)

Prefix / Suffix A dependent, non-conjugational word attached to nouns or the stems of verbs and adjectives in order to form new independent words. Prefixes are attached to the beginnings of nouns, etc. (Ex.(a)), and suffixes to their endings (Ex.(b)).

(a) **超**特急 (superexpress); **副**大統領 (vice-president); **無**関心 (indifference)

(b) 映画**化** (cinematization); 読み**方** (how to read); 高**さ** (height)

Prenominal Form The verb / adjective form which precedes a noun and modifies it. The bold-faced verbs and adjectives in (a), (b), (c) and (d) are prenominal forms.

(a) 私が**読む / 読んだ**新聞
(the newspaper I read)

(b) **大きい / 大きかった**家
(a big house / a house which used to be big)

(c) **立派な / 立派だった**建物
(a magnificent building / a building which used to be magnificent)

(d) **おいしそうな / おいしそうだった**ケーキ
(a delicious-looking cake / a cake which looked delicious)

Punctual Verb A verb that represents a momentary action which either occurs once, as in (a), or can be repeated continuously, as in (b).

(a) 知る (get to know); 死ぬ (die); 始まる (begin); 結婚する (get married); やめる (stop s.t.); 似る (resemble)

(b) 落とす (drop); もぎる (pluck off); ける (kick); 跳ぶ (jump); 打つ (hit)

With the auxiliary verb *iru*, the punctual verbs in (a) express a state after an action was taken, and those as in (b) express either a repeated action or a state after an action was taken. (⇨ Appendix 2 (DBJG: 582–84)

Stative Verb A verb which represents a state of something or someone at some point in time, as in (a). (⇨ Appendix 2 (DBJG: 582–84)

(a) ある (exist (of inanimate things)); いる (exist (of animate things)); いる (need); 出来る (can do)

Subject The subject is an element of a sentence which indicates an agent of an action in active sentences (as in (a)) or an experiencer of an action (as in (b)) or someone or something that is in a state or a situation (as in (c), (e) and (f)). The subject is normally marked by the particle *ga* in Japanese unless it is the sentence topic.

(a) **ジョン**がりんごを食べた。
(John ate an apple.)

(b) **メアリー**が先生にほめられた。
(Mary was praised by her teacher.)

(c) ナンシーはきれいだ。
(Nancy is pretty.)

(d) ドアが開いた。
(The door opened.)

(e) 机が一つある。
(lit. One table exists. (= There is a table.))

(f) 空が青い。
(The sky is blue.)

Subordinate Clause A clause which is embedded into a main clause with a subordinate conjunction. Typical subordinate conjunctions are *ba* 'if,' *kara* 'because,' *node* 'because,' *keredo* 'although' and *noni* 'although.' Thus, in (a) below, the bold-faced clause with the subordinate conjunction *node* is embedded into the main clause *Nakayama-san wa gakkō o yasunda*, 'Mr. Nakayama was absent from school.'

(a) 中山さんは**頭が痛かったので**学校を休んだ。
(Mr. Nakayama was absent from school because he had a headache.)

The informal form of a verb / adjective is usually used in a subordinate clause.

Suffix (⇨ Prefix / Suffix)

***Suru*-verb** A verb which is composed of a noun and *suru* (Exs.(a) and (b)) or a single word and *suru* (Ex.(c)). Nouns preceding *suru* are mostly Chinese-origin words. *Suru*-verbs conjugate in the same way as *suru*.

(a) 勉強**する** (to study); 掃除**する** (to clean); 夜更かし**する** (to stay up late)

(b) ノック**する** (to knock); サイン**する** (to sign)

(c) 熱**する** (to heat); 察**する** (to guess)

Transitive Verb A verb that requires a direct object. It usually expresses an action that acts upon s.o. or s.t. indicated by the direct object. Actions indicated by transitive verbs include *real causatives* (such as *ikaseru* 'make/let s.o. go,' *korosu* 'kill,' *miseru* 'show,' *nakasu* 'make s.o. cry,' *noseru* 'put, place'), *exchange* (such as *ageru* 'give,' *morau* 'receive,' *kureru* 'give'), *creation* (such as *tsukuru* 'make,' *kaku* 'write,' *kangaeru* 'think'), *communication* (such as *hanasu* 'speak,' *oshieru* 'teach,' *tsutaeru* 'convey a message') and others. Note that some English transitive verbs are intransitive in Japanese.

(a) 私は車が**ある**。
(lit. With me a car exists. (= I have a car.))

(b) 僕はお金が**いる**。
(lit. To me money is necessary. (= I need money.))

(c) スミスさんは中国語が**分かる**。
(lit. To Mr. Smith Chinese is understandable. (= Mr. Smith understands Chinese.))

(d) 私はフランス語が少し**出来る**。
(lit. To me French is a bit possible. (= I can speak French a little.))

(e) 木下さんは東京でお父さんに**会った**。
(Mr. Kinoshita met his father in Tokyo.)

(f) 私にはベルが**聞こえなかった**。
(lit. To me the bell wasn't audible. (= I wasn't able to hear the bell.))

(g) ここからは富士山が**見えます**よ。
(lit. From here Mt. Fuji is visible. (= We can see Mt. Fuji from here.))

(h) 私達は新幹線に**乗りました**。
(We rode a bullet train.)

(i) 私は母に**似ている**らしい。
(It seems that I resemble my mother.)

Verbal A sentence element which indicates the action or state of the subject. A verbal is either a verb, an adjective, or a noun followed by a copula, as in (a) – (c).

(a) 私は今学期漢字をたくさん**勉強した**。
(I studied many kanji this term.)

(b) この試験はとても**難しい**。
(This exam is very difficult.)

(c) これは多分**イタリア語だ**。
(This is probably Italian.)

Volitional Sentence A sentence in which a person expresses his will. The main verb in such sentences is in the volitional form, as in (a).

(a) 僕が**行こう / 行きましょう**。
(I will go.)

Wh-question A question that asks for information about *who*, *what*, *where*, *which*, *when*, *why* and *how*, as exemplified by (a) – (f) below.
(cf. Yes-No Question)

(a) **誰**が来ましたか。
(Who came here?)

(b) **何**を食べますか。
(What will you eat?)

(c) **どこ**に行きますか。
(Where are you going?)

(d) **いつ**大阪へ帰りますか。
(When are you going back to Osaka?)

(e) **どうして**買わないんですか。
(How come you don't buy it?)

(f) 東京駅へは**どう**行きますか。
(How can I get to Tokyo Station?)

Wh-word An interrogative word which corresponds to English words such as *who, what, where, which, when, why* and *how*. The following are some examples.

(a) 誰 (who); 何 (what); どこ (where); いつ (when); どうして / なぜ (how come / why); どう (how)

Note that Japanese Wh-words are not always found in sentence-initial position; they are frequently found after a topic noun phrase, as shown in (b) and (c) below.

(b) 昨日(きのう)のパーティーには**誰**が来(き)ましたか。
(lit. To yesterday's party, who came there? (= Who came to yesterday's party?))

cf. **誰**が昨日のパーティーに来ましたか。
(Who came to yesterday's party?)

(c) 日本(にほん)では**何**をしましたか。
(lit. In Japan what did you do? (= What did you do in Japan?))

cf. **何**を日本でしましたか。
(What did you do in Japan?)

Yes-No Question A question that can be answered by *hai / ē* 'yes' or *ie* 'no.' (cf. Wh-question)

Examples follow:

(a) A: 上田(うえだ)さんは来(き)ましたか。
(Did Mr. Ueda come?)

B: はい，来ました。
(Yes, he did.)

(b) A: 鈴木(すずき)さんは学生(がくせい)ですか。
(Is Mr. Suzuki a student?)

B: いいえ，そうじゃありません。
(No, he isn't.)

Special Topics in Intermediate Japanese Grammar

1. Discourse Grammar

(1) Mechanism of Cohesion: Inter-sentential Reference

When two or more sentences are recognized as a cohesive sequence (i.e., discourse) rather than a collection of unrelated sentences, in many instances the discourse involves certain linguistic mechanisms to maintain cohesiveness between sentences.* Among such mechanisms, inter-sentential reference is one of the most common ones.**

Inter-sentential reference (ISR) is a kind of reference in which an element in a sentence refers to something or someone mentioned in another sentence. Specifically, when reference is made to an entity mentioned in a previous sentence, it is called "anaphoric reference" or "anaphora." Anaphora is the most common ISR. Examples of anaphora are given in (1). In this discourse the bold-faced parts (i.e., anaphoric elements or anaphors) refer to persons or things mentioned in previous sentences.

(1) これは清兵衛と云う子供と瓢箪との話である。**この出来事**以来**清兵衛**と

---

*Cohesiveness is also maintained by the information each sentence carries. In general, a sequence of sentences is recognized as a cohesive unit when the sentence contains a "common thread" in terms of the information they carry. For example, a set of sentences is recognized as a cohesive unit if the sentences have a common topic. Similarly, if sentences are put together to perform a common function (e.g., making a request), they are recognized as a cohesive unit.

**Another mechanism to maintain cohesiveness between sentences is the conjunction. As a matter of fact, conjunctions (or conjunction equivalents) such as those shown in (i) create a cohesive sentence sequence by connecting sentences directly.

(i) そして (and (then)); そこで (therefore); しかし (however); 一方 (on the other hand); 例えば (for example); ついでながら (incidentally); その結果 (as the result of that)

(⇨ Appendix 4. Conjunctions)

瓢簞とは縁が断れて了ったが，間もなく**清兵衛**には**瓢簞**に代わる物が出来た。**それ**は絵を描く事で，**彼**は嘗て**瓢簞**に熱中したように今は**それ**に熱中している。

(志賀直哉『清兵衛と瓢簞』)

(This is a story about a child named Seibei and gourds. After this incident, the tie between Seibei and gourds was severed. However, he soon found something to substitute for gourds—painting. He is now as devoted to it as he once was to gourds. (Shiga Naoya: *Seibei and the Gourds*))

As seen in (1), various kinds of elements can appear as anaphors, including pronouns, repeated nouns, and related nouns. In addition, anaphors are ellipted in some situations.

A. Pronouns

Pronouns can be classified into two groups: personal pronouns (e.g., *watashi* 'I,' *kanojo* 'she,' *kare-ra* 'they') and demonstrative pronouns (e.g., *kore* 'this,' *sore-ra* 'those,' *soko* 'that/the place').

Anaphoric personal pronouns are limited to third-person pronouns, including *kare* 'he,' *kanojo* 'she,' and their plural forms. (1) presents an example of *kare*.

Among demonstrative pronouns, only the *so-* and *ko-* series can be anaphoric. (1) gives examples of *sore* and (2) an example of *kore*.*

(2) A社がM型ワープロの五パーセント値下げに踏み切った。**これ**は，最近低下している同社のワープロシェアの巻き返しを狙ったもの(である)。
(Company A has decided to reduce the price of M-type word-processors by five percent. Their aim is to regain (lit. This is to aim at regaining) their recently declining share of the word-processor market.)

**Are* 'that' can be used in conversation to refer to something which is known to both the speaker and the hearer, as in (i).

(i) A: ここにあった英和辞典，知らない?
(Do you know where the English-Japanese dictionary is which was here?)

B: ああ，**あれ**は今山田さんが使ってるよ。
(Oh, that one; Yamada is using it now.)

B. Repeated Nouns

An anaphoric noun is, in many instances, a repetition of its antecedent.

Proper nouns

If an antecedent is a proper noun, the most direct way to refer to the same entity in a later sentence is to repeat the same proper noun. For example, in (1), *Seibei* is repeated in the second sentence.

Common nouns

When an antecedent is a common noun, the same noun may appear as an anaphor in certain situations. For example, if an antecedent refers to generic entities, the same noun can be repeated with no modifier (e.g., *hyōtan* 'gourds' in the second and third sentences in (1)). If an antecedent refers to a specific entity, on the other hand, the same noun may appear in later sentences either with or without a demonstrative adjective (i.e., *sono* 'that/the' or *kono* 'this'). A demonstrative adjective is necessary if the referent would be otherwise interpreted as non-anaphoric because of a lack of sufficient context to interpret it as anaphoric. For example, in (3) the *apāto* 'apartment' in the second sentence does not refer to the same apartment mentioned in the first sentence, while in (4) *sono apāto* 'that apartment' does refer to the same apartment mentioned in the first sentence.

(3) 昨日ボストンの**アパート**を見た。ジョンも今日**アパート**を見た。
(I saw an apartment in Boston yesterday. John also saw an apartment today.)

(4) 昨日ボストンの**アパート**を見た。ジョンも今日**そのアパート**を見た。
(I saw an apartment in Boston yesterday. John also saw that apartment today.)

In (5), on the other hand, there is sufficient context to interpret the *kozukai* 'janitor' in the second sentence as anaphoric; therefore, no demonstrative adjective is necessary.

(5) さて，教員は清兵衛から取り上げた瓢簞を汚れた物ででもあるかのように，捨てるように，年寄った学校の**小使**にやって了った。**小使**はそれを持って帰って，くすぶった小さな自分の部屋の柱へ下げて置いた。

(志賀直哉『清兵衛と瓢簞』)

(Later, the teacher gave the gourd he had taken from Seibei to an old janitor as if it was a filthy object. The janitor took it home and hung it on a pillar in his small dingy room. (Shiga Naoya: *Seibei and the Gourds*))

When reference is made in a later paragraph, the anaphoric noun often appears with a relative clause which reiterates identifying information about the referent mentioned earlier. For example, in the story of *Cinderella*, one of Cinderella's shoes comes off when she runs down the stairs of the palace to hurry home. When this shoe is referred to in a later paragraph, the reference could look like (6).

(6) **シンデレラが階段(かいだん)で落(お)として行(い)った靴(くつ)**を手(て)がかりに，王子様(おうじさま)はシンデレラを探(さが)させました。
(Using the shoe Cinderella lost on the stairs as a clue, the prince had his men look for her.)

C. Related Nouns

Anaphoric reference often occurs with nouns (or noun phrases) which are not the same as but are related to their antecedents. There are three situations in which "related nouns" appear as anaphors:

(a) Situations where an anaphor and its antecedent refer to the same entity (direct anaphora);
(b) Situations where an anaphor refers to part of its antecedent's referent (semi-direct anaphora); and
(c) Situations where an anaphor refers to an entity inferred from previous context (indirect anaphora).

Direct anaphora

In direct anaphora, reference can be made by nouns which refer to larger categories than their antecedents refer to. For example, in (7) the *hana* 'flower' in the second sentence refers to the *sakura* 'cherry (blossoms)' in the first sentence. In this case, a demonstrative adjective is mandatory.

(7) **桜(さくら)**は日本(にほん)のシンボルだ。{**この** / *ø} **花(はな)**はみんなに愛(あい)されている。

(Cherry blossoms are the symbol of Japan. They (lit. These flowers) are loved by everyone.)

Additional examples of direct anaphora can be seen in (8) and (9).

(8) 昨日**山田**が訪ねて来た。**この男**は私の高校時代のクラスメートだった。
(Yamada came to see me yesterday. This guy was one of my classmates in my high school days.)

(9) **山下和仁**のギターを聞いた。**この天才ギタリスト**は16歳の時にヨーロッパの三つの国際コンクールで優勝した。
(I heard Kazuhito Yamashita play guitar (lit. Kazuhito Yamashita's guitar). This genius guitarist won three international competitions in Europe when he was sixteen.)

Semi-direct anaphora

In semi-direct anaphora, an anaphoric noun refers to part (or an element) of its antecedent's referent. For example, in (10), the *yuka* 'floor' in the second sentence refers to the floor of the apartment mentioned in the first sentence. In this case, the anaphor does not require a demonstrative adjective.

(10) 昨日ボストンの**アパート**を見た。**床**に少し傷があったがいいアパートだった。
(Yesterday I saw an apartment in Boston. Although there were some scratches on the floor, it was a good apartment.)

Indirect anaphora

In indirect anaphora, there is no explicit antecedent. The referent of an anaphor is inferred from a previous sentence(s). For example, in (11), the *gen'in* 'cause' in the second sentence does not refer to anything which is directly mentioned in the first sentence. Rather, it refers to something which is inferred from that sentence. In this case, the anaphor does not require a demonstrative adjective.

(11) 昨日神戸の小学校で火事があった。警察が今**原因**を調べている。
(Yesterday there was a fire at an elementary school in Kobe. The police are investigating the cause now.)

D. Anaphor ellipsis (Zero anaphora)

In some situations, anaphors are ellipted. Such anaphoric reference is called "zero anaphora." This can be seen in (12).

(12) 清兵衛が時々瓢箪を買って来る事は両親も知っていた。ø 三四銭から十五銭位までの皮つきの瓢箪を十程も持っていたろう。
(志賀直哉『清兵衛と瓢箪』)

(Seibei's parents were aware that he bought gourds once in a while. (He) had some ten gourds with skins costing from three or four to fifteen cents. (Shiga Naoya: *Seibei and the Gourds*))

In (12), Seibei *wa* or *kare wa* 'he' is ellipted in the second sentence. Because of this "invisible anaphora," the two sentences in (12) form a cohesive sequence.

(2) Phenomena of Tense and Formality Switchings

A. Tense Switching

Usually a series of past events are narrated in the past tenses. But primarily in written Japanese discourse that narrates a past event, past tenses often switch to nonpast tenses. The following is a passage from a famous novel called *Yama no Oto* 'The Sound of the Mountain' by Yasunari Kawabata. Everything that is being described in this passage concerns past events. So the English native reader/writer, for example, expects the author to use nothing but the past tense.

(1) [1]八月の十日前だが，虫が鳴いている。[2]木の葉から木の葉へ夜露の落ちるらしい音も聞こえる。[3]そうして，ふと信吾に山の音が聞こえた。[4]風はない。[5]月は満月に近く明るいが，しめっぽい夜気で，小山の上を描く木々の輪郭はぼやけている。[6]しかし，風に動いていない。[7]鎌倉のいわゆる谷の奥で，波が聞こえる夜もあるから，信吾は海の音かと疑ったが，やはり山の音だった。[8]遠い風の音に似ているが，地鳴りとでもいう深い底力があった。[9]自分の頭の中で聞こえるようでもあるので，信吾は耳鳴りかと思って，頭を振ってみた。[10]音はやんだ。[11]音がやんだ後で，信吾ははじめて恐怖におそわれた。[12]死期が告知されたのではないかと寒気がした。[13]風の音か，海の音か，耳鳴りかと，信吾は冷静に考えたつもりだったが，そんな音などしなかったのではないかと思われた。[14]しかし確かに山の音は聞こえていた。

([1] It *is* ten days before the month of August, but insects *are* already crying. [2] The sound of night dew dropping from a leave to another *is* audible. [3] All of a sudden Shingo heard the sound of the mountain. [4] There *is* no wind. [5] The moon *is* almost a full moon and bright, yet the moist night air *blurs* the outline of the tree tops of the small mountain. [6] But the trees *are* not moving in the wind. [7] At the so-called inner part of the valley of Kamakura, some nights Shingo *is* able to hear the sound of waves, so he suspected that it was the sound of the sea, but it turned out to be the sound of the mountain. [8] It *is* like the distant sound of the wind, but it *had* deep power like that of the earth rumbling. [9] He *feels* as if it were in his head, so he thought it was his ears ringing and he *shook* his head. [10] The sound *stopped*. [11] After the sound stopped Shingo was *overtaken* by fear for the first time. [12] A chill ran through his spine as if the hour of his death had been proclaimed. [13] Shingo had tried to figure out objectively if it was the sound of the wind or the sound of waves or ringing in his ears, and he *thought* it was possible that there wasn't any sound. [14] But there was no doubt that he *had* heard the sound of the mountain.)

Logically speaking, the author could have written every sentence in the past tense. Nevertheless, the author sometimes used the past tense and sometimes the nonpast tense. In this passage, 5 sentences (i.e., Sentences 1, 2, 4, 5, 6) out of 14 sentences are in the nonpast tense shown by the double underline. (In the translation the original nonpast predicate is translated using the nonpast tense and italicized.) In other words, a switch from the past tense to the nonpast has occurred in those 5 sentences.

An examination of the 5 sentences in the nonpast tense reveals that these sentences describe a circumstance that surrounds Shingo, the main character of the story. The rest of the sentences (i.e., sentences 3, 7–14) describe in the past tense whatever Shingo did or felt in the given circumstances. To put it in general terms, tense switching is a strategy available to the writer to differentiate a stage and a set of chronological events that occur within that stage. The stage is certainly important in that it defines a space in which a drama develops, but it is less important than the drama itself. So, important, dramatic information is described in the past tense, whereas relatively unimportant circumstantial information is described in the nonpast tense. The use of such nonpast tenses has an effect of creating a vivid sense of immediateness for the reader.

A principle that appears to govern Tense Switching goes as follows:

Principle of Tense Switching

A part of a past event (often a state rather than an action) can be described using the nonpast tense, if the writer perceives it to be relatively unimportant circumstantial information that has no direct bearing upon the major story line.

B. Formality Switching

By *formality switching* is meant switching from formal style to informal style or less frequently switching from informal style to formal style. The latter, i.e., switching from informal style to formal style, occurs in spoken Japanese. The informal style is a suitable style to be used when the speaker / writer wants to express his feeling, his knowledge or his conviction in a straightforward manner. So, in a formal setting which requires the speaker / writer to use the formal style, the style can switch from formal to informal as shown in the following examples (2a, b, c).

(2) a. 日本という国は外国人の目にはとても閉ざされた国という印象を与えているんですね。日本に行けばガイジン，つまり，外の人と言われ，お客様扱いに終始してしまう。なかなか親しい友人が出来ない。同僚との付き合いも大変だ。会社の昇進にも限界がある。とにかく，日本は，もっと，開かれた社会にならなければなりませんね。

(Japan is giving foreigners an impression of a country very much closed. Foreigners are called "gaijin," that is to say, outsiders and they are always treated like guests. And they cannot make good friends easily. Association with colleagues is tough. There is also a limit to their promotion. Anyway, Japan has to become a society more open to foreigners.)

b. 日本は犯罪が少ないですよね。日本人が犯罪を犯そうとした場合，刑罰は別として，それを止める契機が二つある。女房，子供の顔が浮かぶ。会社のことが気になる。だから，悪いことが出来ないんですよ。
(There are not many crimes committed in Japan, you know. When a Japanese is about to commit a crime there are at least two factors that will deter him from committing it, aside from punishments. The faces of his wife and children come to his mind. He thinks of his company. That's why he cannot do evil things, you know.)

c. いろいろの意味で生きることが困難な今日の日々を，あなたはどのように生きておられますか。生きることが困難なのは，何も今に始まったことではない。昔から，人生は，少なくともそれをまじめに受け取った人にとっては，いつも苦しみに満ちたものだったに違いありません。(……中略……) わたしたちの人生はまことに取るに足りない，小さなものであり，わたしたちの一人一人はまことに哀れな，つまらないもの，そして，時にはいたたまれないほどに醜いものです。しかし，だからといって，この人生，この自己以外にわたしたちは生きる場所はない。ですから，一回限りの人生，かけがえのない自己を大切にしようではありませんか。

(矢内原伊作『自己について』)

(How are you living your life these days when life is difficult in all sorts of ways? The difficulty of living has not just started now. From ancient times, human life must have been full of difficulties at least for those who dealt with it seriously. (. . . omitted . . .) Our lives are truly insignificant, such tiny things, and each one of us is truly miserable, mundane and sometimes unbearably ugly. But even so, we have no other place than ourselves in which we can live. So, shall we value this irreplaceable self in this life that we have but once?) (Isaku Yanaihara "On Self")

The speaker of both (2a) and (2b) is talking to a person in the rather formal situation of a round-table discussion. This is a situation where a formal style is required, but instead of using a formal style all the way, he has switched his style from formal to informal style as indicated by the double underlines.

The writer of (2c) employs formal style all the way with intermittent informal style. In (2c) there are two double-underlined predicates in which formality switching has taken place. In both cases the writer expresses something appendixed to what follows either in a coordinated or subordinated way. In fact, in both cases, the sentences that are in an informal style can turn into a coordinate clause or a subordinate clause like (3a) and (3b), respectively. Whatever is expressed in an appendix to the major clause is usually distanced from the hearer/reader, and therefore tends to be expressed usually in informal style. Also to be noted here is the statistical tendency for formality switching to occur when the sentence is a negative sentence.

(3) a. 生きることが困難なのは，何も今に始まったことではないのであって，昔から，人生は，少なくともそれをまじめに受け取った人にとっては，いつも苦しみに満ちたものだったに違いありません。

b. しかし，だからといって，この人生，この自己以外にわたしたちは生きる場所はないのだから，一回限りの人生，かけがえのない自己を大切にしようではありませんか。

An extreme case of formality switching is instanced by the following example.

(4) 今日(きょう)はこれからコンピュータチップのお話(はなし)をします。まず，コンピュータチップの構造(こうぞう)ですが，(A bee stings the speaker's head) あっ，{痛(いた)い / *痛いです}！

(Today I am going to give a talk on computer chips. First of all, regarding the structure of the chip, ouch!)

The speaker of (4) is giving a public talk in which he is required to use formal speech. However, at the point when he is stung by a bee, he automatically switches his style from formal to informal, because his expression is an exclamation which is a most straightforward expression of his physiological feeling.

Although much less frequent than formal-to-informal switching there are cases of informal-to-formal switching as shown in (5).

(5) A: 僕とドライブに行かない?
(Don't you want to come for a drive with me?)
B: そうねえ，どうしようかしら。
(Mm, I wonder what I should do.)
A: ドライブに行こうよ，ね。
(You must come with me.)
B: あなた，運転が荒っぽいでしょ。
(You are a reckless driver, aren't you?)
A: そんなことはありません。君とドライブする時は，優しく運転します。
(Not at all. When I go for a drive with you, I will drive considerately.)

In this example, a couple is talking very informally. The speaker A wants to persuade B to come for a drive with him, but the persuasion has not been successful, so by switching the style he wants to teasingly indicate that their relationship does not deserve intimate, informal style. Therefore, he intentionally switches his style from informal to formal.

The Principle of Formality Switching

Formal style may be switched to informal style when the speaker / writer wants to express his/her feeling, knowledge or conviction in a straightforward manner.

2. Newspaper Grammar

Japanese newspapers use certain sentence forms, phrases, and words which are not common to other writing.

(1) Headlines

A. Ellipsis of particles and verbals

In newspaper headlines the topic marker *wa* and case markers are often dropped. (Particularly, ellipsis of the subject marker *ga* and the direct object marker *o* is common.) Predictable verbals are also dropped.

Examples:

(1) a. 地球資源衛星(**が**)軌道に(**乗る**)
(Earth resource satellite goes into orbit)

b. 公立高(**が**)授業料(**を**)値上げ(**する**)
(Public high schools to raise tuition)

c. 東アジア重視(**が**)鮮明に(**なる**)
デュポンジャパン(**が**)初の日本人社長(**を**)(**任命する**)
(Emphasis on East Asia becomes clear / Du Pont Japan appoints first Japanese president)

d. 政府は土地価格の問題解決に努力を(**せよ**)[社説]
(Government should make an effort to solve land price problems) [Editorial]

(For examples of *wa*-omission, see (4a) and (4b).)

Note: As seen in (1d), particles are not dropped in imperative sentences.

B. Ellipsis of *no*

The noun connector *no* is often dropped in long noun compounds (particularly, in those which contain more than one *no*).

Examples:

(2) a. 企業(**の**)交際費(は)5兆6,274億円(に)(上る)——昨年分

(Companies' social expenses reached (lit. reach) ¥5,627.4 billion last year)

b. 90年の世界(の)ビール消費量(を)
キリンビール(が)発表(する)
(Kirin announces the world's beer consumption in '90)

C. *Suru*-verbs

The *suru* of *suru*-verbs is usually dropped.

Examples:

(3) a. 米(が), フロン(を)95年(に)全廃(**する**)
(US to totally abolish CFCs (chloro-fluorocarbons) in '95)

b. 衛星事業(が)海外市場(の)開拓に着手(**する**)
(Satellite industry begins foreign market development)

D. *Da* after N and Adj(*na*)stem

Da after nouns and *na*-adjective stems is usually dropped.

Examples:

(4) a. 交通死者(は)1万1,105人(**だ**)——昨年度
(11,105 killed in traffic accidents last year)

b. プラント輸出(は)東南アジア向け(が)好調(**だ**)
(Plant export to SE Asia flourishes)

E. Tense

In headlines past events are represented using the nonpast tense (e.g., (1a), (1c)). Because the nonpast tense also represents future events, whether an event is a future one or a past one is known from other headline elements (e.g., (2a), (3a)) or from the text (e.g., (1b), (3b)).

F. Abbreviations

a. Country names

Country names are often abbreviated.

Examples:

(5) 日 (Japan); 米 (America); 英 (Great Britain); 仏 (France); 独 (Germany); 伊 (Italy); 加 (Canada); 豪 (Australia); 中 (China); 台 (Taiwan); 韓 (Korea); 南ア (South Africa)

b. Groups, companies, institutions

The complete names of groups, companies, and institutions are often abbreviated.

Examples:

(6) 安保理 = 安全保障理事会 (the Security Council)
公取委 = 公正取引委員会 (the Fair Trade Commission)
都銀 = 都市銀行 (city banks)
東電 = 東京電力 (Tokyo Power Company)
京大 = 京都大学 (Kyoto University)

Note: Some abbreviations in this category are commonly used in spoken as well as written language.

c. Special abbreviations
Some English acronyms and letters are commonly used in headlines to save space.

Examples:

(7) EC (European Community); IC (integrated circuit); KO (knock-out); NY株 (New York stocks); W杯 (World Cup); 初V (first victory)

(2) Bodies

A. *Suru*-verbs

The conjugated part of a *suru*-verb connective form (i.e., *-shi*) is often dropped. *-suru* or *-shita* of a *suru*-verb in sentence-final position is also dropped in some situations.

Examples:

(8) 昨年，全国の医療機関で入院または外来で診療を受けた患者は，一日当たり約八百三十六万人と国民の十四・八人に一人に上り，前回の昭和六十二年調査からさらに増加(**し**)，毎年約一兆円伸び二十一兆円にも達した医療費の膨張を数字で裏付けていることが，二十八日厚生省がまとめた平成二年患者調査で分かった。(中略)調査は三年に一度実施され，今回は全国で計一万二千五十四カ所の病院，診療所，歯科診療所を無作為に抽出(**した**)。十月十六日～十八日のうちの一日を調査日に指定(**し**)，外来や入院患者の状況を調べ全国推計した。

(東京新聞12. 29. 91朝刊)

(A survey of patients in 1990 compiled by the Ministry of Health and Welfare on December 28, has revealed that the number of patients who had medical examinations at medical institutions in the nation last year as either hospitalized patients or outpatients was about 8,360,000 (one in every 14.8 Japanese) a day—a further increase since the last survey in 1987. The survey also shows through figures the soaring medical and medicare expenses, which have increased by ¥1 trillion every year since 1987, reaching ¥21 trillion. . . . This survey is conducted once every three years. In this survey a total of 12,054 hospitals, clinics, and dental clinics were randomly selected and their patients were surveyed on one of the designated dates from October 16–18.)

Note: Because the stems of most *suru*-verbs are also used as nouns, the parts of speech must be carefully identified when *-shi* is omitted.

B. *Da* after nouns

Da after nouns is often dropped, the result being a noun-ending sentence.

Examples:

(9) a. 大蔵省と文部省は二十一日午前，国立大学の授業料を年額三万六千円引き上げることで合意した。1993年四月の入学者から適用する。私立大学との格差が鮮明になってきたうえ，理工系の研究設備の近代化が急務になってきたことなどが値上げの理由(**だ**)。

(日本経済新聞12. 21. 91夕刊)

(The Ministry of Finance and the Ministry of Education agreed on the morning of the 21st that the tuition of national universities will be raised by ¥36,000 a year. The new tuition will come into effect from April 1993. The reasons for the raise include the obvious gap between the tuition of private universities and that of national universities and the urgent need to modernize facilities for science and engineering research.)

b. 平成二年度に全国の高校で起きた校内暴力は，四百九十校，千四百十九件に上り，いずれも過去最悪を記録したことが二十五日，文部省の「児童生徒問題行動実態調査」で分かった。特に教師に対する暴力が急増しているのが特徴(**だ**)。

（日本経済新聞12. 26. 91朝刊）

(“A Survey of Problematic Behaviors by K-12 Students” released by the Ministry of Education on December 25 has revealed that the number of cases of school violence which took place at high schools across the country in 1990 reached 1,419, involving 490 schools. Both figures are the worst on record. One of the characteristics is that there is a sharp rise in violence towards teachers.)

3. Conversational Strategies

In order to become proficient in advanced Japanese conversation it is necessary to be able to use conversational strategies. They include (A) *Aizuchi* ('back-channel' responses), (B) Fillers, (C) Rephrasing, (D) Topic Shift and Topic Recovery and (E) Avoidance of Decisive Expressions, among others.

A. *Aizuchi* ('back-channel' responses)

Aizuchi ('back-channel' responses) is an interjection to indicate that the hearer is involved with what the speaker has said up to that point of the conversation. The most common *aizuchi* expressions include はい 'yes,' ええ 'yes,' うん 'yeah,' そう 'oh, yeah?', そうですか 'Is that so?', へえ 'wow,' そうですね 'that's right,' ほんとう(に) 'really,' それで 'so?', それから 'and then?' Examples are given below. (*Aizuchi* expressions are given in double parentheses.) In Japanese the hearer uses such *aizuchi* now and then at phrase-final and sentence-final positions. Phrase endings are often signaled by the particle 'ne.'

(1) [A male superior talking to his subordinate] ちょっと，明日，香港に飛ばなくちゃならないんでね，((はい)) この報告書ね，((はい)) あさってまでに完成しておいてくれないかね。((はい))
(lit. I have to fly to Hong Kong tomorrow ((yes)), so complete this report ((yes)) by the day after tomorrow, will you?)

(2) [A male speaker talking to his male friend] 暮れから正月の七日にかけてね，オーストラリアのシドニーに出かけてね，((へえ)) 真夏の太陽の下で，泳いできたんだ。((そう))
(lit. From the end of the year till January 7, I went to Sydney in Australia ((wow!)) I swam under the midsummer sunshine. ((oh, yeah?)))

(3) [A female speaker talking to her female friend] 昨日銀座を歩いていたらね，((うん)) 万里子を見かけたのよ。((ほんとに)) それで，声をかけたらね，((うん)) 知らん顔をしてそっぽ向いちゃったの。((ええ，ほんとう？))
(Yesterday when I was walking on the Ginza street ((yeah)) I saw Mariko ((really?)) So I called her. ((Yeah)) She pretended not to recognize me and looked the other way ((Oh, yeah?)))

(4) [A male superior to his subordinate] このごろとても忙しいだろう。

《そうですね》だから，息抜きに旅行をしたいと思って，交通公社に行ってみたんだけどね，《ええ》，切符がなかなか手に入らなかったんだ。《そうですか》，それで，結局は旅行をやめてしまったわけ。《そうなんですか》

(You know I've been terribly busy these days. ((right)) So, I wanted to make a trip for a change. And I went to a travel agent ((yes)), but I couldn't get the ticket easily. ((Is that right?)) So in the end I gave up the idea. ((Is that right?)))

It should be noted that in English *aizuchi* (typically 'uh-huh' or 'yeah') is seldom used. In fact, frequent use of *aizuchi* creates an impression that the hearer is not paying serious attention to what is being said. Not only verbally, but also nonverbally, the Japanese hearer nods very frequently to indicate his / her involvement with what the speaker has to say.

B. Fillers

While *aizuchi* is a strategy available for the hearer, a filler is a strategy available for the speaker.

First, the particle *ne* in (5) and (6) is a typical filler that indicates the speaker's attempt to involve the hearer. (5) is an example of informal speech, and (6) is an example of formal speech in which *ne* is preceded by *desu*. This use of *desu ne* is most commonly used in business Japanese.

(5) 昨日ね，トムが突然アメリカからやって来てね，僕の家に一晩泊まったんだよ。

(lit. Yesterday, y'know, Tom suddenly came here from the States, y'know, and stayed overnight at my house.)

(6) これがですね，先日お話ししておりました新しいソフトでして，もし，お時間がおありでしたらですね，試験的に，お使いくださるとありがたいんですが。

(This is the new software I mentioned the other day, and if you have time I'd appreciate it if you could use it on an experimental basis.)

However, too many *ne*'s in a single sentence makes the sentence very awkward, as shown in (7).

(7) ??? 僕はね，今日ね，成田空港にね，友達をね，迎えにね，車でね，行ったんだよ。
(??? Today, y'know, I, y'know, went to Narita Airport, y'know, by car, y'know, to pick up my friend, y'know.)

Secondly, the filler *anō* is used to signal the speaker's hesitation about saying something embarrassing, as in (8a). In (8b) *anō* is used to signal the speaker's search for the right word or phrase. Too many *anō*'s in a single sentence sounds very awkward as shown in (8c).

(8) a. A: どうしたんですか。
(What happened?)

B: あのう，財布を忘れてしまったんです。
(Uhh . . . , I forgot my wallet, you know.)

b. どこだっけ，あのう，昨日買って来た本は。
(Where is it? Eh . . . I mean the book I bought yesterday.)

c. *あのう，昨日，あのう，母が，あのう，京都からやって来て，あのう，久しぶりに，あのう，話して，あのう，帰りました。
(Ah, uh, yesterday, y'know, my mother, y'know, came from Kyoto, y'know, talked with me after a long while, y'know, and went home, y'know.)

Thirdly, the phrase '*nan to iu* X *deshita ka*' 'What was X called?' in (9) becomes '*nan te iu* X *datta kke*' in informal speech. The phrase can be used whenever the speaker has forgotten an exact name.

(9) 新宿に有名な本屋がありますね，何という本屋でしたか，ああそうだ，紀伊国屋だ。あそこで，日本の経済の本を四冊買いました。
(There is a famous bookstore in Shinjuku—what was the name? . . . Oh yeah, Kinokuniya. I bought four books on the Japanese economy there.)

Fourthly, the interjection *ēto* used in (10) is used when the speaker is trying to remember something. Just like the case of *anō*, too many *ēto*'s in a single sentence makes it very awkward.

(10) ロシア共産主義が崩壊したのは，ええと，1991年の十二月でした，たしか。

(The fall of Russian communism was, let's see, December of 1991, if I remember correctly.)

Fifthly, the phrase '*nan to ittara ii deshō* (*ka*)' in (11) and its informal equivalent '*nan to ittara ii ka na/ne*' are used when the speaker is looking for the right expression.

(11) 最近の世界的な思考傾向は，何と言ったらいいのでしょうか，ボーダーレスの思考なんですね。
(The recent tendency in world ideology is, how shall I put it? Borderless thinking.)

Sixthly, the interjection *mā* is used primarily to avoid making a definite statement, as shown below.

(12) a. A: この大学は学生数はどのぐらいですか。
(What's the student population at this college?)

B: まあ，一万五千人ぐらいでしょうか。
(Somewhere around 15,000, I suppose.)

b. A: 最近はお元気ですか。
(Have you been in good health lately?)

B: まあ，そうですね。
(I guess so.)

c. 日本食は，まあ，何でも食べますが，納豆だけはどうもにおいが強すぎて嫌いですね。
(I can eat practically all Japanese food, but *natto* (= fermented soybeans) has too strong a smell for me and I don't like it.)

C. Rephrasing

Just as native speakers of Japanese know how to rephrase words using other explanatory expressions when they cannot recall the most suitable words, intermediate learners of Japanese, too, should start to learn how to rephrase words they don't know or cannot remember. By doing so embarassing pauses can be avoided. A common way to rephrase a noun is by means of a noun modification, as shown in (13a, b).

(13) a. [The speaker A cannot remember / doesn't know the word *geta*, traditional footwear in Japan.]

A: ほら，日本人が着物を着る時履くものがあるでしょ。あれ，何て言ったかな。
(You know the stuff Japanese people put on when they wear kimono—what do they call it?)

B: ああ，下駄のことだね。
(Oh, you mean *geta*?)

b. [The speaker cannot remember / doesn't know the word *genkan*, Japanese version of a foyer.]

日本の家では，ああ，何と言ったかな，ほら，家に上がる前に靴を脱ぐところ，あそこは，面白いスペースですよね。
(In a Japanese house, ah, what do you call it? The place where people take off their shoes before entering the house, that's an interesting space, you know.)

When a word that needs rephrasing is a verb or an adjective, the speaker can rephrase it by using more basic words or phrases, as shown in (14a, b).

(14) a. [The speaker cannot remember / doesn't know the verb *hōsōsuru* 'to broadcast'.]

このFMクラシック番組は毎日同じ時間に放，放，あのう，聞けるんですか。
(Is this FM classic music program broad, broad, ah, can we hear it every day at the same time?)

b. [The speaker cannot remember / doesn't know the *na*-adjective *nihonteki*(*na*) 'Japan-like.']

あの女性は日本人，日本人，日本人らしい雰囲気がありますね。
(That lady has a Japanese, Japanese, Japanese-like atmosphere, doesn't she?)

When the speaker wants to get the word which he cannot remember / doesn't know, he can use ~ *koto* / *hito* / *yōsu*, etc. *o nan to iimasu ka*, as shown in (15a, b).

(15) a. [The speaker cannot remember / doesn't know the verb *nesugosu* 'oversleep'.]

A: 朝，予定より遅くまで寝ることを何と言いますか。
(What do you say when you sleep longer than you planned in the morning?)

B: 「寝過ごす」と言います。
(We say *nesugosu*.)

b. [The speaker cannot remember / doesn't know the adjective *gaikōteki* 'social'.]

A: 人と話すのが大好きで，どこへでも積極的に出かけて行く人のことを何と言いますか。
(What do you call a person who loves to talk with people and goes out willingly no matter where it is?)

B: 「外向的」と言います。
(We call it *gaikōteki*.)

D. Topic Shift and Topic Recovery

In any language the speaker cannot shift the topic of conversation abruptly; there are ways to signal a topic shift. Some of the most common Japanese ways to signal a topic shift are given below.

(16) a. ところで
(By the way)

b. 話は違いますが,
(lit. The story is different, but . . .)

c. ちょっと話がそれますが,
(lit. The story deviates a little bit, but . . .)

d. 話題が変わりますが,
(lit. The topic is going to change, but . . .)

e. Xと言えば / Xって(言えば)
(Speaking of X)

When the speaker wants to get back to the former topic, he can signal his desire to recover the old topic. Some of the standard ways to signal it are as follows:

(17) a. さっきXって言ったけどさ [highly informal]
(A while ago I / you said X, but)

b. さっきの話ですが / さっきのXの話ですが
(Let me get back to the topic / X that we were talking about a while ago.)

c. 先ほど申し上げたことですが [very formal, polite]
先ほどの件ですけど [formal, polite]
(Regarding what I told you a while ago)

E. Avoidance of Decisive Expressions

To a far greater degree Japanese language uses indecisive expressions especially when the speaker/writer expresses his own opinions. The strategy that Japanese native speakers use to make their statements less forceful and more humble is the use of an indirect expression at the end of the sentence. Suppose that the speaker/writer wants to state "Japanese people avoid using decisive expressions," he could say or write very straightforwardly as in (18) or indirectly as in (19) and (20).

(18) 日本人は断定を避ける(よ)。
(Japanese avoid using decisive expressions.)

(19) a. 日本人は断定を避けるの {では / じゃ} ありませんか。
(Isn't it the case that Japanese avoid using decisive expressions?)

b. 日本人は断定を避けるの {では / じゃ} ないでしょうか。
(I wonder if Japanese wouldn't avoid using decisive expressions.)

c. 日本人は断定を避けるの {では / じゃ} ないだろうか。
(I wonder if Japanese wouldn't avoid using decisive expressions.)

d. 日本人は断定を避けるの {では / じゃ} なかろうか。
(I wonder if Japanese wouldn't avoid using decisive expres-

sions.)

(20) a. 日本人は断定を避けると思います。
(I think that Japanese avoid using decisive expressions.)

b. 日本人は断定を避けると思います {が / けど}。
(I think that Japanese avoid using decisive expressions, but . . .)

c. 日本人は断定を避けるの {では / じゃ} ないかと思います。
(I wonder if Japanese wouldn't avoid using decisive expressions.)

d. 日本人は断定を避けるの {では / じゃ} ないかと思います {が / けど}。
(I wonder if Japanese wouldn't avoid using decisive expressions, but . . .)

e. 日本人は断定を避けるのではないかと思われます {が / けど}。
(It seems to me that Japanese will avoid using decisive expressions, but . . .)

f. 私には日本人は断定を避けるのではないかと思われるのですが，いかがなものでしょうか。
(It seems to me that Japanese will avoid using decisive expressions, but what would you say?)

In (19) and (20), in which the same core statement is made, the longer the sentence is, the less decisive the expression is / tends to be. When a Japanese speaker opposes what his superior has said his expression definitely has to avoid straightforward expressions. There are some set phrases that can be prefixed to the speaker's statement of an opposing view, as shown in (21).

(21) a. そうかなあ。[informal]
(Well, I doubt it. (lit. I wonder if that is so.))

b. それでもいい(です)けど。
(That's fine, too, but . . .)

c. それはそう {です / だ} けど。
(That's true, but . . .)

d. もちろんそうなん {です / だ} けどね。
(Of course it is true, but . . .)

e. 言っていることは分かるん {です / だ} けどね。
(I understand what you are saying, but . . .)

f. 反対している {のでは / んじゃ} ないんですが。
(I'm not disagreeing with you, but . . .)

g. 別に反対するつもりはないんですが。
(I don't have any particular intention to disagree with you, but . . .)

h. お言葉を返すようで何ですが… [highly formal and polite]
(lit. Sorry to return words to you, but . . .)

i. 確かにおっしゃる通りだとは思いますが，しかし… [formal, polite]
(What you have said is indeed correct, but . . .)

4. Toward Better Reading Comprehension: Analyzing Sentences Accurately

Reading comprehension involves a variety of mental processes, from understanding the meanings of words and grasping the structures of sentences to identifying the referents of pronouns and understanding inference. If the reader fails in these processes, correct interpretation cannot be attained. One of the most problematic areas here is sentence structure. This section provides aids to improve skills for accurate sentence structure analysis.

(1) Basics

A. Structure of Simple Sentences

Before tackling complex sentence structures, it is essential to understand the basic structure of Japanese sentences. First, let us consider the following sentence.

(1) 私(わたし)は昨晩(ゆうべ)友達(ともだち)のアパートでテレビを見(み)ていた。
(Last night I was watching TV in my friend's apartment.)

(1) is a simple sentence (i.e., a sentence with a single verbal). The structure of this sentence can be diagramed as follows.

(2)
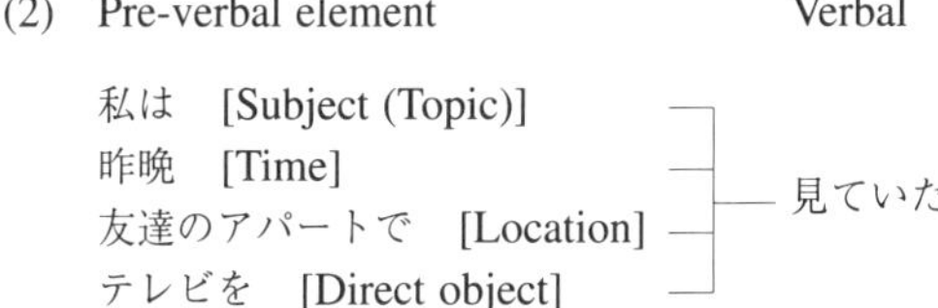

As (2) illustrates, Japanese simple sentences usually consist of a verbal and some pre-verbal elements. Complete sentences in Japanese must contain a verbal, and in some instances simple sentences have only verbals (e.g., imperative sentences). Thus, verbals are considered to be the "hub" of sentences. As a matter of fact, sentences are constructed in such a way that the verbals are modified by pre-verbal elements. The general structure of Japanese simple sentences is provided in (3).

(3) Sentence-initial element   Pre-verbal element   Verbal

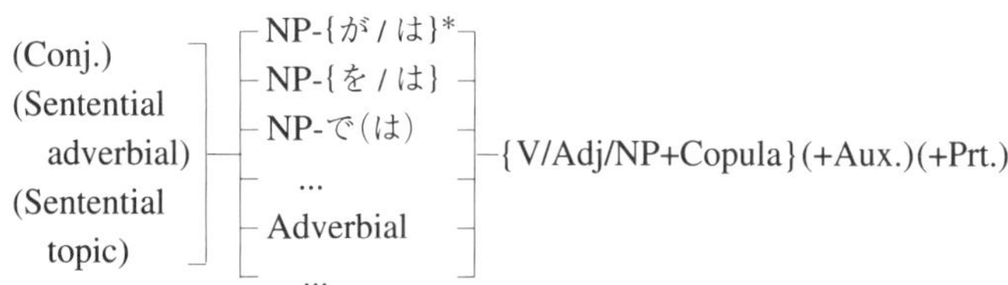

As (3) illustrates, a verbal is either a verb, an adjective, or a noun with a copula (e.g., *sensei da*) and sometimes involves other elements such as auxiliaries (e.g., (V*te*) *iru*) and/or sentence particles (e.g., *ka*, *yo*). A pre-verbal element is either an NP (i.e., noun or noun equivalent) with a particle(s) or an adverbial (i.e., adverb or adverb equivalent). Verbals indicate either an action or state while pre-verbal elements indicate such things as subject, direct object, time, location, and manner. Simple sentences sometimes contain sentence-initial elements such as sentence-initial conjunctions (e.g., *shikashi* 'but') and/or sentential adverbials (e.g., *omoshiroi koto ni* 'interestingly'). As seen later, more complex sentences, such as compound sentences and complex sentences, are composed of two or more simple sentences which have the basic structures shown in (3).

B. Key Elements

The key elements of sentences are verbals, NPs, pre-verbal adverbials, and sentence-initials.

1. *Verbals*

In sentence-final position various forms of verbs, adjectives, and NPs with a copula appear. They are sometimes followed by auxiliaries and/or sentence particles. (4) provides some examples.

---

*In terms of position, NP-(Prt.)-*wa* normally appears before other pre-verbal elements and sometimes even before a sentence-initial element. However, when NP-(Prt.)-*wa* is the sentence subject, direct object, etc., we consider this element to be pre-verbal rather than sentence-initial because, unlike other sentence-initial elements, NP-(Prt.)-*wa* modifies the verbal. (See 4.3. Sentential topic.)

(4) a. 彼は泣いた。
V
(He cried.)

b. 私も行き たい。
V Aux.
(I want to go, too.)

c. 安いです か。
Adj(*i*) Prt.
(Is (it) cheap?)

d. 便利な ようだ ね。
Adj(*na*) Aux. Prt.
(It seems convenient, doesn't it?)

e. 彼女は先生 だった そうだ。*
N Cop. Aux.
(I heard that she was a teacher.)

2. *NPs*

As seen in (3), NPs appear as either pre-verbal elements (with a particle) or verbal elements (with a copula). There are varieties of NP structures, as seen below. Long and complex sentences often include large NPs composed of NPs with different types of structures; therefore, understanding these structural variations is essential for accurate sentence structure analysis.

2.1. Nouns / Pronouns

Single nouns, pronouns, and compound nouns are in this category.

Examples:

(5) 本 (book); 山田さん (Mr. Yamada); 私 (I); これ (this); 入学試験制度 (entrance examination system)

---

*When certain auxiliaries follow an NP with a copula, the copula drops, as in (i).

(i) 彼女は先生 かも知れない。
N Aux.
(She might be a teacher.)

2.2. Pre-nominal element + Noun

There are several patterns in this category.

2.2.1. Demonstrative adjective + Noun

(6) この本 (this book); あの学生 (that student); こんな辞書 (such a dictionary; a dictionary like this)

2.2.2. Adjective + Noun

(7) 難しい宿題 (difficult homework); きれいなドレス (a pretty dress); 普通の家 (an ordinary house)*; 安くて便利なアパート(a cheap and convenient apartment)

2.2.3. Noun (+ Prt.) の Noun

(8) a. 東京の地下鉄
(the subway system in Tokyo)

b. 鈴木さんのお父さんの会社
(Mr. Suzuki's father's company)

c. 先生からの手紙
(a letter from my teacher)

d. 漢字，カタカナなどの問題
(problems such as kanji and katakana)

(⇨ ***no***[1] (DBJG: 312–15))

2.2.4. {Noun / Verb} + Compound particle (pre-nominal form) + Noun

(9) a. 日本語文法に関する論文
(a paper on Japanese grammar)

b. (この仕事を)するに当たっての注意
(precautions before doing (this job))

---

*There are a handful of adjectives that have prenominal forms ending with *no* rather than *i* (*i*-adjectives) or *na* (*na*-adjectives). More examples:

(i) 遠くの (distant); 近くの (nearby); 多くの (many); 一定の (constant); 最新の (the newest)

2.2.5. Relative clause + Noun*

(10) a. (これは)友子が作ったケーキ(だ。)
((This is) a cake which Tomoko made.)

b. 私の一番好きな作曲家(はベートーベンだ。)
(The composer that I like the most (is Beethoven.))
(⇨ **Relative Clause** (DBJG: 376–80))

2.2.6. Noun/Sentence という Noun

(11) a. 鈴木という学生
(a student named Suzuki)

b. 日本語はあいまいな言葉だという考え(は珍しくない。)**
(The idea that Japanese is an ambiguous language (is not uncommon.))
(⇨ ***~ to iu*** (DBJG: 486-87))

2.2.7. Sentence + Nominalizer

(12) a. 光子がピアノを弾いているの(を聞いた。)
((I heard) Mitsuko playing the piano.)
(⇨ ***no***[3] (DBJG: 318-22))

b. ジョーンズさんが今日来ること(を知らなかった。)
((I didn't know) that Mr. Jones was coming today.)
(⇨ ***koto*** (DBJG: 193–96))

---

*In Japanese, restrictive relative clauses and non-restrictive relative clauses are not distinguished by form. For example, the noun phrase in (i) is ambiguous.

(i) よく働く日本人
((1) the Japanese, who work hard; (2) Japanese people who work hard)
A proper context is necessary to make this phrase unambiguous.

**There are some variations of "S *to iu* N," as in (i).

(i) 日本語はあいまいな言葉だ {といった / というような / とかいう} 考え
(such ideas that Japanese is an ambiguous language)

2.3. Noun と Noun

Two or more nouns are connected with noun connecting particles such as *to* and *ya* to form a larger noun equivalent. A comma can also be used to connect nouns. Examples:

(13) a. 漢字とカタカナ(と)
(kanji and katakana)
(⇨ ***to***[1] (DBJG: 473–76))

b. 皿やナイフやフォーク(や)
(plates, knives, and forks (among others))
(⇨ ***ya*** (DBJG: 536–38))

c. 天ぷらとかさしみとか
(tempura, sashimi, and so on)

d. アメリカ，ドイツ，フランスなど
(America, Germany, France, etc.)

e. ペンか鉛筆(か)
(a pen or a pencil)

f. 日本語，韓国語，または中国語
(Japanese, Korean, or Chinese)

2.4. Embedded interrogative sentences

An interrogative sentence embedded in another sentence is a noun equivalent, as in (14).

(14) a. 誰がそれをするか(が問題だ。)
(Who will do that (is the question.))

b. 読書がいかに大切か(を教える必要がある。)
((It is necessary to teach) how important reading is.)

3. *Pre-verbal adverbials*

There are several kinds of words and phrases which function as pre-verbal adverbials.*

3.1. Adverbs / Adverbial nouns

(15) ゆっくり (slowly); 今日 (today)

3.2. Adverbial forms of adjectives

(16) 早く (quickly); 静かに (quietly)

3.3. Adverbial forms of auxiliary adjectives

(17) 分かりやすく (in an easy-to-understand fashion); 悲しそうに (sadly)

3.4. Quantifiers

(18) a. たくさん(食べる)
((eat) a lot)

b. (ビールを)三本(飲む)
((drink) three (beers))

3.5. Phonomimes, phenomimes, and psychomimes

(19) a. (犬が)ワンワン(鳴く)
((a dog) bowwows)

b. (日本語を)すらすら(読む)
((read Japanese) easily)

c. おどおど(する)
((be) nervous)

3.6. Quotation + と**

(20) a. 「おはよう」と(言う)
((say) "Good morning")

---

*The contrastive *wa* may be affixed to pre-verbal adverbials.

**A quotation can be a complete sentence or part of a sentence.

b. 難しいと(思う)
((think) that s.t. is difficult)

(⇨ ***to***[3] (DBJG: 478–80))

3.7. Noun / Verb + Compound particle (pre-verbal form)

(21) a. 日本の文化について(話す)
((talk) about Japanese culture)

b. (年を)とるにつれて(記憶力が衰える。)
(As one grows old, (one's memory fails.))

3.8. V*te*

(22) 歩いて (on foot); 急いで (hurriedly)

(⇨ ***-te*** (DBJG: 464–67))

3.9. V*masu* + に

(23) (友達に)会いに(来た)
((came) to see (s.o.'s friend))

(⇨ ***ni***[5] (DBJG: 297–99))

4. *Sentence-initial elements*

Sentence-initial elements modify the clause which follows. They include sentence-initial conjunctions, sentence adverbials, sentential topics, and sentence-initial clauses. Sentence-initial clauses are elements of complex sentences. (See E. Complex Sentences.)

4.1. Sentence-initial conjunctions

Some conjunctions appear in the sentence-initial position.

(24) a. 確かにこれは難問だ。**しかし**，解決策はあるはずだ。
(This is truly a difficult problem. But there should be a way to solve it.)

b. その仕事は私一人でするには大きすぎた。**そこで**，何人かの友達に応援を頼んだ。
(That job was too big for me to do by myself, so I asked for help from some of my friends.)

4.2. Sentence adverbials

Sentence adverbials are usually phrases, as seen in (25).

(25) a. **面白いことに**，上級のクラスの方が出来が悪かった。
(Interestingly, the advanced class did a poorer job.)

b. **うかつにも**，カメラを持って来るのを忘れた。
(It was stupid that I forgot to bring my camera.)

4.3. Sentential topics

Unlike the pre-verbal NP-(Prt.) marked by *wa*, sentential topics modify the entire sentence which follows.

(26) a. **京子は**父親が弁護士をしている。
(Speaking of Kyoko, her father practices law.)

b. **この問題に関しては**，これ以上議論しても無駄だ。
(With regard to this problem, it is no use to discuss it further.)

4.4. Sentence-initial dependent clauses

Sentence-initial dependent clauses are internal sentences which are dependent on the clauses which follow. Sentence-initial dependent clauses represent such things as condition, time, reason, purpose, and manner. (27) provides examples.

(27) a. **小林さんが来たら**知らせて下さい。
(Please let me know if Mr. Kobayashi comes in.)

b. **私がそこにいた時には**異常はなかった。
(There was nothing unusual when I was there.)

c. **友達が訪ねて来るので**うちを空けるわけにいかない。
(Because a friend of mine is coming to see me, I cannot leave my house.)

d. 私は**日本に留学するために**日本語を勉強しています。
(I'm studying Japanese in order to study in Japan.)

If a sentence-initial dependent clause and the following clause have a common element, the element usually appears only once. In (27d), for example, the sentence-initial dependent clause and the following clause (in this case, the main clause) share the same subject *watashi* 'I.' Thus, *watashi* appears only once (in this case, as the topic).

C. Verbal Connective Forms

When two verbals are connected through an "AND-relation" in a sentence, the first verbal must be in the connective form, as in (28).*

(28) a. 私は朝六時に**起き**，夜十時ごろ寝る。
(I get up at six in the morning and go to bed around ten in the evening.)

b. この辞書は**安くて**便利だ。
(This dictionary is cheap and useful.)

c. 吉田さんは三十二歳**で**独身です。
(Mr. Yoshida is thirty-two and single.)

The affirmative and negative connective forms of different verbals are given in (29) and (30), respectively.**

(29) Affirmative connective forms:

a. Verb: V*te* (e.g., 起きて); V*masu* (e.g., 起き)

---

*If two verbals are connected through a "BUT-relation," the connective forms are not used, as in (i).

(i) a. 私は魚は好きですが野菜は好きじゃありません。
(I like fish but I don't like vegetables.)

b. この辞書は安いけれどもなかなか便利だ。
(This dictionary is cheap but pretty useful.)

As seen in (29), there are two kinds of connective forms. In general, the first kind (i.e., *te*-forms) are used when the first verbal is strongly related to or dependent on the second verbal. In (i), for example, the first verbal *yasukute* '(it is) cheap' gives the reason why the speaker feels that the apartment is good (the second verbal). In this case, the *te*-form is used. (⇨ **V*masu*)

(i) このアパートは {安くて / *安く} いい。
(This apartment is cheap and (therefore) good.)

b. Adj(*i*): Adj(*i*)*te* (e.g., 安くて); Adj(*i*)stem + く (e.g., 安く)

c. Adj(*na*): Adj(*na*)*te* (e.g., 便利で); Adj(*na*)*te* + あり (e.g., 便利であり)

d. N + Cop.: N + Cop.*te* (e.g., 学生で); N + Cop.*te* + あり (e.g., 学生であり)

(30) Negative connective forms:

a. Verb (neg.): Vneg なくて (e.g., 行かなくて); Vneg {ないで / ず} (e.g., 行かないで; 行かず)

(⇨ ***~ nai de*** (DBJG: 271–73))

b. Adj(*i*) (neg.): Adj(*i*)stem くなく(て) (e.g., 高(たか)くなく(て))

c. Adj(*na*) (neg.): Adj(*na*)stem で(は)なく(て) (e.g., 便利で(は)なく(て))

d. N + Cop. (neg.): N で(は)なく(て) (e.g., 学生で(は)なく(て))

D. Compound Sentences

If a sentence involves two (or more) simple sentences (i.e., clauses) and these sentences are conjoined by means of coordinate conjunctions such as *ga* 'but' or continuative forms of verbs, adjectives or the copula such as V*te*, Adj.*te* and Cop.*te* to mean 'and,' the whole is called a "compound sentence." The clauses in a compound sentence are connected through the AND-relation or the BUT-relation. (31) provides examples.

(31) a. ワンさんは中国人(ちゅうごくじん)でキムさんは韓国人(かんこくじん)だ。
(Mr. Wong is Chinese and Mr. Kim is Korean.)

b. 家内(かない)はフランス語を話せるが私は話せない。
(My wife can speak French but I cannot.)

When the clauses in a compound sentence have an element in common (e.g., the subject, the direct object, the verbal), the element usually appears only once. For example, in (28a-c) the subjects are shared and in (31b) the direct object is shared. (32) provides an example of a shared verbal.

(32) ジョンは機械工学を，ナンシーは電気工学を専攻している。
(John is majoring in mechanical engineering and Nancy in electrical engineering.)

The structures of compound sentences can be generalized as in (33). ([S] represents a clause.)

(33) a. AND-relation:
[S_1]–[S_2] ([S_1] ends with a verbal continuative form.)

b. BUT-relation:
[S_1]–"BUT-conj."–[S_2] ("BUT conj." is a non-sentence initial conjunction such as *ga*.)

E. Complex Sentences

If a sentence involves a clause which is dependent on another element or clause in the sentence, the sentence is called a "complex sentence." (34) provides complex sentences which include different kinds of dependent clauses (or subordinate clauses).

(34) a. Relative clauses (See 2.2.5. Relative clause + Noun):

これは友子が作ったケーキだ。 (= (10a))
(This is a cake which Tomoko made.)

b. Internal sentences before "という Noun" (See 2.2.6. Noun/Sentence という Noun):

日本語はあいまいな言葉だという考えは珍しくない。 (= (11b))
(The idea that Japanese is an ambiguous language is not uncommon.)

c. Internal sentences before Compound particles (pre-nominal form) (See 2.2.4. {Noun/Verb} + Compound particle (pre-nominal form) + Noun):

ここにこの仕事をするに当たっての注意が書いてある。
(Precautions for doing this job are written here.)

d. Nominalized sentences (See 2.2.7. Sentence + Nominalizer):

ジョーンズさんが今日来ることを知らなかった。(= (12b))
(I didn't know that Mr. Jones was coming today.)

e. Embedded interrogative sentences (See 2.4. Embedded interrogative sentences):

誰がそれをするかが問題だ。 (= (14a))
(Who will do that is the question.)

f. Clauses before adverbial forms of auxiliary adjectives*
(See 3.3. Adverbial forms of auxiliary adjectives):

みんながよく聞こえるように，マイクを使って下さい。
(Please use a microphone so that everybody can hear well.)

g. Internal sentences as indirect quotations (See 3.6. Quotation と):

ジョージは漢字は難しくないと言っている。
(George says that kanji are not difficult.)

h. Internal sentences before compound particles (pre-verbal form)
(See 3.7. Noun/Verb + Compound particle (pre-verbal form)):

人は年をとるにつれて記憶力が衰える。
(One's memory fails as one grows old.)

i. Sentence-initial dependent clauses (See 4.4. Sentence-initial dependent clauses):

質問されてもだまっていて下さい。
(Please remain silent even if you are asked questions.)

The structures of complex sentences can be generalized as in (35).

*The adverbial forms of auxiliary adjectives preceded by clauses are sometimes classified as conjunctions (e.g., *yōni*).

(35) Sentence-initial element | Pre-verbal element | Verbal

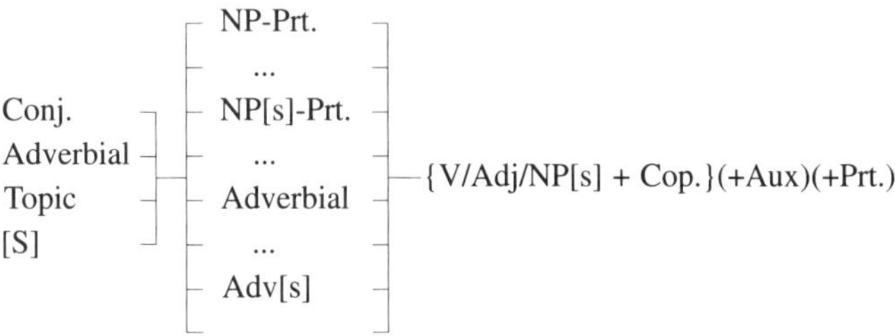

[S]: Clause
NP[s]: NP containing [S]
Adv[s]: Adverbial containing [S]

That is, a sentence which contains at least one of the elements containing [S] in (35) is a complex sentence.

F. Missing Elements

Such sentence elements as illustrated in (35) are not always explicitly present. In fact, sentence element ellipsis is very common in Japanese. When clauses have shared elements (e.g., subjects), the shared element is usually ellipted in the second (and following) clause(s). Sentence elements are also dropped when they have been mentioned in a previous sentence, are contextually known, or situationally known, or when they indicate a generic agent such as "they" and "we." (36) provides examples.

(36) a. Shared by two clauses:

沢田(さわだ)さんがそのことを聞いても[そのことを][彼に]教えないで下さい。

(Even if Mr. Sawada asks about that, please do not tell [him] [about it].)

b. Mentioned in a previous sentence:

昨日ステーキを食べた。[それは]とてもおいしかった。
(I had a steak yesterday. [It] was very good.)

c. Contextually known:

ジェーンが [私に]ホームメードのクッキーをくれた。
(Jane gave [me] some home-made cookies.)

d. Situationally known:

Watching the hearer eating ice cream:
[それは]おいしいですか。
(Is [it] good?)

e. Indicating a generic agent:

[我々(われわれ)は]地球(ちきゅう)を守(まも)るために環境(かんきょう)を破壊(はかい)しないエネルギー源(げん)を開発(かいはつ)しなければならない。
(In order to protect the earth, [we] must develop a new energy source which does not destroy the environment.)

(2) Guidelines

With the basics of Japanese sentence structure presented above, the reader should be able to grasp the structure of a given sentence by following the guidelines illustrated below.

Guideline 1: Identify major clause breaks.

Major clause breaks can be identified by looking for verbal connective forms (See (1) C. Verbal Connective Forms), conjunctions such as *ga* 'but,' *ba* 'if,' *to* 'if; when,' *kara* 'because,' and *node* 'because,' and other conjunction equivalents such as *ni mo kakawarazu* 'in spite of the fact that,' *tame ni* 'in order to; because,' and *no ni taishite* 'while; whereas.'

In the following examples, clause breaks are marked by "//"

(37) 英国(えいこく)の天文学者(てんもんがくしゃ)グループが，太陽系以外(たいようけいいがい)で初(はじ)めて惑星(わくせい)を発見(はっけん)したと，昨年(さくねん)七月の英科学誌(えいかがくし)『ネイチャー』で発表(はっぴょう)したが，//これは計算(けいさん)ミスで，//惑星は存在(そんざい)しないことが分(わ)かった。
(朝日新聞(あさひしんぶん)1. 6. 92 夕刊(ゆうかん))

Vocabulary notes:

英国	Great Britain
天文学者	astronomer
太陽系	the solar system
～以外で	other than ~
惑星	planet
発見する	to discover
科学誌	science journal
発表する	to announce
計算ミス	miscalculation
存在する	to exist

(38) …プラネットBは一年余飛行して，*//97年十月，火星周回軌道に到着し，//二年以上にわたり，観測を続ける予定だ。

(日本経済新聞12. 21. 91 朝刊)

Vocabulary notes:

プラネットB	"Planet B"
～余	a little more than ~
飛行する	to fly
火星	Mars
周回軌道	circling orbit
到着する	to arrive
～にわたり	over
観測	observation
続ける	to continue
予定	schedule

(39) 一方，オプトエレクトロニクスのこれまでの進展を顧みると，//光ファ

---

*The connective form V*te* with the preceding NP(s) often functions as an adverbial to represent manner or reason. In this case, V*te* does not mark a clause break. In (i), for example, ~ *o mochiite* is better interpreted as 'by using . . .' than as 'use . . . and,' as the English equivalent shows. Compare this V*te* with the V*te* in (38).

(i) 従来の情報伝送，処理は，電波や電子を用いて行ってきた。

（島田・土田『入門オプトエレクトロニクス』p. 19）

(The conventional information transmission and processing have been performed (lit. we have performed . . .) by using electric waves and electrons.)

イバー通信(つうしん)が大(おお)きな推進力(すいしんりょく)になってきたと言(い)える。
(島田・土田『入門(にゅうもん)オプトエレクトロニクス』p. 19)

Vocabulary notes:
一方　on the other hand
オプトエレクトロニクス　opto-electronics
これまで　up to now
進展　progress
顧みる　to look back; to examine
光ファイバー通信　optic fiber communication
推進力　thrust

Guideline 2: Identify the skeleton of each clause.

For each clause, identify the skeleton, i.e., the major elements, such as the subject, the direct object, and the verbal, elements which tell "who did what," "what is what," etc. Note that major elements are sometimes shared with another clause or are not present explicitly (See (1) F. Missing Elements).

In the following examples, the major elements are underlined and missing elements are supplied in parentheses. (Dotted underlining indicates elements to be examined in the following step, Guideline 3. These elements include constructions such as "NP[S]-Prt. + Verbal" (e.g., [S] *koto ga wakatta* 'it was understood that [S]'), "Adv[S] + Verbal" (e.g., [S] *to ieru* 'it can be said that [S]'), and "NP[S] + Cop." (e.g., [S] *yotei da* 'it is scheduled that [S]'))

(40) 英国の天文学者グループが，太陽系以外で初めて惑星を発見したと，昨年七月の英科学誌『ネイチャー』で発表したが，//これは 計算ミスで，//惑星は存在しない ことが分かった。(= (37))

(41) …プラネットBは一年余飛行して，//(プラネットBは)97年十月，火星周回軌道に到着し，//(プラネットBは)二年以上にわたり，観測を 続ける予定だ。(= (38))

(42) 一方，(我々が)オプトエレクトロニクスのこれまでの進展を 顧みると，//光ファイバー通信が大きな推進力になってきたと言える。(= (39))

By identifying the skeleton of each clause in a sentence, the idea of the whole sentence becomes clear. For example, (40) conveys the idea that "a British astronomy group announced something, but it was a miscalculation and a/the planet does not exist."

It should be noted that in identifying major elements, the entire NP or verbal does not need to be examined. For example, if an NP contains a long relative clause, examining the head noun should be enough at this stage. The important thing in this step is to grasp a rough idea of each clause identified in the previous step.

Guideline 3: Identify the scope of key elements, including conjunctions, nouns, nominalizers, quotative markers, and auxiliaries.

The scope of an element X is defined as the range of a sentence part which is dependent on X. (See DBJG, Appendix 8 Improving Reading Skill by Identifying an 'Extended Sentential Unit.')

In the following examples, the key elements to be identified and examined are set off by boxes. "[ ]" identifies the scope of the boxed element which follows.

(43) 英国の天文学者グループが，[太陽系以外で初めて惑星を発見した] と，昨年七月の英科学誌『ネイチャー』で発表したが，//これは計算ミスで，//[惑星は存在しない] こと*が分かった。(= (37))

(A British astronomy group announced in last July's issue of *Nature*, a British science journal, that [they had for the first time discovered a planet outside the solar system,] but this was due to a miscalculation (lit. this was a miscalculation) and it turned out that [the planet does not exist.])

(44) …プラネットBは[一年余飛行して，//(プラネットBは) 97年十月，火星周回軌道に到着し，//(プラネットBは) 二年以上にわたり，観測を続ける] 予定だ。(= (38))

(Planet B is scheduled [to travel for a little more than a year, reach Mars' circling orbit in October 1997, and continue its observation for over two years.])

It should be noted that in this example, the scope of *yotei* 'schedule' extends beyond the immediate clause break.

*In (43), the scope of *koto* can extend from "*wakusei wa*" or from "*kore wa*."

(45) ［一方，(我々が)オプトエレクトロニクスのこれまでの進展を顧みる］ と，// ［光ファイバー通信が大きな推進力になってきた］ と言える。(= (39))
(When [we examine the progress in opto-electronics up to the present, on the other hand,] we can say that [optic fiber communication has been a major thrust (in terms of progress).])

(46) 社長が出席できないから //［明日の会議は中止になり］ そうだ。
(Because our president cannot attend, it looks like [tomorrow's meeting will be cancelled.])

(47) 1992年の東京モーターショーでは，［[3] 低燃費エンジンや［[2] ［[1] ガソリンに代わる］［[1] 新しい］ エネルギー [1]*を利用した］ エンジン [2]を搭載した］ 車 [3]が多数出展された。**
(In the Tokyo Motor Show in 1992, many autos[3] were exhibited [which contain (lit. mounted) fuel-efficient engines and engines[2] [which utilized new energy[1] [to replace gasoline.][1]][2]][3])

Guideline 4: Identify the modifying and modified elements accurately when an NP contains an ambiguous modification relationship.

(48) provides examples of NPs which contain ambiguous modification relationships.

(48) a. {S / Adj / N_1の} N_2 の N_3

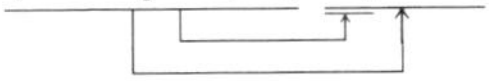

b. {S / Adj / N_1の} N_2 と N_3

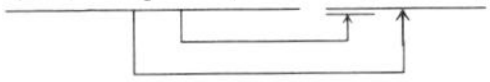

c. N_1 と N_2 の N_3

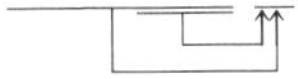

*Here, *Energī* 'energy' has a double modifier.

**When a structure is complex, using scope identification numbers may be helpful, as in (47).

(48a) is ambiguous because {S / Adj / N_1 *no*} can modify either N_2 or "N_2 *no* N_3." (48b) is ambiguous because {S / Adj / N_1 *no*} can modify only N_2 or it can modify both N_2 and N_3. (48c) is ambiguous because N_3 can be modified either by "N_2 *no*" or by "N_1 *to* N_2 *no*." In these cases, the ambiguity can be resolved either by context or by the reader's knowledge of the world. (49) provides examples of the situation in (48a).

(49) a. 難(むずか)しい 日本語(にほんご)の 宿題(しゅくだい)
X Y Z

((1) difficult homework in Japanese [X modifies "Y の Z," i.e., X [Y の Z]]; (2) homework in Japanese, a language which is difficult [X modifies Y and "X Y の" modifies Z, i.e., X [Y] の [Z]])

b. 京都(きょうと)にある Y高校(こうこう)の 分校(ぶんこう)
X Y Z

((1) Y High School's branch campus which is in Kyoto [X modifies "Y の Z," i.e., X [Y の Z]]; (2) A branch campus of Y High School, which is in Kyoto [X modifies Y and "X Y の" modifies Z, i.e., X [Y] の [Z]])

The interpretation of (49a) depends on the context and the interpretation of (49b) depends of the reader's knowledge of Y High School's location.

The ambiguity in (48b) can be illustrated by (50).

(50) 新材料(しんざいりょう)の 開発(かいはつ)と マーケティング
X Y Z

((1) the development of new materials and the marketing of those materials [X modifies Y and Z, i.e., X [Y と Z]]; (2) the development of new materials (for something) and the marketing (of that thing) [X modifies only Y, i.e., X [Y] と Z])

Whether (50) is interpreted as (1) or (2) depends on the context in which this sentence is used.

(51) provides examples of (48c).

(51) a. 洋一と 加代子の 子供
X Y Z

((1) Yoichi's and Kayoko's child [X and Y modify Z, i.e., X と Y の [Z]]; (2) Yoichi and Kayoko's child [Only Y modifies Z, i.e., X と Y の [Z]])

b. P社と Q社 の 合弁会社
X Y Z

((1) a joint corporation consisting of P Corporation and Q Corporation [X and Y modify Z, i.e., X とY の [Z]]; (2) P Corporation and a joint corporation including Q Corporation [Only Y modifies Z, i.e., X とY の [Z]])

Once again, whether (51a) is interpreted as (1) or (2) depends on the context in which this phrase is used. There is little ambiguity in (51b), on the other hand. This is because a joint corporation constituting two or more companies is common knowledge; therefore, (1) is the likely interpretation.

Guideline 5: Accurately identify each element's modified constituents.

Particularly important is whether an element modifies a noun or a verbal. As an example, an explanation of modification in (52) is shown in (53).

(52) このソフトウェアによって文書の作成に必要な基本の操作を覚えて下さい。

(53)

A	modifies B
このソフトウェアによって (by means of this software)	覚えて下さい (please learn)
文書の作成に (for the creation of documents)	必要な (necessary)
必要な (necessary)	基本の操作 (basic operation)
基本の操作を (basic operation [Direct Object])	覚えて下さい (please learn)

Note here that *ni yotte* is a form which modifies verbs; thus, in (52), it modifies *oboete kudasai*. (See Appendix 3 Compound Particles.)

(54) indicates the scope of *sōsa* and (55) provides the English equivalent of (52).

(54) このソフトウェアによって［文書の作成に必要な基本の］操作を覚えて下さい。

(55) With this software, please learn the basic operation necessary for creating documents.

Compare (52) with (56), where *sofutowea* is followed by *ni yoru* rather than *ni yotte*. (57) illustrates the modification relations among the sentence elements.

(56) このソフトウェアによる文書の作成に必要な基本の操作を覚えて下さい。

(57)

A	modifies B
このソフトウェアによる (by means of this software)	文書の作成 (creation of documents)
文書の作成に (for the creation of documents)	必要な (necessary)
必要な (necessary)	基本の操作 (basic operation)
基本の操作を (basic operation [Direct Object])	覚えて下さい (please learn)

Note here that *ni yoru* is a form which modifies nouns (or noun phrases); thus, in (56), it modifies *bunsho no sakusei*.

(58) indicates the scope of *sōsa* and (59) provides the English equivalent of (56).

(58) ［このソフトウェアによる文書の作成に必要な基本の］操作を覚えて下さい。

(59) Please learn the basic operation necessary for creating documents with this software.

As shown in the above examples, misunderstanding a modified element can lead to an entirely wrong interpretation.

A DICTIONARY OF INTERMEDIATE JAPANESE GRAMMAR

(Main Entries)

Seiichi Makino and Michio Tsutsui

日本語文法辞典〈中級編〉

amari あまり *conj.* <w>

a conjunction which marks a cause that involves excessive action

because of too much ~; because ~ too much; so ~ that ~
【REL. *sugiru*】

◆Key Sentences

(A)

	Noun			
私はその晩	**興奮**	の	あまり	寝られなかった。
(I was so excited that I couldn't sleep that night.)				

(B)

Topic	Subordinate Clause			Main Clause
		Vinf		
この教科書は	文法を	**重視する**	あまり	面白くないものになってしまった。
(This textbook has turned out to be an uninteresting one because it stressed grammar too much.)				

Formation

(i) N のあまり

心配のあまり (because of too much anxiety)

(ii) Vinf あまり

用心するあまり (s.o. is so cautious that)

Examples

(a) 秋子は恐怖のあまり声も出なかった。
(Akiko was so frightened that she couldn't even make a sound.)

(b) 私は喜びのあまり思わず隣の人に抱きついてしまった。
(I was so happy that I hugged the person beside me without thinking.)

(c) 日本の英語教育は文法が強調されるあまり会話力の養成が疎かになっているようだ。
(As for English education in Japan, it seems that because grammar is emphasized too much, the development of conversational skills is neglected.)

(d) 今度の会合は形式を重んずるあまり内容が乏しくなってしまった。
(The last meeting ended up having little content because it focused too much on formalities.)

Notes

1. Clauses and phrases involving the conjunction *amari* can be rephrased using the adverb *amari* and the conjunction *node* or *tame ni*, as in (1).

 (1) a. 私はその晩**あまり**興奮した {**ので** / **ために**} 寝られなかった。(=KS(A))

  b. この教科書は**あまり**文法を重視した {**ので** / **ために**} 面白くないものになってしまった。(=KS(B))

(⇨ ***amari*** (DBJG: 72–73))

2. Adj(*i*) and Adj(*na*) cannot precede *amari*, as seen in (2) and (3).

 (2) 私は {**悲しみの** / ***悲しい**} あまり涙も出なかった。
 (I was so sad that I couldn't even cry (lit. even tears didn't come out).)

 (3) 彼らは {**心配の** / ***心配な**} あまり食事も喉を通らない様子だった。
 (It looked like they were so anxious that they couldn't even eat (lit. even foods didn't go through their throats).)

3. Vinf can be either past or nonpast when it represents a past action or event, as in (4), although the nonpast form is more common.

 (4) この教科書は文法を重視した**あまり**面白くないものになってしまった。(=KS(B))

【Related Expression】

The auxiliary verb *sugiru* expresses a similar idea. For example, KS(A) and (B) can be rephrased using *sugiru*, as in [1].

[1] a. 私はその晩興奮 {**のあまり** / **しすぎて**} 寝られなかった。(=KS(A))

b. この教科書は文法を重視 {**するあまり** / **しすぎて**} 面白くないものになってしまった。(=KS(B))

However, there are some differences between *amari* and *sugiru*. First, *amari* is always a part of an adverbial clause or phrase which expresses a cause. *Sugiru*, however, does not always express cause and can be in the predicate of a main clause. Second, *amari* is used only when the verb or noun represents a psychological action or state. Thus, the following sentences are unacceptable.

[2] *昨日ビールを**飲むあまり**今日頭が痛い。
(Yesterday I drank too much beer and I have a headache today.)

cf. 昨日あまりビールを**飲んだ** {**ので** / **ために**} 今日頭が痛い。

[3] ***疲れのあまり**食欲がない。
(I am so tired that I have no appetite.)

Third, *sugiru* is used in both spoken and written Japanese while *amari* is limited in use to formal written Japanese.

(⇨ ***sugiru*** (DBJG: 423–25))

B

~ ba ~ hodo　～ば～ほど　*str.*

a structure indicating that s.t. happens in proportion to the increase of extent / degree of action or state

the ~, the ~
【REL. ***hodo***】

◆Key Sentences

(A)

Topic	Sentence$_1$	Sentence$_2$
日本語(にほんご)は	**勉強(べんきょう)すれ**ば(**勉強**)**する**ほど	面白(おもしろ)くなります。
(The harder you study Japanese, the more interesting it will become.)		

(B)

Topic	Sentence$_1$	Sentence$_2$
パーティーは	人(ひと)が**多(おお)けれ**ば**多い**ほど	楽(たの)しい。
(At a party the more the merrier.)		

(C)

Topic	Sentence$_1$	Sentence$_2$
機械(きかい)は	**簡単(かんたん)**｛**であれ**ば**ある** / なら**簡単な**｝ほど	壊(こわ)れにくい。
(A machine is harder to break, the simpler it is.)		

Formation

(i) V_1cond V_2inf·nonpast ほど　(where $V_1=V_2$)

話(はな)せば話すほど　(the more s.o. talks, the more ~)

(ii) Adj(i)$_1$cond Adj(i)$_2$inf·nonpast ほど　(where Adj(i)$_1$=Adj(i)$_2$)

高ければ高いほど (the more expensive s.t. is, the more ~)

(iii) Adj(*na*)$_1$stem {であればある / なら Adj(*na*)$_2$stem な} ほど
(where Adj(*na*)$_1$=Adj(*na*)$_2$)

{静かであればある / 静かなら静かな} ほど (the quieter s.t. / s.o. is, the more ~)

Examples

(a) この酒は飲めば飲むほどおいしくなります。
(The more you drink this sake, the tastier it becomes.)

(b) 大学はよければよいほど入るのが難しいです。
(The better the university, the harder it is to get in.)

(c) アパートは駅に近ければ近いほど (家賃が) 高い。
(The closer apartments are to the station, the more expensive they are (to rent).)

(d) 普段元気なら元気なほど体に気を付けた方がいいですよ。
(The healthier you are, the more careful you should be about your health.)

Notes

1. The construction of ~ *ba* ~ *hodo* is very close in meaning to *the more ~, the more ~* construction in English.

2. Other conditionals *tara* and *to* cannot be used in this construction. Thus, the following use of *to* and *tara* are ungrammatical.

   (1) 授業料は {**安ければ** / ***安いと**} 安いほどいい。
   (As for the tuition, the cheaper the better.)

   (2) 玄米は {**かめば** / ***かんだら**} かむほど味が出る。
   (As for brown rice, the more you chew it, the tastier it becomes.)

3. When the verb is a *suru*-verb as in KS(A), it takes the form of either N-*sureba* N-*suru hodo* or N-*sureba suru hodo* as in KS(A). If the verb is not a *suru*-verb as in Ex.(a), it always takes the form of Vcond Vinf·nonpast *hodo*.

B

4. The conditional form *nara* is used only with Adj(*na*). So, the following sentences are ungrammatical.

   (3) *この酒は飲む**なら**飲むほどおいしくなる。(cf. Ex.(a))

   (4) *アパートは駅に近い**なら**近いほど（家賃が）高い。(cf. Ex.(c))

~ bakari ka ~ (sae) ～ばかりか～（さえ） *comp. prt. / conj.*

a compound particle / conjunction which is used to connect two nouns or two sentences, the first of which is s.t. normally expected and the second of which is s.t. normally unexpected

not only ~ but also
【REL. ~ *bakari de* (*wa*) *naku* ~ (*mo*); ~ *dake de* (*wa*) *naku* ~ (*mo*); *dokoroka*】

◆Key Sentences

(A)

Topic	Noun		Noun		
日本では	**子供**	ばかりか	**大人**	さえ	漫画を読(よ)んでいる。
(In Japan not only children but even adults are reading comic books.)					

(B)

Topic	Sentence_1		Sentence_2
あの人は	**絵を見て楽しむ**	ばかりか,	**自分でも絵を描く。**
(He not only enjoys looking at pictures; he also draws them.)			

Formation

(i) {V / Adj(*i*)}inf ばかりか

{話す / 話した} ばかりか (not only does / did s.o. speak)

{高い / 高かった} ばかりか (not only {is / was} s.t. high)

(ii) Adj(*na*)stem {な / だった} ばかりか

{静かな / 静かだった} ばかりか (not only {is / was} s.t. / s.o. quiet)

(iii) {N / N だった} ばかりか

{先生 / 先生だった} ばかりか (not only {is / was} s.o. a teacher)

Examples

(a) アメリカでは大学生ばかりか，中学生，高校生さえ日本語を勉強している。
(In America not only college students but even junior and senior high school students are studying Japanese.)

(b) 僕の寮の部屋は狭いばかりか，窓さえないんです。
(My room in the dorm is not just small; it doesn't even have a window.)

(c) トムは漢字が読めないばかりか，平仮名さえ読めない。
(It's not just kanji that Tom cannot read; he cannot read even hiragana.)

(d) 父は食べるのが大好きなばかりか，料理をするのも大好きです。
(My father not only loves to eat, he also loves to cook.)

Notes

1. Before *bakari ka* comes s.t. / s.o. normally expected and after *bakari ka* comes s.t. / s.o. normally unexpected. If the order of the two is reversed an unacceptable sentence like the following results.

    (1) *トムは平仮名が読めないばかりか，漢字さえ読めない。
    (cf. Ex.(c))

2. The particle *sae* can be replaced by the particle *mo* esp. in spoken Japanese.

(2) 僕の寮の部屋は狭いばかりか，窓**も**ないんです。(cf. Ex.(b))

(3) トムは漢字が読めないばかりか，平仮名**も**読めない。
(cf. Ex.(c))

【Related Expressions】

I. The phrases *bakari de* (*wa*) *naku* ~ (*mo*) and *dake de* (*wa*) *naku* ~ (*mo*) are very similar to *bakari ka* ~ (*sae*). Among those three constructions *bakari ka* ~ (*sae*) expresses the highest degree of unexpectedness between the content of S_1 and S_2. If such unexpectedness is missing, the *bakari ka* ~ (*sae*) construction sounds awkward. Examples follow.

[1] a. あの人は勉強 {**だけ / ばかり**} **で**(**は**)**なく**スポーツ**も**よく出来(でき)る。
(He is not only good scholastically; he is also good at sports.)

b. ??あの人は勉強**ばかりか**，スポーツ**さえ**出来る。

[2] a. この本(ほん)は面白(おもしろ)い {**だけ / ばかり**} **で**(**は**)**なく**，とてもためになる。
(This book is not only interesting but also educational.)

b. ??この本は面白い**ばかりか**ために**さえ**なる。
(⇨ ***dake de*** (***wa***) ***naku*** **~** (***mo***) (DBJG: 97–100))

II. S_1 *dokoroka* S_2, a construction indicating that s.o. / s.t. is very far from a/n (un)desirable state, is quite different from S_1 *bakari ka* S_2, when S_1 is affirmative and S_2 is negative or when S_1 is negative and S_2 is affirmative. Examples follow.

[3] 私(わたし)は日本語が話せる {**どころか / *ばかりか**}，一度(いちど)も勉強したことがありません。
(I am far from being able to speak Japanese; I haven't studied it at all.)

[4] スミスさんは日本語が書(か)けない {**どころか / *ばかりか**}，日本語で小説(しょうせつ)さえ書ける。

(Mr. Smith is far from being unable to write Japanese; he can even write a novel in Japanese.)

If both S_1 and S_2 are affirmative or negative, the two constructions are interchangeable.

[5] クラークさんは日本語が話せる{**どころか** / **ばかりか**}，韓国語(かんこくご)さえ話せる。
(Mr. Clark is not only able to speak Japanese; he can even speak Korean.)

[6] ジムは日本語で会話(かいわ)が出来ない{**どころか** / **ばかりか**}，簡単(かんたん)な挨拶(あいさつ)も出来ない。
(Jim is not only unable to converse in Japanese; he cannot even make simple greetings.)

bekida べきだ *aux.*

an auxiliary which expresses the speaker's judgment that s.o. / s.t. should do s.t. or should be in some state

should; ought to
【REL. *hazu*; *hōga ii*; *mono da*; *-nakereba naranai*】

◆Key Sentences

(A)

	Vinf·nonpast	
この論文(ろんぶん)は	**書(か)き直(なお)す**	べきだ。
(This thesis should be rewritten.)		

B

(B)

	Vinf·nonpast	
そんなことを人(ひと)に	**言(い)う**	べき {では / じゃ} ありません。
(You shouldn't say that kind of thing to people.)		

(C)

	Vinf·nonpast	
君(きみ)も	**来(く)る**	べきでしたよ。
(You should have come, too.)		

(D)

	Vinf·nonpast	
山田(やまだ)には	**話(はな)す**	べき {では / じゃ} なかった。
(I shouldn't have told that to Yamada.)		

(E)

Relative Clause		Noun		
Vinf·nonpast				
話す	べき	こと	は	全部(ぜんぶ)話しました。
(I told you everything I should tell you.)				

Formation

(i) Vinf·nonpast べきだ

行(い)くべきだ (should go)

(Exception: する → {す / する} べきだ (should do))

(ii) {Adj(*na*)stem / N} であるべきだ

積極的であるべきだ (s.o. should be positive)

目的であるべきだ (s.t. should be an objective)

Examples

(a) 自分のことは自分です(る)べきだ。
(You should look after yourself. (lit. You should do your own business by yourself.))

(b) 今，家を買うべきじゃないよ。
(You shouldn't buy a house now.)

(c) それは課長にも言っておくべきだったね。
(We should have told that to our boss, too, shouldn't we?)

(d) 彼は結婚なんかす(る)べきじゃなかったんだ。
(He shouldn't have married.)

(e) 我々はもっと創造的であるべきだ。
(We should be more creative.)

(f) この状態が現実であるべきだ。
(This state should be the reality.)

(g) 調査の結果，驚くべきことが分かった。
(As a result of the investigation, a surprising thing (lit. something one should be surprised at) was discovered.)

(h) 田中は全く軽蔑すべき男だ。
(Tanaka is indeed a despicable man (lit. a man whom one should despise).)

(i) あるべき所に記述がない。
(There's no description where there should be one.)

Notes

1. Tense and negation are expressed by conjugating *bekida*. (See KS (A) – (D) and Exs.(a) – (d).)

2. The prenominal form of *bekida* (i.e., the form which modifies a noun) is *beki*. (See KS(E) and Exs.(g) – (i).)

3. *Bekida* usually expresses the idea that s.o. / s.t. should do s.t. or be in some state because it is his / her responsibility or duty, because it is the right thing or a good thing to do, or because it is the right state or a good state to be in. (See KS(A) – (E), Exs.(a) – (f) and (i).)

4. *Bekida* also expresses the idea that s.o. is expected to do s.t. (See Exs. (g) and (h).)

5. Adj(*i*)stem + *ku aru-bekida*, as in (1), is a possible form but this form is not commonly used.

   (1) 体は年をとっても心は**若くあるべきだ**。
   (Even if one's body gets old, one's mind should be young.)

6. *Bekida* is not used when the speaker is younger than the hearer or lower than the hearer in status. For example, (2) is not appropriate in the given situation.

   (2) [From a student to his / her professor]
   ??先生，それはお忘れになる**べきです**。
   (Professor, you should forget it.)

[Related Expressions]

I. *Mono da* also expresses the idea that one should do s.t. as one's duty, as in [1].

   [1] 学生は勉強する**ものだ**。
   (Students should study.)

   However, *mono da* is used only in a generic statement to express a social norm. Thus, in a specific situation, as in [2], it cannot be used.

   [2] 君は勉強する｛**べき** / ***もの**｝だ。
   (You should study.)

(⇨ ***mono*** **(*da*)** (DBJG: 257–61))

II. In terms of forcefulness, *bekida* is weaker than *nakereba naranai* and stronger than *ta hō ga ii*, as in [3].

[3] a. 君はもっと勉強**しなければならない**。 stronger
(You must study harder.)

b. 君はもっと勉強**すべきだ**。
(You should study harder.)

c. 君はもっと勉強**した方**(ほう)**がいい**。
(You'd better study harder.) weaker

(⇨ ***~ nakereba naranai*** (DBJG: 274–76); ***hō ga ii*** (DBJG: 138–40))

III. *Hazu* also expresses the idea of "should." However, *hazu* is used when the speaker's expectation is involved. Compare the following sentences.

[4] a. このレポートは山田さんが書き直す**はずだ**。
(Yamada should rewrite this report. (= I expect that Yamada will rewrite this report.))

b. このレポートは山田さんが書き直す**べきだ**。
(Yamada should rewrite this report. (= Rewriting this report is Yamada's duty.))

[5] a. この本(ほん)はここの図書館(としょかん)にある**はずだ**。
(This book should be in this library. (= I expect that this book is in this library.))

b. この本はここの図書館にある**べきだ**。
(This book should be in this library. (= This library is responsible for having this book in its collection.))

(⇨ ***hazu*** (DBJG: 133–35))

B

-bun 分 *suf.*

a suffix which indicates the amount of s.t.

for ~; ~ worth; amount equivalent to ~; portion
【REL. *-mae*】

◆Key Sentences

(A)

	Number + Counter		
ガソリンを	**十ドル**	分	入れておきました。
(I put in ten dollars worth of gas.)			

(B)

	Number + Counter			Noun	
私は今日	**三日**	分	の	仕事	を片付けた。
(Today I did three days worth of work.)					

(C)

	Noun		
現金の	**不足**	分	は小切手で払います。
(I'll pay the remaining amount (lit. the amount for which cash is short) by check.)			

Formation

(i) Number + Counter 分（のN）

五人分の食糧 (food for five people)

(ii) Noun 分

減少分 (the amount by which s.t. decreased)

Examples

(a) 会議の資料を六人分用意しておいて下さい。
(Please get six sets of materials ready for the meeting.)

(b) ここは後でサインをしますので二行分あけておいて下さい。
(Please leave two lines (of space) here because someone will sign there later.)

(c) 私達は四か月分のボーナスをもらった。
(We were paid a bonus equivalent to four months pay.)

(d) トラック三台分のごみが出た。
(Three truckfuls of garbage came out.)

(e) 政府は十万人分の食糧を被災地に送った。
(The government sent food for 100,000 people to the disaster-stricken area.)

(f) 学校当局は諸経費の増加分を授業料の値上げでカバーしようとしている。
(The school authorities are trying to cover the increase in expenses by raising tuition.)

Note

Either a number + counter or a noun precedes *-bun*. When a number + counter precedes, it means s.t. worth that amount (e.g., KS(A)) or equivalent to that amount (e.g., KS(B)). When a noun precedes *-bun*, it means the amount or portion of something represented by the noun (e.g., KS(C)).

【Related Expression】

The suffix *-mae* also expresses a portion of something, as in [1], but this use is limited to food. A number + *nin* precedes *-mae*.

[1] 吉田はすしを**五人前**平らげた。
(Yoshida ate five orders of sushi.)

daga だが *conj.* <w>

a conjunction that expresses s.t. that is contrasted with what is expressed in the previous sentence

but; however; yet; nevertheless 【REL. *dakedo*; *demo*; *ga*; *keredo*(*mo*); *noni*; *shikashi*】

◆Key Sentences

(A)

$Sentence_1$		$Sentence_2$
日本の経済力は伸びている。	だが，	いつまで続くかは分からない。
(Japanese economic power is growing. But we can't tell how long it will last.)		

(B)

$Sentence_1$		$Sentence_2$
都会の生活は便利だ。	だが，	ストレスが多すぎる。
(Urban life is convenient. But there are too many stresses.)		

Formation

S_1inf。だが，S_2inf。

あの人の話は面白い。だが，内容がない。
(His talk is interesting, but there is no content.)

Examples

(a) 私は彼女とは初めて会った。だが，前から知っていたような親しみを感じた。
(I met her for the first time; but I felt close to her as if I had known her for a long time.)

(b) 山本は医者に何度もたばこをやめるように言われた。だが，やめる気はないらしい。
(Yamamoto was told by his doctor to quit smoking, but he doesn't seem to have any intention of quitting.)

(c) あの人には才能がある。だが，その才能を使っていない。
(He is talented, but he is not using his talents.)

(d) 今日の試験のために寝ないで勉強した。だが，さっぱり出来なかった。
(I studied hard for today's exam without sleeping, but I couldn't do it at all.)

(e) 妹はよく勉強するし，頭もいい。だが，成績はなぜかよくない。
(My younger sister studies hard and she is intelligent, but somehow her grades are not good.)

Note

Daga is not used in spoken Japanese unless it is followed by *ne* as in (1).

(1) A: あの男はなかなか切れるな。
(That guy is really sharp, isn't he?)

B: **だがね**，奴は性格が悪いんだ。
(But, he has a bad character, you know.)

In spoken Japanese it is usually replaced either by *keredo*(*mo*) or by *demo*. The formal version *desu ga* can be used in both spoken and written Japanese.

(2) A: 仕事はお忙しいでしょう。
(Your job must keep you busy.)

B: ええ，{**でも / ですが / けれども**}，面白いんです。
(Yes, but it is interesting.)

(3) 日本へ行きたくて仕方がないんです。{**でも / ですが / けれども**}，お金がないから，行けません。
(I'm dying to go to Japan. But I don't have money, so I can't go there.)

【Related Expression】

D

The first difference between *daga* and *ga* / *keredo(mo)* / *noni* / *shikashi* / *dakedo* / *demo* is the way they combine two sentences. *Daga*, *dakedo*, *shikashi* and *demo* are always used as a sentence-initial conjunction, but *ga* and *noni* are normally used as a non-sentence-initial conjunction, and *keredo(mo)* is used either as a sentence-initial conjunction or a non-sentence-initial conjunction.

Sentence-initial conjunctions:

a. S_1。だが S_2。　　*S_1 だが，S_2。
b. S_1。だけど S_2。　　*S_1 だけど，S_2。
c. S_1。しかし S_2。　　*S_1 しかし，S_2。
d. S_1。でも S_2。　　*S_1 でも，S_2。

Non-sentence-initial conjunctions:

e. S_1 が，S_2。　　???S_1。が S_2。
f. S_1 のに，S_2。　　*S_1。のに S_2。

(Non-)Sentence-initial conjunction:

g. S_1 けれど(も)，S_2。　　S_1。けれど(も)，S_2。

The second difference concerns semantic difference. *Ga* and *keredo(mo)* can be used to in two senses of 'but' and 'and.'

[1] 今東京に来ています{が / けれど / *のに}，東京は，やはり，活気がありますね。
(I'm in Tokyo now, and I feel that Tokyo is full of energy, after all.)

For the difference between *keredo(mo)* and *noni*, see DBJG: 333-35. Among the four sentence-initial conjunctions, the most colloquial is *demo*, followed by *dakedo* and the least colloquial one is *daga*, followed by *shikashi*.

dakara to itte　だからと言って　*conj.*

a coordinate conjunction indicating that even if one accepts a premise expressed in the preceding sentence(s) one cannot jump to an expected conclusion from the premise

However, it doesn't follow from this that ~; But it doesn't mean that ~; because of that 【REL. ***kara to itte***】

◆Key Sentences

(A)

Sentence$_1$	Sentence$_2$
チェンさんは日本語が苦手だ。	テストではいつも半分も出来ない。
	Sentence$_3$
だからと言って，	頭が悪いわけではない。
(Mr. Cheng is not good at Japanese. On a test he cannot even finish half of it. But it doesn't follow from this that he is not smart.)	

(B)

Sentence$_1$	Sentence$_2$	
吉田さんは日本人だ。	しかも，小説家だ。	だからと言って，
Sentence$_3$		
日本語が教えられるとは限らない。		
(Ms. Yoshida is Japanese. And she is a novelist. But she may not be able to teach Japanese.)		

Formation

S_1。(S_2。...) だからと言って S_n。（where S_n often ends with わけではない or とは限らない）

彼は若い。経験も浅い。だからと言って教えられない {わけではない / とは限らない}。

(He is young. He has little experience. But it doesn't follow from this that he cannot teach.)

Examples

(a) ジョンは奥さんのことをちっとも褒めない。時々口をきかないこともある。だからと言って，奥さんを愛していないわけではない。

(John does not praise his wife at all. Sometimes he doesn't talk with her. But it doesn't mean that he doesn't love her.)

(b) 僕は毎日運動をしている。食べ物にも注意している。しかし，だからと言って，長生きする保証はない。

(I am doing exercise every day. I am also paying attention to what I eat. But it doesn't guarantee that I will live long.)

(c) 日本人は集団行動が好きだと言われる。何をするにも一緒にやる。しかし，だからと言って，個人行動が全くないわけではない。

(They say that Japanese like group activities. Whatever they do, they do together. But it is not the case that there are no individual activities.)

(d) 魚は健康にいい。しかし，だからと言って，魚ばかり食べていたら，体に悪いはずだ。

(Fish is good for you. But if you ate nothing but fish, it would be bad for you.)

(e) 日本語はよく難しい言語だと言われる。文法が複雑だし，漢字を覚えるのも大変だ。だからと言って，外国人が学べないわけではない。

(Japanese is often said to be difficult. The grammar is complex and kanji are hard to memorize. But that doesn't mean foreigners cannot learn it.)

Notes

1. *Dakara to itte* is a conjuction which indicates that while the speaker / writer accepts an assertion / fact in the preceding sentence, he argues that what is normally expected from the assertion / fact is not (necessarily) applicable. Thus, for example, S_1 and S_2 of KS(A) may lead to an assertion that Mr. Cheng is not smart. But the speaker denies that extrapolation in S_3. To paraphrase it, it is something like: 'Mr. Cheng is poor at Japanese and he can't even get half way through tests. So you probably think he is not smart, but I don't think that's true.'

2. *Dakara to itte* often occurs with *wake de wa nai* or *to wa kagiranai*, as shown in all the examples except Ex.(d).

dake de だけで *phr.*

a phrase which expresses the idea that just doing s.t. is enough for s.t.	just V-ing is enough; can just ~; just by V-ing

◆Key Sentences

(A)

		Vinf		
君(きみ)は	ここに	**座(すわ)っている**	だけで	よい。
(You can just sit (lit. be sitting) here.)				

(B)

		Vinf		
私は	筆跡を	**見た**	だけで	誰が書いたか分かった。
(I knew who wrote it just by looking at the handwriting.)				

Formation

Vinf だけで

{読む / 読んだ} だけで　(just by reading)

Examples

(a) この植木は二週間に一度水をやるだけでよい。
(Watering just once every other week is enough for this plant.)

(b) この用紙にサインしていただくだけで結構です。
(It will be enough if you just sign this form.)

(c) 本当に来るだけでいいんですか。
(Are you sure that I don't have to do anything except attend?)

(d) その会議では私はただ座っているだけでよかった。
(At that meeting all I had to do was sit there.)

(e) 村上君は一週間勉強しただけであの試験に通ったそうだ。
(I heard that Murakami passed that exam just by studying for one week.)

(f) お金を入れてボタンを押すだけで温かいラーメンが出てくる自動販売機がある。
(There is a vending machine which serves hot *ramen* (lit. from which hot *ramen* comes out) just by inserting coins and pushing a button.)

(g) 頭金一万円を払うだけで品物をお届けします。
(If you just pay 10,000 yen as deposit, we'll deliver the product.)

(h) 聞くだけで胸が悪くなるような話だ。

(Just hearing that story makes me sick. (lit. It is a story that makes me sick just by hearing it.))

Note

The choice of the tense of the verb before *dake* depends on (1) whether or not the action expressed by the verb (Action 1) was taken in the past, and (2) whether or not the action/event expressed by the verb (Action 1) precedes the action/event expressed by the main verbal (Action 2). If A1 precedes A2 and A1 is a past action, the verb must be in the past tense (e.g., KS(B) and Ex.(e)). If A1 precedes A2 and A1 is not a past action, the verb is commonly in the nonpast tense, although the past tense is also acceptable (e.g., Exs.(f) – (h)). If A1 does not precede A2 and A1 is a past action, the verb is commonly in the nonpast, although the past tense is also acceptable (e.g., Ex.(d)). If A1 does not precede A2 and A1 is not a past action, the verb must be in the nonpast (e.g., KS(A) and Exs.(a) – (c)).

(⇨ ***dake*** (DBJG: 93–97))

-darake だらけ *suf.*

a suffix that indicates that s.t. / s.o. is covered or filled with s.t. undesirable

full of; filled with; covered with
【REL. *-mamire*】

◆Key Sentences

(A)

Topic		Noun			Noun	
スミスさんは	いつも	泥(どろ)	だらけ	の	靴(くつ)	を履(は)いています。
(Mr. Smith is always wearing shoes covered with mud.)						

(B)

Topic	Noun		
この作文は	**間違い**	だらけ	です。
(This composition is full of mistakes.)			

Formation

(i) N_1 だらけの N_2

ごみだらけの部屋 (a room filled with rubbish)

(ii) N_1 は N_2 だらけだ

部屋はごみだらけだ (The room is full of rubbish.)

Examples

(a) 長いこと掃除をしていなかったらしく，床も机の上もほこりだらけだった。
(Apparently they have not cleaned the room for a long time and the floor and the tables were covered with dust.)

(b) 病院に担ぎ込んだ時，その男の顔は血だらけだった。
(When we carried him into the hospital, the man's face was covered with blood.)

(c) 泥だらけの足で入って来ないで。
(Don't come in with muddy feet.)

(d) 借金だらけの生活をしています。
(I am living a life with many debts.)

(e) この貝は砂だらけで食べにくい。
(This shellfish contains a lot of sand, and eating is difficult.)

Note

-darake is used when s.t. is covered with s.t. undesirable, but if s.t. is covered with s.t. desirable *-darake* cannot be used.

(1) 床の上｛には札束がゴロゴロしていた / *は札束**だらけ**だった｝。
(On the floor were scattered bundles of money.)

(2) その学生の論文｛にはいいアイディアがいっぱいあった / *はいいアイディア**だらけ**だった｝。
(In the student's paper there were a lot of good ideas.)

【Related Expression】

The difference between *-darake* and *-mamire* is that the latter means 'totally covered / mixed with dirty liquid / powder such as blood, sweat, mud or dust,' excluding intangible objects, whereas the former can be used not only with liquid / powder but also to cover holes / pimples, and intangible objects, as in KS(B) and Ex.(d). More examples to show the difference follow:

[1] 私の作文は訂正｛**だらけ / *まみれ**｝だった。
(My composition was full of corrections.)

[2] 僕のズボンは穴｛**だらけ / *まみれ**｝だ。
(My pants are full of holes.)

[3] 少年の顔はにきび｛**だらけ / *まみれ**｝だった。
(The boy's face was covered with pimples.)

[4] 凸凹｛**だらけ / *まみれ**｝の道を三時間も運転して，疲れてしまった。
(I got tired after driving on a bumpy road for as long as three hours.)

de で *prt.*

a particle which indicates a basic quantity, for each of which certain amount is associated	for; per 【REL. *ni tsuki*】

◆Key Sentence

Topic				
この翻訳は	**一ページ**	で	**二千円**	お払いします。
(We will pay 2,000 yen per page for this translation.)				

Examples

(a) このアルバイトは一時間で千円払ってくれます。
(They will pay me 1,000 yen per hour for this part-time job.)

(b) 昨日は一日で本を五百ページ読んだ。
(Yesterday I read 500 pages in a day.)

(c) 食べて飲んで，五人で，七万円ぐらいでした。
(We ate and drank and it cost us about 70,000 yen for five persons.)

(d) このりんごは一山で二百円です。
(These apples are 200 yen for one pile.)

Note

De can be omitted if the relation between the basic amount and the associated amount is more or less fixed as in KS, Exs.(a) and (d). In Ex.(b) five hundred pages for one day is not fixed, so it is impossible to say *ichi-nichi gohyaku pēji.* The same is true of Ex.(c) in which the cost of 70,000 yen for five people is not fixed.

【Related Expression】

In the sense of 'per,' the particle *de* can be replaced by *ni tsuki*, if the relation between the basic amount and the associated amount is fixed as in KS, Exs.(a) and (d). There is also a stylistic difference: *ni tsuki* is more formal than *de*.

[1] この翻訳は一ページ｛**で** / **につき**｝二千円お払いします。(=KS)

[2] このアルバイトは一時間｛**で** / **につき**｝千円払ってくれます。(=Ex.(a))

[3] このりんごは一山｛**で** / **につき**｝二百円です。(=Ex.(d))

de arō であろう *aux.* <w>

an auxiliary which indicates the writer's conjecture which is not based on any particular information or evidence	probably 【REL. *darō*; *mai*】

◆Key Sentence

Sinf	
日本経済は今後も成長を**続ける**	であろう。
(The Japanese economy will probably still keep growing (lit. from now on, too).)	

Formation

Sinf であろう
(Exceptions: {Adj(*na*)stem / N} であろう)

{話す / 話した} であろう (will probably talk / probably talked)

{高い / 高かった} であろう (is / was probably expensive)

{静か / 静かだった} であろう (is / was probably quiet)

{先生 / 先生だった} であろう (is / was probably a teacher)

Examples

(a) このようなブームはもう二度と起こらないであろう。
(Such a boom will probably not happen again.)

(b) この次に起こる地震は非常に大きいであろうと予想される。
(It is expected that the next earthquake will (probably) be very strong.)

(c) その交渉は極めて困難であろう。
(That negotiation will probably be very difficult.)

(d) この辺りは昔，湖だったであろうと思われる。
(I think that this area was probably a lake a long time ago.)

Note

De arō is originally the conjecture form of the copula *de aru*, but it is used as an auxiliary of conjecture. This is used only in written Japanese.

(⇨ ***de aru***)

【Related Expressions】

I. *Darō*, a less formal auxiliary of conjecture, has the same meaning and function as *de arō* except that *de arō* can appear before a noun as part of a relative clause but *darō* cannot, as in [1].

[1] 私達はいつか起こる｛**であろう** / ***だろう**｝**大地震**に対して備えておかなければならない。
(We must be prepared for a strong earthquake, which will probably take place someday.)

(⇨ ***darō*** (DBJG: 100–02))

II. *Mai* can be used to express a negative conjecture. However, it can be used only with Vinf·nonpast·aff.

[2] 彼はもうここへは**来るまい**。(＝彼はもうここへは来ないであろう。)
(He probably won't come here any more.)

(⇨ ***mai***)

de aru である *cop.* <w>

a copula which is used in formal writing and formal speech	be 【REL. *da*】

◆Key Sentences

(A)

Topic (subject)	Noun	
『坊っちゃん』は	**漱石の初期の代表作**	である。
(*Botchan* is representative of Soseki's early work.)		

(B)

Topic (subject)		Adj(*na*)stem	
今年の水不足は	極めて	**深刻**	である。
(The water shortage this year is extremely serious.)			

Formation

(i) N である

先生である (be a teacher)

(ii) Adj(*na*)stem である

静かである (be quiet)

Examples

(a) 人間は考える葦である。
("Man is a thinking reed.")

(b) 日本語があいまいな言語であるというのは誤りである。
((The idea) that Japanese is an ambiguous language is wrong.)

(c) 大型車に一人で乗るのは不経済である。
(Using a big car for one person is uneconomical.)

(d) 彼に何度も手紙を書いたが無駄であった。
(I wrote him many letters but it was useless.)

(e) 日本語では文脈(ぶんみゃく)から分(わ)かることは原則(げんそく)として言(い)わないのである。
(In principle, in Japanese we do not say what is understood from context.)

(f) 彼らが出来(でき)ないのは練習(れんしゅう)していないからである。
(It is because they haven't practice that they can't do it.)

Notes

1. The conjugation of *de aru* is as follows:

Plain Form			
	nonpast	past	conjecture
Affirmative	である	であった	であろう
Negative	ではない	ではなかった	ではなかろう

Polite Form			
	nonpast	past	conjecture
Aff.	であります	でありました	でありましょう
Neg.	ではありません	ではありませんでした	ではないでしょう

2. The plain forms are used in formal writing, for example, in professional articles and editorials. Although the *de aru* style is more formal than the *da* style, the two styles are often used together. Note that the *de aru* style and the *da* style cannot be used with the *desu* style.

3. In writing, the formality level of the copula is as follows:

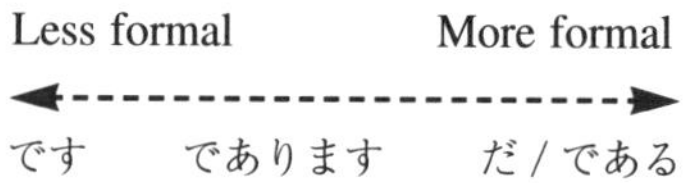

4. The polite forms of *de aru* (i.e., *de arimasu*, *de arimashita*, etc.) are sometimes used in formal speech, for example, in public speaking. In speech, the formality level of the copula is as follows:

Informal ◄------------------------► Formal

ø / だ　　　です　　　であります

【Related Expression】

Although *da* and *de aru* mean the same thing, there are some syntactic differences between them. First, N *da* cannot be used as the prenominal form while N *de aru* can, as in [1].

[1] a. 漱石の代表作 {**である / の / *だ**}『**坊っちゃん**』は明治三十九年に書かれた。
(*Botchan*, which is Soseki's representative work, was written in the 39th year of Meiji.)

b. 彼が一級のピアニスト {**である / *だ**} **こと**は疑う余地がない。
(That he is a first-class pianist is not questioned.)

Second, {N / Adj(*na*)stem} *da* cannot appear before expressions of uncertainty such as *rashii* and *ka mo shirenai*. {N / Adj(*na*)stem} *de aru* does not have this restriction, as in [2].

[2] a. これは漱石の書いたもの {**である / ø / *だ**} {**らしい / かもしれない**}。
(This {seems to / might} be Soseki's writing.)

b. この方法の方が効果的 {**である / ø / *だ**} {**らしい / かもしれない**}。
(This method {seems to / might} be more effective.)

(⇨ **~ *wa* ~ *da*** (DBJG: 521–24))

dokoroka どころか *conj.*

a conjunction indicating that s.o. / s.t. is very far from an expected state

far from; not just; even
【REL. ~ ***bakari ka*** ~ (***sae***)】

◆Key Sentences

(A)

Sentence$_1$		Sentence$_2$
私は日本語が**話せる**	どころか,	一度も勉強したことがありません。
(I am far from being able to speak Japanese. I haven't studied it at all.)		

(B)

Sentence$_1$		Sentence$_2$
ジムは日本語の会話が**出来ない**	どころか,	簡単なあいさつも出来ない。
(Jim is not just unable to converse in Japanese; he cannot even make simple greetings.)		

Formation

(i) {Vinf / Adj(*i*)}inf·nonpast どころか

食べるどころか (far from eating)

大きいどころか (far from being big)

(ii) {Adj(*na*)stem (な) / N} どころか

元気(な)どころか (far from being healthy)

病気どころか (far from being ill)

Examples

(a) スミスさんは日本語の新聞が読めるどころか，平仮名も知らない。
(Mr. Smith is far from being able to read a Japanese newspaper; he doesn't even know hiragana.)

(b) ジョンソンさんは漢字が書けないどころか，平仮名も書けない。
(Mr. Johnson is not just unable to write kanji; he cannot write even hiragana.)

(c) スミスさんは日本語が書けないどころか，日本語で小説が書けるぐらいだ。
(Mr. Smith is far from being unable to write Japanese; he can even write a novel in Japanese.)

(d) クラークさんは刺し身が食べられるどころか，納豆まで食べられる。
(Mr. Clark is not just able to eat sashimi; he can even eat *nattō*.)

(e) あの人は本を読むどころか，新聞も読まない。
(He is far from reading books; he doesn't even read newspapers.)

(f) 父は運動をするどころか，家から一歩も出ない。
(My father is far from doing exercises; he doesn't even step out of the house.)

(g) 今年の八月は暑いどころか，寒かった。
(This August was far from being hot; it was cold.)

(h) 私の父は丈夫(な)どころか，寝たきりです。
(My father is far from being healthy; he is bedridden.)

(i) 食事はご馳走どころか，豚のえさみたいだった。
(The meal was far from being a feast; it was like food for pigs.)

Notes

1. In S_1 *dokoroka* S_2 is used to indicate that s.o. / s.t. is very far from an expected state. In S_2 appears a situation quite different from the situation expressed in S_1.

2. In S_1 *dokoroka* S_2, the distribution of affirmative / negative predicates is as follows.

	S_1	S_2	Examples	
Type 1	Aff.	Aff.	Ex.(d)	'not just; even'
Type 2	Aff.	Neg.	KS(A), Exs.(a), (e) – (i)	'far from'
Type 3	Neg.	Aff.	Ex.(c)	'far from'
Type 4	Neg.	Neg.	KS(B), Ex.(b)	'not just; even'

dōmo どうも *adv.*

an adverb to indicate that one cannot make a definite statement about s.t. due to lack of hard evidence

I don't know why but; I cannot manage to; just; from what I gather; seem; no matter how ~; I gather that ~; for some reason

◆Key Sentences

(A)

	Predicate		
			Neg.
この文の意味が	どうも	よく分から	ない。
(I tried, but I cannot understand the meaning of this Japanese sentence very well.)			

(B)

	Predicate		
			Aux.
鈴木(すずき)さんは	どうも	京都大学(きょうとだいがく)に入(はい)りたい	らしい。
(I gather that Mr. Suzuki wants to enter Kyoto University.)			

(C)

	Predicate		
			Neg.
あの先生(せんせい)の授業(じゅぎょう)は	どうも	面白(おもしろ)く	ない。
(I don't know why, but that instructor's class is uninteresting.)			

Formation

(i) どうも～ {V / Adj(*i* / *na*)}neg

どうも話(はな)せない (no matter how one tries, s.o. can't talk)

どうも食(た)べられない (no matter how one tries, s.o. doesn't eat)

どうもよくない (I don't know why but s.t. isn't good.)

どうも上手(じょうず)じゃない (I don't know why, but s.o. is not good at s.t.)

(ii) どうも～ {V / Adj(*i*)}inf {らしい / ようだ}

どうも話す {らしい / ようだ} (I gather that s.o. is going to talk.)

どうも食べる {らしい / ようだ} (I gather that s.o. is going to eat.)

どうも高(たか)い {らしい / ようだ} (I gather that s.t. is expensive.)

(iii) どうも～ Adj(*na*)stem {らしい / ようだ} or どうも～ Adj(*na*)stem だった{らしい / ようだ}

どうも静(しず)か {らしい / なようだ} (I gather that s.t. is quiet.)

Examples

(a) このごろどうも体の調子がよくないんです。
(I don't know why, but lately I don't feel very good.)

(b) あの人の日本語はどうも聞きにくい。
(I don't know why, but his Japanese is hard to listen to.)

(c) 先生，この問題の意味がどうもつかめないんです。
(Professor, I can't manage to grasp the intent of this problem.)

(d) こんな田舎に住むのはどうも不便だ。
(It is just inconvenient to live out in the country like this.)

(e) うちの子はテレビばかり見て，どうも本を読まない。
(I don't know why, but our kids are always watching TV and do not read books.)

(f) あの先生はどうも厳しいようだ。
(That teacher seems strict to me.)

(g) ジョンは日本語を話すのは上手だが，読むのはどうも下手なようです。
(John is good at speaking Japanese but for some reason he seems poor at reading it.)

(h) その男がどうも犯人に違いないと思っていたが，やっぱりそうだった。
(I gathered that he must be the one who did it, and my guess was right.)

(i) 父は症 状からしてどうもがんになったらしい。
(Judging from the symptoms my father seems to have cancer.)

(j) 彼女が今朝電車の中で僕に言ったことがどうも気になった。
(What she said to me this morning in the train somehow bothered me.)

Notes

1. *Dōmo* is an adverb that indicates the speaker / writer cannot make a definite statement about s.t., because s/he cannot identify / pinpoint the reason. For example, in KS(A) the speaker has made an effort to comprehend the meaning of the sentence but s/he cannot pinpoint the meaning; in KS(B) the speaker has no solid evidence about Suzuki's

entrance to Kyoto University. In KS(C), the instructor's class is boring but the speaker / writer cannot identify the reason.

2. The final predicate is overtly negative, as in KS(A), (C), Exs.(a) – (c) and (e), or covertly negative as in Exs.(d) and (j). When the final predicate is not negative, it normally ends with an auxiliary adjective *-rashii* or *-yōda*, as in KS(B) and Exs.(f) – (i).

3. *Dōmo* is used with *arigatō* (*gozaimasu*) to mean 'Thank you very much,' or with *sumimasen* to mean 'I'm very sorry.' *Dōmo* alone can mean a very casual 'Thank you' or 'Sorry' without the following *arigatō* (*gozaimasu*) or *sumimasen*. Examples follow:

   (1) 先日(せんじつ)は**どうも**（ありがとうございました）。
   (lit. Thank you very much for what you did for me the other day.)

   (2) **どうも**（すみません）。
   (I'm sorry.)

donnani ~ (koto) ka どんなに～(こと)か *str.*

a structure that indicates an exclamation about the degree to which an action or state takes / took place	how ~ (!) 【REL. *dorehodo ~ (koto) ka*; *ikani ~ (koto) ka*】

◆Key Sentences

(A)

Sentence	
兄(あに)は病気(びょうき)が治(なお)ってどんなに**うれしかった**	ことか。
(How glad my elder brother was when he recovered from his illness!)	

(B)

Sentence	
父は母をどんなに**愛していた**	ことか。
(How dearly my father loved my mother!)	

(C)

	Embedded Question	
日本へ行くまで	日本がどんなに**狭い**か	分からなかった。
(I didn't realize how small Japan was until I got to Japan.)		

Formation

(i) どんなに〜(こと)か

どんなに難しいことか。 (How difficult s.t. is!)

(ii) どんなに〜か Predicate

どんなに面白いか知らない。 (S.o. doesn't know how interesting s.t. is.)

Examples

(a) 英夫は由美子に結婚を断られた時にどんなに残念に思ったことか。
(How disappointed Hideo must have felt when Yumiko refused to marry him.)

(b) 勉強が嫌いだった良夫には大学に入るのがどんなに難しかったか。
(For Yoshio, who didn't like to study, how hard it was to enter college!)

(c) 圭子はどんなにフランスに留学したかったことか！
(How strongly Keiko wanted to go to France!)

(d) 学生達はその厳しい先生をどんなに強く憎んだことか！
(How strongly the students hated their strict teacher!)

(e) 駅前のアパートはどんなに便利だったことか！
(How convenient my apartment right in front of the station was!)

(f) 一郎は親のもとを離れた時，親がどんなに寂しがったか分からなかった。
(Ichiro didn't realize how lonely his parents must have felt when he left them.)

Notes

1. In the exclamatory structure of *donna ni ~ koto ka*, Adj(*i* / *na*) or psychological / physiological verb is used before *koto ka*. The psychological verbs include, among others, *aisuru* 'love,' *nikumu* 'hate,' *konomu* 'like' and the physiological verbs include, among others, *tsukareru* 'get tired,' *ase o kaku* 'sweat,' *furueru* 'shiver.'

2. When the structure is used as an embedded question, *koto* is omitted, as in KS(C) and Ex.(f).

【Related Expression】

Ikani ~ (koto) ka and *dorehodo ~ (koto) ka* can be used exactly the same way as *donnani ~ (koto) ka*. The only difference is that the former is a more formal written style.

dōse どうせ *adv.*

an adverb that indicates the speaker / writer's feeling that no matter what s/he does or how s/he does it, the situation will not change

in any case; anyway; at all events; after all; at all

◆Key Sentences

(A)

受けても,	どうせ	駄目だから, 文部省の留学生試験を受けないことにしました。
(I decided not to try for the Education Ministry's Scholarship, because I'd be doomed to failure.)		

(B)

どうせ	外国旅行をするんなら, 若いうちにした方がいい。
(If you make a trip abroad at all, it's better to do it when you are young.)	

Examples

(a) どうせこんなたくさんの宿題, 出来るわけがないから, 遊ぶことにしたよ。
(I cannot do this much homework anyway, so I've decided to play.)

(b) 人間はどうせ死ぬんだから, あくせく働いても仕方がない。
(Since we humans are bound to die, it is no use working hard.)

(c) どうせ捨てられるのに, どうして彼の後を追うの?
(Why are you following him, when you are well aware that you are going to be dumped after all?)

(d) どうせあの女性とは結婚出来ないよ。早くあきらめた方がいいよ。
(You cannot marry that woman anyway. You'd better give her up as soon as possible.)

(e) A: 君はこんなことが分からないのかい?
(Don't you understand this simple matter?)

B: どうせ私はばかですよ。

(I'm stupid, as you know.)

(f) どうせ来週日本へ行きますから，その辞書は日本で買います。

(I'm going to Japan next week anyway, so I'll buy that dictionary over there.)

Note

The adverb *dōse* often indicates the speaker feels helpless and / or angry that nothing can be done to change a given situation, but as exemplified by KS(B) and Ex.(f), the adverb can also be used to suggest finality of one's decision.

fū ni 風に *phr.*

with an appearance / style / tone / manner of ~

in ~ manner; after ~ style; à la ~; like
【REL. *yōni*】

F

◆Key Sentences

(A)

	Noun		
私の家の庭は	**日本**	風に	大きい石が置いてあります。
(The yard of my house has big rocks arranged in Japanese style.)			

(B)

あんな	風に	勉強していたらいい成績は取れないだろう。
(If he studies like that, he won't get good grades.)		

(C)

	Adverbial Clause			
	Quote			
私は先生に	**頭がいいんだからもっと勉強しろ**	という	風に	よく言われた。
(I was often told by my teacher that I have to study harder because I am smart.)				

Formation

(i) {N / こんな / そんな / あんな / どんな} 風に (like {N / this / that / that ~ over there}, in what manner?)

西洋風に (in Western style)

こんな風に (like this)

(ii) Sinf という風に (like)

行かないという風に(聞いている) ((I hear) that s.o. doesn't go there)

今日はデート，明日はコンサートという風に (like a date one day and a concert the next)

Examples

(a) A: これはどんな風に持ったらいいんですか。
(How should I hold this?)

B: こんな風に持って下さい。
(Please hold it like this.)

(b) あんな風に毎日飲んでいたら，きっと病気になるでしょう。
(If he keeps drinking like that every day, he will surely become ill.)

(c) このカレーライスはインド風に，とても辛くしてあります。
(We have made this curried rice very spicy like an Indian version.)

(d) ジェミーが日本風のお辞儀をした時にはびっくりした。
(I was surprised when Jemmy bowed in Japanese style.)

(e) 京子は，今日はお花，あすはダンスという風に，毎日何かを習いに行っている。
(Kyoko goes out every day to take lessons, like flower arrangement one day and dance, the next.)

(f) お母さんが入院なさったという風に人から伺いましたが，いかがですか。
(I heard that your mother has been hospitalized, but how is she?)

(g) 教育改善のためなら，いくらお金を使ってもいい，という風になればいいんですがね。
(I wish things could change in such a way that we can spend as much money as we want to, if it is for educational improvement.)

Notes

1. The adverbial phrase *fū ni* includes the noun *fū* 'wind' which has extended meanings of 'appearance,' 'style,' 'manner' or 'tone.' That is why the adverbial phrase {N / *konna* / *sonna* / *anna* / *donna*} *fū ni* indicates appearance / style / manner in which s.t. is done.

2. S *to iu fū ni* (as in KS(C) and Ex.(f)) is used when one wants to quote s.t., as if to evoke in the mind of the listener the manner in which the original communication was made. The meaning is 'the content to the effect that ~.'

3. S *to iu fū ni* (as in Exs.(e) and (g)) has a meaning of 'in such a way that ~,' in contrast to a quotation case of Note 2.

4. N_1 *fū no* N_2 as in Exs.(c) and (d) means N_2 with a style of N_1. More examples follow:

   (1) a. ヨーロッパ風の建築(けんちく)
   (European-style architecture)

   b. バッハ風の音楽(おんがく)
   (Bach-style music)

   c. モンロー風の女(おんな)
   (a woman like Monroe)

【Related Expression】

The adverbial phrase *fū ni* can be replaced by *yōni*, if the construction is S *to iu fū ni*. If the construction is {*konna* / *sonna* / *anna* / *donna*} *fū ni*, it has to be replaced by {*kono* / *sono* / *ano* / *dono*} *yōni*. N *fū ni* has to be replaced by N *no yōni*.

[1] これは{**どんな風** / **どのよう**}**に**持ったらいいんですか。(=Ex.(a))

[2] {**あんな風** / **あのよう**}**に**毎日飲んでいたら，きっと病気になるでしょう。(=Ex.(b))

[3] このカレーライスは{**インド風** / **インドのカレーのよう** / ***インドのよう**}**に**，とても辛くしてあります。(=Ex.(c))

-gachi -がち *suf.*

a suffix to express an undesirable tendency in s.o. or s.t.

tend to; be prone to; be apt to; be liable to; be subject to; often 【REL. *-gimi*】

◆Key Sentences

(A)

Topic		V*masu*		
田中君は	最近授業を	**休み**	がち	だ。
(Tanaka tends to miss classes these days.)				

(B)

Topic	Relative Clause				Noun	
		V*masu*				
それは	日本に短期間滞在した外国人に	**あり**	がち	な	誤解	だ。
(That's a kind of misunderstanding that foreigners who stay in Japan for a short period of time are subject to.)						

(C)

Topic		Noun		
私は	小さい時	**病気**	がち	でした。
(I was often ill when I was very young.)				

(D)

	Noun			Noun	
この辺(あた)りは昼間(ひるま)	**留守**(るす)	がち	の	家(いえ)	が多(おお)い。
(Around here many people are often away from their houses during the day. (lit. Around here there are many houses which residents are often away from during the day.))					

Formation

(i) V*masu* がちだ

忘(わす)れがちだ (tend to forget)

(ii) N がちだ

留守がちだ (tend not to be home)

Examples

(a) 夏(なつ)はややもすると塩分(えんぶん)が不足(ふそく)しがちだ。
(Our bodies are apt to lack salt in the summer.)

(b) この時計(とけい)は最近(さいきん)遅(おく)れがちだ。
(This watch tends to lose time these days.)

(c) 人(ひと)はともすると自分(じぶん)の都合(つごう)のいいように物事(ものごと)を考(かんが)えがちだ。
(People tend to think (about things) in a way that suits themselves.)

(d) 若(わか)いうちはとかく物事を一途(いちず)に考えがちだ。
(Young people tend to think (about things) too seriously and narrow-mindedly.)

(e) 私は最近週末(しゅうまつ)もうちを空(あ)けがちです。
(These days I seldom stay home even on weekends.)

(f) これはアメリカ人の学生(がくせい)が犯(おか)しがちな間違(まちが)いだ。
(This is the kind of mistake which American students are apt to make.)

(g) 明日は曇りがちの天気でしょう。
(It will be mostly cloudy tomorrow.)

(h) 私のクラスには病気がちの学生が何人かいる。
(There are some students in my class who often get ill.)

(i) 彼女は遠慮がちに話した。
(She talked hesitantly (lit. with a tendency to hesitate).)

Notes

1. *-gachi* is usually used to express an undesirable tendency in someone or something. Thus, *-gachi* is not acceptable in such contexts as in (1).

    (1) a. *いいアイディアはくつろいでいる時に**思いつきがち**だ。
    (Good ideas tend to occur to us when we are relaxed.)

    b. *明日は**晴れがち**の天気でしょう。
    (It will be mostly fine tomorrow.)

2. When *-gachi* modifies a noun, two forms are possible, as in (2).

    (2) a. 休みがち {**な** / **の**} 学生
    (a student who tends to miss classes)

    b. 病気がち {**な** / **の**} 子供
    (a child who often gets ill)

3. *-gachi* can be paraphrased using the adverbs *yoku* 'often' or *shibashiba* 'frequently,' as in (3).

    (3) a. 田中君は最近 {**よく** / **しばしば**} 授業を休む。(=KS(A))

    b. 私は小さい時 {**よく** / **しばしば**} 病気をした。(=KS(C))

4. *-gachi* is often used with such adverbs as *yayamosuruto*, *tomosuruto*, and *tokaku* for emphasis (e.g., Exs.(a), (c), and (d)).

【Related Expression】

The suffix *-gimi* can also express the idea of "tend to" in some contexts. The major difference between *-gachi* and *-gimi* is that *-gachi* usually describes a general tendency in someone or something while *-gimi* describes a visible indication of a tendency. For example, in [1a], Taeko has a general tendency to gain weight but she is not necessarily overweight at the moment of speech. In [1b], on the other hand, Taeko is showing signs of being overweight.

[1] a. 妙子(たえこ)は最近太(ふと)り**がち**だ。
(Taeko tends to gain weight these days.)

b. 妙子は最近太り**ぎみ**だ。
(Taeko is showing a tendency to gain weight these days.)

In addition, *-gimi* also expresses the idea of "touch of" or "a little," as in [2]. *-gachi* does not have this meaning.

[2] 私は今日(きょう)ちょっと風邪(かぜ)**ぎみ**です。
(I have a slight cold today.)

-gatai がたい *aux. adj(i)* <w>

an auxiliary adjective which expresses the idea that for s.o. to do s.t. is virtually impossible or impossible

cannot; un—able; can hardly; difficult to; impossible
【REL. ***-kaneru***; *-nikui*; *-zurai*】

◆Key Sentences

(A)

Topic	V*masu*	
彼(かれ)のしたことは	**許(ゆる)し**	がたい。
(What he did is unforgivable.)		

(B)

	Relative Clause			Noun	
		V*masu*			
この旅行は	私にとって	**忘れ**	がたい	思い出	になるだろう。
(This trip will be an unforgettable one (lit. memory) for me.)					

Formation

V*masu* がたい

信じがたい　(hard to believe ; unbelievable)

Examples

(a) 彼の行為は理解しがたい。
(His behavior is hard to understand.)

(b) あの先生は偉すぎて私には近寄りがたい。
(That professor is so respected that I can hardly approach him.)

(c) この二つの作品は甲乙付けがたい。
(Between these two works, it is hard to say that one is better than the other.)

(d) このプロジェクトは成功したとは言いがたい。
(It is hard to say that this project was a success.)

(e) ジョーンズ氏は得がたい人物だ。
(Mr. Jones is an irreplaceable person (lit. a person hard to get).)

(f) 我々は彼の犯行に関する動かしがたい証拠をつかんだ。
(We obtained an indisputable piece of evidence concerning his crime.)

(g) 私は過去に彼から耐えがたい屈辱を受けた。
(I was intolerably humiliated by him in the past. (lit. received an intolerable humiliation from him.))

Note

-gatai is used when it is virtually impossible for s.o. to do s.t. Thus, KS(A), for example, is equivalent to (1).

(1) 彼のしたことは許せない。
(I / We cannot forgive his conduct.)

【Related Expressions】

-gatai, *-nikui*, and *-zurai* express a similar idea, i.e., "difficulty in doing s.t." However, their usage is significantly different. First, *-gatai* is usually used only in written language or formal speech, but *-nikui* and *-zurai* can be used both in spoken and written language. Second, unlike *-gatai*, *-nikui* and *-zurai* do not imply virtual impossibility. For example, in [1], where Mr. Yamada's handwriting is hard, but not impossible, to read, *-nikui* and *-zurai* can be used but *-gatai* cannot.

[1] 山田さんの字は読み **{にくい / づらい / *がたい}**。
(Yamada's handwriting (lit. characters) is hard to read.)

Third, while *-gatai* and *-zurai* can be used only with verbs which require an agent, *-nikui* can be used with verbs which do not require an agent, as in [2].

[2] a. この戸は**開き {にくい / *づらい / *がたい}**。
(This door doesn't open easily.)

b. この木は**燃え {にくい / *づらい / *がたい}**。
(This wood doesn't burn easily.)

(⇨ ***-nikui*** (DBJG: 307–08))

Fourth, *-zurai* is used when doing s.t. is physically (sometimes psychologically) hard on the agent. Thus, *-zurai* always describes undesirable situations, as in [3].

[3] a. このコピーは字が薄くて**読み {づらい / にくい / *がたい}**。
(The letters in this copy are weak and hard to read.)

b. 歯が悪いので堅いステーキは**食べ {づらい / にくい / *がたい}**。
(Because I have bad teeth, tough steaks are hard to eat.)

If the situation is desirable, *-zurai* cannot be used, as in [4].

[4] 単語(たんご)は例文(れいぶん)と一緒(いっしょ)に覚(おぼ)えれば**忘れ** {**にくい / *づらい / *がたい**}。
(You will not forget vocabulary items easily if you remember them in sentences.)

In the sentences in [3] and [4], *-nikui* can also be used. However, *-gatai* cannot be used in these sentences because they do not convey the idea of (virtual) impossibility.

gyaku ni 逆に *adv.*

an adverb to introduce an event which takes place contrary to one's expectation / intention, or an action or event which is converse to that stated in the preceding sentence or clause

contrary to one's expectation; contrary to one's intention; conversely
【REL. *kaette*】

◆Key Sentences

(A)

Subordinate Clause		Main Clause	
薬(くすり)を飲(の)ん	だら,	逆(ぎゃく)に	熱(ねつ)が出(で)た。
(Contrary to expectations, when I took medicine, I got a fever.)			

(B)

Subordinate Clause		Main Clause	
叱られると思った	のに，	逆に	ほめられた。
(I expected to be scolded but, contrary to my expectation, I was praised.)			

(C)

Sentence$_1$
会話を強調すると文法が不正確になる。
(If we emphasize conversation, their grammar becomes inaccurate.

Sentence$_2$	
逆に	文法を強調すると話せなくなる。
Conversely, if we emphasize grammar, they are (lit. become) unable to speak.)	

Examples

(a) しばらく練習をしなかったら，逆に成績が伸びた。
(I didn't practice for some time; then, contrary to expectations, my performance improved.)

(b) 寝すぎると，元気にならないで，逆に疲れてしまう。
(If you sleep too much, you don't feel well; instead (lit. conversely), you feel tired.)

(c) 文句を言ってやろうと思っていたら，逆に文句を言われてしまった。
(I was thinking of complaining; then, contrary to my intention, I had to listen to complaints.)

(d) 一生懸命仕事をしたのに，逆に仲間に嫌われてしまった。
(I worked very hard, but, contrary to expectations, my peers hated me.)

(e) ガールフレンドを喜ばせようとしたのに，逆に怒らせてしまった。
(I tried to please my girlfriend, but, contrary to my intention, I made her angry.)

(f) その試験に落ちるだろうと思っていたのに，逆に一番で通ってしまった。
(I was expecting to fail the exam, but, contrary to my expectation, I passed it in first place.)

(g) 人に親切にすることは一般にいいことだと考えられている。しかし，親切にすることが，逆に人を傷つけることもある。
(In general, being kind to people is considered to be a good thing. However, contrary to one's intention, being kind sometimes hurts people.)

(h) あの子は優しくすると付け上がる。逆に厳しくするとすぐ泣く。
(If I try to be gentle to the boy, he takes advantage of my gentleness. Conversely, if I try to be strict, he cries readily.)

(i) いい演技をするためには緊張しすぎてはいけない。しかし，逆にリラックスしすぎてもいい演技は出来ない。
(In order to perform well, you mustn't be too tense. But, conversely, if you are too relaxed, you cannot perform well, either.)

Notes

1. The basic meaning of *gyaku ni* is "conversely." However, it is often used when something takes place contrary to one's expectation or intention.

2. When *gyaku ni* is preceded by a clause, the clause often involves *tara*, *to*, or *noni*, as in KS(A), (B), and Exs.(a) – (f).

【Related Expression】

When *gyaku ni* expresses the idea of "contrary to one's expectation / intention," it can be paraphrased as *kaette*, as in [1].

[1] a. 薬を飲んだら，{**逆に / かえって**} 熱が出た。(=KS(A))

b. 叱られると思ったのに，{**逆に / かえって**} ほめられた。(=KS(B))

However, if *gyaku ni* simply means "conversely" without the sense of "contrary to one's expectation / intention," *kaette* cannot be used, as in [2].

[2] 会話を強調すると文法が不正確になる。{**逆に / *かえって**} 文法を強調すると話せなくなる。(=KS(C))

hodo ほど *prt.*

a particle which indicates the extent or the degree to which s.o. / s.t does s.t. or is in some state

the ~, the ~; as; to the extent
【REL. ~ *ba* ~ *hodo*; ***kurai***】

◆Key Sentences

(A)

Topic		Adj(*i*)inf·nonpast		
この音楽(おんがく)は	舞台(ぶたい)に	**近(ちか)い**	ほど	聞(き)きやすい。
(The closer (you sit) to the stage, the easier this music is to hear.)				

(B)

	Vinf·nonpast		
上空(じょうくう)に	**行(い)く**	ほど	酸素(さんそ)が薄(うす)くなる。
(Oxygen is less dense at higher altitudes. (lit. Oxygen becomes thinner as you go higher / the extent to which you go higher in the air.))			

(C)

	Adj.	Noun		
私(わたし)は	**難(むずか)しい**	**仕事(しごと)**	ほど	やる気(き)が出(で)てくる。
(I get more motivated by a harder job.)				

Formation

(i) {V / Adj(*i*)}inf·nonpast ほど

勉強(べんきょう)するほど (the more s.o. studies)

高(たか)いほど (the more expensive s.t. is)

(ii) Adj(*na*)stem {な / である} ほど

便利 {な / である} ほど (the more convenient s.t. is)

(iii) Relative Clause + N ほど

考え方が論理的な人ほど (the more logical a person's way of thinking is)

よく勉強する学生ほど (a student who studies harder ; the harder a student studies)

Examples

(a) 子供は小言を言うほど反発するものだ。
(The more you nag children, the more they disobey you.)

(b) 私は静かなほど落ち着かない。
(The quieter it is, the more uneasy I feel.)

(c) 駅に近くなるほど家賃が高くなる。
(The closer to the station, the higher the rent.)

(d) 運動するほど体の調子が変になる。
(The more I exercise, the worse I feel.)

(e) 元気な人ほど無理をしがちだ。
(Stronger people tend to strain themselves more.)

(f) あまり働かない者ほど不平が多い。
(Lazier people complain more.)

Notes

1. *Hodo* can express the idea of "the ~, the ~" as well as "(not) as ~ as ~" and "so ~ that ~." (⇨ ***hodo*** (DBJG: 135–38))

2. Sentences of the pattern KS(C), which involve noun phrases before *hodo*, can be rewritten using the pattern KS(A). For example, (1) is equivalent to KS(C) in meaning.

   (1) 私は**仕事が難しいほど**やる気が出てくる。
   (The harder the job is, the more motivated I become.)

【Related Expression】

~ *ba* ~ *hodo* also expresses the idea of "the ~, the ~". For example, KS(A), (B), and (C) can be paraphrased as [1], [2] and [3], respectively.

[1] この音楽は舞台に**近ければ近いほど**聞きやすい。(=KS(A))

[2] 上空に**行けば行くほど**酸素が薄くなる。(=KS(B))

[3] 私は難しい**仕事であればあるほど**やる気が出てくる。(=KS(C))

(⇨ **~ *ba* ~ *hodo***)

igai 以外 *n.*

a dependent noun which means "s.t. / s.o. other than"

other than; except (for); but; besides; as well as
【REL. *hoka*】

I

◆Key Sentences

(A)

Noun			Noun		
山田さん	以外	の	人	は	みんなそのことを知っています。
(Everybody except Yamada knows it.)					

(B)

Noun			
日本語	以外	に	何か外国語が話せますか。
(Can you speak any foreign language besides Japanese?)			

(C)

Topic	Sinf			
私には	**酒を飲む**	以外	に	何も楽しみがない。
(I have nothing to enjoy other than drinking.)				

Formation

(i) N 以外(のN)

コーヒー以外(の飲み物) ((drinks) other than coffee)

(ii) Sinf 以外 (*Da* after Adj(*na*)stem and N changes to *de aru*.)

勉強する以外　(besides studying)

高い以外　(besides the fact that s.t. is expensive)

便利である以外　(besides the fact that s.t. is convenient)

先生である以外　(besides the fact that s.o. is a teacher)

Examples

(a) 私は日本酒以外の酒は飲まない。
(I do not drink any alcohol but sake.)

(b) 我々の会社では現在オーストラリア以外の国と取引はない。
(At present our company is not dealing with any countries but Australia.)

(c) アメリカ以外の国からもたくさん研究者が来た。
(Many researchers came from countries other than America, too.)

(d) 原因はこれ以外に考えられない。
(I can't think of any causes other than this.)

(e) 私は散歩以外にも毎日軽い運動をしている。
(I take (other) light exercise every day as well as taking a walk.)

(f) ここで待っている以外ない。
(There is nothing to do but wait here. (lit. There is no other way but waiting here.))

(g) 安い以外に何かいいことがありますか。
(Is there any merit besides the price (lit. besides the fact that it is cheap)?)

(h) この文は少し漢字の間違いがあるが，それ以外は完全だ。
(This sentence (or passage) contains a few kanji mistakes, but other than that, it is perfect.)

(i) 従業員以外立入禁止。[Door sign]
(Employees only. (lit. Entry of those other than employees is prohibited.))

Notes

1. "X *igai no* Y" refers to the referent of Y excluding the referent of X, a member of Y. In "X *igai no* Y," "*no* Y" is often omitted, as in (1).

 (1) a. 山田さん**以外(の人)**はみんなそのことを知っています。 (=KS(A))

 b. 私は日本酒**以外(の酒)**は飲まない。(=Ex.(a))

 c. 我々の会社では現在オーストラリア**以外(の国)**と取引はない。 (=Ex.(b))

I

2. "X *igai ni*" means 'besides X.' In this phrase, *ni* is often omitted, as in (2).

 (2) a. 日本語**以外(に)**何か外国語が話せますか。(=KS(B))

 b. 私には酒を飲む**以外(に)**何も楽しみがない。(=KS(C))

 c. 原因はこれ**以外(に)**考えられない。(=Ex.(d))

 Note that if *ni* is followed by *mo*, *ni* cannot be omitted.

 (3) 私は散歩**以外 {に / *ø} も**毎日軽い運動をしている。(=Ex.(e))

【Related Expression】

Hoka can sometimes be used in place of *igai*. For example, *igai* in the following examples can be paraphrased using *hoka*.

 [1] a. 山田さん {**以外(の人) / のほか**} はみんなそのことを知っています。(=KS(A))

 b. 日本語 {**以外 / のほか**} に何か外国語が話せますか。(=KS(B))

 c. 私には酒を飲む {**以外 / ほか**} に何も楽しみがない。(=KS(C))

 d. 原因は {**これ以外 / このほか**} に考えられない。(=Ex.(d))

Note that N *igai* can be followed by *no* N, as in [1a], but N *no hoka* cannot.

The difference between *hoka* and *igai* is that *hoka* can be used as an independent noun while *igai* is always used as a dependent noun. Thus, *hoka* can appear in sentence initial position but *igai* cannot, as in [2].

[2] a. {**ほか / *以外**} の日は空いていませんか。
(Are you available on other days?)

b. {**ほか / *以外**} (のもの)は問題ありません。
(There's no problem with the others [other things].)

c. {**ほか / *以外**} に何か質問はありませんか。
(Do you have any other questions?)

Another difference between *hoka* and *igai* is that *igai* can be followed by copula conditional forms such as *nara*, *dattara*, and *deareba* but *hoka* cannot, as in [3].

[3] a. お金 {**以外 / *のほか**} {**なら / だったら / であれば**} 何でも貸してあげるよ。
(I will lend you anything except money. (lit. I will lend you anything if it is something other than money.))

b. 麻雀 {**以外 / *のほか**} {**なら / だったら / であれば**} 何でもやります。
(I play everything except mahjong. (lit. I play anything if it is not mahjong.))

Finally, *igai* can be followed by case markers such as *de* and *to* but *hoka* cannot, as in [4].

[4] a. 金持ち {**以外 / *のほか**} **と**は付き合わないことにしている。
(I make it a practice to socialize only with rich people. (lit. I make it a practice not to socialize with people other than rich people.))

b. この部屋 {**以外 / *のほか**} **で**物を食べないで下さい。
(Please do not eat in rooms other than this one.)

ijō (**wa**) 以上(は) *conj.*

a conjunction indicating the speaker / writer's feeling that there should be a very strong logical / natural connection between what precedes the conjunction and what follows it

since; now that; once; if ~ at all; as long as; so long as
【REL. *kagiri* (*wa*); *kara ni wa*】

I

◆Key Sentences

(A)

Sentence$_1$			Sentence$_2$
	Vinf		
日本(にほん)に	**来(き)た**	以上(いじょう)(は),	日本語(にほんご)をしっかり勉強(べんきょう)したい。
(Since I have come to Japan, I would like to study Japanese hard.)			

(B)

Sentence$_1$			Sentence$_2$
Noun			
学生(がくせい)	**である**	以上(は),	勉強すべきだ。
(So long as you are a student, you should study.)			

Formation

(i) Vinf 以上(は)

{話(はな)す / 話した} 以上は (since s.o. talks / talked)

(ii) N である以上は (as long as s.o. / s.t. is N)

先生(せんせい)である以上は (as long as s.o. is a teacher)

Examples

(a) 日本語を始めた以上，よく話せて，聞けて，読めて，書けるようになるまで頑張ります。
(Now that I have begun to study Japanese, I will hang in there until I can speak and understand what I hear, and read and write well.)

(b) 新車を買う以上は，出来るだけ燃費のいいのを買いたいです。
(If I buy a new car at all, I would like to buy one with good gas mileage.)

(c) 親である以上，子供の教育に関心があるのは当然でしょう。
(If you are any sort of parent, you should be interested in your child's education.)

(d) もらった以上は，あなたが何と言おうと，私の物です。
(Now that you have given this to me, it is mine, no matter what you say.)

(e) 体をよく動かしている以上は，人間の体は衰えないらしい。
(So long as you are very active, your body seems to stay strong.)

(f) 人と約束した以上は，それを守らなければならない。
(Once you have made a promise to someone, you have to keep it.)

Notes

1. The construction S_1 *ijō* (*wa*), S_2 can be used when one feels strongly that there should be a close, necessary connection between S_1 and S_2. The structure cannot be used to express an objective causal relation. Examples follow:

   (1) *三時間も歩いた**以上**，とても疲れている。

   (2) *今朝は五時に起きた**以上**，とても眠い。

   (3) *よく勉強した**以上**，試験がよく出来た。

2. S_1 of this construction always ends in a verb or *dearu*; it never ends in an adjective.

【Related Expressions】

I. When S_1 *ijō* S_2 means 'so long as' as in KS(B) and Ex.(e), it can be replaced by S_1 *kagiri* (*wa*) S_2.

[1] 学生である {**以上**(**は**) / **限り**(**は**)}, 勉強すべきだ。(=KS(B))

[2] 体をよく動かしている {**以上**(**は**) / **限り**(**は**)}, 人間の体は衰えないらしい。(=Ex.(e))

(⇨ ***kagiri***[1])

II. S_1 *ijō* S_2 cannot be replaced by S_1 *kara ni wa* S_2, if the former means 'as long as,' otherwise the replacement is possible.

[3] 体をよく動かしている {**以上は** / ***からには**}, 人間の体は衰えないらしい。(=Ex.(e))

[4] 僕が生きている {**以上** / ***からには**}, お前に不自由をさせないよ。
(As long as I live, I won't let you go without anything.)

[5] 酒を飲み続けている {**以上** / ***からには**}, 病気は治らないよ。
(So long as you keep drinking, your illness won't be cured, you know.)

[6] 日本語のラジオを聞いている {**以上** / ***からには**}, 日本語を聞く力は低下しないでしょうね。
(So long as you listen to Japanese radio, your listening skills won't deteriorate, I presume.)

ikanimo いかにも *adv.*

an adverb that indicates the speaker / writer's emotive conviction	really; truly; indeed 【REL. *hontō ni*; *tashika ni*】

◆Key Sentences

(A)

アメリカ人の目から見ると，日本の社会は	いかにも	閉鎖的だ。
(From an American perspective, Japanese society is indeed closed.)		

(B)

外は雪が降っていて，	いかにも	寒そうだ。
(It is snowing outside, and it looks really cold.)		

(C)

彼の書斎の本棚には古今東西の本が詰まっていて，	いかにも	学者の部屋らしい。
(The bookshelves of his study room are packed with books of all ages and countries, and it surely looks like a scholar's room.)		

(D)

先生は最近	いかにも	お忙しいよう / 様子だ。
(These days the professor appears to be really busy.)		

(E)

Sentence$_1$			Sentence$_2$
日本人は集団行動が	いかにも	好きではあるが,	個人行動をしないわけではない。
(The Japanese indeed like group behavior, but it is not the case that they do not do behave individually.)			

(F)

Sentence$_1$			Sentence$_2$
彼は	いかにも	紳士であるかのように振る舞っているが,	なかなかの策士だ。
(He is behaving as if he were truly a gentleman, but he is quite calculating.)			

Examples

(a) 彼の発想はいかにも日本的だ。
(His manner of thinking is very Japanese.)

(b) その教授の知識はいかにも百科全書的だ。
(The professor's knowledge is really encyclopaedic.)

(c) デーヴィッドは文部省の奨学金がもらえて，いかにもうれしそうだった。
(David was able to get a Ministry of Education scholarship and he looked really happy about it.)

(d) 父は退院して，いかにも元気そうになった。
(My father left the hospital and became really healthy-looking.)

(e) 彼女は明るく，陽気で，いかにもアメリカ人らしい。
(She is light-hearted and cheerful, and is truly like an American.)

(f) 僕の大学の友人はいかにも金持ちらしく，いつもしゃれた物を着ている。
(A friend of mine in college appears to be truly rich, and is always wearing fancy clothes.)

(g) ジョンは恋人と別れて，いかにも落ち込んでいるようだった。
(John split up with his girlfriend and looked truly depressed.)

(h) みゆきは母を失って，いかにも悲しんでいる様子だった。
(Miyuki lost her mother and looked really saddened.)

(i) いかにもおっしゃる通りです。
(It is exactly as you have said.)

(j) 日本語はいかにも難しい言語ではあるが，マスター出来ないわけではない。
(Japanese is indeed a difficult language, but it is not the case that you cannot master it.)

(k) 彼はいかにも全部分かっているかのように話しているが，その実何も分かっていない。
(He is talking as if he truly understood everything, but in reality he understands nothing.)

Note

The adverb *ikanimo* is used when the speaker / writer wants to express his emotive conviction. The adverb often occurs with such conjectural expressions as ~ *sōda* (as in KS(B), Exs.(c) and (d)), *rashii* (as in KS(C), Exs.(e) and (f)) and *yōda* / *yōsuda* (as in KS(D), Exs.(g) and (h)). Also it occurs with the conjunction *ga* (as in KS(E), Exs.(j) and (k)).

【Related Expressions】

I. Every use of *ikanimo* in KS and Exs. can be replaced by another adverb *hontō ni* 'truly' without changing the meaning. The only difference between the two is that the former is slightly more formal than the latter.

[1] a. アメリカ人の目から見ると，日本の社会は｛**いかにも** / **本当に**｝閉鎖的だ。(=KS(A))

b. 外は雪が降っていて，｛**いかにも** / **本当に**｝寒そうだ。(=KS(B))

c. 彼の書斎の本棚には古今東西の本が詰まっていて，｛**いかにも** / **本当に**｝学者の部屋らしい。(=KS(C))

II. The adverb *tashika ni* can replace *ikanimo* when the latter is used in the pattern of *ikanimo* S_1 *ga* S_2, as in KS(E) and Ex.(j).

[1] 日本人は集団行動が**確**(たし)**かに**好きではあるが，個人行動をしないわけではない。(cf. KS(E))

[2] 日本語は**確かに**難しい言語ではあるが，マスター出来ないわけではない。(cf. Ex.(j))

Imperative

verb forms which indicate commands or requests

(Don't) V.; No -ing; (not) to V 【REL. *koto*; *-nasai*; *te wa ike-nai*】

◆Key Sentences

(A)

	Vcond	
もう	よせ	よ。
(Stop it now.)		

(B)

	Quotation			
		Vcond		
ここには	十二月三十一日(じゅうにがつさんじゅういちにち)までに	払(はら)え	と	書(か)いてある。
(It says here to pay before December 31.)				

Formation

(A) Affirmative

(i) Gr. 1 Verbs: Vcond
書け (Write!)

(ii) Gr. 2 Verbs: Vstem {ろ [Spoken] / よ [Written]}

答えろ (Answer!)

答えよ (Answer.)

(iii) Irr. Verbs:

来い (Come!)

しろ [Spoken] (Do!)

せよ [Written] (Do.)

(B) Negative

Vinf·nonpast な

話すな (Don't talk!)

食べるな (Dont't eat!)

(⇨ ***na*** (DBJG: 266–67))

Examples

(a) 黙れ！
(Shut up!)

(b) 動くな！
(Don't move!)

(c) 山中首相は即時退陣せよ！ [A demonstrator's placard]
(Yamanaka must go! (lit. Prime Minister Yamanaka must leave his office immediately!))

(d) 次の文を英訳せよ。[An examination direction]
(Translate the following sentences into English.)

(e) 次の質問に答えよ。[An examination direction]
(Answer the following questions.)

(f) 乗るなら飲むな。飲んだら乗るな。
(If you drive, don't drink. If you drink, don't drive.)

(g) 現金は送るなと書いてある。
(It says (lit. is written) not to send cash.)

(h) 課長にあまりタクシーは使うなと言われた。
(I was told by my boss not to use taxis often.)

Notes

1. Imperatives without sentence particles are rarely used in daily conversation. In spoken Japanese they are usually used when the speaker is angry with or threatening the hearer or when the speaker shouts slogans in demonstrations, as in Exs.(a) – (c).

2. Imperatives with the sentence particle *yo* are used by male speakers in very casual situations (e.g., between close friends, between a father and his child), as in KS(A).

3. Imperatives without sentence particles are frequently used in directions in written examinations and mottos, as in Exs.(d) – (f).

4. Imperatives without sentence particles are used in indirect speech, as in KS(B), Exs.(g) and (h). In this case, the corresponding direct quotations are not necessarily imperative. For example, the direct quotations of KS(B) and Ex.(h) may be:

   (1) 十二月三十一日までに**払って下さい**。
   (Please pay by December 31.)

   (2) あまりタクシーは**使わないでくれないか**。
   (Would you mind not using a taxi often?)

【Related Expressions】

I. V*masu* + *nasai* and V*te* + *wa ikenai* / *ikemasen* are milder than the imperatives introduced here; therefore, they are frequently used in daily conversation. Examples follow:

[1] もっと勉強(べんきょう)しなさい。
(Study harder.)

(⇨ ***~ nasai*** (DBJG: 284–85))

[2] 遅刻(ちこく)をしてはいけない / いけません。
(Don't be late for class.)

(⇨ ***~ wa ikenai*** (DBJG: 528))

II. *Koto* also expresses a command, but it is used only in written rules and regulations.

[3] a. 本(ほん)は一週間以内(いっしゅうかんいない)に返(かえ)すこと。
(Books must be returned within a week.)

b. 閲覧室(えつらんしつ)では話(はなし)をしないこと。
(No talking in the reading room.)

(⇨ ***koto***)

I

ippō de (wa) ~ tahō de (wa) ~ 一方で(は)～ 他方で(は)～ *str.*

a structure used to describe two concurring, contrastive actions / states of s.o. or s.t.

on the one hand ~, on the other hand

◆**Key Sentence**

神田先生は，	一方では	大学で物理学を教えながら，
他方では	日本語の研究をなさっている。	
(Prof. Kanda teaches physics at college on the one hand and does research on Japanese language on the other.)		

Formation

N は，一方では S_1 Conj.，他方では S_2。

この薬は，一方では症状を軽くするが，他方では強い副作用がある。
(This medicine, on (the) one hand, alleviates symptoms but on the other hand, it has strong side effects.)

Examples

(a) あの男は，一方では静かな日本画を描いたりしているが，他方ではサッカーのような激しいスポーツをしている。
(That man draws quiet Japanese paintings on the one hand, but plays a very competitive sport like soccer on the other.)

(b) X氏は，一方で慈善事業をやりながら，他方でかなりあくどい商売をしているという噂だ。
(On one hand, Mr. X is engaged in charities, but, on the other hand, rumor has it that he is engaged in a ruthless business.)

(c) あの大統領は，一方では減税を約束しておきながら，他方では側近の税金の無駄使いをあまり重要視していない。
(The President has promised tax-cuts. But on the other hand he doesn't think much about waste of tax-payers' money by his entourage.)

(d) 留守番電話は，一方ではかかる方にもかける方にも便利な面もあるが，他方ではお互いに直接話が出来ないから，不自然な面もある。
(The answering machine is, on the one hand, very convenient for both a person who calls and a person who is called, but, on the other hand, unnatural because you can't talk directly with the other person.)

(e) ストレスは，一方では害になることもあるが，他方では生活のいい刺激にもなるそうだ。
(It is said that stress is sometimes harmful for humans, but, on the other hand, it also seems to be a good stimulus for human life.)

(f) 外国生活は，一方では新しい文化に接することが出来て楽しい面もあるが，他方ではカルチャーショックで大変困ることもある。
(Life in a foreign country is, on the one hand, enjoyable because one can encounter new culture, but, on the other hand, it is sometimes hard because of culture shock.)

Note

The construction is used to give two contrasting facts about a given topic. In other words, it is used to show both sides of the same coin so that the hearer / reader can get a total picture of an action / state.

-jō -上 *suf.*

a suffix which indicates the idea of "from the viewpoint of," "for the sake of," "for the reason," or "in terms of"

from the viewpoint of; for (the sake of); for (the reason); in (terms of); relating to; in -ing 【REL. ***no ue de wa***】

J

◆Key Sentences

(A)

	Noun		
この映画(えいが)は	**教育**(きょういく)	上(じょう)	よくない。
(This film is not good from an educational point of view.)			

(B)

Noun		
便宜(べんぎ)	上	私(わたし)がこの部屋(へや)の鍵(かぎ)を預(あず)かっているんです。
(I keep the key to this room for the sake of convenience.)		

(C)

	Noun		
時間(じかん)の	**制約**(せいやく)	上	細(こま)かい説明(せつめい)は省略(しょうりゃく)させていただきます。
(I will skip a detailed explanation for lack of time (lit. time limitation).)			

(D)

Noun			
計算	上	は	これで正しい。
(In terms of calculation, this is correct.)			

(E)

Noun			Noun	
健康	上	の	理由	で引退することにした。
(I've decided to retire for health reasons (lit. for a reason relating to my health).)				

(F)

Noun			Noun	
「**使用**	上	の	注意」	をよく読んで下さい。
(Read "Warnings for Use" carefully.)				

Formation

N 上

衛生上　(from the viewpoint of hygiene)

Examples

(a) このような行為は道義上許せない。
(Such conduct cannot be forgiven from an ethical point of view.)

(b) この条件はこれからの取引上極めて不利だ。
(This condition is extremely disadvantageous for our future business.)

(c) 仕事の都合上こんな高いマンションに住んでいるんです。
(I live in such an expensive condominium because it's convenient for

commuting to work (lit. for business convenience).)

(d) 仕事の関係上，今この町を離れるわけにはいかないんです。
(For business-related reasons, I cannot leave this town.)

(e) 理論上はこうなるはずなのだが，実際どうなるかは分からない。
(In theory it should turn out like this, but it's not known how it will actually turn out.)

(f) 法律上は彼の行為は罪にならない。
(Legally his conduct is not criminal.)

(g) この製品にはデザイン上の欠陥がいくつかある。
(This product has some design defects.)

(h) 彼女は一身上の都合で会社を辞めることになった。
(She is going to quit her company for personal reasons.)

(i) この部品は製作上いくつかの問題がある。
(There are some problems in manufacturing this part.)

Note

-jō can be interpreted in several ways depending on the context. More specific phrases can be used in place of *-jō*, as in (1) – (6).

(1) [Viewpoint] (KS(A), Ex.(a))

この映画は教育｛**上** / **の点から言って**｝よくない。(=KS(A))

(2) [Purpose] (KS(B), Ex.(b))

便宜｛**上** / **のために**｝私がこの部屋の鍵を預かっているんです。(=KS(B))

(3) [Reason] (KS(C), Exs.(c), (d))

時間の制約｛**上** / **のために**｝細かい説明は省略させていただきます。(=KS(C))

(4) [Domain] (KS(D), Exs.(e), (f))

計算｛**上は** / **の上では** / **の範囲では**｝これで正しい。(=KS(D))

(5) [Relation] (KS(E), Exs.(g), (h))

健康｛**上の** / **に関する**｝理由で引退することにした。(=KS(E))

(6) [Time] (KS(F), Exs.(b), (i))

「使用｛**上の** / **時の** / **に際しての** / **における**｝注意」をよく読んで下さい。(=KS(F))

kaette かえって *adv.*

contrary to one's expectation an opposite result comes about

on the contrary; rather
【REL. *mushiro*】
(Ant. *yahari*; *yappari*)

◆Key Sentence

Subordinate Clause	Main Clause	
薬を飲んだら，	かえって	病気がひどくなった。
(I took medicine, and the illness got worse (contrary to my expectation)).		

Examples

(a) A: 一時間も泳いで，疲れたでしょう。
(You must be tired after swimming as long as one hour.)

B: いや，かえって元気になったよ。
(No, on the contrary, I feel fit now.)

(b) 日本へ行ったら日本語が上手になるかと思って，日本へ行ったんですが，日本人と英語でばかり話していたので，かえって，下手になって帰って来ました。
(I went to Japan, believing that my Japanese would improve (if I go) there, but I spoke only English with the Japanese there, so (contrary to my expectation) my Japanese became worse when I came back here.)

(c) 就職のことで三人の先生にアドバイスをしてもらったのですが，アドバイスが全然違うので，かえって，分からなくなってしまいました。
(I was given advice on job searching from three professors, but their advice was so different that I am rather at a loss.)

(d) いわゆる一流大学で勉強するより小さな私立大学で勉強する方が，かえって，いい教育を受けることが出来る。

((Contrary to your expectation) if you study at a small, private college, you can receive better education than to study at a so-called first-rate university.)

(e) アルコールも適量飲めば，かえって，体にいいそうだ。
(Alcohol is said to be rather good for your health if you drink it in moderate quantity.)

Note

The adverb *kaette* is used when one describes a situation / event that occurs contrary to one's expectation.

【Related Expression】

The adverb *mushiro* 'rather' can replace all the uses of *kaette* in KS and Exs.

[1] a. 薬を飲んだら, {**かえって / むしろ**} 病気がひどくなった。(=KS)

b. 日本へ行ったら日本語が上手になるかと思って，日本へ行ったんですが，日本人と英語でばかり話していたので，{**かえって / むしろ**}，下手になって帰って来ました。(=Ex.(b))

c. いわゆる一流大学で勉強するより小さな私立大学で勉強する方が，{**かえって / むしろ**}, いい教育を受けることが出来る。(=Ex.(d))

However, there are many cases in which *mushiro* cannot be replaced by *kaette* because the former is used when between the alternate choice between action / situation / characterization one is judged to be better than the other, but the latter lacks this particular meaning.

[2] a. あの人は学者というよりは {**むしろ / *かえって**} 教育者だと思う。
(I believe him to be an educator rather than a scholar.)

b. 今日は涼しいというよりは {**むしろ / *かえって**} 寒いです。
(Today it is cold rather than (comfortably) cool.)

c. 京都(きょうと)へ行くのは冬(ふゆ)より {**むしろ** / ***かえって**} 春(はる)の方がよくありませんか。
(Isn't it better to go to Kyoto in spring rather than in winter?)

kagiri[1] 限り *conj.*

a conjunction which expresses the idea "as long as (a certain condition is met)" or "as long as (= to the extent)"

as long as; as far as; while; to the extent; until; unless
【REL. *aida wa*; *uchi wa*】

K

◆Key Sentences

(A)

Subordinate Clause			Main Clause
	Vinf·nonpast		
私(わたし)がここに	**いる**	限(かぎ)り	心配(しんぱい)は無用(むよう)です。
(As long as I am here, you don't have to worry.)			

(B)

Subordinate Clause			Main Clause
	Vinf·nonpast		
田中(たなか)さんが	**来(こ)ない**	限り	この会議(かいぎ)は始(はじ)められない。
(As long as Mr. Tanaka is not here (lit. does not come), we cannot begin this meeting.)			

(C)

Subordinate Clause				Main Clause
	Noun			
これが	**事実**	**である**	限り	彼は有罪を免れないだろう。
(As long as this is the fact, he probably cannot escape being found guilty.)				

Formation

(i) Vinf 限り

見る限り (as far as s.o. sees)

調べた限り (as long as s.o. examined)

読まない限り (as long as s.o. does not read; until s.o. reads)

出来る限り (as long as s.o. can do; to the extent s.o. can do)

(ii) N で {ある / ない} 限り

学生である限り (as long as s.o. is a student; while s.o. is a student)

日本人でない限り (as long as s.o. is not Japanese; unless s.o. is Japanese)

Examples

(a) 今の状態が続く限りプロジェクトは始められない。
(As long as the present situation continues, we cannot start our project.)

(b) この事件に関する限り彼は無実だ。
(As long as this incident is concerned, he is innocent.)

(c) 私の知っている限り彼は正直者です。
(As far as I know, he is an honest man.)

(d) その書類は私が読んだ限り誤りはなかった。
(As far as I read, the document contained no errors.)

(e) 教育者である限りそんなことは口にすべきではない。
(While you are an educator, you shouldn't say things like that.)

(f) この試験に通らない限り上級クラスには入れません。
(Until you pass this exam, you cannot enroll in the advanced class.)

(g) 事態が変わらない限り今以上の援助は不可能です。
(Until the situation changes (lit. As long as the situation doesn't change), we cannot provide additional support.)

(h) アメリカ人でない限りこの仕事には就けない。
(Unless you are an American, you cannot be employed for this job.)

(i) 私達は力の続く限り漕いだ。
(We rowed as long as our strength lasted (lit. to the extent that our strength lasted).)

(j) 出来る限りやってみます。
(I will try my best (lit. to the limit of my ability).)

Notes

1. Adjectives cannot precede *kagiri*.

   (1) ***面白い**限り続けるつもりだ。(Acceptable form: 面白いうちは……)
   (As long as I find it interesting, I will continue to do it.)

   (2) ***上手な**限り誰でもいいです。(Acceptable form: 上手{だったら / であれば / なら} ……)
   (As long as the person is good at it, it doesn't matter who does it.)

2. Nouns before the conjunction *kagiri* must be followed by the copula *de aru* (or *de nai*), as in (3).

   (3) これが事実 {**である** / ***の**} 限り彼は有罪を免れないだろう。
   (=KS(C))

【Related Expression】

Aida wa 'while' and *uchi wa* 'while' are used in similar contexts. In fact, *aida wa* and *uchi wa* can be used in place of *kagiri* if the *kagiri* clause indicates a time interval.

[1] a. 私がここにいる{**限り** / **うちは** / **間**(あいだ)**は**}心配は無用です。 (=KS(A))

b. 田中さんが来ない{**限り** / **うちは** / **間は**}この会議は始められない。(=KS(B))

However, *aida wa* and *uchi wa* can occur with adjectives while *kagiri* cannot, as in [2]. (See Note 1.)

[2] a. 面白い{**うちは** / **間は** / ***限り**}続けるつもりだ。(=(1))

b. 便利(べんり)な{**うちは** / **間は** / ***限り**}借(か)りておくといいでしょう。
(It would probably be a good idea to borrow it (and keep it) while it is convenient.)

K

-kagiri[2] 限り *suf.*

a suffix which expresses the idea of "(last) only until" or "limited"

the last; only until; from ~ on; limited to; only

◆Key Sentences

(A)

Noun (time)			
今度(こんど)	限(かぎ)り	で	彼(かれ)のパーティーには行(い)かないつもりだ。
(This is the last time I am going to any of his parties.)			

(B)

	Number + Counter		
切符は一人	**二枚**	限り	です。
(Tickets are limited to two per person.)			

Formation

(i) N (time) 限り

今週限り (limited to this week; This week is the last week.)

(ii) Number + Counter 限り

一度限り (limited to one time; only once)

Examples

(a) この映画館は今月限りで閉館されます。
(This movie house is open only until the end of this month.)

(b) 今日限りで酒もたばこもやめます。
(From today on I will give up both drinking and smoking.)

(c) セールは明日限りです。
(Tomorrow is the last day of the sale.)

(d) その場限りの約束はしない方がいい。
(You'd better not make an empty promise (lit. a promise limited to the moment).)

(e) 貸し出しは一回三冊限りです。
(Check-out is limited to three books at a time.)

(f) 書き直しは一回限りです。
(You can rewrite only once. (lit. Rewriting is limited to one time.))

Notes

1. -*kagiri* is preceded by either a noun or a number with a counter. Nouns before -*kagiri* are usually those which indicate a certain time.

2. N-*kagiri* is used when a repeated or on-going action, event, or state lasts only until a certain time.

~ ka ~ ka 〜か〜か *str.*

a structure to mark two choices or possibilities about which the speaker / writer is not sure	whether ~ or ~; or

◆Key Sentences

(A)

来年日本へ**行ける**	か	**行けない**	か	まだ分かりません。
(I don't know whether or not I can go to Japan next year.)				

(B)

傘を**駅に置き忘れたの**	か	**事務所に忘れたの**	か,	はっきり覚えていません。
(I don't remember well whether I left my umbrella at the station or in my office.)				

Formation

(i) {V_1 / Adj(*i*)$_1$}inf か {V_2 / Adj(*i*)$_2$}inf か

{遊ぶ / 遊んだ} か {勉強する / 勉強した} か

(whether s.o. plays / played or studies / studied)

{面白い / 面白かった} か {つまらない / つまらなかった} か
(whether s.t. is / was interesting or boring)

(ii) {Adj(*na*)$_1$stem / N$_1$} {ø / だった} か {Adj(*na*)$_2$stem / N$_2$} {ø / だった} か

{便利 / 便利だった} か {不便 / 不便だった} か
(whether s.t. is / was convenient or inconvenient)

{男 / 男だった} か {女 / 女だった} か
(whether s.o. is / was a man or woman)

(iii) {Adj(*na*)$_1$stem / N$_1$} {ø / だった} か {Adj(*na*)$_2$stem / N$_2$}neg か
(where Adj(*na*)$_1$ = Adj(*na*)$_2$, N$_1$ = N$_2$)

{便利 / 便利だった} か便利 {じゃ / で} {ない / なかった} か
(whether s.t. is / was convenient or not)

{男 / 男だった} か男 {じゃ / で} {ない / なかった} か
(whether s.o. is / was a man or not)

Examples

(a) 大学を出てから就職するか大学院に入るかまだ決めていません。
(I haven't decided yet whether to get a job or go to graduate school after graduation from college.)

(b) お客さんが肉が好きか魚が好きか，聞いておいて下さい。
(Please ask the guest in advance whether he likes meat or fish.)

(c) 夏休みにはヨーロッパを旅行するか，ソウルで仕事をするか，まだ決めていません。
(I haven't yet decided whether I should travel in Europe or work in Seoul during the summer break.)

(d) 会議が木曜日だったか金曜日だったか，忘れてしまいました。
(I forgot whether the meeting was on Thursday or Friday.)

(e) 初めてタマラと会ったのがパーティーでだったか，プールでだったか，覚えていません。

(I don't remember whether it was at a party or at the pool that I first met Tamara.)

(f) 木村さんが大学で経済を専攻したのか，政治を専攻したのか，知っていますか。
(Do you know whether Mr. Kimura majored in economics or politics at college?)

(g) 最近は男か，男でないか，分からないような男が多い。
(Lately, it's hard to tell whether a lot of men are men or not.)

(h) 会議は月曜か水曜(か)にして下さい。
(Please make the meeting Monday or Wednesday.)

Notes

1. The ~ *ka* ~ *ka* construction is used when one is not sure about two choices or possibilities. (⇨ ***ka***[1] (DBJG: 164–66))

2. Normally the construction is used to deal with two choices or possibilities, but when one lists the choices and possibilities more than two *ka*'s can be used as in (1).

   (1) 春休みは，家にいる**か**旅行をする**か**研究所で働く**か**，まだ決めていません。
   (I haven't decided whether to stay here or make a trip or work at the research institute during the spring break.)

3. If the same verb is repeated as in KS(A), the second one can be replaced by *dō ka* as follows. (⇨ ***ka*** (***dō ka***) (DBJG: 168–70))

   (2) 来年日本へ行けるか**どうか**，まだ分かりません。

kana かな *prt.* <s>

a sentence-final particle that indicates a self-addressed question or a question addressed to an in-group member	I wonder if ~

◆Key Sentences

(A)

	Vvol·inf	
今週末には何を	**しよう**	かな。
(I wonder what I should do this weekend.)		

(B)

	Vinf	
この問題，君に	**分かる**	かな。
(Can you figure out this problem?)		

Formation

(i) {V / Vvol}inf かな

{話す / 話した / 話そう} かな (I wonder if s.o. talks / if s.o. talked / if I should talk.)

(ii) Adj(*i*)inf かな

{大きい / 大きかった} かな (I wonder if s.t. is / was big.)

(iii) {Adj(*na*)stem / N} {ø / だった} かな

静か {ø / だった} かな (I wonder if s.t. is / was quiet.)

先生 {ø / だった} かな (I wonder if s.o.is / was a teacher.)

(iv) Wh-word {ø / だった} かな

いつ {ø / だった} かな (I wonder when s.t. is / was.)

Examples

(a) 今日は何曜日だったかな。
(I wonder what day of the week today is.)

(b) 来学期から日本語を始めようかな。
(I wonder if I should start Japanese next semester.)

(c) 日本での生活はどうかな。
(I wonder what life is like in Japan.)

(d) 今日の晩ご飯は何かな。
(I wonder what today's dinner will be.)

(e) アパートの家賃は高いかな。
(I wonder if the apartment rent is high.)

(f) 先生はお元気かな。
(I wonder if my teacher is in good health.)

(g) 音楽会の切符があるんだけど，君は行けるかな。
(There is a concert ticket, but I wonder if you can go.)

Notes

1. The sentence-final particle *kana* is used when one asks himself about s.t. In essence *kana* is a marker of monologue question, so this cannot be used as a straightforward question addressed to others. Compare the following:

    (1) どこへ行き**ましょうか**。
    (Where shall we go?)

    (2) どこへ行き**ますか**。
    (Where are you going?)

    (3) どこへ行こう**かな**。
    (I wonder where I should go.)

The questions of (1) and (2) are straightforward questions addressed to others, but (3) is a monologue question which does not need to be answered. However, if it is a yes-no question and if the addressee is an equal or younger one, *kana* can be used as a question addressed to others, as shown in KS(B) and Ex.(g).

2. If one asks himself what one should do,Vvol has to be used as in KS(A) and Ex.(b)

3. *Kana* is normally used by a male speaker, but it is often used by a female speaker, too, in casual spoken Japanese. The normal counterpart is *kashira*. (⇨ ***kashira*** (DBJG: 181–82))

K

kanarazushimo 必ずしも *adv.*

an adverb that indicates that the proposition expressed in the sentence is not always true

not always; not necessarily
【REL. *itsumo wa ~ nai*; *minna wa ~ nai*; *subete wa ~ nai*; *zenbu wa ~ nai*】

◆Key Sentences

(A)

		Vinf	
頭(あたま)のいい人(ひと)が	必(かなら)ずしも	**成功(せいこう)する**	とは限(かぎ)らない。
(A bright person does not always succeed.)			

(B)

		Adj(*i*)inf	
高(たか)い料理(りょうり)が	必ずしも	**おいしい**	わけではない。
(Expensive dishes are not always delicious.)			

(C)

			Adj(*na*)	
記憶力(きおくりょく)のいい人が	必ずしも	外国語(がいこくご)が	**上手(じょうず)だ**	とは言(い)えない。
(One cannot always say that people with good memories are good at foreign languages.)				

(D)

		Noun		
日本人(にほんじん)が	必ずしも	**いい日本語の先生(せんせい)**	**だ**	とは思(おも)わない。
(I don't think that a Japanese is always a good Japanese language teacher.)				

Formation

(i) 必ずしも {Vinf / Adj(*i*)} とは {限ら / 言え / 思わ} ない

必ずしも {話(はな)す / 大(おお)きい} とは限らない
(s.o. does not always talk / s.t. is not always big)

(ii) 必ずしも {Vinf / Adj(*i*)}neg

必ずしも {話しはしない / 大きくはない}
(s.o. does not always talk / s.t. is not always big)

(iii) 必ずしも {Adj(*na*)stem / N} だとは {限ら / 言え / 思わ} ない

必ずしも {静(しず)か / 先生} だとは限らない
(s.t. is not always quiet / s.o. is not always a teacher)

(iv) 必ずしも {Adj(*na*)stem / N} ではない

必ずしも {静か / 先生} ではない
(s.t. is not always quiet / s.o. is not always a teacher)

Examples

(a) 結婚(けっこん)しても必ずしも幸福(こうふく)になるとは言えない。
(One cannot always say that marriage brings happiness.)

(b) 運動(うんどう)をよくする人が必ずしも長生(ながい)きするとは限らない。
(People who exercise regularly do not always live long.)

(c) 日本へ行(い)った学生(がくせい)が日本語が上手になるかというと，必ずしもそうではない。
(Students who have been to Japan do not always become proficient in Japanese.)

(d) お金(かね)は人を必ずしも幸福にはしない。
(Money does not always bring happiness to people.)

(e) 優(すぐ)れた研究者(けんきゅうしゃ)が必ずしも優れた教育者(きょういくしゃ)であるわけではない。
(It is not always the case that an able researcher is an able educator.)

(f) 良薬(りょうやく)は口(くち)に苦(にが)しと言うが，苦い薬(くすり)が必ずしもいいとは限らない。
(They say good medicine is bitter, but bitter medicine is not always good.)

(g) めがねをかけて，カメラを下(さ)げて，集団(しゅうだん)で歩(ある)いている東洋人(とうようじん)が必ずしも日本人ではない。
(An oriental wearing glasses, carrying a camera and walking in a group is not always a Japanese.)

Notes

1. The adverb *kanarazushimo* is used with a negative predicate. Typically, the final predicate is *to wa kagiranai* (lit. ‘not limited to ~’).

(⇨ ***to wa kagiranai***)

2. *Kanarazushimo ~ nai* is often used in a proverbial expression in which the tense of the final predicate is usually nonpast. However, *kanarazushimo* can be used with the past tense as in (1) below.

(1) a. その夏日本に行った学生は必ずしも日本語が上手にはならなかった。
(The students who went to Japan that summer did not always become proficient in Japanese.)

b. ピアノの名手ウラジミール・ホロビッツの演奏は必ずしも完璧ではなかった。
(The performances of the virtuoso pianist Vladimir Horowitz were not always perfect.)

【Related Expression】

Kanarazushimo ~ nai expresses a partial negative. The partial negative can also be expressed by other expressions such as *minna wa ~ nai*, *zenbu wa ~ nai*, *subete wa ~ nai*, *itsumo wa ~ nai*. Examples follow:

[1] 光る物が｛**みんな / 全部 / すべて**｝金で**はない**。
(All that glitters is not gold.)

[2] 私は**いつも**元気だというわけ**じゃない**。
(It is not the case that I am always healthy.)

[3] あの先生の話は｛**みんな / 全部 / すべて**｝**は**分から**ない**。
(It is not the case that I understand everything that the professor has to say.)

Among these partial negative expressions, *Kanarazushimo* and *subete* are much less colloquial than the rest. Note also that *minna* 'all,' *zenbu* 'all,' *subete* 'all,' and *itsumo* 'always' do not always require a negative ending; whereas *kanarazushimo* always requires a negative ending. Examples follow:

[4] a. 友達は｛**みんな / *必ずしも**｝結婚している。
(My friends are all married.)

b. 宿題は｛**全部 / *必ずしも**｝やってしまった。
(I've done all the homework.)

c. 私は｛**いつも** / ***必ずしも**｝元気だ。
(I'm always healthy.)

-kaneru かねる *aux. v.* (*Gr.* 2)

an auxiliary expressing that s.o. cannot do s.t. even if s/he wants to do it

cannot; be not in a position to; hardly possible; hard; hesitate to do
【REL. *-gatai*; *-nikui*】

K

◆Key Sentences

(A)

	V*masu*		
そのことは私(わたし)には	**分(わ)かり**	かねます	から，部長(ぶちょう)にお聞(き)きになって下(くだ)さい。
(I am not in a position to figure out that matter, so please ask the departmental chief.)			

(B)

	V*masu*	
あの男(おとこ)はどんなばかなことでも	**やり**	かねない。
(He might (lit. can) do any stupid thing.)		

Formation

V*masu* かねる / かねない

飲(の)みかねる (s.o. cannot drink s.t.)

飲みかねない (it is possible for s.o. to drink s.t. / s.o. might drink s.t.)

Examples

(a) 来週はロンドンへ出張しますので，誠に申し訳ございませんが，名古屋での会議には出席できかねます。
(Next week I am making a business trip to London, so I cannot attend the meeting in Nagoya.)

(b) これだけの書類を一月では処理いたしかねますが。
(I cannot handle this many documents in a month.)

(c) 大変遺憾に存じますが，ご依頼には応じかねます。
(It is a great regret, but we cannot comply with your request.)

(d) こんな高価な贈り物，頂きかねます。
(I cannot accept such an expensive gift.)

(e) 彼は私の気持ちを量りかねているようだ。
(He appears to find it hard to understand my feelings.)

(f) 非常に言いにくいことなので，さすがの部長も切り出しかねている。
(It is such a delicate matter, so even the departmental chief finds it hard to break the ice.)

(g) みどりさん，ご主人がお待ちかねよ。
(Midori, your husband is waiting for you with impatience (lit. cannot wait).)

(h) あいつはとんでもないことを言いかねないから，注意した方がいいよ。
(He might say outrageous things, so watch out.)

(i) あの男はちょっとしたことで暴力を振るいかねない。
(That man might use violence at the slightest provocation.)

(j) この事件は内閣総辞職にも発展しかねない。
(It is possible for this incident to develop into resignation of the entire cabinet.)

(k) 暴動すら起こりかねないような緊迫した情況だった。
(It was such a tense situation that even a riot could have taken place.)

Notes

1. V*masu kaneru* (*Gr.* 2) is often used in formal spoken or written Japanese to express politely that the speaker / writer cannot do s.t. owing to some circumstance, as shown in KS(A) and Exs. (a) – (d).

2. The negative version, i.e., V*masu kanenai* is actually a double negative, so it literally means 'can do s.t.,' but it actually means 'it is very possible' or 'might.'

3. The verb that can take *-kaneru* is a verb that takes a first person human subject. So verbs such as *kowareru* 'break,' *aru* 'exist,' *kawaku* 'dry up,' *hareru* 'clear up,' *kumoru* 'become cloudy,' etc., cannot take *-kaneru*. In contrast, the verb that can take *-kanenai* can take either the third person human subject (as in Exs.(h) and (i)) or the third person non-human subject (as in Exs.(j) and (k)).

K

4. None of the regular potential forms can take *-kaneru* either, because it creates double potential meaning.

   (1) a. *そのご依頼には，**応じられかねます**。
   (I cannot comply with your request.)
   → そのご依頼には，**応じかねます**。

   b. *この仕事(しごと)は**引(ひ)き受(う)けられかねます**。
   (I cannot accept this job.)
   → この仕事は**引き受けかねます**。

   However, there are two exceptions: *wakaru* 'can figure out' and *dekiru* 'can' (used with a Sino-Japanese compound) can take *-kaneru*, as shown in KS(A) and Ex.(b), respectively.

5. Ex.(g) is an idiomatic case which comes from V*masu* of *machi-kaneru* 'cannot wait' and is exceptional in that it takes a third person subject unlike other cases of the V*masu kaneru*. No other new combination like *o-machi-kane* is possible.

6. As explained in Note 3, *-kaneru* takes the first person, but when the

main predicate is in the progressive form, *-kaneru* can take the third person, as in Ex.(e) and (f).

【Related Expressions】

There are two auxiliaries similar to *-kaneru*. They are V*masu nikui* and V*masu gatai*. The crucial difference is that *-kaneru* conveys the meaning of 'cannot,' but the other two don't; rather, they convey the meaning of 'hard to do s.t.' The auxiliary *-gatai* is used in written Japanese, so it sounds very awkward in [1b] but is acceptable in [1a].

[1] a. そのような条件には応じ{**かねる** / **にくい** / **がたい**}。
(It is hard for me to accept such a condition.)

b. そいつはちょっと賛成し{**かねる** / **にくい** / ??**がたい**}な。
(It's hard to agree to that, you know.)

(⇨ ***-gatai***)

~ kara ~ ni itaru made　〜から〜に至るまで　*str.*　<w>

a structure that expresses a wide range of things

starting with ~ ending with ~; from ~ to ~
【REL. ~ *kara* ~ *made*】

◆Key Sentence

	Noun		Noun		
スミスさんは	**週刊誌**	から	**学術書**	に至るまで,	幅広い日本語が読める。
(Mr. Smith can read Japanese widely, ranging from weekly magazines to scholastic books.)					

Examples

(a) その新聞記者は首相の公の生活から私生活に至るまで，何でも知っている。
(That newspaper reporter knows everything about the premier, ranging from his public life to his private life.)

(b) 私が日本へ行った時，友人の山田さんは空港への出迎えからホテルの予約に至るまで，実に親切にしてくれた。
(When I went to Japan, my friend Mr. Yamada was very kind to me. He did everything from picking me up at the airport to making the hotel reservation for me.)

(c) その女の人は私に家族のことから自分の悩みに至るまで，細かに話した。
(That lady told me everything in detail, starting with her family and ending with the worries of her life.)

(d) 社長が現れた時には，守衛から副社長に至るまで，門の前で待っていた。
(When the president of the company arrived, everyone from the guards to the vice-president was waiting in front of the gate.)

(e) ルーシーは靴から帽子に至るまで，緑の装束だった。
(Lucie was dressed in green, from her shoes to her hat.)

Note

The construction ~ *kara* ~ *ni itaru made* is used to express a wide range of coverage. The construction is primarily used in written Japanese.

【Related Expression】

~ *kara* ~ *ni itaru made* is replaced by ~ *kara* ~ *made* in spoken Japanese. Thus, for example, KS, Exs.(a) and (b) change to, [1], [2], and [3], respectively. (⇨ ***kara***[1] (DBJG: 176); ***made*** (DBJG: 225–28))

[1] スミスさんは週刊誌**から**学術書**まで**，幅広い日本語が読める。 (cf. KS)

[2] その新聞記者は首相の公の生活**から**私生活**まで**，何でも知っている。 (cf. Ex.(a))

[3] 私が日本へ行った時，友人の山田さんは空港への出迎え**から**ホテルの予約**まで**，実に親切にしてくれた。(cf. Ex.(b))

Since ~ *kara* ~ *ni itaru made* cannot express range of physical distance or time, ~ *kara* ~ *made* has to be used in that case.

[4] 東京（とうきょう）から京都（きょうと）{**まで / *に至るまで**} 新幹線（しんかんせん）で三時間（さんじかん）かかる。
(It takes three hours by bullet train from Tokyo to Kyoto.)

[5] 昨日（きのう）は朝九時（あさくじ）から十一（じゅういち）時ごろ {**まで / *に至るまで**} テニスをした。
(Yesterday morning I played tennis from 9 o'clock till about 11 o'clock.)

K

~ kara ~ ni kakete　～から～にかけて　*str.*

a structure that expresses coverage from one time / location into the other

through ~ into ~; through ~ on to; from ~ till / to
【REL. ~ *kara* ~ *made*】

◆Key Sentence

	Noun (time / location)		Noun (time / location)		
今年（ことし）の夏（なつ）,	**七月**（しちがつ）	から	**八月**（はちがつ）	にかけて	中国大陸（ちゅうごくたいりく）を旅行（りょこう）した。
(This summer I travelled on the Chinese continent from July through August.)					

Formation

N から N にかけて

一（いち）月から二（に）月にかけて　(from January through February)

Examples

(a) 今週は木曜から金曜にかけて雪が降るでしょう。
(This week it will probably snow from Thursday through Friday.)

(b) 日本は六月から七月にかけて梅雨が続く。
(In Japan the rainy season continues through June and July.)

(c) 高気圧が朝鮮半島から九州にかけて張り出している。
(High atmospheric pressure extends from the Korean Peninsula up through Kyushu.)

Note

The *kakete* of ~ *kara* ~ *ni kakete* is V*te* of the verb "*kakeru*" whose basic meaning is 'to hang s.t. over s.t. else.' This basic meaning is reflected in the meaning of the structure, that is, 'extended span of time / space across time / spatial boundaries.'

【Related Expression】

~ *kara* ~ *made* is similar to ~ *kara* ~ *ni kakete*, but not exactly. The former indicates a spatial / temporal / quantitative beginning, and the end point is clear, but the latter indicates a spatial / temporal beginning and the end point is not clear. So, as shown in [1], ~ *kara* ~ *ni kakete* is ungrammatical or marginal, because the end point is clear.

[1] a. 午前九時**から**午後五時｛**まで** / ***にかけて**｝水道が止まります。
(The water will be shut off from 9 a.m. till 5 p.m.)

b. JRは新宿駅**から**渋谷駅｛**まで** / ??**にかけて**｝不通になっています。
(JR trains are held up from Shinjuku through Shibuya.)

(⇨ ***made*** (DBJG: 225–28))

kara to itte からと言って *conj.*

a conjunction which introduces the reason for s.o.'s action or for s.o.'s having some idea, and conveys disapproval of the action or idea

just because; even if; even though

【REL. *kara*; *tatte*; *te mo*】

◆Key Sentences

(A)

Subordinate Clause		Main Clause (negative)
Sinf		
子供だ	からと言って	許すわけにはいかない。
(I cannot forgive him just because he is a child.)		

(B)

Subordinate Clause		Main Clause (negative)
Sinf		
何も不平を言わない	からと言って	現状に満足しているわけではない。
(Even though I don't complain, it doesn't mean that I'm satisfied with the present situation.)		

(C)

Subordinate Clause		Main Clause (negative)
Sinf		
試験に受からなかった	からと言って	そんなに悲観することはない。
(You don't have to be so pessimistic because you didn't pass the exam.)		

Formation

Sinf からと言って

高いからと言って　(because / even if / even though it is expensive)

Examples

(a) 弁償したからと言って済む問題ではない。
(It is not a problem which will be solved because you have paid / will pay compensation.)

(b) 上司の命令だからと言って黙って従うわけにはいかない。
(I cannot obey the order without asking questions even if it is from my boss.)

(c) アメリカへ行ったからと言って勝手に英語が上手になるものではない。
(Your English will not improve (by itself / automatically) even if you go to America.)

(d) 毎日授業に出ているからと言って真面目に勉強していることにはならない。
(Even though he goes to class every day, it doesn't mean that he is studying seriously.)

(e) こんなことを言うからと言って別に批判しているわけではない。
(Even though I tell you such a thing, it doesn't mean that I'm criticizing you.)

(f) 自分の問題じゃないからと言って知らん顔をしているのはよくない。
(It's not right for you to be indifferent just because it's not your problem.)

(g) 女だからと言って侮ってはいけない。
(Don't take her lightly just because she is a woman.)

Notes

1. *Kara to itte* occurs with a main clause in the negative form. "S_1 *kara to itte* S_2 {*wake ni wa ikanai / koto wa nai* / etc.}" is used in the following situations:

(1) When the speaker expects the hearer (or someone else) to think S_2 because of S_1 but disagrees with it (e.g., KS(A) and Exs.(a) – (d)) or denies it (e.g., KS(B) and Ex.(e)).

(2) When the hearer (or someone else) does something because of S_1, but the speaker disagrees with that action (e.g., KS(C), Exs.(f) and (g)).

2. *Kara to itte* can be contracted to *karatte* in conversation, as in (3).

(3) ちょっと出来る**からって**，そんなに威張らなくてもいいでしょう。
(You shouldn't boast that much just because you are better than others.)

【Related Expressions】

I. *Kara* cannot be used in place of *kara to itte*. Compare [1] and KS(A).

[1] 子供だから許すわけにはいかない。
(I can't forgive him just because he is a child.)

The difference is that the scope of *wake ni wa ikanai* in [1] is *yurusu* '(I) forgive him' while that of *wake ni wa ikanai* in KS(A) is *kodomo da kara yurusu* '(I) forgive him because he is a child.'

II. *Te mo* and *tatte* are similar to *kara to itte*. However, unlike sentences with *kara to itte*, sentences with *te mo* or *tatte* do not convey the speaker's disapproval of using S_1 as a justification for S_2. (See Note 1.) Compare [2a] with KS(C), and [2b] with Ex.(a).

[2] a. 試験に受から｛**なくても** / **なくたって**｝そんなに悲観することはない。
(You don't have to be so pessimistic even though you didn't pass the exam.)

b. 弁償｛**しても** / **したって**｝済む問題ではない。
(The problem will not be solved even though you have paid compensation / even if you pay compensation.)

karō かろう *aux.* <w>

an auxiliary indicating the writer's conjecture which is not based on any particular information or evidence	probably 【REL. *darō*】

◆Key Sentence

	Adj(*i*)	
十年後の自分を予想するのは	**難し**	かろう。
(It is probably difficult to predict what one's self will be like in ten years time.)		

Formation

(i) Adj(*i*)stem かろう

面白かろう (s.o. / s.t. is probably interesting)

よかろう (s.o. / s.t. is probably good)

なかろう (s.o. / s.t. does not probably exist)

(ii) {Adj(*i*)stem く(は) / {Adj(*na*)stem / N} では} なかろう (s.o. / s.t. is probably not ~)

面白く(は)なかろう (s.o. / s.t. is probably not interesting)

困難ではなかろう (s.t. is probably not hard)

学者ではなかろう (s.o. is probably not a scholar)

Examples

(a) この研究を一年で完成するのは極めて難しかろう。
(It is probably extremely difficult to complete this research in one year.)

(b) 日本人の中にも創造性のない教育に反対する人は多かろう。
(Even among the Japanese, there are probably a lot of people who oppose education without creativity.)

(c) 私のように文化は宗教のようなものだと考えている人は少なかろう。
(Few people probably think, as I do, that culture is something like religion.)

(d) アメリカの大学のように，日本の大学でも学生に教師の評価をさせるとよかろう。
(It would probably be good if Japanese universities allowed students to evaluate instructors as American universities do.)

(e) 人種偏見ほど人間に根深いものはなかろう。
(Nothing is probably as deep-rooted in humans as racial prejudices.)

(f) 近い将来に日米関係に大きな変化はなかろう。
(There will probably not be a big change in the US-Japan relationship in the near future.)

(g) あの二人の間柄は親しくはなかろう。
(The relationship between the two is probably not close.)

(h) 残業手当てを要求することは無理ではなかろう。
(It is probably not unreasonable to ask for pay for overtime work.)

(i) 彼にはアリバイがあるのだから，犯人ではなかろう。
(He has an alibi, so he is probably not the culprit.)

Notes

1. The conjectural auxiliary *karō* is the contracted form of the no longer used Adj(*i*) *ku arō*, and *arō* is the conjectural form of *aru*. (⇨ ***yō***)

2. The auxiliary *karō* is connected only with an Adj(*i*). When Adj(*na*) and N are connected with *karō*, they have to be negative, because the negative *nai* is an Adj(*i*).

3. V cannot be connected with *karō*, as shown in (1).

    (1) *私達は来年もこの共同研究を続ける**かろう**。

(We will probably continue this joint research next year.)
→ 私達は来年もこの共同研究を続ける**だろう**。

【Related Expression】

Another auxiliary *darō* can replace *karō* without any change of meaning, as in [1]. Note that the connections for the two auxiliaries are different: the ones for *darō* are {V / Adj(*i*)inf} *darō* and {Adj(*na*)stem / N} {ø / *datta*} *darō*, whereas the ones for *karō* is Adj(*i*)stem *karō*. (See Formation.)

[1] a. 十年後の自分を予想するのは難しい**だろう**。(cf. KS(A))

b. この研究を一年で完成するのは極めて難しい**だろう**。(cf. Ex.(a))

c. 日本人の中にも創造性のない教育に反対する人は多い**だろう**。(cf. Ex(b))

Also to be noted is the fact that *karō* cannot be connected with the past tense, but *darō* can, as shown in [2].

[2] a. ジョンには日本滞在(たいざい)は興味深(きょうみぶか)かった {(**だ**)**ろう** / ***かろう**}。
(For John the stay in Japan was probably intriguing.)

b. 北海道(ほっかいどう)の冬(ふゆ)は寒(さむ)かった {(**だ**)**ろう** / ***かろう**}。
(The winter in Hokkaido was probably cold.)

The most basic difference between *darō* and *karō* is that *darō* can be used in both spoken and written Japanese, but *karō* can be used only in written Japanese.

(⇨ ***darō*** (DBJG: 100–02))

-kata o suru 方をする *phr.*

a phrase to indicate a manner of doing s.t.

do s.t. in a ~ fashion / manner / way

【REL. *yōni*】

◆Key Sentences

(A)

	Adj(*i*)inf	V*masu*	
林田先生は	**厳しい**	**教え**	方をする。
(Prof. Hayashida teaches in a strict manner.)			

(B)

	Vinf	Noun		V*masu*	
昭は	**変わった**	**もの**	の	**見**	方をする。
(Akira views things in a peculiar fashion.)					

(C)

	Noun		V*masu*	
ブラウンさんは	**日本人**	のような	**考え**	方をする。
(Mr. Brown thinks like the Japanese.)				

(D)

	Vinf		V*masu*	
誰にでも	**分かる**	ような	**書き**	方をして下さい。
(Please write in such a way that anyone can understand it.)				

Formation

(i) {Adj(*i*)inf / Adj(*na*)stem な / Vinf} + (Noun の) + V*masu* 方をする

ひどい負け方をする (lose in a terrible way)

ユニークなものの見方をする (view things in a unique fashion)

よく分かる教え方をする (teach clearly (lit. in a way one can understand well))

(ii) N のような + (Noun の) + V*masu* 方をする

子供のようなものの言い方をする (talk like a child (lit. talk in a child-like manner))

(iii) Vinf ような + (Noun の) + V*masu* 方をする (Adjectives rarely occur before ような)

人が感動するような話し方をする (speak in such a way that people are impressed)

Examples

(a) あのピッチャーは面白い投げ方をする。
(That pitcher throws (a ball) in an interesting way.)

(b) 吉田君は乱暴な運転のし方をするので乗せてもらうのが怖い。
(I'm afraid of getting a ride from Yoshida because he drives carelessly (lit. in a wild fashion).)

(c) 正はほかの学生と違った勉強のし方をしているようだ。
(Tadashi seems to study in a different way from other students.)

(d) 私には野村先生のような考え方は出来ない。
(I cannot think like Prof. Nomura.)

(e) 勉強が楽しくなるような教え方をしてほしい。
(We'd like to be taught in such a way that we (come to) like studying.)

(f) この問題について私と同じような考え方をする人は多くないでしょう。

(There wouldn't be many people who think about this problem in the same way as I do.)

(g) 田村(たむら)はその大臣(だいじん)をよく知(し)っているような話し方をする。
((1) Tamura's talk sounds like he knows the minister well. (2) Tamura talks as if he knew that minister well.)

Notes

1. *-kata o suru* is used to indicate a manner in which someone does something. When this phrase is used in a main clause, the manner is under focus.

2. When a *suru*-verb is involved in V*masu-kata*, the noun part of the verb is followed by *no*, as in (1).

   (1) a. 運転 {の / *ø} し方
   (the way s.o. drives; how to drive)

   b. ノック {の / *ø} し方
   (the way s.o. knocks (on the door); how to knock (on the door))

   (⇨ ***-kata*** (DBJG: 183–87))

3. The direct object of the verb in V*masu-kata* is marked by *no*, not by *o*, as in (2). Thus, when the verb is a *suru*-verb, *no* occurs twice in the phrase, as in (2b).

   (2) a. フットボール {の / *を} 投げ方
   (the way s.o. throws a football; how to throw a football)

   b. クレーン {の / *を} 運転のし方
   (the way s.o. operates a crane; how to operate a crane)

4. The expressions like *yōna hanashi-kata o suru* or *yōna mono no ii-kata o suru* can be interpreted in two ways in some contexts, as in Ex.(g).

【Related Expressions】

I. In some cases, the manner in which someone does something is expressed by the adverbial form of an adjective, as in [1].

K

[1] 米田先生は文法を {**うまく / 上手に**} 教える。
(Mr. Yoneda is good at teaching grammar (lit. teaches grammar skillfully).)

(⇨ **Appendix 1** (DBJG: 581))

However, "Adj(*i* / *na*) V*masu-kata o suru*" and "Adverbial form of Adj(*i* / *na*) V" are not always interchangeable. First, the adverbial forms of some adjectives cannot be used as manner adverbs (i.e., an adverb to mean "in such and such a manner"), as in [2].

[2] a. *あのピッチャーは**面白く**投げる。(Acceptable form: ……面白い投げ方をする。)
(That pitcher throws (a ball) in an interesting way.)

b. *和男は**変に**笑った。(Acceptable form: ……変な笑い方をした。)
(Kazuo smiled strangely (lit. smiled in a strange manner).)

Second, "Adj(*i* / *na*) V*masu-kata o suru*" cannot be used when the manner can be described objectively without involving any personal impression, as in [3].

[3] a. ***まっすぐな**歩き方をして下さい。(Acceptable form: まっすぐに歩いて下さい。)
(Please walk straight.)

b. *私 達は**丸い**座り方をした。(Acceptable form: ……丸く座った。)
(We sat in a circle.)

Third, "Adj(*i* / *na*) V*masu-kata o suru*" cannot be used to describe how a person feels, as in [4].

[4] a. *私は**うれしい**思い方をした。(Acceptable form: ……うれしく思った。)
(I was pleased.)

b. *紀子は**悲しい**感じ方をした。(Acceptable form: ……悲しく感じた。)
(Noriko felt sad.)

II. "X *yōni* V" and "X *yōna* V*masu-kata o suru*" both indicate a manner in which someone does something. However, "X *yōni* V" is used when expressing an exact likeness. Compare [5a] and [5b].

[5] a. 私が言う**ように**書いて下さい。
((1) Please write it down just like I tell you. (2) Please write it in the way I tell you.)

b. 私が言う**ような**書き方をして下さい。
(Please write it in a way similar to the way I tell you.)

Similarly, [6a] implies that Mr. Green's command of Japanese is like that of a native Japanese. [6b], on the other hand, implies that some aspects of Mr. Green's way of speaking Japanese are like native Japanese speakers.

[6] a. グリーンさんは日本人の**ように**日本語を話す。
(Mr. Green speaks Japanese like a native Japanese.)

b. グリーンさんは日本人の**ような**日本語の話し方をする。
(Mr. Green speaks Japanese in a way similar to the way Japanese people speak.)

Because of the "exactness" that "X *yōni* V" implies, this expression is unnatural if it is unreasonable to expect that someone does something exactly in the way indicated in X, as in [7].

[7] a. ??ブラウンさんはハリスさんの**ように**ものを見る。
(Mr. Brown views things just like Mr. Harris.)

b. ブラウンさんはハリスさんの**ような**ものの見方をする。
(Mr. Brown views things similarly to the way that Mr. Harris does.)

(⇨ ***yōni***[1, 2] (DBJG: 553-56))

K

ka to iu to かと言うと *conj.*

a conjunction to indicate the speaker's assertion that a popular belief is not right	you would think that ~ but (that is not right)

◆Key Sentence

Sentence$_1$		Sentence$_2$	Sentence$_3$
日本人はみんなすしが好き	かと言うと，	そうではない。	嫌いな人もいる。
(You would think that all the Japanese like sushi, but that is not true. Some Japanese don't like it.)			

Formation

(i) ~ {V / Adj(*i*)}inf かと言うと，S。

{話す / 話した} かと言うと (you would think that s.o. talks / talked but ~)

{高い / 高かった} かと言うと (you would think that s.t. is / was expensive but ~)

(ii) ~ {Adj(*na*)stem / N} {ø / だった} かと言うと，S。

{静か / 静かだった} かと言うと (you would think that s.t. is / was quiet but ~)

{先生 / 先生だった} かと言うと (you would think that s.o. is / was a teacher but ~)

Examples

(a) がんは治らない病気かと言うと，そうではない。早期発見をすれば治ると言われている。
(You would think that cancer is not curable, but that is not true. If it is detected early it is said to be curable.)

(b) 日本に行って，二，三年住めば日本語が上手になるかと言うと，そうでもないようだ。かえって下手になることもある。

(You'd think that if you went to Japan and lived there for a few years, your Japanese would become good, but that doesn't seem to be true. On the contrary, your Japanese may become worse than before.)

(c) 大学の時にいい成績の学生が社会で成功するかと言うと，必ずしもそうではないようだ。

(You'd think that a college student with good grades would be successful in society, but that doesn't always seem to be the case.)

(d) 毎日運動をすれば長生きをするかと言うと，そうでもなさそうだ。

(You'd think that if you did exercise every day, you would live long, but that does not seem to be true.)

(e) 日本語は難しいかと言うと，話したり聞いたりすることはそんなに難しくない。

(You'd think that Japanese would be hard, but speaking and listening are not that hard.)

(f) ボストンでの車なしの生活が不便だったかと言うと，全然そうではなかったんです。

(You'd think that my life without a car in Boston must have been inconvenient, but it wasn't at all.)

Note

The conjunction can be used when one makes an assertion that a popular belief or what the listener / reader may believe is not always true. In S_1 *ka to iu to* S_2, what the listener / reader is expected to believe is expressed in S_1. S_2 is often *sō de wa nai* or its variations as shown in KS and Exs. However, the S_2 part is sometimes omitted as in the following examples.

(1) 日本人はみんなすしが好きかと言うと，全然すしを食べない日本人も時々いる。

(You would think that all Japanese liked sushi, but you sometimes encounter Japanese who don't like sushi.)

(2) 漫画はくだらないかと言うと，中にはとてもいい漫画もある。
(You would think that comic books are trash, but some of them are really good.)

K

(no) kawari ni (の)代わりに *conj. / comp. prt.*

an action / state that is expressed in the subordinate clause is balanced by another action / state expressed in the main clause, or s.t. / s.o. that is replaced by s.t. / s.o. else

instead of; instead; but (to make up for ~); so (to make up for ~); in place of
【REL. *ga*; *kara*; *keredo*(*mo*); *-nai de*; *node*; *shikashi*; *-zu ni*】

◆Key Sentences

(A)

Sentence$_1$ (Subordinate Clause)			Sentence$_2$ (Main Clause)
	Vinf		
昼間	**遊ぶ**	代わりに	夜勉強するつもりだ。
(I am going to enjoy myself in the daytime, so / but (to make up for it) I will study at night.)			

(B)

Sentence$_1$ (Subordinate Clause)			Sentence$_2$ (Main Clause)
	Vinf·past		
山田さんにはちょっと余分に	**働いてもらった**	代わりに	特別手当てを出した。
(Mr. Yamada worked for us a bit extra, so / but (to make up for it) we paid him special compensation.)			

(C)

Sentence$_1$ (Subordinate Clause)			Sentence$_2$ (Main Clause)
	Adj(*i*)inf		
前のアパートは設備が	**悪かった**	代わりに	家賃が安かった。
(The former apartment had bad facilities, so / but (to make up for it) the rent was cheap.)			

(D)

	Noun		
今朝は,	**コーヒー**	の代わりに	ココアを飲んだ。
(This morning I drank cocoa instead of coffee.)			

Formation

(i) {V/Adj(*i*)}inf 代わりに

話す代わりに (instead of talking)

高い代わりに (instead of being expensive)

(ii) Adj(*na*)stem {な / だった} 代わりに

静か {な / だった} 代わりに (is / was quiet but (to make up for ~))

(iii) N {の / だった} 代わりに

先生の代わりに (in place of the teacher)

いい先生だった代わりに (s.o. was a good teacher, but (to make up for ~))

Examples

(a) 今日は図書館で勉強する代わりに寮の部屋で勉強した。
(Today I didn't study in the library. Instead, I studied in my dorm room.)

(b) 私はトムに日本語を教えてあげた代わりに彼に英語を教えてもらった。
(I taught Tom Japanese, so (to make up for it) he taught me English.)

(c) 高い長距離電話をかける代わりに，手紙をよく書いています。
(Instead of making expensive long distance calls I often write letters.)

(d) 私のアパートは家賃が高い代わりに，駅に近くてとても便利です。
(My apartment is expensive, but it is close to the station and very convenient.)

(e) 私達の日本語の先生は厳しい代わりに学生の面倒見がいい。
(Our teacher is strict, but (instead) he takes good care of his students.)

(f) 大学の先生は給料が低い代わりに自由がある。
(College professors' salaries are low, but (instead) they have freedom.)

(g) 父は体が弱い代わりに意志がとても強い。
(My father is physically weak, but (instead) he has a very strong will.)

(h) この辺は静かな代わりに，店も遠くて不便です。
(This area is quiet, but (instead) it's inconvenient because the stores are far away.)

(i) 日本語の授業にいつもの山田先生の代わりに田中という新しい先生がいらっしゃった。
(To our Japanese class came a new teacher Ms. Tanaka instead of our regular teacher Ms. Yamada.)

Notes

1. The conjunction / particle *kawari ni* indicates s.t. being compensated by s.t. else. If the idea of balancing is missing *kawari ni* cannot be used. (⇨ **Related Expressions**)

   (1) *図書館に行った**代わりに**閉まっていた。
   → 図書館に行ったが，閉まっていた。

   (2) *この本はつまらない**代わりに**読んでしまいました。
   → この本はつまらないけれど，読んでしまいました。

2. Vnonpast before *kawari ni* indicates an action that has not taken place; whereas Vpast *kawari ni* indicates an action that has already taken place. Consider the difference in meaning among the sentences (3) below:

   (3) a. 昼間**遊ぶ**代わりに夜遊ぶつもりだ。
   (I intend to play at night instead of having fun in the daytime.)

   b. 昼間**遊んだ**代わりに夜勉強した。
   (I played in the daytime, but (to make up for it) I studied at night.)

   c. 昼間**遊んだ**代わりに夜勉強するつもりだ。
   (I played in the daytime, so (to make up for it) I intend to study at night.)

   d. 昼間**遊ぶ**代わりに夜遊んだ。
   (I played at night instead of playing in the daytime.)

   In (3a) and (3d), the speaker doesn't or didn't play in the daytime, respectively but in (3b) and (3c), the speaker played.

   In the case of adjectives before *kawari ni*, whatever is expressed by the adjective holds true, but Adj_1 inf·past *kawari ni* Adj_2 inf·nonpast is unacceptable, as shown in (4).

   (4) a. アパートは**高い**代わりに**便利だ**。
   (The apartment is expensive but it is convenient.)

K

b. アパートは**高い**代わりに**便利だった**。
(The apartment was expensive but it was convenient.)

c. *アパートは**高かった**代わりに**便利だ**。
(The apartment was expensive but it is convenient.)

d. アパートは**高かった**代わりに**便利だった**。
(The apartment was expensive but it was convenient.)

【Related Expressions】

If an action / state expressed in S *kawari ni* does not actually occur as in Exs.(a) and (c), the entire sentence can be rewritten by using *-nai de* or *-zu ni*, as shown in [1a]. If an action / state expressed in the subordinate clause actually occurs and the subordinate clause is connected with the main clause with the meaning of 'so' or 'but,' the entire sentence can be rewritten by *kara / node* or *ga / keredo*(*mo*) / *shikashi*, as shown in [1b] and [1c]. However, the choice of *kawari ni* will make the meaning of compensation much clearer.

[1] a. 今日は図書館で勉強 {**しないで** / **せずに**} 寮の部屋で勉強した。 (cf. Ex.(a))

b. 山田さんにはちょっと余分に働いてもらった {**から** / **ので** / **が** / **けれど** / **。しかし**}，特別手当てを出した。(cf. KS(B))

c. 前のアパートは設備は悪かった {**から** / **ので** / **。しかし** / **が** / **けれど** / **のに**}，家賃は安かった。(cf. KS(C))

The crucial difference between *-nai de*, *-zu ni*, *ga*, *keredo*(*mo*), *shikashi* on one hand, and *kawari ni* (as a subordinate conjunction) on the other hand is that the former can be used even when no meaning of balancing is intended, but the latter cannot be used if balancing is not implied. That is why all the following sentences would become unacceptable if *-nai de*, *-zu ni*, *ga*, *keredo*(*mo*), and *shikashi* were replaced by *kawari ni*.

[2] 今朝は朝ご飯を {食べ**ないで** / 食べ**ずに** / *食べる**代わりに**} 会社に行った。
(I went to the company without eating my breakfast.)

[3] 友達(ともだち)に電話(でんわ)した {**が** / **けれど** / ***代わりに**}, あいにく, 家(いえ)にいなかった。
(I called my friend, but to my regret, he wasn't at home.)

[4] スミスさんは日本に行ったことがない {。**しかし** / ***代わりに**}, 日本語が上手(じょうず)だ。
(Mr. Smith has never been to Japan. Yet he is good at Japanese.)

kekka 結果 *n.*

a noun which expresses the idea of "as a result of"

as a result of; after; upon

◆Key Sentences

(A)

Noun			Main Clause (result)
投票(とうひょう)	の	結果(けっか),	その提案(ていあん)は反対多数(はんたいたすう)で否決(ひけつ)された。
(As a result of the vote, the proposal was rejected by the majority's opposition.)			

(B)

	Vinf·past		Main Clause (result)
妻(つま)と	**相談**(そうだん)**した**	結果,	家(いえ)を買(か)うことにした。
(After my wife and I discussed it, we decided to buy a house.)			

Formation

(i) Nの結果

試験(しけん)の結果 (as a result of an exam)

(ii) Vinf·past 結果

話した結果 (upon / after talking)

Examples

(a) 相談の結果，今回の旅行は延期することになった。
(After discussion, it's been decided that the planned trip will be postponed.)

(b) 検査の結果，妻の体はどこにも異状がないことが分かった。
(As a result of the examination, my wife was found to be healthy (lit. it was found that there was no abnormality with my wife's body).)

(c) 調査の結果，新しい事実が発見された。
(As a result of the investigation, new facts emerged.)

(d) 警察で調べた結果，原因はたばこの火の不始末と分かった。
(As a result of the police investigation, it was determined that the cause (of the fire) was the careless handling of a cigarette butt.)

(e) 特別のダイエットをした結果，十キロの減量に成功した。
(I've succeeded in losing ten kilos as the result of a special diet.)

(f) 新しい教科書を使った結果，学生の成績が著しく伸びた。
(As a result of using a new textbook, the students improved their performance remarkably (lit. the performance of the students improved remarkably).)

(g) ゴルフの個人指導を受けた結果，自分の問題点が明らかになった。
(Upon taking a private golf lesson, my problems became clear.)

Note

Kekka can be interpreted as 'as a result of' or 'after / upon doing s.t.' only when it is not followed by a particle. Otherwise, *kekka* is a common noun, as seen in (1).

(1) a. 試験の**結果**は来週知らせます。
(I will let you know the result of the exam next week.)

b. 私が特別のダイエットをした**結果**をまだ誰も知らない。
(No one knows the result of my special diet yet.)

kekkō 結構 *adv.* <s>

an adverb that indicates that s.t. exceeds the speaker's and / or hearer's expectation to a considerable degree

quite; rather; pretty
【REL. *angai*; *igai to*; *wariai*】

◆Key Sentence

ここのすしは，	結構	おいしいね。
(The sushi in this place is quite good, isn't it?)		

Examples

(a) この車は古いんだけど，結構よく走りますよ。
(This car is old, but it runs quite well, you know.)

(b) あの人は間抜けに見えるでしょう。でも，結構 頭がいいんです。
(He looks dumb, but he is quite sharp.)

(c) 四月だというのに，結構寒いね。
(It is April, but it is rather cold, isn't it?)

(d) 小さい町なのに，結構いいレストランがあるね。
(There are quite a few good restaurants in this small town, aren't there?)

(e) この料理は量は少ないけど，結構胃にもたれるね。
(This dish is small in quantity, but it is pretty heavy on the stomach.)

(f) 今日は日曜日なのに高速が結構混んでいるね。
(Today is Sunday, but the highway is rather crowded, isn't it?)

(g) 父は楽天的な人でしたが，失 職した時には結構悩んだようです。
(My father was an optimist, but when he lost his job, I think he suffered quite a bit.)

(h) カラオケは初めてだったが，結構楽しかった。
(It was my first *karaoke*, but it was rather enjoyable.)

Notes

1. The adverb *kekkō* is used in colloquial speech when something exceeds the speaker's and / or hearer's expectation to a considerable degree. In the sentences that end in *ne* the adverb indicates that s.t. exceeds both the speaker's and the hearer's expectation (as in KS and Exs.(c) – (f)). The adverb *kekkō* indicates that s.t. exceeds the hearer's expectation (as in Exs.(a) and (b)) or the speaker's expectation (as in Exs.(g) and (h)).

2. The adverb can be used with a verb that expresses an undesirable state as in Exs.(e) – (g) but it cannot be used easily with an adjective that expresses an undesirable state as shown below:

(1) a. ??この雑誌は結構**つまらない**です。
(This magazine is quite boring.)
→ この雑誌は思ったより**つまらない**です。

b. ??このケーキは結構**まずい**です。
(This cake is rather tasteless.)
→ このケーキは思ったより**まずい**です。

For that matter *kekkō* cannot be used with any negative predicate.

(2) a. *この雑誌は結構**面白くない**です。
(This magazine is quite uninteresting.)
→ この雑誌は思ったより**面白くない**です。

b. *このケーキは結構**おいしくない**です。
(This cake is quite tasteless.)
→ このケーキは思ったより**おいしくない**です。

3. The verb predicate that is modified by *kekkō* is subject to degree interpretation. For example, *yoku hashiru* 'run well' (in Ex.(a)), *i ni motareru* 'heavy on the stomach' (in Ex.(e)), *komu* 'get crowded' (in Ex.(f)) and *nayamu* 'suffer' (Ex.(g)).

【Related Expressions】

I. Another adverb *angai* is used to express unexpectedness about an action or a state. Since *kekkō* also expresses unexpectedness about s.t., there are cases where *kekkō* can be replaced by *angai*, as shown in [1].

[1] a. ここのすしは，**案外**(あんがい)おいしいね。(cf. KS)

b. あの人は間抜けに見えるでしょう。でも，**案外**頭がいいんです。(cf. Ex.(b))

c. 今日は日曜日なのに高速が**案外**混んでいるね。(cf. Ex.(f))

d. 父は楽天的な人でしたが，失職した時には**案外**悩んだようです。(cf. Ex.(g))

However, when the modified verb does not indicate s.t. that is subject to degree interpretation such as *kekkon-suru* 'get married,' *kuru* 'come,' *tsuku* 'arrive,' etc., *kekkō* is out of the question as shown in [2].

[2] a. {**案外** / ***結構**} あの二人(ふたり)は結婚(けっこん)するかもしれないよ。
(The two might get married contrary to our expectation.)

b. あいつはパーティーにはたいてい来(こ)ないけど，今日は夏休(なつやす)みの前(まえ)だし，{**案外** / ***結構**} 来(く)るかもしれないぞ。
(That guy usually doesn't show up at a party, but today is right before the summer break so he might come contrary to our expectation.)

c. {**案外** / ***結構**}，彼(かれ)の方(ほう)が先(さき)に着(つ)いているかもしれませんよ。
(He may have arrived there earlier than us, contrary to our expectation, you know.)

K

When degree interpretation is possible, both *kekkō* and *angai* are both acceptable, as already shown in [1]. In other words, *kekkō* has to be used with a predicate that is subject to degree interpretation, but the degree interpretation is irrelevant to *angai*.

II. There is another adverb *igai to* 'unexpectedly,' 'to one's surprise' which is very similar to *kekkō*. *Igai to* means that s.t. totally beyond one's expectation occurs. Since both *kekkō* and *igai to* express unexpectedness they are interchangeable when the predicate is subject to degree interpretation.

[3] a. ここのすしは，**意外**(いがい)**と**おいしいね。(cf. KS)

b. あの人は間抜けに見えるでしょう。でも，**意外と**頭がいいんです。(cf. Ex.(b))

c. 今日は日曜日なのに高速が**意外と**混んでいるね。(cf. Ex.(f))

d. 父は楽天的な人でしたが，失職した時には**意外と**悩んだようです。(Ex.(g))

Just like *angai*, *igai to* cannot be replaced by *kekkō* when the predicate is not subject to degree interpretation.

[4] a. {**意外と** / ***結構**} あの二人は結婚するかもしれないよ。
(The two might get married contrary to our expectation.)

b. あいつはパーティーにはたいてい来ないけど，今日は夏休みの前だし，{**意外と** / ***結構**} 来るかもしれないぞ。
(That guy usually doesn't show up at a party, but today is right before the summer break so he might come contrary to our expectation.)

c. {**意外と** / ***結構**}，彼の方が先に着いているかもしれませんよ。
(He may have arrived there earlier than us, contrary to our expectation, you know.)

III. Another adverb *wari(ai) to / ni* or *wariai* 'a little more than one has expected' expresses a slight gap between expectation and reality. In other words, the speaker has some expectation about something, and believes that reality is relatively higher or lower than his expectation. *Kekkō* in the KS and Exs. can be all replaced by *wari(ai) to / ni* or by *wariai*.

[5] a. ここのすしは，**割(合)と**おいしいね。(cf. KS)
(The sushi served here is rather good.)

b. あの人は間抜けに見えるでしょう。でも，**割と**頭がいいんです。(cf. Ex.(b))
(He looks dumb, but he is rather smart.)

c. 今日は日曜日なのに高速が**割合**混んでいるね。(cf. Ex.(f))
(Today is Sunday, but the highway is rather crowded, isn't it?)

K

The replaced versions express the speaker's comparison between the expectation and the reality. So, for example, in [5a], the speaker expected that sushi served at the restaurant would not be delicious because the store did not look good or the price was cheap. But he is pleasantly surprised that sushi served there is pretty good. If such comparison between the expectation and the reality is difficult the replacement becomes impossible as shown in [6] below.

[6] *父は楽天的な人でしたが，失職した時には**割に**悩んだようです。(cf. Ex.(g))

kono この *dem. adj.*

a demonstrative adjective which indicates a time or time period around the moment of speech	the last; this past; this; this coming

◆Key Sentences

(A)

		Noun	
秋山さんは	この	**春**	結婚します。
(Miss Akiyama will marry {this spring / this coming spring}.)			

(B)

		Number + Counter	
山下君は	この	**一週間**	授業を休んでいます。
(Yamashita has been absent from class for the past (one) week.)			

Formation

(i) この N

この秋 (this autumn ; this coming autumn)

(ii) この Number + Counter

この一年 (this past year ; this coming year)

Examples

(a) この間吉岡さんに会いました。
(I met Mr. Yoshioka the other day.)

(b) このたびこの会の会員に加えていただきました。
(I became a member of this club at this time.)

(c) この際車を買おうか。
(Shall we buy a car given this occasion?)

(d) この辺で妥協したらどうですか。
(Why don't we compromise now (lit. around this time)?)

(e) この夏は日本の女流作家の研究をしています。
(This summer I'm doing research on Japanese female writers.)

(f) この一週間は忙しくて何もできないだろう。
(I'll be busy this coming week and probably won't be able to do anything (else).)

(g) この次はいつお目にかかれますか。
(When could I meet you next?)

Notes

Kono followed by a certain noun or a number with a certain counter is used as a temporal phrase. The time or time period indicated by the phrase differs depending on the noun which follows and the context.

(1) One time in the past (Exs.(a) and (b)):

この間 (the other day; a while ago); この前 (last time); このたび (on this occasion; at this time); この程 (at this time; recently); この{二月 / 春} (this February / spring)

(2) From one time in the past through the moment of speech (KS(B)):

この頃(these days); この所(these days); この一{週間 / か月 / 年} (this past week / month / year)

(3) Around the moment of speech (Exs.(c) and (d)):

この際 (on this occasion); この辺で (around this time); この辺りで (around this time)

(4) A period of time including the moment of speech (Ex.(e)):

この春 (this spring); この {週 / 月} (this week / month); この一{週間 / か月 / 年} (this week / month / year)

(5) From the moment of speech on (Ex.(f)):

この後(after this); この先(from now on); この一{週間 / か月 / 年} (the following week / month / year)

(6) One time in the future (KS(A) and Ex.(g)):

この次 (next time); この{日曜日 / 二月 / 春} (this coming Sunday / February / spring)

kō shita こうした *dem. adj.*

a demonstrative which refers to s.o. or s.t. mentioned as an example in previous discourse

such; like this

【REL. *ā shita*; *kō itta*; *kō iu*; *konna*; *kono yōna*; *sō shita*】

K

◆Key Sentence

	Noun		
こうした	**問題**	は	この国では聞かれないようである。
(We do not seem to hear about problems like this in this country.)			

Formation

こうした N

こうした人々 (such people)

Examples

(a) こうした行為がどのような結果を招くかは誰の目にも明らかだ。
(It is clear to anyone what kind of result such behavior brings about.)

(b) こうした経験は日本へ行ったことのある者なら誰にでもあるはずだ。
(Anyone who has been to Japan would have had such an experience.)

(c) 私はこうした話には耳を貸さないことにしている。
(I make it a rule not to listen to such stories.)

Note

Kō shita is an adjectival (i.e., pre-noun) form. The adverbial form is *kō shite*. Example:

(1) 私達の活動は**こうして**始まった。
(Our activity started like this.)

【Related Expressions】

I. *Kono yōna* and *konna* (the contracted form of *kono yōna*) mean the same as *kō shita*. However, *kō shita* and *kono yōna* are more formal than *konna* and, therefore, mostly used in written Japanese. The adverbial form of *kono yōna* is *kono yōni*. *Konna* has no adverbial form.

II. The demonstratives *kō iu* and *kō itta* also express the idea "such; like this." However, these expressions do not have corresponding adverbial forms like *kō shite*. (See Note.)

III. *Sō shita* 'like that' and *ā shita* 'like that' are similar to *kō shita* in meaning. However, *sō shita* and *ā shita* cannot be used to refer to s.o. or s.t. from previous discourse.

[1] アメリカでは景気が悪くなると，大企業が大量の労働者を解雇することがよく行われる。{**こうした** / ***そうした** / ***ああした**} 問題はこの国ではあまり聞かれないようである。
(In America, when the economy goes bad, it often happens that big companies lay off a lot of workers. We do not seem to hear about problems like this very often in this country.)

In general, *sō shita* is used to refer to s.o. or s.t. mentioned by a second person, as in [2], and *ā shita* is used to refer to s.o. or s.t. mentioned by a third person, as in [3].

[2] A: アメリカでは景気が悪くなると，大企業が大量の労働者を解雇することがよく行われます。
(In America, when the economy goes bad, it often happens that big companies lay off a lot of workers.)

B: そうですか。{**そうした** / ***ああした** / ***こうした**} 問題はこの国ではあまり聞かれないようです。
(Is that so? We do not seem to hear about problems like that very often in this country.)

[3] [After watching a news report on a massive layoff by an American company on TV, A talks to B]

{**ああした / *こうした / *そうした**} 問題はこの国ではあまり聞かれないようです。
(We do not seem to hear about problems like that very often in this country.)

It should be noted that in [3] *kō shita* is acceptable if A talks to B while watching the report.

K

koso こそ *prt.*

a particle which emphasizes a word, phrase, or clause

the very ~; It is ~ that ~; only (when, after, because, etc.); in particular; precisely; definitely; [an italicized or underlined word]

◆Key Sentences

(A)

Noun		
これ	こそ	我々(われわれ)が探(さが)し求(もと)めていたものだ。
(This is the very thing that we've been looking for.)		

(B)

A:	B:	Noun		
どうもすみませんでした。	いいえ，	**こちら**	こそ	すみませんでした。
(I'm very sorry.)	(No, it's me who should say that (lit. be sorry).)			

(C)

	V*te*		
一人で	**やって**	こそ	勉強になるのだ。
(You can learn something only when you do it by yourself.)			

(D)

Subordinate Clause (cause / reason)			Main Clause
君が正直に**話してくれた**	から	こそ	問題は最小で済んだんだ。
(We could minimize the problem only because you explained (lit. told) it to us honestly.)			

Formation

(i) N (particle) こそ

この人こそ (this man in particular)

彼にこそ (to him in particular)

(ii) V*te* こそ

ここへ来てこそ (only when / after s.o. comes here)

(iii) Sinf からこそ

知らないからこそ (only because s.o. doesn't know)

Examples

(a) A: 一体一週間も何をしていたんだ。
(What on earth were you doing for a whole week?)

B: そう言う君こそ何をしていたんだ。
(You say that but what were *you* doing?)

(b) こんな時(に)こそ全員で力を合わせて問題を解決しなければならない。
(On this kind of occasion, in particular, we all have to cooperate in order to solve the problem.)

(c) 今年こそこの試験に通ってみせる。
(I will pass this exam definitely this year.)

(d) それでこそ我々のリーダーだ。
(That is precisely the kind of behavior we expect from our leader.)

(e) ここにいてこそいい仕事も見つかるのだ。
(You can find a good job only by being here.)

(f) 親友だからこそこんなことまで君に言うんだよ。
(It's because you are my friend that I can tell you (even) such a thing.)

(g) 出来ないからこそ人より余計に練習しなければならないのだ。
(It's precisely because you can't do it that you have to practice more than others do.)

Note

The particles *ga* and *o* are dropped when *koso* follows (e.g., KS(A) and Ex.(a)). The ellipsis of *e* and the temporal, directional, and locational *ni* before *koso* is optional, as in Ex.(b), and (1) and (2).

(1) ロンドン(**へ** / **に**)**こそ**行くべきだ。
(Lodon is the place you shouldn't miss.)

(2) この大学(**に**)**こそ**求めているような学者がいるはずだ。
(This university should be the place to find the type of scholar we are looking for.)

Other particles are not dropped when *koso* follows.

koto こと *aux. n.* <w>

an auxiliary noun to express a command	(Don't) V; should (not); (not) ought to; may not 【REL. **Imperative**】

◆Key Sentences

(A)

	Vinf·nonpast·aff	
発表は十五分以内で	**行う**	こと。
(Each presentation should be completed (lit. done) within fifteen minutes.)		

(B)

	Vinf·nonpast·neg	
プールサイドを	**走らない**	こと。
(Do not run on the pool deck.)		

(C)

	VN		
詳細は二十三ページ(を)	**参照**	の	こと。
(See page 23 for details.)			

Formation

(i) Vinf·nonpast·aff / neg こと

話すこと (should speak)

話さないこと (should not speak)

(ii) VN のこと

使用のこと (should use)

Examples

(a) 私語は慎むこと。
(Refrain from whispering.)

(b) 先に必ずテープを聞くこと。
(Be sure to listen to the tape beforehand.)

(c) 辞書は見ないこと。
(You may not consult any dictionaries.)

(d) 裸足で歩き回らないこと。
(Do not walk around barefoot.)

(e) 弁当(を)持参のこと。
(Bring your own lunch.)

(f) 制服(を)着用のこと。
(Wear uniforms.)

Notes

1. Vinf·nonpast *koto* and VN *no koto* are used only in written Japanese. They often appear in rules and regulations.

2. In sentences involving VN *no koto*, the particles *ga*, *o*, and *ni* are often dropped, as in KS(C), Exs.(e), (f), and (1).

(1) a. 願書は本人(**が**)提出**のこと**。
(The application should be submitted by the applicant in person.)

b. 明朝八時(**に**)東京駅(**に**)集合**のこと**。
(Meet (lit. gather) at Tokyo Station at eight o'clock tomorrow morning.)

koto de ことで *comp. prt.*

a compound particle which indicates a means or a cause

by V-ing; because; result in; cause
【REL. *kara*; *koto ni yori / yotte*; *node*; *tame (ni)*】

◆Key Sentences

(A)

	Means			
		Vinf · nonpast		
私(わたし)は	週末(しゅうまつ)にゴルフを	**する**	ことで	気分転換(きぶんてんかん)を図(はか)っています。
(I try to lift my spirits by playing golf on weekends.)				

(B)

Sinf* (cause)		
彼(かれ)が仲裁(ちゅうさい)の場(ば)に**出(で)ていった**	ことで	事態(じたい)は余計(よけい)にこじれた。
(His appearance at the mediation scene complicated the situation even more. (lit. The situation got even more complicated because he appeared at the mediation scene.))		

*Exceptions: Adj(*na*)stem なことで; N であることで

Formation

(i) Means

Vinf · nonpast ことで

行(い)くことで (by going)

(ii) Cause

Sinf ことで

{行く / 行った} ことで (because s.o. will go / went)

{高い / 高かった} ことで (because s.t. is / was high)

Exceptions: Adj(*na*)stem なことで ; N であることで

便利なことで (because s.t. is convenient)

女であることで (because s.o. is a woman)

Examples

(a) 私が十万円出すことで問題は解決した。
(The problem was solved by my paying 100,000 yen.)

(b) 彼女はものを言わないことで私へ精一杯の抵抗を示しているのです。
(She is demonstrating her utmost resistance to me by not talking.)

(c) 朝晩簡単な体操をするだけのことですばらしい健康が保てます。
(You can maintain wonderful health just by taking simple exercise in the morning and evening.)

(d) 私が参加することであなたに迷惑はかかりませんか。
(Wouldn't my participation cause you trouble?)

(e) 彼のパーティーに行かなかったことで彼の気持ちを害したのでなければよいが。
(I hope I didn't hurt his feelings because I didn't go to his party (lit. by not having gone to his party).)

(f) 私は英語が下手なことで時々損をしている。
(I am sometimes put at a disadvantage because I am poor at English.)

(g) この国では外国人であることで得をすることがある。
(In this country there are times when you benefit from being a foreigner.)

Note

When *koto de* represents a means, the preceding element must be a nonpast verb regardless of the tense of the main clause. When *koto de* represents a cause, the preceding element can be a verb, an adjective, or a copula in either the past or nonpast tense.

【Related Expressions】

I. *Koto ni yori / yotte* expresses the same idea as *koto de*.

[1] 私は週末にゴルフをすること｛**で** / **によって** / **により**｝気分転換を図っています。(=KS(A))

[2] 彼が仲裁の場に出ていったこと｛**で** / **によって** / **により**｝事態は余計にこじれた。(=KS(B))

II. *Tame ni*, *node*, and *kara* can also indicate a cause. One difference between these conjunctions and *koto de* is that "S_1 *koto de* S_2" can be used only when the events, actions, or situations in S_1 and S_2 take place at the same time, as in [3a]. *Tame ni*, *node*, and *kara*, on the other hand, do not have this restriction, as in [3b].

[3] a. 私は学生の時あまり勉強しなかった**ことで**｛**よく親に叱られた** / ***今とても苦労している**｝。
(Because I didn't study very hard when I was a student, {my parents often told me off / I am in trouble now}.)

b. 私は学生の時あまり勉強しなかった｛**ために** / **ので** / **から**｝｛**よく親に叱られた** / **今とても苦労している**｝。
(Because I didn't study very hard when I was a student, {my parents often told me off / I am in trouble now}.)

It should also be noted that *tame ni* indicates a cause, a reason, and a purpose and that *node* and *kara* indicate a cause and a reason, while *koto de* indicates a cause and a means, but not a reason.
(⇨ ***tame*** (***ni***) (DBJG: 447–51); ***node*** (DBJG: 328–31); ***kara***[3] (DBJG: 179–81))

koto ni naru ことになる *phr.*

> a phrase which indicates that an action or event leads to a certain situation or logical conclusion

end up (with); cause; come to mean that

◆Key Sentences

(A)

Topic					
Sinf				Vinf	
これ以上聞く	の	は	彼を余計に	**苦しめる**	ことになる。
(Asking more than this will cause him to suffer too much.)					

(B)

Scond		Adj.	
今これをしておかなかったら	後で	**大変な**	ことになる。
(If we don't do this now, we will end up with an awful situation later.)			

(C)

Scond		Noun		
この手形が落ちなければ	会社は	**倒産**	という	ことになる。
(If we cannot have this draft cashed, our company will end up in bankruptcy.)				

(D)

Topic				
Sinf			Sinf*	
こんな結果(けっか)になった	ということ	は	**我々(われわれ)の準備(じゅんび)に手落(てお)ちがあった**	ことになる。
(Ending up with such a result means that there was something wrong with our preparation.)				

*See Formation (v).

(E)

Topic			
Sinf			Sinf
今回(こんかい)何(なに)も起(お)こらなかった	ということ	は	**このシステムで大丈夫(だいじょうぶ)だ**
という	ことになる。		
(The fact that nothing happened this time means that the system is alright (lit. the situation is alright with this system).)			

K

Formation

(i) Vinf·nonpast ことになる

行(い)くことになる (end up going; lead s.o. to go)

(ii) Adj(*i*)inf·nonpast ことになる

難(むずか)しいことになる (end up with a difficult situation)

(iii) Adj(*na*)stem なことになる

大変なことになる (end up with an awful situation)

(iv) N ということになる

失敗ということになる (end up with a failure; come to mean that s.t. is a failure)

(v) Sinf ことになる (Exceptions: Adj(*na*)stem だ → Adj(*na*)stem な or Formation (vi); N だ → N である or Formation (iv) or (vi))

間違っていたことになる (come to mean that s.t. was wrong)

大丈夫なことになる (come to mean that s.t. is alright)

外国人であることになる (come to mean that s.o. is a foreigner)

(vi) Sinf ということになる

大丈夫だということになる (come to mean that s.t. is alright)

Examples

(a) 今怠けていると試験の時ひどいことになるよ。
(If you don't work now, you'll end up with a terrible situation when you take the exam.)

(b) そんなことをしたら二度と人前に出られないことになる。
(If I / you do such a thing, I / you will end up not being able to appear in public again.)

(c) A 社が百 万円寄付してくれれば合計一千万円に達することになる。
(If Company A donates one million yen, the total sum will become (lit. end up with) ten million yen.)

(d) すべてがうまくいけば来年卒 業ということになります。
(If everything goes well, (it means that) I will graduate next year.)

(e) 葉書が戻って来たということは彼はもうこの住 所には住んでいないことになる。
(That the postcard came back means that he doesn't live at this address any longer.)

(f) これが一キロ二千円ということはこちらの方が高いということになる。
(That this costs 2,000 yen a kilo means that this is more expensive.)

Notes

1. X *koto ni naru* is usually preceded by a topic clause (e.g., KS(A), (D), and (E)) or a conditional clause (e.g., KS(B) and (C)). This clause represents an action or an event which leads to a certain situation or logical conclusion represented by X.

2. A conditional clause before X *koto ni naru* can be either a *tara*-conditional (KS(B) and Ex.(b)), a *ba*-conditional (KS(C), Exs.(c) and (d)), or a *to*-conditional (Ex.(a)).

3. In another context, S *koto ni naru* means 'it will be decided that.'

(⇨ ***koto ni naru*** (DBJG: 202–03))

K

koto ni yoru ことによる *phr.* <w>

a phrase which is used to present an event as the cause of s.t.

be due to the fact that; be caused by; be brought about by; be the result of; because
【REL. *kara da*; *tame da*】

◆Key Sentences

(A)

Topic			
Noun (result)		Clause (cause)	
今回(こんかい)の失敗(しっぱい)	は	事前(じぜん)の話(はな)し合(あ)いが不十分(ふじゅうぶん)だった	ことによる。
(The failure this time is the result of insufficient discussion beforehand (lit. due to the fact that the preceding discussion was insufficient).)			

(B)

Topic				
Clause (result)			Clause (cause)	
進が非行に走った	の	は	**両親の愛情が不足していた**	ことによる。
(Susumu's delinquency was caused by his parents' lack of affection. (lit. The fact that Susumu ran to juvenile delinquency is because his parents were not affectionate enough with him.))				

Formation

Sinf ことによる (Exceptions: Adj(*na*)stem なことによる; N であることによる)

家賃が高いことによる (because the rent is expensive)

表現が不正確なことによる (because the expression is inaccurate)

母が日本人であることによる (because one's mother is Japanese)

Examples

(a) 彼の現在の成功は平生の努力を怠らなかったことによる。
(His present success is due to the fact that he worked hard every day (lit. did not neglect daily effort).)

(b) 彼らの離婚は二人の価値観があまりに違っていたことによる。
(Their divorce was caused by the fact that their value systems were very different.)

(c) 彼が負けたのは勝ちを焦りすぎたことによる。
(His loss is due to the fact that he tried to win quickly.)

(d) 彼の才能がこれ程までに開発されたのは鈴木氏に師事したことによる。
(That his talent was developed to this degree is due to the fact that he studied with Mr. Suzuki.)

Note

S *koto ni yoru* is usually preceded by a topic phrase or clause. S represents the cause of the result represented by the topic phrase or clause.

【Related Expression】

Tame da or *kara da* are also used to present a cause. Thus, KS(B), for example, can be paraphrased as [1].

[1] 進が非行に走ったのは両親の愛情が不足していた {**ことによる / ためだ / からだ**}。(=KS(B))

It should be noted that "X *wa* S *tame da*" and "X *wa* S *kara da*" can be used for "X *wa* S *koto ni yoru*" only when X is a clause. When X is a noun phrase, *tame da* and *kara da* are unnatural, as in [2].

[2] 今回の失敗は事前の話し合いが不十分だった {**ことによる / ?ためだ / ?からだ**}。(=KS(A))

Compare [2] with [3], where X is a clause.

[3] 我々(われわれ)が今回失敗したのは事前の話し合いが不十分だった {**ことによる / ためだ / からだ**}。
(It was because we didn't have enough discussion beforehand that we failed this time.)

It should also be noted that *koto ni yoru* represents only a cause. *Kara da*, on the other hand, represents a reason as well as a cause and *tame da* represents a reason, a purpose, or a cause, as in [4] and [5].

[4] 彼がパーティーに来(こ)なかったのは忙(いそが)しかった {**ためだ / からだ / *ことによる**}。[Reason]
(The reason that he didn't come to the party was that he was busy.)

[5] 彼がパーティーへ来(く)るのは春子(はるこ)に会(あ)う {**ためだ / *からだ / *ことによる**}。[Purpose]
(It is to see Haruko that he is coming to the party.)

(⇨ ***kara***[3] (DBJG: 179–81); ***tame*** (***ni***) (DBJG: 447–51))

K

koto wa nai ことはない *phr.*

a phrase which expresses the idea that there is no need to do s.t. or that there is no possibility of doing s.t.

There is no need to; not necessary; there is no possibility that; there is no chance to 【REL. *hazu wa nai*】

◆Key Sentences

(A)

	Vinf · nonpast	
あんな男の言うことを	**聞く**	ことはない。
(There's no need to listen to a man like that.)		

(B)

	Vinf · nonpast		
彼女が今日の会議を	**忘れる**	ことはない	と思います。
(I think that there is no possibility that she will forget today's meeting.)			

Formation

Vinf · nonpast · aff ことはない

行くことはない (there's no need to go / there is no possibility that s.o. will go)

Examples

(a) あんな奴に親切にしてやることはない。
(There is no need to be kind to a guy like that.)

(b) 何もそんなに慌てることはない。
(There is no need at all to be in such a hurry.)

(c) 君が来ることはないと思います。
((1) I don't think it will be necessary for you to come here. (2) I think that there is no possibility that you will come here.)

(d) 彼がわざわざ出て行くことはないでしょう。
((1) There will probably be no need for him to take the trouble to go out there. (2) There is no possibility that he will go out there.)

(e) もうお目にかかることはないかもしれませんね。
(I might not have a chance to see you again.)

(f) 多分 私が教えることはないと思います。
(I don't think there is a possibility that I will teach.)

Notes

1. Vinf·nonpast + *koto wa nai* is used as an expression equivalent to Vinf·nonpast + *hitsuyō wa nai* 'there is no need to V' or Vinf·nonpast + *kanōsei wa nai* 'there is no possibility that ~.'

2. In some cases *koto wa nai* can be interpreted as either 'no need' or 'no possibility' (e.g., Exs.(c) and (d)). The interpretation depends on the context or situation.

3. Vinf·nonpast + *koto ga/wa aru* does not mean 'there is a need to' or 'there is a possibility that ~.' (⇨ ***koto ga aru***[2] (DBJG: 198–99))

4. In Vinf·nonpast + *koto wa nai*, V must be affirmative.
(⇨ ***nai koto mo/wa nai***)

【Related Expression】

Vinf + *hazu wa nai* is very similar in meaning to Vinf + *koto wa nai* 'there is no possibility that ~.' Vinf + *hazu wa nai* is used when the speaker feels that an event is not impossible but that it is unlikely. Compare KS(B) and [1].

[1] 彼女が今日の会議を忘れる**はずはない**。
(It is unlikely that she will forget today's meeting.)
(⇨ ***hazu*** (DBJG: 133–35))

-ku く *inflectional ending* <w>

a continuative form of an *i*-type adjective	and ; so 【REL. *-kute*】

◆Key Sentences

(A)

	Adj(*i*)stem		
加奈子の性格は	**明る**	く，	無邪気だった。
(Kanako's personality was cheerful and innocent.)			

(B)

		Adj(*i*)stem		
せっかく講演をしに行ったのに，	聴衆が	**少な**	く，	がっかりした。
(I went all the way to give a lecture, but the audience was so small that I felt discouraged.)				

Examples

(a) カルフォルニアの空は青く，美しかった。
(The Californian sky was blue and beautiful.)

(b) トムの東京のアパートの部屋は暗く，狭い。
(Tom's apartment room in Tokyo is dark and small.)

(c) バッハの音楽は歯切れがよく，幾何学的だ。
(Bach's music is very crisp and geometrical.)

(d) ニューヨークタイムズは質が高く，購読者の数も多い。
(The New York Times is high in quality and has many subscribers.)

(e) 世界の平和は得られにくく，維持しにくい。
(World peace is hard to achieve and hard to maintain.)

(f) あの哲学者の思想は分かりやすく，文章も簡潔だ。
(That philosopher's ideas are easy to understand and his writing is simple, too.)

(g) 去年の冬は雪が多く，車の運転が大変だった。
(Last winter there was much snow and it was hard to drive around.)

(h) 私は失敗が恐ろしく，新しいことが何も出来ない。
(I'm afraid of failure, and I can't do anything new.)

(i) 洋子は一人でいるのが寂しく，最近猫を飼い始めた。
(Yoko felt lonely living alone, so she got a pet cat recently.)

Notes

1. Adj(*i*)stem *ku* is used in written Japanese to function as a continuative form. When the *ku*-form connects two predicates, the relationship between the two is either a cumulative relationship as in KS(A) and Exs.(a) – (f) or a cause / reason relationship as in KS(B) and Exs.(g) – (i).

2. As the following examples show it appears that the compound adjective V*masu tai* cannot be used to express a cause / reason relationship as shown in (1), although other compound adjectives can be used that way as shown in (2).

(1) a. ??私は自分の研究を出版**したく**，いくつかの出版社に連絡してみた。
(I want to publish my own research so I contacted several publishers.)

→ 私は自分の研究を出版**したくて**，いくつかの出版社に連絡してみた。

b. ??僕は若い頃から，小説が**書きたく**，うずうずしていた。
(I was restless, wanting to write a novel since my younger days.)

→ 僕は若い頃から，小説が**書きたくて**，うずうずしていた。

(2) a. その作家の文章はとても読み**にくく**，途中で読むのをあきらめてしまった。
(The writer's writings are very hard to read, and I gave up reading it halfway.)

b. 小林先生の文法の説明は分かり**やすく**，とても助かる。
(Professor Kobayashi's grammar explanation is easy to understand, and it is a great help to me.)

K

c. 少女は恋をしている**らしく**，はつらつとしていた。
(The girl appears to be in love with someone, and looks animated.)

3. Adj(*i*) *ku* cannot carry its own tense. Its tense is determined by the tense of the main predicate.

【Related Expression】

Adj(*i*)stem *-kute* can replace all the uses of Adj(*i*)stem *-ku*. The difference between the two are the following. First, *-kute* can be used in both spoken and written Japanese, but *-ku* is restricted to written Japanese. Secondly, *-ku* can be used as an adverb as in [1], but *-kute* cannot be used that way.

[1] a. 字をもっと大き｛**く**／***くて**｝書いて下さい。
(Please write characters larger.)

b. 日本語が面白｛**く**／***くて**｝なってきた。
(Japanese has become interesting.)

Thirdly, as shown in (2) in Notes, *-kute* can be used where *-ku* is not acceptable.
(⇨ **V*masu***; ***te*** (DBJG: 464–67))

kurai くらい *prt.*

a particle which is used to express the degree of a state

to the extent that; so ~ that ~ (almost) ~; at least; the only ~; rather than ~
【REL. *hodo*】

◆Key Sentences

(A)

Topic	Sinf		
私達は	**一歩も歩けない**	くらい	疲れていた。
(We were so tired that we couldn't even take a step. (lit. We were tired to the extent that we couldn't even walk one step.))			

(B)

	Sinf		
今晩は暖かいので	**ストーブが要らない**	くらい	だ。
(It is so warm this evening that we (almost) don't need a heater.)			

(C)

Relative Clause			Noun		Predicate (neg)
Noun					
山田さん	くらい	よく物を忘れる	人	は	いない。
(There's no one who is as forgetful as Yamada (lit. who forgets things as much as Yamada does).)					

(D)

	Noun			
私は料理は下手ですが,	**ご飯**	くらい	(は)	炊けます。
(I am a poor cook (lit. bad at cooking), but I can at least cook rice.)				

(E)

Sinf		Noun		
今この仕事が出来る	のは	**彼**	くらい	のものだ。
(He is the only person who can do this job now. (lit. The person who is capable enough to do this job is he.))				

(F)

	Vinf・nonpast			Vinf・past	
そんなことを	**する**	くらい	なら	死んだ	方がましだ。
(I would rather die than do such a thing.)					

Formation

(i) Sinf くらい (the same as relative clause connection rules)

泳げるくらい (to the extent that one can swim)

(先生も)出来なかったくらい (to the extent that (even our teacher) couldn't do it)

恐ろしいくらい (to the extent that (I) am frightened)

気の毒なくらい (to the extent that (I) feel sorry)

(ii) N くらい

山田さんくらい (to Yamada's degree)

Examples

(a) その家は直しようがないくらい傷んでいた。
(That house was so damaged that it couldn't be repaired. (lit. That house was damaged to the extent that it couldn't be repaired.))

(b) 次郎はひどく酔っていて立っていられないくらいだった。
(Jiro was so drunk that he couldn't hold himself upright.)

(c) こんな本，十ドルでもまだ高いくらいだ。
(Even ten dollars would still be too expensive for a book like this.)

(d) 内田さんくらいかわいそうな人はいない。
(There's no one who is as pitiful as Uchida.)

(e) あの時くらい苦しかった時はない。
(I have never suffered as much as I did that time.)

(f) 信頼していた人に裏切られる(こと)くらい辛いことはない。
(There is nothing as painful as being betrayed by someone you have trusted.)

(g) いくら安い所でもシャワーくらい付いているでしょう。
(Even though it is a cheap place, there should at least be a shower.)

(h) そんな物に二万円も出すのはあなたくらいのものですよ。
(You are the only person who would pay as much as 20,000 yen for such a thing.)

(i) あんな男の下で働くくらいなら乞食になった方がましだ。
(I would rather be a beggar than work under such a man.)

Notes

1. *Kurai* can be replaced by *gurai* without a change in meaning.

2. *Kurai* expresses the degree of some state, as in KS(A), (B) and Exs. (a) – (c). (⇨ ***kurai*** (DBJG: 212–13))

3. *Kurai* with a negative predicate expresses a superlative, as in KS(C) and Exs.(d) – (f). KS(C), for example, can be restated as (1).

   (1) 山田さんは一番(いちばん)よく物を忘れる。
   (Mr. Yamada is the most forgetful.)

4. *Kurai* expresses the idea of 'at least,' as in KS(D) and Ex.(g). X *kurai* in this use implies that the degree of a state is such that one cannot expect much more than X from that state.

5. S *no wa* X *kurai no mono da* expresses the idea that the speaker cannot think of anyone or anything else but X that meets the description in S. In other words, X meets the description in S to the highest degree among those the speaker can think of. (See KS(E) and Ex.(h).)

K

6. V_1 *kurai nara* V_2 *hō ga mashi da* expresses the idea that one would rather V_2 than V_1. (This structure literally means that if the speaker's situation is such that he might V_1, it would be better for him to V_2.) (See KS(F) and Ex.(i).)

【Related Expression】

Kurai as used in KS(A) – (C) can be replaced by *hodo* without changing meaning.

[1] 私達は一歩も歩けない**ほど**疲れていた。(=KS(A))

[2] 今晩は暖かいのでストーブが要らない**ほど**だ。(=KS(B))

[3] 山田さん**ほど**よく物を忘れる人はいない。(=KS(C))

Kurai as used in KS(D) – (F) cannot be replaced by *hodo*.

kuse ni くせに *conj.*

a conjunction which expresses the speaker's contempt, anger, or disagreement about s.o.'s action, behavior, or state

although; in spite of the fact that; and yet; but
【Rel. *ni mo kakawarazu*; *noni*】

◆Key Sentences

(A)

Topic	Noun			
山田(やまだ)さんは	**日本人(にほんじん)**	の	くせに	あまり漢字(かんじ)を知(し)らない。
(Although Mr. Yamada is Japanese, he doesn't know many kanji.)				

(B)

Topic (subject)	Subordinate Clause		Main Clause
山内(やまうち)は	**よく知っている**	くせに	何(なに)も教(おし)えてくれない。
(In spite of the fact that Yamauchi knows a lot about it, he doesn't tell me anything.)			

Formation (the same as relative clause connection rules)

(i) N のくせに

子供(こども)のくせに (Although ~ is a child)

(ii) {V / Adj(*i*)}inf くせに

{出来(でき)る / 出来た} くせに (Although ~ can / could)

{弱(よわ)い / 弱かった} くせに (Although ~ is / was weak)

(iii) Adj(*na*)stem {な / だった} くせに

{下手(へた)な / 下手だった} くせに (Although ~ is / was bad at s.t.)

Examples

(a) 彼は大学生のくせに漫画ばかり読んでいる。
(Although he is a college student, all he does is read comics.)

(b) 良子はまだ学生のくせに高いマンションに住んでいる。
(Although Yoshiko is still a student, she lives in an expensive condominium.)

(c) 隆司は下手なくせに私とテニスをしたがる。
(Takashi is a bad (tennis) player, and yet he wants to play with me.)

(d) 怖いくせに無理するなよ。
(You are afraid. Don't pretend to be strong.)

(e) 孝男はお金もないくせに外車を欲しがっている。
(Takao doesn't have money, and yet he wants a foreign car.)

(f) 吉田は前は私を見ても挨拶もしなかったくせに，私が部長になった途端に急に愛想がよくなった。
(Before (the time I became a division chief), Yoshida never greeted me when he saw me, but he suddenly became friendly when I became a division chief.)

(g) 昨日まで見習いだったくせに大きな口をきくな。
(Don't talk big! You were only a trainee until yesterday!)

Notes

1. *Kuse ni* is used only when the main clause and the subordinate clause share the same subject. Thus, in the following sentence, *kuse ni* cannot be used.

   (1) *良子はまだ学生のくせに 両 親は彼女に高いマンションを買ってやった。
   (Acceptable forms: 良子はまだ学生 {**なのに / にもかかわらず**} 両親は…)
   (Although Yoshiko is still a student, her parents have bought her an expensive condominium.)

2. *Kuse ni* is not used when the subject is the first person. In the following, *kuse ni* cannot be used.

   (2) *私は日本人のくせに日本の国歌(こっか)が歌(うた)えない。
   (Acceptable forms: 私は日本人 {**なのに / にもかかわらず**} 日本の国歌が…)
   (Although I am Japanese, I cannot sing the Japanese national anthem.)

3. In conversation, main clauses often drop, as in (3) and (4).

   (3) 何だ，何も知らない**くせに**。
   (Come on! You don't know anything! (So, keep your mouth shut!))

   (4) まあ，男の**くせに**。
   (Gee, aren't you a man! (You are so sissy!))

K

【Related Expressions】

I. *Noni* is similar to *kuse ni*. In fact, *noni* can replace *kuse ni* in KS(A), (B) and Exs.(a) – (f). *Noni*, however, does not express the speaker's emotion as strongly as *kuse ni*. Thus, *noni* is not suitable in contexts as Ex.(g), (3), and (4), where the speaker swears at the hearer. In addition, the restrictions in Notes 1 and 2 do not apply to *noni.*
(⇨ ***noni***[1] (DBJG: 331–35))

II. *Ni mo kakawarazu* expresses an idea similar to *noni* and *kuse ni*. However, *ni mo kakawarazu* is a highly formal and bookish expression and it expresses no emotion. Therefore, it cannot be used in highly emotive situations as in Ex.(g), (3), and (4). Note that the formation rules are different from those of *kuse ni*, as in [1].

[1] (i) {V / Adj(*i*)}inf にもかかわらず

{出来る / 出来た} にもかかわらず (in spite of the fact that s.o. can / could)

{高い / 高かった} にもかかわらず (in spite of the fact that s.t. is / was expensive)

(ii) {Adj(*na*)stem / N} {ø / だった} にもかかわらず

{不便 / 不便だった} にもかかわらず (in spite of the fact that s.t. is / was inconvenient)

{子供 / 子供だった} にもかかわらず (in spite of the fact that s.o. is / was a child)

(⇨ ***ni mo kakawarazu***)

made mo nai までもない *phr.*

There is no point in going as far as to do s.t.

not necessary (to bother) to; do not need (to go as far as) to; do not have to
【REL. *hitsuyō wa nai*; *hodo no koto mo nai*; *ni wa oyobanai*】

◆Key Sentences

(A)

	Vinf·nonpast	
これは簡単な計算だから計算器を	**使う**	までもない。
(This is a simple calculation, so it is not necessary (to bother) to use a calculator.)		

(B)

Vinf·nonpast		
言う	までもなく	ジョージ·ワシントンはアメリカの初代大統領だ。
(Needless to say, George Washington was the first president of the United States.)		

Formation

Vinf·nonpast までもない

話すまでもない (not necessary (to bother) to talk)

Examples

(a) 彼がみんなに尊敬されたのは言うまでもない。
(It goes without saying that he was respected by everybody.)

(b) 大した用事じゃないからあなたがわざわざ行くまでもないでしょう。
(It is not important business, so it is probably not necessary for you to (take the trouble to) get there.)

(c) 行けば分かることですから電話して聞くまでもありません。
(We can find out when we get there, so we don't need to call and ask about it.)

(d) 今更申すまでもありませんが，山中先生はこの分野では指導的な立場にあるお方です。
(Needless to say (now), Prof. Yamanaka is a leading figure in this field.)

(e) それは説明するまでもなく明らかなことだ。
(It is so obvious that no explanation is necessary.)

(f) 待つまでもなく妻は買い物から帰ってきた。
(My wife came back from shopping without my having to wait for her.)

Note

M

The adverbial form *made mo naku* is also frequently used. (See KS(B), Exs.(e) and (f).)

【Related Expressions】

I. *Hitsuyō wa nai* is similar to *made mo nai* in meaning.
However, the former lacks the sense of going as far as to do s.t. or bothering to do s.t.

[1] これは簡単な計算だから計算器を使う**必要はない**。
(This is a simple calculation, so it is not necessary to use a calculator.)

In addition, *no hitsuyō wa nai* can be preceded by a noun, as in [2].

[2] このレストランは予約**の必要はない**。
(No reservation is necessary at this restaurant.)

II. *Hodo no koto mo nai* and *ni wa oyobanai* are very similar to *made mo nai* except that *ni wa oyobanai* is usually not used in the adverbial form.

[3] これは簡単な計算だから計算器を使う {**までもない / ほどのこともない / には及ばない**}。(=KS(A))

[4] 待つ {**までもなく / ほどのこともなく / *には及ばず**} 妻は買い物から帰ってきた。(=Ex.(f))

Ni wa oyobanai can be preceded by a noun, as in [5] and [6].

[5] **お礼**(れい)には及びません。
(You don't need to thank me.)

[6] **ご心配**(しんぱい)には及びません。
(You don't need to worry.)

III. *No wa iu made mo nai* 'It goes without saying that ~' and *iu made mo naku* 'needless to say' are idiomatic phrases; there are no substitute phrases for these expressions.

mai まい *aux.* <w>

an auxiliary which expresses the speaker's negative volition or conjecture

will not; will probably not; be probably not

◆Key Sentences

(A)

	Vinf·nonpast	
もう橋本(はしもと)には何(なに)も	**頼む**(たの)	まい。
(I will not ask any more favors of Hashimoto.)		

(B)

	Vinf·nonpast	
これは恐らく誰も気が	**付く**	まい。
(Probably no one will notice this.)		

(C)

	Adj(*i*)stem	
参加者はそれほど	**多く**	はあるまい。
(There probably won't be many participants.)		

(D)

	Adj(*na*)stem	
この教え方はあまり	**効果的**	ではあるまい。
(This teaching method is probably not very effective.)		

(E)

	Noun		
これは何かの	**間違い**	ではあるまい	か。
(I have a feeling that this is some kind of mistake. (lit. Is this not some kind of mistake?))			

Formation

(i) Vinf·nonpast まい

行くまい ((I) will not go; probably won't go)

教えるまい ((I) will not teach; probably won't teach)

(ii) Adj(*i*)stem くはあるまい

高くはあるまい (s.t. is probably not expensive)

(iii) {Adj(*na*)stem / N} ではあるまい

静かではあるまい (s.t. is probably not quiet)

先生ではあるまい (s.o. is probably not a teacher)

Examples

(a) 清のパーティーにはもう行くまい。
(I will not go to Kiyoshi's parties any more.)

(b) 日本へ行こうか行くまいか迷った。
(I couldn't decide whether I should go to Japan or not.)

(c) 彼は多分誰の言うことも聞くまい。
(He probably won't listen to anyone.)

(d) それは今我々には必要ではあるまい。
(It is probably not necessary for us now.)

(e) この問題はこの学校の学生にはそれほど難しくはあるまい。
(This problem is probably not very difficult for these students.)

(f) ジョージが真相を知っているのではあるまいか。
(I have a feeling that George knows the truth.)

Notes

1. *Mai* is basically a written form. It is usually used in formal writing.
(⇨ ***darō*** (DBJG: 100–02) ; ***mashō*** (DBJG: 240–43))

2. For Gr. 2 verbs, V*masu* is occasionally used instead of Vinf·nonpast. For irregular verbs, *sumai* and *komai* are sometimes used instead of *surumai* and *kurumai*, respectively.

(1) 彼はもう英語は**教えまい**。
(He probably won't teach English any more.)

(2) 彼女はそんなことは**すまい**。
(She probably won't do such a thing.)

(3) こんな機会は二度と**来まい**。
(Such an opportunity probably won't recur (lit. come again).)

3. Vinf·nonpast *mai* expresses the speaker's negative volition. Like Vvol, *mai* does not have a past form. The past tense is expressed by other verbs, as in (4) – (5).

(4) 清のパーティーにはもう**行くまい**と思った。(cf. Ex.(a))
(I decided (lit. thought) that I would not go to Kiyoshi's parties any more.)

(5) もう橋本には何も**頼むまい**と心に決めた。(cf. KS(A))
(I am determined not to ask any more favors of Hashimoto.)

(⇨ ***~ yō to omou*** (DBJG: 569–71))

4. The volition of someone other than the speaker can be expressed by *mai*, as in (6).

(6) 恵子は清のパーティーにはもう**行くまい**と思った。
(Keiko decided (lit. thought) that she would not go to Kiyoshi's parties any more.)

Note that *to omou* 'think that' is used to express the volition of someone other than the speaker. Thus, (7) expresses the speaker's conjecture rather than Keiko's volition.

(7) 恵子は清のパーティーにはもう**行くまい**。
(Keiko probably won't go to Kiyoshi's parties any more.)

5. Vinf·nonpast *mai to suru* expresses the idea of "try not to V."

(8) 彼は私のハンドバッグを取ろうとしたが，私は**取られ(る)まいとして**脇の下に強くはさんだ。
(He tried to take my bag, but I held it tightly under my arm, trying to keep it from being taken.)

(⇨ ***miru*** (DBJG: 246–47))

When this structure is used in a subordinate clause, *suru* is often omitted, as in (9).

(9) 私は**負け(る)まい**と頑張(がんば)った。
(I hung in there, trying not to lose (the game).)

6. Vvol *ka* Vinf·nonpast *mai ka* expresses the idea "whether (I) will V or not," as in Ex.(b).

7. When *mai* expresses the speaker's conjecture, its meaning is similar to *nai darō*. *Mai*, however, is more formal.

8. Because *mai* is seldom used in conversational Japanese, *ja* (the contracted form of *de wa*) *aru mai* rarely occurs.

M

masaka まさか *adv.*

an adverb that indicates the speaker's strong belief that s.t. is not expected to (have) become a reality

incredible; never thought; never dreamed; surely not; impossible; don't tell me that ~; not at all likely; absolutely not 【REL. *yomoya*】

◆Key Sentences

(A)

まさか	美智子(みちこ)があんな男(おとこ)と結婚(けっこん)する	とは思(おも)わなかった。
(I never dreamed that Michiko would marry that kind of a guy.)		

(B)

まさか	あたしの誕生日を忘れた	んじゃないでしょうね。
(Don't tell me that you forgot my birthday!)		

(C)

まさか	彼がこんな寒い日に来る	はずはないですよ。
(Surely he won't show up on such a cold day!)		

(D)

最近父から手紙が来ないけれど,	まさか	具合が悪い	のではあるまい。
(Lately I haven't heard from my father, but God forbid that he might be ill.)			

(E)

A: 七十のおじいさんが高校に入ったんだって。	B: まさか。
(A: I heard that an old man of 70 entered a high school. B: Incredible!)	

Formation

(i) まさか S とは {思わなかった / 考えてもみなかった}。

まさか雪が降るとは {思わなかった / 考えてもみなかった}。
({I didn't believe / I never thought} that it would snow.)

(ii) まさか S {んじゃ / のでは} ないだろうね。

まさか会社を辞める {んじゃ / のでは} ないだろうね。
(Don't tell me that you are going to quit the company.)

(iii) まさか S はずがない。

まさか四月に雪が降るはずがない。
(It is not at all likely that it will snow in April.)

(iv) まさか S まい。

まさか雪は降るまい。 (Don't tell me it's going to snow.)

Examples

(a) まさか自分が交通事故に巻き込まれるとは思いませんでしたよ。
(I never thought that I would be involved in a traffic accident.)

(b) まさか司法試験に一度でパス出来るとは考えてもいなかった。
(I never dreamed that I could pass the bar examination on my first attempt.)

(c) 青い顔をしているけど，まさか病気じゃないでしょうね。
(You look pale. Are you sure you are not ill?)

(d) まさかこんな高いダイヤモンドの指輪を買ってくれたんじゃないでしょうね。
(I don't believe that you bought me such an expensive diamond ring!)

(e) まさかあんないい人が人を殺すなんてあるはずがない。
(Don't tell me a good person like that killed someone.)

(f) まさか彼が日本語の先生になるとは考えてもみなかった。
(I never thought that he would become a Japanese language teacher.)

(g) まさかあの人がそんなことを言うはずはないでしょ。
(It's not at all likely that she has said such a thing!)

(h) もう五月なのだから，まさか雪は降るまい。
(Since it is May it is very unlikely that it will snow.)

(i) 母は入院中だから，まさか私の結婚式に出席するわけにはいくまい。
(Because my mother is in the hospital right now, it is impossible to expect her to attend my wedding.)

(j) A: スミスさんは日本語を一年しか勉強していないのに，ペラペラですよ。
(Smith has studied Japanese for only one year, but he is fluent, you know.)

B: まさか。 (Impossible!)

Notes

1. The adverb *masaka* is used to express the speaker's strong belief that an action or a state is not expected to become or to have become a reality. The action or the state is usually s.t. that is not desirable for the speaker, but not always. Take Ex.(b), for example: no doubt it was a very desirable thing for the speaker to have passed the bar examination on his first attempt. The adverb *masaka* simply emphasizes that he did not expect to pass it.

2. The final predicate is either a thinking verb, a conjecture expression *darō*, or an expectation expression *hazu*, (*wake ni wa iku*) *mai*, and all take a negative form, as shown in Formation.

3. As shown in KS(E) and Ex.(j), *masaka* can be used by itself as an exclamation meaning 'incredible!' or 'impossible!'

4. There is a set phrase *masaka no toki*, meaning 'the time of need.'

   (1) **まさかの時**に備えて貯金をしておいた方がいいよ。
   (You'd better provide against the time of need.)

【Related Expression】

The adverb *yomoya* can express the same idea as *masaka*. The difference between the two is that *yomoya* cannot be used as an exclamation.

[1] A: 七十のおじいさんが高校に入ったんだって。

B: {**まさか** / ***よもや**}。

[2] A: スミスさんは日本語を一年しか勉強していないのに，ペラペラですよ。

B: {**まさか / *よもや**}。

Except for the two examples above, all the uses of *masaka* in KS and Exs. can be rephrased with *yomoya*.

mashida ましだ *adj.* (*na*)

a phrase indicating that although s.o. / s.t. (or some situation) is not satisfactory it is better than s.o. / s.t. else

better; less objectionable; preferable; might as well ~
【REL. *ii*】

◆Key Sentences

(A)

	Vinf·nonpast		Vinf·past		
こんな給料(きゅうりょう)を	もらう	(くらい)なら	辞(や)めた	方(ほう)が	ましだ。
(If this is the salary, it would be better to quit.)					

(B)

今度(こんど)の日本語(にほんご)の先生(せんせい)は	前(まえ)の先生より	ずっと	ましだ。
(This new Japanese teacher is much better than the former teacher.)			

(C)

もう少し	ましな	コーヒーは	ありませんか。
(Isn’t there coffee that’s a bit better?)			

Examples

(a) こんな大学に入るくらいなら，仕事をした方がましだ。
(I might as well work as enter such a college.)

(b) こんな苦しい生活をするくらいなら，死んだ方がましだ。
(It is better to die than to lead such a life.)

(c) 学校へ行くくらいなら家でテレビでも見ていた方がましだ。
(It’s better to watch TV at home rather than going to school.)

(d) こんなまずいご飯を食べるくらいなら何も食べない方がいい。
(It’s better not to eat anything rather than eating such an untasteful meal.)

(e) あのレストランよりこのレストランの方がましだ。
(This restaurant is better than that restaurant over there.)

(f) ここの夏も暑いですが，東京の夏よりましですね。
(Summer here is hot, too, but it’s better than summer in Tokyo.)

(g) 僕の車もとても古いけど，君のよりましだ。
(My car is also very old, but it is better than yours.)

(h) 給料は二万円でも，ないよりましだ。
(Although the salary is just 20,000 yen it’s better than nothing.)

(i) お宅は狭いと言っても私の家に比べたらずっとましですよ。
(You say your house is small, but it is much better than our house, you know.)

(j) もう少しましな人間になろうと思っています。
(I am thinking of becoming a slightly better person.)

(k) このホテルはひどいですね。この辺(へん)にもう少しましなホテルはないんでしょうか。
(This hotel is awful. Isn't there a slightly better hotel around here?)

Note

Mashi is an Adj(*na*) which is used to indicate that s.t. / s.o. or a situation is better than s.t. / s.o. else or another situation even though it / he / she is not satisfactory. As for the use of *mashida*, it is exactly like any other Adj(*na*).

【Related Expression】

Mashida in all KS and Exs. can be replaced by *ii*, but the former always implies that s.o. or s.t. is not satisfactory but better, whereas the latter simply means that s.o. or s.t. is better.

[1] a. こんな給料をもらう(くらい)なら辞めた方が**いい**。(cf. KS(A))

b. 今度の日本語の先生は前の先生よりずっと**いい**。(cf. KS(B))

c. このホテルはひどいですね。この辺にもう少し**いい**ホテルはないんでしょうか。(cf. Ex.(k))

M

mata wa または *conj.* <w>

a conjunction which connects two choices or possibilities expressed by noun phrases or sentences

or; either ~ or ~
【REL. ~ *ka* ~; ~ *ka* ~ *ka dochiraka*; *soretomo*】

◆Key Sentences

(A)

Noun			Noun	
現金	(か),	または	**小切手**	でお払い下さい。
(Please pay either in cash or by check.)				

(B)

Noun			Noun		
A	(か),	または	**B**	のどちらか	を選びなさい。
(Select either A or B.)					

(C)

Sinf			Sinf	
電話番号を聞き違えた	か,	または	**もうこの電話は使われていない**	のだろう。
(I guess that either I misunderstood the phone number or this number (lit. phone) is no longer in use.				

Formation

(i) N (か), または N

日本語 (か), または英語 (either Japanese or English)

(ii) Sinf か, または Sinf

手紙を書くか, または電話をする (either write a letter or make a phone call)

Examples

(a) 黒(か), または青のボールペンを使って下さい。
(Please use a black or blue ball-point pen.)

(b) 三年以下の懲役(か)，または百万円以下の罰金。
(Imprisonment up to three years or a penalty up to one million yen.)

(c) 昼は仕事があるから，夜間コースを取るか，または家庭教師を探すしかない。
(I have to work during the day, so I have no choice but to take a night course or look for a tutor.)

(d) 二週間前に出したはずの手紙がまだ先方に着いていない。私の秘書が出し忘れたか，または郵便局が間違えたのだろう。
(A letter that I assumed was mailed two weeks ago has not reached the addressee yet. It is probably that my secretary forgot to mail it or that the post office made a mistake.)

Note

When *mata wa* connects two noun phrases, *ka* after the first noun phrase is optional, as in KS(A), (B), Exs.(a) and (b).

【Related Expressions】

I. *Soretomo* is similar to *mata wa* in that it connects two possibilities, as in [1].

[1] 電話番号を聞き違えたか, {**または / それとも**} もうこの電話は使われていないのだろう。(=KS(C))

However, *soretomo* can connect questions whereas *mata wa* cannot.

[2] 車で行きますか。{**それとも / *または**}, 飛行機で行きますか。
(Will you go by car? Or will you go by plane?)
(⇨ ***soretomo*** (DBJG: 421–22))

II. N (*ka*) *mata wa* N can be paraphrased as N *ka* N, as in [3] and [4]. N *ka* N is more informal.

[3] 現金 {(**か**)，**または / か**} 小切手でお払い下さい。(=KS(A))

[4] 黒 {(**か**)，**または / か**} 青のボールペンを使って下さい。(=Ex.(a))
(⇨ ***ka***[1] (DBJG: 164–66))

III. Sinf *ka, mata wa* Sinf can be paraphrased as Sinf *ka* Sinf *ka*, *dochiraka* . . ., as in [5] and [6].

[5] 電話番号を聞き違えた**か**，もうこの電話は使われていない**か**，**どちらか**なのだろう。(=KS(C))

[6] 昼は仕事があるから，夜間コースを取る**か**，家庭教師を探す**か**，**どちらか**しかない。(=Ex.(c))

M

-me 目 *suf.*

a suffix which represents an ordinal number

-th; -th one

◆Key Sentences

(A)

	Starting Point		Number + Counter		
私(わたし)の車(くるま)は	右(みぎ)	から	**二台(にだい)**	目(め)	です。
(My car is the second one from the right.)					

(B)

	Starting Pt.		Number + Counter			Noun	
それは	上(うえ)	から	**三(みっ)つ**	目	の	引(ひ)き出(だ)し	に入(はい)っています。
(It is in the third drawer from the top.)							

Formation

Number + Counter 目

四人目(よにんめ)　(the fourth (person))

Examples

(a) 山本先生(やまもとせんせい)は前(まえ)から二列目(にれつめ)，左(ひだり)から三人目(さんにんめ)の人(ひと)だ。
(Mr. Yamamoto is the person third from the left in the second row.)

(b) 一回目(いっかいめ)は失敗(しっぱい)した。
(I failed the first time.)

(c) この日本語(にほんご)プログラムは今年(ことし)で五年目(ごねんめ)になる。
(This Japanese program is in its fifth year (this year).)

(d) 五週目(ごしゅうめ)からは林(はやし)先生がこのクラスをお教(おし)えになります。
(From the fifth week on Mr. Hayashi will teach this class.)

(e) 上野(うえの)さんは一番目(いちばんめ)に演奏(えんそう)する。
(Miss Ueno will perform first.)

(f) A: 今(いま)のバイオリンは何台目(なんだいめ)ですか。
(How many violins have you used so far?)

B: 六台目(ろくだいめ)です。
(The present one is my sixth.)

Notes

1. *-me* in this use is always preceded by a number and a counter.

2. The counter *-tsu* changes to *-ban* for numbers larger than nine, as in (1).

(1) . . . , **八(やっ)つ**目，**九(ここの)つ**目，**十番**目，**十一番**目，. . .
(. . . , eighth, ninth, tenth, eleventh, . . .)

-men 面 *suf.*

a suffix which forms a compound that means a side of X, or an aspect of X

(on) the side of; (from) the aspect of; (from) the standpoint / viewpoint of; in terms of
【REL. ***ten*** (***de***)】

◆Key Sentence

	Noun			Noun		
彼は	**学業**	面	では優秀だが,	**精神**	面	に少し弱さがあるようだ。
(He is excellent in terms of his academic performance (lit. from the standpoint of his academic performance) but he seems to have some psychological weakness (lit. have some weakness from the standpoint of his psychology).)						

Formation

N 面

運営面 (the aspect of operation; the standpoint of operation)

Examples

(a) この食堂は衛生面によく気を配っている。
(This restaurant pays close attention to hygiene (lit. the hygienic aspect).)

(b) 藤田さんは技術面からのみものを見る傾向がある。
(Mr. Fujita tends to view things from the technical standpoint alone.)

(c) ここの土地所有者は税金面で優遇措置を受けている。
(The land owners here receive favorable treatment in terms of tax.)

(d) あの候補者の演説は政策面での説得力に欠ける。
(That candidate's speech is not convincing (lit. lacks persuasive power) from the standpoint of policy.)

(e) 彼女は日本へ行っても語学面は心配しなくてもいい。
(She does not need to worry about language (lit. the aspect of language) when she goes to Japan.)

(f) この車は性能面を高く評価された。
(This car was highly regarded in terms of performance.)

Notes

1. *-men* is typically followed by the case particles *de*, *ni*, and *kara,* and the topic marker *wa. Wa* may appear alone or with other case particles (e.g., KS and Ex.(e)) with the exception of *ga* and *o*.

2. *Men* can also be used as an independent noun and has the same meaning as the suffix *-men*, as in (1).

   (1) 彼の研究はいろいろの**面**で高い評価を受けている。
   (His studies have been rated high in various aspects.)

miseru みせる *aux. v* (*Gr.* 2)

the speaker's strong determination to achieve s.t. for others to see

can manage to; will definitely do; am determined to

◆Key Sentence

		V*te*	
僕は小説を書いて，	芥川賞を	**取って**	みせる。
(I will definitely write a novel and get the Akutagawa Prize.)			

Formation

V*te* みせる (*Gr.* 2)

読んでみせる (I will definitely read it / I will show you how to read it.)

Examples

(a) 僕はこの会社の社長になってみせる。
(I am determined to become the president of this company.)

(b) 私はあのハンサムな男の子と結婚してみせるわ。
(I can manage to marry that handsome guy.)

(c) 三百ページの本を一時間で読んでみせるぞ。
(I will definitely read a 300-page book in one hour.)

(d) 今年こそは修士論文を書き上げてみせる。
(This year I will definitely finish writing my M.A. thesis.)

(e) 一男は百メートルを十一秒で走ってみせた。
(Kazuo managed to run 100 meters in 11 seconds.)

Notes

1. V*te miseru* expresses primarily the speaker's strong determination to demonstrate his / her ability to accomplish s.t.

2. When *miseru* retains the literal meaning of 'show' a particular action, the tense of *miseru* can be either nonpast or past as shown in (1) and (2) below, but if *miseru* does not retain the original meaning, the tense of the verb cannot be past, as shown in (3) and (4) below.

    (1) 私はその酒を一息で飲みほして**みせた**。
    (I drank up the sake in one gulp (lit. in one breath) for others to see.)

    (2) 一男は百メートルを十一秒で走って**みせた**。(=Ex.(e))

    (3) *僕はこの会社の社長になって**みせました**。(cf. Ex.(a))

    (4) *私はあのハンサムな男の子と結婚して**みせました**。(cf. Ex.(b))

3. Since V*te miseru* expresses the speaker's own determination to do something, the subject can be neither the second person nor the third person.

(5) *この会社の社長になって**みせます**か。
(Are you determined to become the president of this company?)

(5′) *山田さんはこの会社の社長になって**みせます**。
(Mr. Yamada is determined to become the president of the company.)

(6) ??百メートルを十一秒で走って**みせます**か。
(Are you determined to run 100 meters in 11 seconds?)

(6′) ??スミスさんは百メートルを十一秒で走って**みせます**。
(Smith is determined to run 100 meters in 11 seconds.)

The reason why (6) and (6′) are better than (5) and (5′) is that in the former *miseru* partially retains the original meaning of 'show' as a volitional verb. In fact, (7) is a good sentence.

(7) 百メートルを十一秒で走って**みせて**くれませんか。
(Won't you show us that you can run 100 meters in 11 seconds?)

mo も *prt.*

a particle which implies that s.t. else is also (not) the case

also; too; (not) either; (not) even

◆Key Sentences

(A)

		V*masu*		
吉岡さんは今年七十歳だが，毎日一キロ走る。	時々	**泳ぎ**	も	する。
(Although Mr. Yoshioka is seventy this year, he runs one kilometer every day. He occasionally swims, too.)				

(B)

	Adj(*i*)stem			
この本(ほん)は有益(ゆうえき)で，その上(うえ)，	**面白**(おもしろ)	く	も	ある。
(This book is beneficial and, on top of that, it is also interesting.)				

(C)

	Adj(*na*)stem			
この映画(えいが)は面白(おもしろ)くないし，特(とく)に	**教育的**(きょういくてき)	で	も	ない。
(This movie is not interesting and not particularly educational, either.)				

M

(D)

	Noun			
奥田氏(おくだし)は弁護士(べんごし)であり，	**作家**(さっか)	で	も	ある。
(Mr. Okuda is a lawyer and also a novelist.)				

(E)

	V*masu*		
由利子(ゆりこ)は最近廊下(さいきんろうか)ですれ違(ちが)っても	**見向**(みむ)**き**	も	しない。
(Recently Yuriko does not (even) look at me even if we pass each other in the hall.)			

Formation

(i) V*masu* もする / もしない

読(よ)みもする (also read)

読みもしない (do not read, either ; do not even read)

(ii) Adj(*i*)stem くもある / くもない

安くもある (s.t. is also cheap)

安くもない (s.t. is not cheap, either ; s.t. is not even cheap)

(iii) {Adj(*na*)stem / N} でもある / でもない

便利でもある (s.t. is also convenient)

便利でもない (s.t. is not convenient, either ; s.t. is not even convenient)

先生でもある (s.o. is also a teacher)

先生でもない (s.o. is not a teacher, either ; s.o. is not even a teacher)

Examples

(a) 猿だっておかしければ笑いもするでしょう。
(Apes also laugh if something is funny, right?)

(b) 健一は新婚早々三日も家を空けたが，和代は泣かなかった。そして，怒りもしなかった。
(Ken'ichi didn't go home for three days right after their marriage, but Kazuyo didn't cry. She didn't get mad, either.)

(c) あのアパートはあまり便利ではないし安くもない。
(That apartment is not convenient and not inexpensive, either.)

(d) 周遊券は便利な上，経済的でもある。
(Excursion tickets are convenient ; on top of that, they are also economical.)

(e) 田口さんなんて友達でもないのに，どうしてそんなにしてあげるの。
(Mr. Taguchi is not even a friend. How come you do so much for him?)

(f) 安くもないのに，どうしてそんなものを買うんですか。
(Why are you going to buy a thing like that which is not even cheap?)

Notes

1. Verbals with *mo* embedded in them (i.e., V*masu mo suru*/*shinai*,

Adj(*i*)stem *ku mo aru/nai*, {Adj(*na*)stem / N} *de mo aru/nai*) are used in the following situations.

(1) A is X and A is Y, too, or A is not X and A is not Y, either. (Here, X and Y are different adjectives or nouns.) (e.g., KS(B), (C), Exs.(c) and (d))

(2) A does X and A does Y, too, or A does not do X and A does not do Y, either. (Here, X and Y are different verbs and Y is not accompanied by a noun with the particle *ga*, *o*, *e*, or *ni*.) (e.g., KS(A), Exs.(a) and (b))

When the second verb is accompanied by a noun marked by the particle *ga*, *o*, *e*, or *ni*, *mo* marks the noun instead of the verb, as in (3).

(3) a. 吉岡さんは今年七十歳だが，十キロ走れる。柔道**も**出来る。(*Ga* is replaced by *mo*.)
(Although Mr. Yoshioka is seventy this year, he can run ten kilometers. He can also do judo.)

b. 吉岡さんは今年七十歳だが，毎日一キロ走る。時々エアロビクス**も**する。(*O* is replaced by *mo*.)
(Although Mr. Yoshioka is seventy this year, he runs one kilometer every day. He occasionally does aerobics, too.)

c. 吉岡さんは今年七十歳だが，毎日一キロ走る。時々ジム{**に** / **へ**}**も**来る。
(Although Mr. Yoshioka is seventy this year, he runs one kilometer every day. He occasionally comes to the gym, too.)

Compare the above examples with (4).

(4) 吉岡さんは今年七十歳だが，毎日一キロ走る。時々{ディスコで / 夫人と} **踊りも**する。
(Although Mr. Yoshioka is seventy this year, he runs one kilometer every day. He occasionally dances {at discos / with his wife}, too.)

Here, the verb is accompanied by a noun marked by *de* or *to*. In this case, *mo* must mark the verb rather than the noun. If *mo* marks the noun, the discourse becomes unacceptable, as in (5).

(5) 吉岡さんは今年七十歳だが，毎日一キロ走る。時々 {***ディスコでも / *夫人とも**} 踊る。
(Although Mr. Yoshioka is seventy this year, he runs one kilometer every day. He occasionally dances {at discos, too (as well as other places) / with his wife, too (as well as other women)}.)
(⇨ ***mo***[1] (DBJG: 247–50); ***mo***[2] (DBJG: 250–53))

2. *Mo* sometimes appears with no specific reference, as in (6), a typical opening in written correspondence.

(6) 桜の便り**も**聞かれる今日このごろですが，いかがお過ごしですか。
(How are you during cherry blossom season? (lit. Cherry blossom information is also heard these days. How are you?))

In this situation, the *mo* indicates that other things which herald the arrival of spring are implied while the cherry blossom news is being reported.

3. *Mo* is often used in double negative sentences, which can be paraphrased as *nai koto mo nai*, as in (7).

(7) a. 行きたく**なくもない**。(=行きたく**ないこともない**。)
(It's not that I do not want to go.)

b. 彼の言うことは分から**なくもない**が，賛成は出来ない。
(=. . . 分から**ないこともない**が, . . .)
(It's not that I don't understand what he says; I just can't agree with it.)
(⇨ ***~ mo ~ mo*** (this volume; DBJG: 255–57))

~ mo ~ ba 〜も〜ば *str.*

a structure which expresses the idea that a certain amount of s.t. is sufficient to do s.t.

be enough to/for; if ~ at least; if ~ as much/many as ~, it will be enough to

◆Key Sentence

	Number + Counter		Vcond	
この美術館は	**三時間**	も	**あれ**ば	全部見られる。
(Three hours are enough to see everything in this art museum. (lit. If you have as many as three hours, you can see everything in this art museum.))				

Formation

Number + Counter も Vcond

五人も来れば (if five people come, it will be enough to ~)

Examples

(a) 二万円も持って行けば足りるでしょう。
(20,000 yen will probably be enough. (lit. If you take as much as 20,000 yen with you, it will probably be sufficient.))

(b) ビールは二ダースも買っておけば大丈夫だ。
(As for beer, if we buy two dozen, it will be enough (lit. we will be all right).)

(c) 一週間もすれば歩けるようになります。
(It will take no more than a week until you can walk (lit. until you become able to walk).)

(d) 二，三回も聞けば大体分かる。
(Listening two or three times is / will be sufficient for understanding most of it.)

Note

~ *mo* ~ *tara* can also be used to express this idea, although it is less common.

(1) この美術館は三時間**も**あっ**たら**全部見られる。(=KS)

M

~ mo ~ mo ～も～も *str.*

a structure which presents two states or actions of s.o. or s.t.

both ~ and ~; neither ~ nor ~; also; (not) either

◆Key Sentences

(A)

	V*masu*		V*masu*		
腰が痛くて	**立ち**	も	**座り**	も	出来ない。
(Because I have a backache, I can neither stand nor sit still.)					

(B)

	V*masu*				V*masu*	
私は俳句が大好きで，よく	**読み**	も	するし	自分で	**作り**	もする。
(Loving *haiku*, I read them a lot and I write them myself (too).)						

(C)

	Adj(*i*)stem			Adj(*i*)stem			
あのアパートは	**よ**	く	も	**安**(やす)	く	も	ない。
(That apartment is neither good nor cheap.)							

(D)

	Adj(*i*)stem				Adj(*i*)stem			
彼(かれ)の作品(さくひん)は	**面白**(おもしろ)	く	も	あり	**読みやす**	く	も	ある。
(His writings are interesting and also easy to read.)								

(E)

	Adj(*na*)stem			Adj(*na*)stem			
彼女(かのじょ)の英語(えいご)は特(とく)に	**上手**(じょうず)	で	も	**下手**(へた)	で	も	ない。
(Her English is neither particularly good nor bad.)							

(F)

	Noun				Noun			
彼は	**親戚**(しんせき)	で	も	なければ	**友達**(ともだち)	で	も	ない。
(He is neither a relative nor a friend.)								

(G)

	Noun			Noun		
私達(わたしたち)のクラスには	**中国人**(ちゅうごくじん)**の学生**(がくせい)	も	いれば	**スペイン人の学生**	も	いる。
(In my class, there are Chinese students and there are Spanish students too.)						

Formation

(i) a. V*masu* も V*masu* もする / しない

読みも書きもする (both read and write)

読みも書きもしない (neither read nor write)

b. V*masu* も {し / するし / すれば} V*masu* もする

読みも{し / するし / すれば}書きもする (read and also write)

c. V*masu* も {せず / しないし / しなければ} V*masu* もしない

読みも {せず / しないし / しなければ} 書きもしない (do not read and do not write, either)

(ii) a. VN も VN もする / しない

料理も掃除もする (both cook and clean)

料理も掃除もしない (neither cook nor clean)

b. N も {し / するし / すれば} N もする

料理も {し / するし / すれば} 掃除もする (cook and also clean)

c. N も {せず / しないし / しなければ} N もしない

料理も {せず / しないし / しなければ} 掃除もしない (does not cook and does not clean, either)

(iii) a. Adj(*i*)stem くも Adj(*i*)stem くもある / ない

うれしくも悲しくもある (both happy and sad)

うれしくも悲しくもない (neither happy nor sad)

b. Adj(*i*)stem くも {あり / あるし / あれば} Adj(*i*)stem くもある

うれしくも {あり / あるし / あれば} 悲しくもある (happy and also sad)

c. Adj(*i*)stem くも {なく / ないし / なければ} Adj(*i*)stem くもない

うれしくも {なく / ないし / なければ} 悲しくもない
(not happy and not sad, either)

(iv) a. {Adj(*na*)stem / N} でも {Adj(*na*)stem / N} でもある / ない

便利でも経済的でもある (both convenient and economical)

便利でも経済的でもない (neither convenient nor economical)

b. {Adj(*na*)stem / N} でも {あり / あるし / あれば} {Adj(*na*)stem / N} でもある

便利でも {あり / あるし / あれば} 経済的でもある (convenient and also economical)

c. {Adj(*na*)stem / N} でも {なく / ないし / なければ} {Adj(*na*)stem / N} でもない

便利でも {なく / ないし / なければ} 経済的でもない (not convenient and not economical, either)

Examples

(a) 私はドイツ語なら読みも話しも出来る。
(When it comes to German, I can both read it and speak it.)

(b) この教科書は難しすぎもせずやさしすぎもせず，ちょうどいい。
(This textbook is not too difficult and not too easy, either; it's just right.)

(c) ボブの奥さんは料理もしなければ掃除もしない。
(Bob's wife does not cook and does not clean (the house), either.)

(d) この物語は面白くもなければおかしくもない。
(This story is not interesting and not funny, either.)

(e) 奥田氏は弁護士でもあり，作家でもある。
(Mr. Okuda is a lawyer and also a novelist.)

(f) その言葉の意味は字引も引いたし友達にも聞いたが結局分からなかった。

(I checked the word in the dictionary and also asked my friend, but I didn't get the meaning after all.)

(g) あの人(ひと)は頭(あたま)もいいしハンサムでもあるが，どうも好(す)きになれない。
(That man is smart and handsome, too, but I'm unable to like him for some reason.)

Notes

1. As the rules in Formation (ii) show, when *suru*-verbs such as *benkyō-suru* are used in this structure, *mo* follows the verb stem (i.e., VN) rather than V*masu* (i.e., VN *shi*), as in (1).

    (1) a. 太郎(たろう)はよく勉強(べんきょう)も {**し / するし / すれば**} 運動もする。
    (Taro studies hard and he also does a lot of exercise, too.)

    b. *太郎はよく勉強しも {**し / するし / すれば**} 運動しもする。

2. As in KS(G), Exs.(f) and (g), when a clause contains a noun other than the topic, *mo* marks the noun rather than the predicate.

(⇨ **~ *mo* ~ *mo*** (DBJG: 255–57))

mono (da) もの(だ) *n.* <w>

a dependent noun which is used to create a sentence structure which presents a characteristic of s.t.	(is) that which ~; (is) something which ~; (are) those which ~

◆Key Sentences

(A)

Topic	Relative Clause
現在のコンピュータのほとんどは	フォン・ノイマン型と呼ばれている

もの	である。

(Most of the present computers are those which are called (lit. things which are called) the von Neuman model.)

(B)

Sentence$_1$
C社が盲人用障害物感知器の試作品を発表した。
(C Company announced an experimental model of an obstacle detector for the blind.)

Sentence$_2$	
Topic	Relative Clause
この装置は	目の不自由な人が皮膚への刺激を通して，前にある障害物な

Sentence$_2$ (cont.)		
Relative Clause (cont.)		
どを感知出来るようにした	もの	(である)。

(This device enables (lit. is something which has enabled) blind people to recognize (lit. feel) obstacles ahead of them through stimuli to their skin.)

M

(C)

Topic		Vinf			
米国の貿易赤字は	しばらくこのまま	**続く**	もの	と	予想される。
(It is predicted that the U.S. trade deficit will remain as it is for a while.)					

Formation (same as the rules for the relative clauses)

Examples

(a) この本の内容はいかなる人間社会にも当てはまる一般的なものである。
(The content of this book generally applies to any society (lit. is something general which applies to any human society).)

(b) これは革命的発見とも言うべきものだ。
(This is something which should be called a revolutionary discovery.)

(c) D 社が M 型ワープロの五パーセント値下げに踏み切った。これは，最近低下している同社のワープロシェアの巻き返しを狙ったもの(である)。
(D Company has decided to reduce the price of M-type word-processors by five percent. Their aim is to regain (lit. This is to aim at regaining) their recently declining share of the word-processor market.)

(d) 大学入試制度調査会の第一回会合が昨日都内のホテルで行われた。この調査会は，最近しばしば批判の対象になっている，現行の大学入試制度の見直しのために発足したものである。
(The first meeting of the Study Group for University Entrance Examinations was held at a hotel in Tokyo yesterday. This study group was started for the purpose of reviewing the present university entrance examination system which is criticized frequently these days.)

(e) この問題は時期が来れば自然に解決されるものと見られている。
(This problem is expected to solve itself when the time comes.)

(f) エレクトロニクスの世界は今後も急速な進歩を続けていくものと予想される。
(It is predicted that the world of electronics will continue advancing rapidly from now on, too.)

Notes

1. *Mono* (*da*) is used to change the structure "X *wa* VP," which describes an action taken by or received by X, to the structure "X *wa* NP *da*," which is used to present a characteristic of X. Compare the two sentences in (1).

   (1) a. 現在のコンピュータのほとんどはフォン・ノイマン型と呼ばれている。
   (Most of the present computers are called the von Neuman model.)

   b. 現在のコンピュータのほとんどはフォン・ノイマン型と呼ばれているものである。(=KS(A))

   Here, (1a) describes what happens to the referent of the topic (i.e., most of the present computers) while (1b) provides a characteristic of the referent.

2. *Mono* (*da*) as in KS(B), Exs.(c) and (d) frequently appears in newspaper articles. It is used when a sentence provides such information as a purpose, a reason, a cause, or specific information about something introduced in the previous sentence. The copula (e.g., *da*) after *mono* is frequently dropped in this usage.

3. *Mono* followed by the quotative *to*, as in KS(C), Exs.(e) and (f), is used in general statements or opinion. This *mono* could be dropped without a change in meaning. Note that the copula *da* does not follow *mono* in this use.

(⇨ ***mono*** (DBJG: 257–61))

nā なあ *prt.* <s>

an exclamatory sentential particle which is used in informal male speech

How ~!; What ~!; ~!; I wonder; I wish

◆Key Sentences

(A)

Sinf	
彼(かれ)はよく食(た)べる	なあ。
(He eats a lot!)	

(B)

Sinf		
すばらしい映画(えいが)だ	なあ	と思(おも)った。
(I was so impressed by that (wonderful) movie. (lit. What a wonderful movie, I thought.))		

(C)

Sinf		
まだ間(ま)に合(あ)う	か	なあ。
(I wonder if I can still make it in time.)		

(D)

	Vinf·neg		
河合君，早く	**来ない**	か	なあ。
(I wish Kawai would come soon.)			

(E)

	Vinf·past			
車が	**あった**	**ら**	**いい**	なあ。
(I wish I had a car. (lit. It would be nice if I had a car.))				

Formation

(i) Sinf なあ

高いなあ (It's expensive! / How expensive!)

(ii) Sinf かなあ

高いかなあ (I wonder if it's expensive.)

(iii) Vneg·inf かなあ

くれないかなあ (I wish s.o. would give me s.t.)

Examples

(a) よく飲んだなあ。
(We drank a lot! / Did we drink!)

(b) あのけちの吉田がよく金を出したなあ。
(I'm surprised that that stingy guy Yoshida gave money.)

(c) 家が欲しいなあ。
(I want a house so badly.)

(d) 山内さん，今日は来ないかなあ。
(I wonder if Mr. Yamauchi is not coming today.)

(e) 何か面白い映画はないかなあ。
(I wonder if there is (lit. isn't) an interesting movie.)

(f) 彼女，こんなことを言っても怒らないかなあ。
(I wonder if she will (lit. won't) get mad if I say such a thing.)

(g) タイガース，今日勝たないかなあ。
(I wish the Tigers would win today.)

Notes

1. Although it is frequently used by female speakers (particularly, young women), *nā* was originally male speech. The female version of *nā* and *ka nā* are *wa nē* and *kashira*, respectively. The formation rules of *wa nē* and *kashira* are as follows.

(1) a. {V / Adj(*i*)}inf わねえ

きれいに書くわねえ (How beautifully s.o. writes!)

高いわねえ (It's expensive! / How expensive!)

b. {Adj(*na*)stem / N} ねえ (={Adj(*na*)stem / N} だわねえ)

便利ねえ (It's so convenient! / How convenient!)

きれいな星ねえ (The stars are beautiful!)

c. {Adj(*na*)stem / N} だったわねえ

便利だったわねえ (It was so convenient!)

きれいな星だったわねえ (The stars were so beautiful!)

(2) a. {V / Adj(*i*)}inf かしら

行くかしら (I wonder if s.o. will go.)

高いかしら (I wonder if s.t. is expensive.)

b. {Adj(*na*)stem / N} {ø / だった} かしら

便利 {ø / だった} かしら (I wonder if s.t. is / was convenient.)

N

先生 {ø / だった} かしら (I wonder if s.o. is / was a teacher.)
(⇨ ***kashira*** (DBJG: 181–82); ***wa*** (DBJG: 520–21))

2. *Nā* expresses such positive feelings as happiness, thankfulness, and admiration and such negative feelings as unhappiness, envy, pity, ridicule, and contempt. (3) presents some examples.

(3) a. きれいだなあ。[Admiration]
(It's beautiful! / How beautiful!)

b. 面白かったなあ。[Happiness]
(It was great! / It was fun! / What a good time I had!)

c. 僕は幸せ者だなあ。[Thankfulness]
(What a lucky person I am! / How lucky I am!)

d. 高いなあ。[Unhappiness]
(It's expensive! / How expensive!)

e. いいなあ / うらやましいなあ。[Envy]
(I'm envious!)

f. 気の毒だなあ / かわいそうだなあ。[Pity]
(Poor man!)

g. 馬鹿だなあ。[Contempt / ridicule]
(How silly! / Silly man! / You are silly.)

h. ひどいなあ。[Blame]
(How terrible! / It's terrible! / You're terrible!)

3. *Nā* may appear with the quotative marker *to*, as in KS(B), with such verbs as *omou* 'think' ; *kanjiru* 'feel' ; *kanshinsuru* 'be impressed' ; *akireru* 'be astonished' ; *kinodokuni omou* 'feel sorry.' In these situations *nā* is used by both male and female speakers.

4. *Ka nā* expresses the idea of "I wonder . . .," as in KS(C). (⇨ ***kana***)

5. *Nai ka nā* means either "I wonder . . .," as in Exs.(d) – (f), or "I wish . . .," as in KS(D) and Ex.(g).

6. Conditional sentences with *ii nā*, as in KS(E), express the idea "I wish . . ."

7. Sentences with inverted word order are common when *nā* is used, as seen in (4).

(4) a. 楽しかったなあ，あの頃は。
(We had a lot of fun in those days.)

b. よく頑張ったなあ，お互いに。
(We both worked so hard, didn't we?)

c. うらやましいなあ，書斎があって。
(I envy you your den.)

nado to などと *comp. prt.*

a compound particle that indicates an approximate quote of words or ideas

(things) like ~; ~ or something like

◆Key Sentence

Sinf			
日本の文化はユニークだ	など	と	言う人がいるが，私はそうは思わない。
(There are people who say things like Japanese culture is unique, but I don't think so.)			

Formation

(i) {V / Adj(*i*)}inf などと

話すなどと ((say) s.t. like s.o. talks)

つまらないなどと　((say) s.t. like s.t. is uninteresting)

(ii)　{Adj(*na*)stem / N} {だ / だった} などと

便利 {だ / だった} などと　((say) s.t. like s.t. is / was convenient)

学生 {だ / だった} などと　((say) s.t. like s.o. is / was a student)

Examples

(a) お金がないから，日本へ行くなどということは夢です。
(I don't have money, so ideas like going to Japan are just dreams.)

(b) 毎日運動しろなどとは言いませんから，週に二，三度運動したらどうですか。
(I'm not saying you should exercise everyday, but why don't you do it 2 or 3 times a week.)

(c) ジョンソンさんは日本語で何でも話せるなどと言っている。
(Mr. Jonson says things like he can say anything in Japanese.)

(d) 困った時は人が助けてくれるだろうなどと甘く考えてはいけない。
(Don't think indulgently things like people will help you when you are in trouble.)

(e) 日本へ留学しようとしているケントさんは，うまく日本の生活に適応出来るかなどと心配している。
(Mr. Kent, who is about to go to Japan to study, is worried about things like whether he will be able to adjust to Japanese life.)

(f) みんなが君のことをクラブのホープだなどと言っているよ。
(Everybody is saying something like you are the hope of our club.)

(g) 尊敬しています，などと言われると照れくさい。
(When I am told that they respect me, I feel embarassed.)

Notes

1. The particle *nado to* is used to single out an approximate quote of s.o.'s speech or internal monologue.

2. Usually *nado to* occurs with an explicitly negative predicate as in Exs.

(b) and (d), or with a negative implication, as shown in KS and the rest of the Exs. For example, Ex.(f) sounds positive on the surface, but the speaker is saying the sentence with some sarcasm. The only case where a negative meaning is missing is when *nado* is with a noun.

(1) a. 田中さんや小川さん**など**が来ました。
(People like Mr. Tanaka and Mr. Ogawa showed up.)

b. すしやてんぷら**など**を食べました。
(I ate stuff like sushi and tempura.)

(⇨ ***nado*** (DBJG: 267–68))

3. When N of N *nado* is a person it means humbleness if it is the first person pronoun, as shown in (2a); if not, it is a derogatory or downgrading comment, as shown in (2b) and (2c).

(2) a. 私**など**にはこんな仕事は出来ません。
(A person like me cannot do such a job.)

b. 鈴木**など**にこの問題が分かるはずがない。
(There is no reason to believe that Mr. Suzuki, of all people, could understand this problem.)

c. 生卵**など**，食べないよ。
(Stuff like raw eggs, I won't eat, you know.)

nagara(**mo**) ながら(も) *conj.* <w>

a disjunctive conjunction used normally in written Japanese with the meaning of 'although'

although; even though; nevertheless

【REL. *ga*; *keredo*(*mo*); *noni*】

◆Key Sentences

(A)

	Adj(*i*)inf		
この部屋は	**狭い**	ながら(も)	居心地がよい。
(Although this room is small, it is comfortable.)			

(B)

	V*masu*		
山口はそのことを	**知り**	ながら(も)	黙っていた。
(Yamaguchi kept silent, although he knew about the matter.)			

Formation

N

(i) {V*masu* / V*te* い} ながら(も)

言いながら(も) (although s.o. says ~)

分かっていながら(も) (although s.o. understands s.t. / s.o.)

(ii) {Adj(*i*)inf / Adj(*na*)stem / N} ながら(も)

大きいながら(も) (although s.t. is big)

静かながら(も) (although s.t. / s.o. is quiet)

子供ながら(も) (although s.o. is a child)

Examples

(a) あの人は若いながら(も)，なかなか有能だ。
(He is young, but he is very capable.)

(b) 教授のゼミは厳しいながら(も)学ぶところが多かった。
(Although my professor's seminar was tough, I learned a lot from it.)

(c) ベッキーの日本語はたどたどしいながら(も)，言おうとしていることは分かった。
(Becky's Japanese is halting, but I was able to figure out what she had to say.)

(d) この辺は不便ながら(も)，車も少なく，空気がきれいだ。
(This area is inconvenient, but there is little traffic and the air is clean.)

(e) 残念ながら，明日の音楽会には行けません。
(To my regret, I cannot go to tomorrow's concert.)

(f) ひとみは子供ながら(も)，よく考えてものを言う。
(Hitomi is just a child, but she says things very carefully (lit. after thinking hard).)

(g) この車は小型ながら(も)よく走る。
(This car runs well, although it is such a small car.)

(h) 日本の単身赴任のサラリーマンは苦しみながら(も)，会社のために働いている。
(Japanese white-collar workers who have to leave their families behind for work transfers work for the company even though their lives are hard.)

(i) ボブは日本にいながら(も)，洋食ばかり食べている。
(Bob is in Japan, but he eats only Western-style food.)

(j) たばこは体に悪いと分かっていながら(も)，吸ってしまう。
(Even though I know cigarettes are bad for my body, I end up smoking them.)

(k) 弟はたくさん本を買っていながら(も)，少しも読んでいない。
(My younger brother has bought many books, but he has not read any of them.)

(l) 彼は何度も日本へ行っていながら(も)，日本語が少しも話せない。
(Although he has been to Japan many times he cannot speak Japanese at all.)

Notes

1. The disjunctive conjunction *nagara*(*mo*) is a subordinate conjunction

that is used to express the meaning of 'although' by combining two sentences.

2. The conjunction is normally used in written or formal, spoken Japanese.

3. When *nagara* is used as a disjunctive conjunction, the disjunctive meaning is emphasized if *mo* is used. There are cases where *nagara* and *nagaramo* are used as a temporal 'while' and the disjunctive 'although,' respectively, as shown in (1a) and (1b).

(1) a. 彼は倒(たお)れ**ながら**ピストルの引(ひ)き金(がね)を引(ひ)こうとした。
(As he fell down, he tried to pull the pistol trigger.)

b. 彼は倒れ**ながらも**ピストルの引き金を引こうとした。
(Although he fell down, he tried to pull the pistol trigger.)

(⇨ ***nagara*** (DBJG: 269–70))

4. Probably because *zannen nagara* 'to one's regret' in Ex.(e) is an idiomatic phrase, *mo* cannot be attached to it.

【Related Expression】

The crucial differences between *nagara(mo)*, on one hand and *ga*, *keredo (mo)*, *noni*, on the other hand, are: first, the latter can be used in both spoken and written Japanese, whereas the former is normally used only in written or formal spoken Japanese, and secondly, the latter has no restriction on the choice of the subject, but the former normally takes the third person as the subject, apparently because it is usually employed to give the speaker's observation of, or opinion about, a third person. Thus, Ex.(1) cannot take the first nor the second person pronouns.

[1] a. {彼 / *あなた / *僕(ぼく)} は何度も日本へ行ってい**ながら(も)**, 日本語が少しも話せない。

b. {彼 / あなた / 僕} は日本へ何度も行っている {**が** / **けれど** / **のに**}, 日本語が少しも話せない。

(⇨ ***ga*** (DBJG: 120–23); ***keredo(mo)*** (DBJG: 187–88); ***noni*** (DBJG: 331–35))

However, there are cases in which the first person is used as in Exs.(e) and (j).

-nai koto mo/wa nai ないこと も/は ない *phr.*

a double negative phrase used to make a conditional affirmative statement

it isn't the case that ~ not ~; it is not that ~ not ~
【REL. *koto wa*】

◆Key Sentences

A:
日本語の新聞は読まないんですか。
(Don't you read Japanese newspapers?)

B:			
	Vneg		
いいえ,	**読ま**	ないこと {も / は} ない	んですが, 時たまですね。
(I do read them, but very rarely. (lit. It isn't the case that I don't read them, but very rarely.))			

Formation

{V / Adj(*i* / *na*) / Cop}neg. ないこと {も / は} ない

話さないこと {も / は} ない (I do speak, but ~)

高くないこと {も / は} ない (s.t. *is* expensive / high, but ~)

不便 {で / じゃ} ないこと {も / は} ない (s.t. *is* inconvenient, but ~)

学者 {では / じゃ} ないこと {も / は} ない (s.o. *is* a scholar, but ~)

Example

(a) A: この辺は夏涼しくないんですか。
(Isn't it cool around here during the summer?)

B: いや，涼しくないこともないんですが，時々ひどく暑くなります。
(Yes, it *is* cool, but sometimes it gets terribly hot.)

(b) A: お父さんはお元気じゃないんですか。
(Isn't your father in good health?)

B: いや，元気じゃないことはないんですが，血圧が少し高いようです。
(Yes, he *is* healthy, but his blood pressure is a bit high.)

(c) A: 日本語は難しくありませんか。
(Isn't Japanese difficult?)

B: いえ，難しくないこともないんですが，日本語の難しさは強調されすぎていると思いますよ。
(Yes, it *is* difficult, but it seems that the difficulty of Japanese is overemphasized.)

(d) A: 山田さんは政治学者じゃないんですね。
(Mr. Yamada isn't a political scientist, is he?)

B: いや，政治学者じゃないこともないんですが，どちらかというと政治家です。
(Yes, he *is* a political scientist, but he is more of a politician.)

(e) 日本人は集団行動が好きだとよく言われている。確かに，集団行動をしないことはないのだが，個人行動をとる日本人もけっこういる。
(Japanese are said to like group behavior. Certainly, they do behave as a group, but there are quite a few Japanese who behave individually.)

Notes

1. The phrase *-nai koto mo/wa nai* is used when the speaker wants to mildly acknowledge / confirm with a proviso that s.o. has just said or written. The phrase is often followed by *n(o) desu ga*.

2. The phrase expresses a double negative structure that is virtually an affirmative statement.

3. The phrase is an expression of repetition that repeats the same verb, adjective or N + Copula which has just been used in the interlocutor's

question. So, the phrase cannot be used as a discourse-initial sentence. In other words, one cannot start conversation with this phrase. So, for example, in a drinking party situation one cannot utter (1) out of the blue.

(1) 酒(さけ)は飲(の)ま**ないこと｛も／は｝ない**んですが，せいぜいおちょこに二(に)，三杯(さんばい)ですね。
(It isn't that I don't drink sake, but I drink two or three sake cups at most.)

Someone must say something like (2) right before (1).

(2) 酒は飲まないそうじゃありませんか。
(I heard that you don't drink sake.)

4. The difference between *-nai koto mo nai* and *-nai koto wa nai* is that the former is weaker in assertion than the latter. In KS, *yomanai koto wa nai* asserts "I do read it" much more strongly than *yomanai koto mo nai*.

【Related Expression】

The predicate phrase *-nai koto mo nai* and *koto wa* share the same characteristics of not giving an unconditional statement. But the former is used in response to a negative question, whereas the latter is used in response to an affirmative question. Compare [1A] and [2A] with KS(A) and Ex.(a), respectively.

[1] A: 日本語の新聞は読みますか。
(Do you read Japanese newspapers?)

B: そうですね，｛**読むことは読みます／*読まないことはないんです**｝が，時たまですね。
(Yes, I do read newspapers, but very rarely.)

[2] A: この辺は夏涼しいんですか。
(Is it cool around here during the summer?)

B: そうですね，｛**涼しいことは涼しいです／*涼しくないこともないんです**｝が，時々ひどく暑くなります。
(It is cool, but sometimes it gets terribly hot.)

(⇨ ***koto wa*** (DBJG: 206–08))

N

nakanaka なかなか *adv.*

an adverb used to indicate the speaker's feelings that s.t. is impressive or his annoyance at slowness or difficulty in achieving s.t.

quite; fairly; considerably; (not) easily; pretty; (not) readily
【REL. *hijō ni*; *kanari*; *kekkō*; *taihen*; *totemo*】

◆Key Sentences

(A)

		Adj.	
ブラウンさんは日本語(にほんご)が	なかなか	**上手(じょうず)です**	ね。
({Mr. Brown is / Mr. Brown, you are} remarkably good at Japanese.)			

(B)

		Adv.	
この生(い)け花(ばな)は	なかなか	**見事(みごと)に**	生けてある。
(This flower arrangement is done quite nicely.)			

(C)

		Vneg
今年(ことし)は桜(さくら)の花(はな)が	なかなか	**咲(さ)きません。**
(It will be a long time before the cherry blossoms are out this year. (lit. This year the cherry blossoms do not bloom easily.))		

(D)

		Vaff	
あの男(おとこ)は仕事(しごと)が	なかなか	**出来(でき)る**	ねえ。
(That guy does his job quite well, doesn't he?)			

(E)

			N	
山田部長(やまだぶちょう)の奥(おく)さんは	なかなか	(の)	**美人(びじん)**	だ。
(The wife of our departmental chief Yamada is quite a beauty.)				

Formation

(i) なかなか Adj(*i* / *na*)aff

なかなか面白(おもしろ)い (quite interesting)

なかなか便利(べんり)だ (quite convenient)

(ii) なかなか Vaff

なかなかやる (s.o. performs s.t. quite well)

(iii) なかなか Vneg

なかなか分(わ)からない (cannot understand s.t. easily)

(iv) なかなか Adv.

なかなか上手に話(はな)す (s.o. speaks quite well)

(v) なかなか(の) N

なかなか(の)学者(がくしゃ) (quite a scholar)

Examples

(a) この庭園(ていえん)はなかなかきれいですね。
(This garden is quite beautiful, isn't it?)

(b) この数学の問題はなかなか難しそうだ。
(This math problem looks quite difficult, doesn't it?)

(c) 君はなかなかコンピュータに強いそうじゃないか。
(I heard that you are quite good with computers.)

(d) この大学の学生はなかなかよく出来る。
(The students at this college are pretty good.)

(e) あのピアニストはモーツァルトをなかなかうまく弾く。
(That pianist plays Mozart quite well.)

(f) テニスは毎日練習しているのに，なかなか上手にならないんです。
(I am practicing tennis every day, but I cannot become good at it readily.)

(g) 約束の時間になっても友達がなかなか来なかったので家に帰ってしまった。
(The meeting time long passed, but my friend didn't show up for a long time, so I went home.)

(h) あの人はどんなに説明しても，僕の言うことがなかなか分からないようだ。
(No matter how hard I try to explain, he doesn't seem to understand me easily.)

(i) 風邪がなかなか治らないので，困っているんです。
(I'm having a difficult time, because my cold won't go away easily.)

(j) フグは怖くて，なかなか食べられないんだ。
(I am scared of blowfish and cannot eat it easily.)

(k) 中村先生はなかなか話せる先生だ。
(Mr. Nakamura is a teacher who (lit. can talk with us) can understand us.)

(l) 私のルームメートはなかなか(の)勉強家で，かなわない。
(My roommate is such a hard worker that I cannot compete with him.)

Notes

1. *Nakanaka* modifies only adjectives with positive meanings. Thus, *nakanaka* in the following examples is unacceptable.

   (1) この本は{**そんなに / それほど / あまり / *なかなか**}面白くない。
   (This book is not that interesting.)

   (2) この映画は{**全く / 大変 / *なかなか**}つまらない。
   (This movie is very boring.)

   (3) 君のテニスは{**とても / *なかなか**}下手だね。
   (Your tennis is quite bad, isn't it?)

   (4) 十二月になったら，{**とても / *なかなか**}寒くなった。
   (In December it became very cold.)

2. When *nakanaka* occurs with the negative form of a verb it indicates the difficulty or slowness with which s.t. desirable reaches its realization, as shown in KS(C) and Exs.(f) – (j).

3. There are cases in which the affirmative form of a verb can be used as shown in KS(D) and Ex.(k). Notice that in these cases one could say that the adverb *yoku* is understood. The deletion of *yoku* appears to be allowed when it is followed by a verb that already includes the meaning of 'well' like *dekiru* of KS(D) or *hanaseru* of Ex.(k). So, if a verb doesn't include the meaning of 'well', *yoku* cannot be omitted.

   (5) この絵は**なかなか**{**よく / *ø**}描けている。
   (This picture is well painted.)

4. It is not the case that any N can follow *nakanaka*; only those nouns that include the idea of an adjective or adverb can be used with *nakanaka*. For example, *bijin* in KS(E) and *benkyō-ka* in Ex.(l) come from *utsukushii hito* 'a beautiful woman' and *yoku benkyōsuru hito* 'a person who studies well.' Even the loan word *purei-bōi* can be used with *nakanaka*, because it means *yoku onna-no-ko to asobu hito* 'a person who habitually plays with girls.'

(6) 彼(かれ)は**なかなかの**プレーボーイだ。
(He is quite a playboy.)

【Related Expression】

Nakanaka can be used with adjectives that have of positive meaning and with the negative verb when it implies slowness or difficulty. Observe the following examples which contain six adverbs of degree: *nakanaka*, *totemo*, *hijō ni*, *taihen*, *kanari*, and *kekkō*.

[1] a. ブラウンさんは日本語が｛**なかなか** / **とても** / **非常(ひじょう)に** / **大変** / **かなり** / **けっこう**｝上手ですね。(=KS(A))

b. この生け花は｛**なかなか** / **とても** / **非常に** / **大変** / **かなり** / **けっこう**｝見事に生けてある。(=KS(B))

c. 今年は桜の花が｛**なかなか** / ***とても** / ***非常に** / ***大変** / ***かなり** / ***けっこう**｝咲きません。(=KS(C))

d. あの男は仕事が｛**なかなか** / **とても** / **非常に** / **かなり** / **けっこう** / ***大変**｝出来るねえ。(=KS(D))

e. 山田部長の奥さんは｛**なかなか**（**の**）/ **とても** / **非常に** / **かなり** / **大変な** / **けっこう**｝美人だ。(=KS(E))

When *nakanaka* is used with an affirmative predicate, it can be replaced by the five adverbs: *totemo*, *hijō ni*, *kanari*, *taihen*, and *kekkō*. But when *nakanaka* is used with a negative verb as in [1c], it cannot be replaced by either of the five adverbs. The crucial differences among the five adverbs are shown in [2].

[2] a. こんな小(ちい)さい会社(かいしゃ)なのに，｛**けっこう** / **かなり** / ?**とても** / ??**大変**｝質(しつ)のいい製品(せいひん)を出(だ)しているね。
(This is such a small company, but they are turning out a very high quality product, aren't they?)

b. あの人は見(み)かけによらず，｛**けっこう** / **かなり** / ??**とても** / ***大変**｝飲(の)みますね。
(Despite his appearance, he drinks quite a lot.)

c. 東京は日中三十七度もあり，{**とても / 大変 / *けっこう / *かなり**} 暑かった。
(In Tokyo it was 37 degrees in the daytime, and it was very hot.)

The sentences in [2] show that *kekkō* and *kanari* indicate a relatively high degree, wheareas, *totemo* and *taihen* indicate an absolutely high degree. *Kekkō* and *totemo* are more colloquial than *kanari* and *taihen*, respectively.

-naku なく *inflectional ending* <w>

a continuative form of *nai* used in written Japanese (to indicate a reason / cause for what follows if *nai* is attached to Adj(*i* / *na*) and contrast if it is attached to N + Copula)

not ~ and; not ~ but
【REL. *-zu*】

◆Key Sentences

(A)

Sentence$_1$		Sentence$_2$
日本語の期末試験はあまり**難しく**	なく，	ほっとした。
(The Japanese final examination was not very hard, and I felt relieved.)		

(B)

Sentence$_1$		Sentence$_2$
私の研究対象は**現代史では**	なく，	古代史だ。
(My research area is not modern history, but ancient history.)		

Formation

(i) Adj(*i*)stem くなく

大きくなく (s.t. / s.o. is not big and ~)

(ii) {Adj(*na*)stem / N} ではなく

静かではなく (s.t. / s.o. is not quiet and ~)

先生ではなく (s.o. is not a teacher but ~)

Examples

(a) 今年の冬はあまり寒くなく，オーバーも二，三度しか着なかった。
(It wasn't very cold this winter and we wore our overcoats only two or three times.)

(b) 昨日見た映画は実に面白くなく，途中で寝てしまった。
(The movie I saw yesterday was so boring that I went to sleep during it.)

(c) 私には日本語を聞くのが容易ではなく，大分苦労した。
(To listen to Japanese was not easy, and I had quite a difficult time.)

(d) 彼女と別れた時はそれほど悲しくなく，自分でも驚いた。
(I was surprised that I did not feel so sad when I parted with her.)

(e) 私に日本語を教えてくれたのは日本人ではなく，アメリカ人だった。
(The person who taught me Japanese was not a Japanese but an American.)

(f) 僕が好きなのは日本料理ではなくタイ料理だ。
(What I like is not Japanese cuisine, but Thai cuisine.)

Notes

1. Adj(*i*)stem *ku naku* and Adj(*na*) *de wa naku* are used to express a reason / cause for what follows, as shown in KS(A) and Exs.(a) – (d). But the reason / cause there is not stated as precisely as in *kara* / *node*-clauses, just like the English conjunction "and".

(⇨ ***kara***[3] (DBJG: 179–81); ***node*** (DBJG: 328–31))

2. The *-naku* form is used in written Japanese, whereas *-nakute* can be used in both spoken and written Japanese. However, note that the negative continuative form *-naku* cannot be used with a verb except when *naru* follows the *naku* form, as shown in (1) and (2).

(1) a. うちの子は本を {**読まなくて** / ***読まなく**} 困るんです。
(Our child doesn't read books and we don't know what to do.)

b. 主人は酒をあまり {**飲まなくて** / ***飲まなく**} 助かっています。
(My husband doesn't drink much, and it's a relief.)
(⇨ ***nakute*** (DBJG: 279–80))

(2) a. うちの子は本を**読まなく**なりました。
(Our child doesn't read books any more.)

b. 主人は酒を**飲まなく**なりました。
(My husband doesn't drink any more.)

3. If *nai* is attached to N + Copula, it indicates contrast. But, if a noun is a Sino-Japanese compound with an adjectival nature, such as *akusei* (悪性) 'malignant,' *kōhyō* (好評) 'popularity,' it indicates a reason / cause for what follows.

(3) a. 腫瘍が**悪性**でなく，ほっとした。
(The tumor wasn't malignant, and I felt relieved.)

b. 書いた本が**好評**でなく，がっかりした。
(The book I wrote was not popular, and I felt disappointed.)

4. The following chart summarizes the negative and affirmative continuative forms.

	Affirmative		Negative	
		<w>		<w>
Verb	話して 食べて	話し 食べ	話さなくて 食べなくて	話さず 食べず
Adj (*i*)	高くて	高く	高くなくて	高くなく
Adj (*na*)	静かで	静かで	静かでなくて	静かでなく
N + Cop	学生で	学生で	学生でなくて	学生でなく

(⇨ ***te*** (DBJG: 464–67); **V*masu***)

【Related Expression】

The *-naku* form is connected with an Adj(*i* / *na*) or a noun, but it cannot be connected with a verb except when *naru* follows the *-naku* form, as stated in Note 2. However, Vneg *zu* can be used in written Japanese. Vneg usually takes a potential negative form, except when Vneg means 'without doing s.t.' (⇨ ***naide*** (DBJG: 271–73))

[1] a. 日本語の新聞が読め**ず**，困った。
(I was not able to read Japanese newspapers, so I had a difficult time.)

b. 住所も電話番号も分から**ず**，連絡が出来なかった。
(I didn't know the address or the telephone number, so I was not able to contact him.)

c. 簡単な質問に答えられ**ず**，恥をかいた。
(I couldn't answer simple questions, so I felt embarassed.)

nandemo 何でも *phr.*

a phrase that indicates the speaker's uncertainty about s.t.

I don't know for sure, but

◆**Key Sentence**

何(なん)でも	山本(やまもと)さんは奥(おく)さんと別(わか)れて，一人(ひとり)で暮(く)らしている	そうですよ。
(I don't know for sure, but they say that Mr. Yamamoto has separated from his wife and lives alone.)		

Examples

(a) 何でもこの辺(へん)は物価(ぶっか)が非常(ひじょう)に高(たか)いそうですよ。
(I don't know for sure, but they say things are expensive in this neighborhood.)

(b) 何でもあの人(ひと)は株(かぶ)で大分(だいぶ)もうけたようですよ。
(I don't know for sure, but he appeared to have earned a lot of money through stocks.)

(c) 何でも戸田(とだ)さんの息子(むすこ)さんはシカゴ大学(だいがく)で経営学(けいえいがく) 修士(しゅうし)を取(と)ったらしいですよ。
(I don't know for sure, but it seems that Mr. Toda's son received an MBA at the University of Chicago.)

(d) 何でも日本(にほん)とアメリカの西海岸(にしかいがん)を五時間(ごじかん)ぐらいで飛(と)ぶ飛行機(ひこうき)を開発(かいはつ)しているという話(はなし)ですよ。
(I don't know for sure, but there's some talk that they are developing an airplane that flies between Japan and the west coast of the States in about five hours.)

Notes

1. The phrase *nandemo* indicates the speaker's uncertainty about something. It is used at the beginning of the sentence and the final predicate

has to be either a hearsay expression (as in KS, Exs.(a) and (d)) or conjectural expression (as in Exs.(b) and (c)).

2. The sentence remains grammatical without *nandemo*, but it cannot express the idea of uncertainty.

3. Among the conjectural expressions, *darō* / *deshō* cannot be used with *nandemo*, because the speaker is sure about s.t. more than 50% but less than 100% when he uses *nandemo*, whereas he is at most 50% sure about s.t. when he uses *darō* / *deshō*.

    (1) *何でもあの二人(ふたり)は結婚(けっこん)する**でしょう**ね。
    (I don't know for sure, but the two will probably get married.)

    → 何でもあの二人は結婚する {**らしい** / **よう** / **そう**} ですね。
    (I don't know for sure, but the two {seem / appear / have been said} to be getting married.)

(⇨ ***darō*** (DBJG: 100–02))

nanishiro 何しろ *adv.* <s>

> an adverb that indicates the speaker's emotive feeling about some extreme state of affairs

as a matter of fact; no matter what; believe it or not; you may be surprised, but ~; in fact; unbelievably
【REL. *tonikaku*】

◆Key Sentences

(A)

Sentence$_1$		Sentence$_2$
うちの父は頑固なんだ。	何しろ	一度言い出したら絶対に引き下がらないんだから。
(My father is obstinate. As a matter of fact, once he says he will do s.t., he never changes his mind.)		

(B)

A:	B:		
この大学の教育はいいらしいね。	うん,	何しろ	学生六人に先生一人だからね。
(A: I heard that education at this college is good. B: Yeah, you may be surprised, but the instructor-student ratio is 6 to 1.)			

(C)

Sentence$_1$		Sentence$_2$
一日中ボスにがなり立てられるんで,	何しろ,	ストレスが多いんだ。
(Because my boss hollers at me all day long, I'm unbelievably stressed.)		

Examples

(a) あの人は金持ちですよ。何しろベンツを三台も持っているんですからね。
(He is rich, you know. Believe it or not, he has three Mercedes Benz.)

(b) 今年の冬は本当に雪が多かったです。何しろ, 雪の降らない日の方が少ないくらいでしたからね。
(It snowed a lot this winter. In fact, there were less snow-free days than snowy days, you know.)

N

(c) あの人はよくたばこを吸いますよ。何しろ一日に六十本ぐらい吸うんですから。
(He is a heavy smoker. In fact, he smokes about 60 cigarettes a day.)

(d) A: 日本は人が多いねえ。
(Japan is crowded, isn't it?)

B: うん，何しろ，面積はアメリカの二十五分の一なのに，人口は二分の一だからね。
(Yeah, as a matter of fact, the size is one twenty fifth of America but the population is one half, you know.)

(e) 何しろ，忙しいんだ。寝る時間もないんだよ。
(I'm unbelievably busy. I don't have any sleeping time, you know.)

Notes

1. Originally the adverb comes from *nani o shiro* meaning 'do what you may.'

2. *Nanishiro* indicates the speaker's emotive reaction about some extreme state of affairs, so if an unusual situation does not exist the adverb cannot be used.

(1) 今日は休ませて下さい。**何しろ** {頭が割れそうに痛い / *ちょっと頭が痛い} ので。
(Please let me take a day off today, because {I have a severe headache / I have a slight headache}.)

(2) 心配しなくてもいいよ。**何しろ** {警官が二十人も見張っている / *僕がここで見張っている} から。
(Don't worry, because {there are as many as 20 policemen watching / I am watching you}.)

【Related Expression】

Nanishiro in all the KS and Exs. above can be replaced by *tonikaku*. However, *tonikaku* has a meaning of 'any way/at any rate' but unlike *nanishiro* it does not indicate the speaker's emotive feeling. In other words, *nanishiro* is a speaker-oriented expression, but *tonikaku* isn't. So, the latter can be used in highly hearer-oriented request or question sentences but the former cannot.

[1] a. {**とにかく** / ***何しろ**} 会いに来て下さい。
(Come and see me, anyway.)

b. {**とにかく** / ***何しろ**} 手紙を出したらどうですか。
(I'd suggest that you send a letter, anyway.)

c. {**とにかく** / ***何しろ**} たばこをやめますか。
(Are you going to quit smoking anyway?)

naranai ならない *phr.* <w>

a phrase that is used to express insurmountable psychological or physical feelings

cannot help -ing; irresistibly; unbearably
【REL. *tamaranai*】

◆**Key Sentences**

(A)

	Adj(*na*)*te*	
病気の母のことが	**心配で**	ならない。
(I'm very much worried about my sick mother. (Lit. I cannot help worrying about my sick mother).)		

(B)

	Adj(*i*)*te*	
日本の歴史をもっと深く**知り**	**たくて**	ならない。
(I'm dying to know Japanese history more deeply.)		

(C)

	V*te*	
一人で住んでいる母親のことが**気に**	**なって**	ならない。
(I cannot help worrying about my mother who is living alone.)		

Formation

(i) Adj(*i* / *na*)*te* ならない

うれしくてならない (I cannot help feeling happy.)

残念でならない (I cannot help feeling sorry.)

(ii) V*te* ならない

気がせいてならない (I cannot help feeling pressed.)

Examples

(a) 夫が単身赴任しているので，寂しくてなりません。
(My husband has gone alone for work and I cannot help feeling lonely.)

(b) 二人は婚約が決まって，うれしくてならないようだ。
(The couple have decided to get engaged and they look overjoyed.)

(c) 松本清張の推理小説は面白くてならない。
(The mystery novels by Seicho Matsumoto are irresistibly interesting.)

(d) 隣の家のステレオがやかましくてならない。
(Our neighbor's stereo is unbearably noisy.)

(e) 山田先生がこの大学をお辞めになるので，残念でならない。
(Since Prof. Yamada is going to quit this university, I cannot help feeling disappointed.)

(f) 東京の夏は暑くてならない。
(The summer in Tokyo is awfully hot.)

(g) 駅の階段を急いで上がったら，息が苦しくてならなかった。
(When I rushed up the stairs at the station, it became unbearably painful to breathe.)

(h) 買ってきたばかりのテレビがすぐ壊れてしまい，腹が立ってならなかった。
(I got really mad because the TV set which I just bought got broken right away.)

(i) 仕事がうまく行っていないので，気が滅入ってならない。
(I feel helplessly depressed because my business isn't going well.)

Notes

1. *Naranai* is used to express insurmountable psychological or physical feeling. The form is connected with Adj(*i* / *na*) of psychological or physical feeling as shown in KS(A), (B), and Exs.(a) – (g), or with V of psychological feeling as in Exs.(h) and (i). If Adj(*i* / *na*) is neither a psychological nor physical feeling, *naranai* cannot be used.

(1) ??私の家は**狭くてならない**。→ 私の家は**狭すぎる**。
(My house is unbearably small.)

(2) *日本の物価は**高くてならない**。→ 日本の物価は**高すぎる**。
(Prices in Japan are unbearably expensive.)

However, there are some psychological and physiological adjectives that cannot be used with *naranai*.

(3) a. ??久しぶりにジョギングしたら，足が**痛くて**ならなかった。
(I jogged after a long while and my legs hurt unbearably.)

b. *あの先生は厳しいから，**嫌いで**ならない。
(That teacher is strict, so I hate him badly.)

c. *あの人はとても気が優しいから，**好きで**ならない。
(He is very considerate, so I like him a lot.)

When V is connected with *naranai* it is usually an idiomatic verb phrase of psychological feeling, and not of physiological feeling. Thus, for example, (4) is unacceptable, unless *naranai* is replaced by *tamaranai*.

(4) *朝飯を食べて来なかったので，**腹が減って**ならない。
(I came here without eating my breakfast, so I am awfully hungry.)

2. The subject of the *naranai* construction is normally the speaker / writer or whoever the speaker / writer is empathetic with as in (5).

(5) **真知子**はひとみの美貌がうらやましくてならない。
(Machiko cannot help feeling envious of Hitomi's beauty.)

If the subject is other than the speaker / writer and the speaker / writer is not empathetic with the referent of the subject, it is necessary to use expressions such as *yōda*, *rashii*, *yōsu da*, etc, as in Ex.(b).

【Related Expression】

Tamaranai and *shikata ga nai* can be used with any Adj or V of psychological or physical feeling to express its unbearableness, whereas *naranai* is much more restricted in that it has to indicate psychological feeling when used with V, as shown in Note 1 above.

[1] a. 暑いので，**のどが渇いて**｛たまらない / 仕方がない / *ならない｝。
(It's hot and I'm awfully thirsty.)

b. アレルギーのためか，しょっちゅう**くしゃみが出て**｛たまらない / 仕方がない / *ならない｝。
(Probably because of my allergy, I sneeze an awful lot.)

c. 駅まで走ったので**足が痛くて**｛たまらない / 仕方がない / *ならない｝。
(Because I ran to the station, my legs ache a lot.)

The difference between *tamaranai* and *shikata ga nai* is that the former expresses the speaker's feeling of intolerability more strongly than the latter.
(⇨ ***tamaranai*** (DBJG: 445–47))

~ nari ~ nari ～なり～なり *str.*

a phrase to indicate two representative choices / examples

~ or ~ (for example); like ~ or ~
【REL. ~ *ka* ~ *ka*; ~ *-tari* ~ *-tari*; ~ *toka* ~ *toka*】

◆Key Sentences

(A)

	N		N		
文法(ぶんぽう)が分(わ)からなかったら，	**私**(わたし)	なり	**鈴木先生**(すずきせんせい)	なり	に質問(しつもん)しなさい。
(If you don't understand grammar, ask me or Professor Suzuki.)					

(B)

	Vinf·nonpast			Vinf·nonpast		
読(よ)めない漢字(かんじ)は辞書(じしょ)を	**引**(ひ)**く**	なり，	日本人(にほんじん)に	**聞**(き)**く**	なり	しなさい。
(As for kanji you can't read, find out the reading either by looking it up in a dictionary or by asking a Japanese.)						

N

Formation

(i) N_1 なり N_2 なり{が / を}

田中君(たなかくん)なり山田(やまだ)君なり {が / を} (either Tanaka or Yamada)

(ii) N_1 Prt. なり N_2 Prt. なり (where Prt. = other particles than が / を)

山(やま)へなり海(うみ)へなり (to the mountain or to the oceans)

田中君になり山田君になり (either to Tanaka or to Yamada)

(iii) N_1 なり N_2 なり Prt. (where the Prt. is に，へ，と，で，から)

ラジオなりテレビなりで (either on the radio or TV)

(iv) Vinf·nonpast なり (Vinf·nonpast なり)

読むなり，書くなり (reading or writing)

Examples

(a) 私なり山田なりが空港に迎えに参ります。
(Either I or Yamada will go to the airport to pick you up.)

(b) 何か連絡することがありましたら電話なりファックスなりでお願いします。
(If you have something that you want to report, please do it by telephone or by fax.)

(c) 両親なり親友なりに会って，ゆっくり話したいんです。
(I would like to see my parents or a close friend, and talk leisurely.)

(d) 今は忙しくて旅行が出来ないが，春休みなり夏休みなりにするつもりだ。
(Right now I'm so busy that I can't make a trip, but I intend to make one during the spring break or summer vacation.)

(e) テニスがしたかったら，トムなりチャールズなりとしたらいいでしょう。
(If you want to play tennis, why don't you play with Tom or Charles?)

(f) アパートを探しているんなら，不動産屋に行くなり，新聞の広告を見るなりしたらどうですか。
(If you are looking for an apartment, you should go to a realtor or look at the newspaper ads.)

(g) 散歩するなり，泳ぐなり，何か運動をした方がいいですよ。
(You'd better do some exercise, like taking a walk or swimming.)

Notes

1. *~ nari ~ nari* is used to present two choices as examples. The speaker makes a subjective judgment that his / her choice is a reasonable and proper one. That is why it is frequently used in sentences expressing a

command / request as in KS(A), (B), and Exs.(b), or a suggestion / advice as in Exs.(e) – (g), or an intention / desire as in Exs.(a), (c) and (d).

2. Usually *nari* is repeated twice, but it may appear only once in Vinf · nonpast *nari* Vinf · nonpast *nari*.

    (1) 床屋(とこや)に行く**なり**して，もっと髪(かみ)をきちんとしたらどうですか。
    (Why don't you go to the barber's and make your hairstyle neat?)

    (2) *文法が分からなかったら私**なり**に質問しなさい。(cf. KS(A))

3. The main predicate of the structure in question is more often than not in the nonpast tense, because it expresses the speaker's current will, determination, desire or habits as shown in Exs.(a), (c) and (d). But the main predicate can be in the past, if the predicate expresses a habitual determination as shown in (3) below.

    (3) 私は漢字の読み方(かた)が分からない時(とき)は，先生なり日本人なりに聞くようにし**た**。
    (I've made it a rule to ask my teacher or a Japanese when I don't know how to read kanji.)

N

【Related Expressions】

I. The structure ~ *nari* ~ *nari* can be replaced by the conjunction ~ *ka* ~ *ka*, because both can express choice. So, KS(A) and Ex.(a), for example, can be rewritten as [1] and [2], respectively.

    [1] 文法が分からなかったら，私**か**鈴木先生(**か**)に聞いて下(くだ)さい。
    (cf. KS(A))

    [2] 私**か**山田(**か**)が空港に迎えにまいります。(cf. Ex.(a))

The crucial difference between ~ *nari* ~ *nari* and ~ *ka* ~ (*ka*) is that the latter is an exhaustive listing of choices (i.e., 'either ~ or'), but the former is a listing of representatives out of more possible choices.

(⇨ **~ *ka* ~ *ka***; ***ka***[1] (DBJG: 164–66))

II. The expression ~ *-tari* ~ *-tari* can replace ~ *nari* ~ *nari*. For example,

KS(B) and Ex.(f) can be rewritten as [3] and [4].

(⇨ ***~ tari ~ tari suru*** (DBJG: 458–61))

[3] 読めない漢字は辞書を引い**たり**，日本人に聞い**たり**しなさい。(cf. KS(B))

[4] アパートを探しているんなら，不動産屋に行っ**たり**，新聞の広告を見**たり**した方がいいでしょう。(cf. Ex.(f))

Both ~ *nari* ~ *nari* and ~ *-tari* ~ *-tari* list representative examples, but the former sounds more assertive than the latter. (i.e., the speaker feels that his choice is the proper one). So in a situation where the speaker's assertion is due, ~ *-tari* ~ *-tari* is not used.

[5] 分からなかったら，図書館で {**調べるなり** / ***調べたり**}，先生に {**聞くなり** / ***聞いたり**} しろよ。
(If you cannot figure it out, do research at the library or ask your professor.)

In [6a] and [6b] *nari* is ungrammatical, because Vinf·nonpast *nari* Vinf·nonpast *nari* cannot be used with the past tense predicate.

[6] a. 昨日はテニスを {**したり** / ***するなり**} CDを {**聞いたり** / ***聞くなり**} した。
(Yesterday I did things like playing tennis and listening to CDs.)

b. 酒を {**飲んだり** / ***飲むなり**}，歌を {**歌ったり** / ***歌うなり**}，とても楽しかった。
(Doing things like drinking sake and singing songs, we enjoyed very much (lit. was very enjoyable).)

Tari in [7] is ungrammatical, simply because it cannot be connected with a noun.

[7] 文法が分からなかったら，私 {**なり** / ***たり**} 鈴木先生 {**なり** / ***たり**} に質問しなさい。(=KS(A))

In [8] *tari* is ungrammatical, because *tari* expresses X and Y (and others), whereas *nari* expresses X or Y (or s.t.).

[8] 散歩 {**するなり** / ***したり**}, {**泳ぐなり** / ***泳いだり**}, 何か運動をした方がいいですよ。(=Ex.(g))

III. ~ *toka* ~ *toka* is also used to list representative examples. ~ *nari* ~ *nari* can be replaced by ~ *toka* ~ *toka*: the former conveys the speaker's subjective judgment that the choice is the proper one but the latter doesn't. ~ *nari* ~ *nari* in [9d] is unacceptable because it cannot take a verb right after it.

[9] a. 文法が分からなかったら, 私 {**なり** / **とか**} 鈴木先生 {**なり** / **とか**} に質問しなさい。(=KS(A))

b. 読めない漢字は辞書を引く {**なり** / **とか**}, 日本人に聞く {**なり** / **とか**} しなさい。(=KS(B))

c. 私はビール {**とか** / **なり**} ワイン {**とか** / **なり**}, 何か飲み物(もの)がほしいです。
(I'd like something to drink like beer or wine.)

d. 私は政治(せいじ) {**とか** / ***なり**} 宗教(しゅうきょう) {**とか** / ***なり**} いうものは嫌(きら)いです。
(I don't like things like politics or religion.)

N

nari ni なりに *comp. prt.*

in a way / style that is proper to s.o. / s.t.	in one's own way; in one's own style

◆Key Sentences

(A)

Noun		Noun		
あの人	は	**あの人**	なりに	よく考えているらしい。
(He appears to think hard in his own way.)				

(B)

Noun		Noun			
動物	は	**動物**	なりの	コミュニケーション	が出来る。
(Animals are capable of their own communication.)					

Formation

(i) N_1 は N_2 なりに (where $N_1 = N_2$)

学生は学生なりに (students ~ in their own way)

(ii) N_1 は N_2 なりの N_3 (where $N_1 = N_2$)

先生なりの考え (teachers' own idea)

Examples

(a) 小さい大学は小さい大学なりによさがある。
(Small colleges have their own merits.)

(b) 私は私なりに，人生観を持っています。
(I have my own outlook on life.)

(c) 自転車は自転車なりに，車は車なりに，長所，短所がある。
(Both bicycles and cars have good and bad features.)

(d) 健康な人は健康な人なりに，体に気をつけた方がいい。
(Healthy people had better take care of themselves in their own way.)

(e) 私は老人が老人なりに生活を楽しめる社会が好きだ。
(I like a society in which old people can enjoy life in their own way.)

(f) 私は私なりに一生懸命働くつもりです。
(I intend to work very hard in my own way.)

(g) この問題について，父は父なりの考えを持っているようです。
(My father seems to have his own idea about this issue.)

(h) ジャズ音楽はジャズ音楽なりの魅力がある。
(Jazz music has its own charm.)

(i) 金持ちは金持ちなりの悩みがあるのだ。
(Rich people have their own suffering.)

Notes

1. The particle *nari ni* is used to express a way or a style that is proper to s.o. or s.t. The phrase N *wa* N *nari ni* is used when the speaker wants to assert s.t. about N. For example, in KS(A), the speaker wants to assert that he thinks hard in his own way.

2. Along with the adverbial phrase N *nari ni*, there is N *nari no* N as in KS(B) and Exs.(g) – (i).

3. In both N_1 *wa* N_2 *nari ni* and N_1 *wa* N_2 *nari no* N_3, N_2 can be replaced by the pronoun *sore* if N is an inanimate object, as in (1) below.

(1) a. 小さい大学はそれなりによさがある。(cf. Ex.(a))
(Small colleges have their own merits.)

b. ジャズ音楽はそれなりの魅力がある。(cf. Ex.(h))
(Jazz music has its own charm.)

nashi de wa なしでは *comp. prt.*

if s.t. / s.o. is missing

without
【REL. ~ *ga* (*i*)-*nakereba*; *nashi ni wa*】

◆Key Sentence

Noun		
実力	なしでは	世の中は渡れない。
(Without real talents one cannot get along in the society.)		

Formation

N なしでは

先生なしでは (without a teacher)

N

Examples

(a) あなたなしでは生きていけない。
(Without you I cannot keep on living.)

(b) お金なしではいい教育は受けられない。
(Without money we cannot receive good education.)

(c) 暇なしでは人生はつまらなくなってしまう。
(Without leisure time life will become dull.)

(d) 仕事なしでは生活が出来ない。
(Without a job one cannot live a life.)

(e) 基礎研究なしでは科学は発展しない。
(Without basic research science would not develop.)

(f) 車なしではちょっと不便だ。
(Without a car it is a bit inconvenient.)

Notes

1. The compound particle *nashi de wa* is used to express a conditional "if s.t. / s.o. is missing."

2. The particle *nashi de wa* usually appears with a negative predicate. The predicate can be implicitly negative as in Ex.(c).

 (1) a. *あなた**なしでは**生きていける。(cf. Ex.(a))
 →あなた**なしでも**生きていける。
 (Without you I can live a life.)

 b. *実力**なしでは**世の中を渡れる。(cf. KS)
 →実力**なしでも**世の中は渡れる。
 (One can get along in society even without real talents.)

【Related Expressions】

I. *Nashi de wa* can be replaced by *nashi ni wa* in KS and Exs.(a), (b), (d), and (e), but not in the other Exs. It seems that N *nashi de wa* is preferred in a context where N is used as a means of achieving something; whereas N *nashi ni wa* is preferred in a context where the meaning of a means of achieving something is weak. That is why in Exs.(c) and (f) the original *nashi de wa* can hardly be replaced by *nashi ni wa*; the free time is regarded as a means of enriching one's life in Ex.(c) and a car is regarded definitely as a means of transportation in Ex.(f). In [1] below, the same N "*wāpuro*" is regarded as a means in [1a] and not as such in [1b].

 [1] a. ワープロ {**なしでは** / ?**なしには**} いい論文が書けない。
 (Without a word processor one cannot write a good paper.)

 b. ワープロ {**なしには** / ?**なしでは**} 文筆作業は考えられない。
 (One cannot think of writing activities without a word processor.)

II. The adverbial phrase ~ *nashi de wa* can be rephrased by ~ *ga nakereba* or by ~ *ga i-nakereba*. Thus, for example, KS and Ex.(a) can be rewritten into [2] and [3], respectively, without changing their basic meaning.

The only difference between the two versions is that ~ *nashi de wa* version sounds slightly more formal probably due to the archaic form *nashi*.

[2] 実力**がなければ**，世の中を渡れない。(cf. KS)

[3] あなた**がいなければ**生きていけない。(cf. Ex.(a))

However, ~ *ga* (*i*)-*nakereba* cannot be rephrased by ~ *nashi de wa* when the sentence is a question, request, command, suggestion, or volitional sentence. Examples follow.

[4] {仕事**がなければ** / *仕事**なしでは**} {探しなさい / 探してください / 探したらどうですか / 探しましょう}。
(If you don't have a job, look for one / please look for one / why don't you look for one / let's look for one.)

[5] {先生**がいなければ** / *先生**なしでは**} 自分で勉強しなさい。
(If there isn't a teacher, study by yourself.)

[6] {お金**がなければ** / *お金**なしでは**}，どうしたらいいですか。
(If I don't have money, what shall I do?)

-neba naranai ねばならない *phr.* <w>

a phrase that indicates duty, obligation or necessity

must; have to; should
【REL. *-nakereba naranai*】

◆Key Sentences

(A)

	Vinf·neg	
日本を知るためには一度は日本へ	**行か**	ねばならない。
(In order to know Japan one has to go to Japan at least once.)		

(B)

	VN		
日本は市場をもっと広く	**開放**	**せ**	ねばならない。
(Japan has to open its market wider.)			

Formation

Vinf·neg ねばならない

話さねばならない　(s.o. has to talk.)

食べねばならない　(s.o. has to eat.)

せねばならない (irr.)　(s.o. has to do it.)

Examples

(a) 今後も同じ研究を続けねばならない。
(I have to continue the same research from now on.)

(b) 人種偏見をなくさねばならない。
(We should get rid of racial prejudice.)

(c) 会議の内容を帰国後本社に報告せねばならなかった。
(I had to report the agenda of the conference to the main office after returning to my country.)

(d) 自然保護を叫ばねばならない。
(We have to voice preservation of nature.)

(e) 日本はこれから世界をリードせねばなりません。
(From now on Japan has to lead the world.)

Notes

1. Vinf·neg *neba naranai* is used in written Japanese or in formal public speech to express obligation, duty, or necessity.
2. The *neba naranai* form for the irregular verb *suru* is *se-neba naranai.*

【Related Expression】

The only crucial difference between Vinf·neg *-neba naranai* and Vinf·neg *-nakereba naranai* is that the former is used normally in written Japanese, but the latter, in spoken and written Japanese. Connection-wise, the way *-neba naranai* and *-nakereba naranai* are connected with adjectives are different.

[1] a. 理想は高く｛**なければ／あらねば**｝ならない。
(One's ideals should be high.)

b. この問題に関して我々は慎重｛**でなければ／であらねば**｝ならない。
(We have to be cautious about this issue.)

ni に *prt.*

a sentence-final particle that expresses the speaker's feeling of great regret or sympathy

【REL. *noni*】

◆Key Sentences

(A)

Scond	Sinf		
昨日来れば	夏子に**会えた**	でしょう / だろう	に。
(If you had come here yesterday, you could have met Natsuko.)			

(B)

Sinf		
老人が一人で暮らすのはさぞ**寂しい**	でしょう / だろう	に。
(It must be lonely for an old man to live alone.)		

Formation

(i) {V / Adj(*i*)}inf {でしょう / だろう} に

{話す / 話した} {でしょう / だろう} に (would talk / would have talked)

{高い / 高かった} {でしょう / だろう} に (would {be / have been} expensive)

(ii) {Adj(*na*)stem / N} {ø / だった} {でしょう / だろう} に

{静か / 静かだった} {でしょう / だろう} に (would {be / have been} quiet)

いい {先生 / 先生だった} {でしょう / だろう} に (would {be / have been} a good teacher)

Example

(a) 後一年ぐらい日本にいたら日本語がもっと上手になるでしょうに。
(If you could stay in Japan another year or so your Japanese would become more proficient.)

(b) お金がたくさんあればこんな家でも買えるでしょうに。
(If we had a lot of money, we would be able to buy this sort of house.)

(c) 僕にいい仕事があったら美智子さんと結婚出来ただろうに。
(If I had had a good job I could have married Michiko.)

(d) 飛行機で行けば簡単に行ける所でしょうに。
(If you go by plane, you could easily get there.)

(e) 彼はもう少し慎重に金を使えば，貯金出来るだろうに。
(If he uses his money a little more carefully, he could save his money.)

(f) 駅の近くのアパートに住んだら便利でしょうに。
(If you lived in an apartment near the station, it would be convenient.)

(g) 子供を二人も大学に行かせるのにはお金がかかるでしょうに。
(It must cost a lot of money to send two children to college.)

(h) 飛行機の切符をなくして，さぞ困ったことでしょうに。
(You must have had a difficult time when you lost your airplane ticket.)

Notes

1. If the structure is "Scond, ~ {V / Adj}inf·nonpast {*deshō* / *darō*} *ni*," the entire sentence expresses the subjunctive past (i.e., supposition that is counter to the current situation) as in Exs.(a), (b), (d), (e) and (f). "Scond, ~ {V / Adj}inf·past {*deshō* / *darō*} *ni*" expresses the subjunctive past perfect (i.e., supposition that is counter to the past situation) as in KS(A) and Ex.(c). In both the subjunctive past and the past perfect, the entire sentence expresses the speaker's regret. But if the subject of the Scond is the second or third person, it expresses the speaker's sympathy for the second or third person. If Scond is not there, as in KS(B), Exs.(g) and (h), the entire sentence expresses sympathy.

2. The sentence-final particle *ni* always follows *deshō* / *darō*.

【Related Expression】

"Scond, ~ {V / Adj}inf {*deshō* / *darō*}" can be rephrased as "Scond, ~ {V / Adj} inf *noni*," as shown in [1] and [2]. (⇨ ***noni*** (DBJG: 331–35))

[1] 昨日来れば夏子に会えた**のに**。(cf. KS(A))

[2] お金がたくさんあればこんな家でも買える**のに**。(cf. Ex.(b))

The *deshō/darō ni* version indicates uncertainty, whereas the *noni* version does not. Comparison of [3a] and [3b] below will clarify the point.

[3] a. 僕にいい仕事があったら美智子さんと結婚出来た**だろうに**。(=Ex.(c))

b. 僕にいい仕事があったら美智子さんと結婚出来た**のに**。
(If I had had a good job, it is very likely that I could have married her.)

[3a] expresses uncertainty, meaning 'I guess I could have married Michiko,' whereas [3b] doesn't express uncertainty.

ni atatte/atari に当たって / 当たり *comp. prt.* <w>

a compound particle that indicates occasion of doing s.t. or of having done s.t. in formal Japanese

on the occasion of; at; in; before; prior to
【REL. *mae ni*; *ni saishite*; *sai (ni)*; *toki*】

◆Key Sentences

(A)

Noun		
新入(しんにゅう)社員(しゃいん)の入社(にゅうしゃ)	に {当(あ)たって / 当たり}	社長(しゃちょう)はホテルでパーティーを開(ひら)いた。
(On the occasion of new employees' entering the company, the president threw a party at a hotel.)		

(B)

	Vinf·nonpast		
和也は大学を	**卒業する**	に{当たって/当たり},	指導教官に今後の進路について相談した。
(On the occasion of graduating from college, Kazuya consulted with his academic adviser on his future direction.)			

Formation

(i) N に{当たって/当たり}

結婚に{当たって/当たり} (on the occasion of the marriage)

(ii) Vinf·nonpast に{当たって/当たり}

話すに{当たって/当たり} (on the occasion of talking)

Examples

(a) 私の留学に当たり，父は自分の経験を話してくれた。
(On the occasion of my study abroad, my father told me about his own experience.)

(b) 日本の経済を研究するに当たって，国会図書館で資料集めをした。
(Before I did research on the Japanese economy, I collected materials at the National Diet Library.)

(c) 総理はサミット出席に当たり，閣僚と会議をした。
(The Premier had a conference with cabinet members before attending the summit.)

(d) 小説家は時代小説を書くに当たり，その時代の歴史を詳しく調べた。
(Before writing a historical novel, the novelist did an in-depth survey of the history of the period he dealt with.)

Notes

1. *ni atatte/atari* is used to indicate time when one faces s.t. formal. The formality of the compound particle can be shown by (1).

(1) a. 私は就寝**に当たって**少量の洋酒を喫することを習慣にしている。
(It is my custom to drink a small amount of foreign liquor prior to going to bed.)

b. *私は寝る**に当たって**ウイスキーを一杯ひっかける。
(I drink a glass of whisky before going to bed.)

Both (1a) and (1b) express a similar situation, but (1a) is expressed in a more formal way than (1b). Thus, *ni atatte* is acceptable in the formal sentence (1a) but not in the informal sentence (1b).

2. The compound particle is primarily used in written Japanese. When a verb precedes it, the verb is often a Sino-Japanese *suru*-verb as in KS(B) and Ex.(b), because the Sino-Japanese verb is also suitable for written Japanese.

3. The tense of the verb before *ni atatte/atari* is always nonpast regardless of the tense of the final predicate. The nonpast tense expresses an incomplete aspect of an action indicated by the verb. Thus, for example, in KS(B), when Kazuya went to see his academic adviser, he had not yet graduated from college. That is why the phrase can be translated into English as 'before' or 'prior to.'

4. The difference between *ni atari* and *ni atatte* is a matter of style; the former is more formal than the latter.

5. There is a prenominal form ~ *ni atatte no* N used as in (2) below.

(2) 新入社員の入社**に｛当たって／*当たり｝の**パーティーに社長も出席した。
(The president attended the party held on the occasion of new employees' joining the company.) (cf. KS(A))

【Related Expressions】

I. *Toki* is a basic noun which indicates the time when s.o. / s.t will do / does / did s.t. or the time when s.o. / s .t. will be / is / was in some state. It is clear from Note 3 that *toki* cannot be replaced by *ni atari / atatte* when the preceding verb is past. (⇨ ***toki*** (DBJG: 490–94))

[1] 私は日本にいた {時 / *に当たって / *に当たり} 日本語を勉強した。
(When I was in Japan, I studied Japanese.)

[2] 田中さんは大学を卒業した {時 / *に当たって / *に当たり} すぐ会社に入った。
(Mr. Tanaka joined a company soon after graduating from college.)

Toki can be used to express any time, be it formal or informal, whereas *ni atatte/atari* is used only in formal style. This contextual difference is shown in [3].

[3] a. 日本人はご飯を食べる {時 / *に当たって / *に当たり}「いただきます」と言う。
(Japanese people say "*Itadakimasu*" when they eat their meal.)

b. 寝る {時 / *に当たって / *に当たり} シャワーを浴びる。
(Before going to bed I take shower.)

II. The conjunction *mae ni* and the compound particle in question are semantically very close. Both of them allow only Vinf·nonpast because an action indicated by the verb is incomplete. Yet there is one crucial difference between them. *Ni atatte/atari* means 'before s.t. *significant* takes place,' but *mae ni* means 'before s.t. takes place.' The difference can be shown by the following examples. (⇨ ***mae ni*** (DBJG: 231–33))

[4] 伸子は寝る {前に / *に当たって} テレビを見る。
(Nobuko watches TV before she goes to sleep.)

[5] 伸子は入院する {前に / に当たって} 家族といろいろ相談した。
(Nobuko talked about various matters before she entered the hospital.)

III. There is another time expression ~ (*no*) *sai* (*ni*) / ~ *ni saishite* which is used to indicate a special occasion on which s.o. does s.t. The crucial difference between this time expression and ~ *ni attate/atari* is that the latter indicates an occasion in formal sentence, but the former indicates a special occasion. Thus, in the following formal yet non-special sentence the time expression in question cannot be used.

[6] 就寝 {**に当たって / に当たり** / ??**に際して** / ??**の際に**} 少量の洋酒を喫することを習慣にしている。(=(1a) in Note 1)

Practically all the uses of ~ *(no) sai (ni)* / ~ *ni saishite* can be rephrased by ~ *ni atatte/atari*, as long as the sentence is formal.

[7] a. 大阪に転勤する {**に際して / 際に / に当たって / に当たり**}, 妻子は東京に残した。
(When I transferred to Osaka I left my wife and children behind in Tokyo.)

b. 日本の近代化の研究 {**に際して / の際に / に当たって / に当たり**} 日本の国会図書館を利用した。
(At the time of research on Japanese modernization I used the National Diet Library of Japan.)

ni hanshite/hansuru に反して / 反する *comp. prt.* <w>

contrary to or in contrast to

against; contrary to; in contrast to; in violation of; while; whereas
【REL. *ni hikikae*; *ni taishite*; *to gyaku ni*】

◆Key Sentences

(A)

	Noun		
今年の東京国際マラソンは	**大方の予想**	に反して	無名の選手が優勝した。
(Contrary to the majority's expectations, an unknown runner won the Tokyo International Marathon this year.)			

(B)

	Sinf			
我が社は	**テレビの売れ行きが伸びている**	の	に反して	オーディオ製品の売れ行きが下がっている。
(In our company, in contrast to the increase in sales of TV sets, the sales in audio products are decreasing.)				

(C)

Sentence$_1$
日本ではいい大学に入るのは難しいが卒業するのはやさしいと言われている。
(It is said that to enter good universities in Japan is difficult but to graduate from them is easy.)

		Sentence$_2$
これ	に反して,	アメリカではいい大学でも入学は比較的やさしいが卒業するには相当勉強しなければならない。
(In contrast to this, in America even good universities are relatively easy to enter, but students must study quite hard to graduate from them.)		

N

(D)

	Noun		Noun	
妙子(たえこ)は	**意**(い)	に反する	結婚(けっこん)	を押(お)しつけられた。
(Taeko was forced to marry. (lit. A marriage which was against Taeko's will was forced upon her.))				

Formation

(i) N に反して

予想に反して (contrary to expectations)

(ii) Sinf のに反して (Connection rules: the same as のだ)

よく勉強するのに反して (in contrast to the fact that s.o. studies hard)

(iii) Demonstrative pronoun に反して

これに反して (in contrast to this)

(iv) N に反する N

予想に反する結果(けっか) (a result which is contrary to s.o.'s expectation)

Examples

(a) 浩(ひろし)は両親(りょうしん)の期待(きたい)に反して高校(こうこう)を出(で)てからコックになった。
(Contrary to his parents' wishes, Hiroshi became a chef after finishing high school.)

(b) 彼(かれ)は自分(じぶん)の意思(いし)に反して賄賂(わいろ)を受(う)け取(と)ってしまった。
(He was forced to accept a bribe. (lit. He received a bribe against his will.))

(c) この規則(きそく)に反して従業員(じゅうぎょういん)を働(はたら)かせた場合(ばあい)は一(いっ)か月(げつ)の営業停止(えいぎょうていし)になる。
(Your business will be suspended for one month if you work your employees in violation of these rules.)

(d) 奥村(おくむら)さんのうちはご主人(しゅじん)が無口(むくち)なのに反して奥(おく)さんが人一倍(ひといちばい)のおしゃべ

N

りだ。

(In Okumura's family, whereas the husband is quiet, the wife is very talkative.)

(e) 日本での初等教育は生徒に知識を与えることに主眼が置かれている。これに反して，アメリカでは生徒の創造性や個性を伸ばすことに重点が置かれている。

(The principle consideration in elementary education in Japan is to provide students with knowledge. In America, in contrast (to this), emphasis is put on increasing students' creativity and individual talents.)

(f) 今回の選挙は一般の予想に反する結果に終わった。

(The election this time ended up with results which were against the general prediction.)

Notes

N

1. *Te* in *ni hanshite* may be dropped, as in (1).
   (1) 今年の東京国際マラソンは大方の予想**に反し(て)**無名の選手が優勝した。(=KS(A))
2. When *ni hanshite* connects two propositions, the propositions are in opposition, as in KS(B), (C), Exs.(d) and (e).
3. *Ni hansuru* modifies the word which follows, as in KS(D) and Ex.(f).

【Related Expressions】

I. When *ni hanshite* connects two propositions in opposition, it can be paraphrased as *ni hikikae* or *to gyaku ni*, as in [1] and [2].

[1] 我が社はテレビの売れ行きが伸びているの {**に反して / にひきかえ / と逆に**} オーディオ製品の売れ行きが下がっている。 (=KS(B))

[2] 日本ではいい大学に入るのは難しいが卒業するのはやさしいと言われている。これ {**に反して / にひきかえ / と逆に**}，アメリカではいい大学でも入学は比較的やさしいが卒業するには相当勉強しなければならない。(=KS(C))

II. *Ni taishite* can also replace *ni hanshite* when *ni hanshite* connects two propositions in opposition, as in [3] and [4].

[3] 我が社はテレビの売れ行きが伸びているの｛**に反して / に対して**｝オーディオ製品の売れ行きが下がっている。(=KS(B))

[4] 日本ではいい大学に入るのは難しいが卒業するのはやさしいと言われている。これ｛**に反して / に対して**｝，アメリカではいい大学でも入学は比較的やさしいが卒業するには相当勉強しなければならない。(=KS(C))

The difference between the two is that when *ni hanshite* is used, the connected propositions are in opposition but when *ni taishite* is used, the connected propositions are contrastive but not necessarily in opposition. Thus, in [5], where the two propositions are contrastive but not in opposition, only *ni taishite* is acceptable.

[5] A 社が教育産業を重視しているの｛**に対して / *に反して**｝B 社はレジャー産業に力を入れている。
(Company A focuses on products for education (lit. puts importance on the education industry) while Company B focuses on products for leisure (lit. takes great interest in the leisure industry).)

ni hokanaranai にほかならない *phr.* <w>

a phrase that is used to indicate that an action / state mentioned in the topic phrase or clause is nothing but s.t.	be nothing but ~; be simply ~ 【REL. *ni suginai*】

◆Key Sentences

(A)

Topic	Noun	
あの人(ひと)の言葉(ことば)は	**美辞麗句(びじれいく)**	にほかならない。
(His words are nothing but flowery words.)		

(B)

Topic Clause			Sentence (reason)		
日本語(にほんご)を勉強(べんきょう)している	の	は	**将来(しょうらい)日本で仕事(しごと)をしたい**	から	にほかならない。
(The reason that I am studying Japanese is simply because I want to work in Japan in the future.)					

(C)

Topic	Sinf		
外国語学習(がいこくごがくしゅう)は	**ほかの国(くに)の人の考(かんが)え方(かた)を学(まな)ぶ**	こと	にほかならない。
(Foreign language learning is nothing but learning about the ways people in other countries think.)			

Formation

(i) (N は) N にほかならない

(彼(かれ)の話(はなし)は)冗談(じょうだん)にほかならない。 (His talk is nothing but a joke.)

(ii) ～のは～からにほかならない

働(はたら)くのはお金(かね)が欲(ほ)しいからにほかならない。 (The reason that we work is simply because we want money.)

(iii) ～は～ことにほかならない

読書は著者と対話することにほかならない。 (Reading is nothing but a dialogue with the author.)

Examples

(a) モーツァルトの音楽は天使の声にほかならない。
(Mozart's music is nothing but an angel's voice.)

(b) 結婚は人生の墓場にほかならない。
(Marriage is nothing but a graveyard of life.)

(c) 彼の言動は自己宣伝にほかならない。
(His speech and behavior are nothing but self-advertisement.)

(d) 親が子供を厳しくしつけるのは子供を愛しているからにほかならない。
(The reason why parents discipline their children strictly is simply because they love their children.)

(e) 彼女が僕に寄って来るのは僕を利用したいからにほかならない。
(The reason why she comes close to me is simply because she wants to use me.)

(f) 私の日本語がこれほど上達したのは大学の時の日本語の先生のおかげにほかならない。
(The reason why my Japanese made such progress is simply because of my college Japanese instructor.)

(g) この大学の学生の質がいいのは選抜が厳しいからにほかならない。
(The reason why the student quality of this college is so good is simply because the selection is tough.)

(h) 核兵器の使用は人類の破滅を招くことにほかならない。
(The use of nuclear weapons invites nothing but (lit. is nothing but to invite) the annihilation of humanity.)

(i) ほかならない君のためだから，やってあげよう。
(It's for you of all people, so I'll do it.)

Notes

1. The phrase *ni hokanaranai* is used to express that X is nothing but Y,

where Y is either N as in KS(A) and Exs.(a), (b), (c), (f) or *kara*-clause as in KS(B) and Exs.(d), (e), (g) or *koto*-nominalized clause as in KS(C) and Ex.(h).

2. The phrase in question is used in written or very formal spoken Japanese. The final negative *-nai* can be replaced by the archaic negative marker *-nu* in formal written Japanese, as in (1) below:

    (1) 結婚は人生の墓場にほかなら**ぬ**。(cf. Ex.(b))

【Related Expression】

The phrase *ni suginai* which means 'nothing but' sounds very close to *ni hokanaranai* but they are quite different. The former means 's.t. / s.o. is nothing more than what is stated, in terms of amount, degree, status, significance, etc,' whereas the latter means 's.t. / s.o. is nothing other than X.' The former often has downgrading nuance, but the latter lacks this nuance.

[1] a. それは噂**に** {**過ぎない** / ??**ほかならない**}。
(That is nothing but a rumor.)

b. 吉田は平凡な会社員**に** {**過ぎない** / ***ほかならない**}。
(Yoshida is nothing but an average white-collar worker.)

Another crucial difference between the two is that *ni suginai* can be used with a quantity expression but *ni hokanaranai* cannot, as shown in [2] and [3] below:

[2] 僕のアルバイト料は五百円**に** {**過ぎない** / ***ほかならない**}。
(The hourly pay for my part-time job is merely 500 yen. (lit. The hourly pay for my part-time job doesn't exceed 500 yen.))

[3] 私の睡眠時間は四，五時間**に** {**過ぎない** / ***ほかならない**}。
(I usually don't get more than four to five hours' sleep. (lit. My sleeping hours are only 4 to 5 hours.))

Connection-wise, *ni hokanaranai* is attached only to a noun / noun phrase or a *kara*-clause, but *ni suginai* is attached to a noun, a quantity expression and Vinf.

ni kagirazu に限らず *comp. prt.*

not limiting s.t. to ~

not limited to ~ (but also); not only ~ (but also)
【REL. ~ *dake de* (*wa*) *naku* ~ (*mo*)】

◆**Key Sentence**

	Noun		
見合い結婚は	**日本**	に限らず	ほかの国でも行われている。
(Arranged marriage is not limited to Japan; it is practiced in other countries, too.)			

Formation

N に限らず

日本語に限らず (not limited to Japanese)

Examples

(a) 音楽はクラシックに限らず何でも聞きます。
(Talking about music, I listen to any music, not just classical music.)

(b) このバーは男性だけに限らず女性の間にも人気がある。
(This bar is popular not only among men but also among women.)

(c) 果物は何に限らず好きです。
(My preference for fruit is unlimited (lit. not limited to something); I like any kind.)

(d) 何事に限らず仕事は誠意をもって行うことが大切だ。
(Whatever you do (lit. Not limited to anything), it is important to do it with sincerity.)

Note

Kagirazu is a negative continuative form of *kagiru* 'to limit.'

【Related Expression】

~ dake de (*wa*) *naku ~* (*mo*) is used in similar contexts. In fact, KS, Exs.(a) and (b) can be paraphrased using this structure, as in [1] – [3].

[1] 見合い結婚は日本**だけで**(**は**)**なく**ほかの国で**も**行われている。(cf. KS)
(Arranged marriage is practiced not only in Japan but also in other countries, too.)

[2] 音楽はクラシック**だけで**(**は**)**なく**何で**も**聞きます。(cf. Ex.(a))
(When it comes to music, I do not listen just to classical music, I listen to anything.)

[3] このバーは男性**だけで**(**は**)**なく**女性の間に**も**人気がある。(cf. Ex.(b))
(This bar is popular not only among men but also among women.)

However, *~ dake de* (*wa*) *naku ~* (*mo*) cannot be used when an indefinite noun is used in front of *ni kagirazu*, as in Exs.(c) and (d).

ni kagitte　に限って　*comp. prt.*

a compound particle to show that only X is different from others

(X) of all (X's); only

◆Key Sentence

Noun		
うちの子供(こども)	に限って(かぎ)	そんなひどいことはしませんよ。
(Our child, of all children, would not do such a terrible thing.)		

Formation

N に限って

あの日に限って　(only on that day)

あの人に限って　(only that person)

Examples

(a) 中野先生はたいてい研究室にいらっしゃるのに，今日に限っていらっしゃらなかった。
(Prof. Nakano is usually in his office, but today, of all days, he wasn't there.)

(b) 傘を持って来ない日に限って雨が降るんですよ。
(Only on the day when I don't bring my umbrella, it rains, you know.)

(c) 急ぐ時に限って，バスがなかなか来ない。
(Of all times, when I am in a hurry, the bus doesn't come for ages.)

(d) 嫌なことがある時に限って，嫌なことが重なる。
(Only when something unpleasant happens, do other unpleasant things occur.)

(e) この小説家の書いたものに限って，つまらないものはない。
(Only works written by this novelist are never boring.)

Notes

1. The phrase *ni kagitte* is used to express an exclusive focus on topic item X. The predicate is either explicitly negative as in KS and Exs. (a), (c), and (e) or implicitly negative as in Exs.(b) and (d). An explicitly affirmative predicate cannot occur with *ni kagitte*. Examples follow:

   (1) その日**に限って** {??いい天気だった / ??涼しかった / ??元気だった}。
   (Only on that day {the weather was good / it was cool / I was in good spirits}.)

2. The phrase is the particle *ni* with the *te*-form of the verb *kagiru* 'limit.'

ni kanshite/kansuru に関して / 関する *comp. prt.* <w>

related to

concerning; with regard to; about; on
【REL. *ni tsuite*; *no koto*】

◆Key Sentences

(A)

Noun		
消費税	に関して	与野党の意見が対立した。
(With regard to the sales tax, the opinions of the leading party and the opposition parties conflicted.)		

(B)

Noun			
人間の言語習得	に関して	は	まだまだ不明のことが多い。
(Concerning human language acquisition, there are still many unknown things.)			

(C)

	Noun		Noun	
先週，東京で	**超伝導**	に関する	学会	が開かれた。
(Last week a conference on superconductivity was held in Tokyo.)				

Formation

(i) N に関して

首相の訪米に関して (concerning the Prime Minister's visit to the U.S.)

N

(ii) Nに関するN

首相の訪米に関する世論 (public opinion concerning the Prime Minister's visit to the U.S.)

Examples

(a) その学会で吉岡氏の発表に関して多くの批判がなされた。
(There was a lot of criticism concerning Mr. Yoshioka's presentation at the conference.)

(b) その件に関しましては，まだ発表できる段階ではありません。
(With regard to that issue, we are not yet at the stage where we can announce anything.)

(c) 最近老人問題に関する記事が目に付く。
(We see many articles about problems of the elderly these days.)

(d) 大気汚染に関する報告書が委員会に提出された。
(A report concerning environmental pollution was submitted to the committee.)

Notes

1. *Te* in *ni kanshite* may be dropped, as in (1).

   (1) 消費税**に関し**(**て**)与野党の意見が対立した。(=KS(A))

   However, the *te* in *ni kanshite wa*, as in KS(B), cannot be dropped.

2. *Ni kanshi*(*mashi*) *te wa* is used for topic presentation, as in KS(B) and Ex.(b).

3. *Ni kansuru* modifies the noun which follows, as in KS(C), Exs.(c) and (d).

4. The polite form *ni kanshimashite*, as in Ex.(b), can appear in formal speech.

【Related Expressions】

I. *Ni tsuite* can replace *ni kanshite*, as in [1] and [2]; this usage is less formal in tone than *ni kanshite*.

[1] 消費税 {**について / に関して**} 与野党の意見が対立した。 (=KS(A))

[2] 人間の言語習得 {**について / に関して**} はまだまだ不明のことが多い。(=KS(B))

Note that *no* is necessary after *ni tsuite* when *ni tsuite* replaces *ni kansuru*, the prenominal version of *ni kanshite*, as in [3].

[3] 先週，東京で超伝導 {**についての / に関する**} 学会が開かれた。 (=KS(C))

II. *No koto* with a particle and *ni kanshite* express the same idea. However, *no toko* is informal; therefore, it is not appropriate in a formal context. In addition, *no koto* does not have a prenominal version, as in [4].

[4] 先週，東京で超伝導 {**に関する / *のことの**} 学会が開かれた。 (=KS(C))

(⇨ ***no koto***)

N

ni kawatte　に代わって　*comp. prt.*

a compound particle to express replacement or substitution of a regular person / thing by s.o. / s.t.

in place of; replacing; on behalf of
【REL. *kawari ni*】

◆Key Sentence

Noun		
病気の山田先生	に代わって，	鈴木先生が教えて下さった。
(In place of Prof. Yamada, who is ill, Prof. Suzuki taught us.)		

Formation

N に代わって

母(はは)に代わって (in place of my mother)

Examples

(a) 戦後(せんご)ガラスに代わってプラスチックが出(で)てきた。
(After the war plastics became available replacing glass.)

(b) レコードに代わってＣＤが出て，音質(おんしつ)がとてもよくなった。
(In place of records, CDs have become available, and the sound quality has improved a great deal.)

(c) 私(わたし)が父(ちち)に代わって，空港(くうこう)までお客(きゃく)さんを迎(むか)えに行(い)った。
(In place of my father, I went to the airport to pick up our guest.)

(d) 御出 席(ごしゅっせき)の皆様(みなさま)に代わりまして，一言(ひとこと)ご挨拶(あいさつ)を述(の)べさせていただきます。
(On behalf of everyone present here, let me say a word of greeting.)

(e) 申(もう)し訳(わけ)ございませんが，社長(しゃちょう)は今日(きょう)都合(つごう)が悪(わる)いので，私が社長に代わって参(まい)りました。
(I am very sorry that the president was unable to attend, but I have come in his place.)

Notes

1. X *ni kawatte* is used to express replacement / substitution of X by s.t. / s.o. else.

2. X *ni kawatte* which can be used in both spoken and written Japanese. But *ni kawari* is used only in written Japanese.

【Related Expression】

The crucial difference between N *ni kawatte* and N *no kawari ni* is that the former cannot be used when on-the-spot substitution of objects is expressed, as shown in [1a], and the latter cannot be used when 'replacement' is expressed as shown in [2].

N

[1] a. エコノミークラスではガラスの食器 {**の代わりに / *に代わって**} プラスチックの食器が出る。
(In economy class they use plastic wares instead of glass wares.)

b. 戦後ガラス {**に代わって / *の代わりに**} プラスチックが出てきた。(=Ex.(a))

The substitution of s.o. by s.o. else can be expressed by both N *ni kawatte* and N *no kawari ni*.

[2] 病気の山田先生 {**に代わって / の代わりに**}, 鈴木先生が教えて下さった。(=KS)

(⇨ ***kawari ni*** (DBJG: 184–87))

ni kuraberu to/kurabete　に比べると / 比べて　*comp. prt.*

if we compare (it) with / to; comparing (it) with

compared with / to; when compared with / to; in comparison to

◆Key Sentence

Noun		
欧米	に比べて	日本の住宅事情は極めて貧困だ。
(Compared to (the situations) in Europe and the U.S., the housing situation in Japan is extremely poor.)		

Formation

N に比べると / 比べて

去年に比べると / 比べて　(compared with last year)

Examples

(a) 日本に来る前に比べると今は大分日本語でものが言えるようになった。
(I can speak Japanese fairly well now (lit. I have become able to say things in Japanese fairly well) compared to my level before I came to Japan.)

(b) 今年は去年に比べて雨の日が多いようだ。
(In comparison to last year, we seem to have more rainy days this year.)

(c) 十年前の暮らしに比べると今の暮らしは天国です。
(Compared with our life ten years ago, our present life is heavenly (lit. is heaven).)

(d) この新しい(コンピュータ)モデルは，古いモデルと比べて演算が三倍速くなっている。
(When compared with the older (computer) model, the operation speed of this new model is three times as fast.)

Notes

1. *Ni kuraberu to* and *ni kurabete* are interchangeable.

2. The particle *to* can be used instead of *ni* before *kuraberu to/kurabete*, as in Ex.(d).

ni mo kakawarazu にもかかわらず *comp. prt. / conj.* <w>

without any relation to a preceding event / situation

although; though; in spite of; despite; notwithstanding; nevertheless
【REL. *keredo(mo)*; *noni*】

◆Key Sentences

(A)

Noun		
懸命な努力	にもかかわらず,	健一は大学入試に失敗した。
(In spite of his strenuous efforts, Ken'ichi failed the college entrance examination.)		

(B)

	Vinf			
あの人はよく運動を	**する**	(の)	にもかかわらず,	太っている。
(He is fat, although he exercises a lot.)				

(C)

	Adj(*i*)inf			
試験が	**難しかった**	(の)	にもかかわらず,	よく出来た。
(Although the exam was hard, I did well.)				

(D)

	Adj(*na*)stem				
冬山は	**危険**	**な**	の	にもかかわらず,	一郎は山へ出かけた。
		である	(の)		
(Although winter mountains are dangerous, Ichiro left for the mountain.)					

Formation

(i) N {ø / なの / である(の) / だった(の) / であった(の)} にもかかわらず

学生 {なの / である(の) / だった(の) / であった(の)} にもかかわらず
(in spite of being / having been a student)

(ii) Vinf (の) にもかかわらず

{勉強する / 勉強した} (の)にもかかわらず
(in spite of studying / having studied)

(iii) Adj (*i*) inf (の)にもかかわらず

{つまらない / つまらなかった} (の)にもかかわらず
(although s.t. is / was boring)

(iv) Adj (*na*) stem {なの/ である(の)} / だった(の) / であった(の)} にもかかわらず

元気 {なの / である(の) / だった(の) / であった(の)} にもかかわらず
(although s.o. is / was healthy)

Examples

(a) 激しい雨(だった)にもかかわらず，サッカーの試合は続いた。
(In spite of fierce rain, the soccer game continued.)

(b) 安い値段(なの / である)にもかかわらず，その家はまだ売れていない。
(Despite the inexpensive price, that house is not sold yet.)

(c) 宏は美香を愛していた(の)にもかかわらず，結婚しなかった。
(In spite of the fact that Hiroshi loved Mika, he didn't marry her.)

(d) 昨日は徹夜して勉強した(の)にもかかわらず，試験は出来なかった。
(Although I studied all night last night, I didn't do well on the exam.)

(e) キャロルは日本に三年も住んでいた(の)にもかかわらず，日本語は大変下手だ。
(Although Carol lived in Japan for three years, her Japanese is very poor.)

(f) 日本の経済力は強くなっている(の)にもかかわらず，日本人はそれを実感出来ない。
(In spite of the fact that the Japanese economy has become strong, the Japanese people cannot feel the effects.)

(g) 私のアパートは広い(の)にもかかわらず，家賃が安い。
(My apartment is spacious, but the rent is cheap.)

(h) 旅行が好き（なの / である(の)）にもかかわらず，どこに行く暇もない。
(I like to travel, but I don't have time to go anywhere.)

Notes

1. X *ni mo kakawarazu* expresses an idea of 'in spite of X,' where X is an action / state.

2. The verb (i.e. Vinf) and Adj(*i*)inf can be connected directly with *ni mo kakawarazu,* but Adj(*na*) has to be nominalized before it is connected with the conjunction, as shown by KS(D) and Ex.(h). However, if the Adj(*na*) is followed by *de aru*, use of the nominalizer *no* is optional.

   (1) {**健康なの/健康である(の)/*健康な**}にもかかわらず，働かない。
   (Although he is healthy, he does not work.)

【Related Expression】

The conjunctions *noni* and *keredo*(*mo*) can replace *ni mo kakawarazu* with proper adjustments of connections.

[1] a. 激しい雨だった {**のに / けれど**}，サッカーの試合は続いた。
(cf. Ex.(a))

b. あの人はよく運動をする {**のに / けれど**} 太っている。
(cf. KS(B))

c. 試験が難しかった {**のに / けれど**}，よく出来た。(cf. KS(C))

d. 冬山は危険 {**なのに / だけれど**}，一郎は山へ出かけた。
(cf. KS(D))

The basic difference between *noni / keredo*(*mo*) and *ni mo kakawarazu* is that the latter is used in written or formal spoken Japanese. The choice of *ni mo kakawarazu* over *keredo*(*mo*) / *noni* implies the stronger disjunctiveness, that is, the former means 'totally contrary to everybody's expectation,' whereas the latter means 'contrary to everybody's expectation.'

ni motozuite/motozuku　に基づいて / 基づく　*comp. prt.*

with s.t. as a basis

based upon
【REL. *o moto ni* (*shite*)】

◆Key Sentences

(A)

Noun		
事実	に基づいて	お話しします。
(I will give you the facts. (lit. I will talk on the basis of facts.))		

(B)

	Noun		Noun	
これは	**五百年前の史料**	に基づく	研究	だ。
(This is a study based on historical documents from 500 years ago.)				

Formation

(i)　N に基づいて

調査に基づいて　(based on a survey)

(ii)　N に {基づく / 基づいた} N

調査に {基づく / 基づいた} 報告　(a report based on a survey)

Examples

(a)　この製品はアメリカ製だがすべて JIS に基づいて設計されている。
(Although this product is made in America, the design is based entirely on the Japanese Industrial Standards (lit. is designed based entirely on . . .).)

(b) このビルはある有名な建築家の設計に基づいて建てられた。
(This building was (built) based on a famous architect's design.)

(c) この報告は去年行われたアンケート調査に基づいて書かれたものである。
(This report was (written) based on a (questionnaire) survey conducted last year.)

(d) 野村氏の講演は氏の二十年間の教育経験に基づく話で，極めて示唆に富むものであった。
(Mr. Nomura's lecture was based on his 20-year teaching experience (lit. was a talk based on . . .) and was full of suggestions.)

(e) これは一つの仮説に基づいた議論です。
(This is a discussion based on a hypothesis.)

Note

Ni motozuku and *ni motozuita* modify the noun which follows, as in KS(B), Exs.(d) and (e).

【Related Expression】

Ni motozuite can be paraphrased as *o moto ni* (*shite*). The prenominal form of *o moto ni* (*shite*) is *o moto ni shita.*

[1] 事実**を基に(して)**お話しします。(=KS(A))

[2] これは五百年前の史料**を基にした**研究だ。(=KS(B))

ni naru to　になると　*phr.*

a phrase that expresses the time when an uncontrollable state or a habitual action occurs	when it becomes; when it comes to; when; if

◆Key Sentences

(A)

Noun (time)		
夏	になると，	摂氏三十度を越す日が多いです。
(In summer (lit. When it becomes summer), there are many days that exceed 30 degrees Celsius.)		

(B)

	Noun (non-time)		
父は	食べ物のこと	になると，	とてもやかましかった。
(When it comes to the matter of food, my father was very particular.)			

Formation

(i) N (time) になると

八時になると (when it becomes 8 o'clock; at 8 o'clock)

(ii) N (non-time) になると

雨になると (when it becomes rain)

Examples

(a) 四月半ばになると，この辺は桜がきれいに咲きます。
(In this area, in the middle of April, the cherry blossoms are beautiful (lit. the cherry trees bloom beautifully).)

(b) ニューイングランドと言われるアメリカの東北地方は，秋になると，紅葉がとてもきれいです。
(In the north-east area of the U.S. called New England, the fall colors are very beautiful.)

(c) 私は夜十一時になると，頭が働かなくなる。
(At about 11 p.m., my brain stops working.)

(d) 子供の頃，夏になると，両親は僕を海に連れて行ってくれた。
(When I was a child, in summer, my parents took me to the ocean.)

(e) 大学生の時は，休みになると，よく旅行をした。
(When I was a college student, I traveled a lot during vacations.)

(f) 彼はフットボールの話になると夢中だ。
(When the topic of the conversation is football, he is totally absorbed in it.)

(g) 社長は娘のことになると，人が変わったように甘くなる。
(The president becomes lenient as if he were a different person, when it comes to the matter of his daughter.)

(h) 雪になると，この空港はよく閉鎖になる。
(When it turns to snow, this airport is often closed.)

Notes

1. Regardless of whether the noun before *ni naru to* is a time noun or not, the N *ni naru to* as a whole is used to express the time when an uncontrollable state occurs as in KS(A), (B) and Exs.(a) – (c), (f) – (h) or a habitual action occurs as in Exs.(d) and (e).

(⇨ ***to***[4] (DBJG: 480–82))

2. The phrase in question is a subjectless construction because the sentence simply does not have a subject. When the noun / noun phrase that precedes *ni naru to* is a non-time expression, *ni naru to* is used either as a subjectless construction as in KS(B) and Exs.(f) – (h), or as a non-subjectless construction as shown in (1) and (2) below in which *joyū* 'actress' and *haru* 'spring' are not time nouns. Note that the subject of *naru* is *watashi* for (1) and *kisetsu* for (2).

   (1) 私が**女優**になると，両親は嫌がるかもしれません。
   (If I become an actress, my parents might not like it.)

   (2) 季節が**春**になると人の心は自然にはずんでくる。
   (When spring comes human heart jumps for joy.)

ni oite/okeru　において / おける　*comp. prt.*　<w>

> a compound particle which indicates the place of an action / event, a state or time

at; on; in; during
【REL. *de*; *ni*】

◆Key Sentences

(A)

	Noun (place / time)		
来年の総会は	**シカゴのヒルトン・ホテル**	において	行われる。
(Next year's general meeting will be held at the Hilton Hotel in Chicago.)			

(B)

	Noun (place / time)		
コンピュータは	**近い将来**	において	ほとんどの家庭に行き渡るだろう。
(Computers will probably spread to almost every household in the near future.)			

(C)

	Noun (place / time)		Noun	
先月の	**東京**	における	環境保護国際会議	には全世界から大勢の学者が参加した。
(Many scholars from all over the world took part in last month's international conference in Tokyo on environmental protection.)				

Formation

(i) N において

アメリカにおいて (in America)

(ii) N における N

アメリカにおける学生生活 (student life in America)

Examples

(a) 1992年のオリンピックはバルセロナにおいて開催された。
(The 1992 Olympiad was held in Barcelona.)

(b) 過去においてはこのようなことはあまり問題にならなかった。
(Such things were hardly considered to be problems before (lit. in the past).)

(c) この作文は文法においてはあまり問題はない。
(This composition doesn't have many problems in terms of grammar.)

(d) 本校における男女学生の比率は二対一である。
(The ratio of male students to female students at this school is 2 to 1.)

(e) 木村博士は遺伝学における権威者として知られている。
(Dr. Kimura is known as an authority in (the field of) genetics.)

(f) 過去五年間における彼の業 績は実にすばらしいものであった。
(His achievements during the past five years were truly remarkable.)

(g) 十月 十二日における彼のアリバイは成立していない。
(His alibi on the twelfth of October has not been established.)

Notes

1. *Ni oite/okeru* can be used with "non-physical" locations, such as fields of study, as in Exs.(c) and (e).

2. *Ni okeru* modifies the noun which follows, as in KS(C) and Exs. (d) – (g).

3. *Ni okeru* cannot be used to specify existence, as in (1).

(1) *フロリダ {**の** / **にある** / ***における**} ディズニーワールドはとても人気がある。
(Disney World in Florida is very popular.)

4. *Ni oite/okeru* is a highly formal expression. Therefore, it is rarely used for personal activities or trivial events, as in (2) and (3).

(2) 私は昨日ダウンタウンの映画館 {で / ???**において**} 映画を見た。
(I saw a movie at a theater downtown yesterday.)

(3) 山田さんのうち {**での** / ???**における**} 誕生パーティーにはたくさんの友達が集まった。
(Many friends gathered for the birthday party at Yamada's home.)

5. When *ni oite* indicates a time, it cannot be used for a specific time, as in (4).

(4) その会議は1991年 {**に** / ***において**} 開かれた。
(The conference was held in 1991.)

This restriction, however, does not apply to *ni okeru*, the prenominal form of *ni oite*, as in (5).

(5) この表は1991年**における**アジア諸国の GNP を示している。
(This table indicates the GNPs of Asian countries in 1991.)

【Related Expressions】

I. *De* also indicates the place of an action, an event, or a state. Thus, KS(A) and (C), for example, can be paraphrased as [1] and [2], respectively, using *de*.

[1] 来年の総会はシカゴのヒルトン・ホテル**で**行われる。(=KS(A))

[2] 先月の東京**での**環境保護国際会議には全世界から大勢の学者が参加した。(=KS(C))

Note in [2] that with *ni okeru*, the prenominal form of *ni oite*, *no* must follow *de*.

De cannot be used when *ni oite/okeru* is used to indicate a "nonphysical" location, as in [3] and [4].

[3] この作文は文法{**において** / ???**で**}はあまり問題はない。 (=Ex.(c))

[4] 木村博士は遺伝学{**における** / ???**での**}権威者として知られている。(=Ex.(e))

Unlike *ni oite/okeru*, *de* can be used for personal activities and trivial events. (See Note 4.)

(⇨ ***de*** (DBJG: 105))

II. *Ni* also indicates time. Thus, *ni oite* in KS(B), for example, can be paraphrased as [5] using *ni*.

[5] コンピュータは近い将来**に**ほとんどの家庭に行き渡るだろう。 (=KS(B))

Because *ni* is replaced by *no* when N *ni* modifies a noun, *ni okeru* in Ex.(g) is paraphrased as [6] using *no*.

[6] 十月十二日{**の** / ***にの**}彼のアリバイは成立していない。 (=Ex.(g))

Unlike *ni oite*, *ni* can be used for specific times. (See Note 5.)

ni shitagatte/shitagai に従って / 従い *comp. part. / conj.*

s.t. spontaneously and gradually occurs in accordance with some change

as, accordingly; in proportion to; in accordance with; following

【REL. *ni tsurete/tsure*】

◆Key Sentences

(A)

Subordinate Clause			Main Clause
	Vinf·nonpast		
日本の経済力が強く	**なる**	に{従って/従い},	日本語学習者が増えてきた。
(As Japan's economic power has become stronger, the number of Japanese language learners has increased, accordingly.)			

(B)

Noun		
契約	に{従って/従い}	雇用期間を三年とする。
(In accordance with the contract, your tenure shall be three years.)		

N

Formation

(i) Vinf·nonpast に{従って/従い}

その本を読むに{従って/従い} (As s.o. reads the book)

(ii) N に{従って/従い}

指示に{従って/従い} (in accordance with the instructions)

Examples

(a) 収入が増えるに従って，支出も増える。
(As our income increases, our expenditure also increases.)

(b) 年を取るに従い，体力が衰える。
(As you grow older, your physical strength declines.)

(c) 文明が進むに従い，人間のストレスが多くなる。
(As civilization progresses, human stresses increase.)

(d) 日がたつに従って，父の病気は回復してきた。
(As the days went by, my father recovered from his illness.)

(e) 太陽が沈んで行くに従って，温度がどんどん下がった。
(As the sun went down, the temperature went down rapidly.)

(f) 約束に従い，借金を一か月後に返した。
(In accordance with the promise, I returned the loaned money after a month.)

(g) 社長の命令に従って，彼はただちにマニラに飛んだ。
(In accordance with the president's order, he flew to Manila immediately.)

Notes

1. Vinf·nonpast *ni shitagatte/shitagai* is used to express that s.t. beyond human control takes place simultaneously with s.t. else that goes on. The verbs in both main and subordinate clauses do not express a momentary action, but a continuous process. The following sentences are all ungrammatical, because they use momentary verbs and the two events do not occur simultaneously but consecutively.

   (1) *窓を開ける**に従って**，涼しい風が入ってきた。
   → 窓を開けたら，涼しい風が入ってきた。
   (As I opened the window, a cool breeze came in.)

   (2) *たばこを吸うのをやめる**に従って**，体の調子がよくなった。
   → たばこをやめたら，体の調子がよくなった。
   (As I quit smoking, my physical condition improved.)

   In the case of N *ni shitagatte/shitagai*, Note 1 is not applicable. In other words, in this construction what occurs can occur momentarily or non-spontaneously. So in KS(B), Exs.(f) and (g), what is expressed there is nothing spontaneous and gradual.

2. *Shitagatte* and *shitagai* are originally V*te* and V*masu* forms of the verb *shitagau*, respectively, which means 'obey,' 'comply,' or 'follow.'

3. *ni shitagatte/shitagai* cannot be preceded by an Adj(*i* / *na*) or Cop.

(= *da / desu*). And V before *ni shitagatte/shitagai* must be Vinf·nonpast.

4. The difference between *shitagatte* and *shitagai* is stylistical. The latter is usually used in written Japanese whereas the former can be used in both spoken and written style.

【Related Expression】

Vinf·nonpast *ni tsurete/tsure* is an expression very similar to Vinf·nonpast *ni shitagatte/shitagai*. KS and Exs. can all be rephrased by the former without changing the essential meaning except KS(B), Exs.(f) and (g), because the pattern is N *ni shitagatte/shitagai*. The difference seems to be that Vinf·nonpast *ni shitagatte/shitagai* is more of a written style; whereas Vinf·nonpast *ni tsurete/tsure* is more of a spoken style.

N

ni suginai に過ぎない *phr.* <w>

S.t. or s.o. is nothing more than what is stated in terms of amount, degree, status, significance, etc.

nothing more than; not more than; mere; merely; only; just; as little / few as; that's all
【REL. *dake da*; *tada no*】

◆Key Sentences

(A)

	Noun	
これは私(わたし)の	**私見(しけん)**	に過(す)ぎない。
(This is nothing more than my personal opinion.)		

(B)

	Number + Counter	
今期の売り上げの伸びは	**三パーセント**	に過ぎない。
(The sales increase this term is as little as three percent.)		

(C)

	Vinf	
あの男は(ただ)言われたことを	**している**	(だけ)に過ぎない。
(That man is not doing more than what he was told to do.)		

Formation

N

(i) Nに過ぎない

学生に過ぎない (just a student)

(ii) Number + Counter に過ぎない

五人に過ぎない (as few as five people)

(iii) Vinf (だけ)に過ぎない

話している(だけ)に過ぎない (S.o. is doing nothing but talking.)

話した(だけ)に過ぎない (S.o. did nothing more than talk.)

Examples

(a) 彼は私のボーイフレンドの一人に過ぎない。
(He is nothing more than one of my boyfriends.)

(b) これは数ある中のほんの一例に過ぎない。
(This is only one example among many.)

(c) 今言ったことは私の希望に過ぎませんので，あまり深刻に考えないで下さい。

(What I've just told you is nothing more than my hope, so please don't take it too seriously.)

(d) 私の収入はアルバイトを入れても年二万ドルに過ぎない。
(My income is only $20,000 even if I include my side job (income).)

(e) 私を支持してくれる人は身内を入れても五十人程度に過ぎない。
(There are no more than about 50 people who support me (lit. The people who support me are no more than about fifty), even if I include my relatives.)

(f) あの子はまだ十五に過ぎないが，なかなかしっかりしている。
(That girl is only fifteen, but she is quite mature.)

(g) 彼は(ただ)人の意見を受け売りしている(だけ)に過ぎない。
(He is doing nothing more than echoing other people's opinions.)

(h) 彼の演説は(ただ)原稿を読み上げた(だけ)に過ぎない。
(His speech was nothing more than the reading of a prepared manuscript.)

(i) 私と山野氏は初対面の時，簡単な挨拶を交わした(だけ)に過ぎない。
(Mr. Yamano and I did nothing more than exchange simple greetings when we first met each other.)

Notes

1. *Ni suginai* is not commonly used with adjectives although the patterns in (1) are possible.

   (1) a. Adj(*i*)inf だけに過ぎない
   b. Adj(*na*) {な / だった} だけに過ぎない

   To express the idea that someone or something is X and that's all (where X is an adjective), *dake da* is usually used, as in (2).

   (2) この家は大きい**だけだ**。
   (This house is big and that's all.)

   (⇨ ***dake*** (DBJG: 93–97))

2. In Formation (ii), the quantifier can be either a number with or without

a counter, or a word with no number, such as *sukoshi* 'little, few' and *wazuka* 'few.'

【Related Expressions】

I. Vinf *ni suginai* can be paraphrased as Vinf *dake da*, as in [1].

[1] あの男は(ただ)言われたことをしている**だけだ**。(=KS(C))
(The man is just doing what he was told to do, that's all.)
(⇨ ***dake*** (DBJG: 93–97))

II. N *ni suginai* can be paraphrased using *tada no* N *da*, as in [2].

[2] これは私の**ただの**私見**だ**。(=KS(A))
(This is my personal opinion only.)

Note that *tada no*, however, can also mean 'ordinary' depending on the following noun. Therefore, when *tada no* N is interpreted in this way, N *ni suginai* and *tada no* N *da* are not exactly equivalent, as in [3].

[3] a. 彼は高校の先生**に過ぎない**。
(He is no more than a high school teacher.)

b. 彼は**ただの**高校の先生**だ**。
((a) He is an ordinary high school teacher. (b) He is only a high school teacher.)

(⇨ ***tada no***)

III. Quantifier *ni suginai* can be paraphrased as *tada no* (or *tatta*(*no*)) N *da*, as in [4].

[4] 今期の売り上げの伸びは {**ただの** / **たった(の)**} 三パーセント**だ**。
(=KS(B))
(The sales increase this term is only three percent.)

ni taishite/taishi に対して / 対し *comp. prt.*

regarding s.t. / s.o. one opposes, compares, or shows interest in regarding s.t. / s.o. one opposes, compares or shows interest in

toward; to; in contrast to; whereas; in regard to; in; per

【REL. ***ni hanshite / hansuru***】

◆Key Sentences

(A)

	Noun		
これまで日本は	**外国**	に対して	閉鎖的な政策を取ってきた。
(Up until now Japan has taken a closed policy toward foreign countries.)			

(B)

Sinf			
日本の大学は入学するのが難しい	の	に対して,	アメリカの大学は卒業するのが難しい。
(Japanese colleges are hard to enter; whereas American colleges are hard to graduate from.)			

(C)

	Noun		Noun	
アメリカでは	**離婚**	に {対する / 対しての}	考え方	が大分変わってきた。
(In America attitudes toward divorce have greatly changed.)				

Formation

(i) N に対して

先生(せんせい)に対して (towards one's teacher)

(ii) {V / Adj(*i*)}inf のに対して

{話(はな)す / 話した} のに対して (s.o. talks / talked, whereas ~)

{若(わか)い / 若かった} のに対して (s.o. is / was young, whereas ~)

(iii) {Adj(*na*)stem / N} {な / である / だった / であった} のに対して

元気(げんき) {な / である / だった / であった} のに対して (s.o. is / was healthy, whereas ~)

学生(がくせい) {な / である / だった / であった} のに対して (s.o. is / was a student, whereas ~)

(iv) N に {対する / 対しての} N

結婚(けっこん)に {対する / 対しての} 考え方 (one's view of marriage)

N

Examples

(a) 鈴木(すずき)さんは誰(だれ)に対しても丁寧(ていねい)だ。
(Mr. Suzuki is polite to everybody.)

(b) 日本は外国に対して市場(しじょう)をもっと開放(かいほう)すべきだ。
(Japan should open its market more widely to foreign countries.)

(c) 私(わたし)は政治(せいじ)に対して強(つよ)い関心(かんしん)がある。
(I have a strong interest in politics.)

(d) 手数料(てすうりょう)は一万円(いちまんえん)に対して五百(ごひゃく)円です。
(The commission charge will be 500 yen per 10,000 yen.)

(e) 市民(しみん)は増税(ぞうぜい)に対して強く反対(はんたい)している。
(The citizens are strongly opposed to the tax hike.)

(f) 私は高校生(こうこうせい)の時(とき)から，日本の文化(ぶんか)に対して興味(きょうみ)があった。
(Since my high school days, I have had an interest in Japanese culture.)

(g) 去年は自動車事故が少なかったのに対して，今年は大変多かった。
(Last year there were very few car accidents, whereas this year the number was very high.)

(h) 日本人は褒められた時，よく「とんでもない」と言う。これに対して，アメリカ人はよく「ありがとう」と言う。
(When Japanese get compliments, they often say "Oh, not at all." In contrast to this, Americans often say "Thank you.")

(i) 女性の地位は日本ではまだ低いのに対して，欧米では比較的高い。
(Women's position is still low in Japan, whereas in Europe and America it is relatively high.)

(j) 東ヨーロッパの国々が民主化に向かっているのに対して，中国大陸と北朝鮮は民主化がまだ遅れているようだ。
(Eastern European countries are progressing towards democratization, whereas Continental China and North Korea appear to be slower in democratization.)

N

(k) ロシアに対してのアメリカ人の見方は最近友好的になった。
(American views of Russia have recently become friendlier.)

(l) 部長は岡田に対して有利な発言をした。
(The departmental chief made a remark in Okada's favor.)

(m) その経済学者の説に {対する / 対して} 反論はなかった。
(There wasn't a counterargument against the enonomist's thesis.)

Notes

1. N *ni taishite* is used to express s.o.'s attitude / action toward s.o. / s.t. as in KS(A), Exs.(a), (b) and (l), contrast / comparison as in KS(B) and Exs.(g) – (j), confrontation as in Ex.(e), interest as in Exs.(c) and (f), and the sense of 'per' as in Ex.(d).

2. N_1 *ni* {*taisuru / taishite no*} N_2 means 'N_2 in regard to N_1,' as exemplified by KS(C) and Ex.(k) or 'against' as exemplified by Ex.(m).

3. *Taishite* can be replaced by *taishi* in written Japanese or formal speech.

4. N *ni taishite* and N {*na / dearu / datta / deatta*} *no ni taishite* are different in meaning; the latter means 'whereas,' but the former does not, as shown below:

(1) a. 彼(かれ)は女性**に対して**とても親切(しんせつ)だ。
(He is very kind to women.)

b. 淑子(よしこ)が好(す)きな男性(だんせい)は豪快(ごうかい)な男性{**な / である**}**のに対して**,由美子(ゆみこ)が好きな男性は優(やさ)しい男性だ。
(The men Yoshiko likes are spirited; whereas the men Yumiko likes are considerate.)

ni totte にとって *comp. prt.*

N

from the standpoint of; so far as s.o. (or s.t.) is concerned

to; for
【REL. *ni wa*】

◆Key Sentence

	Noun		
これは	**我々**(われわれ)	にとって	無視出来(むしでき)ない問題(もんだい)だ。
(For us this is a problem which cannot be ignored.)			

Formation

N にとって

私(わたし)にとって (to / for me)

Examples

(a) この大学(だいがく)で教(おし)えられることは私にとって極(きわ)めて名誉(めいよ)なことです。
(Being able to teach at this university is a big honor for me.)

(b) 町の人々にとってこの工場の閉鎖は死活問題だ。
(For people in this town, the shutdown of this plant is a matter of life and death.)

(c) 今日は私達にとって忘れられない日になるでしょう。
(Today will be an unforgettable day for us.)

(d) 今度のアメリカの輸入政策は日本企業にとって大きな打撃になる。
(America's policy on imports this time will be a big blow to Japanese companies.)

(e) 今回の合併は我が社にとってあまり益はない。
(There is little benefit for us (lit. for our company) in this merger.)

(f) ここは君にとって一番安全な場所だ。
(This is the safest place for you.)

(g) 今村さんは私にとって遠い親戚に当たる。
(Mr. Imamura is a remote relative of mine.)

Note

Ni totte cannot mark a noun which represents the experiencer or agent (i.e., the semantic subject). In this case, *ni wa* is used, as in (1).

(1) a. この仕事は私 {**には** / ***にとって**} 出来ない。
(I can't do this job.)

b. あの字は私 {**には** / ***にとって**} 見えない。
(I can't see that character (word or letter).)

【Related Expression】

Ni wa can replace *ni totte*, as in [1].

[1] a. これは我々 {**には** / **にとって**} 無視出来ない問題だ。(=KS(A))

b. この大学で教えられることは私 {**には** / **にとって**} 極めて名誉なことです。(=Ex.(a))

Ni totte has a prenominal form *ni totte no*, as seen in [2], but *ni wa* does not.

[2] 太郎{**にとっての / *にはの**}問題は，彼が全然英語が分からないことだ。
(The problem for Taro is that he doesn't understand English.)

In addition, because of the particle *wa*, *ni wa* gives a sense of contrast in some contexts while *ni totte* does not. In [1a], for example, the sentence with *ni wa* can imply that not for others but for us, or at least for us, this is a problem which cannot be ignored. The sentence with *ni totte* does not have this implication.

ni tsuite　について　*comp. prt.*

concerning s.t. / s.o.

about; on; concerning; regarding; with regard to; of
【REL. ***ni kanshite***; *no koto*】

◆Key Sentences

(A)

	Noun		
私は	**日本の政治制度**	について	研究しています。
(I am doing research on the Japanese political system.)			

(B)

	Sinf			
スミスさんは	**日本へ留学する**	こと	について	いろいろ私に尋ねた。
(Mr. Smith asked me various questions about his going to Japan for study.)				

Formation

(i) N について

大学について (concerning college)

(ii) Sinf ことについて

私が行くことについて (concerning my going there)

(iii) {N_1 / Sinf こと} についての N_2

初等教育についての意見 (an opinion about elementary education)

日本へ留学することについての問題点 (problems concerning studying abroad in Japan)

Examples

(a) 御家族について話して下さい。
(Please talk about your family.)

(b) 何について調べているんですか。
(What are you investigating?)

(c) 毎日の生活について聞いてもいいですか。
(May I ask you about your daily life?)

(d) 日本に来る前に，日本についてどんなイメージを持っていらっしゃいましたか。
(What kind of images did you have of Japan before you came to Japan?)

(e) 先生は自分の国について作文を書くようにおっしゃいました。
(Our teacher told us to write a composition on our own country.)

(f) 私はアメリカ人と結婚することについて両親と相談した。
(I talked with my parents regarding my getting married to an American.)

(g) 日本人の宗教についての考え方は西洋人のとはかなり違う。
(Japanese views on religion are quite different from those of Westerners.)

(h) 課長は私が会議に出なかったことについて何か言っていましたか。
(Did the section chief say anything about my absence from the meeting?)

(i) 新聞社が外国人雇用問題についての意見を求めてきた。
(The newspaper company asked about my views on the problem of hiring foreigners.)

(j) 日本が軍隊を平和維持のために海外に派遣することについての是非が盛んに討議された。
(There have been heated discussions as to whether it is right or wrong for Japan to send its army abroad for peace-keeping purposes.)

Note

N_1 *ni tsuite no* N_2 means 'N_2 concerning N_1,' as shown in Ex.(g).

【Related Expression】

The difference between N *ni tsuite* and N *no koto* is that the former means 'about / concerning N,' but the latter, 'things about N.' Compare the following three sentences.

[1] A: 田中さんを知っていますか。
(Do you know Mr. Tanaka?)

B: ええ，昔から。
(Yes, I've known him for many years.)

[2] A: 田中さん**について**知っていますか。
(Do you know about Mr. Tanaka?)

B: ええ，本で読んで，知っています。
(Yes, I know of him through books.)

[3] A: 田中さん**のこと**を知っていますか。
(Do you know (things) about Mr. Tanaka?)

B: 何かあったんですか。
(Did something happen to him?)

[1A] is a straightforward sentence of 'to know s.t.' In other words, [1A] expresses direct knowledge. [2A] has 'N *ni tsuite*' and expresses more indirect knowledge ; [3A] concerns knowledge about circumstances surrounding N (i.e., Tanaka). So, the following combinations are all very awkward: *[1A]–[2B], *[1A]–[3B], *[2A]–[1B], *[2A]–[3B], *[3A]–[1A], *[3A]–[2B].

(⇨ ***koto***[1] (DBJG: 191–93))

ni tsuki につき *comp. prt.*

a compound particle which expresses a rate or ratio	a; per; for; on; to 【REL. *atari*】

◆Key Sentence

	Number + Counter		Number + Counter	
この仕事(しごと)は	**一時間(いちじかん)**	につき	六(ろく)ドル	もらえる。
(This job will pay you six dollars an hour. (lit. You can get six dollars an hour doing this job.))				

Formation

Number + Counter につき

一時間につき　(per hour)

Examples

(a) 一冊(いっさつ)につき百五十円(ひゃくごじゅうえん)の送料(そうりょう)が要(い)ります。
(A hundred and fifty yen is necessary per copy for postage. (lit. Postage of one hundred and fifty yen is necessary per copy.))

(b) 五千円につき四十円の手数料をいただきます。
(We place a forty-yen service charge on five thousand yen.)

(c) 米一カップにつき，しょう油大さじ二杯の割合にします。
(The ratio should be two tablespoons of soy sauce to a cup of rice.)

(d) 切符は一人につき三枚までにして下さい。
(Please limit it to three tickets per person.)

(e) 間違い一つにつき一点減点します。
(I'll take one point off for each mistake.)

Notes

1. Although in most cases the number which precedes *ni tsuki* is one, any number can precede *ni tsuki*, as seen in Ex.(b).

2. When the number before *ni tsuki* is one and a noun does not immediately precede that number, *ni tsuki* may be dropped, as in (1).

(1) a. この仕事は一時間（**につき**）六ドルもらえる。(=KS)

b. 一冊（**につき**）百五十円の送料が要ります。(=Ex.(a))

c. 切符は一人（**につき**）三枚までにして下さい。(=Ex.(d))

If the number before *ni tsuki* is not one or if a noun immediately precedes that number, *ni tsuki* must appear, as in (2).

(2) a. 五千円 {**につき** / *ø} 四十円の手数料をいただきます。
(=Ex.(b))
(We place a forty-yen service charge on five thousand yen.)

b. この仕事は三時間 {**につき** / *ø} 十ドルもらえる。
(This job will pay you ten dollars for three hours.)

c. 米一カップ {**につき** / *ø} しょう油大さじ二杯の割合にします。(=Ex.(c))

3. *Ni tsuite* can be used instead of *ni tsuki*, although *ni tsuite* is less common.

(3) この仕事は一時間**について**六ドルもらえる。(=KS)

【Related Expression】

Atari also means 'per.' The difference between *atari* and *ni tsuki* is that while *atari* can be used with a counter only (i.e., without a number), as in [1], *ni tsuki* requires both a number and a counter. When *atari* appears with a counter only, however, it appears only with certain counters.

[1] a. 時間**当たり**五ドル (five dollars per hour)

b. キロ**当たり**二千円 (two thousand yen a kilo)

Atari is also used in the structure ~ *atari no* N, as in [2].

[2] a. 時間**当たりの**賃金 (wage per hour (i.e., hourly wage))

b. キロ**当たりの**卸値 (wholesale price per kilo)

c. 国民一人**当たりの**年間米消費量 (annual per capita rice consumption (lit. annual rice consumption per citizen))

N

ni tsurete/tsure につれて / つれ *conj. / comp. prt.*

a phrase used to indicate that a change occurs in accordance with another simultaneous change

as; in proportion to; with 【REL. ***ni shitagatte/shitagai***; *~ ba ~ hodo*; ***to tomo ni***】

◆Key Sentences

(A)

	Vinf·nonpast		
日本語が	**上達する**	につれて,	日本人の友達が増えた。
(As my Japanese became more proficient, the number of my Japanese friends increased.)			

(B)

Noun		
時代の変化	につれて，	文化も変わっていく。
(Culture also changes with the change of the times.)		

Formation

(i) Vinf·nonpast につれて

読むにつれて (As one reads s.t.)

(ii) N につれて

気温の変化につれて (with the change of temperature)

Examples

(a) 病気が治ってくるにつれて，食欲が出てきた。
(As I recovered from my illness, I regained my appetite.)

(b) 年を取るにつれて，体力がなくなる。
(As people grow older, they lose their physical strength.)

(c) 日本の生活が長くなるにつれて，日本のよさ，悪さがよく分かってきた。
(As I've spent more time in Japan, I have come to understand the good and bad parts of Japan better.)

(d) 日本の経済力が伸びるにつれて，日本語の学生が増えてきた。
(As Japan's economic strength has grown, Japanese language students have increased.)

(e) 秋が深くなるにつれて，紅葉がきれいになってきた。
(As we've moved further into autumn, the colored leaves have become more beautiful.)

(f) 子供は成長するにつれて，親から離れていく。
(As children grow up, they become independent of their parents.)

(g) 季節(きせつ)の変化につれて，風景(ふうけい)も変わる。
(The scenery also changes with season changes.)

(h) 産業(さんぎょう)の発展(はってん)につれて，公害(こうがい)も増えていく。
(With industrial development, pollution also increases.)

Notes

1. Vinf·nonpast *ni tsurete* (or its more formal version Vinf·nonpast *ni tsure*) is used to express two simultaneously growing changes.

2. Since the conj. / comp. prt. expresses change, the verbs used in the *tsurete/tsure* clause and the main clause have to be a verb of change / process such as *jōtatsusuru* 'become proficient' and *fueru* 'increase' (in KS(A)), *toshi o toru* 'become old' and *naru* 'become' (in Ex.(b)), *seichōsuru* 'grow' and *hanarete iku* 'become independent' (in Ex.(f)). Unless both of the verbs indicate change / process, the sentence is not acceptable, as shown below.

   (1) *日本語を教(おし)える**につれて**，教えることの難(むずか)しさが分かった。
   (As I have taught Japanese, I have come to realize the difficulty of the Japanese language.)

   (2) *その小説(しょうせつ)は読(よ)む**につれて**，味(あじ)があった。
   (As I keep reading the novel, it has become more interesting.)

   In (1) and (2) both verbs in the *tsurete* clause and in the main clause are verbs that do not indicate change, resulting in unacceptable sentences. Even if the main verbs are replaced by verbs of change / process, still the sentences are unacceptable, as shown in (3) and (4).

   (3) *日本語を教える**につれて**，教えることの難しさが分かってきた。

   (4) ??その小説は読む**につれて**，味が出てきた。

   To make the sentences grammatical the verbs in the *tsurete* clause have to be replaced by the verbs of change / process like the following:

   (5) 日本語を教えていく**につれて**，教えることの難しさが分かってきた。

N

(6) その小説は読み進(すす)む**につれて**，味が出てきた。

【Related Expression】

All the cases of Vinf·nonpast *ni tsurete/tsure* can be rephrased with ~ *ba* ~ *hodo* which indicates that in proportion to the increase of extent / degree of action or state, s.t. happens, as in [1] and [2]. However, ~ *ba* ~ *hodo* can be paraphrased by *ni tsurete/tsure* only when the former expresses some change or process.

[1] 日本語が上達すれ**ば**する**ほど**，日本人の友達が増えた。(cf. KS(A))
(The more proficient I become in Japanese, the more Japanese friends I made.)

[2] 年を取れ**ば**取る**ほど**，体力がなくなる。(cf. Ex.(b))
(The older you get, the weaker you will become.)

[3] 日本語を教えれ**ば**教える**ほど**，教えることの難しさが分かった。
(The more I have taught Japanese, the better I have come to understand the difficulty of teaching it.)
→ *日本語を教える**につれて**，教えることの難しさが分かった。 (=(1))
→ 日本語を教えていく**につれて**，教えることの難しさが分かってきた。 (=(5))

[4] その小説は読め**ば**読む**ほど**味があった。
(The more I read the novel the more interesting it became.)
→ *その小説は読む**につれて**，味があった。(=(2))
→ その小説は読み進む**につれて**，味が出てきた。(=(6))

There is another fundamental difference between the two structures under comparison. In front of *ni tsurete/tsure* comes only a verb or noun, but in front of ~ *ba* ~ *hodo* comes not only a verb but also an Adj(*i* / *na*).

(⇨ **~ *ba* ~ *hodo***)

N

ni wa には *conj. / comp. prt.*

a conjunction / compound particle to indicate a purpose for doing s.t.

to; in order to; for; for the purpose of ~
【REL. *ni*; *tame ni*; *no ni*】

◆Key Sentences

(A)

	Vinf·nonpast		
豊かな生活を	**送る**	には	健康が第一だ。
(In order to lead a rich life, health should be your primary concern.)			

(B)

	Noun		
ハイヒールは	**ハイキング**	には	不向きだ。
(High-heeled shoes are unsuitable for hiking.)			

Formation

(i) Vinf·nonpast には

行くには (for going there)

(ii) N には

仕事には (for one's work)

Examples

(a) 日本を知るには日本語を学ぶのが一番だ。
(The best course for getting to know Japan is to study the Japanese language.)

(b) 人生を豊かにするには趣味をたくさん持つことが大事だ。
(To enrich your life it is important is to have many hobbies.)

(c) 人の性格を見抜くには深い洞察力が必要だ。
(In order to see through a person's personality, one needs to have deep insight.)

(d) 外国語の能力を伸ばすにはその国に行くのが一番だろう。
(The best way for developing one's proficiency in a foreign language would be to go to the country of that language.)

(e) 世界の平和を維持するにはエリートの交流より庶民のレベルの交流が肝心だ。
(To maintain world peace, exchange among the general public rather than exchange among elites is essential.)

(f) 期末レポートを書くにはワープロが欠かせない。
(A word processor is a must for writing a term paper.)

(g) あの人を説得するには時間がかかる。
(It takes time to persuade him.)

(h) このクラブの会員になるには会員の推薦状が必要だった。
(In order to become a member of this club a member's letter of recommendation was necessary.)

(i) このかばんは長旅には便利だ。
(This bag is suitable for a long travel.)

(j) この研究にはかなりの時間とお金がかかる。
(This research needs a considerable amount of time and money.)

Notes

1. Vinf·nonpast *ni wa* is used to indicate a purpose for doing s.t. The predicate often expresses the necessity for or importance of using a specific means.

2. Vinf·nonpast may be nominalized by *no*, as in (1) and (2) below.

   (1) 豊かな生活を送る**の**には健康が第一だ。(cf. KS(A))

   (2) 人の性格を見抜く**の**には深い洞察力が必要だ。(cf. Ex.(c))

   There is no difference in meaning between *ni wa* and *no ni wa*.

3. *Ni wa* can take not only a Vinf·nonpast but a noun as shown in KS(B), Exs.(i) and (j). A noun here is a noun of action which can take the verb *suru*. There are two types of such nouns: one is the stem of the so-called *suru*-verb, such as *kenkyū* of *kenkyū-suru* (of Ex.(j)) or the direct object of *suru*, such as *nagatabi* (of Ex.(i)). If a noun is not a noun of action, the sentence does not express a purpose, as shown in (3).

   (3) a. 週末**には**家でテレビを見ています。
   (On weekends I watch TV at home.)
   (⇨ ***ni***[1] (DBJG: 289–91))

   b. 母**には**時々電話をします。
   (I sometimes call my mother.)
   (⇨ ***ni***[2] (DBJG: 291–92))

   c. 黒板**には**漢字が書いてあった。
   (On the blackboard were written kanji.)
   (⇨ ***ni***[4] (DBJG: 295–96))

   d. 事務所**には**誰もいなかった。
   (Nobody was at the office.)
   (⇨ ***ni***[6] (DBJG: 299–302))

   c. 東京**には**一人で行きました。
   (To Tokyo I went alone.)
   (⇨ ***ni***[7] (DBJG: 302))

【Related Expression】

There are at least four similar purpose expressions in Japanese.

[1] a. 私は韓国語の勉強**に**韓国へ行った。
(I went to Korea for the study of Korean.)

b. 私は韓国語を勉強し**に**韓国へ行った。
(I went to Korea to study Korean.)

c. 私は韓国語を勉強する**ために**韓国へ行った。
(I went to Korea in order to study Korean.)

d. 私は韓国語を勉強する {**のに** / ***に**} 韓国へ行った。
(I went to Korea for the purpose of studying Korean.)

[1a] means practically the same as [1b]. However, the latter construction has a restriction on the main verb ; that is, only the verb of motion can be used. The difference between [1a] and [1c] is that the latter has the stronger meaning of purpose. [1a] sounds more casual than [1c]. [1a] is different from [1d] in that the latter puts more weight on the way the speaker learned Korean. In other words, [1d] implies seriousness of the purpose.

(⇨***ni*** [5] (DBJG: 297–99)); ***noni*** [2] (DBJG: 335–37))

ni yotte/yori によって / より *comp. prt.*

a particle that indicates means, cause, agent of passive sentence, or dependency on a situation

according to; due to; owing to; because of; depending on; from ~ to; by means of; on the basis of; with; by
【REL. *ni*; *de*; *no tame ni*】

◆Key Sentences

(A)

Noun		
漢和辞典	によって	知らない漢字を調べる。
(We examine unknown kanji with a Chinese character dictionary.)		

(B)

Noun		
先生（せんせい）	によって，	もちろん，教（おし）え方（かた）が違（ちが）います。
(Teaching methods are, of course, different, depending on the teacher.)		

(C)

Noun		
戦争（せんそう）	によって	父（ちち）を亡（な）くした。
(We lost our father, owing to the war.)		

(D)

	Noun		
この研究所（けんきゅうじょ）は	**文部省**（もんぶしょう）	によって	設立（せつりつ）された。
(This research institute was established by the Ministry of Education.)			

(E)

Embedded Yes-No Question			
奨学金（しょうがくきん）がもらえるか	どうか	によって	大学（だいがく）入学（にゅうがく）を決（き）めます。
(I will decide my entrance to college, depending on whether I can get a scholarship or not.)			

(F)

Embedded Wh-Question		
何を食べるか	によって	健康状態は変わる。
(Our health condition changes according to what we eat.)		

(G)

	Sinf			
我々は	**本を読む**	こと	によって	視野を広げることが出来る。
(We can expand our horizons by reading books.)				

Formation

N

(i) N によって

政府によって (by the government)

(ii) {V / Adj(*i*)}inf かどうかに {よって / より}

{来る / 来た} かどうかに {よって / より} (depending on whether s.o. comes / came or not)

{面白い / 面白かった} かどうかに {よって / より} (depending on whether s.t. is / was interesting or not)

(iii) {Adj(*na*)stem / N} {ø / だった} かどうかに {よって / より}

{静かø / 静かだった} かどうかに {よって / より} (depending on whether s.t. is / was quiet or not)

(iv) Embedded Wh-Question に {よって / より}

何を食べたかに {よって / より} (depending on what s.o. ate)

誰が来るかに {よって / より} (depending on who comes)

Examples

(a) このごろは宇宙中継によって世界のニュースをテレビで見ることが出来る。
(These days we can watch world news on TV via satellite live broadcasting.)

(b) その老人達はわずかの貯金によって生活している。
(The old people are living on little savings.)

(c) その問題は話し合いによって解決出来るはずだ。
(We should be able to solve that problem by means of negotiation.)

(d) 人によって，年のとり方が違う。
(Depending on the person, the aging process differs.)

(e) 僕はその日の気分によって，違う音楽を聞きます。
(Depending on the day's mood, I listen to different music.)

(f) 定年は会社によって違う。
(Retirement ages vary from company to company.)

(g) その青年は麻薬によって青春時代を失ってしまった。
(The young man lost his adolescence because of drugs.)

(h) 彼は難病によって再起不能になった。
(He became unable to come back because of the difficult disease.)

(i) この絵はピカソによって描かれた。
(This picture was painted by Picasso.)

(j) アメリカ大陸はコロンブスによって発見された。
(The American Continent was discovered by Columbus.)

(k) 日本へ行けるかどうかによって，来年の計画が全く変わってきます。
(Depending on whether or not I can go to Japan, my coming year's schedule will become totally different.)

(l) 君と結婚出来るかどうかによって，僕の人生の幸，不幸が決まるんです。
(My fortune will be determined by whether I can marry you or not.)

(m) どの日本語の先生に習うかによって，学習者の進歩が違うはずだ。
(The learner's progress should differ, depending on which Japanese language instructor he learns from.)

(n) 誰が演奏するかによって，同じ曲でも，印象が違う。
(The same musical piece sounds different, depending on who performs it.)

(o) アメリカでは麻薬を厳しく取り締まることによって，犯罪を減らすことが出来るのではないだろうか。
(Would it not be possible to reduce crimes in the U.S. by maintaining strict control of drugs?)

(p) 自動車の事故による死者の数は毎年増えている。
(The number of the people killed in automobile accidents is increasing every year.)

(q) 誤診による手遅れはよくあることだ。
(Belated treatment due to misdiagnosis is a matter of frequent occurrence.)

Notes

1. The particle *ni yotte* indicates the means for doing s.t. (e.g. KS(A), (G), Exs.(a) – (c) and (o)), dependency on a situation / s.t. / s.o. (e.g. KS(B), (E), (F), Exs.(d) – (f) and (k) – (n)), cause for s.t. (e.g. KS(C), Exs.(g) and (h)), and an agent of a passive sentence (e.g. KS(D), Exs.(i) and (j)).

2. When *ni yotte* means dependency on a situation, the preceding element can be an embedded Yes-No question (e.g. KS(E), Exs.(k) and (l)) or a WH-question (as in KS(F), Exs.(m) and (n)).

3. When *ni yotte* means a means for doing s.t., it can be preceded by a clause nominalized by *koto* as in KS(G) and Ex.(o).

4. ~ *ni yotte* can be unconditionally replaced by ~ *ni yori* when it means dependency on a situation / s.t. / s.o., as in KS(B), (E), (F), Exs.(d) – (f) and (k) – (n). The difference between the two is that ~ *ni yori* is used in written Japanese.

(1) a. 日本語の先生の教え方は先生**に｛よって / ??より｝**違いますよ。
(The teaching methods of Japanese teachers differ depending on the teacher.)

b. 日本語の教授法(きょうじゅほう)は教師(きょうし)**に｛よって / より｝**異(こと)なる。
(The Japanese language pedagogy differs depending on the instructor.)

In (1a) *ni yori* is unacceptable, because it is used in spoken Japanese, whereas the same comp. prt. can be used in (1b) which belongs to written Japanese. The replacement is also possible when ~ *ni yotte* means an instrument with which to do s.t.

(2) a. このごろは宇宙中継**により**世界のニュースをテレビで見ることが出来る。(cf. Ex.(a))

b. その問題は話し合い**により**解決出来るはずだ。(cf. Ex.(c))

c. アメリカでは麻薬を厳しく取り締まること**により**，犯罪を減らすことが出来るのではないだろうか。(cf. Ex.(o))

However, when the instrument is a concrete, tangible object *ni yori* cannot be used as in (3).

(3) a. *漢和辞典**により**知らない漢字を調べる。(cf. KS(A))

b. *その老人達はわずかの貯金**により**生活している。
(cf. Ex.(a))

When the particle means a cause or a passive agent, ~ *ni yori* is not used. Thus, the following sentences are all marginal.

(4) a. ??戦争**により**父を亡くした。(cf. KS(C))

b. ??この研究所は文部省**により**設立された。(cf. KS(D))

5. In the prenominal use of N_1 *ni yoru* N_2, the comp. prt. expresses cause as in Ex.(p) and (q), or a means as in (5a) or a passive agent as in (5b).

(5) a. 人文科学の領域でもコンピュータ**による**研究が盛んだ。
(Even in the humanities field research using computers is popular.)

b. ニューヨークでは麻薬常用者**による**殺人事件が多発している。
(In New York City murders by habitual drug users occur frequently.)

In all of these *ni yotte* cannot be used.

【Related Expressions】

I. The particle *de* of means can always replace *ni yotte* of means, as shown below: (⇨ ***de***[2] (DBJG: 106–07))

[1] a. 漢和辞典**で**知らない漢字を調べる (cf. KS(A))

b. このごろは宇宙中継**で**世界のニュースをテレビで見ることが出来る。(cf. Ex.(a))

c. その老人達はわずかの貯金**で**生活している。(cf. Ex.(b))

d. 我々は本を読むこと**で**視野を広げることが出来る。(cf. KS(G))

However, *ni yotte/yori* cannot always replace *de* of means. Examples follow:

[2] a. 僕はバス {**で** / ***によって**} 会社に行っています。
(I am commuting to my company by bus.)

b. 都会のサラリーマンは公共の交通機関 {**で** / **によって**} 通勤している。
(The urban white-collar workers are commuting by public transportation.)

[3] a. 私はワープロ {**で** / ***によって**} 手紙を書いています。
(I am writing a letter with a word processor.)

b. 書類作成業務はワープロ {**で** / **によって**} 処理している。
(Document preparation is handled by a word processor.)

[4] a. すみませんが，原稿をファックス｛**で / *によって**｝送って下さいませんか。
(Could you kindly send the manuscripts by fax?)

b. 最近はファックス｛**で / によって**｝通信連絡するのが常識化されている。
(These days, it is common practice to communicate by fax.)

In [2]–[4], *ni yotte* is totally unacceptable in the (a) sentences and acceptable in the (b) sentences. The crucial difference between (a) and (b) sentences is that the former belongs to spoken Japanese, whereas the latter belongs to more impersonal and formal Japanese. The impersonal and formal aspects of the latter are accented by the use of Sino-Japanese words. In short, the basic difference between *de* and *ni yotte* is a stylistical difference; the former can be used in both spoken and written Japanese, but the latter is usually used only in written Japanese or very formal speech.

II. The difference between the agent marker *ni* and *ni yotte* is grammatical and stylistical. The sentences in [5] show that when the subject of the passive sentence is inanimate (such as 'research institute,' 'painting,' 'American Continent') the agent has to be marked not by *ni*, but by *ni yotte*.

[5] a. この研究所は文部省｛**によって / *に**｝設立された。 (=KS(D))

b. この絵はピカソ｛**によって / *に**｝描かれた。(=Ex.(i))

c. アメリカ大陸はコロンブス｛**によって / *に**｝発見された。 (=Ex.(j))

[6a] and [7a] show examples where *ni* is chosen over *ni yotte*.

[6] a. アリスはジョン｛**に / *によって**｝だまされた。
(Alice was deceived by John.)

b. デモ隊は機動隊｛**に / によって**｝一掃された。
(The demonstrators were dispelled by riot police.)

[7] a. 僕は手紙を両親 {に / *によって} 読まれた。
(I got my letter read by my parents.)

b. 我々は研究所の機密書類を外部の者 {に / によって} 読まれた。
(We got our secret document of the research institute read by unknown outsiders.)

[8] a. 私は日本語の先生 {に / *によって} 発音を直された。
(My Japanese teacher corrected my pronunciation (lit. I am annoyed by the fact that my professor corrected my pronunciation).)

b. 学生達は厳しい日本語教師 {に / によって} 発音矯正をされた。
(The students had their pronunciation corrected by their strict Japanese instructors.)

N

Sentences [6] – [8] show that *ni yotte/yori* can be used in (b) type sentences which have impersonal and formal written style, but not in (a) type sentences which have personal style.

(⇨ ***rareru***[1] (DBJG: (364–69))

III. The particle *ni yotte/yori* of cause has the related expressions *de* and *no tame ni*. KS(C), Exs.(g) and (h) can be rewritten using *de* and *no tame ni* as shown below.

(⇨ ***de***[3] (DBJG: 107–09); ***tame*** (***ni***) (DBJG: 447–51))

[9] a. 戦争 {で / のために} 父を亡くした。(cf. KS(C))

b. その青年は麻薬 {で / のために} 青春時代を失ってしまった。(cf. Ex.(g))

c. 彼は難病 {で / のために} 再起不能になった。(cf. Ex. (h))

As shown in [10], there are cases in which *ni yotte* is unacceptable for some unknown reason.

[10] a. 仕事 {で / のために / *によって} とても疲れた。
(Because of my work I got very tired.)

b. 病気 {**で / のために / *によって**} 会社を休んだ。
(Because of illness, I took a day off from the company.)

c. 停電 {**で / のために / *によって**} 大変困った。
(Because of the power failure we had a difficult time.)

The crucial differences among *de, no tame ni*, and *ni yotte* are: first, *ni yotte* and *no tame ni* are more formal than *de*. That is why abstract Sino-Japanese words go more harmoniously with the former as shown in [11a] below:

[11] a. 日本の経済発展 {**のために / によって / ??で**} 日本語学習者が増えた。
(Because of Japan's economic progress, Japanese language learners have increased.)

b. 日本の経済の発展 {**のために / によって / で**} 日本語学習者が増えた。

In [11b] *de* becomes acceptable, because the inserted *no* makes the entire sentence less formal. Secondly, *de* can be used to mean 'cause' rather loosely, but *ni yotte* can be used only when the focus is sharply placed on a 'cause,' as shown in [12].

[12] a. 金の問題 {**で / ??のために / *によって**} 友達とけんかした。
(Because of money problems I quarrelled with my friend.)

b. つまらないこと {**で / *のために / *によって**} 悩んでいるね。
(You are suffering because of a trivial matter, aren't you?)

no kankei de の関係で *phr.*

a phrase indicating that s.t. takes place or does not take place because of s.t.	because of 【REL. *no tame (ni)*】

◆Key Sentence

	Noun		
ホールさんは今	**仕事**	の関係で	東京に行っています。
(Mr. Hall has gone to Tokyo on a business-related matter.)			

Formation

N の関係で

会社の関係で (because of the company)

天気の関係で (because of the weather)

Examples

(a) 鈴木は単位の関係で今年は卒業出来ないそうだ。
(I heard that Suzuki cannot graduate this year because of insufficient credits / units.)

(b) 時間の関係で，残念ですが，詳しくお話し出来ません。
(Because of the time limit, I am sorry I cannot go into detail.)

(c) 部屋の広さの関係で，四十人以上はお呼び出来ません。
(Because of the size of the room we cannot invite more than 40 people.)

(d) 桃子は年齢の関係で，採用されなかったようだ。
(It seems that Momoko was not hired because of her age.)

(e) レズリーは会社の関係でよく海外に出張するらしい。
(I was told that Leslie makes frequent company-related business trips

abroad (lit. makes frequent trips abroad because of his company).)

(f) みゆきは御主人(ごしゅじん)の仕事の関係でロンドンに三年(さんねん)住(す)むそうだ。
(I heard that because of her husband's work Miyuki is going to live in London for 3 years.)

(g) 予算(よさん)の関係で，そのプロジェクトは中止(ちゅうし)になった。
(Because of the budgetary situation, that project has been cancelled.)

Notes

N *no kankei de* is used to refer to causal relationship in a very indirect way. In fact, the noun *kankei* means 'relationship' and the particle *de* indicates a causal relationship. (⇨ ***de***[3] (DBJG: 107–09))

【Related Expression】

The following sentences are saying virtually the same thing, but they are slightly different from each other.

[1] a. 予算｛**の関係で / のため(に) / *で**｝，そのプロジェクトは中止になった。(=Ex.(g))

b. 予算不足(ぶそく)｛**のため(に) / *で / ??の関係で**｝，そのプロジェクトは中止になった。

c. 予算が不足した｛**から / ので**｝，そのプロジェクトは中止になった。

Among the five choices, N *no kankei de* is the most indirect reference to causal relationship, because it does not need to be specific about the cause (i.e., (lack of) budget funds in [1a] and [1b]). N *no tame* (*ni*) is next most indirect about specification of the cause. Exs.[1b] and [1c] show that the preceding N can be a neutral *yosan* 'budget' or a negative *yosan-busoku* 'lack of budget.' N *de*, *kara* and *node* all requires a specific cause. In this sense they are markers of direct reference to causal relationship. Among *de*, *kara* and *node*, the latter two are markers of more direct reference to causal relationship.

(⇨ ***tame*** (***ni***) (DBJG: 447–51); ***node*** (DBJG: 328–31); ***kara***[3] (DBJG: 179–81))

no koto のこと *phr.*

things of / about

about; in terms of; related to 【REL. ***ni kanshite/kansuru***; ***ni tsuite***】

◆Key Sentences

(A)

	Noun			
私は明日の講義で	**日本文化**	のこと	を	話すつもりだ。
(I'm going to talk about Japanese culture in my lecture tomorrow.)				

(B)

Noun			
彼女	のこと	は	もう忘れた方がいいよ。
(You'd better forget about her now.)			

(C)

Noun			
日本留学	のこと	で	ちょっとご相談があるんですが。
(I'd like to talk to you about studying in Japan.)			

(D)

	Noun		
実は,	**明日の会議**	のこと	なんですが。
(Actually, it's (=The reason I'm calling is / The reason I came to see you is) about tomorrow's meeting.)			

Formation

N のこと

試験のこと　(about an / the exam)

Examples

(a) 昨日荒井さんが君のことをいろいろ聞いていたよ。
(Miss Arai asked various questions about you yesterday.)

(b) レポートは日本の大学生活のことを書こうと思っている。
(For my term paper I'm thinking of writing about college life in Japan.)

(c) 子供のことは私が責任を持ちます。
(I'll take the responsibility for our children (lit. for things related to our children).)

(d) 今回の実習のことでは大変お世話になりました。
(I owe you a lot in terms of my internship this time.)

(e) あのう，お電話したのは，来週のパーティーのことなんですが。
((The reason) I'm calling (is to talk) about the party next week.)

Notes

1. *No koto* literally means 'things of / about.' Thus, X *no koto o kaku*, for example, literally means 'to write things about X.' This phrase often appears with a particle to form a compound particle meaning 'about,' as in KS(A) – (C) and Exs.(a) – (d).

2. X *no koto* (*nan*) *desu ga* is used to introduce the reason for phoning someone or visiting someone, as in KS(D) and Ex.(e), or to introduce a topic to the hearer, as in (1).

(1) A: 先生，レポート**のことなんですが**。
(Professor, I'd like to talk to you (lit. It's) about my term paper.)

B: 何ですか。
(Yes? (lit. What is it?))

A: 締(し)め切(き)りを一日(いちにち)延(の)ばしてもらえないでしょうか。
(Could you give me another day? (lit. Could you extend the due date by one day?))

no koto da kara のことだから *phr.*

because it is a matter of X with which / whom s.t. is habitually the case

because ~ is habitually / usually / often that way; because

◆Key Sentences

(A)

Noun		
中島(なかじま)	のことだから,	今日(きょう)もまた遅(おく)れて来(く)るだろう。
(Because Nakajima is always that way (i.e., comes late), he will probably come late again today. (lit. Because it is a matter of Nakajima (who habitually comes late), . . .))		

(B)

Relative Cl.	Noun		
傷(いた)みやすい	**とうふ**	のことだから,	冷蔵庫(れいぞうこ)に入(い)れておいた方(ほう)がいいですよ。
(Because tofu goes bad quickly, you'd better put it in the refrigerator. (lit. Because it is a matter of tofu, which always goes bad quickly, . . .))			

Formation

N のことだから

岡田(おかだ)さんのことだから (because Okada is habitually that way)

N

Examples

(a) 夏のことだから，食べ物には十分気を付けて下さい。
(Because it is summer (when foods go bad quickly), please be very careful about what you eat.)

(b) お金持ちの日本人のことだから，きっと高くても買いますよ。
(Because they are rich Japanese, I'm sure they will buy them even if they are expensive.)

(c) カラオケの好きな木下さんのことだから，歌い始めたらマイクを離さないんじゃありませんか。
(Because Kinoshita loves *karaoke*, I have a feeling that he will not let go of the microphone once he starts singing.)

(d) 酒好きの山田のことだから，この酒を見たら飲まずには帰らないだろう。
(Because Yamada is a sake lover, if he sees this sake, he will probably not leave until he drinks it (lit. without drinking it).)

Notes

1. Using X *no koto da kara*, the speaker presents a reason for something, based on what habitually occurs with X.

2. When N *no koto da kara* is used, the main clause must represent a future action, event, or state.

nomi のみ *prt.* <w>

a particle which expresses a limit imposed upon an action, event, or a state

only; just; alone
【REL. *dake*】

◆Key Sentences

(A)

Noun		Prt.	
要点(ようてん)	のみ	(を)	話(はな)して下(くだ)さい。
(Please tell me just the main point.)			

(B)

	Noun	Prt.		
これは	吉田先生(よしだせんせい)	に	のみ	話してあります。
(I have told this only to Prof. Yoshida.)				

(C)

	Vinf		
勝(か)てるかどうか分(わ)からないが，ベストを	尽(つ)くす	のみ	だ。
(I don't know whether I can win or not, but I will just do my best.)			

Formation

(i) N のみ (Prt.)

学生(がくせい)のみ(が)来(き)た (Only students came.)

学生のみ(を)呼(よ)ぶ (invite students only)

(ii) N {Prt. のみ / のみ Prt.}

学生 {にのみ / のみに} 話す (talk only to students / talk to students only)

(iii) Vinf のみだ

{行(い)く / 行った} のみだ (only go / went)

Examples

(a) この答えは私のみ(が)知っている。
(Only I know the answer to this.)

(b) 姓のみ記入のこと。
(Write your surname only.)

(c) 私はただ言われたことをするのみだ。
(I will just do what I was told to do.)

(d) ただ実行あるのみ(だ)。
(The only thing we have to do is to put it into practice.)

(e) 外装が終わったのみでまだほかは何も手が着いていない。
(We've just finished the exterior and haven't started anything else yet.)

Notes

1. The case particles *ga* and *o* are optional after *nomi*. Other case particles such as *ni*, *e*, *to*, *de*, and *kara* appear either before or after *nomi*.

2. When the particle *de* appears with *nomi*, the meaning changes according to the position of the two particles, as in (1).

(1) a. 私は日本語**でのみ**説明出来る。
(I can explain it only in Japanese. (i.e., I cannot explain it in other languages.))

b. 私は日本語**のみで**説明出来る。
(I can explain it in Japanese alone. (i.e., I don't need any other languages but Japanese to explain it.))

【Related Expression】

Dake can replace *nomi* without a change in meaning. The main difference between the two is that *dake* can follow adjectives and quantifiers but *nomi* cannot, as in [1].

[1] a. 安い {**だけ / *のみ**} だ (s.t. is cheap, that's all)

b. 静かな {**だけ / *のみ**} だ (s.t. is quiet, that's all)

c. 一つ{だけ/*のみ}買う (buy only one)

Note also that *dake* is used in formal and informal speech and written Japanese while *nomi* is used in formal speech and written Japanese.

(⇨ ***dake*** (DBJG: 93–97))

no moto de の下で *comp. prt.* <w>

under some object; under the control or influence of s.o. or s.t.

under; in; with
【REL. *-ka de*】

◆Key Sentence

	Noun		
私は鈴木先生の	**指導**	の下で	修士論文を書き上げた。
(I finished my master's thesis under Prof. Suzuki's guidance.)			

Formation

N の下で

学部長の指揮の下で (under the direction of the dean)

Examples

(a) さんさんたる太陽の下で開会式が行われた。
(The opening ceremony was held in (lit. under) the brilliant sun.)

(b) 彼はカラヤンの下で指揮法を学んだ。
(He studied conducting under (Herbert von) Karajan.)

(c) 弁護士(の)立ち会いの下で私達の離婚が成立した。
(Our divorce was agreed upon in (lit. under) the presence of attorneys.)

N

(d) 囚人達は厳しい監視の下で強制労働をさせられた。
(The prisoners were forced to work under strict supervision.)

(e) このインフレの下では金を貯めても意味がない。
(With this inflation there's no point in saving money.)

Notes

1. When this phrase refers to physical space, its use is limited to "atmospheric space," for example, the sky and the weather.

2. Some nouns require the particle *ni* rather than *de* after *no moto*, as in (1) and (2).

   (1) 私はもうけは折半という約束**の下に**この仕事をしている。
   (I'm doing this job with the promise that the profit will be divided in half (and one half will be given to me).)

   (2) 田口先生の許可**の下に**この実験室を使っている。
   (We are using this lab with Prof. Taguchi's permission.)

【Related Expression】

-ka de, when combined with some nouns, means the same as *no moto de*, as in [1].

[1] a. ～の指揮**下で** (under the direction of ~)

b. ～の監視**下で** (under the supervision of ~)

no ue de wa　の上では　*comp. prt.*

> as far as ~ is concerned

as far as ~ is concerned; as far as ~ goes; from the viewpoint / standpoint of; according to; in terms of
【REL. *-jō wa*】

◆Key Sentence

	Noun		
この計画は	**書類**	の上では	問題なさそうだ。
(There seems to be no problem with this plan as far as the documents are concerned.)			

Formation

Nの上では

理論の上では　(in theory; on paper; as far as the theory goes)

Examples

(a) 計算の上では二百万円ぐらいもうかることになっている。
(According to the calculations, we are supposed to make a profit of (about) two million yen.)

(b) このプロジェクトは話の上ではうまく行きそうだが，何となく不安だ。
(Although in theory (lit. As far as the story is concerned,) it looks like this project will work out, I feel somewhat uneasy.)

(c) 数字の上では川野の方が倉田より強そうだ。
(Statistically, (lit. As far as the figures are concerned,) Kawano looks stronger than Kurata.)

(d) 大野は仕事の上では完全主義者だが，私生活はだらしがない。
(Ohno is a perfectionist at work (lit. as far as his business is concerned) but messy in his private life.)

(e) 彼の行為は法律の上では罰しようがない。
(There's no way to punish his conduct legally (lit. from the legal point of view).)

Note

No ue de wa is not the same as *no ue de.* (⇨ ***ue de***)

【Related Expression】

-jō wa is used with some nouns in the same way as *no ue de wa*, as in [1].

[1] a. **計算上は** (as far as computation goes; in terms of the calculation)

b. **理論上は** (in theory; on paper; as far as the theory goes)

c. **法律上は** (legally; from the legal point of view)

(⇨ ***-jō***)

~ no wa ~ no koto da　～のは～のことだ　*str.*

a structure which focuses on a time when s.t. takes place

It will be / was ~ when / that ~

◆Key Sentence

Sinf		Noun (time)	
吉田さんと最後に会った	のは	1985年の五月	のことだ。
(It was in May 1985 that I last met Mr. Yamada.)			

Formation

Sinf のは (the same formation as *no da*) N のことだ

話したのは去年のことだ (It was last year when s.o. talked . . .)

Examples

(a) 日本語の面白さが分かり始めたのはごく最近のことだ。
(It was only recently that I began to understand how interesting Japanese is.)

(b) 本格的なロボットが現れたのは1960年代後半のことである。
(It was in the late sixties when genuine robots came out.)

(c) ゲラ刷りが出来るのは来月の終わりのことになるだろう。
(It will be around the end of next month when we get galley proofs.)

(d) 父が公務員だったのは私がまだ学校へ行く前のことだ。
(It was before I went to school that my father was a government worker.)

(e) 日本製品の評判が悪かったのは戦後二十年くらいの間のことだ。
(It was for a period of about twenty years after World War II that the reputation of Japanese products was bad.)

(f) 健一と利子が仲良く歩いているところを見たのはつい一か月ほど前のことなのに彼らはもう別れたという話だ。
(Although it was only (about) a month ago when I saw Ken'ichi and Toshiko walking together intimately, I heard they've already split up.)

Note

This structure is a special form of *~ no wa ~ da* and is used when a particular time is under focus. (⇨ ***~ no wa ~ da*** (DBJG: 337–42))

-nu ぬ *aux.* <w>

an archaic auxiliary that indicates negation

not
【REL. *-nai*; *-zu*】

◆Key Sentences

(A)

	Vneg	
グローバルな時代に自国のことだけを考えるわけには	**いか**	ぬ。
(In the global age we cannot think of our own country alone.)		

(B)

Vneg			Vneg		
知ら	ぬ	ことを	**知ら**	ぬ	と言うには勇気が要る。
(When you don't know something, it takes courage to admit it.)					

Formation

Vneg ぬ (N / Aux)

知らぬ (s.o. doesn't know s.o. / s.t.)

知らぬ人 (a person whom s.o.doesn't know or s.o. who doesn't know s.t.)

知らぬらしい (it appears that s.o. doesn't know s.o. / s.t.)

せぬ (irr.) (does not do s.t.)

おらぬ (irr.) (s.o. does not exist)

Examples

(a) 彼は何を聞いても，知らぬとしか答えぬ。
(No matter what I ask, he answers only that he does not know.)

(b) その日本人は英語が分からぬようだった。
(That Japanese did not seem to understand English.)

(c) 最近は滅多に酒を飲まぬが，若い頃はよく飲んだものだ。
(I seldom drink these days, but I used to drink a lot when I was young.)

(d) 日本語が話せる者はこの辺にはおらぬ。
(In this area there are not people who can speak Japanese.)

Notes

1. *-nu* is an archaic negative marker that corresponds to *-nai*, but is used only with verbs. The archaic *-nu* is used in very stiff written Japanese. That is why there are quite a few proverbial phrases in which *-nu* is used exclusive of *-nai*.

   (1) 転ば {**ぬ** / ***ない**} 先の杖。
   (Prevention is better than cure. (lit. A cane in advance so as not to fall.))

   (2) 知ら {**ぬ** / ***ない**} が仏。
   (Ignorance is bliss. (lit. Not to know is to be a Buddha.))

   (3) 言わ {**ぬ** / ***ない**} が花。
   (Better leave it unsaid. (lit. Not to speak is a flower.))

2. There is no past tense form for *-nu*. See [1a] below.

【Related Expressions】

I. *-nu* is an archaic version of *-nai*. Except in idiomatic phrases mentioned in Note 1 *-nu* can be replaced by *-nai*, but the reverse is not always the case.

[1] a. この本は面白く {**ない** / ***ぬ**}。
(This book isn't interesting.)

b. 朝ご飯を食べ {**ないで** / **ずに** / ***ぬで** / ***ぬに**} 学校へ行った。
(I went to school without eating breakfast.)

(⇨ ***~ nai de*** (DBJG: 271–73))

II. The difference between *-nu* and *-zu* is straightforward. The latter can be used as a continuative form or before *ni* to mean 'without ~.' The former can be used at the end of a sentence or before a noun, auxiliary or a conjunction.

[2] a. 昼ご飯を食べ {**ず** / ***ぬ**} に仕事をした。
(I worked without eating my lunch.)

b. 今日は風邪ぎみで, 会社にも行か {**ず** / ***ぬ**}, 家で寝ていた。
(I felt a cold coming on today, so I stayed in bed at home, without going to work.)

c. そうは思わ {**ぬ** / ***ず**}。
(I don't think so.)

d. 知ら {**ぬ** / ***ず**} ことを知っていると言ってはいけない。
(You shouldn't say you know what you don't know.)

o ~ da お〜だ *phr.*

a phrase which expresses the speaker's respect for someone when describing that person's action or state

【REL. *o ~ ni naru*; *rareru*】

◆Key Sentences

(A)

	V*masu*		
お	**急(いそ)ぎ**	です	か。
(Are you in a hurry?)			

(B)

		V*masu*		Noun		
今(いま)	お	**持(も)ち**	の	カード	は	もう使(つか)えません。
(You can no longer use the card you have now.						

Formation

(i) お V*masu* だ

お待(ま)ちだ (s.o. is waiting)

(ii) ご VN だ

ご研究(けんきゅう)だ (s.o. is doing research)

(iii) お V*masu* の N

今日(きょう)お帰(かえ)りの方(かた) (those who are going back today)

(iv) ご VN の N

ご研究の問題(もんだい) (a problem which s.o. is doing research on)

Examples

(a) もう皆さんお集まりです。
(Everybody is here (lit. has gathered) now.)

(b) 河野さん，課長がお呼びですよ。
(Mr. Kono, the Section Chief wants to see you (lit. is calling you).)

(c) コピーはもうお済みですか。
(Have you already finished copying?)

(d) どんな人をお望みですか。
(What kind of person would you like?)

(e) お客様はまだお帰りじゃありません。
(The guests haven't left yet.)

(f) お疲れでしたらこの部屋でしばらくお休み下さい。
(If you are tired, please take a rest in this room for a while.)

(g) 今お使いのワープロはいつお買いになりましたか。
(When did you buy the word processor you are using now?)

(h) 先生は今何をご研究ですか。
(What are you researching now, Professor?)

(i) 天皇陛下がご訪問の国々はどこですか。
(Which countries is the Emperor going to visit?)

Notes

1. *O* ~ *da* does not express the aspect (i.e., progressive, perfect etc.) of a verb explicitly. Aspect can be determined from context, as seen in (1).

(1) a. お客様がもうすぐ**お**帰り**です**。(＝帰る)
(The guests are leaving soon.)

b. 今何を**お**読み**ですか**。(＝読んでいる)
(What are you reading now?)

c. コピーはもう**お**済み**ですか**。(＝済んだ)
(Have you already finished copying?)

2. *O ~ da* cannot be used with two-syllable Gr. 2 verbs (e.g., *miru* 'look at,' *iru* 'stay,' *kiru* 'wear,' *neru* 'sleep') and irregular verbs (i.e., *suru* 'do' and *kuru* 'come').

   (2) a. *お見だ / *お寝だ

   b. *おしだ / *お来だ

3. As Formation (ii) shows, for *suru*-verbs which require the polite prefix *go-*, *go* VN *da* is used rather than *o* V*masu da*. The *suru*-verbs which require the polite prefix *o-*, such as *sōjisuru* 'clean,' *denwasuru* 'make a call,' *ryōrisuru* 'cook,' and *sentakusuru* 'wash' are not commonly used in this pattern.

   (3) a. ??先生がお一人で部屋をお掃除だ。(Acceptable form: 先生がお一人で部屋を掃除して {**おられる / いらっしゃる**}。)
   (The teacher is cleaning the room by himself.)

   b. ??先生は今学生にお電話です。(Acceptable form: 先生は今学生に電話して {**おられる / いらっしゃる**}。)

(⇨ ***o-*** (DBJG: 343–47))

【Related Expression】

O ~ da is not as polite as *o ~ ni naru* but is politer than passive honorific forms.
(⇨ **Politeness and Formality** (DBJG: 36–44); ***o ~ ni naru*** (DBJG: 358–60); ***rareru***[1] (DBJG: 364–69))

o hajime (to shite) をはじめ(として) *phr.* <w>

a phrase that is used to give a primary example	starting with; not only ~ but also ~ 【REL. ~ *dakede* (*wa*) *naku* ~ (*mo*)】

◆Key Sentence

	Noun		
私のうちでは，	父	をはじめ(として)，	家族全員スポーツが好きだ。
(In my family, starting with my father, all of us like sports.)			

Formation

N をはじめ(として)

先生をはじめ(として) (starting with the teacher)

Examples

(a) キャシーは，すしをはじめとして，日本食なら何でも食べる。
(Starting with sushi, Cathy eats any Japanese cuisine.)

(b) 今年は大阪をはじめ，関西地方はどこも梅雨が短かった。
(This year, starting with Osaka, the rainy season was short in all parts of the Kansai district.)

(c) この会社は，社長をはじめとして，社員一同が同じ食堂で昼ご飯を食べている。
(At this company, starting with the president, all the employees eat lunch in the same cafeteria.)

(d) この事件には，警察をはじめ，近くの住民が皆強い興味を示した。
(Not only the police but also the nearby residents showed a strong interest in this incident.)

Notes

1. N *o hajime to shite* literally means 'by making N the beginning (of s.t.),' an idea very similar to the English phrase 'starting with.'

2. N *o hajime* is an abbreviative version of N *o hajime to shite*.

3. In conversational Japanese N *o hajime* (*to shite*) is not used; instead, *dake de* (*wa*) *naku* ~ (*mo*) is used.

(⇨ ***dake de*** (***wa***) ***naku*** **~** (***mo***) (DBJG: 97–100))

O

【Related Expression】

All the examples can be rephrased by *dake de (wa) nakute ~ (mo)*. In fact, as noted in Note 3, in conversational Japanese *dake de (wa) naku ~ (mo)* is used instead of N *o hajime (to shite)*.

o ~ kudasai　お～下さい　*phr.*

a phrase which expresses a highly polite request	please do s.t. 【REL. *kudasai*】

◆Key Sentences

(A)

		V*masu*	
少々	お	**待ち**	下さい。
(Please wait a moment.)			

(B)

		VN	
電話で	ご	**注文**	下さい。
(Please order by phone.)			

Formation

(i)　お V*masu* 下さい

お話し下さい　(Please talk.)

(ii) ご VN 下さい

ご連絡下さい (Please contact (us).)

Examples

(a) このペンをお使い下さい。
(Please use this pen.)

(b) 時間があまりありませんのでお急ぎ下さい。
(Please hurry because we don't have much time.)

(c) どうぞお気軽にご相談下さい。
(Please feel free to consult with us.)

(d) 便利でお得な周遊券をご利用下さい。
(Please use excursion tickets, which are convenient and economical.)

Notes

1. *O ~ kudasai* cannot be used with two-syllable Gr. 2 verbs (e.g., *miru* 'look at,' *iru* 'stay,' *kiru* 'wear,' *neru* 'sleep') and irregular verbs (i.e., *suru* 'do' and *kuru* 'come').

   (1) a. *お見下さい。/ *お寝下さい。
   (Please look at it. / Please go to bed.)

   b. *おし下さい。/ *お来下さい。
   (Please do it. / Please come.)

2. The *suru*-verbs which require the polite prefix *o*-, such as *denwasuru* 'make a call,' *ryōrisuru* 'cook,' *sōjisuru* 'clean,' and *sentakusuru* 'wash' are not commonly used in this pattern. In fact, the examples in (2) are awkward.

   (2) a. ??ご自分でお掃除下さい。(Acceptable form: ご自分で掃除{して / なさって} 下さい。)
   (Please clean up by yourself.)

   b. ??ぬるま湯でお洗濯下さい。(Acceptable form: ぬるま湯で洗濯 {して / なさって} 下さい。)
   (Please wash in lukewarm water.)

The sentence in (3), however, is acceptable. This sentence is derived from the sentence in (4) ; in (3) the direct object marker *o* has been deleted.

(3) 今晩(こんばん)**お**電話**下さい**。
(Please give me a call tonight.)

(4) 今晩**お**電話**を下さい**。

3. *O ~ kudasai* cannot be used in negative requests.

(5) *このペンはお使わないで下さい。
(Please do not use this pen.)

【Related Expression】

O ~ kudasai is politer than *~ kudasai*. While there are some verbs which cannot be used in the *o ~ kudasai* pattern as mentioned in Notes 1 and 2, any verb can be used in the *~ kudasai* pattern.

[1] a. 見て下さい / *お見下さい。
(Please look at it.)

b. して下さい / *おし下さい。
(Please do it.)

c. ご自分で {掃除して下さい / 掃除なさって下さい / ??お掃除下さい}。
(Please clean up by yourself.)

Note also that *~ kudasai* can be used to make negative requests, but *o ~ kudasai* cannot, as in [2].

[2] この部屋(へや)は {使わないで下さい / *お使わない下さい}。
(Please do not use this room.)

In addition, *~ kudasai* can be used with auxiliary verbs which require verb *te*-forms while *o ~ kudasai* cannot.

[3] a. 見ていって下さい / *お見ていき下さい。
(Please look at it before you go.)

b. 食べてしまって下さい / *お食べてしまい下さい。
(Please finish eating.)

(⇨ ***~ kudasai*** (DBJG: 209–10))

omowareru 思われる *v.* (*Gr.* 2) <w>

> a verb that indicates what the speaker / writer feels spontaneously or his / her hesitation about asserting himself / herself

seem; appear; apparently

◆Key Sentences

(A)

Sinf		
来年の景気は今年よりもいい	ように	思われる。
(It seems that the business conditions of the coming year will be better than those of this year.)		

(B)

Sinf		
この病気の治療は約一か月かかる	と	思われる。
(It appears that the treatment of this disease will take approximately one month.)		

Formation

(i) {V / Adj(*i*)} inf ように思われる。

{来る / 来た} ように思われる。 (It appears that s.o. is coming / came.)

{面白い / 面白かった} ように思える。 (It appears that s.t. is / was interesting.)

(ii) Adj(*na*)stem {な / だった} ように思われる。

元気 {な / だった} ように思われる。 (It seems that s.o. / s.t. is / was healthy / sturdy.)

(iii) N {の / だった} ように思われる。

学生 {の / だった} ように思われる。 (S.o. seems to be / have been a student.)

(iv) Sinf と思われる。

正しくないと思われる。 (It appears that s.t. is not right.)

Examples

(a) 日本の輸出は今後あまり伸びないように思われる。
(It seems that Japanese exports are not going to grow so much in the future.)

(b) 子供の非行を犯罪映画に結び付けるのは短絡的なように思われる。
(It appears too simplistic to relate children's delinquency to crime movies.)

(c) この大学の教育は理工系が特にいいように思われる。
(Education at this university seems to be particularly good in science and engineering.)

(d) 二十一世紀は情報化がもっと進んで，世界が一つの共同体になるだろうと思われる。
(It seems to me that in the 21st century society will become more information oriented, and the world will become one community.)

(e) 日本語を習う時はローマ字を使わない方がよいと思われる。
(When you learn Japanese it seems better not to use romanization.)

(f) 健康管理には毎日三十分ぐらいの運動をするのが効果的だと思われる。
(To look after your health, it is apparently effective to exercise for about 30 minutes every day.)

Notes

1. *omowareru* is the passive form of *omou* 'to feel; to think,' but *omowareru* in the present entry does not have the meaning of passivity; rather it has the meaning of autogenesis, i.e., what the speaker / writer feels / thinks spontaneously. The fact that *omowareru* is different from the real passive use should become clear by the fact that the former does not have the true agent, but the latter does.The true passive by definition involves an agent (= actor) and the agent is marked by *ni* in passive sentences. Thus genuine passive sentences should be grammatical with a *ni*-marked agent. That is why the addition of a *ni*-marked agent to KS(A) and (B) as in (1a) and (2a), respectively, will produce ungrammatical sentences. (1b) and (2b) are grammatical, because here *ni* indicates not an agent 'by' but an experiencer 'to.' Compare (1) and (2) with genuine passives of (3) and (4).

(1) a. *来年の景気は今年よりもいいように {私**に** / 経済学者**に**} 思われる。(cf. KS(A))

b. 私**には**来年の景気は今年よりもいいように思われる。
(To me it seems that the business conditions of the coming year are better than those of this year.)

(2) a. *この病気の治療は約一か月かかると {私**に** / 医者**に**} 思われる。(cf. KS(B))

b. 私**には**この病気の治療は約一か月かかると思われる。
(To me it appears that the treatment of this disease takes approximately one month.)

(3) そんなことをしたら，人**に**ばかだと思われますよ。
(If you do such a thing, you will be regarded as a fool.)

cf. そんなことをしたら，人はあなたのことをばかだと思いますよ。

(If you do such a thing, people will regard you as a fool.)
(= Active version of (3))

(4) 日本は外国人に不思議な国だと思われている。
(Japan is thought to be an enigmatic country by foreigners.)

cf. 外国人は日本のことを不思議な国だと思っている。
(Foreigners consider Japan to be an enigmatic country.)
(= Active version of (4))

(⇨ ***rareru***[1] (DBJG: 364–69))

2. The difference between (5a) which is identical with KS(A) and (5b) cannot be captured by the translation, because both sentences come out the same in the translation.

(5) a. 来年の景気は今年よりもいいように思われる。(=KS(A))

b. 来年の景気は今年よりもいいようだ。

Since *yōda* is a conjecture based on the speaker's reasoning process, if it is used with *omowareru*, a marker of autogenesis, the combination sounds more indirect and even humble.

3. The experiencer of the spontaneous feeling of ~ *omowareru* is usually the speaker / writer, but can be a third person, if the tense is past.

(6) 山田には会社の仕事が単調に思われた。
(To Yamada the company work seemed monotonous.)

(7) 加代子には結婚はまだ夢のように思われた。
(For Kayoko marriage still seemed like a dream.)

Suppose (6) and (7) were sentences in a novel in which the reader can empathize with Yamada or Kayoko: then, the nonpast tense is acceptable.

ori おり *aux. v.* (*Gr.* 1) <w>

Vmasu of the auxiliary verb *oru*

be ~ and
【REL. *ite*】

◆Key Sentence

	V*te*		
この入口は従業員専用に	**なって**	おり,	一般の人はここからは入れない。
(This entrance is for employees only and other people (lit. general people) cannot enter from here.)			

Formation

V*te* おり

話しており (be speaking and)

Examples

(a) 彼は最近プラモデルに凝っており，暇さえあれば模型の飛行機を組み立てている。
(He is crazy about plastic models these days and is assembling model planes whenever he has free time.)

(b) 日本では義務教育がよく行き届いており，識字率はほとんど100パーセントに近い。
(In Japan compulsory education is very thorough (lit. prevails thoroughly) and the literacy rate is almost 100 percent.)

(c) この高校は全寮制になっており，全学生が三つの寮で生活している。
(This high school is a boarding school (lit. total dormitory system) and all the students live in three dormitories.)

Notes

1. V*te ori* is the written version of V*te ite*. Although *ori* is the *masu*-form of the humble auxiliary verb *oru*, when V*te ori* is used in the writing of

documents, articles, papers, etc., it does not express the writer's politeness.

2. V*te ori* is more formal than V*te ite* or V*te i*.

3. V*te oru*, the informal sentence-final form of V*te ori*, is not used in writing in place of V*te iru*.

【Related Expression】

V*te ori* can be replaced by V*te ite* without changing meaning, as in [1].

[1] この入口は従業員専用になっ**ていて**，一般の人はここからは入れない。(=KS)

(⇨ ***iru***[2] (DBJG: 155–57))

O

o tōshite　を通して　*comp. prt.*

a compound particle that is used to indicate a medium through which s.t. is done or time through which s.t. takes place

through; by the medium of; via; throughout
【REL. *o tsūjite*】

◆Key Sentences

(A)

	Noun		
私(わたし)は	**親(した)しい友達(ともだち)**	を通(とお)して	そのピアニストと知(し)り合(あ)いになった。
(I became acquainted with the pianist through a close friend of mine.)			

(B)

	Noun		
私は	**一年**	を通して	五回ぐらい海外に行っている。
(I go abroad about 5 times a year (lit. throughout the year).)			

Formation

N を通して

先生を通して　(through my teacher)

Examples

(a) お書きになった御本を通して，先生のことは存じ上げておりました。
(I knew of you through the books you wrote.)

(b) その事件のことは新聞の記事を通して知っていた。
(I knew about the incident from newspaper articles.)

(c) その政治家は，首相の側近を通して，首相に接近した。
(That politician approached the Prime Minister through his entourage.)

(d) 二人は手紙のやり取りを通して親しくなっていった。
(Through an exchange of letters, the two became close.)

(e) ラジオもテレビも全国の放送網を通して放送される。
(Both radio and television programs are broadcast through the nation-wide network.)

(f) 海外生活の経験を通していろいろなことを学んだ。
(I have learned all sorts of things through my life in foreign countries.)

(g) カーテンを通して室内の様子が見えた。
(What was inside the room was visible through the curtain.)

(h) これらの写真を通して当時の人々の生活を偲ぶことが出来る。
(Through these photos, we can relive the lives of people in those days.)

(i) 現場(げんば)に残された指紋(しもん)を通して犯人(はんにん)が割(わ)れた。
(They found the criminal through the fingerprints left behind at the scene of the crime.)

(j) 父(ちち)は一生(いっしょう)を通して，一度(いちど)も東京(とうきょう)を出(で)たことがない。
(My father has never left Tokyo in his life.)

Note

O tōshite means ‘through the medium of ~’ or ‘through specific duration of time.’

【Related Expression】

Tōshite can be replaced by *tsūjite* in all cases except when the medium is a concrete, physical medium as in Exs.(g) – (i).

-ppanashi っぱなし *aux.*

an auxiliary which expresses the idea that s.o. or s.t. keeps doing s.t., or s.o. leaves s.t. in an improper state

keep -ing; have been -ing; leave

【REL. *mama*; *tsuzuke da*; *tsuzukeru*】

◆Key Sentences

(A)

	V*masu*		
新幹線(しんかんせん)が満員(まんいん)で東京(とうきょう)から京都(きょうと)までずっと	**立(た)ち**	っぱなし	だった。
(The Shinkansen was so crowded that I stood all the way (lit. kept standing) from Tokyo to Kyoto.)			

(B)

	D.O.	V*masu*		
友達(ともだち)にまだ	お金(かね)を	**借(か)り**	っぱなし	だ。
(I borrowed money from a friend of mine and still haven't paid it back.)				

(C)

	D.O.	V*masu*			
和彦(かずひこ)は	ラジオを	**かけ**	っぱなし	で	どこかへ行(い)ってしまった。
(Kazuhiko went out, leaving his radio on.)					

Formation

V*masu* っぱなし

座(すわ)りっぱなし ((vi.) have been sitting)

つけっぱなし ((vt.) leave s.t. on)

P

Examples

(a) ブラジルのバレーボール・チームは今日まで勝ちっぱなしだ。
(Brazil's volleyball team hasn't lost a game up to now. (lit. Brazil's volleyball team has been winning up to today.))

(b) 今日は朝から電話が鳴りっぱなしだ。
(The telephone has been ringing since this morning (lit. since morning today).)

(c) 朝からしゃべりっぱなしで喉が痛い。
(I have been talking since this morning and my throat is sore.)

(d) 車のヘッドライトを一晩中つけっぱなしだったのでバッテリーが上がってしまった。
(Because I left my car headlights on all night, the battery died.)

(e) 光子は水を出しっぱなしで友達と電話で話している。
(Mitsuko is talking with her friend on the phone while leaving the water running.)

(f) 茂はやかんをコンロにかけっぱなしにして出て行った。
(Shigeru went out somewhere leaving a kettle on the stove.)

(g) 開けっぱなしの窓から蚊がたくさん入ってきた。
(Many mosquitoes came in through the window which was left open.)

Notes

1. *-ppanashi* is derived from *hanashi*, the *masu* stem of the verb *hanasu* 'leave.'

2. The meaning of *-ppanashi* differs depending on the kind of verb which precedes it. When the verb is intransitive, *-ppanashi* means that s.o. or s.t. keeps doing something (e.g., KS(A) and Ex.(a)). When the verb is transitive, *-ppanashi* means that s.o. does s.t. to X and leaves X as it is without putting it back to its original state, which is not the proper way (e.g., KS(B) and (C)).

3. *-ppanashi* behaves like a noun; therefore it is followed by the copula *da*

(e.g., KS(A) and (B)) or particles such as *de*, *ni*, and *no* (e.g., KS(C), Exs.(f) and (g)).

【Related Expressions】

I. *Mama* expresses an idea similar to *-ppanashi*. In fact; *-ppanashi* can be rephrased as *mama* in most cases when the preceding verb is transitive, as in [1].

[1] a. 友達にまだお金を｛**借りっぱなし / 借りたまま**｝だ。 (=KS(B))

b. 和彦はラジオを｛**かけっぱなし / かけたまま**｝でどこかへ行ってしまった。(=KS(C))

However, because *-ppanashi* with a transitive verb implies an improper state, *-ppanashi* cannot be used in contexts such as [2].

[2] 彼(かれ)はまだたばこを｛**やめたまま / *やめっぱなし**｝だ。
(He still isn't smoking. (He used to smoke but gave it up.))

Notice also that in [3] *mama* has no negative implication while *-ppanashi* indicates that the speaker disagrees with Haruko's manner.

[3] 春子(はるこ)は帽子(ぼうし)を｛**かぶったまま / かぶりっぱなし**｝で頭(あたま)を下(さ)げた。
(Haruko bowed with her hat on.)

When the preceding verb is intransitive, *mama* cannot always replace *-ppanashi*. For example, *mama* can be used instead of *-ppanashi* in [4], but not in [5].

[4] 新幹線が満員で東京から京都までずっと｛**立ちっぱなし / 立ったまま**｝だった。(=KS(A))

[5] 朝から｛**しゃべりっぱなし / *しゃべったまま**｝で喉が痛い。 (=Ex.(c))

This is because *mama* focuses on the state after a single action (i.e., an action described by a punctual verb) while *-ppanashi* focuses on a continuous action.

Note also that if the preceding verb is intransitive, *-ppanashi* cannot be

P

used in an adverbial phrase, as in [6].

[6] {**座ったまま / *座りっぱなし**} で話して下さい。
(Please remain seated while talking. (lit. Please talk remaining seated.))

-ppanashi in [7] is acceptable because it is not in an adverbial phrase.

[7] 長い間 {**座ったまま / 座りっぱなし**} でお尻が痛い。
(I've been sitting for a long time, so my bottom hurts.)

(⇨ ***mama*** (DBJG: 236–40))

II. V*masu tsuzuke da* also expresses the idea "to keep doing s.t." and can be used in place of V*masu ppanashi* (with intransitive verbs), as in [8].

[8] a. 新幹線が満員で東京から京都までずっと {**立ちっぱなし / 立ち続け**} だった。(=KS(A))

b. ブラジルのバレーボール・チームは今日まで {**勝ちっぱなし / 勝ち続け**} だ。(=Ex.(a))

c. 朝から {**しゃべりっぱなし / しゃべり続け**} で喉が痛い。 (=Ex.(c))

P

V*masu tsuzuke da* cannot replace *-ppanashi* when the preceding verb is transitive.

III. V*masu tsuzukeru* also expresses the idea of "to keep doing s.t." and can be used in place of V*masu ppanashi*, as in [9].

[9] a. ブラジルのバレーボール・チームは今日まで {**勝ちっぱなしだ / 勝ち続けている**}。(=Ex.(a))

b. 朝から {**しゃべりっぱなしで / しゃべり続けて**} 喉が痛い。 (=Ex.(c))

V*masu ppanashi* (with intransitive verbs), however, does not express the actor's volition while V*masu tsuzukeru* does. Thus, V*masu ppanashi* is not acceptable in [10].

[10] 私は苦しかったが {**走り続けた / *走りっぱなしだった**}。
(Although I was in pain, I kept running.)

Conversely, in [11] V*masu ppanashi* is more natural than V*masu tsuzukeru* because standing or sitting was beyond the speaker's control.

[11] 新幹線が満員で東京から京都までずっと{**立ちっぱなしだった** / ??**立ち続けた**}。(=KS(A))

-ppoi っぽい *adj*(*i*) *suf.*

a suffix that indicates s.o. / s.t. has some distinctive characteristic or an attribute identified by a noun, an adjective, or a verb to which the suffix is attached

apt to; easy to; -ish; -like
【REL. *fū no*; *rashii*; *-yasui*; *yōna*】

P

◆Key Sentences

(A)

	Noun		Noun	
サングラスをかけた	**やくざ**	っぽい	男(おとこ)	が街角(まちかど)に立(た)っていた。
(A *yakuza*-like man wearing sunglasses was standing at the corner of the street.)				

(B)

	Adj(*i*)stem		Noun	
その女(おんな)の人(ひと)は確(たし)か	**黒**(くろ)	っぽい	セーター	を着(き)ていたと思(おも)います。
(If I remember correctly, I believe she was wearing a blackish sweater.)				

(C)

	V*masu*		Noun	
彼は	**ほれ**	っぽい	性格	で，どの女の人も好きになってしまう。
(He is apt to fall for women, and falls in love with practically any woman.)				

Formation

(i) N っぽい

子供っぽい (childish)

(ii) Adj(*i*)stem っぽい

安っぽい (cheapish)

(iii) Adj(*na*)stem っぽい

哀れっぽい (pitiful)

(iv) V*masu* っぽい

忘れっぽい (easy to forget, forgetful)

Examples

(a) 昼食時にはこのレストランはサラリーマンっぽい人達で一杯になる。
(During the lunch hour, this restaurant becomes crowded with men who look like salaried workers.)

(b) あの女優は実に女っぽいから好きだ。
(I like the actress, because she is so womanish.)

(c) こんな水っぽい酒，飲めないぞ。
(Who can drink such watery sake?)

(d) あなた，こんな安っぽいソファを買ってきてどうするの？
(What are you going to do with this cheapish sofa that you bought?)

(e) 公園のベンチに座って，きざっぽい男とあだっぽい女が話している。
(Sitting on a bench at the park a foppish man is talking with a coquettish woman.)

(f) うちの息子は飽きっぽいんで，次から次へと新しいことをするんですが，一つとして，ものにならないんですよ。
(Our son gets bored easily, and he tries new things one after another, but doesn't get anywhere with any of them.)

(g) うたぐりっぽい人って，嫌ですね。
(I don't like a person who is distrustful.)

(h) じゅうたんは汚れっぽいから，私は使っていません。
(Carpets get dirty easily, so I'm not using them.)

Notes

1. The Adj(*i*) suffix *-ppoi* is usually used in highly informal speech and writing, meaning something like English "-ish."

2. The suffix *-ppoi* is an Adj(*i*), so it conjugates exactly like other Adj(*i*)'s.

   (1) 黒っぽ**く**｛ありません / ない｝ (s.t. isn't blackish)

   黒っぽ**い**(です) (s.t. is blackish)

   黒っぽ**ければ** (if s.t. is blackish)

   黒っぽ**かった**(です) (s.t. was blackish)

3. The nouns, adjectives, and verbs that can take the suffix *-ppoi* are not unlimited, but quite productive, especially when it is connected with a noun. The following is a list of nouns, adjectives and verbs most commonly used with the suffix.

   (2) Noun + *ppoi*

   学生っぽい (student-like), 先生っぽい (teacher-like), 日本人っぽい (Japanese-like), アメリカ人っぽい (American-like), 商人っぽ

P

い (merchant-like), 不良っぽい (delinquent-like), 大人っぽい (adult-like), 芸者っぽい (geisha-like), 埃っぽい (dusty), いたずらっぽい (mischievous), 浮気っぽい (Don Juan-like), 理屈っぽい (argumentative), 色っぽい (sexy), 灰色っぽい (grayish), 茶色っぽい (brownish), 熱っぽい (feverish / enthusiastic), 愚痴っぽい (peevish)

(3) Adj(*i*)stem + *ppoi* (restricted to adjectives of color and shape except 安っぽい (cheapish))

白っぽい (whitish), 赤っぽい (redish), 黄色っぽい (yellowish), 丸っぽい (roundish), 四角っぽい (squarish)

All the examples except *yasuppoi* can be also grouped under (2).

(4) Adj(*na*) + *ppoi*

あだっぽい (coquettish), きざっぽい (affected), 嫌味っぽい (sarcastic), 皮肉っぽい (cynical), げすっぽい (vulgar), 俗っぽい (vulgar)

(5) V*masu* + *ppoi*

怒りっぽい (quick tempered), 疲れっぽい (easily tired), 慌てっぽい (apt to lose self-control), ひがみっぽい (apt to feel victimized), 湿っぽい (dumpy)

The last example *shime-ppoi* is actually an irregular form, because the expected form is **shimeri-ppoi*.

【Related Expressions】

I. N + *ppoi* can be replaced by N + *no yōna* or by N + *rashii*, and N + *fū no*, as shown in [1] below. Here, the choice of *-ppoi* expresses that the man is manifesting the distinctive character of a *yakuza*. In that sense it is very close to *fū no* which refers to s.o.'s or s.t.'s style. The expressions *no yōna* and *rashii* are quite different from *-ppoi* and *fū no* in that the former are conjectural expressions, whereas the latter are not.

[1] サングラスをかけたやくざ {**っぽい** / **のような** / **らしい** / **風の**} 男が街角に立っていた。(= KS(A))

There are cases where the replacement is restricted as shown in [2] and [3]. Here, *rashii* is acceptable, because it means 's.o. or s.t. is like the ideal model of X.' But *no yōda* and *fūda* which mean 'to look like X' does not make sense in the context. In [3] the meanings of *rashii* and *fū no* do not fit in the context, but *yōna* 'like X' in the sense of 'taste like water' fits in the context.

[2] あの女優は実に女 {**っぽい** / **らしい** / ***のようだ** / ***風だ**} から好きだ。(= Ex.(b))

[3] こんな水 {**っぽい** / **のような** / ***らしい** / ***風の**} 酒，飲めないぞ。(= Ex.(c))

The following N + *ppoi* cannot be replaced either by *no yōna*, *rashii* or *fū no*, because the meaning is very specific and fixed.
zoku-ppoi 'vulgar,' *hokori-ppoi* 'dusty,' *itazura-ppoi* 'mischievous,' *uwaki-ppoi* 'Don Juan-like,' *rikutsu-ppoi* 'argumentative,' *iro-ppoi* 'sexy,' *haiiro-ppoi* 'grayish,' *chairo-ppoi* 'brownish,' *netsu-ppoi* 'feverish'. P

II. Adj(*i* / *na*)stem + *ppoi* can be replaced neither by *no yōna* nor by *rashii* nor by *fū no*.

[4] a. その女の人は確か黒 {**っぽい** / ??**のような** / ***らしい** / ***風の**} セーターを着ていたと思います。(= KS (B))

b. あなた，こんな安 {**っぽい** / ***いような** / ***らしい** / ***風の**} ソファを買ってきてどうするの？ (= Ex.(d))

c. 公園のベンチに座って，きざ {**っぽい** / ***なような** / ***らしい** / ***風の**} 男とあだ {**っぽい** / ***なような** / ***らしい** / ***風の**} 女が話している。(= Ex.(e))

III. V*masu* + *ppoi* can be replaced by Vinf·nonpast + *yasui* as in [5], but depending on the verb with which *-ppoi* is connected, the *-yasui* version becomes marginal, as shown in [6].

[5] a. 私は最近とても疲れ｛**っぽく** / **やすく**｝なった。
(These days I became tired easily.)

b. うたぐり｛**っぽい** / **やすい**｝人って，嫌ですね。(= Ex.(g))

c. じゅうたんは汚れ｛**っぽい** / **やすい**｝から，私は使っていません。(= Ex.(h))

[6] a. 父は年をとってから怒り｛**っぽく** / ??**やすく**｝なった。
(My father has become short tempered since he became old.)

b. うちの息子は飽き｛**っぽい** / ***やすい**｝んで，次から次へと新しいことをするんですが，一つとして，ものにならないんですよ。(= Ex.(f))

(⇨ ***rashii*** (DBJG: 373–75); ***-yasui*** (DBJG: 541–43); ***yōda*** (DBJG: 547–52))

-rai 来 *suf.* <w>

during a certain amount of time (s.t. has continued up until the moment of speech or s.t. has never been like the current state)

for; in; since

【REL. *-buri*; *irai*; *-kan*; *mae kara*】

◆Key Sentences

(A)

	Noun (duration)		
トムは	**二十年**	来	日本語の勉強を続けている。
(Tom has been studying Japanese for the past 20 years.)			

(B)

	Noun (duration)		Noun	
今年の冬は	**五十年**	来の	寒さ	だ。
(This winter is the coldest one in 50 years.)				

Formation

(i) N (duration) 来

三十年来 (for the past 30 years)

(ii) N (duration) 来の N

六十年来の大地震 (the strongest earthquake in 60 years)

Examples

(a) 父は三十年来，同じ会社に勤めています。
(My father has been employed in the same company for the past 30 years.)

(b) 私はこの研究を十年来続けてきました。
(I've been continuing this research for the past 10 years.)

(c) 夜半来の雨が，ようやく上がったようだ。
(The rain which started after midnight appeared to have finally stopped.)

(d) 僕と岡田とは四十年来の友人だ。
(Okada and I have been friends for the past 40 years.)

(e) 今年の夏は六十年来の暑さだそうだ。
(They say that this summer is the warmest in 60 years.)

(f) これは三十年来の大雪です。
(This is the heaviest snow we have had in 30 years.)

Notes

1. When *-rai* is used to mean s.t. has continued up until the moment of speech, the final predicate takes V*te iru* as in KS(A) and Ex.(a) or V*te kuru* as in Ex. (b).

2. X *wa* N (of duration)*-rai no* Y *da* as exemplified by KS(B), Exs.(e) and (f), means that as for X, the speaker has never experienced Y in the specified duration. When Y is a person as in Ex.(d), *-rai* means X has continued to have the status of Y for a certain amount of time.

【Related Expressions】

I. *-rai* is used with an expression of time duration. The following phrases are all ungrammatical because the nouns used here express a point of time. To make them grammatical phrases *-irai* has to be used.

[1] a. *八月二十日来 (cf. 八月二十日**以来** (since August 20))

b. *1990 年来 (cf. 1990 年**以来** (since 1990))

c. *二時半来 (cf. 二時半**以降** (after 2 o'clock))

d. *去年来 (cf. 去年**以来** (since last year))

e. *去年の秋来 (cf. 去年の秋**以来** (since last fall))

f. *先週来 (cf. 先週**以来** (since last week))

g. ??先週末来 (cf. 先週末**以来** (since the end of last week))

h. ??先月来 (cf. 先月**以来** (since last month))

i. ??年末来 (cf. 年末**以来** (since the end of the year))

However, there are exceptional cases where *-rai* can be used with a non-duration expression as in (2):

[2] a. 昨日**来** (since yesterday) cf. 昨日**以来**, *昨日来

b. 昨夜**来** (since last night) cf. 昨夜**以来**, *昨夜来

c. 昨年**来** (since last year) cf. 昨年**以来**

d. 一昨年**来** (since year before last) cf. 一昨年以来

II. When *-rai* indicates continuation of an action / state, it can be replaced by ~ *mae kara*, or *-kan*, as shown in [3a], [3b] below.

[3] a. トムは二十年 {**来** / **前から** / **間**} 日本語の勉強を続けている。(= KS(A))

b. 父は三十年 {**来** / **前から** / **間**}, 同じ会社に勤めています。(= Ex.(a))

-rai can be freely replaced by ~ *mae kara* and *-kan*, but not vice versa, because the latter can be used with an expression of both relatively short and long duration; whereas the former can be used only with a relatively long duration, as shown below:

[4] a. 彼は {**二時間** / **二時間前から** / ***二時間来**} 日本語を勉強している。
(He's been studying Japanese for two hours.)

b. 二日 {**間** / **前から** / ***来**} 雪が降っている。
(It's been snowing for two days.)

When *-rai* is used in X *wa* N(duration)*-rai no* Y *da* construction, *-rai* can be replaced by *-buri da* which means 'after the lapse of ~,' as shown by [4a] and [4b]. Note that Y cannot be a person as in Ex.(d).

[5] a. 今年の冬は五十年｛**来** / **ぶり**｝の寒さだ。(= KS(B))

b. これは三十年｛**来** / **ぶり**｝の大雪です。(= Ex.(f))

rei no 例の *phr.*

a phrase which signals that the referent of the following noun phrase is definite and that the speaker expects the hearer to understand what the referent is

the ~ (in question); that (same); the usual

【REL. *wa*】

◆Key Sentences

(A)

	Noun		
例の	**プロジェクト**	は	どうなりましたか。
(What happened to the project (in question)?)			

(B)

		Noun	
今年の忘年会はまた	例の	**中華料理屋**	だそうだ。
(I heard that this year's year-end party is going to be at that Chinese restaurant again.)			

Formation

例の N

例の問題 (the problem (in question))

Examples

(a) 例のレポートは出来ましたか。
(Have you finished the report (I requested, you mentioned, etc.)?)

(b) 例のコピーが出来ましたよ。
(The copy (you asked for) is ready.)

(c) 例のダイアナ妃の本，さっそく買って読んだよ。
(I bought the book about Princess Diana (everybody is talking about, you recommended, etc.) right away and read it.)

(d) A: 一時に学生が来るんですよ。
(A student is coming at one.)

B: ああ，例のドイツから来た学生ですね。
(Oh, that student from Germany (you mentioned), right?)

(e) A: 今晩，会える？
(Can we meet this evening?)

B: ええ，いいわよ。
(Sure.)

A: じゃ，六時に例の喫茶店で。
(Then, (let's meet) at the usual coffee house at six.)

(f) 吉田さんがまた例の冗談を言ったが誰も笑わなかった。
(Mr. Yoshida told us that (same) joke again, but no one laughed.)

Notes

1. *Rei no* is used in situations where some information is shared by the speaker and the hearer. For example, when A utters KS(A) to B, B must have talked to A about a project at an earlier time. Similarly, when A utters KS(B) to B, A knows that B understands which Chinese restaurant A means, from their shared experience.

2. Because *rei no* is a device to remind the hearer of something experienced or mentioned earlier (although not in the same discourse), *rei no* X can be used without having mentioned X previously in the discourse.

Thus, *rei no* has the "force" to make the hearer recall the referent of the following noun phrase.

3. If there is strong situational and / or contextual support to indicate the referent of the following noun phrase, *rei no* can be omitted, as in (1) and (2). (See Related Expression.)

 (1) レポートは出来ましたか。
 (Have you finished the report?)

 (2) コピーが出来ましたよ。
 (The copy is ready.)

However, if *rei no* in KS(B) is omitted, for example, *chūkaryōri-ya* does not refer to a definite Chinese restaurant, as in (3).

 (3) 今年の忘年会はまた中華料理屋だそうだ。
 (I heard that this year's year-end party is going to be at a Chinese restaurant again.)

【Related Expression】

The topic marker *wa* marks known information. Thus, *wa* and *rei no* have some commonality. As a matter of fact, both X *wa* and *rei no* X are used when X is definite and known to the hearer. However, *wa* alone does not have the force that *rei no* has, a force to make the hearer recall the referent of X. Therefore, [1] might be too abrupt in some situations where KS(A) is perfectly acceptable.

 [1] プロジェクトはどうなりましたか。
 (What happened to the project?)

Note also that the referent of X *wa* can be generic while that of *rei no* X is always definite. Compare [2a] and [2b].

 [2] a. 本は役(やく)に立(た)つ。
 (Books are useful.)

 b. **例の**本は役に立つ。
 (The book (you mentioned) is useful.)

In addition, X *wa* is a topic phrase, while *rei no* X is a simple noun phrase and can appear in any position where a noun can appear.

(⇨ ***wa***[1] (DBJG: 516–19))

Relative Clause

◆Key Sentence

Relative Clause	Noun	
頭(あたま)がよくなる	**薬**(くすり)	はない。
(There isn't medicine which makes you smart.)		

Examples

(a) 日本語(にほんご)に強(つよ)くなる本(ほん)がありますか。
(Is there a book that will make you proficient in Japanese?)

(b) バロック音楽(おんがく)は心(こころ)が静(しず)まる音楽だ。
(Baroque music is music that soothes the mind.)

(c) これは日本の経営法(けいえいほう)がよく分(わ)かる本です。
(This is a book which enables us to understand Japanese management.)

(d) 体重(たいじゅう)が減(へ)る運動(うんどう)を教(おし)えて下(くだ)さい。
(Please recommend any exercise that will reduce my weight.)

(e) 気持(きも)ちが明(あか)るくなる話(はなし)が聞(き)きたいです。
(I would like to listen to hear something that will cheer me up.)

(f) これは太(ふと)らないお菓子(かし)ですから，どうぞたくさん召(め)し上(あ)がって下さい。
(These are non-fattening cakes, so please eat as many of them as you can.)

(g) あの先生(せんせい)の講義(こうぎ)はすぐ眠(ねむ)くなる講義だね。
(That professor's lecture is a lecture that will make you sleepy.)

R

Notes

1. The example of relative clauses given in this entry are all different from those of ordinary relative clauses in that one of the two source sentences includes a topic marker *wa* which carries a conditional meaning. Take KS, for example: it apparently comes from (1a) and (1b).

(1) a. 薬はない。
(There isn't medicine.)

b. その薬**は**頭がよくなる。
(If you take the medicine, you will become smart. (lit. As for the medicine, one will become smart.))

(1b) is a grammatical sentence, meaning 'if you take the medicine you will become smart.' So (1b) is the same as (2) in which the conditional conjunction *ba* is overtly used.

(2) その薬を飲(の)め**ば**, 頭がよくなる。
(If you take the medicine, you will become smart.)

Because the verb *nomu* is missing in KS, it looks as though medicine itself becomes smart. The same explanation is possible with the other example sentences.

R

(3) a. (その本を**読**(よ)**めば**日本語に強くなる)本がありますか。
(cf. Ex.(a))

b. バロック音楽は(その音楽を**聞けば**心が静まる)音楽だ。
(cf. Ex.(b))

c. これは(その本を**読めば**日本の経営法がよく分かる)本です。
(cf. Ex.(c))

d. (その運動を**すれば**体重が減る)運動を教えて下さい。
(cf. Ex.(d))

e. (その話を**聞けば**気持ちが明るくなる)話が聞きたいです。
(cf. Ex.(e))

Since a Japanese relative clause can contain a conditional clause within the relative clause, sentences of (3) are grammatical even if Vcond is retained. So, the following sentences are all grammatical.

(4) a. **飲めば**頭がよくなる薬はない。(cf. KS)
(There isn't medicine which, if taken, will make you smart.)

b. **読めば**日本語に強くなる本がありますか。(cf. Ex.(a))
(Is there a book which, if read, will make you proficient in Japanese?)

c. バロック音楽は**聞けば**心が静まる音楽だ。(cf. Ex.(b))
(Baroque music is music which, if listened to, will make your mind calm.)

2. Exs.(f) and (g) come from (5a) and (5b), respectively.

(5) a. これは(お菓子を**どんなに食べても**太らない)お菓子ですから，どうぞたくさん召し上がって下さい。(cf. Ex.(f))
(These are cakes that will not cause you to gain weight no matter how much you eat them, so please eat a lot of them.)

b. あの先生の講義は(講義を**聞くと**，眠くなる)講義だね。(cf. Ex.(g))
(That professor's lecture is a lecture that will make you sleepy if you listen to it.)

In the process of relative clause formation, the noun in the parentheses identical to the head noun (i.e. *o-kashi* of (5a) and *kōgi* of (5b)) is deleted, but the bold type parts (i.e. *donna ni tabete mo* of (5a) and *kiku to* of (5b)) can stay.

(⇨ **Relative Clause** (DBJG: 376–80))

R

Rhetorical Question

a question which functions as a forceful statement with no expected response

◆Key Sentences

(A)

		Vpot	
そんな	恥ずかしいことが	出来ます	か。
(I could never do such an embarrassing thing! (lit. Could I do such an embarrassing thing?))			

(B)

Sentence (affirmative)	
誰があんな人にお金なんか貸す	もんですか。
(Who would lend money to such a person!)	

(C)

Sentence (affirmative)	
今さら何を隠すことがある	だろう(か)。
(What is there to hide now!)	

(D)

Sentence		
彼女(かのじょ)がこんな所(ところ)へ来(く)る	わけが	ないじゃない(か)。
(There is no reason that she would come to a place like this.)		

(E)

	Sentence	
何(なん)だ,	テレビを見(み)ている	の(か)。
(Oh, you're watching TV!)		

(F)

	Vneg	
早(はや)く	しない	か。
(Do it quickly!)		

Examples

(a) こんなものがお客様(きゃくさま)に出(だ)せますか。
(How could we serve such a thing to guests!)

(b) あんな男(おとこ)に何が出来る(もの)か。 [male, informal]
(What can a man like that do!)

(c) 私(わたし)の気持(きも)ちがあなたなんかに分(わ)かるもんですか。
(You never understand my feelings!)

(d) こんなばかなことってあるでしょうか。
(How can such a ridiculous thing happen!)

(e) どうしてそれが彼(かれ)に分からないことがあろう(か)。
(How could he not understand it!)

(f) 彼にそんな難しいことが分かるはずがないじゃない(か)。
(How could you expect him to understand such a difficult thing!)

(g) なにも泣くことはないじゃない(か)。
(Oh, there's no reason to cry!)

(h) 男は「開け，ゴマ！」と叫んだ。すると，なんと岩の扉が音もなく開いたではないか。
(The man shouted, "Open sesame!" And look what happened: the rock (lit. rock door) opened with no sound!)

(i) ああ，ここにいたの(か)。
(Oh, you are here!)

(j) さっさと歩かないか。
(Walk quickly!)

Notes

1. Rhetorical questions take various forms, as seen in the Key Sentences. Typical endings include potential verbs (KS(A), Exs.(a) and (b)), *mono desu ka* and its variations (KS(B), Exs.(b) and (c)), *darō ka* and its variations (KS(C), Exs.(d) and (e)), (*nai*) *de wa nai ka* and its variations (KS(D) and Exs.(f) – (h), *no ka* and its variations (KS(E) and Ex.(i)) and *nai ka* (KS(F) and Ex.(j)). No matter what form it takes, however, a rhetorical question always uses falling intonation. Note that in Japanese, genuine questions always use rising intonation.

2. Rhetorical questions in some forms are equivalent to their corresponding negative sentences in meaning. For example, KS(A), (B), and (C) are semantically equivalent to (1), (2), and (3), respectively.

   (1) そんな恥ずかしいことは出来ない。
   (I couldn't do such an embarrassing thing.)

   (2) 誰もあんな人にお金なんか貸さない。
   (No one would lend money to such a person.)

   (3) 今さら何も隠すことはない。
   (There is nothing to hide now.)

Note that rhetorical questions are more powerful than their corresponding sentences.

3. A simple negative question can function as a strong command, as in KS(F) and Ex.(j), and is often used for intimidation.

rokuni ~ nai ろくに〜ない *str.*

a structure that is used to indicate that s.t. animate does not or cannot do s.t. satisfactorily / sufficiently / properly	not sufficiently; not satisfactorily; not properly; not well; hardly

◆Key Sentence

		Vneg	Neg.
飛行機の中では	ろくに	**寝られ**	なかった。
(On the plane I couldn't sleep well.)			

Formation

ろくに Vneg ない

ろくに食べない (s.o. doesn't eat properly.)

Examples

(a) ろくに勉強もしないで試験を受けたので，全然出来なかった。
(I took the exam without studying properly, so it was a disaster (lit. I couldn't do well at all).)

(b) 短いパリ滞在だったので，彼女とはろくに会えなかった。
(It was such a short stay in Paris that I hardly met her.)

(c) 彼はフランスのことなどろくに知らないのに，よく知っているような口を利く。
(He hardly knows about France, but he talks as if he knew a lot about it.)

(d) せっかくデパートまで買い物に出かけたのに，買い物中気分が悪くなってろくに買い物もせずに帰って来た。
(I went shopping, and got as far as to a department store, but I came home without doing much shopping (lit. shopping properly) because I felt sick while shopping.)

(e) 僕の犬はろくに芸もしない。
(My dog hardly does any tricks.)

Note

Along with *rokuni ~ nai* there is another structure similar to it; i.e., *rokuna* N ~ *nai* which is used to indicate that s.t. animate does not or cannot do something decent / sufficient / satisfactory. Examples follow:

(1) a. あの男は**ろくな**あいさつもし**ない**。
(He doesn't give us even a decent greeting.)

b. ナンシーは**ろくな**手紙も書け**ない**。
(Nancy cannot write even a satisfactory letter.)

c. あの人達は**ろくな**食事をしてい**ない**らしい。
(It appears that they are not eating decent meals.)

d. あの犬は**ろくな**えさを食べてい**ない**。
(That dog is not eating decent food.)

e. あの先生は**ろくな**先生じゃ**ない**。
(That professor is not a professor to speak of.)

If the prenominal form *rokuna* in all the examples except (1e) is replaced by the adverbial form *rokuni* the meaning will change. The *rokuna* version indicates that an action does occur but not in a satisfactory manner; whereas the *rokuni* version indicates that the action hardly takes place.

(2) a. あの男は**ろくに**あいさつもしない。(cf. (1a))
(He hardly gives us even a greeting.)

b. ナンシーは**ろくに**手紙も書けない。(cf. (1b))
(Nancy can hardly write even a letter.)

c. あの人達は**ろくに**食事もしていないらしい。(cf. (1c))
(It appears that they are hardly eating meals.)

d. あの犬は**ろくに**えさを食べていない。(cf. (1d))
(That dog is hardly eating food.)

sa さ *prt.* <s>

> a sentence-final particle used in highly informal speech by male speakers to express different degrees of assertion ranging from a light touch comment up to opposition or imposition

you know; sure; I tell you
【REL. *ne*; *tomo*; *yo*】

◆Key Sentences

(A)

	Vinf	
A: 就職出来るかな。	B: **出来る**	さ。
(A: I wonder if I can get a job.)	(B: Sure you can.)	

(B)

		Vinf	
A: 君は日本語，読めないよね。	B: いや，	**読める**	さ。
(A: You cannot read Japanese, right?)	(B: Yeah, sure I can.)		

(C)

	NP	
人生は	**長い旅のようなもの**	さ。
(Life is something like a long journey.)		

(D)

Wh-word			
どうして	酒(さけ)を飲(の)んじゃいけない	の	さ。
(How come I can't drink sake?)			

Formation

(i) {V / Adj(*i*)}inf さ

{食(た)べる / 食べた} さ。 (s.o. eats / ate it, you know.)

{やさしい / やさしかった} さ。 (s.t. is / was easy, you know.)

(ii) {Adj(*na*) / N} {ø / だった} さ

{元気(げんき) / 元気だった} さ。 (s.o. is / was healthy, you know.)

{学生(がくせい) / 学生だった} さ。 (s.o. is / was a student, you know.)

(iii) Wh-word ~ のさ

どうして食べないのさ。 (Why don't you eat it?)

(iv) NP さ

これはお茶(ちゃ)さ。 (This is tea, you know.)

Examples

(a) A: 今日(きょう)の日本語のテストは難(むずか)しいかな。
(I wonder if today's Japanese test is difficult.)

B: いや，難しくないさ。
(No, it's not difficult, I tell you.)

(b) A: このスーツケース，持(も)てるかな。
(I wonder if I can carry this suitcase.)

B: 持てるさ。
(I'm sure you can.)

(c) A: お前は車を買う金なんかないよな。
(You don't have money to buy a car with, do you?)

B: いや，あるさ。
(Sure I do.)

(d) A: ニューヨークの一人歩きは危ないだろう。
(Walking alone in New York City must be unsafe!)

B: いや，大丈夫さ。
(No, it's safe, you know.)

(e) A: この問題，君には解けないと思うよ。
(I bet you can't solve this math problem.)

B: こんなもの，やさしいさ。
(This is a cinch, you know.)

(f) 人生とはこんなものさ。
(Such is life, you know.)

(g) 仕事に失敗はつきものさ。
(Work and failure go together, you know.)

(h) どうしてこんな簡単なことが分からないのさ。
(How come you don't understand such a simple thing?)

(i) A: 僕は大学に行くのをあきらめたよ。
(I've given up the idea of going to college, you know.)

B: 何を言っているのさ。
(What are you talking about?)

Notes

1. *Sa* as a sentence-final particle is used usually by male speakers in very informal speech and it expresses the speaker's encouragement as in KS(A), Exs.(a) and (b), or his assertion to negate someone's challenge as in KS(B) and Exs.(c) – (e), or his light touch comment as in KS(C), Exs.(f) and (g), or his irritation about s.o.'s words or behavior as in Ex.(h) or opposition as in KS(D) and Ex.(i). *Sa* is also used by both

males and females to draw the hearer's attention to something. (See Related Expression III.)

2. Note that when a Wh-word is used with *sa*, the predicate part has to be *no*-nominalized. The non-nominalized version is totally unacceptable.

(1) **どうして**酒を飲んじゃいけない {***さ** / **のさ**}。(= KS(D))

(2) **何**を言っている {***さ** / **のさ**}。(= Ex.(i)–B)

【Related Expressions】

I. All the uses of *sa* in the KS and Exs. can be replaced by *yo*.

[1] A: 就職出来るかな。

B: 出来る**よ**。(cf. KS(A))

[2] A: 君は日本語，読めないよね。

B: いや，読める**よ**。(cf. KS(B))

[3] 人生は長い旅のようなもの**よ**。(cf. KS(C))

[4] どうして酒を飲んじゃいけないの**よ**。(cf. KS(D))

Note that [3] and [4] will change to strictly female speech, because *yo* is attached to a noun or to a nominalized clause, respectively, but other than that the crucial difference is that *sa* is far more informal than *yo*. That is why *yo* can be connected with both informal and formal forms but *sa* can be connected only with informal forms.

[5] a. A: 就職できるかな。

B: 出来ます {**よ** / ***さ**}。(cf. KS(A))

b. A: 君は日本語，読めないよね。

B: いや，読めます {**よ** / ***さ**}。(cf. KS(B))

c. 人生は長い旅のようなものです {**よ** / ***さ**}。(cf. KS(C))

Wh-word ~ *yo/sa* is always connected with informal forms, so there is no contrast between *yo* and *sa*.

d. どうして酒を飲んじゃいけないのです {*よ / *さ}。
(cf. KS(D))
(⇨ ***yo*** (DBJG: 543–47))

II. Another sentence-final particle *tomo* can replace *sa* when the latter expresses encouragement or assertion to negate someone's challenge.

[6] a. A: 就職できるかな。

B: {出来る / 出来ます} **とも**。(cf. KS(A))

b. A: 君は日本語，読めないよね。

B: いや，{読める / 読めます} **とも**。(cf. KS(B))

c. 人生は長い旅のようなもの {だ / です} **とも**。(cf. KS(C))

d. *どうして酒を飲んじゃいけないの {だ / です} **とも**。
(cf. KS(D))

[6c] is an acceptable sentence, but the use of *tomo* presupposes s.o.'s insistence that life is not like a long journey, whereas the use of *sa* does not presuppose it.

III. The sentence-final particle *ne* is fundamentally different from *sa*, because the former indicates the speaker's request for confirmation or agreement from the hearer, whereas *sa* indicates a male speaker's assertion. But both can be used in a non-sentence-final position to draw the hearer's attention to something as shown in [7]. *Sa* used this way can be used by both male and female speakers in very informal speech and sounds much more informal than *ne*. The excessive use of such *ne* and *sa* in a single sentence leads to vulgarity.

[7] 昨日(きのう)映画(えいが)を見(み)に行ったら {**ね** / **さ**}，雷(かみなり)で急(きゅう)に停電(ていでん)しちゃって {**ね** / **さ**}，ひどい目(め)に遭(あ)ったんだ。
(Yesterday I went to see a movie, y'know, and there was power failure, y'know, and I had a bad time.)

sae さえ *prt.*

an emphatic particle which expresses the idea of "even" in non-conditional clauses (or sentences) or the idea of "only" in conditional clauses

even; if ~ only; if ~ just; as long as; The only thing ~ need is

【REL. *made*; *mo*; *sura*】

◆Key Sentences

(A)

	Noun		
彼女は現代日本語はもちろん	**古典**	さえ	読める。
(She can read even classical Japanese, not to mention modern Japanese.)			

(B)

	Noun	Prt.		
この研究所には	**アメリカ**	**から**	さえ	研究者が来る。
(Researchers even from America visit this lab.)				

(C)

	Noun	Prt.		
その歌は	**子供**	**で**	さえ	知っている。
(Even children know the song.)				

(D)

Conditional Clause				Main Clause
	V*masu*			
ここに	**置いておき**	さえ	すれば	後はここの人が全部やってくれます。
(If you just leave it here, the people in this place will take care of the rest.)				

(E)

Conditional Clause				Main Clause
Noun		Vpast		
この仕事	さえ	**片付いた**	ら	後は楽なんです。
(If we can only finish (lit. If we only finish) this work, the rest will be easy.)				

Formation

(i) N さえ

鹿さえ出る (even deer appear)

さしみさえ食べる (eat even sashimi)

(ii) N (Prt.) さえ

アフリカ(へ / に)さえ行った (went even to Africa)

(iii) N Prt. さえ

こんな町にさえある (exist even in such a town)

私にさえ分かる (understandable even to me)

学校でさえ教える (teach even at school)

犬とさえ遊ぶ (play even with a dog)

中国からさえ来る (come even from China)

(iv) N (Prt.) でさえ

専門家でさえ分からない (even professionals don't understand (lit. one doesn't understand s.t. even if he is a professional))

果物でさえ食べない (don't eat even fruit (lit. don't eat s.t. even if it is fruit))

私からでさえもらわない (don't accept (s.t.) even from me (lit. don't receive s.t. even if it is from me))

(v) V*te* さえ（いる / もらう / etc.）

読んでさえいない (have not even read)

見てさえ分からない (don't understand even by looking at)

(vi) V*masu* さえする

書きさえする (even write)

(vii) Adj(*i*)stem くさえある

安くさえある (be even inexpensive)

(viii) {Adj(*na*)stem / N} でさえある

便利でさえある (be even convenient)

学者でさえある (be even a scholar)

Examples

(a) 彼はもうおかゆさえのどを通らなかった。
(He was no longer able to eat even porridge.)

(b) 私はその写真を大人にはもちろん子供にさえ見せた。
(I showed the picture even to kids, not to mention adults.)

(c) 彼は私の言うことを聞こうとさえしない。
(He doesn't even try to listen to me.)

(d) 山田にさえ出来たんだから君にも出来るよ。
(Even Yamada could do it, so you can do it, too.)

(e) 先生でさえこの問題を解くのに二時間もかかった。
(Even my teacher took (as much as) two hours to solve this problem.)

(f) クレジットカードさえあればいつでも入会出来ます。
(You can join our club any time if you only have a credit card.)

(g) 君さえ承知してくれたら今すぐこのプロジェクトを始めるつもりだ。
(As long as you agree (to our plan), we are planning to begin this project right away.)

(h) まじめに勉強してさえいれば試験は大丈夫だ。
(As long as you study seriously, you'll do okay on the exam (lit. the exam will be all right).)

(i) 手を上げさえすればすぐ警官が飛んでくる。
(If you just raise your hand, a policeman will rush to you.)

(j) 高くさえなければ売れるはずだ。
(It should sell as long as it's not expensive.)

(k) 通勤に便利でさえあればどんなところでもいいんです。
(Any location will be fine as long as it is convenient for commuting.)

(l) アメリカ人でさえあれば雇ってもらえる。
(The only thing you need in order to be hired is to be American.)

Notes

1. As the Formation shows, the particles *ga* and *o* do not appear with *sae*, the directional particles *e* and *ni* optionally precede *sae*, and the other case particles must precede *sae*.

2. When *sae* is used in a conditional clause, the clause expresses such ideas as "if only," "as long as," and "the only thing someone needs is," as in KS(D), (E), and Exs.(f) – (l). In other words, in "S_1 (conditional with *sae*), S_2" S_1 presents the only condition that must be met in order for S_2 to be true. In this structure, the *ba*-conditional (e.g., KS(D) and Ex.(f)) is most commonly used. The *tara*-conditional (e.g., KS(E) and

Ex.(g)) can be used but is less common. The *nara*-conditional is used only in limited contexts such as (1) and (2).

(1) 君**さえ**承知(してくれる)**なら**今すぐこのプロジェクトを始めるつもりだ。(cf. Ex.(g))
(As long as you agree (to our plan), we are planning to begin this project right away.)

(2) 家族**さえ**無事**なら**後は何もいらない。
(As long as my family is all right, I ask for nothing else.)

The *to*-conditional is unacceptable.

3. In conditional clauses, *sae* can appear in various positions. The focus changes according to the position, as in (3) and (4).

(3) when no auxiliary verb is involved:

a. これ**さえ**読め**ば** (if (you) read only this)

b. これを読み**さえ**すれ**ば** (if (you) only read this)

(4) when an auxiliary verb is involved:

a. これ**さえ**読んでしまえ**ば** (if (you) finish reading only this)

b. これを読み**さえ**してしまえ**ば**
(if (you) finish only reading this)

c. これを読んで**さえ**しまえ**ば**
(if (you) finish only reading this)

d. これを読んでしまい**さえ**すれ**ば**
(if (you) only finish reading)

The pattern in (4b) is not commonly used.

【Related Expressions】

I. *Made* is also used as an emphatic marker and can replace *sae*, as in [1].

[1] a. 彼女は現代日本語はもちろん古典 {**さえ** / **まで**} 読める。
(=KS(A))

b. この研究所にはアメリカから｛**さえ／まで**｝研究者が来る。 (=KS(B))

In the case of *sae* in KS(C), *made* replaces both the *sae* and the *de*.

[2] その歌は子供｛**でさえ／まで／*でまで**｝知っている。 (=KS(C))

Made, however, cannot replace *sae* in negative sentences and conditional clauses, as in [3] and [4].

[3] a. 彼はもうおかゆ｛**さえ／*まで**｝のどを通らなかった。 (=Ex.(a))

b. 彼は私の言うことを聞こうと｛**さえ／*まで**｝しない。 (=Ex.(c))

[4] a. ここに置いておき｛**さえ／*まで**｝すれば後はここの人が全部やってくれます。(=KS(D))

b. この仕事｛**さえ／*まで**｝片付いたら後は楽なんです。 (=KS(E))

(⇨ ***made*** (DBJG: 225–28))

II. The emphatic marker *sura* is very similar to *sae* but *sura* is more literary. *Sura* can replace *sae* except in conditional clauses.

[5] a. ここに置いておき｛**さえ／*すら**｝すれば後はここの人が全部やってくれます。(=KS(D))

b. この仕事｛**さえ／*すら**｝片付いたら後は楽なんです。 (=KS(E))

III. Although it is weaker than *sae*, *made*, and *sura*, the particle *mo* also functions as an emphatic marker in some contexts. First, *mo* functions as an emphatic marker in negative sentences, as in [6].

[6] a. 彼はもうおかゆ｛**さえ／も**｝のどを通らなかった。(=Ex.(a))

b. 彼は私の言うことを聞こうと｛**さえ／も**｝しない。 (=Ex.(c))

Mo can also replace *sae* after *de*, as in [7].

[7] その歌は子供で｛**さえ** / **も**｝知っている。(=KS(C))

As a matter of fact, *de* and *mo* are often used together as an emphatic particle.

Mo in ordinary affirmative sentences does not function as an emphatic marker. Compare [8a] and [8b].

[8] a. この研究所にはアメリカから**さえ**研究者が来る。(=KS(B))

b. この研究所にはアメリカから**も**研究者が来る。
(Researchers visit this lab from America, too.)

In addition, *mo* cannot replace *sae* in conditional clauses.

[9] a. ここに置いておき｛**さえ** / ***も**｝すれば後はここの人が全部やってくれます。(=KS(D))

b. この仕事｛**さえ** / ***も**｝片付いたら後は楽なんです。(=KS(E))

(⇨ ***demo*** (DBJG: 111–13); ***mo***[2] (DBJG: 250–53))

S

sai (ni) 際(に) *n. / conj.*

on the special occasion of / when

when; on the occasion of; at the time of

【REL. *ba'ai*; ***ni attatte/atari***; *ori ni*; *toki ni*】

◆Key Sentences

(A)

	Vinf		
詳しいことは八月に	**上京する**	際に,	お話し致します。
(I will tell you the details when I come down to Tokyo in August.)			

(B)

	Noun			
これは	**大学卒業**	の	際に	父が買ってくれたワープロです。
(This is a word processor which my father bought me on the occasion of my college graduation.)				

(C)

Noun			
私達の結婚	に	際して	過分のお祝い物を頂き恐縮しております。
(I feel much obliged to have received such an unmerited gift on the occasion of our wedding.)			

Formation

(i) Vinf 際(に)

{買う / 買った} 際(に) (when s.o. buys / bought s.t.)

(ii) N の際(に)

試験の際(に) (at the time of an examination)

(iii) N に際して

入学に際して (on the occasion of entering a school)

(iv) {この / その / あの} 際

この際 (on this occasion)

Examples

(a) 大阪に転勤する際に，妻子は東京に残した。
(When I transferred to Osaka I left my wife and children behind in Tokyo.)

(b) 激しい運動をする際には準備運動が必要だ。
(When you engage in strenuous exercise, you need to do stretch exercises.)

(c) 首相はサミット会談に出席した際に国際収支に関する日本側の立場を説明した。
(When the premier attended the summit meeting, he explained Japanese views on balance of international payments.)

(d) 出発の際には，わざわざお見送りに来ていただき，ありがとうございました。
(Thank you very much for taking the time to see me off at the time of my departure.)

(e) 旅行の際には必ずカメラを持って行きます。
(When I go on a trip I always take my camera with me.)

(f) 近くにおいでの際には，ぜひお立ち寄り下さい。
(Please call on us when you happen to be in our neighborhood.)

(g) 日本の近代化の研究に際して日本の国立国会図書館を利用した。
(At the time of my research on Japanese modernization I used the National Diet Library of Japan.)

(h) この際，私が直接社長に話してみます。
(Since this is an important occasion (lit. on this occasion), I will talk directly to the president (and see what happens).)

(i) これは帰国の際ホストファミリーのお父さんがくれた腕時計です。
(This is a wrist watch which my host family father gave me when I left for home.)

Notes

1. ~ *sai* (*ni*) is used to indicate a special occasion on which s.o. does s.t. So, the phrase cannot be used on common occasions as in (1) and (2).

   (1) 朝起きた {**時** / ***際**} 熱があった。
   (When I got up in the morning I had a fever.)

   (2) a. 図書館に行った {**時** / ***際**} 本を三冊借りた。
   (When I went to the library I checked out 3 books.)

   b. 研究費をもらって国立国会図書館へ行った {**時** / **際**}, 本を十二冊借り出した。
   (When I received research money and went to the National Diet Library I checked out a dozen books.)

   Notice that the occasion of going to the library is far more special in (2b) than in (2a). That is why *sai* is acceptable in (2b) but not in (2a).

2. Only Vinf or N or demonstrative adjectives *kono*, *sono*, *ano* can be used before *sai ni*. Vinf · nonpast and Vinf · past indicate incompletion and completion, respectively, in relation to the action in the main clause. *Kono sai* as exemplified by Ex.(h) can be used only when the occasion is special.

3. The particle *ni* of *sai ni* may be dropped. When *ni* is dropped as in Ex.(i), the focus shifts from the occasion to what is described in the main clause.

4. ~ *sai ni* is a formal expression that is often used with Sino-Japanese words, as shown in all the KS and Exs. except Ex.(f). Notice that in Ex.(f), an honorific-polite Japanese verb is used. In the following sentences in which neither a Sino-Japanese verb / noun nor a honorific-polite verb is used *sai ni* is unacceptable.

   (3) a. 詳しいことは八月に来る {**時** / ***際**} に，話します。 (cf. KS(A))

   b. 近くに来た {**時** / ***際**} には，ぜひ寄ってね。(cf. Ex.(f))

5. N *ni saishite* is more formal than N *no sai ni*. When the former is used, N has to express a very special occasion as in KS(C) and Ex.(g). If N expresses an occasion which is not so special as in Ex.(e), N *no sai ni* cannot be replaced by N *ni saishite*.

   (4) 旅行 {**の際には** / ??**に際して**} 必ずカメラを持って行きます。 (= Ex.(e))

【Related Expressions】

I. *Sai ni* indicates the time when s.t. special takes place,whereas *ori ni* indicates an occasion when s.t. ordinary takes place.

   [1] a. 京都にいらっしゃる {**折** / ***際**} にはご連絡下さい。
   (If you have a chance to come to Kyoto, please let me know.)

   b. ビルは結婚する {**際** / ***折**} に両親の許可を得ていなかった。
   (When Bill got married he hadn't obtained his parents' permission.)

For the difference between *toki ni* and *sai ni*, see Note 1 above.

(⇨ ***toki*** (DBJG: 490–94))

II. There is another expression *ba'ai*, 'case,' which is used in the form of Vinf *ba'ai* or N *no ba'ai*.

   [2] a. 先生がいらっしゃる {**場合** / **時** / **際**} は私がお供致します。
   (If you go I will accompany you. / If the teacher goes I will accompany him.)

   b. 雨が降った {**場合** / **時** / ***際**} はハイキングは中止です。
   (If it rains the hiking will be cancelled.)

   c. 火災の {**場合** / **時** / **際**} はエレベーターを使わないで下さい。
   (In case of fire please don't use the elevator.)

Ba'ai means 'a suppositional case,' so an event that precedes it may not take place. So if the event is a real event, *ba'ai* cannot be used.

[3] a. 去年パリに行った{**際** / **時** / ***場合**}ミッシェルに会った。
(When I went to Paris last year, I met Michelle.)

b. 僕が入院した{**際** / **時** / ***場合**}友達が見舞に来てくれた。
(When I was hospitalized, my friend came to see me.)

sasuga　さすが　*adv.*

an adverb that expresses the speaker / writer's strong feeling that s.t. has turned out as s / he expected

as might be expected; after all; it is only natural that ~; naturally; truly; really; indeed; impressive

【REL. *yahari*】

◆Key Sentences

(A)

			Main Clause
ネルソンさんは日本に三年留学していたので,	さすが	に	**日本語が上手です。**
(Because Mr. Nelson has studied in Japan for three years, naturally he speaks Japanese well.)			

(B)

		Noun		
さすが	(は)	**広島のかき**	だ。	実においしい。
(After all, they are Hiroshima oysters. They are really good.)				

(C)

	Noun		
さすが	**元ボートの選手**	だけ {あって / に},	体格がいい。
(After all, he is a former boating man. He has a fine physique.)			

(D)

	Subordinate Clause		
さすが,	**パリで十年暮らした**	だけ {あって / に},	彼は大変なフランス通だ。
(It is only natural that he is well versed in things French, because he lived in Paris for 10 years.)			

(E)

			Noun		
難しい質問に,	さすが	の	**大先生**	も,	困ってしまった。
(The great teacher that he was, even he had a hard time answering the difficult question.)					

Formation

(i) さすがに S

さすがに, 疲れた。 (It is only natural that I got tired.)

(ii) さすが(は) Nだ

さすが(は)日本の車だ。 (After all, it is a Japanese car.)

(iii) さすが {V / Adj(*i*)}inf だけ {あって / に}

さすがよく {勉強する / 勉強した} だけ {あって / に}
(as might be expected from the fact that s.o. studies / has studied hard)

さすが｛面白い / 面白かった｝だけ｛あって / に｝
(as might be expected from the fact that s.t. is / was interesting)

(iv) さすが｛N (ø / だった) / Adj(*na*) (な / だった)｝だけ｛あって / に｝

さすが｛若い人 / 若い人だった｝だけ｛あって / に｝
(as might be expected from the fact that s.o. is / was a young person)

さすが｛きれいな / きれいだった｝だけ｛あって / に｝
(as might be expected from the fact that s.t. / s.o. {is / was} beautiful)

(v) さすがの N も

さすがの天才も　(even a genius)

Examples

(a) 昨日は十時間も運転をしたので，さすがに疲れました。
(Yesterday I drove a car for 10 hours, so I got tired, as might be expected.)

(b) 運動を何もしないで，食べてばかりいたから，さすがに太ってしまった。
(It is only natural that I gained weight, because I was just eating without doing any exercise.)

(c) いつも，CDで音楽を聞いているんですが，生のコンサートはさすがにいいですね。
(I'm always listening to music on CDs, but concerts are good, after all.)

(d) さすが(は)本場のイタリア料理だ。日本のイタリア料理とは味が違う。
(After all, it is authentic Italian cuisine in Italy. It tastes different from the Italian cuisine in Japan.)

(e) さすが(は)科学者だ。観察が鋭い。
(After all, he is a scientist. He makes sharp observations.)

(f) さすが，若い頃山に登っていただけに，今でも足が強い。
(As may be expected of a person who used to climb mountains in his young days, he still has strong legs.)

(g) さすがの父も，今度の入院はこたえたようだ。
(Even on my father the recent hospitalization seemed to have been hard.)

(h) さすがの先生にも，解答が分からなかった。
(The great teacher that he was, even he couldn't figure out the solution.)

(i) 彼は肉が大好物のようで，大きなステーキを二枚も平らげたのはさすがだった。
(He seems to like meat a lot and it was impressive that he ate two large steaks.)

(j) ジョンはさすがだね。ビールを十本も飲んでしまったよ。
(As might be expected of John, he drank 10 bottles of beer.)

Notes

1. *Sasuga* expresses one's strong feeling that s.t. has turned out as one expected, as shown in KS(A) – (D), Exs.(a) – (f), (i) and (j), or that s.t. has turned out to be contrary to one's expectation, as in KS(E), Exs.(g) and (h) as one has not expected.

2. In the structure *sasuga wa* X *da*, *wa* can be omitted.

3. *Sasuga ~ dake* may take either *atte* or *ni* as shown in KS(C), (D) and Ex.(f).

4. In the case of *sasuga no* X *mo*, the speaker wants to say that s.t. has occurred contrary to what one can expect from the characteristics of X, as in KS(E), Exs.(g) and (h).

5. *Sasuga* can be used like an exclamation in conversational Japanese.

   (1) A: 山田は司法試験に一度で受かったそうだよ。
   (I heard that Yamada passed the bar examination on his first attempt.)

   B: **さすが！**
   (I knew he would.)

【Related Expression】

Another adverb *yahari / yappari* is similar to *sasuga*. For examples, *sasuga ni* of KS(A) – (D) can be replaced by *yahari / yappari*. However *yahari* does not express the strong feeling of fulfillment of expectation that is expressed by *sasuga*.

[1] ネルソンさんは日本に三年留学していたので，**やはり**日本語が上手です。(cf. KS(A))
(As expected, Mr. Nelson speaks Japanese well, because he has studied in Japan for three years.)

[2] **やっぱり**広島のかきだ。実においしい。(cf. KS(B))
(After all, they are Hiroshima oysters. They are really good.)

Also to be noted is the fact that *yahari* does not have prenominal nor precopula use, as shown in [3].

[3] a. 難しい質問に，{**さすが** / ***やっぱり**} の大先生も，困ってしまった。(=KS(E))

b. ジョンは {**さすが** / ***やはり**} だね。ビールを十本も飲んでしまったよ。(=Ex.(j))

(⇨ ***yahari*** (DBJG: 538–40))

S

sei せい *n.*

a dependent noun expressing a cause which brings about an undesirable result	because; due to 【REL. *okage*; *tame* (*ni*)】

◆Key Sentences

(A)

	Noun				
今年は	**不況**	の	せい	で	車があまり売れない。
(Because of the depression, cars are not selling well this year.)					

(B)

Noun				
寝不足	の	せい	か	体に力が入らない。
(Because of lack of sleep, I suppose, I feel weak (lit. the body has no power).)				

(C)

Clause (result)			Noun			
私が失敗した	の	は	**彼**	の	せい	だ。
(It is because of him that I failed.)						

(D)

Clause_1 (cause)			Clause_2 (result)
昨夜飲みすぎた	せい	で	今日は頭がふらふらする。
(I am dizzy today because I drank too much last night.)			

Formation

(i) N のせい（で / か / etc.)

過労のせいで (because of overworking)

S

(ii) Sinf せい（で / か / etc.） (the same as the relative clause formation)

働きすぎたせいで (because s.o. worked too hard)

Examples

(a) 最近運動不足のせいで体重が増えた。
(I've gained weight because of lack of exercise these days.)

(b) 雨が少なかったせいで今年は米が不作だそうだ。
(It is reported that becaue there was little rain, we are going to have a bad crop of rice this year.)

(c) 年のせいか最近耳が聞こえにくくなった。
(Due to my age, I suppose, I cannot hear well these days.)

(d) 新しい土地に来て水が変わったせいか近頃おなかの調子がよくない。
(Maybe because I have moved to a new place and the water is different, my stomach is uncomfortable these days.)

(e) 目が悪くなったのは一日中コンピュータを使って仕事をしているせいだ。
(It is because you work with a computer all day that your eyesight has deteriorated.)

(f) 彼はよく自分の失敗を人のせいにする。
(He often blames others for his own failure (lit. claims that his own failure is due to others).)

(g) これは誰のせいでもない。
(This is (due to) no one's fault.)

Notes

1. *Sei* is a dependent noun; therefore, it needs a modifying word, phrase, or clause.

2. *Sei de* is used only when the result is undesirable. Thus, (1a) is acceptable but (1b) is unnatural.

   (1) a. 彼女がいる**せいで**仕事があまり出来ない。
   (Because she is here, I cannot do a lot of work.)

b. 彼女がいる｛**から** / **ので** / **ために** / ???**せいで**｝仕事がよく出来る。
(Because she is here, I can do a lot of work.)

Sei ka, however, is used whether the result is desirable or undesirable, as in (2), KS(B), Exs.(c) and (d).

(2) a. 彼女がいる**せいか**仕事がよく出来る。
(I think it is because she is here that I can do a lot of work.)

b. 排気ガス規制が効を奏した**せいか**近頃空気が前よりきれいになった。
(Because the emission control rules have worked, I suppose, the air has become cleaner than before.)

c. 薬を飲んだら気の**せいか**少し気分がよくなった。
(I feel a little better after taking medicine, although it might be my imagination.)

3. *Sei de* is used when the speaker finds the cause of an undesirable result to be beyond his / her control, as in KS(A). Thus, if the cause is within the speaker's control, *sei de* cannot be used, as in (3).

(3) a. 漢字をあまり知らない｛**から** / **ので** / **ために** / ***せいで**｝新聞が読めない。
(I cannot read newspapers because I don't know many kanji.)

Sei ka has no such restriction as KS(B) and Ex.(c) show.

4. *Sei* cannot be used to express a reason. The following sentences are ungrammatical.

(4) a. 宿題がたくさんある｛**から** / **ので** / **ために** / ***せいで**｝パーティーには行けない。
(I cannot go to the party because I have a lot of homework.)

b. 誰も手伝ってくれない｛**から** / **ので** / **ために** / ***せいで**｝一人でやらなければならない。
(Because no one will help me, I have to do it by myself.)

【Related Expressions】

I. *Okage* and *sei* are similar in that both express a cause. The difference is that *okage* is used when the result is desirable, as in [1]. Note also that *okage* implies that the person who attained the result is thankful for the cause.

[1] a. 安全ベルトの**おかげで**命が助かった。
(The safety belt saved my life. (lit. My life was saved thanks to the safety belt.))

b. 彼女が手伝ってくれた**おかげで**仕事が早く片付いた。
(Because she helped me, I could finish my work quickly.)

c. 学生時代によく英語を勉強しておいた**おかげで**今アメリカにいてもあまり困らない。
(Because I studied English hard when I was a student, I don't have much trouble with my life in America now.)

Okage is sometimes used with an undesirable result for the purpose of sarcasm, as in [2].

[2] a. 君の**おかげで**ひどい目に遭ったよ。
(I had a terrible time thanks to you.)

b. お前が余計なことをしてくれた**おかげで**計画が台無しになった。
(Because you did something unnecessary, thanks to you, our plan was ruined.)

II. *Tame* (*ni*) can also express a cause (as well as a reason), as in [3].

[3] a. 今年は不況の**ために**車があまり売れない。(=KS(A))

b. 寝不足の**ためか**体に力が入らない。(=KS(B))

c. 昨夜飲みすぎた**ために**今日は頭がふらふらする。(=KS(D))

Unlike *sei*, *tame* (*ni*) has no such restrictions as those in Notes 2, 3, and 4.

(⇨ ***tame* (*ni*)** (DBJG: 447–51))

semete せめて *adv.*

an adverb that indicates the speaker / writer's minimally satisfactory level	at least 【REL. *sukunakutomo*】

◆Key Sentences

(A)

		Number + Counter		
百点(ひゃくてん)とは言(い)いませんが,	せめて	**八十点(はちじってん)**	ぐらいは	取(と)りたいです。
(I am not saying that I want to get 100 points, but I would like to get at least 80 points.)				

(B)

	Noun		
せめて	**なべ**	(だけ)でも	あれば，ご飯(はん)が炊(た)けるんですが。
(If we had a pan, at least, we would be able to cook rice.)			

(C)

	Noun	Prt.		
せめて	**両親(りょうしん)**	に	は	分(わ)かってもらいたいんですが。
(I wanted at least my parents to understand me.)				

Formation

(i) せめて Number + Counter (ぐらい)～

せめて二時間(にじかん)ぐらい (at least two hours)

(ii) せめて N {ぐらい/(だけ)でも}

S

せめて新聞 {ぐらい / (だけ)でも} (at least a newspaper)

(iii) せめて N Prt.

せめて妻に (at least to my wife)

Examples

(a) せめて一年に十日ぐらい，休暇が取れるといいんですが。
(I wish I could take at least 10-day's leave each year.)

(b) 日本にいる間に，せめて一度ぐらいは会いに来て下さい。
(Please come and see me at least once while you are in Japan.)

(c) 美人でなくてもいいけど，せめて，可愛らしい女の子と結婚したい。
(It's alright if she is not a real beauty. But I would like to marry at least a cute girl.)

(d) 日本に行くんだから，せめて，日本語だけは勉強して来ようと思っています。
(I am going to Japan, so, I'm thinking of learning at least Japanese.)

(e) せめてもう後一日生きていたら，父の死に目に会えたのに。
(If my father lived at least one day longer I could have been with him when he died.)

(f) あんなに広い家でなくてもいいけど，せめてもう一部屋あるといいのに。
(I don't need that spacious house, but I wish I had at least another room.)

(g) 一月もご厄介になるんですから，せめて，皿洗いぐらいはさせて下さい。
(I'm going to stay at your house for a month, so please let me wash the dishes, at least.)

(h) せめて日本語で日常会話ぐらいは出来るようになりたいです。
(I would like to become able to engage in daily conversation in Japanese.)

Note

Semete indicates the speaker / writer's minimally satisfactory level; he is well aware that he cannot realize an ideal state. Each sentence ends in a direct or indirect expression of desire, such as *-tai* as in KS(A), (C), Exs.(c) and (h), *(to ii) n desu ga* as in KS(B) and Ex.(a), *noni* as in Exs.(e) and (f), *-(sase) te kudasai* as in Exs.(b) and (g) and *-yō to omotte imasu* in Ex.(d). Of these, *noni* of Ex.(e) and (f) express counter-factual desire.

【Related Expression】

Sukunakutomo is another adverb with the meaning of 'at least.' The crucial difference between *sukunakutomo* and *semete* is that the former focuses on rather objective lower limits of number / quantity; whereas the latter on the speaker's strong desire to realize a certain minimum level of satisfaction. So all the KS and Exs. of *semete* can be rephrased by *sukunakutomo*, but the following use of *sukunakutomo* cannot be rephrased by *semete*, because it does not express the speaker's desire; it merely expresses the speaker's estimation of numbers / quantity.

[1] a. この大学の学生数は {**少なくとも / *せめて**} 三万だろう。
(I guess that enrollment at this university is at least 30,000.)

b. この車は {**少なくとも / *せめて**} 三百万円はするだろう。
(This car will cost at least 3,000,000 yen.)

c. 今学期漢字を {**少なくとも / *せめて**} 千字は覚えたはずだ。
(This semester I'm supposed to have memorized at least 1,000 kanji.)

shidai 次第 *conj. / n.*

a conjunction / noun to express that an action indicated by a preceding verb or an action implied by a preceding noun is a prerequisite for another action

as soon as; depend on
【REL. *ni yoru*; *-tara sugu*】

◆Key Sentences

(A)

	V*masu*		
大阪に	**着き**	次第,	お電話を差し上げます。
(As soon as I get to Osaka, I will call you.)			

(B)

	VN		
原稿は	**完成**	次第	お送り致します。
(I will send my manuscipts as soon they are completed.)			

(C)

	Noun	
世の中で成功するかしないかは	**あなたの努力**	次第ですよ。
(Whether you succeed in the world or not depends on your efforts.)		

Formation

S

(i) V*masu* 次第

読み次第 (as soon as s.o. has read s.t.)

帰り次第 (as soon as s.o. has returned)

Exceptions:

いらっしゃり次第 (as soon as s.o. comes / goes there)

おっしゃり次第 (as soon as s.o. says it)

なさり次第 (as soon as s.o. does s.t.)

(ii) VN 次第

帰国次第 (as soon as s.o. comes back to his / her country)

到着次第 (as soon as s.o. / s.t. arrives)

(iii) (X は) N 次第だ / で

(農業は)天気次第だ (Farming depends on the weather.)

給料次第で (depending on the salary)

Examples

(a) 夫は仕事が終わり次第，毎日まっすぐ帰宅します。
(My husband comes straight home every day, as soon as he has finished his work.)

(b) 空港から電話があり次第，お迎えに参ります。
(I will go to pick you up as soon as you call me from the airport.)

(c) 山岸先生がいらっしゃり次第，会議を始めたいと思います。
(As soon as Professor Yamagishi comes here I'd like to begin our meeting.)

(d) 東大を卒業次第，京大の大学院に入学するつもりだ。
(Upon graduation from the University of Tokyo, I intend to enter the Graduate School of Kyoto University.)

(e) お尋ねの件は，判明次第，ご連絡申し上げます。
(On the matter you have inquired about, I will inform you as soon as I find out.)

(f) レセプションが終了次第，晩餐会を始めます。
(As soon as the reception is finished we will start the dinner party.)

(g) 就職はコネ次第ですよ。
(Finding employment depends on connections.)

(h) 「地獄の沙汰も金次第(だ)」ということわざを知っていますか。
(Do you know the proverb "Even affairs in hell depend on money" ?)

(i) ご注文次第で，どんな物でも料理致します。
(Depending on your orders, I will cook you anything you like.)

(j) 条件次第では，その仕事を引き受けたいと思います。
(Depending on the employment terms I would like to accept that job.)

Notes

1. V*masu* / VN *shidai* and N *shidai da/de* mean ‘as soon as’ and ‘depends on / depending on,’ respectively. What is common to both cases is that an action or state indicated by the preceding verb or noun is a prerequisite for another action or state expressed in the main predicate.

2. The V*masu* of V*masu shidai* can hardly be *suru*-verb, probably because it will create a sequence of *shi-shi* which is hard to pronounce.

   (1) ??東大を**卒業し**次第，京大の大学院に入学するつもりだ。
   (cf. Ex.(d))

   (2) ??お尋ねの件は，**判明し**次第，ご連絡申し上げます。
   (cf. Ex.(e))

3. As noted in Formation, as far as V*masu shidai* is concerned, the V*masu* forms of honorific, polite verbs such as *irassharu*, *ossharu*, *nasaru* are not *irasshai-*, *osshai-*, and *nasai-*, but *irasshari-*, *osshari-*, and *nasari-*, respectively.

4. For the *shidai* structure, the main clause cannot be past tense.

   (3) a. ??夫は仕事が終わり次第，毎日まっすぐ帰宅しました。
   (My husband came straight home every day, as soon as he finished his work.)

   → 夫は仕事が終わるとすぐ，毎日まっすぐ帰宅しました。

   b. *空港から電話があり次第，迎えに行った。
   (As soon as I received a call from the airport I went to pick him up.)

   → 空港から電話があってすぐ，迎えに行った。

【Related Expressions】

I. There is another structure *-tara sugu* with the meaning of ‘as soon as.’ The crucial difference between V*masu* / VN *shidai* and *-tara sugu* is that the former expresses a planned sequence of two actions, whereas the latter can express any kind of sequence of two actions. Examples in [1] and [2] show that both forms can be used to express a planned sequence and those in [3] show that V*masu shidai* cannot be used in a non-planned non-controllable sequence. In this case *-tara sugu* is much better than *shidai*, but slightly marginal and should be replaced by *-tara mamonaku*.

[1] a. 空港から電話が｛あり**次第**／あっ**たらすぐ**｝，お迎えに参ります。(=Ex.(b))

b. 山岸先生が｛いらっしゃり**次第**／いらっしゃっ**たらすぐ**｝，会議を始めたいと思います。(=Ex.(c))

[2] a. 原稿は完成｛**次第**／し**たらすぐ**｝お送り致します。 (=KS(B))

b. 東大を卒業｛**次第**／し**たらすぐ**｝，京大の大学院に入学するつもりだ。(=Ex.(d))

[3] a. 家に｛帰っ**たら間もなく**／帰っ**たらすぐ**／*帰り**次第**｝，地震が起きた。
(As soon as I got home there was an earthquake.)

b. 彼は日本に｛行っ**たら間もなく**／行っ**たらすぐ**／*行き**次第**｝病気になった。
(As soon as he got to Japan he got ill.)

II. N *shidai da* in KS(C) and Exs.(g) – (j) can be replaced by N *ni yoru*, as shown in [4].

[4] a. 世の中で成功するかしないかはあなたの努力**によります**よ。 (cf. KS(C))

b. 就職はコネ**によります**よ。(cf. Ex.(g))

c. ご注文**によって**，どんなものでも料理致します。(cf. Ex.(i))

But not all cases of N *ni yoru* can be replaced by N *shidai da*, because the former has a wider meaning: N *ni yoru* indicates 'cause' for s.t. as in [5a], 'means' as in [5b], or 'source' as in [5c]. N *ni yoru* cannot be replaced by N *shidai da* in any of these, simply because the latter lacks these particular meanings.

[5] a. その怪我は不注意 {**による** / ***次第だ**}。
(That injury is due to carelessness.)

b. 彼は政治的手腕 {**によって** / ***次第で**}, 世の中で成功した。
(He succeeded in this world by means of his political skills.)

c. ラジオに {**よると** / ***次第で**} 明日は雪だそうだ。
(According to the radio, it will snow tomorrow.)

(⇨ ***ni yotte*/*yori***)

shika mo しかも *conj.*

a conjunction which is used to provide additional important information

moreover; furthermore; besides; on top of that; what's more; what's worse; more surprisingly; at that; nevertheless; and yet; even so

【REL. *omake ni*; *sono ue*; *sore de ite*; *sore mo*; *sore ni*; (*sore*) *ni mo kakawarazu*】

◆**Key Sentences**

(A)

Topic	Comment$_1$		Comment$_2$
最近(さいきん)のテープレコーダーは	小(ちい)さくて軽(かる)く,	しかも	音(おと)がすばらしくよくなった。
(The tape recorders available these days are compact and light, and on top of that, their sound has improved greatly.)			

(B)

Sentence		Phrase / Sentence
彼(かれ)は家(いえ)を買(か)った。	しかも	大(おお)きい庭付(にわつ)きのを(だ)。
(He bought a house, and more surprisingly, a house with a large yard.)		

(C)

Sentence$_1$		Sentence$_2$
彼はいつも夜遅(よるおそ)くまで勉強(べんきょう)し,	しかも	朝(あさ)は誰(だれ)よりも早(はや)く起(お)きる。
(He studies till late every night; nevertheless, he gets up earlier than anyone else.)		

S

Formation

(i) {V / Adj. / N + Cop.} *te* しかも

結婚(けっこん)していて, しかも子供(こども)までいる (S.o. is married, and what's more, s/he even has a child.)

面白(おもしろ)くて, しかもただだ (S.t. is interesting, and what's more, it is free of charge.)

ハンサムで, しかもお金持(かねも)ちだ (S.o. is handsome, and what's more, he is rich.)

失業中で，しかも病気だ (S.o. is out of work, and what's worse, s/he is ill.)

(ii) V*masu* しかも

よく働き，しかも不平を言わない (S.o. works hard, and yet (*or* nevertheless), s/he does not complain.)

(iii) Adj(*i*)*ku* しかも

値段が安く，しかも丈夫だ (S.t. is cheap; futhermore, it's durable.)

(iv) S_1。しかも S_2。

この仕事は面白い。しかも給料がいい。(This job is interesting. On top of that, the pay is good.)

Examples

(a) 彼女は美人でしかも頭がいい。男子学生が夢中になるのも無理はない。
(She is pretty, and what's more, (she is) smart. It is natural that boys (lit. male students) should be crazy about her.)

(b) 日本語は語彙が英語と全然違うし文法も難しい。しかも，日本語には漢字がある。
(Japanese has entirely different vocabulary from English, and the grammar is also difficult. On top of that, Japanese has kanji.)

(c) あのレストランの定食はおいしくて安い。しかも，ボリュームがあるから学生や若いサラリーマンに人気がある。
(That restaurant's *teishoku* (set meal) is good and reasonable. On top of that, it is substantial (lit. it has volume), so it is popular among students and young white-collar workers.)

(d) 彼はこの大雨の中を出かけて行った。しかも，傘も持たずに。
(He went out in this heavy rain, and more surprisingly, without an umbrella.)

(e) 彼は試験に遅刻してしまった。しかも，三十分も。
(He was late for the exam, and what's worse, as much as thirty minutes late.)

(f) 彼女は英語のほかに四か国語を話す。しかも，すべて母国語話者のように。
(She speaks four languages besides English, and more surprisingly, she speaks all of them like a native speaker.)

(g) 私は風邪を引いてしまった。しかも，大事な試験の前日にだ。
(I caught a cold, and at that on the day before an important exam.)

(h) 彼はどんなつらい仕事でも黙ってこなし，しかも，給料についてほかの者のように不平を言わなかった。
(No matter how hard the job was, he did it quietly, and what's more, he did not complain about his salary like the others did.)

(i) 彼女は何をやっても上手で，しかも，その才能をひけらかさない。
(She is good at everything, but even so, she does not show off her talents.)

Notes

1. Basically, *shika mo* has three uses. First, *shika mo* is used when one provides additional important characteristics of s.o. or s.t., as in KS(A) and Exs.(a) – (c). Second, *shika mo* is used when one adds special information to a statement about a rather uncommon action or state, as in KS(B) and Exs.(d) – (g). Third, *shika mo* is used when one provides information which is rather unexpected from the preceding statement, as in KS(C), Exs.(h) and (i).

2. In the second use, additional information can be provided with an independent phrase, as in Exs.(d) – (f), or with a sentence, as in Ex.(g). However, the version with an independent phrase is more common.

【Related Expressions】

I. *Shika mo* in the first use described in Note 1 can be replaced by *sono ue*, *omake ni*, or *sore ni*, as in [1].

[1] a. 最近のテープレコーダーは小さくて軽く，{**しかも / その上 / おまけに / それに**} 音がすばらしくよくなった。
(=KS(A))

b. 彼女は美人で｛**しかも** / **その上** / **おまけに** / **それに**｝頭がいい。(=Ex.(a))

c. 日本語は語彙が英語と全然違うし文法も難しい。｛**しかも** / **その上** / **おまけに** / **それに**｝, 日本語には漢字がある。(=Ex.(b))

d. あのレストランの定食はおいしくて安い。｛**しかも** / **その上** / **おまけに** / **それに**｝ボリュームがあるから学生や若いサラリーマンに人気がある。(=Ex.(c))

(⇨ ***sono ue***; ***sore ni***)

II. *Shika mo* in the second use described in Note 1 can be replaced by *sore mo*, as in [2].

[2] a. 彼は家を買った。｛**しかも** / **それも**｝大きい庭付きのを(だ)。(=KS(B))

b. 彼はこの大雨の中を出かけていった。｛**しかも** / **それも**｝, 傘も持たずに。(=Ex.(d))

c. 彼は試験に遅刻してしまった。｛**しかも** / **それも**｝, 三十分も。(=Ex.(e))

d. 彼女は英語のほかに四か国語を話す。｛**しかも** / **それも**｝, すべて母国語話者のように。(=Ex.(f))

e. 私は風邪を引いてしまった。｛**しかも** / **それも**｝, 大事な試験の前日にだ。(=Ex.(g))

(⇨ ***sore mo***)

III. *Shika mo* in the third use described in Note 1 can be replaced by *sore de ite* or (*sore*) *ni mo kakawarazu*, as in [3].

[3] a. 彼はいつも夜遅くまで勉強し, ｛**しかも** / **それでいて** / (**それ**)**にもかかわらず**｝朝は誰よりも早く起きる。(=KS(C))

b. 彼はどんなつらい仕事でも黙ってこなし, ｛**しかも** / **それでいて** / (**それ**)**にもかかわらず**｝, 給料についてほかの者のように不平を言わなかった。(=Ex.(h))

S

c. 彼女は何をやっても上手で，{**しかも / それでいて** / (**それ**) **にもかかわらず**}，その才能をひけらかさない。(=Ex.(i))

(⇨ ***ni mo kakawarazu***)

shitagatte したがって *conj.* <w>

a conjunction that is used to indicate that a result / situation follows necessarily from the foregoing situation

therefore; accordingly; consequently

【REL. *da kara*】

◆**Key Sentence**

Sentence$_1$		Sentence$_2$
予算が不足している。	したがって	この計画は実行できない。
(The budget is insufficient. Therefore this plan cannot be implemented.)		

Formation

S$_1$。したがって S$_2$。

雨がよく降る。したがって緑が多い。

(It rains a lot. Therefore there is a lot of greenery.)

Examples

(a) 今週は重役達は朝から晩まで会議で忙しい。したがって好きなゴルフをする暇もない。
(This week the executives are busy attending meetings from morning till night. Therefore they don't even have time for their favorite pastime of golf.)

(b) 運動をすると，エネルギーを使う。したがって太らない。
(If you do exercise, you use energy. Accordingly you don't gain weight.)

(c) 日本の車は故障が少ない。したがってよく売れる。
(Japanese cars have fewer troubles. Therefore they sell well.)

(d) 彼女は日本に五年も住んでいた。したがって日本のことをよく知っている。
(She lived in Japan for five years. Therefore she knows a lot about Japan.)

(e) 日本では父親はあまり家にいない。したがって母親が子供の教育をすることになる。
(In Japan fathers are seldom at home. Therefore mothers are in charge of their children's education.)

Notes

1. "S_1. *Shitagatte* S_2" is used to express that S_2 naturally results from S_1. The focus of the conjunction is more on the result than the cause.
2. *Shitagatte* is used either in written Japanese or in formal speech.
3. If what is expressed in S_1 is a reason for what is expressed in S_2, *shitagatte* cannot be used; *da kara* has to be used.

(1) a. *過半数の人が賛成した。**したがって**私も賛成した。

b. 過半数の人が賛成した。**だから**私も賛成した。
(The majority of the people agreed. Therefore I also agreed.)

【Related Expression】

The conjunction *da kara* can replace *shitagatte* in all the KS and Exs., but not vice versa, because the former can express both reason-action and cause-result relations, but the latter expresses cause-result relation only. (See Note 3.)

[1] a. この本の書評はよかった。{**だから** / ***したがって**} 私は買って読んだ。
(The review of this book was good, so I bought it and read it.)

b. 今日は天気がよかった。{**だから** / ***したがって**} 私はハイキングに出かけた。
(It was a fine day, so I went out hiking.)

sō ka to itte そうかと言って *phr. / conj.*

a structure which expresses that the speaker / writer cannot easily accept the corollary from the preceding statement owing to some circumstances, although he feels like accepting it

but; yet; even so
【REL. (*sō*) *desu ga*; *keredo*(*mo*); *shikashi*】

S

◆Key Sentences

(A)

A:
魚は体にいいそうですよ。
(I hear that fish is good for your health.)

B:	
そうかと言って,	毎日魚ばかりを食べているわけにもいかないでしょう。
(But we couldn't eat just fish every day, you know.)	

(B)

$Sentence_1$			$Sentence_2$
アメリカの方が土地も家も安い	が，	そうかと言って，	簡単に移住するわけにもいかない。
(Land and housing are less expensive in America, but we cannot easily immigrate.)			

Formation

(i) A: S_1。

B: そうかと言って，S_2。

A: 漫画は面白いですね。
(Comic books are fun.)

B: そうかと言って，漫画ばかり読んでいるわけにもいきませんよ。
(But you can't read just comic books, you know.)

(ii) S_1 が，そうかと言って，S_2。

漫画は面白いですが，そうかと言って，漫画ばかり読んでいるわけにもいきませんよ。(Comic books are fun, but you can't read just comic books, you know.)

S

Examples

(a) A: 手ぶらで来て下さいと言っていましたよ。
(He told me not to bring anything.)

B: そうかと言って，何も持って行かないわけにもいかないでしょうね。
(But, we cannot go there empty handed, you know.)

(b) A: 明日の試験はとてもやさしいそうですよ。
(They say that tomorrow's examination is very easy.)

B: そうかと言って，何も勉強しないわけにもいかないでしょう。
(But still, it can't mean that we don't need to study at all.)

(c) A: 来週は連休だから，遊べますね。
(There are consecutive holidays next week, so we can have fun.)

B: そうかと言って，ゴルフばかりしているわけにもいかないね。
(But, I cannot just play golf, you know.)

(d) A: たばこは体に悪いですよ。
(Cigarettes are bad for your health, you know.)

B: そうかと言って，たばこに代わる物が見つからないし。
(Even so, I cannot find a substitute for cigarettes.)

(e) A: 毎日三十分くらい運動するといいそうですよ。
(They say that it's good to exercise for about 30 minutes every day.)

B: そうかと言って，それだけの時間は作れないしね。
(But it is next to impossible to make that amount of free time, you know.)

(f) 漢字をもっと覚えなければならないのは分かっているが，そうかと言って，漢字ばかり覚えているわけにもいかない。
(I know I have to memorize more kanji, but even so, I cannot memorize just kanji.)

(g) 妻子と別れるのはつらいが，そうかと言って，この海外出張を断るわけにもいかない。
(It is painful to leave my wife and kids behind, but I cannot excuse myself from this business trip abroad.)

Notes

1. *Sō ka to itte* is used when one is inclined to accept what one's conversational partner has said as in KS(A) and Exs.(a) – (e), or what has been mentioned in the preceding sentence as in KS(B), Exs.(f) and (g), but this inclination is accompanied by a realization that it is impossible to accept its corollary due to some circumstance.

2. *Sō ka to itte* always occurs with an explicitly or an implicitly negative predicate. It often occurs with ~ *wake ni* {*wa* / *mo*} *ikanai*, but there are

cases where an implicitly negative predicate is used as shown in the following:

(1) a. この町は気に入らないんだが，そうかと言って，引っ越すには**金がかかる**し。
(I don't like this town, but it costs a lot of money to move, so . . .)

b. 僕らは忙しいけど，そうかと言って，彼一人に**任せておけるかい**？
(We are busy, but how can we leave the work to him alone?)

The predicates *kane ga kakaru* 'it costs a lot of money' and *makasete okerukai*, a rhetorical question in informal male speech meaning 'we cannot leave it to him,' are cases of an implicitly negative predicate.

【Related Expression】

Sō ka to itte used in sentence-initial position as in KS(A) and Exs.(a) – (e) can be replaced by disjunctive conjunctions such as *keredo(mo)*, *shikashi*, (*sō*) *desu ga*. The same phrase used in non-sentence-initial position as in KS(B), Exs.(f) and (g) cannot be replaced by such conjunctions.

[1] アメリカの方が土地も家も安いが，{?**しかし** / ??**けれども** / ***だが**}，簡単に移住するわけにもいかない。(cf. KS(B))

[2] 妻子と別れるのはつらいが，{??**けれども** / ??**しかし** / ***だが**}，この海外出張を断るわけにもいかない。(cf. Ex.(g))

Disjunctive conjunctions such as *keredo(mo)*, *shikashi*, etc. cannot be replaced by the structure in question unless *sō ka to itte* satisfies the condition mentioned in Note 1 above. The following example sentences all explain this point.

[3] A: このアパートは広くていいね。
(This apartment is spacious and nice.)

B: {**しかし** / **けれど** / ***そうかと言って**}，高いんだよ。
(But it's expensive, you know.)

[4] A: 酒(さけ)は体によくないよ。
(Alcohol is not good for your health, you know.)

B: {**しかし** / **けれど** / ***そうかと言って**}, 適当(てきとう)に飲(の)めば大丈夫(だいじょうぶ)だよ。
(But it's OK if you drink moderately.)

[5] 漢字は覚えるのが大変(たいへん)だ。{**しかし** / **けれども** / ***そうかと言って**}, 一度(いちど)覚えると便利(べんり)だ。
(It is tough to memorize kanji. But once you have memorized them they are very useful.)

soko de[1] そこで *conj.*

a conjunction which connects a situation presented as a reason and an action taken because of that situation	so; because of that; therefore 【REL. *sore de*】

◆Key Sentence

Sentence$_1$		Sentence$_2$
友達(ともだち)が夕食(ゆうしょく)は簡単(かんたん)なものでいいと言(い)った。	そこで,	ピザを注文(ちゅうもん)した。
(My friend told me that something simple would be fine for supper. So, I ordered a pizza.)		

Formation

S$_1$。そこで，S$_2$。

会議室(かいぎしつ)が使(つか)えなくなった。そこで，食堂(しょくどう)で打(う)ち合(あ)わせをすることにした。
(The conference room has become unavailable. So, we've decided to have the meeting in the cafeteria.)

Examples

(a) 荷物がたくさんあるのに雨が降り出した。そこで，タクシーで行くことにした。

(I had a lot of baggage and it began to rain. Therefore, I decided to go by taxi.)

(b) リーダーの山田さんが来られなくなった。そこで，ミーティングは延期せざるをえなくなった。

(It has turned out that our leader Mr. Yamada can't come, so we have no choice but to postpone the meeting.)

(c) 試験の日に怪我をして学校へ行けなくなった。そこで，先生に電話して別の日に受けられるか聞いてみた。

(I got injured and couldn't go to school on the day of an exam. So, I called my teacher to ask if I could take it another day.)

(d) 彼はすべて私が悪かったような言い方をした。そこで，私も黙っていられなくなって，言い返した。

(He talked as if it were all my fault. Therefore, I couldn't hold my tongue and I talked back.)

(e) 息子が来年大学なんですが英語が苦手で困っているんです。そこで，お願いがあるんですが，息子に英語を教えてやっていただけませんか。

(My son is going to college next year but he is not good at English (lit. and has trouble with it). Therefore, I'd like to ask a favor of you. Could you teach him English?)

S

Notes

1. *Soko de* cannot connect a cause and a result, as in (1).

(1) a. サンフランシスコで大地震があった。***そこで**建物がたくさん壊れた。(Acceptable form: {**そのため / それで**} 建物が…)

(There was a big earthquake in San Francisco. Because of that, many buildings collapsed.)

b. 昨夜安いウィスキーをたくさん飲まされた。***そこで**今日は頭が痛くて起きられない。(Acceptable form: {**そのため** / **それで**} 今日は…)
(I was forced to drink a lot of cheap whiskey last night. Because of that, I have a headache and cannot get up today.)

(⇨ ***tame*** (***ni***) (DBJG: 447–51))

2. In general, when *soko de* is used, the situation presented as a reason is a special situation. For example, (2a) is acceptable, but (2b) is somewhat odd.

(2) a. 明日森田さんのうちでパーティーがあって昔のクラスメートがたくさん来るという。**そこで**，私も行くことにした。
(I heard that there is a party at Morita's tomorrow and many of my old classmates are coming. So, I've decided to go, too.)

b. 明日森田さんのうちでパーティーがあるという。??**そこで**，私も行くことにした。(Acceptable form: **それで**，私も…)
(I heard that there is a party at Morita's tomorrow. So, I've decided to go, too.)

3. In "S_1. *Soko de*, S_2," S_2 usually represents a controllable action. Thus, in the following examples, (3a) is acceptable, but (3b) and (3c) are somewhat unnatural.

(3) a. その毛皮のコートはセールで半額だった。**そこで**，思いきって買った。
(The fur coat was on sale at fifty percent off. So, I made a big decision and bought it.)

b. その毛皮のコートはセールで半額だった。???**そこで**，私も買いたくなってきた。(Acceptable form: **それで**，私も…)
(The fur coat was on sale at fifty percent off. So, I wanted (lit. began to want) to buy it.)

c. その毛皮のコートはセールで半額だった。???**そこで**，私にも買うことが出来た。(Acceptable form: **それで**，私にも…)

(The fur coat was on sale at fifty percent off. So, I could buy it.)

4. In "S_1. *Soko de*, S_2," S_2 cannot be a command, a request, a suggestion, or an invitation, as in (4).

   (4) 明日森田さんのうちでパーティーがあって昔のクラスメートがたくさん来ます。***そこで**, あなたも {ぜひ来て下(くだ)さい / いらっしゃったらどうですか / いらっしゃいませんか}。(Acceptable form: {**だから** / **ですから**} あなたも…)
   (There is a party at Morita's tomorrow and many of our old classmates are coming. So, {please join us by all means. / how about joining us? / would you like to join us?})

(⇨ ***da kara*** in ***sore de*** (DBJG: 413–14))

【Related Expression】

Sore de and *soko de* are similar and are interchangeable in many situations. Some examples follow.

[1] a. 友達が夕食は簡単なものでいいと言った。{**それで** / **そこで**}, ピザを注文した。(=KS)

b. 荷物がたくさんあるのに雨が降り出した。{**それで** / **そこで**}, タクシーで行くことにした。(=Ex.(a))

In addition, like *soko de*, *sore de* cannot be used with a command, a request, a suggestion, or an invitation. (See Note 4.)

Sore de, however, differs from *soko de* in several ways. First, *sore de* can connect a cause and a result while *soko de* cannot, as in [2]. (See Note 1.)

[2] a. サンフランシスコで大地震があった。{**それで** / ***そこで**} 建物がたくさん壊れた。(=(1a))
(There was a big earthquake in San Francisco. Because of that, many buildings collapsed.)

b. 昨夜安いウィスキーをたくさん飲まされた。{**それで** / ***そこで**} 今日は頭が痛くて起きられない。(=(1b))
(I was forced to drink a lot of cheap whiskey last night. Because of that, I have a headache and cannot get up today.)

Second, *sore de* is used to mean 'that's why.' *Soko de* cannot replace *sore de* in this use, as in [3].

[3] a. 昨日(きのう)は風邪(かぜ)を引(ひ)きました。{**それで** / ***そこで**} 学校(がっこう)を休(やす)んだんです。
(I had a cold yesterday. That's why I took a day off from school.)

b. A: 昨日はちょっと大阪(おおさか)で用事(ようじ)がありましてね。
(I had some business in Osaka yesterday.)

B: ああ，{**それで** / ***そこで**} いらっしゃらなかったんですね。
(Oh, that's why you were not here.)

Third, when *sore de* is used, the situation does not have to be a special one, as in [4]. (See Note 2.)

[4] 明日森田さんのうちでパーティーがあるという。{**それで** / ??**そこで**}, 私も行くことにした。(=(2b))

Fourth, when *sore de* is used, the situation does not have to be controllable, as in [5]. (See Note 3.)

[5] a. その毛皮のコートはセールで半額だった。{**それで** / ???**そこで**}, 私も買いたくなってきた。(=(3b))

b. その毛皮のコートはセールで半額だった。{**それで** / ???**そこで**}, 私にも買うことが出来た。(=(3c))

(⇨ ***sore de*** (DBJG: 413–14))

S

soko de[2] そこで *conj.*

a conjunction which connects an event and an action taken at the time of the event	then; at that time

◆Key Sentences

(A)

Subordinate Clause		Main Clause
私が手を振ったら，	そこで	拍手をして下さい。
(When I wave my hand, (lit. then,) please clap your hands.)		

(B)

$Sentence_1$		$Sentence_2$
彼は飲み物を勧めるかもしれません。	そこで	遠慮をしてはいけません。
(He might offer you a drink. At that time you mustn't hesitate.)		

Formation

(i) S_1，そこで S_2。

このランプがついたら，そこで充電を始めて下さい。
(When this light comes on, (lit. then,) start charging it.)

(ii) S_1。そこで S_2。

多分受付が身分証明書を要求するでしょう。そこでこのカードを見せなさい。(The receptionist will probably ask for an ID. Show her this card at that time.)

Examples

(a) 一時間たったら私が「やめ！」と言いますから，そこで書くのをやめて鉛筆を置いて下さい。
(In an hour I will say, "Stop!" Then, stop writing and put your pencils down.)

(b) 私が合図をしたら，そこで皆さんお立ち願います。
(When I give you a signal, (lit. then,) you will all stand up, please.)

(c) 酔ったなと思ったら，そこで飲むのをやめるべきです。
(If you think you are intoxicated, you should stop drinking at that time.)

(d) 小さい子供は時にとんでもないいたずらをする。そこで親は叱らないといけない。
(Little children sometimes get into unbelievable mischief. Their parents must scold them then.)

(e) 矢野先生が学生を叱った。そこでその学生が素直に謝ればよかったのだが，彼は口答えをした。
(Prof. Yano scolded a student. It would have been all right if the student had apologized to him meekly at that time, but the student talked back (instead).)

Notes

1. In "S_1. *Soko de* S_2." S_1 represents an event and S_2 an action at the time of the event.
2. S_2 is often a command, a request, a suggestion, or an invitation.
3. *Soko de* may appear in mid-sentence position in S_2, as in (1).

   (1) a. 私が合図をしたら，皆さんそこでお立ち願います。(=Ex.(b))

   b. 小さい子供は時にとんでもないいたずらをする。親はそこで叱らないといけない。(=Ex.(d))

soko o　そこを　*conj.*

a conjunction used to indicate that in spite of the negative situation mentioned in the previous part of the sentence / discourse some positive effort is made	but; in spite of that

◆Key Sentences

(A)

トムはフットボールの選手としては小さい	が,	そこを	脚力で補っている。
(Tom is small for a football player, but he makes up for it with his swift legs.)			

(B)

A:	
これ以上金を貸すわけにはいかないよ。	
(I cannot loan you more money than this.)	
B:	
そこを	何とかして下さいませんか。
(But, could you do something about it?)	

Examples

(a) 彼は頭はそれほどよくないが, そこを努力で何とかやっている。
(He is not that bright, but he manages to get along on his efforts.)

(b) その女優はもう年齢を隠すことは出来ないが, そこを芸で何とか持たせている。
(The actress cannot hide her age any longer, but she functions somehow because of (lit. using) her acting skills.)

(c) お忙しいとは存じますが, そこを何とか出席していただけないでしょうか。
(I know that you are busy, but I wonder if you could possibly attend it.)

(d) A: こんな成績じゃ, 君, 卒業できないよ。
(With such poor grades, you cannot graduate, you know.)

B: そこを，先生，どうにかしていただけないでしょうか。
(But, could you do something about it, Professor?)

(e) A: こんな企画に予算を付けるわけにはいかないな。
(I cannot allocate a budget for such a project.)

B: 部長，そこを何とか一つお願いします。
(But, chief, could you give me a chance?)

Notes

1. *Soko o* is used to express some positive efforts in spite of some negative situation mentioned either in the first half of the sentence as in KS(A) and Exs.(a) – (c) or in the interlocutor's line as in KS(B), Exs.(d) and (e).

2. *Soko o* is often used to push one's request in spite of an initial negative reaction, as shown in Exs.(c) – (e). In this case, the sentence often takes the form of *Soko o nantoka ~ deshō ka*.

3. *Soko o* can be replaced by *soko no tokoro o* without changing the meaning when *soko o* is used to express the speaker's beseeching, as in KS(B) and Exs.(c) – (e).

   (1) お忙しいとは存じますが，**そこのところを**何とか出席していただけないでしょうか。(cf. Ex.(c))

-sō ni naru　そうになる　*phr.*

a phrase expressing that s.t. almost happens

almost
【REL. *mō sukoshi/chotto de ~ suru tokoro (datta)*】

◆**Key Sentence**

	V*masu*	
冷たい雨の中を傘もささないで歩いていたら，風邪を	引き	そうになった。
(While walking in the cold rain without using an umbrella, I almost caught a cold.)		

Formation

V*masu* そうになる

忘れそうになる (s.o. almost forgets s.t.)

分かりそうになる (s.o. almost understands s.t.)

失職しそうになる (s.o. almost loses his / her job)

Examples

(a) 私は子供の時，プールで危うくおぼれそうになったことがある。
(When I was a child I almost drowned in a swimming pool.)

(b) 昨日もうちょっとで車にひかれそうになった。
(Yesterday I almost got run over by a car.)

(c) 地震で僕の家はつぶれそうになった。
(My house almost got destroyed by an earthquake.)

(d) 庭の古い松の木が台風で倒れそうになった。
(An old pine tree in the yard almost fell down in the typhoon.)

(e) 今日混んだ電車の中で，財布をすられそうになった。
(Today in a crowded train I almost got my purse pickpocketed.)

(f) 数学の試験で最後の問題がもう少しで解けそうになった時に，時間切れになってしまった。
(In the math exam, I was almost able to solve the last problem when the time was up.)

(g) やっと日本へ行けそうになった時に，母が病気になってしまった。
(When I was almost able to go to Japan my mother got ill.)

Notes

1. V*masu sō ni naru* expresses the idea that s.t. almost happens. As shown in Exs.(a), (b) and (f), V*masu sō ni naru* is often used with an extra adverbial phrases such as *ayauku* ‘narrowly,’ and *mō sukoshi/chotto de* ‘a little more, then ~,’ which reinforce the idea of ‘almost.’

2. The verb is restricted to non-volitional verbs, that is, a verb that expresses s.t. that is beyond human control, such as (*kaze o*) *hiku* ‘to catch (a cold)’ (KS), *oboreru* ‘to drown’ (Ex.(a)), *tsubureru* ‘to be destroyed’ (Ex.(c)), *taoreru* ‘to fall down’ (Ex.(d)). Since passive and potential forms are regarded as a non-volitional verb, they can be also used with *sō ni naru*, as shown in Exs.(b), (e) and (g). If the verb is a volitional verb, V*masu sō ni naru* cannot be used if the subject is the speaker himself / herself.

(1) a. *私が昼ご飯を**食べそうになった**時，友達から電話がかかってきた。
(When I was about to eat my lunch I received a call from my friend.)

→ 私が昼ご飯を**食べようとした**時，友達から電話がかかってきた。

b. *僕が大学を**出そうになった**時，母が亡くなりました。
(When I almost graduated from college, I lost my mother.)

→ 僕が大学を**出ようとした**時，母が亡くなりました。

However, if the entire situation expressed by the whole sentence expresses a situation that is beyond human control, a volitional verb can be used even if the subject is the speaker himself as shown in (2): in both (2a) and (2b) the action is not the speaker’s choice. What (2a) and (2b) mean are ‘I was almost forced to eat that poisonous bean-jam bun’ and ‘I was swindled by somebody to use that counterfeit paper money to purchase things.’

(2) a. 私は危うくその毒まんじゅうを**食べそうになった**。
(I almost ate that poisonous bean-jam bun.)

b. 僕はもうちょっとでその偽札で買い物を**しそうになった**。
(I almost bought things with that counterfeit paper money.)

If the subject is s.o. other than the speaker, V*masu sō ni naru* can be used, even if the verb is a controllable verb, because whatever happens to the third person is considered to be beyond the speaker's control.

(2) a. 小さい子供が酒を**飲みそうになった**ので，母親は急いで取り上げた。
(Because a small child almost drank sake, the mother hastily took it away.)

b. 山田が会社を**辞めそうになった**ので，同僚達は懸命に引き留めた。
(Because Yamada almost quit the company, his colleagues retained him with great efforts.)

【Related Expression】

All the examples of V*masu sō ni naru* can be replaced by *mō sukoshi/chotto de ~ suru tokoro datta*, except Exs.(f) – (g) in which V*masu sō ni naru* is used in a dependent clause. The latter expression focuses on both the impending aspect of something and the point of time at which s.t. occurs, but the former focuses only on the impending aspect.

[1] a. 私は子供の時，プールで**もう｛少し / ちょっと｝**でおぼれる**ところだった**。(cf. Ex.(a))

b. 昨日**もう｛少し / ちょっと｝**で車にひかれる**ところだった**。
(cf. Ex.(b))

c. 地震で僕の家は**もう｛少し / ちょっと｝**でつぶれる**ところだった**。(cf. Ex.(c))

d. 庭の古い松の木が台風で**もう｛少し / ちょっと｝**で倒れる**ところだった**。(cf. Ex.(d))

e. 今日混んだ電車の中で，**もう｛少し / ちょっと｝で**財布をすられる**ところだった**。(cf. Ex.(e))

As mentioned in Note 2, the verb of V*masu sō ni naru* is restricted to a non-volitional verb. But *mō sukoshi/chotto de ~ suru tokoro datta* is free of this restriction.

[2] a. 長い論文を**もう｛少し / ちょっと｝**で｛書き上げる**ところだった** / *書き上げ**そうになった**｝。
(I almost finished writing a long thesis.)

b. **もう｛少し / ちょっと｝で**｛家に帰り着く**ところだった** / *家に帰り着き**そうになった**｝が，あいにくと雨が降ってきてしまった。
(I was almost home, but unfortunately it started to rain.)

c. **もう｛少し / ちょっと｝で**出かける**ところ**に友達がやって来た。
(When I was just about to leave, a friend of mine visited me.)

sono ue その上 *conj.*

a conjunction which introduces an additional, emphatic statement

on top of that; besides; moreover; furthermore; what's more; what's worse; not only ~ but also

【REL. *omake ni*; ***shika mo***; *sore ni*; *ue* (*ni*)】

◆Key Sentences

(A)

Topic	Comment_1	
彼は	一緒にアパートを探してくれて，	その上，

Comment_2
引っ越しまで手伝ってくれた。
(He looked for an apartment with me, and moreover, he even helped me move.)

(B)

Topic	Comment_1			Comment_2
この仕事は	給料がいい	し，	その上，	時々外国に行く機会もある。
(This job pays a good salary, and what's more, it offers opportunities to go abroad from time to time.)				

(C)

Sentence_1		Sentence_2	
Topic	Comment_1		Comment_2
バナナは	安い。	その上，	栄養も豊富だ。
(Bananas are cheap. On top of that, they are nutritious.)			

Formation

(i) {V / Adj. / N+Cop.} *te* その上

いつでも使えて，その上，無料だ (You can use it any time, and on top of that, it's free.)

おいしくて，その上，栄養がある (It's delicious, and what's more, nutritious.)

不便で，その上，家賃が高い (It's inconvenient, and moreover, the rent is expensive.)

純金製で，その上，ダイヤがはまっている (It's made of pure gold, and besides, it has a diamond (lit. a diamond is embedded).)

(ii) V*masu* その上

ほめられ，その上，ほうびまでもらった (I was praised, and what's more, I was given an award.)

(iii) Adj(*i*)*ku* その上

話が面白く，その上，読みやすい (The story is interesting, and on top of that, it's easy to read.)

(iv) S し，その上

その仕事はつまらないし，その上，給料が悪い (The job is boring, and what's worse, the pay is bad.)

(v) S。その上

その老人は体が不自由だ。その上，耳が遠い。(The old man is disabled. Furthermore, he is hard of hearing.)

Examples

(a) 彼女は美人で，その上，気立てがいいから，みんなに好かれている。
(Everybody loves her because she is not only pretty but also good-natured (lit. because she is pretty, and what's more, she is good-natured).)

(b) 先生のうちに就職の相談に行ったら，いろいろアドバイスをいただいて，その上，夕食までごちそうになった。
(When I went to my professor's house to consult him about my job, he gave me all kinds of advice, and on top of that, he even served me dinner.)

(c) ジョンのうちに遊びに行ったら，家のペンキ塗りを手伝わされ，その上，芝刈りまでさせられた。
(When I went to see John at his place, he got me to help him paint his house, and what's more, he even got me to mow the lawn.)

(d) このアパートは通勤に便利で家賃も安く，その上，駐車場まである。
(This apartment is convenient for commuting and the rent is reasonable. Moreover, it even has a parking space.)

(e) 日本語は構造が英語とかなり違うし，その上，漢字があるから，アメリカ人には習得が難しい。
(The structure of Japanese is considerably different from that of English, and on top of that, it has *kanji*; therefore, it is difficult for Americans to learn.)

(f) この学校はいい先生が少なく設備もよくない。その上，生徒の非行も多い。
(This school does not have many good teachers and the facilities are not good, either. And besides that, there is a lot of juvenile crime.)

Note

Sono ue is used to introduce an emphatic statement. Thus, an emphatic marker like *made* often appears in the added statement, as in KS(A) and Exs.(b) – (d). (See Related Expression III.)

【Related Expressions】

I. *Ue* (*ni*) can replace *sono ue*, as in [1].

[1] a. 彼は一緒にアパートを探してくれた**上**(**に**)，引っ越しまで手伝ってくれた。(=KS(A))

b. この仕事は給料がいい**上**(**に**)，時々外国に行く機会もある。(=KS(B))

c. バナナは安い**上**(**に**)，栄養も豊富だ。(=KS(C))

(⇨ ***ue* (*ni*)**)

II. *Omake ni* can replace *sono ue* without changing meaning, as in [2], although *omake ni* is slightly more casual.

[2] a. 彼は一緒にアパートを探してくれて，{**その上** / **おまけに**}，引っ越しまで手伝ってくれた。(=KS(A))

b. この仕事は給料がいいし，{**その上** / **おまけに**}，時々外国に行く機会もある。(=KS(B))

c. バナナは安い。{**その上** / **おまけに**}，栄養も豊富だ。(=KS(C))

III. *Sore ni* is similar to *sono ue* except that the added statement is not emphatic. Thus, this statement is often supplementary information. In the following examples, [3a] and [3b] are acceptable but [4a] and [4b] are somewhat unnatural. The reason is that in [3a] and [3b] the second statements are not necessarily emphatic while in [4a] and [4b] the second statements are emphatic as the emphatic marker *made* shows.

[3] a. この仕事は給料がいいし，{**その上** / **それに**}，時々外国に行く機会もある。(=KS(B))

b. バナナは安い。{**その上** / **それに**}，栄養も豊富だ。(=KS(C))

[4] a. 彼は一緒にアパートを探してくれて，{**その上** / ??**それに**}，引っ越し**まで**手伝ってくれた。(=KS(A))

b. ジョンのうちに遊びに行ったら，家のペンキ塗りを手伝わされ，{**その上** / ??**それに**}，芝刈り**まで**させられた。(=Ex.(c))

(⇨ ***sore ni***)

S

sore demo それでも *conj.*

in spite of the circumstance expressed in the preceding sentence

nevertheless; yet; but in spite of that; even so
【REL. (*sore*) *ni mo kakawarazu*; *te mo*】

◆Key Sentence

Sentence$_1$		Sentence$_2$
両親は二人の結婚に反対している。	それでも	二人は結婚するつもりらしい。
(The parents are opposed to the couple's marriage. Nevertheless, they seem intent on marrying.)		

Formation

(i) S$_1$。(しかし)それでも S$_2$。

悪い天気だった。(しかし)それでも私達は出かけた。
(The weather was bad. Nevertheless we went out.)

(ii) S$_1$ {が/けれど(も)/のに}, それでも S$_2$。

悪い天気だった {が/けれど(も)/のに}, それでも私達は出かけた。
(The weather was bad. Nevertheless we went out.)

Examples

(a) 暑いので扇風機をつけたが, それでもまだ暑かった。
(It was so hot that we turned on an electric fan, but it was still hot.)

(b) 父はひどい風邪を引いていた。しかしそれでも旅行に出かけた。
(My father was suffering from a bad cold. Nevertheless, he went on a trip.)

(c) この本はとても高いのに, それでもいい本だから, よく売れている。
(This book is very expensive, yet it is selling well, because it is a good book.)

(d) 彼はとても忙しいのに，それでもジョギングを一日も欠かさない。
(He is very busy, yet he does not miss jogging even a day.)

(e) A: このオーバー，高いねえ。
(This overcoat is expensive, isn’t it?)

B: それでも買うつもり？
(But do you intend to buy it?)

Note

Sore demo means that in spite of the circumstance expressed in the preceding sentence something surprising or contradictory takes place. So if this basic meaning is missing *sore demo* cannot be used.

(1) 今日は仕事がある。{**でも / けれども / しかし / *それでも**} 明日は休みだ。
(I have work to do today. But I can take a day off tomorrow.)

(2) このアパートは広いです。{**でも / けれども / しかし / *それでも**} とても高いんです。
(This apartment is spacious. But it is very expensive.)

(3) 僕はよく運動をする。{**でも / けれども / しかし / *それでも**} 弟は全然しない。
(I do exercise a lot. But my younger brother doesn’t at all.)

【Related Expressions】

I. (*Sore*) *ni mo kakawarazu* also means of ‘in spite of (that)’ and, in fact, it can replace *sore demo* in all the KS and Exs. except Ex.(e). The reason why the replacement is impossible in Ex.(e) is that (*sore*) *ni mo kakawarazu* is used only in written or formal spoken Japanese; therefore, it doesn't fit in a very colloquial use of *sore demo* in Ex.(e).

[1] A: このオーバー，高いねえ。
(This overcoat is expensive, isn’t it?)

B: {**それでも / *それにもかかわらず**} 買うつもり？
(Do you intend to buy it in spite of that?) (= Ex.(e))

[2] 両親は二人の結婚に反対している。{**それでも / それにもかかわ**

らず} 二人は結婚するつもりらしい。
(The parents are opposed to the couple's marriage. In spite of that, they seem to intend to get married.) (= KS)

II. *Sore demo* can be rephrased by *te mo* as in:

[3] a. 両親が二人の結婚に反対してい**ても**，二人は結婚するつもりらしい。(cf. KS)
(Even if the parents are opposed to the couple's marriage, they seem intent on getting married.) (cf. KS)

b. 暑いので扇風機をつけたが，つけ**ても**まだ暑かった。
(cf. Ex.(a))

But Wh-word ~ *te mo* cannot be rephrased by *sore demo*.

[4] a. **何**を食べ**ても**おいしい。
(No matter what I eat, it tastes good.)
cf. *何を食べる。それでもおいしい。

b. 彼は**誰**に対し**ても**同じ態度を取る。
(No matter who he faces, his attitude remains the same.)
cf. *彼は誰に対する。それでも同じ態度を取る。

(⇨ ***te mo*** (DBJG: 468–70))

sore dokoroka それどころか *conj.*

a conjunction that is used to indicate that the level / degree of a fact or a situation expressed in the second sentence is far above or below the level / degree of a fact or a situation expressed in the first sentence

on the contrary; far from that; as a matter of fact
【REL. *dokoroka*】

◆Key Sentences

(A)

Sentence$_1$		Sentence$_2$
スミスさんは漢字(かんじ)が書(か)けない。	それどころか,	平仮名(ひらがな)も満足(まんぞく)に書けない。
(Mr. Smith cannot write kanji. As a matter of fact, he cannot write even hiragana satisfactorily.)		

(B)

A:	B:		
今晩(こんばん)パーティーに行(い)かない?	それどころ	{か, / じゃないよ。}	親父(おやじ)が入院(にゅういん)したんだ。
(Shall we go to the party tonight?)	(No way (lit. Far from it). Dad got hospitalized.)		

Formation

(i) S$_1$。それどころか S$_2$。

暑(あつ)くない。それどころか寒(さむ)い。 (It's not hot. On the contrary, it's cold.)

(ii) A: S。

B: それどころ {か, / ではない。/ じゃない。} S。

A: 疲(つか)れたね。 (Tired, aren't we?)

B: それどころ {か, / じゃないよ。} 死(し)にそうなんだよ。 (Far from it. I'm almost dead.)

Examples

(a) あの人(ひと)は若(わか)くはありませんよ。それどころか, お孫(まご)さんが三人(さんにん)もいるんですよ。
(She is not young. On the contrary, she has as many as three grandchildren.)

S

(b) お金は一銭もありません。それどころか，借金で苦しんでいるんです。
(I don't have a penny. As a matter of fact, I'm suffering from debts.)

(c) ジムは日本語の会話が出来ない。それどころか，簡単なあいさつも日本語で出来ない。
(Jim cannot speak Japanese. In fact, he cannot even make simple greetings in Japanese.)

(d) A: 風邪を引いたんだって？
(Did you have a cold? (lit. I heard that you had a cold, but is it true?))

B: それどころか，肺炎になって，入院していたんだ。
(On the contrary, I had pneumonia and got hospitalized.)

(e) A: 映画を見に行こうか？
(Shall we go see a movie?)

B: それどころじゃないよ。今晩は徹夜しなければならないほど忙しいんだ。
(Are you kidding? (lit. Far from it) Tonight I'm so busy that I have to stay up all night.)

(f) A: 和子，手伝ってくれる？
(Kazuko, can you help me?)

B: それどころじゃないのよ，今宿題で忙しくて。
(No way, I'm busy doing my homework, you know.)

(g) クラークさんは刺身が食べられる。それどころか納豆まで食べられる。
(Clark can eat sashimi. As a matter of fact, he eats even *nattō*.)

Notes

Sore dokoro {ka / de wa nai / ja nai} can indicate a flat rejection of an invitation / request / command of the conversational partner as in KS(B), Exs.(e) and (f). S_2 gives an unusual circumstance which makes it impossible to accept the invitation / request / command.

【Related Expression】

Sore dokoroka can be replaced by {Adj(*i* / *na*) / V}inf · nonpast *dokoroka* or N *dokoroka*, if the negative predicate of S_1 is switched to an affirmative predicate.

[1] a. スミスさんは漢字が {書ける / *書けない} **どころか**, 平仮名も満足に書けない。(cf. KS(A))

b. ジムは日本語の会話が {出来る / *出来ない} **どころか**, 簡単なあいさつも日本語で出来ない。(cf. Ex.(c))

(⇨ ***dokoroka***)

sore ga それが *int.* <s>

an interjection which signals that the speaker is going to provide an unexpected response to a question

well (contrary to your expectation; I'm afraid to say this, but)

【REL. *sore wa*; ***tokoro ga***】

◆Key Sentence

A:		
奨学金(しょうがくきん)はもらえそうですか。		
(Does it look like you can get a scholarship?)		
B:		
(Neg. Int.)		
(いえ,)	それが	難(むずか)しそうなんです。
(Well, (no,) it looks difficult.)		

S

Examples

(a) A: 試験，どうだった？
(How was the exam?)

B: それが，だめだったんだ。
(Well, (I'm sorry to say this, but) it was no good.)

(b) A: 来年は日本で働くんですね。
(You're going to work in Japan next year, aren't you?)

B: いや，それが行けなくなってしまったんです。
(Well, no, it's turned out that I can't go.)

(c) A: 彼女に会って話したんだろう。
(You met her and talked to her, right?)

B: それが，会ったことは会ったんだけど，顔を見たら何も言えなくなってしまって。
(Well, I did meet her, but when I saw her face, I couldn't say anything.)

Notes

1. *Sore ga* can be used with or without an interjection such as *iie*, *ie*, or *iya*. When an interjection is used, *sore ga* follows it, as in KS and Ex.(b).

2. Although *sore ga* is often used when the response is negative, it can be used when the response is positive, as in (1).

A: 試験，だめだったんだろう。
(You didn't pass the exam, I bet.)

B: いや，**それが**，通ったんだよ。
(No, (the fact is that) I passed it!)

3. Because of the nature of the situations where *sore ga* is used, it is often pronounced with a somewhat hesitant tone.

【Related Expression】

In contrast to *sore ga*, *sore wa* is used when the speaker provides an expected response to a question.

[1] A: 彼女に会いたいでしょう。
(You want to see your girlfriend, don't you?)

B: **それは**，会いたいですよ。
(Yes, (naturally,) I do.)

(⇨ ***sore wa***)

sore mo それも *conj.*

a conjunction which is used to add more specific information to information about a rather uncommon action or state

what's more; what's worse; at that; furthermore; moreover; on top of that
【REL. ***shika mo***】

◆Key Sentences

(A)

$AdvP_1$		$AdvP_2$	Verbal		
英語(えいご)**で，**	それも	**早口**(はやくち)**で**	話(はな)された	ので	全然分(ぜんぜんわ)からなかった。
(Because he spoke (lit. I was talked to) in English, and what's worse, rapidly, I didn't understand anything.)					

(B)

	AP_1		AP_2	Noun			
彼女(かのじょ)は	**銀座**(ぎんざ)**の，**	それも	**一流**(いちりゅう)**の**	店(みせ)	で	ばかり	買(か)い物(もの)をする。
(She always does her shopping at shops in Ginza, and moreover, at first-class ones.)							

S

(C)

Clause_1		Clause_2
子供が五人もいて，	それも	**いたずら盛りの男の子ばかり**なので，
野口さんの奥さんは毎日大変忙しいです。		
(Because she has as many as five children, and moreover, they are all very mischievous boys, Mrs. Noguchi is extremely busy every day.)		

Formation

(i) AdvP_1 それも AdvP_2 (Verbal)

日本語で，それもくずし字で書いてある。 (It is written in Japanese, and what's worse, in flowing style.)

(ii) AP_1 それも AP_2 (Noun)

ダイヤ(の)，それも二カラットのダイヤの指輪だ。 (It is a diamond ring, and a 2-karat diamond ring at that.)

(iii) Clause_1 それも Clause_2

新築で，それも駅から五分という便利な所にある。 (It is newly built, and on top of that, it is conveniently located five-minutes from the station.)

Examples

(a) 彼はその場で，それも現金で払ってくれた。
(He paid on the spot, and what's more, in cash.)

(b) 真冬に，それもはだしで走った。
(I ran in midwinter, and what's more, barefooted.)

(c) その銀行は都心の，それも東京駅前の一等地に本社ビルを建てた。
(The bank built their headquarters building in central Tokyo, and moreover, on the best spot, in front of Tokyo Station.)

(d) 彼女は雑誌記者，それもゴシップ雑誌の記者に見つかってしまった。
(She was seen by a magazine reporter, and what's worse, a reporter from a gossip magazine.)

(e) 忙しい学期末に，それも論文の締め切り直前に手紙を訳してくれと頼まれた。
(I was asked to translate a letter when I was busy at the end of the semester, and what's worse, just before the deadline for my term paper.)

(f) 硬貨で十万円，それも十円玉ばかりだったからとても重かった。
(Because it was one hundred thousand yen in coins, and what's worse, (they were) all ten-yen coins, it was terribly heavy.)

Notes

1. The phrases or clauses before and after *sore mo* are connected to the same noun phrase, verbal, or clause which follows, as in KS(A) – (C).

2. *Sore mo* usually appears in mid-sentence position although it can appear as an independent phrase as well, as in (1).

(1) a. 彼女は銀座の店でばかり買い物をする。**それも**一流の店で。(=KS(B))

b. 彼はその場で払ってくれた。**それも**現金で。(=Ex.(a))

sore ni それに *conj.*

a conjunction which introduces an additional item or statement

(and) in addition; moreover; furthermore; what's more; on top of that
【REL. *omake ni*; ***shika mo***; ***sono ue***; ***sore to***】

◆Key Sentences

(A)

	Noun$_1$		Noun$_2$	
ここのモーニングセットは	コーヒー	に	トースト，	それに

Noun$_3$		
ゆでたまご	が	付いている。

(The "morning set" here includes coffee and some toast; in addition, there is a boiled egg (lit. it is accompanied by a boiled egg).)

(B)

Sentence$_1$			Sentence$_2$
車を買っても置く所がない	し，	それに	あまり乗る機会もない。

(Even if we bought a car, there would be no place to park it, and moreover, there would be few occasions to use it.)

(C)

Sentence$_1$	
私は家では仕事の話はしないことにしているんです。	それに，

Sentence$_2$
今晩はとても疲れているので，その話は明日にしてもらえませんか。

(I make it a rule not to discuss business at home. In addition, I'm very tired this evening, so could we discuss it tomorrow?)

Formation

(i) N_1 {と / に /,} N_2 {と / に /,} …それに N_n

テレビ，ステレオ，それにビデオカメラ

(a TV set, a stereo, and, in addition, a video camera)

(ii) S_1 し，それに S_2

その仕事はつまらないし，それに給料が悪い。

(The job is boring, and what's worse, the pay is bad.)

(iii) S_1。それに，S_2。

その老人は体が不自由だ。それに，耳が遠い。

(The old man is disabled. Furthermore, he is hard of hearing.)

Examples

(a) 私のうちには私達夫婦と子供が二人，それにネコとイヌが一匹ずついる。

(My family consists of my wife and me, and two children, and in addition, (there are) a cat and a dog.)

(b) いい仕事がないし，それに子供も日本の学校へ行きたがっているので，日本へ帰ろうと思っている。

(We are thinking of going back to Japan because there are no good jobs here, and what's more, my child wants to go to a Japanese school.)

(c) ピアノなんか買っても誰も弾く者はないし，それにうちは狭いので置く所がありません。

(Even if we bought a piano, no one would play it, and moreover, there would be no place to put it because our place is small.)

(d) このアパートは明るくて清潔だ。それに家賃が安い。

(This apartment is light and clean. Furthermore, the rent is reasonable.)

(e) 昔と違って今は相手がどこにいても電話で簡単に話が出来る。それに，テレビ電話を使うと相手の顔を見ながら話すことも出来る。

(Unlike the old days, we can easily talk with people over the phone these days no matter where they are. Moreover, if we use a TV telephone, we can talk with someone while watching his or her face.)

Notes

1. *Sore ni* introduces an additional non-emphatic item or statement. (See Related Expression.)

2. When *sore ni* is used to introduce an additional statement, the patterns (ii) and (iii) in the Formation are commonly used, as in KS(B) and (C). However, {V / Adj. / N + Cop.}*te*, V*masu*, and Adj(*i*)*ku* can also precede *sore ni*, as in (1) – (3). (V*masu* and Adj(*i*)*ku* are usually used in written language.)

(1) a. 彼女は結婚してい**て**，**それに**子供もある。
(She is married, and what's more, she has children.)

b. とうふは安く**て**，**それに**栄養がある。
(Tofu is cheap, and in addition, it's nutritious.)

c. このアパートは不便**で**，**それに**家賃が高い。
(This apartment is inconvenient, and moreover, the rent is expensive.)

d. 私は近視**で**，**それに**乱視も少し入っている。
(I am near-sighted, and what's more, I have astigmatism.)

(2) 彼は大学で日本語を三年間勉強**し**，**それに**日本で仕事をしたこともある。
(He studied Japanese at college for three years, and in addition, he worked (lit. has worked) in Japan.)

(3) 彼の書く小説はストーリーが面白**く**，**それに**読みやすい。
(The novels he writes have interesting story lines, and on top of that, they are easy to read.)

【Related Expression】

Omake ni and *sore ni* are used in similar situations. The difference is that *omake ni* introduces an emphatic statement while *sore ni* introduces a non-emphatic statement. Thus, in [1] *omake ni* is acceptable because the additional statements can be emphatic.

[1] a. ピアノなんか買っても誰も弾く者はないし，{**それに** / **おまけに**} うちは狭いので置く所がありません。(=Ex.(c))

b. このアパートは明るくて清潔だ。{**それに** / **おまけに**} 家賃が安い。(=Ex.(d))

However, in [2] *omake ni* is not quite acceptable because the additional statement is not as important as the initial one and, therefore, cannot be emphasized.

[2] 車を買っても置く所がないし，{**それに** / ??**おまけに**} あまり乗る機会もない。(=KS(B))

When *omake ni* is used to introduce an item, an emphatic marker like *made* is necessary, as in [3].

[3] ここのモーニングセットはコーヒーにトースト，**おまけに**ゆでたまご {**まで** / ???**が**} 付いている。
(The "morning set" here includes coffee and some toast; in addition, there is even a boiled egg (lit. it is even accompanied by a boiled egg).)

sore to それと *conj.* <s>

S

a conjunction which introduces an additional item or statement

and; also; in addition; as well
【REL. *sore kara*; *sore ni*】

◆Key Sentences

(A)

Noun$_1$		Noun$_2$		Noun$_3$	
リンゴ三つ	と	**オレンジ二つ，**	それと，	**バナナを三本**	下さい。
(Give me three apples and two oranges, and three bananas, as well.)					

(B)

	Sentence$_1$
スポーツはテニスとゴルフをします。	
(Speaking of sports, I play tennis and golf.)	
	Sentence$_2$
それと,	学生時代はアイスホッケーをしていました。
(In addition, I played ice hockey at school (lit. in my school days).)	

Formation

(i) N_1 {と / に /, } N_2 {と / に /, } …それと, N_n

ビールとチーズ, それと, ポテトチップ (beer and cheese, and potato chips as well)

(ii) S_1。それと, S_2。

音楽はコーラスをしています。それと, 学生の頃フルートを少しやりました。 (Speaking of music, I am a member of a chorus. In addition, I played flute a little when I was a student.)

Examples

S

(a) 山田さん, 木下さん, 上野さん, それと, 高橋さんもお見えになります。
(Mr. Yamada, Mr. Kinoshita, and Mr. Ueno are coming. And Mr. Takahashi, too.)

(b) 外国語はドイツ語にフランス語, それと, 日本語が少し話せます。
(Talking about foreign languages, I can speak German and French, and a little Japanese.)

(c) 留守中に山村さんと浜田さんからお電話がありました。それと, 吉田さんからお手紙が来ております。
(There were calls from Mr. Yamamura and Mr. Hamada while you were out. Also, a letter came from Mr. Yoshida.)

(d) 緊急の問題は先生をどうするかということです。それと，もう一つ，教室の問題も考えなければなりません。
(How to get a teacher is the urgent problem. And, for another thing, we have to think about the classrom problem.)

(e) この手紙を昼までにタイプしておいてくれる？ あ，それと，昨日頼んでおいた飛行機の切符，取れた？
(Could you type this letter by noon? Oh, and did (lit. could) you get the air tickets I asked for yesterday?)

Note

Sore to appears only in spoken Japanese. It is often used when the speaker wants to add an item or statement which s/he has forgotten to mention.

【Related Expressions】

I. *Sore ni* is similar to *sore to* in that both introduce an additional item or statement. The crucial difference is that *sore ni* is used when the preceding clause / phrase and the following clause / phrase are closely connected while *sore to* is used when this connection is weak. Therefore, *sore ni* cannot be used when the speaker adds an item or statement which s/he has forgotten to mention.

[1] リンゴ三つとオレンジ二つ。あ，{**それと** / ***それに**}，バナナも三本下さい。
(Give me three apples and two oranges. Oh, and three bananas, too.)

On the other hand, *sore to* cannot be used when the preceding clause or phrase has a continuative ending such as {V / Adj. / N + Cop.}*te*, V*masu*, Adj(*i*)*ku*, and S *shi*, as in [2] – [5].

[2] a. 彼女は結婚してい**て**，{**それに** / ***それと**} 子供もある。
(She is married, and what's more, she has children.)

b. このアパートは不便**で**，{**それに** / ***それと**} 家賃が高い。
(This apartment is inconvenient, and what's more, the rent is expensive.)

S

[3] 彼は大学で日本語を三年間勉強し，{**それに** / ***それと**} 日本で仕事をしたこともある。
(He studied Japanese at college for three years, and in addition, he worked (lit. has worked) in Japan.)

[4] この小説はストーリーが面白く，{**それに** / ***それと**} 読みやすい。
(This novel has an interesting story line, and moreover, it's easy to read.)

[5] その仕事はつまらないし，{**それに** / ***それと**} 給料が悪い。
(That job is not interesting, and what's more, the pay is bad.)

(⇨ ***sore ni***)

II. *Sore kara* can replace *sore to* without changing meaning, as in [6].

[6] a. リンゴ三つとオレンジ二つ，{**それと** / **それから**}，バナナを三本下さい。(=KS(A))

b. スポーツはテニスとゴルフをします。{**それと** / **それから**}，学生時代はアイスホッケーをしていました。(=KS(B))

c. この手紙を昼までにタイプしておいてくれる？　あ，{**それと** / **それから**}，昨日頼んでおいた飛行機の切符，取れた？

(=Ex.(e))

(⇨ ***sore kara*** (DBJG: 416–19))

S

sore wa　それは　*int.*　<s>

an interjection which is used when the speaker emphatically provides an expected response to a question	(yes,) naturally; (yes,) of course; oh, surely 【REL. ***sore ga***】

◆Key Sentence

A:
勝ちたいでしょうね。
(I bet you want to win (the game).)

B:		
(Aff. Int.)		
(ええ,)	それは	勝ちたいですよ。
((Yes,) Of course, I do.)		

Examples

(a) A: 国へ帰りたいと思うことがありますか。
(Are there times when you want to go back to your country?)

B: (ええ,) それはありますよ。
((Yes,) Of course.)

(b) A: この値段だったらみんな買うでしょうか。
(I wonder if they would buy (them) for this price.)

B: それは買いますよ。そんな値段では絶対買えませんから。
(They surely would. They could never buy them (anywhere else) for that price.)

(c) A: もっと給料が高い方がいいでしょう?
(You would prefer a higher salary, right?)

B: そりゃ(あ)そうですが…。
(Naturally, I would, but . . .)

Notes

1. *Sorya*(*a*) in Ex.(c) is the contracted form of *sore wa*.

2. Interjections such as *hai*, *ee* and *un* can be used with *sore wa*. When such an interjection is used, *sore wa* follows it, as in KS and Ex.(a).

3. *Sore wa* in the following examples should not be confused with the *sore wa* presented here. As a matter of fact, *sore* in these examples is a demonstrative pronoun. That is, *sore* in (1) refers to A's idea and *sore* in (2) refers to A's giving a gift.

   (1) A: 彼女(かのじょ)は僕(ぼく)が嫌(きら)いになったのかなあ。
   (Perhaps she doesn't love me any more.)

   B: **それは**違(ちが)うよ。
   (That's not true.)

   (2) [When giving a gift,]

   A: これ，つまらないものですが。
   (This is nothing special, but . . .)

   B: **それは**ご丁寧(ていねい)に。
   (That's very kind of you.)

Note that *sore wa* in these examples cannot be preceded by interjections such as *hai* and *ee*.

S

sorezore　それぞれ　*adv.*

each of two or more things / persons	each; respectively【REL. *meimei*; *ono'ono*】

◆Key Sentences

(A)

山田さんと鈴木さんは，果物とお菓子を	それぞれ	買った。
(Yamada and Suzuki bought fruits and cakes, respectively.)		

(B)

読んだ小説は	それぞれ	面白かった。
(Each of the novels I read was interesting (in its own way).)		

Examples

(a) 好子，美保子，信夫はそれぞれ十五歳，十三歳，九歳です。
(Yoshiko, Mihoko, and Nobuo are 15, 13, and 9 years old, respectively.)

(b) 父は私と妹に，それぞれ，一万円のお小遣いをくれた。
(Father gave me and my younger sister a 10,000 yen allowance each.)

(c) トムは寮の部屋で，僕は図書館で，それぞれ勉強する。
(Tom and I study in the dorm room and at the library, respectively.)

(d) ボブはベスと，一雄はジェミーと，それぞれ出かけた。
(Bob and Kazuo went out with Beth and Jemmy, respectively.)

(e) 私達は兄弟だが，趣味がそれぞれ違う。
(We are brothers, but each of us has different interests.)

(f) 誰でもそれぞれ長所と短所がある。
(Each of us has our strengths and weaknesses.)

(g) このキャンパスの建物はそれぞれ個性がある。
(Each of the buildings of this campus has its own individuality.)

(h) レストランではそれぞれ好きな物を食べました。
(At the restaurant we ate what each of us like.)

(i) 裁判官はそれぞれの席に着いた。
(The judges took their respective seats.)

Notes

1. *Sorezore* is used to express an idea of 'each' or 'respectively.'

2. There are two types of construction that involve *sorezore*. One is the construction that is a condensed version of two or more co-ordinated sentences as in KS(A) and Exs.(a) – (d). For example, KS (A) is a reduction from (1) below:

    (1) 山田さんは果物を買って，鈴木さんはお菓子を買った。
    (Yamada bought fruits and Suzuki bought cakes.)

    This sentence can be condensed either into KS(A), (2) or (3).

    (2) 山田さんは果物を，鈴木さんはお菓子を買った。
    (Yamada bought fruits, and Suzuki, cakes.)

    (3) 山田さんは果物を，鈴木さんはお菓子を，**それぞれ**買った。
    (Yamada bought fruits, and Suzuki, cake, respectively.)

    The other type is a construction that is not a reduction from a coordinated sentence as exemplified by KS(B) and Exs.(e) – (h).

3. *Sorezore* can be used as a pronoun as in Ex.(i). In this case *sorezore* is used in a combination of *sorezore no* N. Two more examples follow:

    (4) オーケストラは**それぞれの**音色を持っている。
    (Orchestras have their own respective sounds.)

    (5) 学生は**それぞれの**自転車で登校する。
    (Students come to school on their own bicycles.)

4. *Sorezore* can be used as a kind of noun as shown in (6) and (7) below.

    (6) 宇宙の星は**それぞれ**が引力で引き合っている。
    (The stars of the universe are each pulling others by gravitation.)

(7) このワインの中にはフランス産とドイツ産が混じっています。匂いをかいだだけで，**それぞれ**を言い当てることが出来ますか。
(In these wines are mixed both French wines and German wines. Can you tell the respective wines by just smelling them?)

【Related Expression】

Meimei and *ono'ono* are similar in meaning to *sorezore*.

[1] 私達は兄弟だが，趣味が｛**それぞれ** / **各々** / **銘々**｝違う。(=Ex.(e))

But they are distinctly different. *Meimei* and *ono'ono* can refer only to a human, but *sorezore* can refer to anything, as shown in [2].

[2] 読んだ小説は｛**それぞれ** / ***各々** / ***銘々**｝面白かった。(=KS(B))

Furthermore, *sorezore* can be used in a condensed structure as in KS(A) and Exs.(a) – (d), but neither *meimei* nor *ono'ono* can be used in this structure, as shown in [3].

[3] 山田さんと鈴木さんは，果物とお菓子を｛**それぞれ** / ***各々** / ***銘々**｝買った。(=KS(A))

sugu すぐ *adv.*

without having much temporal or physical distance

at once; soon; right away; immediately; readily; instantly; easily; right
【REL. *mō sugu*】

◆Key Sentences

(A)

家に帰ったら	すぐ，	寝てしまいました。
(I went to sleep as soon as I got home.)		

(B)

銀行は駅の	すぐ	前です。
(The bank is right in front of the station.)		

Examples

(a) 部長は会社に着くとすぐ，仕事を始めた。
(The departmental head started to work as soon as he arrived at the company.)

(b) 日本に来たらすぐ，電話して下さい。
(Please call me as soon as you come to Japan.)

(c) 話したいから，すぐ来て下さい。
(I want to talk with you, so please come right away.)

(d) 安いテレビを買ったらすぐ，壊れてしまいました。
(I bought a cheap TV and it broke right away.)

(e) あの人はすぐ怒るから，嫌いだ。
(He easily gets angry so I don't like him.)

(f) その数学の問題はすぐ解けた。
(I could solve that math problem easily.)

(g) 私の家はすぐそこです。
(My house is right there.)

(h) 郵便局はスーパーのすぐ隣です。
(The post-office is right next to the supermarket.)

Notes

1. *Sugu* in KS(A) and Exs.(a) – (f) means 'without much temporal distance,' whereas in KS(B), Exs.(g) and (h) it means 'without much spatial distance.'

2. ~ *tara/to sugu* is used to mean 'as soon as ~' as in KS(A), Exs.(a) and (b), if the main verb is a volitional verb. Ex.(d) cannot mean 'as soon as,' because the verb is a non-volitional verb. Another example follows:

   (1) そのエビを食べ**たら**, **すぐ**おなかが痛くなった。
   (I got a stomachache straight after eating that shrimp.)

【Related Expression】

Mō sugu as in [1] is used to mean 's.t. is going to take place very soon since a triggering event has already taken place.' Sentences [2] and [3] are unacceptable because in [2] the triggering event (i.e., a telephone call) has not taken place and in [3] the triggered event (Smith's coming) has already taken place.

[1] スミスさんは電話したから, **もうすぐ**来るよ。
(Because we have called Mr. Smith, he will come pretty soon.)

[2] *スミスさんは電話すれば, **もうすぐ**来るよ。
(*If we call Mr. Smith, he will come pretty soon.)

[3] *スミスさんは電話したら, **もうすぐ**来た。
(*Mr. Smith came pretty soon when we called him.)

tabi ni たびに *conj.*

> a conjunction to express that each time s.o. / s.t. does s.t., s.t. else takes place

every time; each time; on every occasion; whenever
【REL. *itsu* (*de*) *mo*; *to itsu* (*de*) *mo*; *toki* (*ni*) *wa*】

◆Key Sentences

(A)

	Vinf·nonpast		
日本へ	**行く**	たびに	新しいことを学んで帰ります。
(Each time I go to Japan I come home having learned something new.)			

(B)

	Noun			
父は	**旅行**	の	たびに	おみやげを買ってきてくれる。
(On every trip my father comes back with souvenirs.)				

Formation

(i) Vinf·nonpast たびに

食べるたびに (each time s.o. eats s.t.)

勉強するたびに (each time s.o. studies (s.t.))

(ii) N のたびに

試験のたびに (on every examination occasion)

(iii) VN のたびに

勉強のたびに (on every occasion of study)

Examples

(a) あの人と話すたびに心が和みます。
(Each time I talk with her my heart softens.)

(b) この本は読むたびに新しい発見がある。
(Each time I read this book I discover new things.)

(c) 僕は東京に行くたびに恩師のお宅を訪ねることにしている。
(I make it a point of visiting my professor's residence every time I go to Tokyo.)

(d) 私の孫は会うたびに前より大きくなっている。
(Every time I see my grandson, he has become bigger than before.)

(e) モーツァルトの音楽を聞くたびに人生が豊かになった気がする。
(Each time I listen to Mozart's music I feel my life is enriched.)

(f) 誕生日のたびに夫はバラの花を買ってくれます。
(On every birthday my husband buys me roses.)

(g) うちでは給料日のたびに銀座のレストランで食事をします。
(Our family eats at a restaurant in the Ginza every payday.)

Notes

1. The meaning of 'each / every time' is emphasized by inserting *goto* between *tabi* and *ni*.

   (1) a. 日本へ行く**たびごとに**新しいことを学んで帰ります。 (cf. KS(A))

   b. 父は旅行の**たびごとに**おみやげを買ってきてくれる。 (cf. KS(B))

2. The tense of the verb that comes before *tabi ni* is restricted to nonpast.

3. The particle *ni* of *tabi ni* cannot be dropped.

【Related Expressions】

I. Sinf *tabi ni*, N *no tabi ni* and VN *no tabi ni* can be paraphrased by Sinf *toki* (*ni*) *wa itsu* (*de*) *mo*, N *ni wa itsu* (*de*) *mo*, and VN *suru toki wa itsu* (*de*) *mo* respectively, as shown in [1].

[1] a. あの人と話す**時**(とき)**(に)はいつ(で)も**心が和みます。(cf. Ex.(a))

b. 誕生日**にはいつ(で)も**夫はバラの花を買ってくれます。(cf. Ex.(f))

c. 父は旅行 {**する時はいつ(で)も** / ***にはいつ(で)も**} おみやげを買ってきてくれる。(cf. KS(B))

The paraphrasability between the two structures does not always mean that they are synonymous. Since the tense of the verb that comes before *tabi ni* is restricted to nonpast, Ex.(e), for example, is ambiguous as to whether the speaker feels his life is enriched while listening to Mozart or after he has finished listening to it. The two readings of Ex.(e) correspond to [2a] and [2b] below.

[2] a. モーツァルトの音楽を**聞く**時にはいつでも人生が豊かになった気がする。
(When I listen to Mozart's music I always feel my life is enriched.)

b. モーツァルトの音楽を**聞いた**時にはいつでも人生が豊かになった気がする。
(When I have listened to Mozart's music I always feel my life is enriched.)

Such two-way interpretation is also possible with Exs.(a) – (c), but the interpretation is logically impossible for KS(A) and Ex.(d).

(⇨ ***toki*** (DBJG: 490–94))

T

II. Sinf *tabi ni* and N *no tabi ni* can also be paraphrased by Sinf·nonpast *to itsu* (*de*) *mo*. The original and the paraphrased versions again mean practically the same. Notice, however, that unlike Ex.(e), [3] is not ambiguous like [2] above: it means only [2b].

[3] モーツァルトの音楽を聞く**といつ(で)も**人生が豊かになった気がする。

(⇨ ***to***[4] (DBJG: 480–82))

tada ただ *adv.*

an adverb which emphasizes the idea of "only"

only; just; simply; that's all
【REL. *tatta*】

◆Key Sentences

(A)

		One + Counter		Noun		
彼(かれ)の	ただ	**一つ(ひと)**	の	欠点(けってん)	は	時間(じかん)にルーズだということだ。
(His only (one) defect is that he is not punctual (lit. he is slack about time).)						

(B)

			One + Counter			Verbal(neg)
彼女(かのじょ)は	ただ	の	**一度(いちど)**	も	手紙(てがみ)を	くれなかった。
(She didn't write me even once (lit. only once).)						

(C)

		Noun			
彼は	ただ	**弁護士(べんごし)**	だけ	が	頼(たよ)りだ。
(He has no one else to rely on but his lawyer.)					

(D)

		Predicate			
彼女とは	ただ	**お茶を飲んで話をした**	(という)	だけ	だ。
(I just talked with her over a cup of tea; that's all.)					

Formation

(i) ただ *One* + Counter (の N)

ただ一人の息子 (the only son)

ただ一発で (with only one shot)

(ii) ただの *One* + Counter も Verbal(neg)

ただの一日も休んだことがない (have not taken even one day off)

(iii) ただ N だけ (Prt.)

ただ単語だけ(を)覚える (remember only words)

ただ力だけで解決する (solve s.t. only with force)

(iv) ただ Verbal (という)だけ(だ)

ただ読んだ(という)だけ(だ) (S.o. just read it; that's all.)

ただ安い(という)だけ(だ) (S.t. is just cheap; that's all.)

ただ {静かな / 静かだという} だけ(だ) (S.t. is just quiet; that's all.)

ただ大学教授(だ)というだけ(だ) (S.o. is just a college professor ; that's all.)

T

Examples

(a) 彼はただ一人でやってきた。
(He came over alone.)

(b) 私達が困っていた時，助けてくれた者はただの一人もいなかった。
(Not a single person helped us when we were in trouble.)

(c) ただそれだけのことで彼を首にしたんですか。
(Did you fire him only for that reason?)

(d) ただ言われたことだけをやっていても進歩はない。
(There will be no progress if you do only what you are told to do.)

(e) 私はただ頼まれたことをしているだけだ。
(I am just doing what I was asked to do; that's all.)

(f) あの男はただまじめだというだけだ。
(He is just serious; he has no other merit.)

(g) 別に大した意味はないんですが，ただちょっと聞いてみたかったんです。
(It doesn't have any special meaning, but I just wanted to ask.)

(h) ただ人の言うことを鵜呑みにしていては面白い発想は生まれない。
(If you simply swallow what other people say, you won't come up with any interesting ideas.)

Notes

1. *Tada* is a device to emphasize such ideas as "only," "just," and "simply." As a matter of fact, a sentence with *tada* and one without *tada* mean the same thing unless *tada* is followed by *One* + Counter *no* Noun (e.g., *hito-ri no otoko* 'a man,' *ichi-dai no kuruma* 'a car'). For example, the two sentences in (1) and (2) are semantically equivalent. The addition of *tada* however, makes the (a) sentences more emphatic.

   (1) a. 彼女は**ただの一度も**手紙をくれなかった。(=KS(B))

   b. 彼女は**一度も**手紙をくれなかった。

   (2) a. 彼は**ただ弁護士だけ**が頼りだ。(=KS(C))

   b. 彼は**弁護士だけが**頼りだ。

   When *tada* is followed by *One* + Counter *no* Noun, the meaning changes, as in [3].

   (3) a. 彼の**ただ一つの**欠点は時間にルーズだということだ。(=KS(A))
   (His only (one) defect is that he is not punctual.)

b. 彼の**一つの**欠点は時間にルーズだということだ。
(One of his defects is that he is not punctual.)

2. *Tada* can be used in a variety of sentence patterns. Those presented in KS and in Formation are not exhaustive. (See Exs.(g) and (h).)

【Related Expression】

Tatta can be used instead of *tada* when *One* + Counter immediately follows, as in KS(A) and Ex.(a).

[1] a. 彼の {**ただ / たった**} **一つの**欠点は時間にルーズだということだ。(=KS(A))

b. 彼は {**ただ / たった**} **一人で**やってきた。(=Ex.(a))

However, *tatta* cannot replace *tada* in its other uses, as in [2].

[2] a. 彼女は {**ただ / *たった**} **の一度も**手紙をくれなかった。(=KS(B))

b. 彼は {**ただ / *たった**} **弁護士だけが**頼りだ。(=KS(C))

c. 彼女とは {**ただ / *たった**} **お茶を飲んで話をした**(**という**)**だけ**だ。(=KS(D))

On the other hand, *tada* cannot be used to modify a number beyond one or to modify an adverb, as in [3] and [4].

[3] 私はこの夏(なつ) {**たった / *ただ**} **二日(ふつか)しか**休まなかった。
(I took only two days off this summer.)

[4] ジョンは {**たった / *ただ**} **今**帰(いまかえ)ったばかりです。
(John has just left/come back (lit. left/come back just now).)

tada no ただの *phr.*

not deserving to be mentioned

usual; ordinary; plain; common; rank-and-file
【REL. *futsū no*; ***ni suginai***】

◆Key Sentence

		Noun	
私(わたし)は	ただの	**平社員(ひらしゃいん)**	ですから，そんなことは知(し)りません。
(I'm only an ordinary employee, so I'm not aware of that.)			

Formation

ただの N

ただの先生(せんせい) (an ordinary teacher)

Examples

(a) ただの風邪(かぜ)だと思(おも)っていたら，肺炎(はいえん)だった。
(I thought it was an ordinary cold, but it was pneumonia.)

(b) あの人(ひと)はただの学者(がくしゃ)ではないようですね。
(He doesn't appear to be an ordinary scholar, does he?)

(c) ただの集(あつ)まりだと思って，顔(かお)を出(だ)したら，偉(えら)い人達(たち)が出席(しゅっせき)していたのでびっくりした。
(I put in an appearance because I thought it was an ordinary gathering, but to my surprise there were big shots attending.)

(d) A: お父様(とうさま)はお偉い方(かた)だったそうですね。
(I heard that your father was a great man.)

B: いいえ，とんでもありません。ただの大学(だいがく)教師(きょうし)でした。
(No, not at all. He was an ordinary college professor.)

(e) ただの冗談(じょうだん)ですよ。
(I'm just kidding, you know.)

Note

Tada no N is used when the speaker makes nothing out of s.t. / s.o. Therefore, it can be used as a humble expression as in KS and Ex.(d).

【Related Expression】

Tada no N is similar in meaning to *futsū no* N which means 'ordinary N.' The latter does not carry the former's emotive overtone of 'making nothing out of s.t. / s.o.'; it is, rather a neutral term to mean 'not special,' or 'standard.' So when the emotive overtone is strong (including a case of humble expression) *tada no* can hardly be replaced by *futsū no*, as shown below.

[1] a. 私は｛**ただ** / ?**普通**(ふつう)｝**の**平社員ですから，そんなことは知りません。(=KS)

b. いいえ，とんでもありません。｛**ただ** / ??**普通**｝**の**大学教師でした。(=Ex.(d))

c. ｛**ただ** / ***普通**｝**の**冗談ですよ。(=Ex.(e))

tashikani ~ ga 確かに〜が *str.*

a structure which expresses the idea "indeed ~ but"

indeed ~ but; certainly ~ but; truly ~ but; it is true that ~ but; I admit that ~ but; definitely ~ but
【REL. ~ *koto wa* ~ *ga*】

◆Key Sentence

Topic		Comment$_1$		Comment$_2$
この車は	確かに	**魅力的だ**	が,	値段が高すぎる。
(This car is certainly attractive, but the price is too high.)				

Examples

(a) そのパーティーのことは確かに聞いたが，いつだったか思い出せない。
(I certainly heard about the party, but I don't remember when it is going to be.)

(b) 確かに約束はしたが，今すぐとは言わなかった。
(It's true that I promised (to do it), but I didn't say that I would do it right now.)

(c) 彼は確かに第一印象がよくないが，本当はいい男なんだよ。
(He definitely makes a bad first impression, but actually he is a nice man.)

(d) この学校は確かにいい学校だが，僕には向いていない。
(I admit that this is a good school, but it's not suitable for me.)

(e) 確かに僕が悪かったが，そんなに怒ることはないだろう。
(I admit that it was my fault (lit. I was bad.), but you shouldn't be that mad.)

(f) 確かに多くの日本人が海外へ出かけるようになった。外国語を上手に話す人もたくさんいる。しかし，本当の国際人と呼べる人はまだ少ない。
(It it true that many Japanese go abroad now. There are also many who speak other languages (lit. foreign languages) well. However, there are still few who can be called "true internationalists.")

Note

Tashikani ~ ga is usually used when the speaker admits that something is certain or true but wants to say something in opposition to what is admitted.

【Related Expression】

~ koto wa ~ ga can replace *tashikani ~ ga*, as seen in [1]; however, the sentence with *tashikani ~ ga* sounds more subjective.

[1] a. この車は {**確かに魅力的だ / 魅力的なことは魅力的だ**} が値段が高すぎる。(=KS)

b. {**確かに約束はした / 約束したことはした**} が今すぐとは言わなかった。(=Ex.(b))

(⇨ ***koto wa*** (DBJG: 206–08))

ta tokoro de たところで *conj.*

even if an action or a state were realized	even if 【REL. *te mo*】

◆Key Sentence

	Vinf·past		
どんなに低(ひく)く	**見積(みつ)もった**	ところで,	工費(こうひ)は五億円(ごおくえん)を超(こ)えるだろう。
(No matter how low we estimate the construction expense it will go beyond 500 million yen.)			

Formation

Vinf·past ところで

読(よ)んだところで (even if s.o. read s.t.)

飲(の)んだところで (even if s.o. drank s.t.)

Examples

(a) この薬を飲んだところで，風邪がすぐ治るわけじゃない。
(Even if you took this medicine, it would not be the case that your cold would be cured right away.)

(b) この本を読んだところで，日本の経済の全体は分からないだろう。
(Even if you read this book, you wouldn't understand the entire economy of Japan.)

(c) 一週間に一度ぐらい運動したところで，あまり効果はないでしょう。
(Even if you exercise once a week, it won't be very effective.)

(d) どんなに頑張ったところで，この科目では優が取れるはずがない。
(No matter how much I worked, it would be impossible to get an A in this course.)

(e) 休みに天気が良くなったところで，どこかへ出かけるあてもない。
(Even if the weather gets better on the holiday, there is no particular place to go.)

(f) 日本語が話せたところで，日本へ行く金もないので，何にもならない。
(Even if I were able to speak Japanese, it wouldn't amount to anything, because I cannot afford to go to Japan.)

(g) これ以上話し合ったところで，恐らく無駄でしょう。
(Even if we discussed it more, it would probably be futile.)

(h) 問題が起こったところで，君には迷惑はかからない。
(Even if a problem arises, it will not cause you any trouble.)

Notes

1. The conjunction *tokoro de* is used with Vinf·past. The past form is used here not as the past tense marker but as the counterfactual marker. So in every case what is expressed in the *tokoro de* clause has not taken place yet. What the conjunction really means is: 'even if one supposes an action or a state in the clause has already taken place.'

2. The main clause usually takes an explicit negative marker *nai*, but there

are cases like KS and Ex.(g) in which the main clauses express something undesirable.

【Related Expression】

Vinf·past *tokoro de* can always be replaced by V*te mo*.

[1] a. どんなに低く見積もっ**ても**，工費は五億円を超えるだろう。 (cf. KS)

b. この薬を飲ん**でも**，風邪がすぐ治るわけじゃない。(cf. Ex.(a))

c. 一週間に一度ぐらい運動し**ても**，あまり効果はないでしょう。 (cf. Ex.(c))

However, there is a crucial difference between Vinf · past *tokoro de* and V*te mo*. The former has a clear counterfactual meaning, but the latter does not have a clear counterfactual meaning.

There are a lot of cases where V*te mo* cannot be replaced by Vinf · past *tokoro de* owing to the crucial difference. Notice that in [2] below V*te mo* clearly expresses not something counterfactual but something factual.

[2] a. 主人(しゅじん)は私(わたし)が何(なん)度注意(ちゅうい) {**しても** / ***したところで**} たばこをやめない。

(My husband won't quit smoking no matter how many times I advise him.)

b. 僕(ぼく)は何(なに)を {**食**(た)**べても** / ***食べたところで**} 太(ふと)っちゃうんです。

(I gain weight no matter what I eat.)

T

Another crucial difference is that the main clause for Vinf · past *tokoro de* has to be negative either explicitly or implicitly; whereas the main clause for *te mo* can be affirmative. (See Note 2.)

[3] a. この科目を {**取らなくても** / ??**取らなかったところで**} 卒業(そつぎょう)は出来(でき)る。

(I can graduate even if I don't take this course.)

b. 鉛筆(えんぴつ)で {**書**(か)**いても** / ***書いたところで**} いいですか。

(Can I write with a pencil?)

c. ちょっと {**読んでも** / ***読んだところで**} つまらない本だとすぐ分かる。
(Even if you read a little you can tell that it is a boring book.)

(⇨ ***te mo*** (DBJG: 468–70))

te て *te-form*

after / since a point in time at which s.t. takes place

and; since; having done s.t.
【REL. *te kara*】

◆Key Sentence

	V*te*	
こちらに	**いらっしゃって**	もう何年になりますか。
(How long have you been here / How many years is it since you came here?)		

Formation

V*te* N (duration)

来て二年 (it has been two years since s.o. came)

Examples

(a) 二人は結婚して二年後に離婚した。
(The couple got married and two years later they got divorced.)

(b) 会社を辞めてもう久しい。
(It has been a long time since I quit the company.)

(c) この島を訪れてもう何年になるだろうか。
(I wonder how many years have already passed since I last visited this island.)

(d) この会社で働き始めてこれで四年になります。
(It's been four years since I began to work at this company.)

(e) この町に来てまだ一週間目です。
(It's my first week in this town.)

Notes

1. The *te* form in question is followed by a duration.

(⇨ ***-te*** (DBJG: 464–67))

2. The antonym for V*te* + N(duration) is Vinf·nonpast + N(duration) *mae ni* as in (1) below.

   (1) 二人は**結婚する二年前に**お見合いをした。
   (The couple met by arrangement two years before they got married.)

【Related Expression】

All the *te* forms in KS and Exs. can be replaced by *te kara*. The only difference is that *te kara* focuses on the point in time at which s.t. takes place; whereas *te* focuses on the duration of time following *te*.

(⇨ ***kara***[2] (DBJG: 177–78))

te hajimete て初めて *phr.*

a phrase which expresses the idea that s.o. does s.t. or s.t. happens only after s.t. else happens or s.t. else is done

not until; only after; for the first time

◆Key Sentence

	V*te*		
アメリカへ	**来**て	初めて	竜巻を見た。
(It was not until I came to America that I saw a tornado.)			

Formation

V*te* 初めて

読んで初めて　(only after you read)

Examples

(a) 日本で生活して初めて日本人のものの考え方が分かってきた。
(It was not until I lived in Japan that I started to understand how Japanese people thihk.)

(b) 日本語を勉強して初めて外国語を学ぶ面白さを知った。
(I didn't realize how interesting learning a foreign language was until I studied Japanese.)

(c) 考えは文字にしてみて初めてはっきりすることが多い。
(It is often not until you write down your idea that it becomes clear.)

(d) 病気になって初めて健康の有り難さが分かる。
(It is only after you become ill that you realize the value of health.)

(e) 生まれて初めてさしみを食べた。
(I ate sashimi for the first time in my life.)

Note

Umarete hajimete in Ex.(e) is an idiomatic phrase which means 'for the first time in one's life.' Note that it does not mean 'only after one was born' or 'not until one was born.' This phrase also appears in the structure in (1) below.

(1) [Before, while, or just after eating sashimi]

さしみ(を食べるの)は**生まれて初めて**です。
(This is the first time I've had sashimi.)

ten (de) 点(で) *n.*

a noun which expresses the idea of "a point of argument; a point of evaluation; a point of view"

point; respect; regard; aspect; way; in terms of; -wise; in that; as far as ~ is concerned
【REL. *-men*】

◆Key Sentences

(A)

	Dem.			
彼(かれ)は	**そういう**	点(てん)	で	まだ大人(おとな)とは言(い)えない。
(He is not (lit. cannot be called) an adult in that respect.)				

(B)

Adj (*i* / *na*) stem					
使(つか)いやす	**さ**	の	点	では	この辞書(じしょ)はネルソンの漢英辞典(かんえいじてん)に及(およ)ばない。
(This dictionary is no match for Nelson's Japanese-English Character Dictionary in terms of ease of use.)					

(C)

Noun		Adj (*i* / *na*) stem					
通勤(つうきん)	**の**	**便利**(べんり)	**さ**	という	点	では	今(いま)のアパートは最高(さいこう)だ。
(In terms of commuting convenience, the present apartment is the best.)							

(D)

Topic	Clause				
このテーブルは	**手作**(てづく)**りである**	（という）	点	で	値打(ねう)ちがある。
(This table is valuable in that it is handmade.)					

Formation

(i) {Demonstrative / Quantifier} 点(で)

この点で (in this regard)

二(に)，三(さん)の点で (on a couple of points)

(ii) {N / Adj(*i* / *na*)stem さ} の点(で)

値段(ねだん)の点で (in terms of price)

大(おお)きさの点で (in terms of size)

静(しず)かさの点で (in terms of quietness)

(iii) N の Adj(*i* / *na*)stem さという点(で)

頭(あたま)のよさという点で (in terms of brightness)

体(からだ)の柔軟(じゅうなん)さという点で (in terms of body flexibility)

(iv) Sinf という点(で)

性能(せいのう)がいいという点で (in that the performance is good)

Examples

(a) 我が社の製品はすべての点で国外の類似製品より優れている。
(Our product is superior to similar foreign products in every way.)

(b) 学力の点ではこの学生が一番だろう。
(With regard to scholarship, this student is probably the best.)

(c) 住みやすさの点では私はこの町の方が前に住んだ町より気に入っている。
(In terms of livability I like this city better than the one where I lived before (this one).)

(d) 時間の正確さという点では日本の鉄道は世界一でしょう。
(In terms of punctuality the railway systems in Japan are probably the best in the world.)

(e) イルカは言葉を話すという点で他の多くの水生動物より高等であると言える。
(Dolphins can be said to be superior to other aquatic animals in that they speak (language).)

(f) 彼女と私はクラシック音楽が好きだという点で趣味が一致している。
(She and I share the same taste in that both of us like classical music.)

(g) スミス氏は時代を先取り出来るという点で社長に適任だ。
(Mr. Smith is the right person for president in that he can anticipate the trends of the times.)

Notes

Ten can be followed by particles other than *de*, as in (1).

(1) a. 彼女のそういう点**が**人に嫌われるのだ。
(It is that aspect which people dislike about her.)

b. 私は彼の日本語がよく出来る点**を**評価したい。
(I value (lit. I'd like to value) the fact (lit. the point) that he is very good at Japanese.)

c. 私はこの製品が未来を指向している点**に**引かれる。
(I am attracted by this product in that it is future-oriented.)

d. その点**について**何人かの人から質問を受けた。
(I was asked questions on that point by some people.)

【Related Expression】

The suffix *-men* and the noun *ten* express a similar idea. As their original meanings (i.e., *men* 'face, side'; *ten* 'point') suggest, however, *-men* reflects a more general, broader viewpoint than *ten* does, as in [1] and [2].

[1] a. あの会社は {**技術面 / *技術の点**} に問題がある。
(That company has problems in terms of technology.)

b. 我々はその取引において {**値段の点 / *値段面**} で合意出来なかった。
(In that business deal we couldn't agree in terms of the price.)

[2] a. この車は {**性能面 / *性能の点**} を高く評価された。
(This car was highly regarded in terms of performance.)

b. この車は性能が優れている {**点 / *面**} を高く評価された。
(This car was highly regarded in terms of its excellent performance (lit. the point that the performance is excellent).)

(⇨ ***-men***)

te wa てはconj.

a conjunction which presents an action / state as a topic about which a negative comment is given	if; when; because

◆Key Sentences

(A)

	V*te*		
そんなに	勉強(べんきょう)**し**て	は,	体(からだ)をこわしますよ。
(If you study that hard, you will ruin your health.)			

(B)

	Adj(*i*)*te*		
こんなに	**寒(さむ)く**て	は	外出(がいしゅつ)できません。
(We cannot go out in this cold weather (lit. when it is this cold).)			

(C)

	Adj(*na*)*te*		
仕事(しごと)がそんなに	**嫌(きら)い**で	は	困(こま)りますね。
(It's too bad that you hate your work that much.)			

Formation

(i) V*te* は

食(た)べては (when / if one eats; to eat)

(ii) Adj(*i* / *na*)*te* は

大(おお)きくては (when / if s.t. / s.o. is big)

不便(ふべん)では (when / if s.t. is inconvenient)

(iii) N では

病気(びょうき)では(頼(たの)めない) (if s.o. is ill (I can't ask him to do s.t.))

T

あの先生では（話にならない） (that teacher (would be out of the question))

Examples

(a) そんなに遊んでいては，試験に失敗しますよ。
(If you are fooling around like that, you will fail the examination.)

(b) あの男が来ては邪魔になる。
(If he comes he will get in our way.)

(c) こんなに働かされては，病気になってしまうよ。
(If I'm forced to work like this, I will end up by becoming ill.)

(d) こんなに部屋が汚くては，お客さんが見えた時に恥ずかしい。
(Because the room is messy like this, I feel ashamed when I have a guest.)

(e) 人が皆個人主義的では，国はやっていけない。
(If everybody is individualistic, a country cannot get along well.)

(f) こんなに忙しくては，新聞も読めない。
(When one is this busy, one cannot read even the newspaper.)

(g) あんな女性がデートの相手では，彼は小さくなっているだろう。
(If a woman like her is his date, he must feel intimidated.)

Notes

1. The conjunction *te wa* is used to connect an action or state presented as a topic and a negative comment. The information of the *te wa* clause is shared information and often includes the demonstrative adjective *ko-*, *so-*, *a-*, as shown in KS, Exs.(a) – (d), (f) and (g).

2. *te wa* is etymologically V*te* + *wa* (topic marker), but it is used like a conjunction.

3. V*te wa ikenai*, a phrase which indicates prohibition, is a special case of the *te wa* construction. (⇨ ***~ wa ikenai*** (DBJG: 528))

to と *prt.*

a particle which makes an adverbial clause, with a verb of saying / thinking / understood after it

(thinking / saying) that ~; because; like; in such a way that ~

◆Key Sentences

(A)

幸夫(ゆきお)は来年(らいねん)は家(いえ)が買(か)える	と	大変(たいへん) 喜(よろこ)んでいる。
(Yukio is very happy that he can buy a house next year.)		

(B)

S (internal monologue)		
博物館(はくぶつかん)は開(あ)いているかな	と,	電話(でんわ)してみた。
(Wondering if the museum is open I called them.)		

(C)

テニスをしよう	と	出(で)かけたら,	途中(とちゅう)で雨(あめ)が降(ふ)ってきた。
(With the intention of playing tennis (lit. Thinking that I will play tennis) I went out, but on my way it started to rain.)			

T

(D)

父はまだ元気なようだ	と	安心していたが，最近急に弱ってきた。
(I felt at ease, thinking that my father still looked healthy, but suddenly he began to grow weak.)		

(E)

外国語の能力は単語から文，文から段落，そして段落から複段落	と，	伸びていく。
(Foreign language proficiency develops from words to sentences, from sentences to paragraphs, and then from paragraphs to complex paragraphs.)		

Formation

(i) {V / Adj(*i* / *na*)} inf と（思って / 言って）V of psychology

読めると（思って / 言って）うれしがっている (s.o. is happy thinking / saying that s/he can read it)

面白いと（思って / 言って）喜んでいる (s.o. is happy thinking / saying that s.t. is interesting)

便利だと（思って / 言って）うれしがっている (s.o. is happy thinking / saying that s.t. is convenient)

(ii) S (internal monologue) と（思って）

もう会うまいと，縁を切った (thinking that s.o. would not see s.o. else, he severed the relationship)

映画でも見に行こうかなと，出かけた (wondering if I should go see a movie I left home)

(iii) Vvol と（思って / して）

食べようと（思って / して） (thinking that s/he would eat it)

(iv) {V / Adj(*i* / *na*)} inf (conjectural) と(思って)

来ないだろうと(思って) (thinking that s/he might not come)

つまらないかもしれないと(思って)
(thinking that s.t. might be boring)

元気だろうと(思って) (thinking that s.o. might be healthy)

(v) N Prt N, . . . N Prt N (そして) N Prt N と(いう {よう / 風} に) V

男は二階，女は一階と(いう {よう / 風} に)，部屋を分ける
(s.o. divides the rooms in such a way that men are placed upstairs and women in the first floor)

Examples

(a) 友達は長い間飼っていた猫が死んでしまったと，悲しがっていた。
(My friend looked sad, saying that a cat, which she kept for a long time, had died.)

(b) 彼はがんになったかもしれないと心配している。
(He is worried that he may have cancer.)

(c) その学生はもうちょっとで百点が取れたのにと，悔しがった。
(That student felt chagrined that he could almost get 100 points.)

(d) 彼女と会うのもこれが最後かと，寂しかったのです。
(Thinking that this would be the last time to see her, I felt lonely.)

(e) 変な音がしたなと，外に出てみたが，何でもなかった。
(Wondering what the strange noise was, I went outside, but it was nothing.)

(f) 僕は今晩は酒を飲むまいと，まっすぐ家に帰った。
(I came straight home, thinking that I would not drink tonight.)

(g) 年内に論文を仕上げようと，懸命に努力しているところです。
(Thinking that I should complete the paper before the end of the year, I am right now doing my very best.)

(h) 彼にお礼を言おうとやって来たのに，ほかのことばかり話して，お礼を

言うのを忘れてしまった。
(I came here intending to thank him, but I just talked about something else, and forgot to thank him.)

(i) 少しは体にいいだろうと，最近は散歩をしています。
(I thought it would make a small improvent to my body, so I am taking walks these days.)

(j) 宿題を忘れたので先生に叱られるかもしれないと，びくびくしていた。
(I forgot my homework so I feared that I might be scolded by my teacher.)

(k) 日本の四季は，春は三月から五月，夏は六月から八月，秋は九月から十一月，冬は十二月から二月までと，どの季節もほぼ同じ長さになっている。
(In Japan the four seasons are of approximately equal length, in such a way that spring is from March through May, summer from June through August, autumn from September through November, and winter from December through February.)

(l) 彼は朝は和食，昼はめん類，夜は洋食と，食事のパターンが決まっている。
(His eating pattern is fixed so that he has a Japanese style dish for breakfast, noodles for lunch, and a western style dish for dinner.)

(m) 社長は先月はロンドン，今月はモスクワ，来月はソウルと，出張が多い。
(The president is busy making business trips, to London last month, to Moscow this month, to Seoul next month, and so on.)

Notes

1. For all the sentences given in KS and Exs, the verbs of saying, thinking, feeling or doing are ellipted, except KS(E) and Exs.(k) – (m) in which the entire *iu yōni / iu fū ni* is deleted.

(1) a. 幸夫は来年は家が買える**と**｛**思って** / **言って**｝，大変喜んでいる。(cf. KS(A))

b. 博物館は開いているかな**と思って**，電話してみた。(cf. KS(B))

c. テニスをしようと **{思って / して}** 出かけたら，途中で雨が降ってきた。(cf. KS(C))

d. 父はまだ元気なようだ**と思って**安心していたが，最近急に弱ってきた。(cf. KS(D))

e. 外国語の能力は単語から文，文から段落，そして段落から複段落**という {よう / 風} に**，伸びていく。(cf. KS(E))

KS(A) type, i.e., Exs.(a) – (c), KS(B) type, i.e., Exs.(d) – (f), KS(C) type, i.e., Exs.(g), (h), and KS(D) type, i.e., Exs.(i) and (j), usually take *omotte*. They can take *itte*, if the *to*-clause can be interpreted as a quote, as in KS(A) and Ex.(a). Notice that Ex.(a) may take *omotte*, but the meaning is not the same as the original ellipted one. It means 'My friend looked sad, wrongly assuming that a cat which she kept for a long time died.' For that matter, one of the interpretations of KS(A) is 'Yukio is very happy assuming wrongly that he can buy a house next year.' KS(C) type, i.e., Exs.(g) and (h), usually take *omotte* and *shite*. KS(E) type, i.e., Exs.(k) – (m), take *iu* {*yōni* / *fū ni*}.

(⇨ ***to***[3] (DBJG: 478–80))

2. In KS(A) type, the only type which allows ellipsis of *itte* the main verb is usually a psychological verb such as *yorokobu* 'rejoice' of KS(A), *kanashigaru* 'deplore' of Ex.(a), *shinpaisuru* 'worry' of Ex.(b), and *kuyashigaru* 'feel chagrined' of Ex.(c). Another notable thing about this type is that the whole sentence refers not to the speaker's but to a third person's psychological state.

T

(2) a. *僕は来年は家が買えると大変喜んでいる。(cf. KS(A))
(I'm very happy that I can buy a house next year.)

b. *私は長い間飼っていた猫が死んでしまったと，悲しかった。(cf. Ex.(a))
(I was sad that the cat I kept for a long time died.)

The acceptable versions of (2a) and (2b) are (3a) and (3b), respectively.

(3) a. 僕は来年は家が買える **{から / ので}** 大変喜んでいる。

b. 私は長い間飼っていた猫が死んでしまった {**から / ので**} 悲しかった。

3. The *omotte*-ellipsis is possible when the preceding verb expresses the speaker's volition with Vvol as in KS(C), Exs.(g) and (h) or his / her conjecture as in KS(D), Exs.(i) and (j). However, if the preceding verb does not express either volition or conjecture by means of *darō* (as in Ex.(i)), *kamoshirenai* (as in Ex.(j)) and *yōda* (as in KS(D)), the *omotte*-ellipsis does not usually occur.

(4) a. 日本語を日本で勉強するのも面白い**と** {**思って** / *ø}, 去年の夏日本で日本語を勉強した。
(Thinking that it would be interesting to study Japanese in Japan, last summer I studied Japanese in Japan.)

a′. 日本語を日本で勉強するのも面白い**だろうと** {**思って** / ø}, 去年の夏日本で日本語を勉強した。
(Thinking that it might be interesting to study Japanese in Japan, last summer I studied Japanese in Japan.)

(5) a. 太郎は冬休みに海外旅行でもしたい**と** {**思って** / *ø}, 急に家の近くの旅行代理店に出かけた。
(Taro suddenly went to a travel agent near his house, wanting to make a trip abroad during the winter break.)

a′. 太郎は冬休みに海外旅行でも**しようと** {**思って** / *ø}, 急に家の近くの旅行代理店に出かけた。
(Taro suddenly went to a travel agent near his house, wishing to make a trip abroad during the winter break.)

4. The *shite*-ellipsis out of Vvol *to shite* is possible only when the Vvol *to shite* clause appears in a larger construction, as in KS(C), Exs.(g) and (h). For example, in (6a) below, no action is described, so the *shite*-ellipsis is impossible, whereas in (6a′) an action is explicitly mentioned, so the ellipsis is possible.

(6) a. お金を払おう**と** {**して** / *ø}, 財布がないことに気がついた。
(When I tried to pay, I realized that I didn't have my purse.)

a′. お金を払おうと{**して** / ø}, **ポケットに手を突っ込んだ**が, 財布がないことに気がついた。
(I tried to pay and put my hand into my pocket, but I realized that I didn't have my purse.)

5. The *iu* {*yō* / *fū*} *ni*-ellipsis is possible when N Prt + N, . . . N Prt + N (*soshite*) N(Prt) precedes *to iu* {*yō* / *fū*} *ni*, as in KS(E) and Exs. (k) – (m). Otherwise the ellipsis is impossible unless the main verb is a verb of saying or thinking.

(7) a. 社長には問題はなかった**という**{**よう** / **風**}**に**言っておいて下さい。
(Please tell the president that there were no particular problems with it.)

→ 社長には問題はなかった**と**言っておいて下さい。

b. この物語は今の社会を風刺している**という**{**よう** / **風**}**に**は考えられませんか。
(Can't we regard this story as mocking contemporary society?)

→ この物語は今の社会を風刺している**と**は考えられませんか。

(⇨ ***to iu fū ni***)

(8) a. 彼はもう我慢が出来ない**という**{**よう** / **風**}**に**荒々しく立ち上がった。
(He stood up abruptly in a way that showed he could no longer stand it.)

→ *彼はもう我慢が出来ない**と**, 荒々しく立ち上がった。

b. 彼はどうしようもない**という**{**よう** / **風**}**に**首を振った。
(He shook his head in such a fashion as to suggest that there was no way out.)

→ *彼はどうしようもない**と**, 首を振った。

to dōji ni と同時に *comp. prt. / conj.*

a phrase which is used to express the idea that s.o. does s.t. or s.t. takes place at the same time as another action or event, or that s.o. or s.t. is in two states simultaneously

at the same time (as); at the time; when; as; while; as well as ~

【REL. *to tomo ni*; ***totan*** (***ni***)】

◆Key Sentences

(A)

	Noun		
彼は	**大学卒業**	と同時に	銀行に就職した。
(He got a job at a bank at the time of (lit. at the same time as) his graduation from college.)			

(B)

	Vinf·nonpast		
部屋に	**入る**	と同時に	電話が鳴った。
(The telephone rang (lit. at the same time) as I entered the room.)			

(C)

	Noun			Noun	
彼は	**この会社の社長**	**である**	と同時に	大株主	でもある。
(He is the president of this company and, at the same time, a big stockholder.)					

Formation

(i) N と同時に

到着と同時に (at the same time as s.o.'s arrival)

(ii) Vinf·nonpast と同時に

着くと同時に (at the same time as s.o. arrives)

(iii) {Adj(*na*)stem / N} であると同時に {Adj(*na*)stem / N} でもある。

便利であると同時に経済的でもある。
(S.t. is economical as well as convenient.)

フットボールの選手であると同時に野球の選手でもある。
(S.o. is a baseball player as well as a football player.)

Examples

(a) 彼女は結婚と同時に会社を辞めた。
(She quit her company at the time of (lit. at the same time as) her marriage.)

(b) 銃声と同時に警官の一人が倒れた。
(We heard the shot and saw one of the policemen fall. (lit. One of the policemen fell at the same time as the sound of a gun.))

(c) 新しい単語の学習と同時に文法の復習も忘れてはならない。
(You mustn't forget grammar review as well as new vocabulary study.)

(d) 私はルースと同時に日本語の勉強を始めた。
(I started my Japanese study when (lit. at the same time as) Ruth did.)

(e) 電車が止まってドアが開くと同時に客がなだれ込んだ。
(The train came to a halt and as the doors opened the passengers rushed into the train (lit. the passengers rushed into the train at the same time as the doors opened).)

(f) 新社長は就任すると同時に社名を変更した。
(The new president changed the company's name when (lit. at the same time as) he assumed the presidency.)

(g) 外国語を勉強する時は、文法を理解すると同時に文型の口頭練 習もしなければならない。
(When you study a foreign language, while you learn (lit. understand) grammar, you must also practice sentence patterns orally.)

(h) この新しい装置は安全であると同時に効率がいい。
(This new equipment is safe and, at the same time, its performance is good.)

(i) 森鷗外は医者であると同時に小 説家でもあった。
(Mori Ogai was a novelist as well as a doctor.)

Notes

1. *Na*-adjectives and nouns with *to dōji ni* (e.g., KS(C), Ex.(h)) usually appear in written language or formal speech.

2. *I*-adjectives are usually not used with *to dōji ni*, as in (1).

 (1) この設備は {**危険である / *危ない**} **と同時に**効率が悪い。
 (This equipment is dangerous and, at the same time, its performance is bad.)

【Related Expression】

To tomo ni can replace *to dōji ni* when a noun immediately precedes *to dōji ni*, as in [1].

[1] a. 彼は大学卒業**と** {**同時に / 共に**} 銀行に就職した。(=KS(A))

b. 銃声**と** {**同時に / 共に**} 警官の一人が倒れた。(=Ex.(b))

To tomo ni can also replace *to dōji ni* when {Adj(*na*)stem / N} *de aru* precedes to *dōji ni*, as in [2].

[2] a. 彼はこの会社の社長である**と** {**同時に / 共に**} 大株主でもある。 (=KS(C))

b. この新しい装置は安全である**と** {**同時に / 共に**} 効率がいい。 (=Ex.(h))

When a verb precedes *to dōji ni*, *to tomo ni* can replace *to dōji ni* only if the two actions or events are not momentary actions or events. Thus, *to tomo ni* is acceptable in [3] but not acceptable in [4].

[3] 外国語を勉強する時は，文法を理解する**と {同時に / 共に}** 文型の口頭練習もしなければならない。(=Ex.(g))

[4] a. 部屋に入る**と {同時に / *共に}** 電話が鳴った。(=KS(B))

b. 電車が止まってドアが開く**と {同時に / *共に}** 客がなだれ込んだ。(=Ex.(e))

Note that if a noun precedes *to dōji ni*, *to tomo ni* can replace *to dōji ni* even if the two actions or events are momentary, as in [1]. Compare [1] to [5] where verbs precede *to dōji ni*.

[5] a. 彼は大学を卒業する**と {同時に / *共に}** 銀行に就職した。 (cf. KS(A))
(He got a job at a bank when (lit. at the same time as) he graduated from college.)

b. 銃声が鳴る**と {同時に / *共に}** 警官の一人が倒れた。(cf. Ex.(b))
(We heard the shot and saw one of the policemen fall. (lit. One of the policemen fell at the same time as the sound of a gun.))

Note also that *to tomo ni* is usually used in written language.

(⇨ ***to tomo ni***)

T

to itte mo と言っても *phr.*

a phrase which is used to clarify a statement in the preceding discourse which might be misleading	although ~ say / said that ~; even though ~ say / said that ~

◆Key Sentences

(A)

Sentence$_1$	Sentence$_2$			
	Noun			
私には子供がいます。	**子供**	と言っても	もう大学生です	が。
(I have a child. Well, although I said, "child," he is already a college student (lit. he is already a college student, though).)				

(B)

A:
毎日お忙しいんでしょうね。
(You are busy every day, aren't you?)

B:			
	Adj·inf		
いえ,	**忙しい**	と言っても	週末は休んでいますから。
(No, although people may say that I'm busy, I do not work on weekends, so . . .)			

Formation

(i) N と言っても

先生と言っても (although (I) say, "teacher")

(ii) {V / Adj(*i*) / Adj(*na*) / N+Cop.}inf と言っても

{行く / 行った} と言っても (although (I) say that s.o. {will go / went})

{安い / 安かった} と言っても (although (I) say that it is / was cheap)

{静か / 静かだった} と言っても (although (I) say that it is / was quiet)

{病気だ / 病気だった} と言っても (although (I) say that s.o. is / was ill)

Examples

(a) もう三月だ。しかし，三月と言ってもこの辺はまだ寒い。
(It's already March. But even though I say, "March," it is still cold around here.)

(b) 山崎先生はまだお若いですよ。もちろん，若いと言っても五十代ですが。
(Prof. Yamazaki is still young. Of course, even though I said, "young," he is in his fifties (lit. he is in his fifties, though).)

(c) 仕事が見つかりました。と言ってもパートなんですが。
(I've found a job. Well, although I said, "job," it is a part-time job (lit. it is a part-time job, though).)

(d) A: 韓国語をご存知なんでしょう？
(You know Korean, right?)

B: いや，知っていると言っても二年勉強しただけですから大したことはありません。
(No, even though people say that I know it, my knowledge is limited because I studied it only two years.)

(e) A: 辻村さんが手伝ってくれるそうですよ。
(I heard that Mr. Tsujimura will help us.)

B: でも，手伝ってくれると言ってもせいぜい二，三時間でしょう。
(But, even though he says that he will help us, it will probably be for a couple of hours at most.)

(f) A: あの子は強いですよ。
(That boy is strong, you know.)

B: いや，強いと言ってもたかが小学生ですよ。

(Well, even though you say he is strong, he is only an elementary school kid.)

Notes

1. X in X *to itte mo* can be dropped, as in Ex.(c), when the preceding sentence containing X is uttered by the same speaker and *to itte mo* immediately follows the preceding sentence. If *to itte mo* does not immediately follow the preceding sentence, X cannot be dropped, as in (1).

    (1) a. もう三月だ。しかし，{**三月** / *ø} **と言っても**この辺はまだ寒い。(=Ex.(a))

    b. 山崎先生はまだお若いですよ。もちろん，{**若い** / *ø} **と言っても**五十代ですが。(=Ex.(b))

2. X *to itte mo* can be used without a preceding discourse containing X, as in (2).

    (2) 年をとった**と言っても**ビルは元プロ選手だ。私では勝てないだろう。
    (Although (people may say that) Bill has gotten old, (he is still strong because) he used to be a professional athlete. I won't be able to beat him.)

    In this instance, people may or may not actually be saying that Bill has gotten old, but by using *to itte mo* the speaker can avoid making a direct statement like that in (3).

    (3) 年をとってもビルは元プロ選手だ。
    (Although Bill has gotten old, (he is still strong because) he used to be a professional athlete.)

to iu fū ni という風に *phr.*

a phrase which expresses a manner or a way in which s.o. does s.t.

in such a way that; in such a fashion to suggest / show (etc.) that; as if to say / show (etc.) that
【REL. *to iu yōni*】

◆Key Sentences

(A)

	Sinf		
彼(かれ)は	**どうしようもない**	という風(ふう)に	首(くび)を振(ふ)った。
(He shook his head as if to say that there was no way out.)			

(B)

	Sinf		
私(わたし)は	**河村(かわむら)さんは来(こ)られない**	という風に	聞(き)いている。
(I have been informed that Mr. Kawamura cannot come. (lit. I have been informed in such a way that I understand that Mr. Kawamura cannot come.))			

T

(C)

Topic$_1$			Topic$_2$				
浩司(ひろし)	は	**うなぎ,**	**友子(ともこ)**	は	**てんぷら,**	という風に	めいめいが自分(じぶん)の好(す)きなものを注文(ちゅうもん)した。
(Each of them ordered the (different) things they liked—Hiroshi, eel, Tomoko, tempura, and so on.)							

Formation

(i) Sinf という風に

困ったという風に頭を抱えた (S.o. held his head in such a fashion as to suggest that he didn't know what to do.)

(ii) X は A, Y は B という風に

月曜日はピアノ，火曜日はダンスという風に良子は毎日レッスンがある。 (Yoshiko has a lesson every day—piano on Monday, dance on Tuesday, and so on.)

Examples

(a) 彼はもう我慢が出来ないという風に荒々しく立ち上がった。
(He stood up in a violent manner showing that he could no longer bear it.)

(b) 彼女はもうこれ以上聞きたくないという風に両手で耳を被った。
(She covered her ears as if to say that she didn't want to listen to it any more.)

(c) 社長には，特に問題はなかったという風に言っておいて下さい。
(Please tell the president that (lit. tell it to the president in such a way to convey that) there were no particular problems with it.)

(d) この物語は今の社会を風刺しているという風には考えられませんか。
(Can't we think that (lit. think in such a way that) this story mocks contemporary society?)

(e) そういうことは規則に反するから出来ないという風に説明しておけばいい。
(You can explain that (lit. explain it in a way to mean that) we cannot do things like that because they are against the rules.)

(f) 去年はボストン，今年はニューヨークという風に，この協会の大会は毎年東部の大都市で開かれている。
(This association's convention is held in a big city on the East Coast every year: last year Boston; this year New York; and so on.)

(g) ジョンはケートと，マイクはシンディーと，という風にみんながパートナーを見(み)つけてペアになった。
(Everybody found a partner and paired up—John with Kate, Mike with Cindy, and so on.)

Notes

1. *To iu fū ni* is used to express what the manner of a person's action shows or suggests, as in KS(A), Exs.(a) and (b).
2. *To iu fū ni* is used when the speaker does not want to be exact about a message or an idea, as in KS(B) and Exs.(c) – (e).
3. As KS(C), Exs.(f) and (g) demonstrate, *to iu fū ni* is used to present specific examples of the way in which someone (or some people) does something.

【Related Expression】

To iu yōni can replace *to iu fū ni* without changing the meaning of a discourse.

[1] a. 彼はどうしようもない**という｛風／よう｝に**首を振った。 (=KS(A))

b. 私は河村さんは来られない**という｛風／よう｝に**聞いている。 (=KS(B))

c. 浩司はうなぎ，友子はてんぷら，**という｛風／よう｝に**めいめいが自分の好きなものを注文した。(=KS(C))

T

to iu koto wa ということは *phr.*

a phrase which changes a sentence into a topic noun clause	that; the fact that 【REL. *koto*】

◆Key Sentences

(A)

Sinf		
彼がこの集まりに来ない	ということは	考えられない。
(It is unthinkable that he won't come to this meeting.)		

(B)

Sinf		Sinf
手紙が戻って来た	ということは	彼女はもうこの住所にはいないということだ。
(The fact that the letter came back means that she no longer lives at this address.)		

(C)

Sinf	
彼が真面目に日本語を勉強していない	ということは
Sinf	
本気で日本で仕事をする気がない	のだ。
(The fact that he is not studying Japanese seriously means that he is not serious about working in Japan.)	

Formation

Sinf ということは

返事がないということは (the fact that there is no reply)

T

Examples

(a) これだけ丁寧に説明すれば，分からないということはあり得ない。
(If we explain it this thoroughly, it is impossible that they won't understand it.)

(b) 空がこんなに赤いということは何かよくないことが起こる前兆かもしれない。
(This red sky (lit. That the sky is this red) might be an omen that something bad will happen.)

(c) 彼が金を貸してくれたということは私は彼に信用されているということだ。
(The fact that he lent me money means that I am trusted by him.)

(d) 言うことを聞かないということは体罰を与えるしかないということだ。
(The fact that he doesn't listen to us means that there is no alternative but to punish him physically.)

(e) 私がこれだけ言っても分からないということはどういうことなんでしょう。
(What does it mean that he doesn't understand me even though I have talked to him such a lot?)

(f) 彼女がパーティーをするということは試験に通ったのだ。
(That she is having a party must be because she passed the exam.)

(g) 彼が毎日授業に来ているということは勉強を続けることにしたのだろう。
(The fact that he is attending the class every day probably means that he has decided to continue studying.)

Note

S *to iu koto wa* is used when the speaker / writer views the content of S at a conceptual level. Specifically, S *to iu koto wa* is used (1) when S is unlikely or impossible (e.g., KS(A) and Ex.(a)), or (2) when the speaker / writer concludes or attempts to conclude s.t. from S (e.g., KS(B) and (C), and Exs.(b) – (g)).

【Related Expression】

Koto also changes a sentence into a noun clause. The difference between S *to iu koto* and S *koto* is that the former is used when S represents a concept rather than a fact (e.g., KS(A)) or when the speaker / writer views the concrete content of S at a conceptual level (e.g., KS(B) and (C)). On the other hand, S *koto* is used when S represents a fact (or something nearly factual) and the speaker / writer views it at a concrete level. The following examples illustrate this point.

First, S *koto* cannot be used when S is unlikely to happen. In this case, S *to iu koto* is used, as in [1].

[1] a. 彼がこの集まりに来ない {**という** / *ø} **こと**は考えられない。 (=KS(A))

b. これだけ丁寧に説明すれば，分からない {**という** / *ø} **こと**はあり得ない。(=Ex.(a))

Second, if S represents a fact which the speaker / writer knows through his / her direct experience, only S *koto* is acceptable, as in [2].

[2] 彼がその集まりに来なかった {ø / ??**という**} **こと**は事実だ。
(It is a fact that he didn't come to the meeting.)

However, if S represents a fact which the speaker / writer knows through indirect experience (i.e., through secondhand information), S *to iu koto* is acceptable, as in [3].

[3] 彼が離婚した {ø / **という**} **こと**は事実だ。
(It is a fact that he got divorced.)

Third, if S represents something likely to happen, both S *koto* and S *to iu koto* are acceptable, as in [4]. In this case the speaker / writer may view the situation at either a concrete level or a conceptual level.

[4] 彼がこの集まりに来ない {ø / **という**} **こと**は確かだ。
(It is certain that he will not come to this meeting.)

Fourth, when verbs like *kanjiru* 'feel' and *yōkyūsuru* 'request; demand' are used, the content of S should be concrete. In this case, S *koto* is used, as in [5].

[5] a. 何かよくないことが起こりつつある {ø / *という} ことを感じる。
(I feel that something bad is happening.)

b. 我々は社長が謝罪する {ø / *という} ことを要求した。
(We demanded that the president apologize to us.)

However, as in [6], with verbs like *tsutaeru* 'convey; tell' and *kiku* 'hear; listen' both S *to iu koto* and S *koto* can be used because the content of S can be either conceptual or concrete.

[6] a. 彼がこの集まりに来ない {という / ø} ことをみんなに伝えた。
(I told everybody that he would not come to this meeting.)

b. 彼がこの集まりに来ない {という / ø} ことを聞いた。
(I heard that he would not come to this meeting.)

(⇨ ***koto***² (DBJG: 193–96))

to iu noni というのに *conj.*

a conjunction to indicate that an action / state takes place quite contrary to one's expectation

but; although; in spite of the fact that ~
【REL. *noni*】

◆Key Sentence

Subordinate Clause		
Sinf		
四月だ	というのに,	まだ肌寒い。
(It is April, but still chilly (lit. cold on the skin).)		

Formation

Sinf というのに

いい天気だというのに　(although it is a fine day)

人が来るというのに　(although someone is coming)

無駄だというのに　(although it is a waste)

危ないというのに　(although it is dangerous)

Examples

(a) あさってはロンドンへ行かなければならないというのに，まだ何も準備していないんですよ。
(Although I have to go to London the day after tomorrow, I haven't prepared anything yet, you know.)

(b) 彼は母親が危篤だというのに，映画を見に行った。
(He went to see a movie in spite of the fact that his mother is in a critical condition.)

(c) 年末でとても忙しいというのに，うちの人は一体どこへ行ったのだろう。
(It's the end of the year, and we are very busy, but where in the world did my husband go?)

(d) 小学四年生だというのに，あの子はもう中学の数学をやっている。
(The child is a fourth grader, but he is already studying junior high math.)

(e) 先生がわざわざ本を貸して下さったというのに，読んでいないの？
(Your teacher kindly loaned a book to you, but you haven't read it?)

(f) 学生は貧乏だというのに，結構いい車を乗り回しているね。
(Students are said to be poor, but they are driving around in pretty good cars, aren't they?)

Notes

1. Sinf *to iu noni* is used to indicate that an action or state expressed in the main clause takes place quite contrary to one's expectation from an action or a state expressed in the subordinate clause (=Sinf *to iu noni* clause).

2. *Iu* in Sinf *to iu noni* in this heading does not have the original meaning of 'say,' because it does not express a quote. But as in (1a) below, there are cases in which Sinf *to iu noni* expresses a quote. Compare (1a) with (1b) which is a non-quote case.

   (1) a. 市役所は閉まっている**というのに**，妻はそんなことはないと言う。
   (I told my wife that the City Hall is closed, but she says it isn't.)

   b. 市役所は閉まっている**というのに**，その前に人が集まっている。
   (Although the City Hall is closed, a lot of people are gathered in front of it.)

【Related Expression】

All the Sinf *to iu noni* in KS and Exs can be replaced by Sinf *noni* without changing the essential meaning, because both of them express the meaning of 'although.'

[1] a. 四月な**のに**，まだ肌寒い。(cf. KS)

b. あさってはロンドンへ行かなければならない**のに**，まだ何も準備していないんですよ。(cf. Ex.(a))

c. 彼は母親が危篤な**のに**，映画を見に行った。(cf. Ex.(b))

d. 年末でとても忙しい**のに**，うちの人は一体どこへ行ったのだろう。(cf. Ex.(c))

Sinf *to iu noni* is used when something quite contrary to what is expected from S is expressed in the main clause, so if the contrast to one's expectation is not fully expressed as in [2a], the use of Sinf *to iu noni* becomes marginal. In [2b] in which ample information is given to make the contrast clear, *to iu noni* becomes acceptable.

[2] a. 彼はお金がある {**のに** / ??**というのに**} なかなか出さない。
(He has money alright, but he does not part with it readily.)

b. 彼は資産家の息子でお金が余るほどある {**のに** / **というのに**} なかなか出さない。
(He is the son of a man of property, and he has money more than he can use, but he does not part with it readily.)

to iu no wa ~ koto da というのは～ことだ *str.*

a structure which is used in interpreting, explaining, or defining a word, a phrase, or a sentence

mean; the meaning of ~ is; what ~ means is
【REL. *to iu koto wa*】

◆Key Sentences

(A)

Noun		Noun		
パソコン	というのは	**パーソナル・コンピュータ**	の	ことだ。
(*Pasokon* means personal computer.)				

(B)

Noun		VPinf		
過労死	というのは	**働きすぎがもとで死ぬ**	(という)	ことだ。
(*Karōshi* means to die from overwork.)				

(C)

VPinf		Sinf
「足が出る」	というのは	出費が予定していたより多くなる

（という）	ことだ。

(*Ashi ga deru* (lit. a foot sticks out) means that an expense exceeds the amount budgeted.)

(D)

Sinf	
「猿も木から落ちる」	というのは

Sinf		
上手な人でも時には失敗することがある	という	ことだ。

(*Saru mo ki kara ochiru* (lit. even monkeys fall from trees) means that even a skillful person sometimes makes a mistake.)

Formation

(i) N / Adj(*na*)stem というのは

マンションというのは (What *manshon* means is ~)

独創的というのは (*Dokusōteki* means ~)

(ii) {VP / AP / S}inf というのは

「首を切る」というのは (What *kubi o kiru* (lit. to cut one's head off) means is ~)

「おぼれる者はわらをもつかむ」というのは (What *oboreru mono wa*

wara o mo tsukamu (lit. a drowning person clutches even at a straw) means is ~)

(iii) N のことだ

買取りのアパートのことだ (~ means an apartment for purchase)

(iv) V / Adj ことだ (the same as the relative clause formation rules)

(何かをするのが)やさしいことだ (~ means 'easy to do s.t.')

(何かが)大好きなことだ (~ means 'to like s.t. a lot')

(何かが上手に)なることだ (~ means 'to become skillful in s.t.')

(v) {VP / AP / S}inf ということだ

細かい所ばかりを見て全体を見ないということだ (~ means that one sees only details and does not see the whole)

Examples

(a) マイカーというのは個人が持っている車のことだ。
(*Maikā* (lit. my car) means a car owned by an individual.)

(b) 裏口入学というのは試験を受けないで学校に入ることだ。
(*Uraguchi-nyūgaku* (lit. entering school through the back door) means to enter a school without taking an entrance exam.)

(c) 「口が軽い」というのは人に言ってはいけないことをすぐ言ってしまう(という)ことだ。
(*Kuchi ga karui* (lit. one's mouth is light) means easily telling others things one shouldn't.)

(d) 「頭を絞る」というのはいいアイディアを出そうとして一生懸命考える(という)ことだ。
(*Atama o shiboru* (lit. squeeze one's head) means to think hard to get good ideas.)

(e) 「猫の額のような」というのは場所がとても狭い(という)ことだ。
(*Neko no hitai no yōna* (lit. like a cat's forehead) means that a place is very small (as in "a very small yard").)

(f) 「花より団子」というのはきれいなものより食べられる団子の方がいい，外観より実質の方を取るということだ。
(*Hana yori dango* (lit. dumplings rather than blossoms) means that edible dumplings are better than pretty but inedible blossoms; i.e., one should take substance over appearance.)

Notes

1. Although there is no restriction as to what precedes it, *to iu no wa* is usually preceded by N / Adj(*na*)stem or {VP / AP / S}inf. Similarly, any form can precede *to iu koto da*, but it is normally preceded by {VP / AP / S}inf. When *to iu* is not present before *koto da*, N *no* or the pre-noun form of V or Adj. must precede.

2. In X *to iu no wa* Y *to iu koto da*, the presence of the second *to iu* depends on the relationship between X and Y. If Y is the unshortened word of, a definition of, or a synonym for X, *to iu* is not used (e.g., KS(A) and Ex.(a)).

   (1) a. パソコンというのはパーソナル・コンピュータ {**の** / ***という**} ことだ。(=KS(A))

   b. マイカーというのは個人が持っている車 {**の** / ***という**} ことだ。(=Ex.(a))

   If Y is an interpretation or explanation of X, *to iu* should be present (e.g., KS(D) and Ex.(f)).

   (2) a. 「猿も木から落ちる」というのは上手な人でも時には失敗することがある {**という** / ??ø} ことだ。(=KS(D))

   b. 「花より団子」というのはきれいなものより食べられる団子の方がよい、外観より実質の方を取る {**という** / ??ø} ことだ。(=Ex.(f))

   If Y can be interpreted either way, *to iu* is optional. For example, in KS(C), if *to iu* is present, the speaker is explaining the meaning of *ashi ga deru.* If *to iu* is not present, the speaker is providing a definition for the phrase under focus.

3. To request the meaning of a word, a phrase, or a sentence, the following expressions are commonly used.

   (3) [Asking the meaning of a word]
   カラオケというのは何(なん)ですか。
   (What does *karaoke* mean?)

   (4) [Asking the meaning of a phrase or a sentence]
   「首を切る」というのはどういう意味(いみ)ですか。
   (What does *kubi o kiru* mean?)

   Note that the expression is (5) is not used in this situation.

   (5) *カラオケの意味は何ですか。
   (lit. What is the meaning of *karaoke*?)

4. In asking the meaning of X in conversation, X *to iu no wa* is often contracted to X *tte*, as in (6).

   (6) a. カラオケ**って**(=というのは)何ですか。(=(3))

   b. 「首を切る」**って**(=というのは)どういう意味ですか。(=(4))

   In informal conversation simply X *tte* (with rising intonation) is used, as in (7).

   (7) A. カラオケは好きですか。
   (Do you like *karaoke*?)

   B. カラオケ**って**？
   (What's *karaoke*?)

T

【Related Expression】

X *to iu koto wa* Y *to iu koto da* also means that X means Y. However, this structure is used to provide an interpretation of a fact (or something nearly factual), and is not used to provide a definition, an explanation, or an interpretation of a word, a phrase, or a sentence. Thus, *to iu koto wa* is acceptable in [1], but not in [2], and *to iu no wa* is acceptable in [2], but not in [1].

[1] 手紙(てがみ)が戻(もど)って来(き)た {**ということは** / ***というのは**}, 彼女(かのじょ)はもうこの住所(じゅうしょ)にはいないということだ。
(The fact that the letter came back means that she no longer lives at this address.)

[2] a. 「足が出る」{**というのは** / ***ということは**} 出費が予定していたより多くなるということだ。(=KS(C))

b. 「猿も木から落ちる」{**というのは** / ***ということは**} 上手な人でも時には失敗することがあるということだ。(=KS(D))

(⇨ ***to iu koto wa***)

to iu to　と言うと　*phr.*

a phrase which is used when s.t. which s.o. has mentioned causes an involuntary response

when ~ mention; if ~ say that ~; when ~ say that ~; when it comes to
【REL. *to ieba*】

T

◆Key Sentences

(A)

Noun		
サンフランシスコ	と言(い)うと,	あのケーブルカーを思(おも)い出(だ)す。
(When you mention San Francisco, I remember those cable cars.)		

(B)

Sentence$_1$			
Sinf			
日本語を話す	と言うと	聞こえはいいんです	が,

Sentence$_2$
実は簡単な挨拶が出来るだけなんです。
(It sounds impressive when I say that I can speak Japanese, but the fact is that all I can do is exchange simple greetings.)

Formation

(i) N と言うと

長崎と言うと (when it comes to Nagasaki)

(ii) Sinf と言うと

家を買ったと言うと (if I say that I've bought a house)

Examples

(a) パリと言うと，誰でも真っ先にあのエッフェル塔を思い浮かべるだろう。
(When someone mentions Paris, the (lit. that) Eiffel Tower is the first thing likely to come to everyone's mind.)

(b) 柔道と言うと，毎日練習した学生時代を思い出す。
(When it comes to judo, I remember my school days when I used to practice it every day.)

(c) 漫画と言うと馬鹿にする人もあるが，あれはあれで面白いのだ。
(Some people ridicule comics (lit. Some people despise you when you mention comics), but comics are interesting in their own way.)

(d) 東大卒と言うと偉そうに聞こえるが，私は勉強なんか全然しない劣等生だったんです。

T

(It sounds great when I say that I am a graduate of the University of Tokyo, but I was (in fact) a poor student who didn't study at all.)

(e) 会社を辞めたと言うと体裁がいいんですが，彼は本当は辞めさせられたんですよ。
(It sounds good when he says that he quit his company, but the truth of the matter is that he was fired (lit. was made to quit).)

Notes

1. *To iu to* is used when something mentioned evokes some memory, as in KS(A), Exs.(a) and (b), or when the speaker / writer wants to make a remark which is different from what is expected, as in KS(B) and Exs.(c) – (e). In both cases, the clause which follows X *to iu to* is a response (an involuntary action or a state of mind) caused by X.

2. *To iu to* is also used to question the meaning of a word or phrase mentioned by the interlocutor, as in (1).

(1) A: カラオケは好きですか？
(Do you like *karaoke*?)

B: カラオケ**と｛言う / 言います｝と**？
(What do you mean by *karaoke*? (lit. When you mention *karaoke*, (what do you mean by that?))

【Related Expression】

To ieba is similar to *to iu to*. However, *to iu to* is used in the situations mentioned in Note 1, whereas *to ieba* is used when the speaker wants to present what has just been mentioned as a new topic. Compare [1] and [2].

[1] サンフランシスコ｛**と言うと** / ??**と言えば**｝，あのケーブルカーを思い出す。(=KS(A))

[2] A: 今，サンフランシスコから友達が来ているんです。
(I have a friend from San Francisco visiting me now.)

B: サンフランシスコ｛**と言えば** / ***と言うと**｝，田中さんがサンフランシスコに転勤になるそうですよ。

(Speaking of San Francisco, I heard that Mr. Tanaka is going to be transferred there.)

It should also be noted that *to ieba* cannot be used to question the meaning of a word or phrase, as in Note 2.

[3] A: カラオケは好きですか。(=(1) in Note 2)

B: カラオケ {**と言うと** / ***と言えば**} ?

(⇨ **~ *to ieba*** (DBJG: 484–85))

to iu yori (wa) というより(は) *phr.*

a phrase that is used to indicate more accurate characterization of s.o. or s.t.

rather than; more ~ than ~

◆Key Sentences

(A)

Topic	Adj(*i*)inf		Adj(*i*)
今年(ことし)の夏(なつ)は	**涼(すず)しい**	というよりは	**寒(さむ)かった**。
(This summer was cold rather than cool.)			

(B)

Topic	Adj(*na*)stem			Adj
カーラは	**臆病(おくびょう)**	というより(は)	むしろ	**用心深(ようじんぶか)い**。
(Kara is cautious rather than timid.)				

T

(C)

Topic	Noun			Noun	
本田さんは	**教育者**	というより(は)	むしろ	**学者**	に近い。
(Mr. Honda is more of a scholar than an educator.)					

(D)

Topic	VP				VP
		Vinf			
あの人は	**酒を**	**飲む**	というより(は)	むしろ	**酒に飲まれている**と言った方がいい。
(One should say that sake drinks him rather than he drinks sake.)					

Formation

(i) Adj(*i*)inf というより(は),(むしろ) Adj(*i / na*)

涼しいというより(は),(むしろ)寒い (cold rather than cool)

(ii) Adj(*na*)stem というより(は),(むしろ) Adj(*i / na*)

きれいというより(は),(むしろ) かわいい (cute rather than pretty)

(iii) N というより(は),(むしろ) N

青というより(は),(むしろ)紫 (purple rather than blue)

(iv) Vinf というより(は),(むしろ) V

食べるというより(は),(むしろ)飲み込んでいる
(s.o. is swallowing rather than eating)

Examples

(a) 私にはこの音楽は楽しいというよりは,むしろやかましい。
(To me this music is noisy rather than enjoyable.)

(b) あの人は丁寧というよりは,いんぎん無礼だ。

(He is politely insolent rather than polite.)

(c) 彼の説明は簡潔というよりは，むしろ不十分だと言うべきだ。
(We should say that his explanation is insufficient rather than concise.)

(d) 父は，父親というよりは，むしろいい友達という感じでした。
(I felt that my father was a good friend rather than a father.)

(e) 彼は大学教授というよりは，ビジネスマンだ。
(He is a businessman rather than a college professor.)

(f) 私は教師ですが，教えているというよりは，勉強させてもらっています。
(I'm a teacher, but I am learning (lit. I have the privilege of being allowed to study) rather than teaching.)

(g) あの母親は子供を愛しているというよりは，むしろ，甘やかしている。
(That mother is pampering her child rather than loving him.)

(h) 彼と話していると，会話をしているというよりは，一方的に話を聞かされているといった感じだ。
(When I talk with him I feel that unilaterally I am forced to listen to his talk rather than being engaged in conversation.)

(i) 私が呼んだというより，むしろ彼女の方が押しかけて来たんです。
(It's more of a case of her having invited herself than my having invited her.)

Notes

1. X *to iu yori wa* Y is used when the speaker / writer chooses what he believes to be a more accurate characterization of s.o or s.t. over another.

2. X *to iu yori wa* Y usually takes a topic as shown in KS and Exs.(a) – (h) but there are cases when it does not take a topic as in Ex.(i).

3. X *to iu yori wa* Y often takes the form of X *to iu yori wa mushiro* Y. The adverb *mushiro* makes the meaning of 'rather' more explicit.

4. The past tense is usually specified once at the end of the sentence, as shown in Ex.(h).

toka de とかで *conj.*

a conjunction that is used to give an uncertain reason for s.t.

for some reason like ~; saying something like ~; because ~ or something like that
【REL. *kara*; *node*】

◆Key Sentence

	Sinf		
高木さんは	**大阪に出張する**	とかで	パーティーに来なかった。
(Mr. Takagi didn't show up at the party, saying something like he was going to make a business trip to Osaka.)			

Formation

Sinf とかで

日本へ行くとかで (saying something like s.o. is going to Japan)

学校がつまらないとかで (saying something like the school is boring)

Examples

(a) 友人の竹田は大学の授業が面白くないとかで大学を辞めてしまった。
(My friend Takeda quit college, saying something like the college classes weren't interesting.)

(b) ミリアムは日米関係に興味があるとかで，大学で国際関係論を専攻した。
(Miriam majored in international relations saying something like she was interested in Japan-US relations.)

(c) エンジンに故障があったとかで，飛行機の出発が五時間も遅れた。
(The flight departure was five hours late for some reason like there was engine trouble.)

(d) 受講生が少なかったとかで，四年生の日本語のクラスは取りやめになった。
(The 4th-year Japanese class has been cancelled for some reason like the enrollment was low.)

(e) 田村は殺人現場に居合わせたとかで，警察に逮捕された。
(Tamura was arrested by the police allegedly because he happened to be at the scene of the murder or something like that.)

Notes

1. The particle *toka de* is used to give an unconfirmed reason for a given action or state. The particle consists of the quotation marker *to* and the question marker *ka* and the particle of cause / reason *de*.
(⇨ ***to***³ (DBJG: 478–80); ***ka***² (DBJG: 166–68); ***de***³ (DBJG: 107–09))

2. Since *toka de* is used to express what the speaker / writer has heard from someone as a reason for an action / state, the subject cannot be the speaker / writer himself.

   (1) {**ジョン / *私 / *あなた**} は仕事があるとかで映画に行かない。
   (John / *I / *You will not go see the movie, saying something like he has things to do.)

【Related Expression】

Toka de and *kara / node* are crucially different in that the former is used to express an uncertain hearsay reason; whereas the latter two conjunctions for reason / cause have nothing to do with hearsay. Therefore in (1) above *kara / node* can be used regardless of the person (i.e., the first person or the third person) of the subject, as shown in [1].

[1] {**ジョン / 私 / あなた**} は仕事がある {**から / ので**} 映画に行かない。
(cf. (1))
(Because {John has / I have / you have} work to do he / I / you won't go see a movie.)
(⇨ ***kara***³ (DBJG: 179–81); ***node*** (DBJG: 328–31))

T

tokoro ところ *n.* <w>

a dependent noun which is used to express the idea that when s.o. did s.t., s.t. took place as the result	when; then 【REL. *-tara*】

◆Key Sentence

Subordinate Clause			Main Clause
	Vinf·past		
先生に	**相談した**	ところ,	ぜひ大学院に行くよう勧められた。
(When I consulted with my teacher, he strongly advised me to go to graduate school.)			

Formation

Vinf·past ところ

使ったところ (when s.o. used (it))

Examples

(a) 部長に頼んでみたところ，喜んで引き受けてくれた。
(When I asked my boss (lit. department chief), he was glad to do it.)

(b) 友達に話したところ，しばらく考えさせてほしいと言った。
(When I told one of my friends (about that), he said he would like to think (lit. would like me to let him think) (about it) for a while.)

(c) これまでに書いた論文を本にしたところ，意外によく売れた。
(When I published a book of the papers that I had written (lit. till this time), it sold unexpectedly well.)

(d) 人に勧められてヨガを始めたところ，非常に効果があることが分かった。
(I started yoga because someone recommended it; then, I realized it had a great effect.)

(e) 冗談のつもりで言ったところ，思わぬ結果になって驚いている。
(I'm surprised that what I said as a joke had unexpected consequences (lit. that when I said it as a joke, it brought about an unexpected result).)

(f) その仕事に興味のある旨，手紙を出したところ，すぐに面接をしたいとの返事があった。
(When I wrote to them saying that I was interested in the job, I got a letter immediately saying they wanted to interview me.)

Notes

1. Vinf·past *tokoro* is used when someone does something intentionally. Thus, the *tokoro* clause must represent a volitional action. The following sentences are unacceptable. (See Related Expression.)

   (1) a. ***目が覚めた**ところ，もう昼だった。
   (When I woke up, it was already noon.)

   b. ***夕立が通った**ところ，とても涼しくなった。
   (When the shower passed, it became very cool.)

2. The main clause after a *tokoro* clause must represent an event caused by the *tokoro* action. The sentence in (2) are unacceptable. (See Related Expression.)

   (2) a. *図書館に行ったところ，**トムがいた。**
   (When I went to the library, Tom was there.)

   b. *窓を開けたところ，**外は雨だった。**
   (When I opened the window, it was raining outside.)

3. "V *tokoro* S" cannot represent a non-past event, as in (3). (See Related Expression.)

   (3) a. *彼に話したところ，きっと**賛成するだろう。**
   (If I tell him (about that), he will surely agree.)

   b. *私が頼んだところ，彼女はいつも喜んで**してくれる。**
   (When I ask her (to do it), she always does it happily.)

【Related Expression】

V *tara* (i.e., Vinf·past *ra*) can be used in place of Vinf·past *tokoro*, as in [1]. However, V *tokoro* is more formal than V *tara* and is usually used in formal speech and writing, while V *tara* is used in both formal and informal language.

[1] a. 先生に相談した {**ところ / ら**}, ぜひ大学院に行くよう勧められた。(=KS)

b. 部長に頼んでみた {**ところ / ら**}, 喜んで引き受けてくれた。 (=Ex.(1))

It is noted that V *tara* does not have the restrictions listed in Notes 1, 2, and 3. Thus, the following sentences are all acceptable.

[2] a. 目が覚めた {**ら / *ところ**}, もう昼だった。(=(1a) in Note 1)

b. 夕立が通った {**ら / *ところ**}, とても涼しくなった。 (=(1b) in Note 1)

[3] a. 図書館に行った {**ら / *ところ**}, トムがいた。(=(2a) in Note 2)

b. 窓を開けた {**ら / *ところ**}, 外は雨だった。(=(2b) in Note 2)

[4] a. 彼に話した {**ら / *ところ**}, きっと賛成するだろう。 (=(3a) in Note 3)

b. 私が頼んだ {**ら / *ところ**}, 彼女はいつも喜んでしてくれる。 (=(3b) in Note 3)

T

(⇨ **~ *tara*** (DBJG: 452–57))

tokoro ga ところが *conj.*

a conjunction which is used to present what in fact happened or what is in fact the case when something else was / is expected	however; but 【REL. *daga*; *keredo(mo)*; *shikashi*; *sore ga*】

◆Key Sentences

(A)

	Sentence$_1$
	日本式の部屋に泊まりたいと思って旅館を予約した。
	Sentence$_2$
ところが,	通された部屋は洋式だった。
(I wanted to stay in a Japanese-style room and made a reservation at an inn. However, the room I was shown to was a Western-style one.)	

(B)

A:	
	Sentence$_1$
	彼女にプロポーズしたんだろう？　どうだった？
(You proposed to her, right? What happened?)	
B:	
	Sentence$_2$
ところが,	だめだったんだ。
(It didn't work out. (lit. It was no good.))	

Formation

(i) S_1。ところが，S_2。(See KS(A).)

(ii) A: S_1。

B: ところが，S_2。(See KS(B).)

Examples

(a) 私の娘はアメリカにいる時きれいな英語を話していた。ところが，日本へ帰って一年もたたないうちにきれいに忘れてしまった。
(My daughter was speaking beautiful English when she was in America. However, she forgot it completely within a year (lit. even before one year elapsed) after we came back to Japan.)

(b) 日本から来た有名な先生の講演があるというので行ってみた。ところが，その先生は英語が下手で何を言っているのか全然分からなかった。
(Because I heard that there was going to be a lecture by a famous professor from Japan, I went (to listen to it). However, his English was so bad that I didn't understand what he was saying at all.)

(c) 先生は私達に遅刻してはいけないと何度も言った。ところが，次の日，時間通りに行ってみると先生はまだ来ていなかった。
(Our teacher repeatedly told us that we mustn't be late for his class. However, when I went to his class on time the next day, he was not yet there.)

(d) アメリカへ来ればいくらでも仕事はあると言われた。ところが，来てみるとアメリカは不況でどこにも仕事はなかった。
(I was told that if I came to America, there would be a lot of jobs. However, when I came, there were no jobs anywhere because of the depression.)

(e) アメリカではのこぎりは押して切る。ところが，日本では引いて切る。
(In America you push a saw in order to cut; however, in Japan you pull one to cut.)

(f) A: 今晩のパーティー，君も来てくれるね。[male speech]
(You can come to tonight's party, too, can't you?)

B: ところが，あいにく行けないの。[female speech]
(No, I'm afraid I can't.)

(g) A: 彼女は結婚しているんでしょう？ [female or polite male speech]
(She is married, isn't she?)

B: そう見えるでしょう？ ところが，まだ独身なんですって。
[female speech]
(She looks like it, doesn't she? But I heard that she's still single.)

Notes

1. *Tokoro ga* always appears in sentence-initial position.
2. In "S_1. *Tokoro ga* S_2," S_2 represents something one does not expect from S_1, as in KS(A).
3. *Tokoro ga* is used in response to the addressee's utterance, as in KS(B). In this case, the sentence following *tokoro ga* is not what the addressee expects to hear.

【Related Expressions】

I. Although the sense of unexpectedness disappears, the conjunctions *daga*, *keredo*(*mo*), and *shikashi* can replace *tokoro ga* in "S_1. *Tokoro ga* S_2," as in [1].

[1] 日本式の部屋に泊まりたいと思って旅館を予約した。{**ところが / だが / けれども / しかし**}，通された部屋は洋式だった。
(=KS(A))

However, *daga*, *keredo*(*mo*), and *shikashi* cannot replace *tokoro ga* when "*Tokoro ga*, S" is a reply to a question, as in [2].

[2] A: 彼女にプロポーズしたんだろう？ どうだった？

B: {**ところが / *だが / *けれども / *しかし**}，だめだったんだ。
(=KS(B))

Tokoro ga, on the other hand, cannot be used when the situation does not involve unexpectedness, as in [3].

[3] a: この本は高い。{**だが / けれども / しかし / *ところが**} いい本だ。
(This book is expensive. But it is a good book.)

b: 結局負けてしまった。{**だが / けれども / しかし / *ところが**} 我々はベストを尽くした。
(We lost in the end. But we did our best.)

c: ここの冬は寒い。{**だが / けれども / しかし / *ところが**} 夏は涼しい。
(It's cold here in winter. But it's cool in summer.)

(⇨ ***daga***; ***keredomo*** (DBJG: 187–88))

II. *Sore ga* is also used when the speaker is going to provide an unexpected response to a question. In fact, *tokoro ga* in such situations can be replaced by *sore ga*, as in [4].

[4] A: 彼女にプロポーズしたんだろう？ どうだった？

B: {**ところが / それが**}, だめだったんだ。(=KS(B))

However, unlike *tokoro ga*, *sore ga* can be used when the second speaker is not sure what the first speaker expects to hear in the second speaker's response. For example, in [5] *sore ga* can be used even when B is not sure what A expects, while *tokoro ga* can be used only when B knows that A expects a good result. (⇨ ***sore ga***)

[5] A: 試験どうだった？
(How was the exam?)

B: {**それが / ところが**} だめだったんだ。
((Well, you might expect a good result but / Contrary to what you expect) it was no good.)

T

tomo とも *conj.* <w>

a conjunction in written Japanese that is used to express a concession

no matter ~ may be; even if; at ~ -est

【REL. *te mo*; *tatte*】

◆Key Sentences

(A)

	Wh-word		Vvol		
よく勉強したから，試験に	どんな	問題が	**出よう**	とも	大丈夫だ。
(Since I studied hard I feel confident no matter what problem shows up on the test.)					

(B)

Wh-word		Adj(*i*)stem			
いかに	家事が	**忙し**	**く／かろう**	とも	母は文句一つ言わなかった。
(No matter how busy she was with housekeeping, my mother never uttered a single complaint.)					

(C)

Wh-word	Adj(*na*)stem			
どんなに	**健康**	**であろう**	とも，	一年に一回は健康診断を受けるべきだ。
(No matter how healthy you are, you should have a checkup once a year.)				

(D)

	Adj(*i*)stem			
このプロジェクトは	**遅**	く	とも	来年の四月には完了するだろう。
(At the latest, this project will be complete in April of next year.)				

Formation

(i) Wh-word + Vvol とも

どこへ行こうとも (no matter where s.o. may go)

何を食べようとも (no matter what s.o. may eat)

何があろうとも (no matter what may happen)

(ii) Wh-word + Adj(*i*)stem {く / かろう} とも

{いかに / どんなに} 難し {く / かろう} とも (no matter how difficult s.t. may be)

(iii) Wh-word + Adj(*na*)stem であろうとも

{いかに / どんなに} 好きであろうとも (no matter how much s.o. likes s.t.)

(iv) Adj(*i*)stem くとも

早くとも (at the earliest)

Examples

(a) 父は何が起きようともいつも平然としている。
(My father is always very calm no matter what is impending.)

(b) 私は世界のどこに住もうとも一向に構わない。
(I do not care at all where in the world I live.)

(c) 万一失敗しようとも，簡単にあきらめてはいけない。
(Even if by any chance you fail you shouldn't give up easily.)

(d) いかに頭がよ｛く／かろう｝とも，努力しなければいい仕事は出来ない。
(No matter how bright you may be, you cannot do a good job unless you make an effort.)

(e) どんなに品物が安｛く／かろう｝とも，質が悪ければ金を捨てることになる。
(No matter how cheap merchandise may be, if the quality is poor, you will end up throwing away money.)

(f) 金が十分な｛く／かろう｝とも，生活を楽しむことは出来るはずだ。
(Even without enough money we should be able to enjoy life.)

(g) どんなに運動が好きであろうとも，運動のやりすぎはかえって悪い。
(No matter how much one may like exercise, too much of it is bad.)

(h) この手紙はあなたがいくら読みたくとも読ませるわけにはいかない。
(I cannot let you read this letter, no matter how much you want to read it.)

(i) 僕は少なくとも一年に三回は海外出張をしています。
(I make business trips abroad at least three times a year.)

Notes

1. The conjunction usually occurs with a Wh-word as shown in KS and Exs. However, there are cases where Wh-word is not used as in KS(D), Exs.(c), (f) and (i). Note that *naku / nakarō* in Ex.(f) comes from a negative Adj(*i*)*nai*.

2. When *tomo* is connected with an Adj(*i*), the form can be either Adj(*i*)stem *ku to mo* or Adj(*i*)stem *karō to mo*, as shown in Formation (ii). But when Adj(*i*)stem is used with *tomo* as a fixed phrase, as in KS(D) and Ex.(i), only Adj(*i*)stem *ku tomo* is used. The only other commonly used fixed phrases are *hayaku tomo* 'at the earliest' and *tashō tomo* 'more or less.' All this express quantity or degree and can be used in both spoken and written Japanese.

3. Note that *mo* of Vvol *to mo* can be deleted, but *mo* of *te mo* cannot. (⇨ ***te mo*** (DBJG: 468–70)) *Mo* can be also omitted from Adj(*i*)stem *karō tomo* and Adj(*na*)stem *de arō tomo*.

【Related Expression】

Vvol *tomo*, {*karō* / *ku*} *tomo*, Adj(*na*)stem *de arō tomo* can be replaced by *te mo* or *tatte* without changing the meaning. However, *tomo* definitely belongs to written Japanese, and *te mo* belongs to either spoken or written Japanese, and *tatte* belongs to spoken Japanese. However, the fixed phrases such as *osoku tomo* 'at the latest' and *sukunaku tomo* 'at least' are the exceptions.

[1] a. よく勉強したから，試験にどんな問題が {**出ようと(も) / 出ても / 出たって**} 大丈夫だ。(=KS(A))

b. いかに家事が {**忙しくとも / 忙しかろうと(も) / 忙しくても / 忙しくたって**}，母は文句一つ言わなかった。(=KS(B))

c. どんなに健康で {**あろうと(も) / あっても / あったって**}，一年に一回は健康診断を受けるべきだ。(=KS(C))

d. 僕は {**少なくとも / *少なくても / *少なくたって**} 一年に三回は海外出張をしています。(=Ex.(i))

Adj(*i* / *na*)*te mo* can be replaced by Adj(*i*)stem {*ku* / *karō*} *tomo* / Adj(*na*)stem *de arō tomo*, but V*te mo* cannot be replaced by Vvol *tomo*, especially when the verb expresses something controllable. Note that in [2] and [3] below, [2a] and [3a] express something controllable, but [2b] and [3b] express causative passive situations that are beyond human control.

[2] a. 私は四時間(よじかん) {**歩(ある)いても / *歩こうとも**} 疲(つか)れなかった。
(I didn't get tired although I walked for four hours.)

b. 私は四時間 {**歩かされても / 歩かされようとも**} 疲れなかった。
(I didn't get tired although I was forced to walk for four hours.)

[3] a. 何を {**食(た)べても / *食べようとも**} おいしい。
(No matter what I eat, it tastes good.)

b. 何を {**食べさせられても / 食べさせられようとも**} 喜(よろこ)んで食べる。
(No matter what I am forced to eat, I eat it with pleasure.)

to naru となる *phr.* <w>

a phrase which expresses the idea that s.o. or s.t. becomes s.t.	become

◆Key Sentence

	Noun	
吉田さんが	**初代の委員長**	となった。
(Mr. Yoshida has become the first committee chairman.)		

Formation

N となる

必修科目となる (become a compulsory subject)

Examples

(a) その土地は結局国の所有物となった。
(That land eventually became state property.)

(b) 戦後義務教育は九年間となった。
(After the war, (the period of) compulsory education was changed to (lit. became) nine years.)

(c) 彼らの結婚は悲劇的な結果となった。
(Their marriage ended in tragedy (lit. became a tragic result).)

(d) 彼は証拠不十分で無罪となった。
(For lack of evidence, he was found (lit. became) innocent.)

(e) その試合は雨のため中止となった。
(The game was cancelled (lit. became a cancellation) due to rain.)

Notes

1. *To naru* is similar in meaning to *ni naru*. *To naru*, however, is more formal and is used exclusively in written language.

(1) 吉田さんが初代の委員長 {**と / に**} **なった**。(=KS)

2. *Na*-adjectives cannot precede *to naru.*

(2) 図書館(としょかん)が便利(べんり) {**に / *と**} **なった**。
(The library has become very convenient.)

to naru to となると *phr.*

a phrase which expresses the idea "when it comes to" or "if it is true that"

when it comes to; if it is true that ~; if it is the case that ~; if it turns out that ~
【REL. *to suru to*】

◆Key Sentences

(A)

	Noun		
私(わたし)は	**機械(きかい)のこと**	となると	何(なに)も分(わ)からない。
(When it comes to mechanical things, I don't understand anything.)			

(B)

Sinf		
彼(かれ)が手伝(てつだ)ってくれない	となると	誰(だれ)かほかの人(ひと)を頼(たの)むしかない。
(If it's true that he is not going to help us, we'll have no alternative but to ask someone else.)		

Formation

(i) N となると

映画(えいが)となると (when it comes to movies)

T

(ii) Sinf となると (Exception: X が N となると)

彼が来るとなると (if it is true that he is coming)

彼女が病気となると (if it is the case that she is ill)

Examples

(a) 勉はギャンブルとなると人が変わってしまう。
(When it comes to gambling, Tsutomu becomes another person.)

(b) 日本語が出来る科学者となると数がかなり限られてくる。
(When it comes to scientists who can speak Japanese, the number is quite limited.)

(c) 何でも仕事となると楽なものはない。
(Nothing is easy (lit. There is nothing easy) when it comes to work.)

(d) 彼が参加できないとなるとこのプロジェクトは考え直さなければならない。
(If it turns out that he cannot participate (in this project), we'll have to reconsider it.)

(e) 秘密が漏れたとなるとこの計画は変更しなければならない。
(If it is true that the secret (of this plan) has leaked, we must change it.)

(f) 彼が新しい社長になるとなると経営方針がかなり変わるだろう。
(If he turns out to be the new president, the management policy will probably be considerably different.)

(g) この仕事は簡単そうに見えるが，一人でするとなると結構大変だ。
(This job looks easy, but if (it is the case that) you do it by yourself, it will be quite tough.)

Notes

1. When N precedes *to naru to*, it means "when it comes to N."

2. S *to naru to* is used when the speaker / writer has just learned that S is true.

【Related Expression】

To suru to is similar to *to naru to* in that both express a provisional idea. However, S *to suru to* is used when S is hypothetical or uncertain, whereas S *to naru to* is used when the speaker / writer takes S to be true or a reality. Thus, *to naru to* cannot be used in the hypothetical situation in [1].

[1] 今自分の家を建てる {**とすると** / ***となると**} どんな家を建てますか。
(Suppose you were to build your own house now, what kind of house would you build?)

On the other hand, *to suru to* is unacceptable when the situation involves an actual event, as in [2].

[2] 彼が手伝ってくれない {**となると** / ??**とすると**} 誰かほかの人を頼むしかない。(=KS(B))

(⇨ ***to suru to***)

tōri (ni) 通り(に) *n.*

a dependent noun which expresses the idea that s.o. does s.t. or s.t. takes place in the same way as s.t. else

(in) the same way as; (in) the way; as
【REL. *yōni*】

◆Key Sentences

(A)

Noun				
説明書	の	通り	(に)	やったが，うまくいかなかった。
(I did it as the manual shows (lit. in the same way as the manual), but it didn't work.)				

(B)

Vinf			
私の言う	通り	（に）	体を動かして下さい。
(Please move your body as I tell you to (lit. in the same way as I tell you).)			

(C)

Vinf		
思った	通り	彼が一番先に来ていた。
(As I expected (lit. thought), he was the first to come.)		

(D)

	Vinf		
結果はやはり	**予想した**	通り	だった。
(The result was just as I expected, after all.)			

Formation

(i) N の通り（に）

計画の通り（に） (the same way as the plan)

(ii) Vinf 通り（に）

見た通り（に） (the way s.o. saw s.t.)

(iii) Demonstrative Adj. 通り（に）

この通り（に） (the same way as this; this way)

T

Examples

(a) この地図の通り(に)行けば間違いなく行けます。
(If you go as this map shows (lit. in the same way as this map), you can get there without fail.)

(b) 私はただ言われた通り(に)やっているだけです。
(I'm just doing as I'm told (lit. in the way I'm told).)

(c) ここに書いてある通り(に)すれば誰にでも出来ます。
(If you follow what is (lit. do it in the way) written here, anyone can do it.)

(d) 予想した通り誰も宿題をやってこなかった。
(As I expected, none of them did their homework.)

(e) 心配していた通りペンキが足りなくなった。
(As I feared, I ran out of paint.)

(f) 内容はこの間説明した通りです。
(The content is the same as I explained to you the other day.)

(g) これは私が考えていた通りのデザインです。
(This is the same design as the one I have thought about.)

(h) A: これは何語か分かりますか。
(Do you know what language this is?)

B: アラビア語です。
(It's Arabic.)

A: はい，その通りです。
(That's right (lit. the same as you said).)

Notes

1. X *tōri* means either that someone does something in the same way as X (e.g., KS(A) and (B)) [manner], or that something agrees with X (e.g., KS(C) and (D)) [concordance]. In the first case, the particle *ni* may follow *tōri*, but in the second case, no particle follows, as in (1).

(1) 思った**通り** {ø / ***に**} 彼が一番先に来ていた。(=KS(C))

2. *Tōri* is sometimes followed by the object marker *o*. This is the same as *tōri no koto o* 'things which are the same way as.'

(2) 思っている**通り(のこと)を**書いて下さい。
(Please write what you are thinking (lit. things which are the same way as you are thinking).)

3. N with the suffix *-dōri* is more commonly used than N *no tōri*.

(3) a. **指示通り**(=指示の通り)(に)動いて下さい。
(Please move as is directed.)

b. これは**予定通り**(=予定の通り)の行動です。
(This is a scheduled activity (lit. an activity which is the same as we scheduled).)

【Related Expression】

In some contexts, *yōni*, the adverb form of *yōda*, also expresses the idea "in such a way." However, X *yōni* basically means that the way someone does something or something takes place is like X, while X *tōri* means that the way someone does something or something takes place is the same as X. Thus, in contexts where the way is practically the same as X, *yōni* and *tōri* are almost interchangeable; otherwise, they are not. In [1], for example, the *yōni* sentences and the *tōri* sentences mean practically the same thing, except that the *tōri* sentences stress "exactness."

[1] a. 私の言う {**ように / 通り(に)**} 体を動かして下さい。(=KS(B))

b. 予想した {**ように / 通り**} 誰も宿題をやってこなかった。
(=Ex.(d))

In [2], on the other hand, *tōri* is not acceptable.

[2] a. 春になった {**ように / *通り**} 暖かい。
(lit. Today is as warm as if spring had come.)

b. 彼女は日本人の {**ように / *通り**} 日本語を話す。
(She speaks Japanese like a Japanese.)

(⇨ ***yōni***[2] (DBJG: 554–56))

to suru[1] とする *phr.*

a phrase indicating that s.o. assumes s.t.

assume that; regard ~ as; let; suppose
【REL. *ni suru*; *to naru to*】

◆Key Sentences

(A)

		Noun	
温度(おんど)	は	**一定(いってい)(だ)**	とする。
(We assume that the temperature is constant.)			

(B)

	Vinf·nonpast	
一日(いちにち)に五百(ごひゃく)マイル	**運転(うんてん)できる**	とすれば / すると, 何日(なんにち)で着(つ)きますか。
(Assuming that we can drive 500 miles a day, how many days will it take to get there?)		

(C)

	Vinf·past	
温暖化現象(おんだんかげんしょう)がこのまま	**続(つづ)いた**	としよう。
(Suppose the greenhouse effect continued on like this.)		

Formation

(i) N_1 は N_2 (だ)とする

一ドルは百三十円(ひゃくさんじゅうえん)(だ)とする。(We assume that one dollar is 130 yen.)

(ii) Sinf·nonpast とする

山田さんが来られないとすると(ちょっと困る。) (If we assume that Mr. Yamada cannot come, (we are at a bit of a loss.))

日本へ行くとすれば(いつ行ったらいいだろう。) (Assuming that we go to Japan, (I wonder what would be the best time.))

(iii) Sinf·past とする

百万円もらったとしよう。 (Suppose you received ¥1,000,000.)

あと百日の命だと言われたとする。 (Let's suppose that you were told you only had 100 days left to live.)

Examples

(a) 今，空気抵抗は無視できるものとする。
(Now let's assume that we can ignore air resistance.)

(b) 男性の女性に対するこのような行為は性的いやがらせであるとする。
(Let's assume such behavior by men towards women is regarded as a sexual harassment.)

(c) 西洋では日本のいわゆる私小説は小説ではないとされる。
(In the West the Japanese so-called 'I' novels are not regarded as novels.)

(d) 私はアメリカを第二の故郷とすることに違和感を覚えない。
(I don't feel uneasy regarding America as my second home country.)

(e) 夏の九週間集中日本語講座の単位は六単位とする。
(We let the units of the 9-week intensive Japanese course in summer count for 6 units.)

(f) 利息は年 3.5 % とする。
(Let the interest rate be 3.5 % anually.)

(g) 日本経済がこのまま下降線をたどるとすると，日本語ブームもやがては終わるかもしれない。
(If we assume that the Japanese economy keeps going down as it is now, the Japanese language boom may eventually come to an end.)

(h) 日本が集団主義的な国だとすれば，欧米は，やはり，個人主義的な国と言えるだろう。
(If we assume that Japan is a country of groupism, then Europe and the States can be said to be countries of individualism.)

(i) 為替レートを一ドル百円とすれば，この家はいくらになりますか。
(Assuming that the exchange rate is one dollar to 100 yen, how much will this house amount to?)

(j) X + Y = 20 で，X が 8 だとすれば，Y は 12 になる。
(If we assume that X = 8 in X + Y = 20, Y will be 12.)

(k) 一男を養子とすることには依存はない。
(I have no objection to regarding Kazuo as our adopted son.)

(l) 大陸の中国が完全に資本主義社会になったとしよう。中国は何年後に経済大国になるであろうか。
(Suppose that continental China became a completely capitalized society. How long do you think it would take for the country to become an economic giant.)

(m) ニューヨークの物価指数を 100 としよう。
(Let New York's price index be 100.)

Notes

1. The common meaning for all the uses of *suru* in KS and Exs is the speaker's assumption about something. Vinf·past *to suru* is a hypothetical assumption. Excepting the cases where *to suru* is used in the sense of 'regard ~ as ~,' practically all the uses of *to suru* can take both non-past and past tenses.

(1) a. 温度は一定 {**だ / だった**} とする。(=KS(A))

b. 一日に五百マイル運転 {**できる / できた**} とすれば / すると，何日で着きますか。(=KS(B))

c. 温暖化現象がこのまま {**続く / 続いた**} としよう。(=KS(C))

The choice of the past tense over the non-past tense serves to indicate a greater degree of hypothesis, because the past tense expresses s.t. as if a given situation already existed.The similar contrast that is found in basic grammar is ~ *hō ga ii* as in (2).

(2) すぐ｛**行く / 行った**｝**方がいい**よ。
(You should / had better go there right away.)

2. In terms of the choice of particles there are three patterns for the N (*da / dearu*) *to suru* structure: that is, N_1 {*ga / o / wa*} N_2 (*da / dearu*) *to suru*.

(3) a. 温度**は**一定だとする。(=KS(A))

b. 温度**が**一定だとする。

c. 温度**を**一定だとする。

The most basic one is the *ga*-version, i.e., (3b) and it means 'Let's assume that (not something else but) the temperature is constant.' In the *o*-version, i.e., (3c), the original subject of (3b) has been changed to a direct object *o*. The *o*-version translates into English as 'Let's assume the temperature to be constant' in which the original subject has changed to the direct object, just as in the Japanese version. In (3a) 'the temperature' is presented as the topic of the sentence. The similar particle choice is observed in the *omou* construction.

(4) a. その映画**は**面白いと思う。
(As for the movie, I believe that it is interesting.)

b. その映画**が**面白いと思う。
(I believe that (not something else but) the movie is interesting.)

c. その映画**を**面白いと思う。
(I believe the movie to be interesting.)

Note also that in (3) the copula *da* can be dropped in (3a) and (3c), but not in (3b).

【Related Expressions】

I. Compare N *to suru* in [1a] and [2a] and N *ni suru* in [1b] and [2b].

[1] a. 温度は一定**とする**。(=KS(A))

b. 温度は一定**にする**。
(We will make the temperature constant.)

[2] a. 一ドルは三百六十(さんびゃくろくじゅう)円**とする**。
(Let 1 dollar be ¥360.)

b. 一ドルは三百六十円**にする**。
(We will make 1 dollar ¥360.)

The choice of the particle *ni* indicates that the speaker causes the change, whereas the choice of the particle *to* indicates that the speaker simply assumes a certain state of the matter. So if the speaker cannot make an assumption about something, the use of *to* is ungrammatical, as shown in [3] and [4].

[3] 氷(こおり)を水(みず) **{に / *と} する**。
(We make ice into water.)

[4] 魔法使(まほうつか)いはカエルを王子様(おうじさま) **{に / *と} する**。
(The wizard will change a frog into a prince.)

II. *To sureba / suru to* can be contrasted with *to nareba / naru to*, with difference of meaning. The former expresses an assumption, but the latter expresses a reality, as shown in [5] and [6] below:

[5] a. 一日に五百マイル運転できる**と {すれば / すると}**, 何日で着きますか。(=KS(B))

b. 一日に五百マイル運転できる**と {なれば / なると}**, 何日で着きますか。
(If we can drive 500 miles per day, how many days will it take to get there?)

[6] a. 日本経済がこのまま下降線をたどる**と {すれば / すると}**, 日本語ブームもやがては終わるかもしれない。(=Ex.(g))

b. 日本経済がこのまま下降線をたどる**と {なれば / なると}**, 日本語ブームもやがては終わるかもしれない。
(If the Japanese economy keeps going down as it is now,

the Japanese language boom may eventually come to an end.)

(⇨ ***to naru to***)

to suru[2] とする *phr.*

to have a sensory or psychological experience	feel ~; look ~

◆Key Sentence

	Sound Symbolism	
あの人(ひと)はちょっとしたことで	**かっ**	とする。
(That person flares up at the slightest provocation.)		

Formation

Sound Symbolism とする

つるっとする (s.o. feels s.t. slippery)

ほっとする (s.o. feels relieved)

Examples

(a) あの男(おとこ)の人は目(め)がギョロリとしている。
(He has goggling eyes.)

(b) 姉(あね)は足(あし)がすらっとしている。
(My older sister has slender legs.)

(c) 今日(きょう)の天気(てんき)はからっとしていて，気持(きも)ちがいい。
(It is nice and dry today.)

(d) 昔の恋人を東京駅で見かけて，はっとした。
(I was taken aback when I saw my old girlfriend at Tokyo station.)

(e) ジョンは遅刻して先生に叱られたのに，けろっとしていた。
(John was scolded by his teacher when he came in late, but he didn't show any sense of wrong doing.)

(f) 日本語の試験が思ったよりよく出来たのでほっとした。
(I felt relieved because I did better in a Japanese test than I expected.)

(g) 部長は部下に反対された時，むっとした。
(The department chief looked offended when he was opposed by his subordinate.)

(h) 難しいと思っていた日本語の試験がやさしかったのでほっとした。
(The Japanese test which I thought would be difficult turned out to be easy, and I felt relieved.)

(i) 休みの日は何もしないで，ぼうっとしているのが好きです。
(On my days off I like to do nothing and to be completely laid back.)

Note

Sound-symbolical word + *to suru* is used to mean 'to look ~' or 'to feel ~.' The sound-symbolical word (i.e., a phono-mime, pheno-mime and psycho-mime) expresses sensory experience as in Exs.(a) – (c) or psychological experience as in KS and Exs.(d) – (i). The following is an inexhaustive list of such sound-symbolical words that take *to suru*.

ぐにゃっとする (to become limp) すかっとする (to feel very refreshed)
しゅんとする (to feel despondent) つんとする (to look standoffish)
ぎくっとする (to feel shocked) ぎょっとする (to be startled)
じっとする (to stay still) ほろりとする (to be moved to tears)
どきっとする (to be startled) くらっとする (to feel dizzy)
ぞくっとする (to shiver with cold) すうっとする (to feel refreshed)

Unlike the ones listed above, most of the sound symbolical words are based on reduplication, that is, they take the form of X-X as in:

きらきら ((shine) sparklingly) ころころ ((small objects) roll)

ぼたぼた ((large amount of liquid) drips) ぬるぬる (slimy)
ざくざく ((cut) a heavy, thick object) かちかち ((freeze) hard)
しとしと ((it rains) quietly) するする ((slide) smoothly)
くるくる ((turn) round and round) こそこそ ((escape) secretly)

But all the sound symbolical words with reduplication cannot normally fit into the *to suru* pattern.

(1) 今日は春のように，一日中**ぽかぽかして**いた。
(Today all day long it was nice and warm like spring.)

(2) あの女の人は目が**きらきらして**いる。
(That woman's eyes are sparkling.)

(3) もうすぐ日本に行けると思うと，**わくわくする**。
(I get excited when I think that I can go to Japan pretty soon.)

(⇨ ***suru***[1] (DBJG: 428–33); **Characteristics of Japanese Grammar 8** (DBJG: 50–56))

totan (ni) 途端(に) *n. / adv.*

a noun / adverb which expresses the idea that 's.t. occurred the moment s.o. did s.t. or s.t. took place'

the moment; just as; as soon as; then
【REL. *to dōji ni*】

◆Key Sentences

(A)

	Vinf·past			
先生の顔を	**見た**	途端	(に)	宿題があったことを思い出した。
(The moment I saw my teacher, I remembered that there was a homework assignment.)				

(B)

	Vinf·past			
ドアを	**開けた**	ら,	途端に	カレーの匂いがした。
(The moment I opened the door, I smelled curry.)				

Formation

(i) Vinf·past 途端(に)

座った途端(に) (the moment s.o. sat down)

(ii) Vinf·past ら, 途端に

食べたら, 途端に (the moment s.o. ate s.t.)

Examples

T

(a) 部屋に入った途端(に)電話が鳴った。
(Just as I entered my room, the telephone rang.)

(b) その日本の写真を見た途端(に)家族に会いたくなった。
(I wanted to see my family the moment I saw that Japanese photograph.)

(c) 彼女は私の顔を見た途端(に)泣き出した。
(As soon as she saw me, she started to cry.)

(d) コンセントを差し込んだら，途端に家中の電気が消えた。
(The moment I put the plug in, all the lights went out in the house.)

(e) その牛乳を飲んだら，途端に腹が痛み出した。
(As soon as I drank the milk, my stomach started to ache.)

(f) 助かったと思った。その途端(に)，力が抜けて気を失ってしまった。
(I thought I was saved; then (lit. at that moment), my strength was gone and I lost consciousness.)

Notes

1. In "V_1 *totan* (*ni*) ~ V_2," V_2 must represent an uncontrollable action, although when the subject of V_2 is the third person, a controllable verb is acceptable. Compare KS(A) to (1).

 (1) a. *私は先生の顔を見た**途端**，立ち上がった。
 (I stood up the moment I saw my teacher.)

 b. 洋子は先生の顔を見た**途端**，立ち上がった。
 (Yoko stood up the moment she saw her teacher.)

2. The demonstrative adjective *sono* 'that' can precede *totan*, as in Ex.(f). The demonstrative adjectives *kono* and *ano* cannot be used before *totan*.

3. The particle *ni* is optional when *totan* is modified by a verb or by *sono* 'that.'

【Related Expression】

To dōji ni expresses an idea similar to *totan* (*ni*). For example, KS(A) and (B) can be rephrased as in [1] without changing the meaning of the discourse except that *to dōji ni* focuses on simultaneous action and *totan* (*ni*) on suddenness.

 [1] a. 先生の顔を｛**見た途端**(**に**) / **見ると同時に**｝宿題があったことを思い出した。(=KS(A))

 b. ドアを｛**開けたら，途端に** / **開けると同時に**｝カレーの匂いがした。(=KS(B))

To dōji ni, however, does not have the restriction described in Note 1, as seen in [2].

[2] 私は先生の顔を {**見ると同時に / *見た途端,**} 立ち上がった。
(I stood up when (lit. at the same time as) I saw my teacher.)

To dōji ni can also express concurrent states, while *totan (ni)* is used only for actions, as in [3].

[3] 群衆(ぐんしゅう)が遠(とお)くに {**見えると同時に / *見えた途端(に)**} 太鼓(たいこ)の音(おと)も聞(き)こえる。
(A crowd can be seen in the distance and, at the same time, (sounds of) drums can be heard.)

It should also be noted that *to dōji ni* can be preceded by nouns and adjectives while *totan (ni)* occurs only with verbs and the demonstrative *sono* 'that.'

(⇨ ***to dōji ni***)

tōtō とうとう *adv.*

an adverb that is used to express the eventual arrival of an expected situation

finally; at (long) last; eventually; in the end; after all
【REL. *yatto*; *tsui ni*】

T

◆**Key Sentence**

朝(あさ)から降(ふ)りそうだった雨(あめ)が	とうとう	降り出(だ)した。
(It's been threatening to rain since the morning and finally it started to rain. (lit. The rain which threatened to fall from the morning finally started to fall.))		

Examples

(a) 弟は医者の忠告を聞かないでたばこを吸い続け，とうとう肺がんになってしまった。
(My younger brother didn't take his doctor's advice and kept smoking until he finally got lung cancer.)

(b) 日本語の先生が余りにも厳しかったから，その学生はとうとう日本語が嫌いになってしまった。
(Because his Japanese instructor was so strict the student eventually came to hate the Japanese language.)

(c) その数学の問題は何時間かけても解けなかったので，とうとうあきらめてしまった。
(I wasn't able to solve the mathematical problem after spending many hours on it, so I finally gave up.)

(d) ビルは妻との関係がだんだん悪化し，とうとう別れてしまった。
(Bill's relationship with his wife gradually deteriorated and they eventually separated.)

(e) この会社で働くのもとうとう今日が最後となった。
(At long last this is the last day I work at this company.)

(f) 十五年も飼っていた猫がとうとう老衰で死んでしまった。
(The cat we had kept for 15 years finally died of old age.)

(g) とうとう博士論文を書いてしまった。
(At long last I finished writing a Ph.D. dissertation.)

(h) 私達の結婚の日がとうとうやって来た。
(Our wedding day has finally come.)

Notes

1. The adverb *tōtō* is used to express that an expected situation has come about after an extended period of time. The resulted situation is often negative in nature, but not always, as shown in Exs.(g) and (h).

2. The main verb that is used with *tōtō* often takes V*te shimau*, an auxil-

iary verb that indicates completion of something about which the speaker is emotive. (⇨ ***shimau*** (DBJG: 403–06))

【Related Expressions】

I. *Tōtō* is crucially different from *yatto* in that the former often indicates a negative situation that came about spontaneously, but the latter indicates a positive situation that has been realized with the greatest efforts. So, every *tōtō* in the KS and Exs. cannot be replaced by *yatto*, except Exs.(g) and (h).

[1] a. 弟は医者の忠告を聞かないでたばこを吸い続け，{**とうとう / *やっと**} 肺がんになってしまった。(=Ex.(a))

b. 日本語の先生が余りにも厳しかったから，その学生は {**とうとう / *やっと**} 日本語が嫌いになってしまった。 (=Ex.(b))

However, if the final verb is a verb that expresses s.t. positive that has resulted by human efforts, then *yatto* can be used but not *tōtō*. Note that the final verbs in [2a] and [2b] are non-volitional verbs. If the verbs are volitional as in [2a′] and [2b′], both *yatto* and *tōtō* become acceptable. In this case *yatto* and *tōtō* indicate difficulty in the process and the sense of accomplishment, respectively.

[2] a. 三時間も考えて {**やっと / *とうとう**} 数学の問題が解けた。
(I was able to solve a mathematical problem eventually after working on it for three hours.)

b. 探していた本が神田の古本屋で {**やっと / ??とうとう**} 見つかった。
(I finally found a book I'd been looking for at a second-hand bookstore in Kanda.)

a′. 三時間も考えて {**やっと / とうとう**} 数学の問題を解いた。
(I solved the problem eventually after working hard at it for three hours.)

b′. 探していた本を神田の古本屋で {**やっと / とうとう**} 見つけた。

(I finally found a book I had been looking for at a second-hand bookstore in Kanda.)

As explained in Note 1 above, *tōtō* tends to occur with a negative statement, so for example in [3a] the choice of *tōtō* indicates the speaker / writer's dislike of the winter, whereas, the choice of *yatto* indicates his liking of the winter. In [3b] the choice of *tōtō* indicates the speaker / writer's unhappiness about the man's quitting the job, whereas the choice of *yatto* indicates his happiness about the guy's quitting the job.

[3] a. 冬が {**とうとう / やっと**} やって来た。
(The winter finally came.)

b. その男は会社を {**とうとう / やっと**} 辞めた。
(The man quit the company in the end.)

Note also that *yatto* cannot be used with a negative predicate, as follows.

[4] a. スミスさんは {**とうとう / *やっと**} パーティーに来ませんでした。
(Smith didn't show up at the party after all.)

b. なくした財布は {**とうとう/*やっと**} 見つかりませんでした。
(The purse I lost was not found after all.)

II. Another similar adverb *tsui ni* can replace *tōtō* and *yatto*, when the main verb is affirmative, but when it is negative, it can replace only *tōtō*.

[5] 待ちに待った夏休みは {**ついに/とうとう/やっと**} やって来た。
(The long-waited summer vacation has finally arrived.)

[6] a. キャシーは {**ついに / とうとう / *やっと**} パーティーに現れなかった。
(Cathy didn't show up at the party after all.)

b. エドには {**ついに / とうとう / *やっと**} 会うことが出来なかった。
(I couldn't see Ed after all.)

Tsui ni focuses on the final moment, whereas *tōtō* focuses on the process that leads to the final moment, but in actual use they are virtually interchangeable.

to tomo ni と共に *phr.* <w>

a phrase which is used to express the idea that A and B share a common property or do the same thing together, that two things take place at the same time, or that s.o. or s.t. possesses two properties

as well as; with; along with; at the same time; when, as; while

【REL. *ni shitagatte*; *ni tomonatte*; *ni tsurete*; ***to dōji ni***; *to issho ni*; *to narande*; *to onajiku*】

◆Key Sentences

(A)

	Noun		
スタインベックは	**ヘミングウェイ**	と共(とも)に	アメリカの代表的作家(だいひょうてきさっか)の一人(ひとり)だ。
(Steinbeck, as well as Hemingway, is a writer representative of American writers.)			

(B)

	Noun		
私(わたし)は	**職場(しょくば)の同僚達(どうりょうたち)**	と共に	そのデモに参加(さんか)した。
(I took part in the demonstration with my office colleagues.)			

T

(C)

Subordinate Clause			
	Vinf·nonpast		
病気(びょうき)が	**回復(かいふく)する**	と共に	食欲(しょくよく)も出(で)てきた。
(As I'm recovering from my illness, my appetite is coming back.)			

(D)

	Noun			
彼(かれ)は	**科学者(かがくしゃ)**	**である**	と共に	哲学者(てつがくしゃ)でもあった。
(He was a philosopher as well as a scientist.)				

Formation

(i) N と共に

山田先生(やまだせんせい)と共に (as well as Mr. Yamada; with Mr. Yamada)

退職(たいしょく)と共に (at the same time as one's retirement)

気候(きこう)の変化(へんか)と共に (with the climate change; as the climate changes)

(ii) Vinf·nonpast と共に

景気(けいき)が回復すると共に (as business recovers)

(iii) {N / Adj(*na*)stem} であると共に

医者(いしゃ)であると共に (as well as being a doctor)

経済的(けいざいてき)であると共に (as well as being economical)

(iv) Adj(*i*)inf·nonpast と共に

興味深(きょうみぶか)いと共に (as well as being interesting)

T

Examples

(a) 原子力は石油と共に重要なエネルギー源だ。
(Atomic energy, as well as petroleum, is an important energy source.)

(b) 轟音と共にジェット機が飛び去った。
(A jet flew off with a roaring sound.)

(c) 武士階級は封建制と共に滅びた。
(The samurai class died with the feudal system.)

(d) 終戦と共に激しいインフレが人々を襲った。
(Severe inflation hit people when the war ended (lit. with the end of the war).)

(e) 景気の回復と共に失業率が下がってきた。
(As business is recovering (lit. With the recovery of business), the unemployment rate is coming down.)

(f) 年をとると共に耳が遠くなってきた。
(As I get older, I am losing my hearing.)

(g) 調査が進むと共に新しい事実が次々に明らかになっていった。
(As the investigation progressed, one new fact after another was revealed.)

(h) 文法を復習すると共に漢字の勉強も忘れてはならない。
(While you review grammar, you must not forget to study *kanji*.)

(i) 現在のエネルギー利用技術を改良すると共に新しいエネルギー源を探すことが急務である。
(It is urgent that we improve current energy utilization technology while looking for a new energy source.)

(j) その提案は建設的であると共に革命的であった。
(The discovery was revolutionary as well as constructive.)

Note

The meaning of *to tomo ni* changes depending on the sentence pattern and context.

(1) When A and B share the common property C in "A *wa* B *to tomo ni* C," *to tomo ni* means 'as well as' (e.g., KS(A) and Ex.(a)).

(2) When A and B are the actors of the action C in "A *wa* B *to tomo ni* C," *to tomo ni* means 'with ; along with' (e.g., KS(B), Exs.(b) and (c)).

(3) When *to tomo ni* is preceded by a noun representing an event or action, *to tomo ni* means either 'at the same time as ; when' or 'as; with' depending on the event or action represented by the noun (e.g., Exs.(d) and (e)).

(4) When *to tomo ni* is preceded by a verb, *to tomo ni* means 'as ; while' (e.g., KS(C) and Exs.(f) – (i)).

(5) When *to tomo ni* is preceded by N / Adj(*na*)stem *de aru*, *to tomo ni* means 'as well as' (e.g., KS(D) and Ex.(j)).

【Related Expressions】

I. When *to tomo ni* means 'as well as' [(1) in Note], it can be rephrased as *to onajiku* or *to narande*.

[1] スタインベックはヘミングウェイ｛**と共に / と同じく / と並んで**｝アメリカの代表的作家の一人だ。(=KS(A))

II. When *to tomo ni* means 'with ; along with' [(2) in Note], it can be rephrased as *to issho ni*.

[2] 私は職場の同僚達｛**と共に / と一緒に**｝そのデモに参加した。(=KS(B))

Note, however, that *to issho ni* is more colloquial than *to tomo ni*.

III. When *to tomo ni* means 'as' [(3) and (4) in Note], it can be rephrased as *ni tsurete*, *ni tomonatte*, or *ni shitagatte*.

[3] 景気の回復｛**と共に / につれて / に伴って / に従って**｝失業率が下がってきた。(=Ex.(e))

[4] 病気が回復する｛**と共に / に従って / につれて / に伴って**｝食欲も出てきた。(=KS(C))

(⇨ ***ni shitagatte/shitagai***; ***ni tsurete/tsure***)

to wa kagiranai とは限らない *phr.*

a phrase which expresses the idea "not necessarily"

not always; not necessarily

◆Key Sentences

(A)

Sinf	
体の弱い人が早く死ぬ	とは限らない。
(Frail people do not necessarily die young.)	

(B)

Sinf			
高い物が	いつも / 必ずしも	安い物よりいい	とは限らない。
(Expensive things are not always / necessarily better than inexpensive ones.)			

(C)

Sinf		Sinf	
日本に長く住んでいる	から(と言って)	日本語が上手だ	とは限らない。
(It is not necessarily the case that people are good at Japanese because they have lived in Japan a long time.)			

(D)

Sinf		
Sconc		
日本に行っても	日本語が上手になる	とは限らない。
(You will not necessarily become good at Japanese even if you go to Japan.)		

(E)

Sinf		
Scond		
お金があれば	幸福になれる	とは限らない。
(You will not (lit. cannot) necessarily be happy if you have money.)		

Formation

Sinf とは限らない

よくなるとは限らない　(s.o. will not necessarily get well)

Examples

(a) 漫画が子供の教育にとって有害だとは限らない。
(Comics are not necessarily harmful to children's education.)

(b) 日本人の使う日本語がいつも正しいとは限らない。
(The Japanese used by Japanese people is not always correct.)

(c) スポーツ選手が必ずしも健康だとは限らない。
(Athletes are not necessarily healthy.)

(d) 技術の進歩が必ずしも我々に繁栄をもたらすとは限らない。
(Progress in technology does not necessarily bring us prosperity.)

(e) 先生がそう言ったからと言ってそれが正しいとは限らない。
(It is not necessarily correct just because the teacher said so.)

(f) 薬を飲んだからと言ってよくなるとは限らない。
(You do not necessarily get better because you take medicine.)

(g) 頭がよくても人生に成功するとは限らない。
(You do not necessarily succeed in your life even if you are smart.)

(h) 実力があっても失業しないとは限らない。
(It is not necessarily true that you won't lose your job even if you have ability.)

(i) 悪い家庭環境に育てば必ず悪い子供になるとは限らない。
(It is not necessarily true that children become bad if they grow up in a bad family environment.)

(j) 時間がたくさんあればいい論文が書けるとは限らない。
(It is not necessarily true that you can write a good paper if you have a lot of time.)

Note

S *to wa kagiranai* literally means that (cases) are not limited to S. Although the idea of "necessarily" or "always" is included in this phrase, the adverbs *kanarazushimo* 'necessarily' or *itsumo* 'always' can also be used (e.g., KS(B) and Exs.(b) – (d)).

T

tsumari つまり *adv.*

an adverb that is used to summarize or rephrase what has been mentioned / stated in the preceding context	that is (to say); namely; in short; to sum up; in other words; after all; that means 【REL. *kekkyoku*; *sunawachi*; *yōsuru ni*】

◆Key Sentences

(A)

Sentence			Sentence
ベルリンの壁が崩れた。	これは	つまり，	民主化の嵐が始まったということだ。
(The Berlin Wall fell apart. This means that the storm of democratization has started.)			

(B)

NP		Noun	
私の母の弟，	つまり，	叔父	が最近離婚した。
(My mother's younger brother, that is to say, my uncle, has recently divorced.)			

Formation

(i) S_1。(S_2 . . .) つまり，Sn。

金がない。つまり，貧乏なんです。
(I don't have money. In other words, I'm poor.)

(ii) NP，つまり，N / NP

母の姉の子供，つまり，私のいとこ
(The child of my mother's older sister, my cousin, that is.)

Examples

(a) アメリカに一年間一人で出張するんです。つまり，単身赴任ということですよ。
(I'm going without my family to work for the company in America for one year. In other words, I'm becoming a *tanshin-funin* worker.)

(b) 運動をした後は気分がよくなりますね。つまり，運動でストレスがなくなるということなんですよ。

(You feel good after exercise, right? That means, stress is eliminated by exercise.)

(c) A: 部長，このプロジェクトは出来ますか。
(Chief, can we do this project?)

B: そうだね。いいプロジェクトだと思うけど，予算がどうもねえ。
(Well, I think it's a fine project, but you know how the budget is.)

A: つまり，出来ないということですね。
(In short, we cannot do it, right?)

(d) 日本の父親は子供がまだ寝ている時に家を出て，子供達が寝てから家に帰って来る。つまり，父親不在ということだ。
(Japanese fathers leave home while their children are still asleep and come home after they have gone to sleep. This is, in short, an absence of fathers.)

(e) A: 彼女，僕が会いに行っても，あまり話してくれないんですよ。
(I go to see her, but she doesn't talk much to me, you know.)

B: それは，つまり，君のことが嫌いなんだよ。
(That means, she doesn't like you.)

(f) 産業化のために自然が破壊されること，つまり，環境破壊は人類の問題だ。
(The destruction of nature by industrialization, that is to say, environmental destruction, is a problem of mankind.)

(g) 私の母の妹の娘，つまり，私のいとこが来週バンコクから来ます。
(The daughter of my younger sister, my cousin, that is, is coming from Bangkok next week.)

(h) 女性を女性だからといって差別すること，つまり，性差別の問題はどこへ行ってもある。
(To discriminate against a woman simply because she is a woman, in short, sexual discrimination, exists no matter where you go.)

(i) つまり，誰も悪くないということだよ。
(Nobody is to blame, after all.)

Notes

1. The adverb *tsumari* is used when the speaker / writer wants to summarize or rephrase s.t. that has been mentioned / stated in the preceding discourse.

2. *Tsumari* is often used in *tsumari ~ to iu koto da* as in KS(A), Exs.(a) – (d) and (i).

3. *Tsumari* can be used to rephrase the preceding noun phrase as in KS(B) and Exs.(f), (g) and (h).

【Related Expressions】

I. *Tsumari* can be replaced by *sunawachi* ‘namely’ in all the examples except Exs.(c), (e) and (i) where *tsumari* is used to summarize what the conversational partner has said.

[1] a. ベルリンの壁が崩れた。これは {**つまり / すなわち**}，民主化の嵐が始まったということだ。(=KS(A))

b. 運動をした後は気分がよくなりますね。{**つまり / すなわち**}，運動でストレスがなくなるということなんですよ。(=Ex.(b))

c. {**つまり / *すなわち**}，出来ないということですね。(=Ex.(c))

d. それは，{**つまり / *すなわち**}，君のことが嫌いなんだよ。(=Ex.(e))

II. *Tsumari* can be replaced by another similar adverb *yōsuru ni* in “S_1. *Tsumari* S_2,” but not in “NP, *tsumari* N / NP.”

[2] a. ベルリンの壁が崩れた。これは {**つまり / 要**(よう)**するに**}，民主化の嵐が始まったということだ。(=KS(A))

b. {**つまり / 要するに**}，出来ないということですね。(=Ex.(c))

c. 私の母の弟，{**つまり / *要するに**}，叔父が最近離婚した。(=KS(B))

T

d. 産業化のために自然が破壊されること，{**つまり** / ***要するに**}，環境破壊は人類の問題だ。(=Ex.(f))

III. *Tsumari* can also be replaced by *kekkyoku* only when it means ‘after all.’ For example, *tsumari* in [3] means ‘this means that ~,’ so it cannot be replaced by *kekkyoku*; however, *tsumari* in [4] means ‘after all’; therefore it can be replaced by *kekkyoku*.

[3] a. ベルリンの壁が崩れた。これは {**つまり** / ***結局**(けっきょく)}，民主化の嵐が始まったということだ。(=KS(A))

b. 運動をした後は気分が良くなりますね。{**つまり** / ***結局**}，運動でストレスがなくなるということなんですよ。(=Ex.(b))

[4] a. {**つまり** / **結局**}，誰も悪くないということだよ。(=Ex.(i))
(After all, nobody is to blame.)

b. {**つまり** / **結局**} お金(かね)を出(だ)したくないんだろう。
(After all, you don’t want to give money, do you?)

tsutsu つつ *aux. / conj.* <w>

(1) an auxiliary which expresses an action in progress; (2) a conjunction which is used to present two concurrent actions

-ing; while; although
【REL. *iru*; *nagara*】

◆Key Sentences

(A)

	V*masu*		
台風(たいふう)が九州(きゅうしゅう)に	**接近(せっきん)し**	つつ	ある。
(A typhoon is approaching Kyushu.)			

(B)

	V*masu*		
彼女(かのじょ)は夫(おっと)の無罪(むざい)を	**信(しん)じ**	つつ	息(いき)を引(ひ)き取(と)った。
(She died believing that her husband was innocent.)			

(C)

	V*masu*		
たばこは体(からだ)によくないと	**分(わ)かり**	つつ	なかなかやめられない。
(Although I know that smoking is harmful to my health, I just cannot quit.)			

Formation

V*masu* つつ

思(おも)いつつ　(while thinking)

Examples

(a) 新(あたら)しい本社(ほんしゃ)ビルが完成(かんせい)しつつある。
(The new headquarters building is drawing to completion.)

(b) オリンピックの施設(しせつ)が出来(でき)つつある。
(The Olympic facilities are being completed.)

T

(c) この大学は現在キャンパスの移転を検討しつつある。
(This university is considering moving its campus now.)

(d) 甘い物を食べると太ると分かりつつ，つい手が出てしまう。
(Although I know that eating sweets makes me gain more weight, I unintentionally reach out for them.)

(e) 悪いことと知りつつ，友達にうそをついてしまった。
(Knowing that it was a bad thing, I told my friend a lie.)

(f) 早く論文を書かなければいけないと思いつつ，今日もテレビを見てしまった。
(Although I was thinking that I had to write the paper soon, I watched TV today, too.)

(g) 私は父の無事を祈りつつ病院に急いだ。
(I hurried to the hospital hoping that my father was all right.)

(h) 彼は最後まで自分の学説が正しいことを主張しつつこの世を去った。
(He died while insisting until the last moment that his theory was correct.)

Notes

1. *Tsutsu aru* always expresses an action in progress (e.g., KS(A) and Exs.(a) – (c)).

2. V_1 *tsutsu* V_2 expresses concurrent actions by the same person (e.g., KS(B), (C) and Exs.(d) – (h)). *Tsutsu* cannot be used when concurrent actions are performed by different individuals, as in (1).

   (1) ルームメートがテレビを {**見ている間** / ***見つつ**}，私は日本語を勉強した。
   (I studied Japanese while my roommate watched TV.)
   (⇨ ***aida* (*ni*)** (DBJG: 67–71))

3. *Tsutsu* is not used to describe such everyday actions as those in (2) and (3).

   (2) a. ??私は今，晩ご飯を**食べつつある**。
   (I'm eating my dinner.)

b. ??デイブは今，友達に電話を**かけつつある**。
(Dave is calling his friend now.)

(3) a. ??私はビールを**飲みつつ**テレビを見た。
(I watched TV while drinking beer.)

b. ??太郎は**歩きつつ**アイスクリームを食べている。
(Taro is eating ice cream while walking.)

4. The auxiliary verb *iru* cannot precede *tsutsu*, as in (4).

(4) a. たばこは体によくないと{**分かり** / ***分かってい**} **つつ**なかなかやめられない。(=KS(C))

b. 悪いことと{**知り** / ***知ってい**} **つつ**，友達にうそをついてしまった。(=Ex.(e))

c. 彼女は毎日あれだけ仕事を{**し** / ***してい**} **つつ**，一言も苦情を言わない。
(Even though she does (lit. is doing) that much work every day, she doesn't complain a bit.)

【Related Expressions】

I. The auxiliary verb *iru* also expresses an action in progress. However, *iru* cannot be used with punctual verbs and movement verbs to express an action in progress, as in [1]. In this case, *tsutsu* is used, as in [2].

[1] a. 舞台の幕が**開いている**。
(The (stage) curtain is up (lit. open). / *The (stage) curtain is opening.)

b. 難民は自分達の国に**帰っている**。
(The refugees are back in their own country. / *The refugees are returning to their own country.)

[2] a. 舞台の幕が**開きつつ**ある。
(The (stage) curtain is going up.)

b. 難民は自分達の国に**帰りつつ**ある。
(The refugees are returning to their country.)

(⇨ ***iru***[2] (DBJG: 155–57))

T

II. *Nagara* also expresses concurrent actions by one person. Thus, *nagara* and *tsutsu* in this use are interchangeable, as in [3].

[3] a. 彼女は夫の無罪を信じ {**ながら / つつ**} 息を引き取った。 (=KS(B))

b. たばこは体によくないと分かり {**ながら / つつ**} なかなかやめられない。(=KS(C))

Note, however, that *nagara* can be preceded by adjectives and nouns to express the concurrent states of one entity, while *tsutsu* cannot, as in [4]. (Note that *de ari* in [4b] is the continuative form of the copula *de aru*.)

[4] a. ジムは経験が**浅い** {**ながら / *つつ**} なかなかいい仕事をする。
(Although Jim doesn't have much experience, he does a pretty good job.)

b. 彼はこの事故の**責任者であり** {**ながら / *つつ**} 責任を逃れようとしている。
(Despite the fact that he is the person responsible for this accident, he is trying to avoid his responsibility.)

Note also that *nagara* can be preceded by Vneg *nai* and V*te i* while *tsutsu* cannot, as in [5].

[5] a. 私は英語が**分からない** {**ながら / *つつ**} そのショーを十分楽しめた。
(Even though I don't understand English, I could fully enjoy the show.)

b. 彼女は毎日あれだけ仕事を**してい** {**ながら / *つつ**} 一言も苦情を言わない。(=(4c) in Note 4)

(⇨ ***nagara*(*mo*)** (this volume; DBJG: 269–70))

(no) ue de　(の)上で　*comp. prt.*

a compound particle that is used to express a preparatory action for a relatively important action

upon ~; after ~
【REL. *te kara*】

◆Key Sentences

(A)

	Vinf·past		
よく	**考えた**	上で	御返事いたします。
(I will reply upon careful consideration.)			

(B)

Noun		
話し合い	の上で	結論を出したいと思います。
(I would like to draw a conclusion after discussion.)		

Formation

(i) Vinf·past　上で

読んだ上で　(upon reading)

研究した上で　(upon conducting research)

(ii) Nの上で

調査の上で　(after investigation)

討議の上で　(after discussion)

Examples

(a) よく問題を話し合った上で決めたらどうでしょうか。
(Why don't we decide after discussing the matter?)

(b) 実験をした上で，理論の正しさを証明しなければならない。
(We have to prove the correctness of the theory after conducting an experiment.)

(c) 日本文学のスミス先生と相談した上で，修士論文の題目を決めました。
(I decided the topic of my M.A. thesis after consulting with Japanese literature Professor Smith.)

(d) 彼女とはお見合いをして，一年間交際した上で，結婚に踏み切りました。
(I decided to get married after meeting her through an arranged match and dating her for one year.)

(e) 日本の生活は高くつくと知った上で，日本へ留学した。
(I went to Japan to study, knowing that life is expensive there.)

(f) 十冊ぐらい本を読んだ上で，学期末のレポートを書き上げた。
(I finished writing my term paper after having read about 10 books.)

(g) 面談の上で，採否を決めます。
(After an interview we will decide whether or not to approve the adoption.)

(h) 二人は協議の上で離婚した。
(The two got divorced after reaching an agreement.)

Notes

1. Vinf·past *ue de* is used to express an idea that someone will do something rather important (quite often decision-making) after they have done something as a preparatory action. The image is that the action expressed in the main clause is *on top of* the accompanying action, as shown in the following diagram.

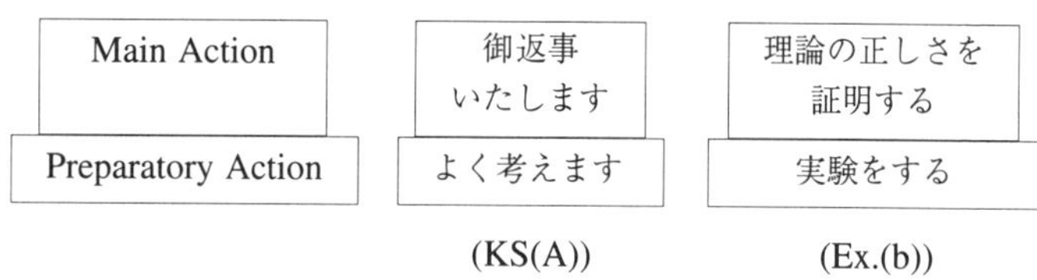

2. The verbs of the main and preparatory actions are non-passive, volitional verbs.

(1) a. 彼は新しい仕事｛**を見つけた / *が見つかった**｝上で，彼女と結婚した。
(He married her after he found a new job / a new job was found.)

b. 彼は財産を全部整理した上で，｛**自殺した / *死んだ**｝。
(He killed himself / died after he had sorted out all of his assets.)

Compare the following four sentences in which main and preparatory actions are stated in active or passive predicates.

(2) a. ??この問題はよく**調査された**上で，結論が**出される**べきだ。
(For this problem a conclusion should be drawn after a careful investigation has been conducted.) [passive-passive]

b. ?この問題はよく**調査した**上で，結論が**出される**べきだ。
(For this problem a conclusion should be drawn after we have conducted a careful investigation.) [active-passive]

c. *この問題はよく**調査された**上で，結論を**出す**べきだ。
(For this problem a conclusion should be drawn after a careful investigation has been conducted.) [passive-active]

d. この問題はよく**調査した**上で，結論を**出す**べきだ。
(For this problem we should draw a conclusion after we have made a careful investigation. [active-active]

3. N in N *no ue de* as exemplified by KS(B), Exs.(g) and (h) is typically a noun of investigation, interview, discussion and the like. And the noun is usually a Sino-Japanese noun that takes (*o*) *suru*.

【Related Expression】

V*te kara* is close in meaning to Vinf·past *ue de*, in that both express two actions in sequence. In fact, all the KS and Exs. can be rephrased using V*te kara*, as long as the verbs are volitional. See Note 2.

[1] a. よく考え{**た上で** / **てから**}，御返事いたします。(=KS(A))

b. よく問題を話し合っ{**た上で** / **てから**}，決めたらどうでしょうか。(=Ex.(a))

c. 実験をし{**た上で** / **てから**}，理論の正しさを証明しなければならない。(=Ex.(b))

However, there is a crucial difference between the two constructions: V*te kara* is used solely to indicate time sequence but Vinf·past *ue de* is used to indicate a preparation for a relatively important action. Therefore, there are cases of V*te kara* which cannot be rephrased by Vinf·past *ue de* as in [2]. In these examples, V*te kara* part lacks the sense of prerequisite. That is why the use of Vinf·past *ue de* is impossible.

[2] a. ジョーンズさんは必ずシャワーを浴び{**てから** / ***た上で**}寝る。
(Mr. Jones always goes to bed after taking a shower.)

b. 雪子は晩ご飯を食べ{**てから** / ***た上で**}映画に行った。
(After eating her supper, Yukiko went to a movie.)

c. 私達がこの家を買っ{**てから** / ***た上で**}もう十年になる。
(It's already been 10 years since we bought this house.)

If V*te kara* indicates a preparation, then, the rephrasing is alright as in [3].

[3] a. 電話をし{**てから** / **た上で**}友達を訪ねた。
(I visited with my friend after calling him.)

b. 彼は必ず翌日の予定表を調べ{**てから** / **た上で**}床につく。
(He always goes to bed after looking at the following day's schedule.)

(⇨ ***kara***[2] (DBJG: 177–78))

ue (ni) 上(に) *conj.*

a conjunction which introduces an additional, emphatic statement

as well; in addition; besides; furthermore; moreover; not only ~ but also
【REL. ~ *bakari de* (*wa*) *naku* ~ (*mo*); ***bakari ka*** **~** (***sae***); *dake de* (*wa*) *naku* ~ *mo*; ***sono ue***】

◆**Key Sentences**

(A)

Topic		Adj(*i*)·inf		
この映画(えいが)は	話(はなし)の筋(すじ)が	**面白(おもしろ)い**	上(うえ)(に)	配役(はいやく)がいい。
(Besides the fact that this movie has an interesting storyline, the cast is good.)				

(B)

Topic		Vinf		
彼(かれ)は	仕事(しごと)を	**見(み)つけてくれた**	上(に)	お金(かね)まで貸(か)してくれた。
(Not only did he find me a job, he even lent me some money.)				

(C)

Topic		Noun			
彼女(かのじょ)は	フランス語(ご)が	**専門(せんもん)**	**の**	上(に)	パリにしばらく住(す)んでいたから, フランス語がペラペラだ。
(She is fluent in French because she majored in French and, in addition, she lived in Paris for a while.)					

U

Formation

S 上(に)　(the same as the relative clause connection rules)

Examples

(a) 吉岡さんは奥さんに離婚された上(に)仕事まで失った。
(Not only was Mr. Yoshioka divorced by his wife, he also (lit. even) lost his job.)

(b) 私は年をとっている上(に)特に技能もないので，なかなか仕事が見つからない。
(Because I am not only old but also have no special skills, it is hard to find a job.)

(c) この車は故障が少ない上(に)燃費がいいので，よく売れている。
(This car sells well because (besides the fact that) it seldom needs repairs (lit. seldom has trouble) and furthermore it gets good mileage.)

(d) 私のアパートは狭い上(に)家具がたくさんあるので，お客さんが来た時，寝てもらう場所がない。
(Besides being small, my apartment has a lot of furniture, so there is no space for guests to sleep when they come.)

(e) 私のアパートは通勤に便利な上(に)家賃が安い。
(My apartment is convenient for commuting to work and, furthermore, the rent is inexpensive.)

(f) 田中先生は教え方が上手な上(に)学生の面倒をよく見るから，とても人気がある。
(Ms. Tanaka is very popular because she is good not only at teaching but also at taking care of her students.)

(g) 彼はスピード違反で捕まった時，無免許の上(に)酒に酔っていた。
(When he was caught for speeding, he had no driver's license (i.e., he was not licensed) and, moreover, he was drunk.)

Note

Ni after *ue* is optional.

【Related Expression】

Ue (*ni*) can be rephrased using *bakari de* (*wa*) *naku* ~ (*mo*) or *dake de* (*wa*) *naku* ~ (*mo*), as in [1].

[1] a. この映画は話の筋が面白い｛**上**(**に**) / **ばかりで**(**は**)**なく** / **だけで**(**は**)**なく**｝配役もいい。(=KS(A))

b. 彼は仕事を見つけてくれた｛**上**(**に**) / **ばかりで**(**は**)**なく** / **だけで**(**は**)**なく**｝お金まで貸してくれた。(=KS(B))

c. 彼女はフランス語が専門である｛**上**(**に**) / **ばかりで**(**は**)**なく** / **だけで**(**は**)**なく**｝パリにもしばらく住んでいたから，フランス語がペラペラだ。(=KS(C))

(⇨ ***dake de* (*wa*) *naku* ~ (*mo*)** (DBJG: 97–100))

uru/**eru** 得る(うる / える) *aux. v.* (*Gr.* 2) <w>

an auxiliary verb that expresses possibility

can; possible; -able
【REL. *koto ga dekiru*; *rareru*】

◆Key Sentence

	V*masu*		
二十一世紀に日本語は国際語に	**なり**	得る	と思う。
(I think it's possible for the Japanese language to become an international language in the 21st century.)			

Formation

V*masu* うる / える

起こり {うる / える} (can happen)

あり {うる / える} (can exist)

Examples

(a) 株の変動はいつでも起こり得る。
(The fluctuation of stocks can happen any time.)

(b) ほとんどのがんは予防し得る。
(The majority of cancers are preventable.)

(c) 一度に記憶し得る単語の数は限られている。
(The number of vocabulary items one can memorize at one time is limited.)

(d) 運動をすることによって健康を維持し得る。
(By doing exercise one can maintain one's health.)

(e) 日本語の基礎はだいたい二年間で学び得る。
(One can learn the basics of Japanese in roughly two years.)

(f) 日本の経済が不況になることだって十分にあり得る。
(It is quite possible that the Japanese economy will go into a slump.)

Notes

1. The auxiliary verb *uru/eru* is used primarily in written Japanese, but it can be used in formal speech as well, as in:

 (1) キャンパスでそんな事件が起こり**得る**なんて思いませんでしたね。
 (We never thought that such an incident could occur on campus.)

2. The basic conjugation pattern is as follows.

起こり {え / *う} ない
{え / *う} ます
{うる / える}。
{うれ / *えれ} ば
{え / *う} よう

起こり {え / *う} て
{え / *う} た

【Related Expression】

The auxiliary verb *uru/eru* can be replaced either by Vinf·nonpast *koto ga dekiru* or by *rareru*, except when the verb is totally non-controllable, such as *okiru* 'to take place' or *aru* 'to exist,' as in Exs.(a) and (f).

[1] a. 二十一世紀には日本語は国際語に {**なり得る / なれる / なることが出来る**} と思う。(=KS)

b. ほとんどのがんは予防 {**し得る / 出来る / することが出来る**}。(=Ex.(b))

c. 日本語の基礎はだいたい二年間で {**学び得る / 学べる / 学ぶことが出来る**}。(=Ex.(e))

[2] a. 株の変動はいつでも {**起こり得る / *起これる / *起こることが出来る**}。(=Ex.(a))

b. 日本の経済が不況になることだって十分に {**あり得る / *あれる / *あれることが出来る**} (=Ex.(f))

Since the basic meaning of *uru/eru* is the existence of possibility (not ability), it cannot be used in a sentence that expresses pure ability as shown in [3].

[3] a. 彼は日本語を {**話せる/話すことが出来る / *話し得る**}。
(He can speak Japanese.)

(⇨ ***koto ga dekiru*** (DBJG: 200–01); ***rareru***[2] (DBJG: 370–73))

U

V*masu* *v.*

a continuative form of a verb which means “V and . . .”	and; -ing 【REL. V*te*】

◆Key Sentences

(A)

	V*masu*	
ジョンは日本で	**生まれ,**	十歳まで日本の学校で勉強した。
(John was born in Japan and studied at a Japanese school until he was ten.)		

(B)

Topic$_1$		V*masu*	Topic$_2$	
父は	銀行に	**勤め,**	母は	うちの近くでブティックを開いている。
(My father works for a bank and my mother has a boutique near my house.)				

Examples

(a) みんながお金を出し合い，京子の出産祝いを買った。
(Everybody contributed some money and bought a present for Kyoko’s new baby.)

(b) エビは殻をむき，サラダ油で軽く炒めます。
(As for shrimp, you take their shells off and fry them lightly in salad oil.)

(c) 日本では一週間前から梅雨に入り，毎日うっとうしい日が続いています。
(In Japan we’ve been in the rainy season for a week (lit. since a week ago) and had gloomy days every day.)

(d) 本校の五十周年を記念し，祝賀パーティーを開きます。
(Commemorating this school's fiftieth anniversary, we are going to have a celebration party.)

(e) 長男は医者になり，次男は弁護士になった。
(My first son became a doctor and my second, a lawyer.)

(f) 男が荷車の前の綱を引っ張り，女が後ろを押した。
(The man pulled the strap in front of the cart and the woman pushed it from behind.)

【Related Expression】

The *te*-forms of verbs (V*te*) are also used to mean 'V and ~.' The difference between V*masu* and V*te* is as follows.

Basically, in "V_1*te* ~ V_2" there is a close relationship between the action in V_1 and that in V_2. No such relationship exists between V_1 and V_2 in "V_1*masu* ~ V_2." Usage restrictions differ depending on the subjects of V_1 and V_2.

A. When the subjects of V_1 and V_2 are the same:

A–1. V*te*

In general, "V_1*te* ~ V_2" is used when the two actions are closely related and the sequence is important. More specifically, V*te* is used in situations like those in [1] – [3].

[1] When one action (V_2) cannot take place until another action (V_1) takes place, as in (a) and (b):

a. 私は今日デパートへ｛**行って** / ***行き**｝買い物をしなければならない。
(I have to go to the department store to do some shopping today.)

b. 実物を｛**見て** / ***見**｝買うかどうか決めたい。
(I'd like to decide whether to buy it or not after I see the real thing.)

[2] When V_1 represents the cause of V_2 (a special case of [1]), as in (a) and (b):

a. 彼は {**働きすぎて** / ???**働きすぎ**} 体を壊してしまった。
(He damaged his health by overworking.)

b. 赤ん坊は私の顔を {**見て** / ???**見**} 急に泣き出した。
(Seeing my face, the baby suddenly began to cry.)

[3] When V_1 represents a means or manner of doing V_2, as in (a) and (b):

a. 京子は毎日自転車に {**乗って** / ???**乗り**} 学校へ行く。
(Kyoko goes to school by bicycle (lit. by riding a bicycle) every day.)

b. 私は手袋を {**はめて** / ???**はめ**} その仕事をした。
(I did the work with gloves on.)

A–2. V*masu*

In general, "V_1*masu* . . . V_2" is used when two actions or states are not directly related. More specifically, V*masu* is used when the times of two independent actions or states overlap, as in [4] and [5].

[4] Overlapping actions

a. 幸男はよく {**働き** / ***働いて**}, よく遊ぶ。
(Yukio works hard and plays a lot.)

b. みんなはその知らせに {**驚き** / ***驚いて**}, 悲しんだ。
(Everybody was surprised and saddened by the news.)

[5] Overlapping states

a. 次郎はクラシック音楽を {**好み** / ***好んで**}, 演奏家もよく知っている。
(Jiro likes classical music and knows many performers, too.)

b. 我々は平和を {**愛し** / ***愛して**}, 戦争を憎む。
(We love peace and hate war.)

A–3. Additional information before V_2 and acceptability of V_1*masu*

When the action of V_1 precedes that of V_2, V*te* is preferred. However, when additional information precedes V_2, V*masu* is acceptable even when the action of V_1 occurs before that of V_2 (e.g., KS(A) and Exs.(a) – (c)). Compare (a) and (b) in [6] and [7].

[6] a. エビは殻を {**むいて / *むき**}, ø 炒めます。
(As for shrimp, you take their shells off and fry them.)

b. エビは殻を {**むいて / むき**}, サラダ油で軽く炒めます。
(=Ex.(b))

[6] a. これは炭火で {**焼いて / *焼き**} ø 食べます。
(You eat this after grilling it over charcoal. (lit. This, you grill it over charcoal and eat it.))

b. これは炭火で {**焼いて / 焼き**}, しょう油を {**付けて / *付け**} ø 食べます。
(You eat this with soy sauce after grilling it over charcoal. (lit. This, you grill it over charcoal, dip it into soy sauce, and eat it.))

The acceptability of V_1*masu* in this situation may be due to the fact that when additional information occurs before V_2, the focus shifts from the relationship between the two verbs to the additional information before V_2.

A–4. Stylistic use of V*masu*

In sentences involving a series of verbs, V*masu* is often used in situations where either form can occur. This choice is stylistic and avoids the overuse of the V*te* form. For example, in [8], V_1–V_5 can be *te*-form verbs. However, because V_1, V_3 and V_5 must be *te*-forms (See [1]), the V*masu* form would more commonly be used for V_2 and V_4.

[8] 私は今日，まず，デパートへ {**行って / *行き**} (=V_1) 買い物をし (=V_2)，その後，銀行に {**寄って / *寄り**} (=V_3) 新しい口座を**開き** (=V_4)，帰りに喫茶店で友達に {**会って / *会い**} (=V_5) 本を返す予定だ。
(Today I'm planning to go to the department store first to do some

shopping, then, to stop by the bank to open a new account, and on my way back, to meet a friend of mine at a coffee shop to return her book.)

In conversation, however, such stylistic control is difficult and, therefore, *te*-forms often occur for every verb. This is the reason why in some situations the use of V*te* sounds colloquial and the use of V*masu* sounds formal.

A–5. V*te* / V*masu* and controllability

In "V_1*te* ~ V_2," because the action in V_1 is closely related to the action of V_2, both verbs must be either controllable or non-controllable, as in [9] and [10]. This is not the case with V*masu*.

[9] a. 私はボブに**会って**，ジェーンのことを**尋ねた**。

[Both controllable]

(I met Bob and asked him about Jane.)

b. 私はたまたまボブに {**会い** / ?**会って**}，ジェーンのことを**尋ねた**。

[Non-controllable and controllable]

(I saw Bob accidentally and asked him about Jane.)

[10] a. スリは刑事に**見つかって**，**逮捕された**。[Both non-controllable]

(The pickpocket was found by a detective and was arrested.)

b. スリは刑事に {**見つかり** / ?**見つかって**}，電車から**飛び降りた**。

[Non-controllable and controllable]

(The pickpocket was found by a detective, and he (= pickpocket) jumped off the train.)

B. When the subjects of V_1 and V_2 are different:

When two different subjects are involved in "V_1*te* ~ V_2," the action of V_1 has not necessarily been completed before that of V_2, as in [11].

[11] 勉がピザを焼いて，利子がサラダを作った。

(Tsutomu baked a pizza and Toshiko fixed a salad.)

(⇨ ***-te*** (DBJG: 464–67))

V*masu* as a Noun *n.*

V*masu* used as a regular noun

◆Key Sentences

(A)

	V*masu* (=N)	
彼はまだ若いから，	**考え**	が浅い。
(Because he is still young, his thoughts are shallow.)		

(B)

	V*masu*·V*masu* (=N)	
日本語は，話すのは比較的やさしいが，	**読み書き**	は難しい。
(It is relatively easy to speak Japanese, but reading and writing are hard.)		

Examples

(a) 終わりがよければ，全体がよくなる。
(If the end is alright, all becomes good.)

(b) 遊びのない生活はつまらない。
(Life without play is boring.)

(c) お金の貸し借りはしない方がいい。
(It is better not to borrow or lend money.)

(d) 東京ディズニーランドに車で行って来たが，行き帰りに五時間以上もかかった。
(We went to Tokyo Disneyland but it took more than five hours to get there and back.)

(e) 人生は勝ち負けの連続だ。
(Life is a series of wins and losses.)

Notes

1. The V*masu* of practically all the verbs can be used as a noun, except Sino-Japanese *suru*-verbs. Some of the verb stems (V*masu*) are treated like real nouns and listed as such in dictionaries, taking the topic marker *wa*, the subject marker *ga*, the direct object marker *o*, etc. It is strongly suggested that the non-native speaker / writer check each use of V*masu* as a noun in the dictionary.

(1)

におい	'smell'	代わり	'replacement'
考え	'thought'	別れ	'leave-taking'
通り	'street'	思い	'feeling / love'
育ち	'upbringing'	感じ	'feeling'
話	'talk'	望み	'hope'
決まり	'rule / regulation'	続き	'continuation / sequel'
始まり	'beginning'	休み	'holiday / rest'
終わり	'end'	答え	'answer'
変わり	'change'	出会い	'encounter'

2. Some verb stems (V*masu*) can be used in a compound of the V*masu* V*masu* form as exemplified by KS(B) and Exs.(c) – (e). In this case, the two V*masu* show contrastive meaning. More examples follow:

(2)

上り下り	'ups and downs'
行き来	'comings and goings'
やりとり	'give and take'
出し入れ	'taking in and out / depositing and withdrawing'
寝起き	'sleeping and waking up / living'
浮き沈み	'up and down' (lit, floating and sinking)

3. Some V*masu* cannot be used as a noun in isolation, but can be used as such in a compound.

(3) 物知り　'an erudite person'

そぞろ歩き　'slow walking'

犬死に　'dying in vain'

花見　'the viewing of cherry blossoms'

wa は *prt.*

a particle which emphatically affirms or negates the proposition represented by the preceding verbal and other related elements

[emphatic] {*do* / *does* / *did*} V; *will* V; {*am* / *are* / *is* / *was* / *were*} Adj. / N; (*not*) V / Adj. / N

【REL. *koto wa*】

◆**Key Sentences**

(A)

Sentence$_1$				Sentence$_2$
V*masu*				
行(い)き	は	します	が,	何(なに)も手伝(てつだ)えませんよ。
(I *am* going (there) but I cannot help you, all right?)				

(B)

Sentence$_1$				Sentence$_2$
V*te*				
疲(つか)れて	は	いる	が,	まだ休(やす)みたくない。
(I *am* tired but I don't want to take a break yet.)				

(C)

	V*masu*		
あの男(おとこ)には説明(せつめい)しても	**分(わ)かり**	は	しない。
(That guy would *not* understand even if you explained it to him.)			

(D)

Sentence$_1$						Sentence$_2$
Topic	Adj (*i*) stem					
あのズボンは	安	く	は	ある	が，	ちょっと時代遅れだ。
(Those pants *are* cheap but they are a little too old-fashioned.)						

(E)

Topic		Adj (*i*) stem			
この本は	内容を考えれば決して	高	く	は	ない。
(This book is *not* expensive at all when you consider its content.)					

Formation

(i) V*masu* は {する(が) / しない}

話しは {する(が) / しない} (s.o. *will* tell (but) / will *not* tell)

(ii) V*te* は {いる(が) / いない}, {みる(が) / みない}, etc.

食べては {いる(が) / いない} (s.o. *is* eating (but) / is *not* eating)

(iii) Adj(*i*)stem くは {ある(が) / ない}

面白くは {ある(が) / ない} (s.t. *is* interesting (but) / is *not* interesting)

(iv) {Adj(*na*)stem / N} では {ある(が) / ない}

便利では {ある(が) / ない} (s.t. *is* convenient (but) / is *not* convenient)

学生では {ある(が) / ない} (s.o. *is* a student (but) / is *not* a student)

W

Examples

(a) 酒は飲みはするが，それほど好きではない。
(I *do* drink but don't like it very much.)

(b) 彼は日本語を読めはするが，話せはしない。
(He *can* read Japanese but cannot speak it.)

(c) 彼女はベッドに横になってはいるが，目は開いている。
(She *is* lying in bed but her eyes are open.)

(d) 試験を受けてはみるが，通る自信は全然ない。
(I *will* take the exam (and see what will happen), but I have no confidence that I will pass it.)

(e) 彼は何を言っても聞きはしない。
(He does *not* listen, no matter what we tell him.)

(f) この花瓶は高くはあるが，それだけの値打ちはある。
(This vase *is* expensive but it is valuable to that extent.)

(g) この問題はよく考えれば難しくはないはずだ。
(If you think carefully, this problem should *not* be difficult.)

(h) あの男は優秀ではあったが，不正なことをしたので首になった。
(He *was* smart but he was fired because he did something illegal.)

(i) 彼は日本人ではあるが，あまり日本語を話せない。
(He *is* Japanese but cannot speak Japanese well.)

Notes

1. Affirmative forms such as V*masu wa suru*, Adj(*i*)stem *ku wa aru*, and {Adj(*na*)stem / N} *de wa aru* often appear with the conjunction *ga* in contrastive sentences. (⇨ ***wa***[1] (DBJG: 516–19))

2. Adj(*na*)stem *de wa nai* and N *de wa nai* are, in fact, the ordinary negative forms of Adj(*na*) and N + Copula and do not express any special emphasis.

3. When auxiliaries occur with V*te*, *wa* follows V*te*, as in Formation (ii).

When auxiliaries occur with V*masu*, however, *wa* follows the auxiliaries, as in (1).

(1) a. 遊(あそ)びたい → 遊びたく**は**ある(が)
(want to play)

b. 落(お)ちそうだ → 落ちそうで**は**ある(が)
(looks like it's about to fall down)

c. しゃべりすぎる → しゃべりすぎ**は**する(が)
(talk too much)

4. In casual conversation sound changes may occur in V*masu wa shinai*, as in (2).

(2) a. Gr. 1 verbs:
~ (C)V *wa shinai* → ~ (C) *ya shinai*
(C: consonant; V: vowel)

Exs. 行き**ゃしない** (*iki wa shinai* → *ikya shinai*)
買(か)**やしない** (*kai wa shinai* → *kaya shinai*)

b. Gr. 2 verbs and irregular verbs:
(C)V *wa shinai* → ~ (C)V*ya shinai*

Exs. 見(み)**やしない** (*mi wa shinai* → *miya shinai*)
食べ**やしない** (*tabe wa shinai* → *tabeya shinai*)
し**やしない** (*shi wa shinai* → *shiya shinai*)
来(き)**やしない** (*ki wa shinai* → *kiya shinai*)

【Related Expression】

Sentences with the emphatic particle *wa* can be rephrased using the structure X *koto wa* X, as in [1]; however, X *koto wa* X is more emphatic than *wa*.

[1] a. **行くことは行きます**が何も手伝えませんよ。(=KS(A))

b. **疲れていることは**(**疲れて**)**いる**がまだ休みたくない。(=KS(B))

c. あのズボンは**安いことは安い**がちょっと時代遅れだ。(=KS(D))

This structure is usually not used for negative sentences.

(⇨ ***koto wa*** (DBJG: 206–08))

W

wa iu made mo naku は言うまでもなく　*adv. phr.*　<w>

an adverbial phrase that conveys the meaning of 'not to speak of s.t. / s.o.'

not to speak of; let alone; not to mention; to say nothing of
【REL. ~ *bakari de* (*wa*) *naku* ~ (*mo*); *wa iu ni oyobazu*; *wa mochiron*】

◆Key Sentence

	Noun		Noun	
大統領の職務は	**頭脳**	は言うまでもなく,	体力	も要求される。
(The duty of the presidency requires physical strength, not to mention brains.)				

Formation

N は言うまでもなく

スポーツは言うまでもなく　(not to speak of sports)

Examples

(a) 日本は土地は言うまでもなく，家も非常に高い。
(In Japan houses are very expensive, not to mention land.)

(b) この大学は教育内容は言うまでもなく，設備も抜群に優れている。
(This university excels in facilities, to say nothing educational programs.)

(c) 彼は平日は言うまでもなく，週末や祭日も仕事をしている。
(He is working even on weekends and holidays, not to speak of weekdays.)

(d) ジュリアンは菜食主義者なので，牛肉は言うまでもなく，魚も鳥肉も食べない。
(Julian is a vegetarian, so he doesn't eat fish or chicken, let alone beef.)

(e) あの学生(がくせい)は漢字(かんじ)は言うまでもなく，平仮名(ひらがな)，片仮名(かたかな)さえ知(し)らない。
(That student doesn't know even hiragana and katakana, let alone kanji.)

Note

The adverbial phrase X *wa iu made mo naku* is a continuative form of ~ *wa iu made mo nai*, which means 'it is needless to say X; it goes without saying X' as in:

(1) 読書(どくしょ)が大事(だいじ)なこと**は言うまでもない**。
(It is needless to say that reading books is very important.)

(2) 人生(じんせい)に浮(う)き沈(しず)みがあるの**は言うまでもない**。
(It goes without saying that there are ups and downs in life.)

【Related Expression】

Both ~ *bakari de* (*wa*) *naku* ~ (*mo*) 'not only ~,' *wa mochiron* 'of course ~' and *wa iu ni oyobazu* 'to say nothing of ~' can replace *wa iu made mo naku*.

[1] a. 大統領の職務は頭脳｛**ばかりで（は）なく / はもちろん / は言うに及(およ)ばず**｝，体力も要求される。(cf. KS)

b. 彼は平日｛**ばかりで（は）なく / はもちろん / は言うに及ばず**｝週末も祭日も仕事をしている。(cf. Ex.(c))

The only difference is that X *wa iu made mo naku* is used primarily in written Japanese, whereas ~ *bakari de* (*wa*) *naku* ~ (*mo*) and *wa mochiron* can be used in both spoken and written Japanese. *wa iu ni oyobazu* is not used in casual speech.

wake da わけだ *phr.*

> a phrase which presents a fact or truth known to the hearer as an introduction to a following statement, or which gives emphasis to a fact or truth which the hearer might not know

as you know; the fact is that ~; the truth of the matter is that ~
【REL. *no da*】

◆Key Sentences

(A)

Sentence$_1$		
福田先生の死で私達はリーダーを失ってしまった	わけです	が,
Sentence$_2$		
今後は私達自身でこの会を発展させていかなければなりません。		
(As you know, we lost our leader with Prof. Fukuda's death. From now on we have to advance this group by ourselves.)		

(B)

Sentence$_1$	
戦争は大きな犠牲を伴う	わけで,
Sentence$_2$	
我々は何としてもこれを避けなければならない。	
(War is accompanied by great sacrifice, as you know, and we have to avoid it at any cost.)	

(C)

Sentence$_1$	
今でこそ地球が丸いことは子供でも知っている	が,

Sentence$_2$		
コロンブス以前は誰もが地球は平らだと思っていた	わけ	だ。
(Today, even children know that the earth is round, but the truth of the matter is that before Columbus everybody thought that it was flat.)		

Formation

(i) {V / Adj(*i*)} わけだ

{話す / 話した} わけだ (s.o. will talk / talked, as you know)

{高い / 高かった} わけだ (s.t. is / was expensive, as you know)

(ii) Adj(*na*)stem {な / だった} わけだ

{静かな / 静かだった} わけだ (s.t. is / was quiet, as you know)

(iii) N {である / だった(or であった)} わけだ

彼の責任 {である / だった(or であった)} わけだ (s.t. is / was his responsibility, as you know)

Examples

(a) 残念ながら今回の交渉はこういう結果になってしまったわけですが，これからも交渉は続けていくつもりです。
(Unfortunately, the negotiation this time, as you know, ended up with a result like this, but we are planning to keep negotiating from now on, too.)

(b) 我々は多くの技術を日常生活に取り入れてきたわけだが，それらがすべて我々に幸福をもたらしたかどうかは疑問である。
(We have incorporated a lot of technology into our everyday life, as

you know, but whether or not all of it has brought us happiness is questionable.)

(c) 私は動物のコミュニケーションを研究しているわけですが，この研究からいろいろ面白いことが分かります。
(I've been doing research on animal communication, as you know, and various interesting facts have become known from this research.)

(d) 何事をするにも基本がしっかり出来ているかどうかが進歩の鍵となるわけで，外国語学習についても同じことが言えるわけです。
(As you know, whatever you do, whether or not you have built a firm foundation for that is a key to your progress, and in fact, you can say the same thing about foreign language study.)

(e) 赤ん坊は自分ではものを言わないが，話しかけられている時に言葉を学習しているわけだ。
(Babies, themselves, do not talk, but the truth of the matter is that they are learning language when they are spoken to.)

(f) 我々は今コンピュータを取り上げられるとたちどころに困ってしまうけれども，今から十年程前はコンピュータなしでやっていたわけです。
(We would be in trouble immediately if computers were taken away from us now, but the fact is that we were getting by without them a decade ago.)

Notes

1. In casual conversation *wake*, an informal form of *wake da*, is used quite frequently to give slight emphasis to a fact when the speaker does not expect the hearer to know about it. (1) presents an example.

   (1) 私が帰ったらね，いとこの政ちゃんが来てた**わけ**。で，話してるうちにディスコへ行こうということになって，友達に電話した**わけ**。
   (When I got back home, my cousin Masa was there. While we were talking, we decided to go to a disco and I called some friends of mine.)

2. *Wake da*, as introduced here, should not be confused with the use in which two propositions X and Y have the relationship "given X, one is

logically led to Y," as in (2). In this use, *wake da* is interpreted as "it means that ~," "you mean that ~," "that's why," "no wonder," "that is," "in other words," etc.

(2) a. Teacher: 私は来週一週間日本に行きます (=X)。
(I'll be in Japan for a week beginning next week.)

Student: じゃ，来週は授業が**ない** (=Y) **わけです**か。
(So, you mean there will be no classes next week?)

b. ジョーンズさんは日本に十年もいたんだ (=X) そうだ。日本語が**上手な** (=Y) **わけだ**。
(I heard that Mr. Jones was in Japan for ten years. That's why he speaks Japanese well.)

c. ジョーンズさんは日本語が**上手な** (=Y) **わけだ**。日本に十年もいたんだ (=X) そうだ。
(No wonder Mr. Jones speaks Japanese well. He was in Japan for ten years, I heard.)

(⇨ ***wake da*** (DBJG: 531–34))

【Related Expression】

In some situations *no da* also conveys the idea "the fact is that ~." For example, KS(A) and (C) could be rephrased as [1] and [2], respectively, only [1] does not convey as strongly the speaker's expectation that the proposition represented by the preceding sentence is known to the hearer and [2] does not give as much emphasis to the fact represented by the preceding sentence.

[1] 福田先生の死で私達はリーダーを失ってしまった**のです**が，今後は私達自身でこの会を発展させていかなければなりません。
(We lost our leader with Prof. Fukuda's death, and from now on we have to advance this group by ourselves.)

[2] 今でこそ地球が丸いことは子供でも知っているが，コロンブス以前は誰もが地球は平らだと思っていた**のだ**。
(Today even children know that the earth is round, but before Columbus, everybody thought that it was flat.)

Wake de cannot be rephrased as *no de*, however, because *no de* conveys a sense of reason or cause. [3], for example, does not mean the same thing as KS(B).

[3] 戦争は大きな犠牲を伴う**ので**，我々は何としてもこれを避けなければならない。
(Because war is accompanied by great sacrifice, we have to avoid it at any cost.)

On the other hand, *wake da* cannot be used to provide or ask for an explanation of, or a reason for, information shared by the speaker and the hearer, as in [4] and [5].

[4] 今日のパーティーには行けません。宿題がたくさんある **{ん / の / *わけ} です**。
(I can't come to today's party. I have a lot of homework.)

[5] [Looking at someone doing something]

A: 何をしている **{ん / *わけ} です**か。
(What are you doing?)

B: 日本語を勉強している **{ん / *わけ} です**。
(I'm studying Japanese.)

(⇨ ***no da*** (DBJG: 325–28))

wake de wa nai わけではない *phr.*

W

a phrase which is used to deny what is implied in the previous or following statement

It does not mean that ~; I don't mean that ~; It is not that ~; It is not true that ~; It is not the case that

◆Key Sentences

(A)

Sentence₁	
この問題を解決するのは非常に難しい。	

	Sentence₂			
	Adj (*na*) stem			
しかし,	**不可能**	(だ)	という	わけではない。
(It is very difficult to solve this problem. But that does not mean that it is impossible (to solve).)				

(B)

Sentence₁			
	Vinf		
君の考えに	**反対する**	わけではない	が,

Sentence₂
そのやり方でうまくいくだろうか。
(I don't mean to oppose your idea, but I wonder if things will go well using that approach.)

(C)

Sentence		
結果さえよければいい	という	わけではない。
(Obtaining a good result is not enough. (lit. It is not that it is all right if just the result is good.))		

Formation

(i) {V / Adj(*i*)}inf（という）わけではない

{分かる / 分かった}（という）わけではない (It does not mean that s.o. understands / understood s.t.)

{悪い / 悪かった}（という）わけではない (It does not mean that s.t. is / was bad.)

(ii) Adj(*na*)stem {な / だった} わけではない

{駄目な / 駄目だった} わけではない (It does not mean that s.t. is / was no good.)

(iii) Adj(*na*)stem {(だ) / だった} というわけではない

{駄目(だ) / だった} というわけではない (It does not mean that s.t. is / was no good.)

(iv) N だったわけではない

失敗だったわけではない (It does not mean that s.t. was a failure.)

(v) N {(だ) / だった} というわけではない

{失敗(だ) / だった} というわけではない (It does not mean that s.t. is / was a failure.)

Examples

(a) 私は最近あまりたくさん食べないが，食欲がないわけではない。
(I do not eat much these days, but it doesn't mean that I have no appetite.)

(b) この二，三年本を書いていないが，スランプというわけではない。
(I haven't written a book for the last few years, but it doesn't mean that I am in a slump.)

(c) このプロジェクトは資金不足のため中止されることになった。しかし，今までしてきたことが全く無駄になるわけではない。
(It's been decided that this project is going to be stopped because of a

lack of funds. However, it doesn't mean that what we have done up to now is going to be a total waste.)

(d) いくら日本語が出来ないと言っても全然話せないわけではない。
(Although I say that I cannot speak Japanese, it doesn't mean that I cannot speak it at all.)

(e) 君の言うことが分からないわけではないが，やっぱりこの計画は止めた方がいいと思う。
(I don't mean that I don't understand what you are saying, but I think you'd better give up this plan after all.)

(f) 全然見込みがないわけではないが，あまり期待はしない方がいいでしょう。
(I don't mean that there is no hope, but you'd better not expect too much.)

(g) あの人が嫌いだというわけではないんですが，結婚したいとは思いません。
(I don't mean that I don't like him, but I do not want to marry him.)

(h) 言われたことだけしていたらそれでいいというわけではない。
(Doing only what you are told to do is just not enough.)

(i) A: この病人は全く助からないんですか。
(Can't this patient be saved (lit. at all)?)

B: いや，そういうわけではありません。
(No, it is not that he can't be saved.)

Notes

1. *Wake de wa nai*, the negative form of *wake da*, denies what is implied either in the previous statement (e.g., KS(A) and Exs.(a) – (d)) or in the following statement (e.g., KS(B) and Exs.(e) – (g)). In either case, *wake de wa nai* sentences and the previous (or following) sentences are often connected by conjunctions like *ga* and *shikashi*.
(⇨ ***wake da*** (this volume; DBJG: 531–34))

2. In some situations the ideas whose implications are denied by *wake de*

wa nai are not stated (e.g., KS(C) and Ex.(h)). For example, KS(C) denies an implication of (1), the idea which is not stated in KS(C).

(1) 結果がいいことは大切(たいせつ)だ。
(It is important that the result is good.)

wake ga nai わけがない *phr.*

a phrase which negates the existence of a reason to believe that s.o. does s.t. or is in some state, or that s.t. takes place; or which negates a possibility of s.o.'s doing s.t. or being in some state, or s.t.'s taking place

There is no reason why ~; It is impossible (for ~) to ~; cannot 【REL. *hazu ga nai*】

◆Key Sentences

(A)

Sinf·nonpast	
こんなやさしい仕事(しごと)が君(きみ)に出来(でき)ない	わけがない。
(There is no reason why you cannot do such an easy job.)	

(B)

Sinf·nonpast	
日本語(にほんご)がそんなに速(はや)くマスター出来る	わけがない。
(It is impossible to be able to master Japanese that quickly.)	

Formation

(i) {V / Adj(*i*)}inf·nonpast わけがない

分かるわけがない (It is impossible to understand)

面白いわけがない (It is impossible for s.t. to be interesting)

(ii) {Adj(*na*)}stem なわけがない

きれいなわけがない (It is impossible for s.t. to be clean)

(iii) N であるわけがない

先生であるわけがない (It is impossible for s.o. to be a teacher)

Examples

(a) そんなことをしていいわけがない。
(No one is allowed to do that kind of thing. (lit. There is no reason why it is all right to do such a thing.))

(b) そんなことを言って人が喜ぶわけがない。
(There is no reason for people to be pleased if you say such a thing to them.)

(c) 彼女がそんなひどいことを言うわけがない。
(There is no reason for her to say such a terrible thing. / It is impossible for her to say such a terrible thing.)

(d) 彼はあんなに酔っていて大丈夫なわけがない。
(Being that drunk, he cannot be all right.)

(e) あの店の物がこんなに安いわけがない。
(Things at that shop cannot be this cheap.)

(f) 彼女がこの時間にこんな所にいるわけがない。
(It is impossible for her to be in such a place at this time (of the day).)

(g) 彼がこの学校の卒業生であるわけがない。
(It is impossible for him to be a graduate of this school.)

Note

Wake ga nai basically negates either (a) the existence of a reason to believe that someone will do / does something, will be / is in some state, or something will happen / happens, or (b) a possibility of someone's future / present action or state, or a future / present event. Thus, sentences before *wake ga nai* are always nonpast. However, *wake ga nai* can indirectly negate the existence of a reason to believe that someone did something or was in some state, or that something happened, or negate the possibility of a past action or state by presenting the negation in a statement about a common belief, a habitual action or state, or one's ability. For example, KS(B) can be used in a context as in (1).

(1) A: チャールズが一年(いちねん)で日本語をマスターしたそうだよ。
(I heard that Charles mastered Japanese in a year.)

B: 冗談(じょうだん)だろう。日本語がそんなに速くマスター出来る**わけがない**。 (=KS(B))
(You are kidding! It is impossible to be able to master Japanese that quickly.)

【Related Expression】

Hazu ga nai expresses an idea very similar to *wake ga nai*. Thus, the key sentences above can be rephrased, as in [1].

[1] a. こんなやさしい仕事が君に出来ない{**わけ** / **はず**}**がない**。 (=KS(A))

b. 日本語がそんなに速くマスター出来る{**わけ** / **はず**}**がない**。 (=KS(B))

However, *hazu ga nai* can be used with past sentences and it negates the possibility of a past action, state, or event, as in [2]. (See Note.)

[2] a. 彼女がそんなことを**した**{**はず** / ???**わけ**}**がない**。
(It is impossible for her to have done such a thing.)

b. 彼が優等生(ゆうとうせい)**だった**{**はず** / ???**わけ**}**がない**。
(It is impossible for him to have been an excellent student.)

(⇨ ***hazu*** (DBJG: 133–35))

wake ni wa ikanai わけにはいかない *phr.*

a phrase which is used to indicate that one cannot do s.t. due to an external circumstance

cannot; cannot but ~; cannot help -ing; have no (other) choice but to ~
【REL. *koto ga dekiru*; *-nakereba naranai*; *rarenai*】

◆Key Sentences

(A)

	Vinf·aff·nonpast	
来週は期末試験があるから，今週末は	**遊んでいる**	わけにはいかない。
(There will be final examinations next week, so I cannot fool around this weekend.)		

(B)

	Vinf·neg·nonpast	
親友の結婚式だから，	**出席しない**	わけにはいかない。
(Since it is the wedding of my close friend I have no other choice but to attend it.)		

Formation

(i) Vinf·nonpast わけにはいかない

行くわけにはいかない (s.o. cannot go)

(ii) Vinf·neg·nonpast ないわけにはいかない

読まないわけにはいかない (s.o. has no other choice but to read s.t.)

W

Examples

(a) こんな高価な物を頂くわけにはいきません。
(I have no reason to receive such an expensive gift.)

(b) 私のような若い者がそんな会議に出席するわけにはいきません。
(A young person like me cannot attend such a meeting.)

(c) まだ定職もないんだから，結婚するわけにはいかないんですよ。
(I don't have a regular job, so I cannot get married.)

(d) これから運転しなければなりませんから，酒を飲むわけにはいきません。
(I have to drive from now, so I cannot drink.)

(e) まだ仕事が残っているので，帰るわけにはいきません。
(I still have work to do, so I cannot go home.)

(f) これは秘密なので，話すわけにはいきません。
(This is a secret, so I cannot talk about it.)

(g) この論文は重要だから，読まないわけにはいかない。
(This paper is important, so I have no choice but to read it.)

(h) 上司の命令なのだから，報告書を書かないわけにはいかない。
(It is my boss's order, so I cannot avoid writing the report.)

Notes

1. *Wake ni wa ikanai* is used to express the meaning that one cannot do s.t. because of an external circumstance. So, the phrase cannot be used to indicate a simple fact of incompetence. For example, (1a) presents a simple case incompetence, whereas (1b) presents a case in which one cannot play the piano owing to some circumstance (e.g. a baby is asleep). Actually (1b) presupposes that the speaker can play the piano.

(1) a. 僕はピアノが**弾けない**。
(I cannot play the piano.)

b. 僕はピアノを**弾くわけにはいかない**。
(I cannot play the piano (owing to some circumstance).)

2. *-nai wake ni wa ikanai* is used to express the meaning that 's.o. has no other choice but s.t.,' as shown in KS(B), Exs.(g) and (h).

3. There is no affirmative counterpart of *wake ni wa ikanai.*

(2) 今日はいい天気だから，テニス｛**が出来る / *をするわけにいく**｝。
(It's a fine day, so we can play tennis.)

【Related Expressions】

I. Regular expressions of potential, (i.e., *rareru* and *koto ga dekiru*) can replace *wake ni wa ikanai* as shown in [1].

[1] a. 来週は期末試験があるから，今週末は｛**遊べない / 遊ぶことは出来ない**｝。(cf. KS(A))

b. これから運転しなければなりませんから，酒を｛**飲めません / 飲むことは出来ません**｝。(cf. Ex.(d))

c. まだ仕事が残っているので，｛帰れません / 帰ることは出来ません｝。(cf. Ex.(e))

But *rareru* and *koto ga dekiru* cannot replace *wake ni wa ikanai* unless an external circumstance which blocks s.o. from doing s.t. exists, as noted in Note 1.

(⇨ ***rareru***[2] (DBJG: 370–73); ***koto ga dekiru*** (DBJG: 200–01))

II. *-nai wake ni wa ikanai* can be rephrased by *-nakereba naranai*, but notice that the latter expresses obligation, responsibility and necessity, whereas the former expresses the idea of 'to have no other choice but to do s.t.'

[2] a. 親友の結婚式だから，**出席しなければならない**。(cf. KS(B))

b. この論文は重要だから，**読まなければならない**。(cf. Ex.(g))

(⇨ ***~ nakereba naranai*** (DBJG: 274–76)

yaru[1] やる　*v.* (*Gr.* 1)

to cause s.t. / s.o. to move to a place or to do / eat / drink s.t.

send; give; do; play; operate; eat; drink
【REL. *suru*】

◆Key Sentences

(A)

			Noun(place)		
貧乏(びんぼう)な家庭(かてい)は	子供(こども)	を	**大学(だいがく)**	に	やれない。
(Poor families cannot send their children to college.)					

(B)

			Noun		
僕(ぼく)は	弟(おとうと)	に	**自転車(じてんしゃ)**	を	やるつもりだ。
(I intend to give a bike to my younger brother.)					

(C)

	Noun(sports / game)		
午後(ごご),	**テニス**	を	やりませんか。
(Won't you play tennis this afternoon?)			

(D)

	Noun(occupation)		
今(いま)アメリカで	**日本語(にほんご)の教師(きょうし)**	を	やっています。
(I'm now (lit. doing) a Japanese instructor in the U.S.)			

(E)

		Noun(role)	
三船敏郎の	やる	**役**	は正義感の強い男だ。
(The role played by Toshiro Mifune is a male with a strong sense of justice.)			

(F)

	Noun(cigarette/alcoholic drink)		
先月まで	**たばこ**	を	やっていました。
(I was smoking up until last month.)			

Formation

(i) s.o. が s.o. を place にやる

私が息子を外国にやる。 (I will send my son to a foreign country.)

(ii) s.o. が s.o. に s.t. をやる

僕が妹に人形をやる。 (I will give my younger sister a doll.)

(iii) s.o. が s.t.をやる

友達が弁護士をやる。 (My friend is (lit. doing) a lawyer.)

Examples

(a) 息子を郵便局にやって，切手を買って来させた。
(I sent my son to the post office and had him buy stamps.)

(b) 猫にこのえさをやってね。
(Give this food to the cat, OK?)

(c) 宿題をやりましたか。
(Did you do your homework?)

(d) チェスをやろうか。
(Shall we play chess?)

(e) 来月クラス会をやります。
(We will have (lit. do) a class reunion next month.)

(f) ちょっと遅れるから，先に(食事を)やっていて下さい。
(I'm coming in a bit late, so please start eating without me.)

(g) 私は酒もたばこもやりません。
(I neither drink nor smoke.)

(h) 私は去年から生け花をやっています。
(I have been learning flower arrangement since last year.)

(i) 僕は小さい時いろいろな病気をやりました。
(When I was a kid I suffered from various diseases.)

(j) 友達がジャズ喫茶をやっている。
(My friend is running a jazz cafe.)

Notes

1. The meaning of the transitive verb *yaru* depends on the structure in which it is used and on the meaning of the direct object noun.

Structure	Meanings	Examples
a) s.o. *ga* s.o. *o* N(place) *ni yaru*	'send'	KS(A), Ex.(a)
b) s.o. *ga* s.o. *ni* N *o yaru*	'give'	KS(B), Ex.(b)
c) s.o. *ga* N(sports / game) *o yaru*	'play'	KS(C), Ex.(d)
d) s.o. *ga* N(occupation) *o yaru*	'work as'	KS(D)
e) s.o. *ga* N(role) *o yaru*	'play a role'	KS(E)
f) s.o. *ga* N(food / alcoholic drink / cigarette) *o yaru*	'eat / drink / smoke'	KS(F), Ex.(f), (g)
g) s.o. *ga* N(work / task) *o yaru*	'do'	Ex.(c)
h) s.o. *ga* N(event) *o yaru*	'hold'	Ex.(e)
i) s.o. *ga* N(hobby / subject) *o yaru*	'learn'	Ex.(h)
j) s.o. *ga* N(illness) *o yaru*	'suffer from'	Ex.(i)
k) s.o. *ga* N(store / company) *o yaru*	'run'	Ex.(j)

Note that the structures for c through k are identical. The only crucial difference among them is the meaning of '*yaru*' depending on the meaning of the direct object nouns.

(⇨ ***ageru***[1]; ***ageru***[2] (DBJG: 63–67))

2. *Yaru* has the meaning of 'drink,' 'eat,' and 'smoke' but the usage is very much restricted, as shown in (1).

(1) a. 昨日はおいしいすしを {**食べました** / ***やりました**}。
(Yesterday I ate delicious sushi.)

b. ここではたばこを {**吸って** / ***やって**} はいけません。
(You shouldn't smoke here.)

c. 毎朝僕はオレンジジュースを一杯 {**飲みます** / ***やります**}。
(Every morning I drink one cup of orange juice.)

Besides KS(F), Exs.(f) and (g), there are only a few expressions which can be used correctly.

(2) a. 今晩僕と一杯**やりませんか**。
(Won't you drink with me tonight?)

b. どうぞ皿のものを**やって下さい**。
(Please help yourself to the dishes.)

【Related Expressions】

I. *Yaru* can be replaced by *suru* in the cases of c, d, e, g, h and j of the chart in Note 1. That is, *suru* lacks the meanings of 'send,' 'give,' 'learn' and 'eat / drink / smoke.' When *yaru* can be replaced by *suru*, the difference between *yaru* and *suru* is a matter of style: the former is more informal and colloquial.

[1] a. 午後，テニスを**しませんか**。(cf. KS(C))

b. 今アメリカで日本語の教師を**しています**。(cf. KS(D))

c. 三船敏郎の**する**役は正義感の強い男だ。(cf. KS(E))

d. 宿題を**しましたか**。(cf. Ex.(c))

e. 来月クラス会を**します**。(cf. Ex.(e))

f. 僕は小さい時いろいろな病気を**しました**。(cf. Ex.(i))

[2] a. 息子を郵便局に {**やって** / ***して**}, 切手を買って来させた。 (=Ex.(a))

b. 猫にこのえさを {**やって** / ***して**} ね。(=Ex.(b))

c. 私は去年から生け花を {**やって** / ***して**} います。(=Ex.(h))

d. 私は酒もたばこも {**やりません** / ***しません**}。(=Ex.(g))

II. *Suru* can be replaced by *yaru* only when it means 'play,' 'work as,' 'eat / drink / smoke.' That is, *yaru* lacks the meanings of 'make,' 'wear,' 'have,' 'feel,' and 'cost.'

[3] a. 先生(せんせい)はテストをやさしく {**した** / ***やった**}。
(The teacher made the test easy.)

b. 京子(きょうこ)はきれいなスカーフを {**している** / ***やっている**}。
(Kyoko is wearing a beautiful scarf.)

c. 洋子(ようこ)は長(なが)い足(あし)を {**している** / ***やっている**}。
(Yoko has long legs.)

d. 子供の声(こえ)が {**しました** / ***やりました**}。
(I heard children's voices.)

e. この時計(とけい)は十万円(じゅうまんえん) {**する** / ***やる**}。
(This watch costs 100,000 yen.)

(⇨ ***suru***[1] – ***suru***[4] (DBJG: 428–37))

yaru[2] やる *aux. v.* (*Gr.* 1)

an auxiliary verb which expresses the idea that s.o. does s.t. undesirable to s.o. else when he / she knows his / her action will cause hardship or trouble

(knowing that it will cause s.o. trouble / difficulty)

【REL. *kureru*; *morau*】

◆Key Sentence

	V*te*	
私は正を	**からかって**	やった。
(I teased Tadashi.)		

Formation

V*te* やる

いじめてやる ((I) will bully s.o.)

Examples

(a) ルームメートが部屋を全然掃除しないので，文句を言ってやった。
(Because my roommate never cleans our room, I complained (to her about it).)

(b) 彼にあまり腹が立ったので，どなりつけてやった。
(I was so mad at him that I shouted at him.)

(c) 会社の付けで飲んでやった。
(I had drinks at my company's expense.)

(d) 浩はテレビゲームばかりしてちっとも勉強しないんですよ。一度叱ってやって下さい。
([From a wife to her husband] Hiroshi always plays video games (lit. TV games) and doesn't study at all. Will you talk to him (lit. tell him off) about it (lit. once)?)

(e) 言うことを聞かなかったら少し脅してやれ。
(If he doesn't listen, threaten him a little.)

Notes

1. *Yaru* is one of the "giving" auxiliary verbs meaning 'do s.t. for s.o.' However, it is also used when A does something undesirable to B knowing that A's deed will cause B difficulty. For example, KS states that the speaker teased Tadashi, with the implication that he knew that it would make trouble for Tadashi. Compare KS with (1), which is a neutral statement and conveys no such implication.

   (1) 私は正を**からかった**。
   (I teased Tadashi.)

   (⇨ ***ageru***[2] (DBJG: 65–67))

2. The subject of V*te yaru* is the first person in declarative sentences and the second person in interrogative sentences, commands, requests, or suggestions. (2) is ungrammatical unless the speaker / writer is totally empathetic with Taro.

   (2) *太郎は次郎を**からかってやった**。
   (Taro teased Jiro.)

【Related Expressions】

I. The auxiliary verb *kureru*, which usually means 'do s.t. for me,' is also used when an action causes difficulty, as in [1]. Here, *kureru* expresses strong feelings of unhappiness, anger, etc., on the side of the person who is affected by the action.

   [1] a. ジェリーはとんでもないことを**してくれた**。
   (Jerry did a terrible thing to me.)

   b. よくも恥を**かかせてくれた**わね。[female speech]
   (You really disgraced me!)

Y

Note that in the above sentences the verb phrases *tondemonai koto o suru* 'to do a terrible thing' and *haji o kakaseru* 'to disgrace' represent undesirable actions. If a verb phrase does not represent an undesirable action, *kureru* means 'do s.t. for me' as in [2].

[2] ケイトは私の魚(さかな)を**食(た)べてくれた**。
(Kate ate my fish for me.)

(⇨ ***kureru***[2] (DBJG: 216–19) ; ***rareru***[1] (DBJG: 364–69))

II. The "receiving" verb *morau* (not the auxiliary verb *morau*) can also be used when the sentence object is something undesirable, as in [3].

[3] a. テッドに風邪(かぜ)を**もらった**。
(I got a cold from Ted.)

b. 課長(かちょう)に大変(たいへん)な仕事(しごと)を**もらってしまった**。
(I got an awful assignment from my boss (lit. section chief).)

(⇨ ***morau***[1] (DBJG: 261–63))

yatto やっと *adv.*

an adverb to indicate that s.t. desirable has been finally achieved or will be eventually achieved though with great difficulty

finally; at last; barely
【REL. *karōjite*; *nantoka*; *tōtō*; *yōyaku*】

◆Key Sentences

(A)

日本史(にほんし)の期末(きまつ)レポートを	やっと	**書(か)き終(お)えた。**
(I finally finished writing my Japanese history term paper.)		

Y

(B)

この道(みち)は車(くるま)が	やっと	**一台通(いちだいとお)れる**	くらいの狭(せま)さです。
(This street is so narrow that one car can barely go through.)			

(C)

	Vinf·nonpast				
私(わたし)の日本語(ご)の力(ちから)ではあいさつを	**する**	の	が	やっと	です。
(My Japanese language ability is barely enough to make greetings.)					

(D)

やっと	のことで,	**家(いえ)が買(か)えた。**
(At long last, I could buy a house.)		

Formation

(i) やっと Vinf

やっと {会(あ)える / 会えた} (I am / was finally able to meet him.)

(ii) やっと Vinf

やっと {乗(の)れる / 乗れた} (can / could barely ride)

(iii) Vinf·nonpast のがやっと {だ / だった}

そう言(い)うのがやっと {だ / だった} (s.o. can / could barely say so)

(iv) やっとのことで V

やっとのことで {着(つ)く / 着いた} (At long last, s.o. gets / got there)

Examples

(a) 半年の長い冬が終わって，やっと暖かい春になった。
(The long winter that lasted for half a year has ended and finally the warm spring is here.)

(b) 日本で一年間日本語を勉強したら，やっと，日本語が通じるようになった。
(After I studied Japanese for a year in Japan, I finally reached the point where I could make myself understood in Japanese.)

(c) あの二人はずいぶん長い間付き合っていたが，やっと結婚したようだね。
(The couple have been together for a very long time, but it seems that they finally got married.)

(d) 長い間の夢だった海外旅行にやっと行けそうだ。
(It seems that finally I can travel abroad which was a dream I cherished for a long time.)

(e) 家から駅まで走って，やっと，七時半の電車に間に合った。
(I ran to the station from my house, and I just caught the 7:30 train.)

(f) 家族四人がやっと住めるような小さいアパートに入った。
(We moved into a small apartment which can barely accommodate a family of four.)

(g) 父は腰を痛めているので，家のまわりを散歩するのがやっとです。
(My father is suffering from pain in the lower back, and he can barely walk around the house.)

(h) やっとのことで，富士山の頂上に着いた。
(With the greatest effort, we reached the top of Mt. Fuji.)

Notes

1. The adverb *yatto* can be used with Vinf when s.t. desirable has been finally achieved, as exemplified by KS(A) and Exs.(a) – (d). If s.t. negative has been brought about the adverb cannot be used.

(1) a. 彼は四年間癌の治療を受けていたが，{***やっと / とうとう / ついに**} 死んでしまった。
(He was receiving treatment for cancer for four years, but he finally died.)

b. 彼らは夫婦仲が前から悪かったが，{***やっと / とうとう / ついに**} 別れてしまった。
(They have been unhappily married for some time, but finally they got divorced.)

2. The adverb can also mean 'barely' as in KS(B), (C), Exs.(e), (f) and (g).

3. *Yatto no koto de* is a set phrase that emphasizes the time and efforts it takes for s.t. positive to come about, as exemplified by KS(D) and Ex.(h). The English translations are 'at long last,' 'with the greatest effort,' 'with the greatest trouble.'

【Related Expressions】

I. *Yatto* and *yōyaku* are very close in that both of them indicate eventual completion of something positive; the only difference is that *yōyaku* sounds more formal and is usually written.

[1] {**ようやく / *やっと**} 蛍雪の功なって，ここに卒業の段となりましたことを心からお祝い申し上げます。
(From the bottom of my heart I would like to congratulate you on your graduation today after long diligent study.)

II. *Yatto* can be replaced by adverbs *nantoka* and *karōjite* as shown in [2]. Both *nantoka* and *karōjite* mean that s.t. positive has been luckily accomplished in spite of difficulty. But the latter implies that almost insurmountable difficulty has been cleared.

[2] a. 日本史の期末レポートを {**やっと / 何とか / かろうじて**} 書き終えた。(=KS(A))

b. この道は車が {**やっと / 何とか / かろうじて**} 一台通れるくらいの狭さです。(=KS(B))

However, when *yatto* indicates that it is a matter of a long wait before s.t. desirable is realized, it cannot be replaced either by *karojite* or by *nantoka* as shown in [3].

[3] a. 半年の長い冬が終わって，{**やっと** / ***かろうじて** / ***何とか**} 暖かい春になった。(=Ex.(a))

b. 十時(じゅうじ)になって，{**やっと** / ***かろうじて** / ***何とか**} 事務所(じむしょ)が開(ひら)いた。
(Ten o'clock came round and finally the office opened.)

c. つまらない講演(こうえん)が {**やっと** / ***かろうじて** / ***何とか**} 終わった。
(The boring lecture finally came to an end.)

III. *Tsui ni* is another adverb which indicates that either s.t. desirable or undesirable has finally come about or will come about after a relatively long process. It can replace *yatto* in KS(A), Exs.(b) and (c). If the result is a natural one as in Ex.(a) *yatto* is preferable to *tsui ni*. Also, if the focus is placed more on current difficulty rather than on a long process as in KS(B), (C), Exs.(f) and (g), the replacement is impossible. (See Note 1.)

-yō[1] よう *suf.*

a noun-forming suffix which means a way (of doing s.t.)

a / the way to; a / the way of -ing; the way (s.o. does s.t.)
【REL. *-kata*】

◆Key Sentences

(A)

	V*masu*			
この作文(さくぶん)は	**直(なお)し**	よう	が	ない。
(There is no way to correct this composition.)				

(B)

NP / Adj(*na*)stem		V*masu*			
この成績(せいせき)	じゃ / では	**救(すく)い**	よう	が	ない。
(There is no way to save (him) with this grade.)					

(C)

	{V / Adj.}*te*		V*masu*			
こんなに	壊(こわ)れてしまって	は	**直し**	よう	が	ない。
(We cannot fix it now that it is broken to this extent.)						

(D)

	{V/Adj. / N+Cop.}inf·past		V*masu*			
みんなで同時(どうじ)に	攻(せ)めて来(き)た	ら	**防(ふせ)ぎ**	よう	が	ない。
(There is no way to defend ourselves if all of them attack us at the same time.)						

Formation

V*masu* よう

書(か)きよう　(a way to write)

Examples

(a) これ以外(いがい)に考えようがない。
(There is no other way to think (about it).)

(b) 日本語(にほんご)があんなに下手(へた)じゃどうしようもない。
(There is no hope to do with such poor Japanese. (lit. There is no way even to do if his Japanese is that poor.))

(c) 漢字(かんじ)が読(よ)めないんじゃ(＝のでは)仕事(しごと)のさせようがない。
(There is no way to have him work if he cannot read kanji.)

(d) こんなに学生(がくせい)が多(おお)くては教(おし)えようがない。
(There is no way to teach if there are this many students.)

(e) そんな聞(き)き方(かた)をされたら答(こた)えようがない。
(I cannot answer if you ask (lit. I am asked) that way.)

(f) 私(わたし)に謝(あやま)ってもらってもしようがない。
(There is no point apologizing to me (lit. even if you apologize to me).)

(g) ほかにやりようはないのだろうか。
(Isn't there any other way to do it, I wonder?)

(h) 見(み)つからないのは探(さが)しようが悪(わる)いんだよ。
(It's because your way of searching (for it) is wrong that you cannot find it.)

(i) 読みようによってはこの手紙(てがみ)は遺書(いしょ)ともとれる。
(Depending on how you read it, this letter can be taken as a suicide note.)

Notes

1. *Vmasu-yō* is most commonly used with *ga nai* 'there is no way to V; cannot V.'

2. Although V*masu-yō* can be used in affirmative sentences (e.g., Exs.(h) and (i)), it is most commonly used in negative sentences.

Y

3. *Vmasu-yō* often appears with conditional clauses ending in *-te wa*, *-tara*, or *-te mo*, as in KS(B) – (D) and Exs.(b) – (f).

【Related Expression】

V*masu-kata* also means 'a / the way to V; a / the way of V-ing.' However, V*masu-kata* cannot be used with *ga nai* to mean 'there is no way to V; cannot V,' as in [1].

[1] a. この作文は**直し**｛**よう** / ***方**｝がない。(=KS(A))

b. この成績じゃ(=では)**救い**｛**よう** / ***方**｝がない。(=KS(B))

c. みんなで同時に攻めて来たら**防ぎ**｛**よう** / ***方**｝がない。(=KS(D))

Unlike V*masu-kata*, V*masu-yō* cannot be used to mean 'how to V,' as in [2].

[2] a. すしの**作**(つく)**り**｛**方** / ***よう**｝を教えて下(くだ)さい。
(Please show me how to make sushi.)

b. 漢字の勉強(べんきょう)の**し**｛**方** / ***よう**｝が分(わ)からない。
(I don't know how to study kanji.)

It is also noted that V*masu-kata* is used to mean 'way' either in terms of method or manner, as in [2] and [3], while *Vmasu-yō* is usually used to mean 'method.'

[3] a. 私は彼女(かのじょ)の**話**(はな)**し**｛**方** / ??**よう**｝が好(す)きだ。
(I like the way she talks.)

b. 彼(かれ)は面白(おもしろ)い**食**(た)**べ**｛**方** / ??**よう**｝をする。
(He eats in a funny fashion.)

(⇨ ***-kata*** (DBJG: 183–84))

-yō[2] -よう *aux.* <w>

> an auxiliary verb that expresses the writer's conjecture about some potentiality or his certainty about a given state of affairs

probably; likely; must be; should; ought; naturally
【REL. *darō*; *deshō*】

◆Key Sentences

(A)

	V*masu* of Vpot	
この程度の文章なら日本語の一年生でも	**読め**	よう。
(Even the first year students of Japanese (probably) can read a passage of this level.)		

(B)

			Vvol
こんな寒い日にオーバーも着ないで歩き回れば,	**風邪**	**も**	**引こ**う。
(If you walk around without wearing an overcoat on such a cold day, it is a matter of course that you will catch a cold.			

(C)

	Adj(*na*)stem	
この政治的問題を解決するのは	**容易**	であろう。
(It is probably / must be easy to solve this political problem.)		

Formation

(i) Vvol (V: non-controllable verb)

書けよう (s.o. (probably) can write s.t.)

出来よう (s.o. (probably) can do s.t.)

(ii) (Noun + Prt) Vvol (V: non-controllable verb)

目も覚めよう (it is natural that one wakes up)

日本語が分かろう (s.o. probably understands Japanese)

(iii) Adj(*na*)stem であろう

便利であろう (s.t. is probably / must be convenient)

Examples

(a) この問題についてはいろいろ政治的解決が考えられよう。
(Regarding this problem, all sorts of political solutions can (probably) be considered.)

(b) このピアノソナタだったら子供にも弾けよう。
(Even a child should be able to play this piano sonata.)

(c) この報告書は来週の金曜日までには書けよう。
(We should be able to write this report by next Friday.)

(d) あのタワーに上れば，町全体がよく見えよう。
(If you go up that tower, you should be able to see the entire city.)

(e) 米ソ関係の改善で，世界の平和は維持出来よう。
(With the improvement of U.S.-Russia relations, it is likely that world peace can be maintained.)

(f) あんなにひどいことをされたら，腹も立とう。
(If you are treated as badly as that you naturally get mad.)

(g) あれだけむちゃくちゃに働けば，病気にもなろう。
(If you work as crazy as that, you will naturally get ill.)

(h) この辺りでは夜の一人歩きは危険であろう。
(In this neighborhood it is probably / must be dangerous to walk alone at night.)

Notes

1. The auxiliary verb *-yō* is used to express either the writer's conjecture that s.t. can be done or his belief that s.t. should happen. The structure ~ N + Prt + Vvol, always expresses certainty, as shown in KS(B), Exs.(f) and (g). Adverbs such as *sazo* 'surely' and *kitto* 'certainly' also indicate conjecture with a feeling of certainty. Otherwise, the auxiliary verb is subject to either interpretation.

2. The auxiliary verb *-yō* is primarily used in written Japanese.

3. The Adj(*na*) version of *-yō* is Adj(*na*)stem + *dearō*. For the Adj(*i*) version, see *karō* of this volume.

4. The negative versions of *-yō* are Vinf·nonpast *mai* (V: a non-controllable verb), Adj(*i*)stem + *ku arumai*, Adj(*na*)stem + *de wa arumai*, respectively.

(1) a. こんな難しい文章は小学生には分かる**まい**。
(An elementary school child might not comprehend such a difficult passage.)

b. 彼の講演は面白**くあるまい**。
(His lecture might not be interesting.)

c. 経済の回復は不可能**ではあるまい**。
(Economic recovery might not be impossible.)

(⇨ ***mai***)

【Related Expression】

Darō, the informal, spoken / written form of *deshō*, is a contracted form of *dearō* and can replace all the uses of the *-yō* without changing the meaning. *Deshō*, the formal spoken version of *darō* also can replace all the uses of *-rō*.

(⇨ ***darō*** (DBJG: 100–02))

[1] a. この程度の文章なら日本語の一年生でも読める｛**だろう / でしょう**｝。(cf. KS(A))

b. こんな寒い日にオーバーも着ないで歩き回れば，風邪も引く｛**だろう / でしょう**｝。(cf. KS(B))

c. この政治的問題を解決するのは容易｛**だろう / でしょう**｝。(cf. KS(C))

yori より *adv.*

an adverb which forms the comparative of an adjective or an adverb to mean 'more ~ than now or than otherwise'

more ~ (than now; than s.t. at present; than otherwise)
【REL. *motto*】

◆Key Sentences

(A)

Topic			Adj.	
私達は	いつも，	より	**よい**	サービスの提供に努めています。
(We are always trying to offer better services.)				

(B)

Topic	Scond		Adv.
外国語は	新しい技術を利用すれば	より	**効果的に**教えることが出来る。
(We can teach foreign languages more effectively if we utilize new technology.)			

Y

(C)

Sinf*			Adj.
子供達に自分で考えさせる	方が	より	**教育的だ。**
(It is more educational to have children think for themselves.)			

*Adj(*na*) and N + Cop. must be in the prenominal forms.

Formation

(i) より Adj.

より面白い (more interesting)

(ii) より Adv.

より正確に (more accurately)

Examples

(a) 今後もより速い，より大容量の記憶装置の開発が続くだろう。
(The development of faster and larger (lit. of a larger capacity) storage devices will continue from now on, too.)

(b) 私達はより多くの人々にこの施設を利用してもらいたいと思っています。
(We would like more people to use this facility.)

(c) この車は車体をより軽くするためにアルミの合金を使っている。
(In order to make the body lighter, aluminum alloy is used for this car.)

(d) 「より軽く，より薄く，より小さく」が我が社のモットーだ。
("Lighter, thinner, and smaller" is our company's motto.)

(e) 原色を使うと，より刺激的になる。
(Using original colors would make it more stimulating.)

(f) 電話回線を利用すれば，より広い地域のユーザーにこのサービスが提供出来る。
(If we utilize telephone lines, we can offer this service to users in a larger region.)

(g) 集中管理システムの方がより効率的だろう。
(A centralized system would probably be more efficient.)

(h) バスで通勤する方がより経済的です。
(Commuting to work by bus is more economical.)

Notes

1. The adverb *yori* was derived from the particle *yori* 'than.' *Yori* Adj. / Adv. expresses the idea 'more Adj. / Adv. than now or than otherwise' and is used to make a general comparison rather than a comparison between two specific entities. For example, KS(A), (B), and (C) are equivalent to (1), (2), and (3), respectively.

    (1) 私達はいつも**今より**よいサービスの提供に努めています。
    (We are always trying to offer better services than (we do) now.)

    (2) 外国語は新しい技術を利用すれば，**そうしないより**効果的に教えることが出来る。
    (If we utilize new technology, we can teach foreign languages more effectively (lit. than not doing so).)

    (3) 子供達に自分で考えさせる方が，**そうしないより**教育的だ。
    (To have children think for themselves is more educational (lit. than not doing so).)

    (⇨ ***yori***[1] (DBJG: 564–67))

2. If X (*no*) *hō ga* is present, as in KS(C), the sentence is comparative without *yori*. In this case, *yori* is used for emphasis.

    (⇨ ***~ hō ga ~ yori*** (DBJG: 140–44))

【Related Expression】

Motto also expresses the concept of 'more.' However, *motto* is more colloquial than *yori*. Thus, the combination of *motto* and *yoi*, the literal version of *ii* 'good,' is awkward, as in [1].

[1] 私達はいつも，{**より** / ?**もっと**} **よい**サービスの提供に努めています。
(=KS(A))

On the other hand, *motto* can be used when a specific item of comparison *kore / are / sore yori* 'than this / that / that' is known from the situation or context, whereas *yori* is unacceptable in this situation, as in [2].

[2] a. {**もっと / *より**} 大きいのはありませんか。
(Do you have a bigger one (than this)?)

b. あの映画は {**もっと / *より**} 面白いと思っていたのだが，期待外れだった。
(I thought that that movie would be more interesting (than that), but it was disappointing.)

c. {**もっと / *より**} (たくさん)召し上がって下さい。
(Please have more (than that).)

Note also that when X *hō ga* 'X is (more)' is present, *motto* implies 'much more,' while *yori* is simply for emphasis. (See Note 2.) Compare [3a] and [3b].

[3] a. バスで通勤する**方がもっと**経済的です。
(Commuting to work by bus is much more economical.)

b. バスで通勤する**方がより**経済的です。(=Ex.(h))

zaru o enai ざるを得ない *aux.* <w>

an auxiliary indicating that there is no other choice but to do s.t.

cannot help -ing; cannot (help) but; have no choice but to ~; have to

【REL. *-nai wake ni (wa) ikanai*; *-nakereba naranai*; *shika nai*】

◆Key Sentence

	Vneg	
それは高かったが，教科書だったから	**買わ**	ざるを得なかった。
(It was a textbook so I had no choice but to buy it, although it was expensive.)		

Formation

Vneg ざるを得ない

食べざるを得ない (s.o. cannot help eating s.t.)

行かざるを得ない (s.o. cannot help going there)

Exception:

せざるを得ない (s.o. cannot help doing s.t.)

Examples

(a) 日本へ行けば，日本の習慣に従わざるを得ない。
(If you go to Japan you cannot help but adapt yourself to Japanese customs.)

(b) 上司に飲みに行こうと言われれば，部下は行かざるを得ない。
(If a subordinate is told by his superior to go out drinking he cannot help going with him.)

(c) これだけの人が拳銃で殺されているのだから，拳銃所持をより厳しくコントロールせざるを得ないと思う。
(Because this many people have been murdered by guns, I feel that we cannot help but control possession of guns more strictly.)

(d) ジョンは一年で日本語がすらすら話せて，新聞が楽に読めるようになったのだから，語学の天才と言わざるを得ない。
(Since John was able to speak Japanese fluently and read newspapers with ease in one year we cannot help calling him a genius of language learning.)

(e) 日本は天然資源の乏しい国だから，経済発展のためには輸出に依存せざるを得ないのである。
(Since Japan is a country lacking natural resources, she cannot help relying on exports.)

Notes

1. Vneg *zaru o enai* is used in written Japanese to express an idea of 'cannot help -ing.'

2. The irregular verb *suru* changes to *se* before *zaru o enai*, as shown in Formation and Exs.(c) and (e).

3. Just like its English counterpart, the verb that can be used in Vneg *zaru o enai* has to be a volitional verb, so a non-volitional verb such as *wakaru* 'understand,' *dekiru* 'can,' *tsukareru* 'get tired,' *komaru* 'get into trouble,' *mieru* 'can see' and not every potential form can be used with Vneg *zaru o enai.*

【Related Expressions】

I. Vneg *zaru o enai* can be replaced by Vneg *nakereba naranai* when the latter means 'have to do s.t. because there is no other choice.'

[1] a. それは高かったが，教科書だったから買わ**なければならなかった**。(=KS)

b. 日本へ行けば，日本の習慣に従わ**なければならない**。
(=Ex.(a))

c. これだけの人が拳銃で殺されているのだから，拳銃所持をより厳しくコントロールし**なければならない**。(=Ex.(c))

When Vneg *nakereba naranai* is used in a context where one has to do s.t. because s/he has an obligation to do it, it cannot be replaced by Vneg *zaru o enai,* as shown in [2]. In [2] the writer had made a promise with s.o. to go see a movie and as a result of that had to leave home right away. In such a case Vneg *zaru o enai* cannot replace Vneg *nakereba naranai*.

[2] 映画に行く約束があったので，すぐ出かけ｛**なければならなかった / *ざるを得なかった**｝。
(I had to leave my home right away, because I had arranged to go to a movie.)

But if the same predicate is used in a situation where there is no choice but to leave a place right away, Vneg *zaru o enai* can replace Vneg *nakereba naranai*, as shown in [3].

[3] 社長からの命令だったので，すぐ出かけ｛**なければならなかった / ざるを得なかった**｝。
(Because it was the president's order, I had to leave right away.)

The crucial difference between the two structures is: Vneg *zaru o enai* is used to express only a no-choice situation but Vneg *nakereba naranai* is used to express either a no-choice situation or an obligation situation.

(⇨ **~ *nakereba naranai*** (DBJG: 274–76))

II. Vneg *zaru o enai* can be also replaced by Vneg *wake ni* (*wa*) *ikanai* and V *shika nai* as shown in [4].

[4] a. それは高かったが，教科書だったから｛**買わざるを得なかった / 買わないわけに(は)いかなかった / 買うしかなかった**｝。(=KS(A))

b. 日本へ行けば，日本の習慣に｛**従わざるを得ない / 従わないわけに(は)いかない / 従うしかない**｝。(=Ex.(a))

Vneg *wake ni* (*wa*) *ikanai* can be used in both no-choice and obligation situations, and implies the speaker's unwillingness to do s.t. indicated by the verb, whereas both Vneg *zaru o enai* and V *shika nai* are used only in a no-choice situation. So in an obligation situation as in [2] above, Vneg *wake ni* (*wa*) *ikanai* can be used but not V *shika nai*.

zo ぞ *prt.* <s>

a sentence-final particle that emphasizes a male speaker's emotion about s.t. in his monologue or his strong desire to draw s.o. else's attention

I tell you; I'm telling you; you know
【REL. *yo*】

◆Key Sentences

(A)

	Sinf	
あれ,	財布がどこかへ行ってしまった	ぞ。
(Hey, my purse has gone somewhere!)		

(B)

Sinf	
急がないとバスに乗り遅れる	ぞ。
(If you don't hurry, you'll be late for the bus, you know.)	

Formation

{V / Adj(*i*)}inf ぞ

食べるぞ。 (Hey, s.o. is going to eat it.)

食べたぞ。 (Hey, s.o. ate it.)

まずいぞ。 (Yuck!)

まずかったぞ。 (It was yucky.)

{Adj(*na*) / N} {だ / だった} ぞ

元気だぞ。 (S.o. is healthy.)

元気だったぞ。 (S.o. was healthy.)

Examples

(a) 今日はあの子とデートが出来るぞ。
(Wow! I can date that girl today.)

(b) 変だぞ。女房の顔が猫の顔に見える。
(Strange indeed! My wife's face looks like a cat's face.)

(c) 今度こそ文部省の奨学金をもらってやるぞ。
(By God, this time I will get the Education Ministry's Scholarship.)

(d) 今日の日本語の試験はうまくいったぞ。
(Thank God, today's Japanese exam went well!)

(e) 今日は寒いから，オーバーを着て行った方がいいぞ。
(It's cold today, so you'd better go out with an overcoat on.)

(f) このケーキ，食べないなら，俺が食べちゃうぞ。
(If you don't eat this cake, I will.)

(g) 同じ間違いをもう一度したら，許さないぞ。
(If you make the same mistake again, I'm not going to forgive you.)

(h) おい，この酒，熱くないぞ。
(Hey, this sake isn't hot enough!)

(i) 予告もなしに来るなんて失礼だぞ。
(It's rude of you to come here without any advance notice. Do you know that?)

Notes

1. The sentence-final particle *zo* is used only by male speakers in informal speech to express either the speaker's strong feeling about something in a monologue or a strong desire to draw the hearer's attention to something.

2. KS(A) and Exs.(a) – (d) are examples of a monologue in which the male speaker is expressing his emotion such as dismay (KS(A)), joy (Ex.(a)), surprise (Ex.(b)), determination (Ex.(c)), etc. KS(B) and Exs. (e) – (i), on the other hand, are examples of other-directed speech in which the speaker wants to draw the hearer's attention to something assumed to be unknown to the hearer. For example, in KS(B), a father can be the speaker who wants to draw his wife's or children's attention to the fact that the bus's scheduled time for departure is drawing near.

3. The particle *zo* is used in informal speech only. When it is used to draw s.o.'s attention to s.t., the addressee has to be either the male speaker's equal or inferior. So, for example, a male child cannot use *zo* to his parents.

【Related Expression】

There are four differences between the sentence-final particles *zo* and *yo*. First, the latter cannot be used in a monologue but the former can, as shown in [1] below.

[1] a. *あれ，財布がどこかへ行ってしまった**よ**。(cf. KS(A))

b. *今日はあの子とデートが出来る**よ**。(cf. Ex.(a))

c. *変だ**よ**。女房の顔が猫の顔に見える。(cf. Ex.(b))

In other words, *yo* is always other-directed, but *zo* can be used either self-directed or other-directed way. Therefore, in all the other-directed examples *zo* can be replaced by *yo*.

[2] a. 急がないとバスに乗り遅れる**よ**。(cf. KS(B))

b. 今日は寒いから，オーバーを着て行った方がいい**よ**。(cf. Ex.(e))

c. 予告もなしに来るなんて失礼だ**よ**。(cf. Ex.(i))

The choice of *yo* in the above sentences sounds much less persuasive and informal than the choice of *zo*. Note that the sentences of [1] are all unacceptable as self-directed sentences (i.e., monologues) but acceptable if they are other-directed sentences. The second difference between the two sentence-final particles is that *yo* can be used by both male and female speakers but *zo* is used only by male speakers. The third difference is shown in [3] below. In the sentence-final combination of *yo ne* (assertion + confirmation) *yo* cannot be replaced by *zo*.

[3] a. 最近日本の政治はずいぶん変わった{**よね** / ***ぞね**}。
(Japanese politics has undergone tremendous change, hasn't it?)

b. 日本人は世間体を気にする{**よね** / ***ぞね**}。
(Japanese people are concerned about how they appear to the world, aren't they?)

The fourth and the last difference stems from the fact that *zo* can be used only with informal forms as indicated in Formation. In contrast, the particle *yo* can be used either with informal or formal forms.

[4] a. この本は面白いです{**よ** / ***ぞ**}。
(This book is interesting, you know.

b. 彼は日本人です{**よ** / ***ぞ**}。
(He is a Japanese, you know.)

c. 酒を飲み過ぎると，病気になります{**よ** / ***ぞ**}。
(If you drink too much sake, you'll get ill, you know.)

(⇨***yo*** (DBJG: 543–47))

Appendixes

Appendix 1 ***Katakana* Word Transcription Rules**

Katakana words, or borrowed words spelled in *katakana*, make up a significant portion of Japanese vocabulary. When the original foreign words are used as Japanese words, certain phonological rules apply to them, usually yielding somewhat different pronunciations from the original.

The following is a list of correspondences between English vowels and Japanese vowels to show how a particular English vowel is perceived by a native Japanese. English is used here, because the majority of borrowed words are now coming from English. Phonetic symbols are given in brackets.

(A) English [æ] (c*a*t, s*a*lmon) [ʌ] (c*u*t, c*o*me), and [ə] (s*u*ppose, *a*head) → Japanese [a]
(A′) English vowels [ɑː] (f*a*ther, c*a*lm), [əːr] (s*er*vice, f*ur*), and [ər] (doct*or*, bett*er*) → Japanese [aː]
(B) English [i] (s*i*t, b*u*sy) → Japanese [i]
(B′) English [iː] (b*ea*t, ch*ie*f) → Japanese [iː]
(C) English [u] (b*oo*k, p*u*t) → Japanese [u]
(C′) English [uː] (s*ou*p, r*u*le) → Japanese [uː]
(D) English [e] (g*e*t, fr*ie*nd) → Japanese [e]
(E) English [ɔ] (h*o*t, y*a*cht) → Japanese [o]
(E′) English [ɔː] (*a*ll, ch*a*lk) → Japanese [oː]

The following rules can be used to interpret unfamiliar *katakana* words or to transcribe foreign words in *katakana*.

Rule 1: Both [s] and [θ] (the sound for *th*) are represented by サ シ ス セ ソ.

Exs. service → サービス
seat → シート
switch → スイッチ
sex → セックス
socks → ソックス

thank you → サンキュー
think tank → シンクタンク
theory → セオリー

Rule 2: Both [z] and [ð] (the voiced version of [θ]) are represented by ザ ジ ズ ゼ ゾ.

Exs. Zambia → ザンビア
zigzag → ジグザグ
zoom → ズーム
zero → ゼロ
zone → ゾーン

godfather → ゴッドファーザー

Rule 3: Both [r] and [l] are represented by ラ リ ル レ ロ.

Exs. rice → ライス
radio → ラジオ
lamp → ランプ
rule → ルール
list → リスト

Rule 4: [tʃ] (chur*ch*, *ch*eese) and [dʒ] (ju*dge*, *ge*sture) are represented by チ and ジ, respectively.

Exs. cheese → チーズ
kitchen → キッチン

judge → ジャッジ
exchange → エックスチェンジ

Rule 5: [ti] and [di] are represented by チ / ティ or デ / ディ, respectively.

Exs. party → パーティー
ticket → チケット

dilemma → {ジ / ディ}レンマ
diesel → {ジ / ディ}ーゼル

Rule 6: [tu] is represented by ツ.

Exs. tool → ツール
two → ツー

Note: Some Japanese can now pronounce [tu].

Rule 7: [tʃ] (*ch*urch, *c*ello) and [dʒ] (sol*di*er, *g*esture) / [ʒ] (mea*s*ure, deci*s*ion) are represented by チャ チュ チェ チョ and ジャ ジュ ジェ ジョ, respectively.

Exs. Chinatown → チャイナタウン
chewing gum → チューインガム
chocolate → チョコレート

jumbo jet → ジャンボジェット
juice → ジュース
Johnson → ジョンソン

Rule 8: Word-final consonants or two or more consonants in succession are pronounced and written with a vowel placed after each consonant.

8-1: The vowel [o] is added to a word-final [t] or [d].

Exs. bat → バット
post → ポスト
test → テスト
note → ノート

pound → ポンド
poolside → プールサイド
Polaroid → ポラロイド
shade → シェード

(Exception: salad → サラダ)

8-2: The vowel [u] comes after [p], [b], [f], [v], [k], [ŋ], [s], [z], [θ], [ts], [l] and [m].

Exs. grape → グレープ
Bob → ボブ
knife → ナイフ

drive → ドライブ
mask → マスク
king → キング
bus → バス
Lions Club → ライオンズクラブ
bathroom → バスルーム
sports → スポーツ
single → シングル
game → ゲーム

The vowel [i] comes after [k].

cake → ケーキ（*ケーク）
steak → ステーキ（*ステーク）
strike → ストライキ 'workers' strike'
(cf. ストライク 'strike in baseball')

8-3: The vowel [i] comes after [tʃ] and [dʒ].

Exs. speech → スピーチ
coach → コーチ
judge → ジャッジ
page → ページ

Rule 9: Long vowels and diphthongs are represented by the lengthening marker ー.

Exs. [əːr] girl → ガール
skirt → スカート
curtain → カーテン
service → サー{ビ / ヴィ}ス

[iː] queen → クイーン
Peter → ピーター
beef → ビーフ
cheese → チーズ

[uː] group → グループ
coupon → クーポン
rule → ルール

blue → ブルー

[ei] paper → ペーパー
image → イメージ
inflation → インフレーション
date → デート

[ɔː] chalk → チョーク
story → ストーリー
hall → ホール
ball → ボール

[ɔː*r*] form → フォーム
sports → スポーツ
cord → コード
pork → ポーク

[ou] boat → ボート
show → ショー
note → ノート
coat → コート

Note: The diphthong [ai] can be represented not by the lengthening marker by Japanese [ai] as in:

spy → スパイ
wine → ワイン
pie → パイ

Rule 10: If the original English word has a word structure of [. . . Short Vowel + Consonant . . .], then ッ is inserted before the consonant. The original consonants are [p, t, d, k, s, tʃ, dʒ, ʃ, ts] at a word-final position and [p, t, k, s, tʃ, ʃ] at a word-medial position.

10.1: [. . . Short Vowel + p . . .]

Exs. slipper [slipə*r*] → スリッパ
zipper [zipə*r*] → ジッパー
top [tɑp] → トップ

10.2: [. . . Short Vowel + t / d . . .]

Exs. motto [matou] → モットー
bat [bæt] → バット
pet [pet] → ペット

(Exception: butter [bʌtər] → バター)

bed [bed] → ベッド
thoroughbred [θəːrəbred] → サラブレッド
deadball [dedbɔːl] → デッドボール

10.3: [. . . Short Vowel + k . . .]

Exs. slacks [slæks] → スラックス
black [blæk] → ブラック
kick [kik] → キック
cracker [krækər] → クラッカー

(Exception: necktie [nektai] → ネクタイ)

10.4: [. . . Short Vowel + s . . .]

Exs. message [mesidʒ] → メッセージ
essay [esei] → エッセー
kiss [kis] → キ(ッ)ス

(Exception: dress [dres] → ドレス)

10.5: [. . . Short Vowel + tʃ / dʒ . . .]

Exs. watch [watʃ] → ウォッチ
switch [switʃ] → スイッチ
kitchen [kitʃin] → キッチン

judge [jʌdʒ] → ジャッジ
college [kalidʒ] → カレッジ
badge [bædʒ] → バッジ

10.6: [. . . Short Vowel + ʃ . . .]

Exs. cash [kæʃ] → キャッシュ
fishburger [fiʃbəːrgər] → フィシュバーガー

rush hour [rʌʃauər] → ラッシュアワー
pressure [preʃər] → プレッシャー

10.7: [. . . Short Vowel + ts . . .]

Exs. cats [kæts] → キャッツ
guts [gʌts] → ガッツ

Notes 1. If the original English word has a word structure of [. . . Long Vowel / Diphthong + Consonant . . .], the consonant is not represented by the small ツ in Japanese as shown by:

speech [spiːtʃ] → スピーチ
beach [biːtʃ] → ビーチ
peak [piːk] → ピーク
jeep [dʒiːp] → ジープ
concert [kɑnsərt] → コンサート
rate [reit] → レート
coach [koutʃ] → コーチ
out [aut] → アウト
date [deit] → デート

(⇨ Rule 9)

2. If a given word has a word structure of [. . . Short Vowel + Consonant + Short Vowel + Consonant], not the word-medial consonant but the word-final consonant is represented by ツ as shown by:

rocket [rɑkit] → ロケット, pocket [pɑkit] → ポケット,
racket [rækit] → ラケット, ticket [tikit] → チケット,
topic [tɑpik] → トピック, classic [klæsik] → クラシック

Rule 11: The nasal sounds, [m], [n] or [ŋ], in [. . . Vowel + Nasal + Consonant) . . .] and [. . . Vowel + Nasal] are represented by ン. If the nasal sound in [. . . Vowel + Nasal] is [ŋ], it is represented not by ン but by ング.

Exs. pink [pink] → ピンク
pin [pin] → ピン
tent [tent] → テント

campus [kæmpəs] → キャンパス
companion [kəmpænjən] → コンパニオン
lamp [læmp] → ランプ

song [sɔːŋ] → ソング
gang [gæŋ] → ギャング
singer [siŋgər] → シンガー

(Exceptions: Hong Kong [hɑŋkɑŋ] → ホンコン
ping-pong [piŋ-pɑŋ] → ピンポン

Note: If [m] occurs word-finally, [m] is represented not by ン but by ム as in:

cream [kriːm] → クリーム
dream [driːm] → ドリーム
game [geim] → ゲーム

Rule 12: There is a set of new spellings which attempt to transcribe the original sound more faithfully.

Note: The *katakana* word in parentheses represents the older transcription.

12-1: [fæ], [fai], [fi], [fe], [fɔ], [fou] by ファ, ファイ, フィ, フェ, フォ, フォー, respectively.

Exs. fight [fait] → ファイト
fashion [fæʃən] → ファッション
feet [fiːt] → フィート
fiancé [fiːɑːnsei] → フィアンセ
feminism [femənizm] → フェミニズム
festival [festəvəl] → フェスティバル
folk dance [fouk dæns] → フォークダンス
forum [fɔːrəm] → フォーラム

12-2: [və], [vai], [vi], [ve] and [vou] by ヴァ, ヴァイ, ヴィ, ヴェ and ヴォー, respectively.

Exs. vacation [vəkeiʃən] → ヴァケーション (バケーション)
violin [vaiəlin] → ヴァイオリン (バイオリン)

violet [vaiəlit] → ヴァイオレット（バイオレット）
victory [viktəri] → ヴィクトリー（ビクトリー）
Venus [viːnəs] → ヴィーナス（ビーナス）
Venice [venis] → ヴェニス（ベニス）
vocal [voukəl] → ヴォーカル（ボーカル）

12-3: [wi], [we] and [wo] by ウィ, ウェ and ウォ.

Exs. wit [wit] → ウィット（ウイット）
wink [wiŋk] → ウィンク（ウインク）
Western [westərn] → ウェスタン（ウエスタン）
waitress [weitres] → ウェイトレス（ウエートレス）
water [wɔːtər] → ウォーター（ウオーター）

12-4: [qui], [que] and [quo] by クィ, クェ and クォ.

Exs. queen → クィーン（クイーン）
Quaker → クェーカー（クエーカー）
quarterback → クォーターバック（クオーターバック）

12-5: [ti], [di], [du] and [tsə] by ティ, ディ, デュ and ツァ.

Exs. tea [tiː] → ティー
disco [diskou] → ディスコ
duet [d(j)uːet] → デュエット
pizza [piːtsə] → ピッツァ

Rule 13: The correspondences between the Japanese palatalized sounds and their English counterparts are as follows:

English	Japanese (palatalized sounds)	Examples
[kæ]	キャ	cash [kæʃ] → キャッシュ
[kju]	キュ	cute [kjuːt] → キュート
[ʃæ]	シャ	chandelier [ʃændəliə] → シャンデリア
[ʃu]	シュ	shoot [ʃuːt] → シュート
[ʃɑ]	ショ	shop [ʃɑp] → ショップ
[tʃæ]	チャ	challenge [tʃælindʒ] → チャレンジ
[tju]	チュ	tube [tjuːb] → チューブ

[tʃɔ]	チョ	choice [tʃɔis] → チョイス
[nju]	ニュ	New York [njuːjɔrk] → ニューヨーク
[gæ]	ギャ	gap [gæp] → ギャップ
[dʒæ]	ジャ	jam [dʒæm] → ジャム
[dʒu]	ジュ	juice [dʒuːs] → ジュース
[dʒou]	ジョ	joke [dʒouk] → ジョーク

In addition to the pronunciation-based rules give above, there are spelling-based rules.

Rule 14: English [ə] → Japanese [a], if [ə] is spelled *a*.

Exs. oper*a* [ɑpərə] → オペラ
b*a*nan*a* [bənænə] → バナナ
p*a*rade [pəreid] → パレード

Rule 15: English [ə] → Japanese [i], if [ə] is spelled *i*.

Exs. ident*i*ty [aidentəti] → アイデンティティ
personal*i*ty [pəːrsənæləti] → パーソナリティ
stam*i*na [stæmənə] → スタミナ

Rule 16: English [ə], [d] or [de] → Japanese [e], if [ə] is spelled *e* or *de*.

Exs. gar*de*n [gɑːrdn] → ガーデン
cam*e*ra [kæmərə] → カメラ
mo*de*l [mɑdl] → モデル

Rule 17: English [ə] → Japanese [o], if [ə] is spelled *o*.

Exs. lem*o*n [lemən] → レモン
inflati*o*n [infleiʃən] → インフレーション
communicati*o*n [kəmjuːnəkeiʃən] → コミュニケーション

Rule 18: English spellings -age, -ate and -wer are spelled [eː] ージ, [eː] ート and ワー, respectively.

Exs. im*age* → イメージ
percent*age* → パーセンテージ

chocol*ate* → チョコレート
priv*ate* → プライベート

tow*er* → タワー
show*er* → シャワー

Appendix 2 **Compound Verbs**

A compound verb is a verb that consists of two verbs creating a specific meaning not always predictable from the meanings of each element. The compound verb has only one accentual peak and no other elements can enter between the two verbs. The compound verb is either V*te* + V as in *katte ageru* 'to buy s.t. for s.o.,' *katte miru* 'to buy s.t. on an experimental basis,' *katte oku* 'to buy s.t. in advance,' or V*masu* + V. In this segment only the latter will be exemplified and explained.

The V*masu* to which another verb is affixed acquires additional meaning such as 'to start to do s.t.,' 'to finish doing s.t.,' 'to continue to do s.t.,' etc. On one hand there are some compound verbs that are so productive (i.e., they can be almost freely produced according to the pattern) that they are not listed in a dictionary. For example, V*masu* + *hajimeru* 'to begin to do s.t.,' V*masu* + *sugiru* 'to do s.t. too much' are not listed in a dictionary. On the other hand, there are other verb compounds that are so unproductive that they are listed in a dictionary. For example, *tori-kaeru* 'to exchange,' *kaki-naosu* 'to rewrite,' etc.

The following are a list of frequently used compound verbs with the pattern of V_1 (= V*masu*) + V_2. For each compound verb given below the basic meaning is given in brackets and the conjugation type is given in parentheses, followed by English glosses (which are omitted when there is no close equivalent). The symbols v.i. and v.t. stand for an intransitive verb and a transitive verb, respectively. Generally speaking, the entire compound verb is an intransitive verb, if V_1 is intransitive, and a transitive verb if V_1 is transitive.

～合う v.i. / v.t. [to do s.t. mutually] (Gr. 1) do s.t. together; do s.t. with each other

a. 喜び**合って**くれる人，悲しみ**合って**くれる人が本当の友達だ。
(A person who will rejoice with you and grieve with you is a true friend.)

b. 二人は小さなことで言い**合って**いた。
(The two were arguing with each other over a trifle.)

c. この家庭では両親と子供達がよく話し**合う**。
(In this family the parents and the children frequently talk with each other.)

d. 僕達はお金を出し**合って**，アパートを借りている。
(We jointly contribute money to rent an apartment.)

e. 男女が公園のベンチで抱き**合って**いる。
(A man and a woman are embracing on a bench in the park.)

～上がる v.i. [an action takes place upward] (Gr. 1) ~ up

Note: V_1 is an intransitive verb and is almost limited to a movement verb.

a. 男は立ち**上がって**，来客と握手をした。
(The man stood up and shook hands with the visitor.)

b. 私が知らないでしっぽを踏んだら猫は飛び**上がった**。
(When I accidentally stamped on its tail, the cat jumped up.)

c. 私はお寺の階段を駆け**上がった**。
(I ran up the stairs of the temple.)

d. 曇っていた空が急に晴れ**上がった**。
(The cloudy sky suddenly cleared up.)

～飽きる v.i. [to get tired of doing s.t.] (Gr. 2) get tired of ~

Note: V_1 is almost limited to *taberu* 'eat,' *miru* 'see' and *kiku* 'hear.'

a. 毎日すしを食べていたのに，すしは食べ**飽きない**。
(I've been eating sushi every day, but I am not tired of eating it.)

b. このワインはもう飲み**飽きた**よ。
(I'm tired of drinking this wine.)

c. あの人の話はいつも同じなので，聞き**飽きた**。
(His talk is always the same, so I am tired of listening to it.)

d. このビデオは何度も見たので，見**飽きた**よ。
(I saw this video many times, so I got tired of watching it.)

～上げる v.t. [to cause an action to take place upward or to finish up s.t.] (Gr. 2)

Note: V_1 has to be a transitive verb.

a. すみません，この箱を持ち**上げて**下さいませんか。
(Excuse me, but could you kindly lift this box, please?)

b. 卒業論文をようやく書き**上げた**。
(At long last I finished up writing the senior thesis.)

Note: If the connected verb is a verb that indicates s.t. that directly involves a person, *-ageru* implies politeness, as shown below.

c. 先生のお名前は前々から存じ**上げて**おりました。
(I have known your name for a long time.)

～合わせる v.i. / v.t. [to bring two things/persons together] (Gr. 2)

Note: When V_1 is a v.t., it means 'to put things/persons together' and if it is a v.i., it means 'for two things/persons to be accidentally brought together.'

a. 「女」という漢字と「子」という漢字を組み**合わせる**と，「好(き)」という漢字になる。
(If you put the Chinese characters 女 'woman' and 子 'child' together, you get the character 好 'like.')

b. 私はオートミールとヨーグルトとバナナを混ぜ**合わせて**，食べています。
(I mix oatmeal, yogurt and banana together and eat it.)

c. 僕は彼女と駅前の喫茶店で待ち**合わせた**。
(I met her at a coffee shop in front of the station.)

d. 私達二人は同じ空港のロビーに居**合わせた**。
(The two of us happened to be together at the lobby of the same airport.)

e. 私達は偶然同じバスに乗り**合わせた**。
(We happened to ride the same bus together.)

～入れる v.i. / v.t. [to get s.t. into some place] (Gr. 2) in; into

a. ピアノを家に運び**入れる**のが大変だった。
(It was hard to carry the piano into the house.)

b. ここに住所と電話番号を書き**入れて**下さい。
(Please write in here the address and the telephone number.)

c. 地下鉄がやがてこの辺りにも乗り**入れる**はずだ。
(The subway is expected to extend into this area, too.)

d. 明治時代に日本は西洋からいろいろな物を取り**入れた**。
(During the Meiji era Japan adopted all sorts of things from the West.)

e. 社長は私の辞職を聞き**入れなかった**。
(The president didn't accept my resignation.)

～得る (⇨553–55)

～送る v.t. [to send or send off after doing s.t.] (Gr. 1) send; ~ off

Note: V_1 is very much limited.

a. 母に手紙を書き**送った**。
(I sent a letter to my mother.)

b. 友達を空港で見**送った**。
(I saw my friend off at the airport.)

c. 先方にはその旨言い**送り**ましょう。
(I will write them to that effect.)

～落ちる v.i. [s.t./s.o. falls down in a certain manner] (Gr. 2)

a. コンクリートの天井が急に崩れ**落ちて**来た。
(The concrete ceiling suddenly collapsed on us.)

b. 火事でデパートが焼け**落ちた**。
(The department store burned down in a fire.)

c. 祖母が階段を転げ**落ちた**。
(My grandmother fell down the stairway.)

d. 地震で本が棚から滑り**落ちた**。
(The books slipped off the bookshelves because of the earthquake.)

～降りる v.i. [to descend in a certain manner] (Gr. 1) down

Note: V_1 is very much limited.

a. 僕は山を駆け**降りた**。
(I ran down the mountain.)

b. 地震の時，窓から飛び**降りた**。
(At the time of the earthquake I jumped out of the window.)

～下ろす v.t. [to lower s.t./s.o. in a certain manner] (Gr. 1) ~ down

a. 木に登った猫を引き**下ろした**。
(I pulled down the cat that had climbed up the tree.)

b. 警官はデモ隊に棍棒を打ち**下ろした**。
(The policemen struck down demonstrators with their clubs.)

c. 私の家は湖を見**下ろす**所に立っている。
(My house stands at a place that overlooks a lake.)

d. 山の方から冷たい風が吹き**下ろして**来る。
(A cold wind blows down from the mountain.)

Note: The following example has the specific meaning of 'to write a new novel or play.'

e. 小説家は新しい小説を書き**下ろした**。
(The novelist wrote a new novel.)

～終わる / 終える v.t. [a process of doing s.t. comes to its end] (Gr. 1) finish

Note: ~ *owaru* can be replaced without changing the meaning by using ~ *oeru*.

a. 博士論文をやっと書き {**終わった / 終えた**}。
(I finally finished writing my doctoral dissertation.)

b. トルストイの『戦争と平和』を読み {**終わった** / **終えた**}。
(I finished reading Tolstoy's *War and Peace*.)

c. 映画を見 {**終わった** / **終えた**} 時，もう夜中を過ぎていた。
(When I finished watching the movie it was already past midnight.)

Note: ～終える cannot be used in spoken Japanese.

d. この新聞，もう読み {**終わった** / ***終えた**}?
(Have you finished reading this newspaper?)

～返す v.t. [to do s.t. again (and again)] (Gr. 1) ~ again; ~ back

Note: *-kaesu* is used with a controllable action verb.

a. 昔読んだ漱石の小説を読み**返して**みた。
(I reread Soseki's novels that I had read a long time ago.)

b. 大事な物を持って行かれそうになったので，あわてて取り**返した**。
(Someone was about to take away my valuable articles, so I hastily retrieved them.)

c. 殴られたから，殴り**返した**。
(Someone hit me, so I hit him back.)

d. そいつがひどいことを言ったので，俺も言い**返した**んだ。
(Because that guy said an awful thing, I talked back.)

Note: In the following example the V_1 has lost its original meaning of 'to reel threads' using a weaving machine.

e. あの男は同じことを何度も繰り**返す**。
(He repeats the same thing again and again.)

～換える v.i. / v.t. [to replace s.t./s.o. by s.t./s.o. else] (Gr. 2) change; re-

Note: *-kaeru* means replacement of s.t. by s.t. else but *-naosu* means redoing of the same thing. For example, *ki-kaeru/ki-gaeru* means to put on different clothing, but *ki-naosu* means to put on the same clothing again, so that it is worn properly.

a. 買ったばかりのテレビの調子が悪いので，取り**換えて**もらった。
(The TV set which I just bought didn't work well, so I had it exchanged.)

b. ソファーの位置が変だったので，置き**換えて**みた。
(The position of the sofa was strange, so we changed the position.)

c. 本棚の本を入れ**換えた**。
(I replaced the books on the shelves.)

d. 新宿で JR 山手線に乗り**換えた**。
(At Shinjuku we transferred to the JR Yamanote Line.)

e. 彼女はきれいな洋服に着**換えた**。
(She changed into a beautiful dress.)

〜かかる[1] v.i. [an event is about to take place] (Gr. 1) begin to ~; be about to ~; almost ~

Notes: 1. The verb is usually a v.i.
2. The verb has to be a non-volitional, punctual verb.
3. ~ *kakaru* can be replaced by ~ *kakeru* without substantial change in meaning. For example, *shini-kakatta* means 'faced death' and *shini-kaketa* means 'was half dead.'

(⇨ ~ *kakeru*[1])

a. 父は若い時に，海でおぼれ**かかった**そうだ。
(I heard that my father almost drowned in the ocean when he was young.)

b. ドアが開き**かかった**が，また閉まってしまった。
(The door began to open, but it closed again.)

c. 僕は車の事故で死に**かかった**。
(I almost died in a car accident.)

d. 森の上に月が出**かかった**。
(The moon was about to come out over the forest.)

e. 月曜日に始めた仕事も金曜日には出来**かかって**いた。
(The work I started on Monday was almost finished on Friday.)

～かかる[2] v.i. [a directed movement works on s.t. / s.o.] (Gr. 1) at; on

a. 道を歩いていたら，男が僕に殴り**かかって**きた。
(When I was walking along the street, a man came to hit me.)

b. 花子は太郎の肩にもたれ**かかった**。
(Hanako leaned on Taro's shoulder.)

c. 犬が子供に飛び**かかった**。
(A dog jumped at a child.)

～かける[1] v.i. / v.t. [an action or a state is about to take place] (Gr. 2) begin to; be about to; almost ~

a. ご飯を食べ**かけた**時に，地震が起きた。
(When I {was about to / just started to} eat my meal, the earthquake occurred.)

b. 父は若い時に，海でおぼれ**かけた**そうだ。
(I was told that my father almost drowned in the ocean when he was young.)

c. 雨が降り**かけた**が，また天気になった。
(It started to rain, but it became fine again.)

d. 飲み**かけた**ビールのコップがテーブルの上にあった。
(There was a glass of beer that someone didn't finish drinking.)

e. ドアが開き**かけた**が，また閉まってしまった。
(The door began to open, but it closed again.)

f. 卒論を書き**かけた**んですが，まだ完成していません。
(I started to write my senior thesis, but I haven't finished it yet.)

～かける[2] v.i. [a communicative action directed toward s.o.] (Gr. 2) at; to

a. 電車で，向こう側に座っていた美人が僕に笑い**かけた**。
(A beautiful lady sitting opposite me in the train smiled at me.)

b. 彼は日本人に会うと日本語で話し**かける**ことにしている。
(He always addresses Japanese people in Japanese when he meets them.)

c. 大統領候補が道行く人に呼び**かけていた**。
(The presidential candidate was speaking to passers-by.)

〜きる v.i. / v.t. [to do s.t. completely] (Gr. 1)

a. トルストイの『戦争と平和』を読み**きった**。
(I read Tolstoy's *War and Peace* completely.)

b. 今月の予算を全部使い**きって**しまった。
(I have used up my entire budget for this month.)

c. これだけの漢字を覚え**きれます**か。
(Can you memorize this many kanji?)

d. 彼女は25マイルマラソンを走り**きった**。
(She finished running the 25-mile marathon.)

〜比べる v.t. [to compare things/persons in a certain manner] (Gr. 2) ~ and compare

a. いろいろなレストランでカレーライスを食べ**比べた**。
(Visiting various restaurants I ate and compared curried rice.)

b. 世界のビールを飲み**比べて**みた。
(I drank (various) kinds of beer from all around the world to compare them.)

c. 子供はケーキの大きさをよく見**比べて**から，大きい方を取った。
(The child compared the size of the cakes with her eyes and took the larger one.)

d. いろいろな新聞を読み**比べて**みたが，やっぱり，ニューヨークタイムズが一番いい。
(I have read various papers and compared them, but after all the New York Times is the best.)

〜消す v.t. [to cancel or negate s.t. in a certain manner] (Gr. 1) cancel; deny

a. 風邪を引いたので，今日の出張を取り**消し**たいんですが。
(I've caught cold, so I would like to cancel today's business trip.)

b. 山田氏は自分から醜聞にからんでいることを強く打ち**消した**。

(Mr. Yamada strongly denied his involvement with the scandal.)

c. 歩行者は吸っていたたばこを足でもみ**消した**。
(The pedestrian rubbed out with his foot the cigarette he was smoking.)

～込む v.i. / v.t. [an action takes place deep in s.t./s.o.] (Gr. 1) into; deeply

a. 知らない男が部屋に入り**込んで**来た。
(A male stranger came into the room.)

b. 昨日は風邪で寝**込んで**しまった。
(Yesterday I was completely down in bed because I had a cold.)

c. 友達と夜遅くまで話し**込んだ**。
(I was deep in conversation with my friend until late at night.)

d. 私 達は朝七時の新幹線に乗り**込んだ**。
(We got into the 7 a.m. bullet train.)

e. 子供がキャンディーを飲み**込んだ**。
(The child swallowed the candy.)

～下げる v.t. [to lower s.t. in a certain manner] down; lower ~

a. 妻はブラインドを引き**下げた**。
(My wife pulled down the blind.)

b. 日本銀行は金利を引き**下げた**。
(The Bank of Japan lowered the interest rate.)

c. 原告は訴 訟 を取り**下げた**。
(The plaintiff withdrew the case.)

～さす v.t. [to leave s.t. half done] (Gr. 1) half ~

Note: V_1 is very much limited.

a. ビールを飲み**さした**コップがテーブルの上にたくさんある。
(On the table are many glasses of beer only half drunk.)

b. 僕は読み**さした**本を膝に置いて寝てしまった。
(I fell asleep with a half-read book on my lap.)

Note: It sounds more natural to say *nomi-sashi no bīru no koppu, yomi-sashi no hon* in (a) and (b), respectively.

〜過ぎる (⇨DBJG: 423–25)

〜過ごす v.t. [to let s.t. negative happen] (Gr. 1) overlook ~; let pass by ~

a. 私は小さな文法の間違いは見**過ごす**。
(I overlook small grammatical errors.)

b. 初めの電車がとても混んでいたので，やり**過ごした**。
(The first train was so crowded that I let it pass by.)

c. 疲れてバスの中で寝ていたら，自分の停留所を乗り**過ごして**しまった。
(I was tired and was sleeping in the bus and ended up by passing my bus stop.)

d. 今朝は寝**過ごして**しまった。
(I overslept this morning.)

〜進む v.i. / v.t. [to go on doing s.t. or to proceed in a certain manner] (Gr. 1) keep on -ing; progress

a. その本は面白いので，どんどん先を読み**進んだ**。
(It was interesting, so I kept on reading it at a fast pace.)

b. 警官は犯人を追いかけて，林の中を突き**進んだ**。
(The policeman dashed through the forest in pursuit of the culprit.)

c. 彼は小説を半分ぐらいまで書き**進んで**きた時，病気になってしまった。
(After he had progressed half way through writing his novel, he fell ill.)

〜進める v.t. [to go on doing s.t.] keep on -ing

Note: V_1 is very much limited.

a. 気が向くままに，小説を書き**進めて**いった。
(I kept on writing the novel as I pleased.)

b. この海底トンネルを完成するために，深さ300メートルまで掘り**進**

めていった。
(To complete this undersea tunnel they kept on digging down till they reached a depth of 300 meters.)

c. この理論の枠組みで研究を推し**進めて**いくつもりだ。
(I intend to continue my research using this theoretical framework.)

～損なう v.i. / v.t. [to fail to do s.t. or to come near doing s.t.] (Gr. 1) fail ~

a. 昨日は忙しくて，パーティーに行き**損ないました**。
(I failed to go to the party, because I was busy last night.)

b. 寝坊していつもの電車に乗り**損なった**。
(I overslept and failed to catch the regular train.)

c. ニューヨークフィルのコンサートを聞き**損なった**。
(I failed to listen to the New York Philharmonic Orchestra's concert.)

Note: In the following example ~ *sokonau* has a meaning of 'almost.'

d. 彼は交通事故で死に**損なった**。
(He was almost killed in a traffic accident.)

～足す v.t. [to do s.t. additionally] (Gr. 1) additionally; add

a. ちょっと付け**足し**たいことがあるんですが，いいですか。
(I have something to add, but is it alright?)

b. 一度書いてから，大分書き**足した**。
(After writing once I have added (in writing) quite a bit.)

c. リンゴを六つ買ったが，あと三つ買い**足した**。
(I bought six apples, then I bought three more.)

～出す[1] (⇨DBJG: 102–04)

～出す[2] v.t. [to take out s.t. in a certain manner] (Gr. 1) ~ out

Note: If V_1 indicates a movement or a process that causes s.t. to come out in the open, any verb can be used with *-dasu*.

a. 男はポケットからナイフを取り**出して**，飛びかかってきた。
(The man took out a knife from his pocket and jumped upon me.)

b. スーパーに買い物に行きますから，買って来て欲しい物を書き**出して**下さい。
(I'm going to the supermarket, so please list the items you want me to buy.)

c. 人々は窓から身を乗り**出して**パレードを見ている。
(People are leaning out of the windows, looking at the parade.)

d. このアイディアは誰が考え**出した**んですか。
(Who came up with this idea?)

e. 彼女に最初に会ったのがどこだったか思い**出せない**。
(I cannot remember where I met her first.)

f. 図書館で日本史の本を借り**出した**。
(I checked out a Japanese history book from the library.)

～立つ v.i. [whatever has been figuratively lying down stands up] (Gr. 1) ~ up

a. あの人の話を聞くと気持ちが奮い**立つ**。
(When I listen to his talk my mind gets stirred up.)

b. 彼女は仕事でパリに向けて飛び**立った**。
(She flew off to (lit. flew up toward) Paris on business.)

c. 父は思い**立つ**とすぐ実行する人だ。
(When my father thinks of doing something, he puts it into practice right away.)

d. 今日は妻と連れ**立って**，映画を見に行った。
(Today I went to see a movie in the company of my wife.)

～足りる v.i. [to be sufficient] (Gr. 2) sufficient; enough

Note: If ~ *tariru* is affirmative, then *michi-tariru* is the only combination, but if ~ *tariru* is negative, V_1 can be any verb, except **shini-tarinai*.

a. 私の生活は満ち**足りて**いる。
(I am fully content with my life.)

b. これだけでは食べ**足りない**。
(This is not enough to eat.)

c. 僕は推理小説が大好きだから，一冊では読み**足りない**。
(I love mystery novels, so it is not enough for me to read just one.)

d. 私は七時間では寝**足りない**。
(For me seven hours of sleep is not sufficient.)

〜違える [to make an error in doing s.t.] (Gr. 2) make a mistake in -ing

a. 私は手紙の趣旨を取り**違えて**いた。
(I misunderstood the point of the letter.)

b. 住所を書き**違えた**ために，手紙は着かなかった。
(Because I made a mistake in writing the address, the letter didn't get there.)

c. 彼女は見**違える**ほどきれいになった。
(She has become so beautiful that I cannot recognize her.)

〜散らす v.t. [to do s.t. without any sense of direction or discretion] (Gr. 1)

a. そんなにどなり**散らさない**で下さい。
(Please don't rant and rave.)

b. 父は機嫌の悪い時は誰にでも当たり**散らした**。
(When my father was in a bad mood, he worked off his bad temper on everybody.)

c. 私の大事な書類に子供が漢字を書き**散らした**。
(My child scribbled kanji on my important papers.)

〜継ぐ v.i. / v.t. [to continue on to s.t. else without a break] (Gr. 1)

Note: V_1 is very much limited.

a. 新宿で成田エクスプレスに乗り**継いで**，成田空港まで行った。
(I transferred to the Narita Express at Shinjuku and went to Narita

Airport.)

b. 川端康成はエピソードをいくつか書き**継いで**『雪国』を完成したそうだ。
(Kawabata Yasunari is said to have completed his *Snow Country* by writing several episodes successively.)

～付ける v.i. / v.t. [to be accustomed to doing s.t.] (Gr. 2)

Notes: 1. V_1 can be any verb as long as it indicates a repeatable action.
2. *tsukeru* in examples (a) and (b) retain the original meaning of 'to attach s.t. to s.t. else.'

a. このタイヤを取り**付けて**くれる？
(Will you put this tire on?)

b. 約束の日を手帳に書き**付けた**。
(I wrote the appointment date in my notebook.)

c. あの町は行き**つけて**いるから，迷いません。
(I'm familiar with that town, so I won't get lost.)

d. 食べ**つけない**ものは食べない方がいい。
(It's better not to eat things you are not used to eating.)

e. このコンピュータは使い**つけて**いるから，問題ありません。
(I'm used to this computer, so there is no problem.)

f. 飛行機は乗り**つけて**いないから，すぐ酔ってしまいます。
(I'm not used to flying, so I get sick easily.)

～続ける v.i. / v.t. [an action continues] (Gr. 2) keep -ing; continue

a. 私は一時間も泳ぎ**続けた**ので，疲れてしまった。
(I kept swimming for as long as one hour, so I got tired.)

b. 今年の梅雨は長い間 雨が降り**続けた**。
(During the rainy season this year it kept raining for a long time.)

c. 私はこれからも日本語を勉強し**続ける**つもりです。
(I intend to keep studying Japanese even from now on.)

〜つぶす v.i. [to crush s.t. in a certain manner or to use s.t. until it becomes useless] (Gr. 1)

Note: ~ *tsubusu* means literally 'to crush s.t. in a certain manner' as in (a)–(c) or it means 'to use s.t. until it becomes useless' as in (d) and (e).

a. ラッシュアワーの電車の中で私は押し**つぶされ**そうになった。
(I almost got crushed in a rush hour train.)

b. 子供が手に持っていたバナナを握り**つぶして**しまった。
(The child crushed the banana he was holding.)

c. 私は台所のゴキブリを踏み**つぶした**。
(I smashed a cockroach in the kitchen by treading on it with my foot.)

d. 僕は今までに車を十台ぐらい乗り**つぶした**。
(Up until now I've gone through (lit. driven and worn out) about ten cars.)

e. 私はジョギングを始めてから，靴を何足履き**つぶした**か知らない。
(Since I started jogging I don't know how many shoes I've worn out.)

〜通す v.i. / v.t. [to continue doing s.t. until the last moment] (Gr. 1) ~ through; finish -ing

a. この本は読み**通す**のに一週間かかってしまった。
(It took me one week to read through this book.)

b. 僕はついに30マイルを走り**通した**。
(I finally finished running 30 miles.)

c. 彼は大学の四年間アルバイトをしながら，頑張り**通した**。
(While working part time, he stuck out four years in college.)

d. その政治家は自分の考えを押し**通した**。
(The politician pushed his ideas through.)

e. ピストルの弾が彼の心臓を突き**通した**。
(The bullet of the pistol pierced through his heart.)

～直す v.i. / v.t. [to do s.t. all over again because of failure or dissatisfaction] (Gr. 1) re-; ~ again

Note: The verb used with *-naosu* is a controllable action verb.

a. 作文を書き**直しました**。
(I rewrote my composition.)

b. 文を読み**直して**みたが，まだ意味がよく分からなかった。
(I read the sentence again, but I still couldn't understand the meaning properly.)

c. 計算が間違っていたようなので，計算をし**直した**。
(My calculation appeared to be wrong, so I did the calculation again.)

d. まだ早かったので，寝**直した**。
(It was still early, so I went to sleep again.)

～流す v.t. [to let s.t. go by] (Gr. 1)

a. ジョギングの後の汗をシャワーで洗い**流した**。
(After jogging I washed away the sweat in the shower.)

b. その子は母親の話を聞き**流して**いた。
(The child paid no attention to what his mother had to say.)

c. 濁流が家屋を押し**流した**。
(The muddy water swept away the houses.)

d. スミス先生は筆で日本語の手紙を書き**流せる**。
(Professor Smith can write letters in Japanese with a brush with ease.)

～慣れる v.i. / v.t. [to be used to do s.t.] (Gr. 2) get used to

a. 住み**慣れた**シカゴを出て，テキサス州のダラスにやって来た。
(I left Chicago, where I had gotten accustomed to living, and came to Dallas, Texas.)

b. 方言は聞き**慣れる**まで時間がかかる。
(It takes time to get used to a dialect.)

c. お母さん，見**慣れない**人達がうちの近くにいたよ。
(Mother, there were strangers near our house.)

d. 履き**慣れない**靴で旅行しない方がいい。
(It is better not to go on a trip wearing shoes you are not used to.)

e. 使い**慣れた**ワープロが壊れてしまった。
(The word processor I am used to got broken.)

f. 通い**慣れた**四キロの道を毎日会社まで自転車で行く。
(I go to the company every day riding a bike on the street I am used to.)

g. ホームステイの小さい子供達とも話し**慣れて**きた。
(I've become used to talking with the small children in my home stay family.)

～抜ける v.i. [to go through some place by doing s.t.] through

Note: V_1 is a verb of motion. If V_1 isn't a verb of motion, the compound has a metaphorical meaning.

a. 大きな公園を走り**抜ける**と，オフィス街だった。
(When I ran through the big park, there was an office area.)

b. 正門を通り**抜ける**と，正 面に講堂があります。
(If you go through the front gate, there is an auditorium in front of you.)

c. トンネルをくぐり**抜け**たら，海が見えてきた。
(When we passed through the tunnel, the ocean came into view.)

d. この困難を切り**抜ける**ためにはかなりの努 力が必要だ。
(To pull through this difficulty we need to make enormous efforts.)

e. ジョンはメアリーの嘘が見**抜け**なかった。
(John was not able to see through Mary's lies.)

～残す v.t. [to leave s.t./s.o. behind after doing s.t.]

Note: V_1 is almost limited to *taberu* 'eat,' *kaku* 'write,' *iu* 'say' and *toru* 'take.'

a. 食べ**残して**はいけません。
(Don't leave your food half-eaten.)

b. 書き**残した**ことがあるから，明日また書きます。
(There are some things I omitted writing about, so I will write you again tomorrow.)

c. 言い**残した**ことが一つあります。
(There is one thing that I failed to say.)

d. せめて新聞ぐらい読まないと，時代に取り**残されて**しまいますよ。
(If you do not at least read newspapers, you will be left behind the times.)

e. 昨日ビデオで見**残した**部分を今晩見るつもりだ。
(I intend to watch the portion of the video I didn't watch yesterday.)

f. 人生を十分楽しんだから，思い**残す**ことは一つもない。
(I have nothing to regret, because I have enjoyed my life very much.)

〜残る v.i. [to remain where s.o./s.t. is now] (Gr. 1)

a. 私は会社に十一時ごろまで居**残って**仕事をした。
(I stayed behind at the office till about 11 o'clock and did my work.)

b. その飛行機事故で生き**残った**人はたった三人だった。
(The survivors of the plane crash were just three.)

c. 九月だというのに，藤の花がまだ咲き**残って**いる。
(Even though it is September, the wisteria flowers are still in bloom.)

d. デパートでは売れ**残った**夏の衣服の安売りをしていた。
(At the department store they were selling unsold summer clothing at cheap prices.)

e. 私の母校は高校野球の試合で準決勝まで勝ち**残った**。
(My alma mater won its way to a semifinal game in the high

school baseball tournament.)

～始める (⇨DBJG: 131–33)

～回る v.i. [to move around] (Gr. 1)

Note: V_1 is limited to a movement verb such as *aruku* ‘walk,’ *tobu* ‘fly,’ *hashiru* ‘run’ and *ugoku* ‘move.’

a. 今日は忙しくて一日中都内を歩き**回ってい**た。
(I was very busy today walking around the city of Tokyo all day long.)

b. 彼は証券会社に勤めていて，世界を飛び**回ってい**る。
(He is working for a securities company and flying around the world.)

c. アメリカの大学のキャンパスでは，リスが走り**回ってい**る。
(On American college campuses squirrels are running around.)

d. よく動き**回る**ことは健康にいい。
(To be always on the go is good for your health.)

～戻す v.i. [to bring s.o./s.t. back to an original place in a certain manner] (Gr. 1) ~ back

Note: V_1 is almost limited to *yobu* ‘call,’ *harau* ‘pay’ and *okuru* ‘send.’

a. 社長はニューヨークに出張中の部下を東京に呼び**戻した**。
(The president recalled his subordinate to Tokyo from New York where he was sent on business.)

b. 一度買ったコンサートの切符は払い**戻して**くれませんよ。
(Once you buy a concert ticket they will not refund it, you know.)

c. 友達に送った小包が住所不明で送り**戻されて**来た。
(The package I sent to my friend came back because the address could not be located.)

d. 一度売った車を買い**戻した**。
(I bought back the car which I once sold.)

～止む v.i. [s.t. uncontrollable comes to its end] (Gr. 1) stop -ing; ceases to ~

Note: V_1 is very much limited.

a. 雨が降り**止んだ**。
(It stopped raining.)

b. 赤ん坊が泣き**止んだ**。
(The baby stopped crying.)

c. 雷が鳴り**止んだ**。
(The thunder stopped rolling.)

～寄る v.i. [to approach s.o. closely in a certain manner] (Gr. 1)

a. 男は女にしつこく言い**寄った**。
(The man persistently wooed the woman.)

b. 犬がしっぽを振りながら走り**寄って**来た。
(A dog came running toward me wagging his tail.)

c. 日米関係はお互いに歩み**寄らなければ**改善されない。
(The Japan-US relationship won't improve unless both countries move closer to each other.)

d. お暇な時にお立ち**寄り**下さい。
(Please drop by when you have time.)

(⇨DBJG: Appendix 4B (589–90) & F (593))

～分ける v.t. [to distinguish s.t. in a certain manner] (Gr. 2)

Note: V_1 is often a verb of perception such as *kiku* 'hear,' *miru* "see,' *kagu* 'smell' and *nomu* 'drink.' But the verb of perceptions such as *kanjiru* 'feel,' *fureru* 'touch' and *ajiwau* 'taste' cannot be the V_1.

a. 私は東京方言と大阪方言は聞き**分けられる**。
(I can tell the difference (by hearing) between the Tokyo dialect and the Osaka dialect.)

b. 中国人，韓国人，日本人を見**分ける**のは難しい。

(It is hard to tell the difference (by looking) among Chinese, Korean and Japanese people.)

c. 彼女は香水をかぎ**分けられる**。
(She can identify perfumes by smelling them.)

d. スミスさんはアメリカのいろいろな方言が使い**分けられる**。
(Mr. Smith can use various American dialects properly.)

e. いろいろなご馳走が盛り**分けられて**，出てきた。
(Various delicacies came out served on separate dishes.)

～忘れる v.t. [to forget to do s.t.] (Gr. 2)

a. 答案に名前を書き**忘れた**。
(I forgot to write my name on the answer sheet.)

b. 言い**忘れましたが**，今晩うちでパーティーがありますから，どうぞいらして下さい。
(I forgot to mention that there is a party at our home. Please come along.)

c. ああそうだ。電話番号を聞き**忘れた**。
(Oh, yeah. I forgot to ask the telephone number.)

d. 電気を消し**忘れた**。
(I forgot to turn off the light.)

e. 鍵をかけ**忘れた**。
(I forgot to lock it.)

Note: The following example doesn't mean to 'forget to do s.t.' but it has a specific meaning of 'misplace.'

f. 電車の網棚にかばんを置き**忘れた**。
(I left my bag on the rack of the train.)

Appendix 3 **Compound Particles**

a. Definition

While "content words," such as nouns, verbs, and adjectives, convey content information about people, things, their actions and states, etc., "function words," such as particles and conjunctions, indicate grammatical relations between sentence elements or propositional relations between statements. Compound particles are function words which consist of two or more words and function as single particles in that they are interpreted as a unit rather than word by word.

b. Common structures

Common structures for compound particles are as follows:

(1) Prt. + V*te*（の）/ V*masu* / Vinf·nonpast. (Exs. に関(かん)して(の); に関し; に関する)

(2) Prt. + N + Prt. （Exs. のために; を中心(ちゅうしん)に）

(3) N + Prt. （Exs. 次第(しだい)で; 上(うえ)で）

c. Preceding elements

Many compound particles mark only nouns; some compound particles mark verbs or sentences as well as nouns; [N _], [V _], [S _], and [Sq _] indicate what element precedes the compound particle. (Sq indicates an interrogative sentence.)

d. Forms

Compound particles appear either in preverbal or prenominal forms. Compound particles in preverbal forms modify the following verbal, and compound particles in prenominal forms modify the following noun. Prenominal forms are listed with N at the end of the compound particle (e.g., に関するN).

e. Topic marker

Some preverbal compound particles are followed by the topic marker *wa* to introduce topical phrases. (Exs. にかけては; については)

f. Formal forms

In formal speech, Prt. + V*masu mashite* is occasionally used instead of Prt. + V*te*. (Exs. におきまして; につきましては)

g. More notations

＝: Expressions which are interchangeable

≈: Expressions which are similar but not always interchangeable

---

The entries below are listed in *a-i-u-e-o* order.

上で [V _] upon; after; in -ing

よく考えた**上で**御返事します。

(I will respond to you after thinking it over.)

この辞書は日本語を勉強する**上で**大変役に立つ。

(This dictionary is very useful in studying Japanese.)

(⇨ ***ue de***)

ことで [V _] by V-ing; because; result in; cause

私は週末にゴルフをする**ことで**気分転換を図っています。

(I try to lift my spirits by playing golf on weekends.)

彼が仲裁の場に出ていった**ことで**事態は余計にこじれた。

(The situation got even more complicated because he appeared at the mediation scene.)

(⇨ ***koto de***)

ことに{よって / より} ＝ことで

次第で [N _] depending on

努力**次第で**日本の小説が原文で読めるようになりますよ。

(Depending on your effort, you can (lit. will become able to) read Japanese novels in Japanese.)

と逆に; と逆のN [N _] against; contrary to; reverse; opposite

風が我々の進行方向**と逆に**吹いている。

(The wind is blowing against us (lit. against the direction of our course).)

彼は私**と逆の**見方をした。

(He viewed it in the opposite way from me.)

と比べ(て) = に比べ(て)

と{異なって / 異なり}; と異なるN / と異なったN = と{違って / 違い}; と違うN / と違ったN

Note: と異なって is more formal than と違って.

として [N _] as; in the capacity of

田中さんはセールスマン**として**採用された。

(Mr. Tanaka was hired as a salesman.)

プラスチックはガラスに代わる材料**として**広く利用されている。

(Plastic is widely used as a substitute (lit. a substitute material) for glass.)

(⇨ ***to shite*** (DBJG: 501))

としては [N _] for

これは日本のアパート**としては**大きい方です。

(For a Japanese apartment, this is one of the bigger ones.)

(⇨ ***to shite wa*** (DBJG: 502–03))

と{違って / 違い}; と違うN / と違ったN [N _] unlike; different from

野口さんは私**と違って**手先が器用だ。

(Unlike me, Mr. Noguchi is skilled with his hands.)

ジョンは私**と違った**考えを持っている。

(John has different ideas from mine.)

と同時に [N / V _] at the (same) time; when; as; while; as well as

彼女は結婚**と同時に**会社を辞めた。

(She quit her company at the time of her marriage.)

部屋に入る**と同時に**電話が鳴った。

(The telephone rang as I entered the room.)

彼はこの会社の社長であると**同時に**大株主でもある。
(He is the president of this company and, at the same time, a big stockholder.)

(⇨ ***to dōji ni***)

と共に [N / V _] as well as; with; along with; at the same time; when; as; while

原子力は石油**と共に**重要なエネルギー源だ。
(Atomic energy, as well as petroleum, is an important energy source.)

武士階級は封建制**と共に**滅びた。
(The *samurai* class died with the feudal system.)

病気が回復する**と共に**食欲も出てきた。
(As I recover from my illness, my appetite is coming back.)

(⇨ ***to tomo ni***)

と{並んで / 並び}; と並ぶN [N _] as well as

サッカーは今や野球**と並んで**日本の代表的スポーツだ。
(Soccer, as well as baseball, is now one of the major sports in Japan.)

鷗外は漱石**と並ぶ**日本文学の巨峰だ。
(Ogai, as well as Soseki, is a giant in Japanese literature (lit. a giant peak in Japanese literature who stands side by side with Soseki).)

と並行して [N _] parallel to

ハイウェーが鉄道**と並行して**走っている。
(The highway runs parallel to the railway.)

なしで(は) [N _] without

この町では車**なしでは**生活できない。
(In this town you cannot live without a car.)

(⇨ ***nashi de wa***)

なしに(は) [N _] without

政府の援助**なしには**この事業は進められない。
(This project cannot be advanced without support from the govern-

ment.)

(⇨ ***nashi de wa***)

に{当たって / 当たり}; に当たってのN ≈ に際し(て)

[N / V _] when; at; in; on the occasion of; before; prior to

ドイツ留学**に当たって**田中先生の助言を受けた。
(Before studying in Germany, I received advice from Prof. Tanaka.)

新しい事業を始める**に当たって**，二千万円ほどの資金を確保しなければならない。
(Before starting a new business, I have to secure ¥20,000,000 in funds.)

新社長の就任**に当たっての**あいさつは社員に感銘を与えたようだ。
(The new president's speech (lit. greeting) on the occasion of the assumption of his duties appears to have moved the employees.)

緊急**に{*当たって / 際して}の**処置をよく習得しておいて下さい。
(Please master how to deal with (the situation in case of) an emergency.)

(⇨ ***ni atatte/atari***)

に合わせて [N _] according to; to

予算**に合わせて**家具を選んだ。
(We selected furniture according to our budget.)

私達は音楽**に合わせて**踊った。
(We danced to the music.)

において; におけるN / においてのN [N _] at; on; in; during

来年の総会はシカゴのヒルトン・ホテル**において**行われる。
(Next year's general meeting will be held at the Hilton Hotel in Chicago.)

コンピュータは近い将来**において**ほとんどの家庭に行き渡るだろう。
(Computers will probably spread to almost every household in the near future.)

木村博士は遺伝学**における**権威者として知られている。
(Dr. Kimura is known as an authority in (the field of) genetics.)

(⇨ ***ni oite/okeru***)

に応じ(て); に応じたN / に応じてのN [N _] in proportion to; in accordance with; according to; depending on; in compliance with; in response to

業績**に応じて**従業員全員にボーナスが支給された。

(Bonuses were paid to all the employees according to their performances.)

組合の要求**に応じて**標準就業時間が短縮されることになった。

(In compliance with the union's request, it has been decided that the standard working hours will be reduced.)

収入**に応じた**住居を選ぶべきです。

(You should choose a house according to your income.)

にかかわらず ≈ によらず

[N / Sq _] regardless of; independently of; whether or not

この会社では性別**にかかわらず**，同様に昇進できる。

(In this company people can be promoted equally regardless of sex.)

我々は助成金が下りるかどうか**にかかわらず**，このプロジェクトを進めるつもりだ。

(We will advance this project whether we get a grant or not.)

誰に{***かかわらず / よらず**}，規則を犯した者は罰せられる。

(Regardless of who it is, a person who violates the rules will be punished.)

にかかわるN [N _] related to; concerning

これは生死**にかかわる**重大事だ。

(This is an important matter which concerns life and death.)

に限らず [N _] not limited to; not only

見合結婚は日本**に限らず**，ほかの国でも行われている。

(Arranged marriage is not limited to Japan; it is practiced in other countries, too.)

(⇨ ***ni kagirazu***)

に限って [N _] the last; particular; only

彼**に限って**そんなことはしない。
(He is the last person to do such a thing.)

その日**に限って**妙子は留守だった。
(It was one of the rare days when Taeko was not home.)

忙しい時**に限って**よく電話がかかってくる。
(I get a lot of phone calls only when I am busy.)

(⇨ ***ni kagitte***)

にかけて(は) [N _] to; over; when it comes to; in; at; in the matter of; as for

今日，東海から関東**にかけて**，大雨が降った。
(There was heavy rain today covering Tokai and Kanto (lit. from Tokai to Kanto).)

週末**にかけて**ワシントンに行きます。
(I'm going to Washington, D.C. over the weekend.)

金もうけ**にかけては**，正男は天才だ。
(When it comes to money-making, Masao is a genius.)

に{代わって / 代わり}; に代わるN / に代わってのN [N _] for; in place of; instead of; replacing; on behalf of

病気の山田先生**に代わって**，鈴木先生が教えて下さった。
(In place of Prof. Yamada, who is ill, Prof. Suzuki taught us.)

科学者は石油**に代わる**エネルギー源を探している。
(Scientists are looking for an energy source to replace oil.)

(⇨ ***ni kawatte***; ***kawari ni*** (DBJG: 184–87))

に関し(て(は)); に関するN / に関してのN [N _] concerning; with regard to; with respect to; regarding; about; on; as for; as to; in terms of; in connection with; in reference to

消費税**に関して**与野党の意見が対立した。
(With regard to the sales tax, the opinions of the leading party and the

opposition parties conflicted.)

人間の言語習得**に関しては**まだ不明のことが多い。

(Concerning human language acquisition, there are still many unknown things.)

先週東京で超伝導**に関する**学会が開かれた。

(Last week a conference on superconductivity was held in Tokyo.)

(⇨ ***ni kanshite/kansuru***)

に関する限り [N _] as far as ~ is concerned

この事件**に関する限り**彼は無実だ。

(As far as this incident is concerned, he is innocent.)

(⇨ ***kagiri***[1])

に比べ(て) [N _] compared with / to; when compared with / to; in comparison to

今年は去年**に比べて**雨の日が多いようだ。

(In comparison to last year, we seem to have more rainy days this year.)

(⇨ ***ni kuraberu to/kurabete***)

に加え(て) [N _] in addition to

彼女は美貌**に加えて**演技力がすばらしい。

(In addition to her beauty, she has superb acting talent.)

に際し(て); に際してのN ≈ に{当たって / 当たり}; に当たってのN

[N / V _] in case of; on; when; at; in

この実験**に際して**何人かのアメリカの専門家の協力を得た。

(In this experiment we obtained cooperation from some American experts.)

日本を離れる**に際し**家財道具を全部処分した。

(When leaving Japan, I got rid of all my household goods.)

緊急**に{際して / *当たって}の**処置をよく習得しておいて下さい。

(Please master how to deal with (the situation in case of) an emergency.)

に{従って / 従い} [N / V _] as; with; in accordance with; in proportion to; following

沢田は社長の命令**に従って**ただちにマニラに飛んだ。

(In accordance with the president's order, Sawada flew to Manila immediately.)

日本の経済力が強くなる**に従って**日本語学習者が増えてきた。

(As Japan's economic power gets stronger, the number of Japanese language learners has increased.)

(⇨ ***ni shitagatte/shitagai***)

にしては [N / V _] for; considering that

今日は八月**にしては**涼しい。

(For August, it's cool today.)

彼はアメリカの大学で学位を取った**にしては**英語が下手だ。

(Considering that he received a degree from an American university, his English is poor.)

(⇨ ***ni shite wa*** (DBJG: 309–10))

に沿って; に沿ったN / に沿ってのN [N _] along; by; parallel to; in accordance with

道路は海岸**に沿って**走っている。

(The road runs along the shore.)

指導書**に沿った**教え方をして下さい。

(Please teach in accordance with the teacher's manual.)

に対し(て(は)); に対するN / に対してのN [N _] toward; to; for; against; in; per; in contrast with / to; compared with; while; whereas; with regard to; about

日本は外国**に対して**閉鎖的な政策を取ってきた。

(Japan has adopted a closed policy toward foreign countries up to now.)

アメリカでは離婚**に対する**考え方が大分変わってきた。

(People's views about divorce have changed considerably in America.)

日本人はグループや社会を大切にするの**に対し**，アメリカ人は個人を大切にする。
(While the Japanese value groups and society, Americans value individuals.)

(⇨ ***ni taishite***)

に{ついて(は) / つき}; についてのN　　[N _]　about; on; over; concerning; regarding; with regard to; respecting; with respect to; as to; as for

日本の選挙制度**について**話していただけませんか。
(Could you talk about the Japanese election system?)

明治天皇**についての**資料を集めています。
(I'm gathering (research) materials on Emperor Meiji.)

(⇨ ***ni tsuite***)

につき　　[N _]　a; per; for; on; to

この仕事は一時間**につき**六ドルもらえる。
(This job will pay you six dollars an hour.)

間違い一つ**につき**一点減点します。
(I'll take one point off for each mistake.)

(⇨ ***ni tsuki***)

につれ(て)　　[N / V _]　as; with; in proportion to; accompanied by

このあたりは季節の変化**につれて**景色がいろいろに変わる。
(The scenery changes in a variety of ways here as the seasons change.)

年をとる**につれて**体力が衰えてくる。
(As one grows old, one loses physical strength.)

(⇨ ***ni tsurete***)

にとって　　[N _]　to; for

これは我々**にとって**無視出来ない問題だ。
(For us this is a problem which cannot be ignored.)

吉岡博士を失ったことは我々のプロジェクト**にとって**致命的な打撃だ。
(The loss of Dr. Yoshioka is a fatal blow to our project.)

(⇨ ***ni totte***)

に反し(て); に反するN [N _] contrary to; in contrast to; against; in violation of; while; whereas

会議は予想**に反して**出席者が少なかった。

(Contrary to expectations, few people attended the meeting.)

テレビは輸出が伸びているの**に反して**国内の売れ行きが伸び悩んでいる。

(In contrast to the increase in exports of TV sets, the increase in domestic sales is slow.)

今回の選挙は一般の予想**に反する**結果に終わった。

(The election this time ended up with results which contradicted the general prediction.)

(⇨ ***ni hanshite/hansuru***)

に{伴って / 伴い}; に伴うN [N / V _] as; along with; with; accompanying; attendant upon

人口の急増**に伴って**, いろいろの問題が出てきた。

(With the rapid increase in population, various problems emerged.)

景気が回復する**に伴い**失業率が下がってきた。

(As the economy recovers, the unemployment rate is decreasing.)

医者はその手術**に伴う**危険を患者の家族に説明した。

(The doctor explained the risks of the operation to the patient's family.)

には [N / V _] for; to; in order to

外国語の勉強**には**テープレコーダーが欠かせない。

(A tape recorder is indispensable for foreign language studies.)

頭痛**には**この薬がよく効きます。

(This medicine works well for headaches.)

そこへ行く**には**地下鉄が一番便利です。

(The subway is the most convenient way to get there.)

(⇨ ***ni wa***)

に比し(て) = に比べ(て)

Note: に比し(て) is more formal than に比べ(て).

に向かって [N _] toward; to; at; heading for

台風は時速三十キロの速さで北**に向かって**進んでいる。

(The typhoon is advancing toward the north at a speed of 30 kilometers per hour.)

に向け(て); に向けてのN [N _] toward; for; aimed at

和男は来年の大学入試**に向けて**猛勉強している。

(Kazuo is working very hard for the college entrance exams next year.)

現在，石油に代わる新しいエネルギー開発**に向けての**研究が進められている。

(Research aimed at the development of new energy to replace oil is presently underway.)

にもかかわらず [N / S _] in spite of; despite; although; though

激しい雨**にもかかわらず**，サッカーの試合は続いた。

(Despite the fierce rain, the soccer game continued.)

弘は美樹を深く愛していた**にもかかわらず**，結婚しなかった。

(In spite of the fact that Hiroshi loved Miki deeply, he didn't marry her.)

(⇨ ***ni mo kakawarazu***)

に{基づいて / 基づき}; に基づくN / に基づいたN [N _] based on

この報告はアンケート調査**に基づいて**書かれたものである。

(This report was (written) based on a (questionnaire) survey.)

これは五百年前の史料**に基づく**研究だ。

(This is a study based on historical documents from 500 years ago.)

(⇨ ***ni motozuite/motozuku***)

に{よって / より}; によるN [N / Sq _] due to; owing to; because of; according to; depending on; from ~ to ~; by; by means of; with; on the basis of

戦争**によって**父を亡くした。
(I lost my father due to the war.)

先生**によって**教え方が違う。
(Teaching methods differ from teacher to teacher.)

どこに泊まるか**によって**費用が大分変わる。
(The cost differs considerably depending on where you stay.)

この研究所は日本政府**によって**設立された。
(This research institute was established by the Japanese government.)

武力ではなく，話し合い**による**解決が望まれる。
(A resolution not by force but by discussion is hoped for.)

によらず ≈ にかかわらず

[N _] regardless of; independently of; (what)ever it may be; whether or not

この会社は学歴**によらず**，実力さえあれば大きな仕事をさせてくれる。
(If you are capable, this company assigns you important tasks regardless of your educational background.)

採否**によらず**結果は連絡します。
(We'll inform you of the results whether we hire you or not.)

誰に｛**よらず / *かかわらず**｝規則を犯した者は罰せられる。
(Regardless of who it is, a person who violates the rules will be punished.)

によると [N _] according to

新聞**によると**，昨日フロリダに雪が降ったそうだ。
(According to the newspaper, it snowed in Florida yesterday.)
(⇨ ***sōda***[1], Note 2 (DBJG: 409))

に｛わたって / わたり｝; にわたるN / にわたってのN [N _] extending for / over / through; for; over

百メートル**にわたって**堤防が崩れた。
(The break in the levee extended for 100 meters. (lit. The levee was

broken extending over100 meters.))

そのドラマは一週間**にわたり**放映された。

(The drama was telecast for one week.)

二か月**にわたる**ミュージカルの興行が先週終わった。

(The musical, whose run was extended for two months, ended last week.)

の上で(は) [N _] as far as ~ is concerned; as far as ~ goes; from the viewpoint of; according to; in terms of

この計画は書類**の上では**問題なさそうだ。

(There seems to be no problem with this plan as far as the documents are concerned.)

(⇨ ***no ue de wa***)

の代わりに; の代わりのN = に代わって / 代わり; に代わるN / に代わってのN

(⇨ ***kawari ni*** (DBJG: 184–87))

の結果 [N _] as a result of; after; upon

相談**の結果**，今回の旅行は延期することになった。

(After discussion, it's been decided that this trip will be postponed.)

調査**の結果**，新しい事実が発見された。

(As a result of the investigation, new facts emerged.)

(⇨ ***kekka***)

の際(に) [N _] at the time of; when

入室**の際に**身分証明書の提示を求められた。

(I was asked to show my ID when I entered the room.)

お出かけ**の際に**は鍵をフロントにお預け下さい。

(Please leave your key at the front desk when you go out.)

(⇨ ***sai*** (***ni***))

のせいで [N _] because of; due to

今年は不況**のせいで**車があまり売れない。

(Because of the recession, cars are not selling well this year.)

(⇨ ***sei***)

の度に [N _] every time; each time

私は試験**の度に**漢字を復習しなければならない。

(I have to review kanji every time we have a test.)

(⇨ ***tabi ni***)

のため(に); のためのN [N _] for the purpose of; in order to; because of; owing to; for the benefit of; for the sake of; on behalf of

来年研究**のために**日本へ行く予定です。

(I'm planning to go to Japan for research next year.)

州の財政難**のために**学校が閉鎖された。

(The school was closed because of the state budget shortage.)

田中先生は日本へ行く学生**のために**オリエンテーションをした。

(Prof. Tanaka gave an orientation for the students who are going to Japan.)

今外国人**のための**和英辞典を書いています。

(I'm writing a Japanese-English dictionary for foreigners.)

(⇨ ***ni yotte/yori***, Related Expression III; ***tame*** (***ni***) (DBJG: 447–51))

のほかに [N _] besides; other than

日本語と英語**のほかに**何か話せますか。

(Can you speak any languages other than Japanese and English?)

の下で [N _] in; with; under

私は鈴木先生の指導**の下で**修士論文を書き上げた。

(I finished my master's thesis with Prof. Suzuki's guidance.)

(⇨ ***no moto de***)

をおいて [N _] except; but; other than

この仕事が出来る人はブラウンさん**をおいて**ほかにない。

(There is no one else but Mr. Brown who can do this job.)

を介し(て); を介したN / を介するN / を介してのN ≈ を通し(て); を通し

たN / を通してのN

[N _] by way of; through

私達は弁護士**を介して**その問題を協議した。

(We discussed the matter through our lawyers.)

私は友達**を介して**この仕事を紹介してもらった。

(I was introduced to this job through one of my friends.)

通訳**を介して**の話し合いだったので，こちらの意図が十分相手に伝わったかどうか心もとない。

(Because it was a discussion using (lit. through) an interpreter, we are unsure about whether or not our ideas were fully conveyed to the other party.)

これらの写真**を{*介して / 通して}**当時の人々の生活を偲ぶことが出来る。

(Through these photos we can relive the lives of people in those days.)

を中心に [N _] around; with ~ as the center

地球は太陽**を中心に**回っている。

(The earth revolves around the sun.)

今度の台風は関東**を中心に**大雨を降らせた。

(The last typhoon brought heavy rain around the Kanto area.)

を通じ(て); を通じてのN ≈ を通し(て); を介し(て); を通したN / を通してのN; を介したN / を介してのN

[N _] through; throughout

知り合い**を通じて**木村氏に面会を申し込んだ。

(I asked for an interview with Mr. Kimura through an acquaintance.)

これは上司**を通じて**の申し込みなので断るわけにはいかない。

(Because this request was delivered by my boss, I cannot turn it down.)

壁**を{*通じて / 通して}**隣の部屋の話し声が聞こえる。

(I hear conversations from next door through the wall.)

この島は一年**を{通じて / *介して}**気候が温暖だ。

(This island's climate is warm throughout the year.)

を通し(て); を通したN / を通してのN ≈ を通じ(て); を介し(て); を通じてのN; を介したN / を介するN / を介してのN

[N _] through; throughout; by means of; via

知り合い**を通して**木村氏に面会を申し込んだ。

(I asked for an interview with Mr. Kimura through an acquaintance.)

電話**を通した**声は肉声と大分違う。

(Sounds (lit. Voices) via the telephone are considerably different from natural ones.)

壁を{**通して / *通じて**}隣の部屋の話し声が聞こえる。

(I hear conversations from next door through the wall.)

この島は一年**を**{**通して / *介して**}気候が温暖だ。

(This island's climate is warm throughout the year.)

(⇨ ***o tōshite/tsūjite***)

を{除いて / 除き}; を除くN / を除いたN [N _] excluding; except (for); but

私**を除いて**ここには誰も日本語の分かる者がいない。

(Except for me, there is no one who understands Japanese here.)

ケンとスーザン**を除いた**クラスの全員が留学経験者だ。

(Everyone in the class but Ken and Susan have study-abroad experience.)

をはじめ(として); をはじめとするN / をはじめとしたN [N _] including; and other; starting with

レーザーは，CD**をはじめ(として)**，我々の身の回りのものにも広く応用されている。

(Laser (technology) is widely applied to commodities around us, too, including CDs.)

アメリカ**をはじめとする**先進国の首脳がその会議に出席した。

(The leaders from America and other advanced countries attended the meeting.)

(⇨ ***o hajime (to shite)***)

を経て [N _] by way of; via; through

その飛行機はロンドン**を経て**ベルリンへ向かう。
(The plane is going to Berlin via London.)

クリントン氏はアーカンソー州知事**を経て**大統領になった。
(Mr. Clinton became president after serving as governor of Arkansas.)

を目指し(て); を目指したN / を目指してのN [N _] aiming at; heading for; toward; for

健二は国立大学**を目指して**勉強している。
(Kenji is studying to enter (lit. aiming at) a state university.)

我々はクリーンなエネルギー**を目指した**研究に取り組んでいる。
(We are engaged in research into (lit. aiming at) clean energy.)

をもって [N _] with; by means of; using; as of

この領収書**をもって**保証書に代えさせていただきます。
(We use this receipt as a warranty (lit. replace a warranty with this receipt).)

これ**をもって**本大会を閉会します。
(With this we will close this meeting.)

島田氏は一月一日**をもって**我が社の社長に就任されます。
(Mr. Shimada will become our company president as of January 1.)

を基に(して); を基にしたN / を基にしてのN = に{基づいて / 基づき}

Appendix 4 **Conjunctions**

There are two types of conjunctions: *coordinate conjunctions* which serve to connect independent sentences and *subordinate conjunctions* which serve to connect two sentences into a single complex sentence. The coordinate conjunctions of S_1. *Conj.* S_2 structure as instanced by Exs.(1a, b) below are particularly important, because the proper use of such conjunctions is essential for forming a paragraph, a discourse unit consisting of meaningfully arranged independent sentences.

(1) a. 私は今朝ひどく頭が痛かった。**だから**，会社に行かなかった。
(I had a severe headache this morning. So I didn't go to work.)

b. 日本へ行って日本語を勉強したい。**しかし**，旅費が高くて行けない。
(I want to study Japanese in Japan. But the travel cost is so expensive that I cannot go there.)

In view of the importance of the coordinate conjunctions in discourse, this segment addresses specifically the classification, meaning / function and uses of the coordinate conjunctions that combine independent sentences. For the subordinate conjunctions, see the following items in DBJG and in this volume:
ato de (DBJG: 78–80), *ba* (DBJG: 81–83), *kagiri*[1] (82–85), *kara*[2] (DBJG: 177–78), *kara*[3] (DBJG: 179–81), *kara to itte* (103–05), *ka to iu to* (114–16), (*no*) *kawari ni* (116–21), *kekka* (121–23), *keredo*(*mo*) (DBJG: 187–88), *kuseni* (155–58), *mae ni* (DBJG: 231–33), *nagara* (DBJG: 269–70), *nagara*(*mo*) (199–202), *nara* (DBJG: 281–84), *ni atatte/atari* (237–41), *ni mo kakawarazu* (257–60), *ni shitagatte/shitagai* (268–71), *ni tsurete* (285–88), *ni wa* (289–92), *node* (DBJG: 328–31), *noni*[1] (DBJG: 331–35), *noni*[2] (DBJG: 335–37), *sai* (*ni*) (369–74), *tabi ni* (442–44), *-tara* (DBJG: 452–57), *tatte* (DBJG: 461–63), *te mo* (DBJG: 468–70), *te wa* (461–63), *to*[4] (DBJG: 480–82), *to dōji ni* (471–74), *to itte mo* (474–77), *to iu noni* (484–87), *to iu yori* (*wa*) (495–97), *to naru to* (512–14), *to tomo ni* (532–35), *totan* (*ni*) (525–28), *uchi ni* (DBJG: 512–15), (*no*) *ue de* (547–50), and *ue* (*ni*) (551–53)

The coordinate conjunctions are further classified according to their general meanings into eight subcategories:

(A) Conjunctions which indicate CAUSE & EFFECT, REASON & RESULT, SITUATION & RESULT:

かく(し)て，こうして，したがって，すると，そこで，その結果，そのため(に)，それで，それ故(に)，だから，ですから

(B) Conjunctions which mean 'BUT':

(だ)けど，けれども，しかし，そのくせ，それでも，それなのに，それにしては，それにしても，だが，だからと言って，ただ，ただし，ですが，ですけ(れ)ども，でも，ところが，とは言うものの，とは言え，とは言っても，(それ)にもかかわらず，もっとも

(C) Conjunctions which mean 'AND':

おまけに，しかも，そ(う)して，その上(に)，それから，それと，それに，そればかりか，そればかりでなく，また

(D) Conjunctions which mean 'OR':

あるいは，それとも，または

(E) Conjunctions which mean 'TO CHANGE THE SUBJECT':

さて，それはそうと，ときに，ところで，話変わって，話は変わります{が / け(れ)ど}

(F) Conjunctions which indicate PARAPHRASING:

言い換えると，言い換えれば，結局，つまり，要するに

(G) Conjunctions which mean 'FOR EXAMPLE':

例えば，例を挙げると

(H) Conjunctions which mark A REASON FOR SOMETHING:

と言いますのは，と言うのは，なぜかって言うと，なぜかと言うと，なぜかと言えば，なぜなら(ば)

(I) Conjunctions which indicate CONTRAST:

一方，他方，それに対して

Examples and meanings of the eight types of coordinate conjunctions are given. (For the items already explained in DBJG or in this volume, the page number is given.)

(A) Conjunctions which indicate CAUSE & EFFECT, REASON & RESULT, SITUATION & RESULT:

かく(し)て / manner & result <w> /

プリンストンの町はアメリカ独立戦争の古戦場の一つだった。しかし，1756年にプリンストン大学が移ってからは静かな大学町として発展してきた。{**こうして** / **かく(し)て**}，今では，高等研究所をはじめ，研究機関の所在地としてよく知られている。

(The town of Princeton was one of the battlefields during the War of Independence. It has developed as a quiet college town since Princeton University moved there in 1756. As a result of this, now it is well known as a site of research institutes, including the Center for Advanced Studies.)

こうして / manner & result /

したがって / reason & result <very fml> / (395–97)

先学期はあまり勉強しなかった。**したがって**，成績も悪かった。
(Last semester I didn't study much. So my grades were bad.)

すると / events & unexpected situations; situation & prediction / (DBJG: 437–39)

私が別れようと言った。**すると**彼女は泣き出した。
(I told her that we should break up. Then she started to cry.)

そこで / situation & result / (401–05)

おじいさんが大学卒業の日に，3,000ドルくれた。**そこで**，僕は日本へ行くことにした。
(My grandfather gave me $3,000 on my college graduation day. So I decided to go to Japan.)

その結果 / cause & effect; reason & result /

不況が続いている。**その結果**，失業者の数が急激に増えている。
(The depression is continuing. As a result of that, the number of unemployed is rapidly on the increase.)

そのため(に) / cause & effect; reason & result /

去年の冬は例年より寒かったんです。**そのために**，暖房費が高かったんです。
(Last winter it was colder than the ordinary year. That's why the heating cost was high.)

それで / cause & effect; reason & result / (DBJG: 413–14)

昨日は京都へ出張していました。**それで**，うちにいなかったんです。
(Yesterday I was in Kyoto on a business trip. That's why I wasn't at home.)

それ故(に) / cause & effect; reason & result <w> /

日本は資源に乏しい。**それ故(に)**，日本の経済は底が浅い。
(Japan lacks natural resources. Therefore, the Japanese economy has no firm base (lit. is shallow).)

だから / cause & effect; reason & result / (DBJG: 414)

日本語を勉強すると役に立つ。**だから**日本語を勉強している。
(If we study Japanese, it will be useful. That's why I am studying Japanese.)

ですから / cause & effect; reason & result <fml> / (DBJG: 414)

その日本語の文章には分からない言葉がたくさんありました。**ですから**和英辞典を使いました。
(In that Japanese passage there were a lot of words which I don't understand. So I used a Japanese-English dictionary.)

(B) Conjunctions which mean 'BUT':

(だ)けど / disjunctive <inf, s> / (DBJG: 122)

けれども / disjunctive / (DBJG: 187–90)

彼はノーベル賞をもらった学者だ。**けれども**，とても謙虚だ。
(He is a scholar who won the Nobel Prize. But he is very humble.)

しかし / disjunctive <fml> / (DBJG: 122, 186)

したいことはたくさんある。**しかし**，人生は短い。
(There are so many things that I want to do. But life is short.)

そのくせ / disjunctive, accusatory, contemptful /

彼は権利ばかり主張している。**そのくせ**，義務を果たさない。
(He is insisting on his rights. But he does not perform his duties.)

彼女は人の前ではいいことばっかり言っている。**そのくせ**，陰では悪口を言っているのだ。
(She is saying nothing but nice things in front of people. But behind their backs she is speaking ill of them.)

それでも / highly disjunctive / (418–20)

（それ）にもかかわらず / highly disjunctive; accusatory; surprise; dissatisfaction <w> /

それなのに / highly disjunctive, accusatory; surprise; dissatisfaction /

彼の生活は多忙を窮めている。**それ｛でも／にもかかわらず／なのに｝**，一日一時間運動をしている。
(His life is extremely busy. Yet he exercises one hour every day.)

それにしては / disjunctive, unexpectedness /

彼は日本経済の専門家だそうだ。**それにしては**，彼の講演はお粗末だったね。
(I was told that he is an expert on the Japanese economy. But his lecture was awful, wasn't it?)

あなたは昨日まで入院していたんでしょ。**それにしては**，ずいぶん元気ですね。

(You were hospitalized until yesterday, right? But you look so healthy!)

それにしても / disjunctive, partial acceptance of S_1 content /

あの人はいつも遅く来るんですよ。**それにしても**，今日はずいぶん遅いですねえ。

(He always shows up late. But he's very late today, isn't he?)

不況の時にレイオフがあるのは仕方がない。**それにしても**，従業員の一割が首になるとはひどい。

(During a depression we cannot do without some layoffs. But it's too much for 10% of the workers to be fired.)

だが / disjunctive <inf in <s> but can be fml in <w>> / (DBJG: 122)

エイズのワクチンはまだ見つかっていない。**だが**，遅かれ早かれ，見つかると思う。

(They haven't yet discovered a vaccine for AIDS. But I believe that sooner or later they will.)

だからと言って / disjunctive, partial acceptance of S_1 content / (21–23)

卵はコレステロールがたくさんある。**だからと言って**，卵を食べるのを一切やめるのはおかしい。

(There is a lot of cholesterol in eggs. But it is absurd to stop eating eggs completely.)

音楽は生がいいと思う。**だからと言って**，コンサートにばかり行くわけにもいかないから，CD で我慢している。

(I like live music. But I cannot afford to go to every concert, so I put up with CDs.)

ただ / disjunctive, partial acceptance of S_1 / (445–48)

あの先生は教え方はいいね。**ただ**，性格がよくない。

(That teacher is good at teaching. But his personality is not good.)

ただし / disjunctive, supplementary explanation, condition, exception /

お酒，飲んでもいいわよ。**ただし**，飲み過ぎないでね。

(You can drink sake. But don't drink too much.)

ですが / disjunctive <polite> /

漢字は確かに面白いです。**ですが**，大変覚えにくいです。

(Kanji are indeed interesting. But it is hard to memorize them.)

ですけ(れ)ども / disjunctive <polite> /

日本語で簡単なことは言えます。{**だ / です**} **け(れ)ど(も)**，難しい話はだめなんです。

(I can say simple things in Japanese. But I cannot handle difficult conversation.)

でも / disjunctive <inf, s> / (DBJG: 122)

姉は結婚しています。**でも**，兄はまだ独身なんです。

(My older sister is married. But my older brother is still single.)

ところが / disjunctive, unexpectedness /

アメリカ人はみんなハンバーガーが好きだと思っていた。**ところが**，ロバートさんは嫌いだった。

(I thought all Americans loved hamburgers. But Robert didn't like them.)

とは言うものの / disjunctive, partial acceptance of S_1 content <w> /

とは言え / disjunctive, partial acceptance of S_1 content <w / s> /

とは言っても / disjunctive, partial acceptance of S_1 content /

去年から毎週五時間日本語を習っている。**とは** {**言え / 言っても / 言うものの**}，少しも上手にならない。

(I have been studying Japanese five hours each week since last year. But my Japanese isn't getting any better.)

もっとも / disjunctive, condition; limitation; exception /

この万年筆はとても書きやすいですよ。**もっとも**値段もいいですが。

(This fountain pen is very easy to write with. But the price is high, you know.)

彼の現在の結婚生活は幸福なようです。**もっとも**，彼は前に三回離婚していますけど。

(He seems to be happy about his current married life. But he has divorced three times before.)

(C) Conjunctions which mean'AND':

おまけに / addition <inf> /

今日は明日からの出 張の準 備で忙しかったよ。**おまけに**，来 客まであってさ，大変だったんだ。

(Today I was busy preparing for the business trip for tomorrow. To make matters worse, I had guests, you know. Gee, it was a tough day!)

彼女は美人なんだよな。**おまけに**，頭がいいときている。

(She is a beauty, isn't she? And she's smart at that.)

しかも / addition / (390–95)

あのレストランはとても安いよ。**しかも**，ボリュームも味も最高なんだ。

(That restaurant is very inexpensive. Moreover, the amount they serve and the taste are super!)

そ(う)して / a sequence of actions / (DBJG: 422–23)

僕は駅前の喫茶店に行った。**そ(う)して**そこで友達を待っていた。

(I went to the coffee shop in front of the station. And there I waited for my friend.)

その上(に) / addition, surprise / (413–17)

あの人は頭がいい。**その上(に)**，性格もとてもいい。

(He is bright. On top of that, he has such a nice personality.)

それから / event & event; action & action; state & state <chronology> / (DBJG: 416–19)

八時まで日本語の宿 題をした。**それから**，映画を見に出かけた。

(I did my Japanese language homework until 8 o'clock. And then I went out to see a movie.)

それと / addition / (431–34)

スポーツはテニスをします。**それと**，学生の頃バレーボールを少ししていました。

(Speaking of sports, I play tennis. In addition I played volleyball a little when I was a student.)

それに / addition / (427–31)

今日はピクニックに行けません。ちょっと体の調子が悪いんです。**それに**，来週は期末テストがあるし。

(I cannot go on a picnic today. I feel kind of ill. And what's more, there is a final test next week.)

そればかりでなく / addition /

そればかりか / addition /

ホストファミリーは成田空港まで迎えに来てくれた。{**そればかりでなく** / **そればかりか**} 毎日いろいろ面白い所に連れて行ってくれた。

(My host family kindly came to pick me up at Narita Airport. And it didn't stop there. They also took me around every day to all sorts of interesting places.)

また / addition /

彼は研究を盛んにやっている。**また**，人とも親しく付き合って，なかなか社交的だ。

(He is doing research vigorously. Moreover, he is quite outgoing, associating with people very closely.)

(D) Conjunctions which mean 'OR':

それとも / alternative /

または / alternative / (171–74)

あるいは / alternative /

この絵は彼が描いたのでしょうか。{**それとも** / **あるいは** / **または**} どこかから買って来たのでしょうか。
(Did he draw this painting? Or did he buy it somewhere?)

ビールにしますか。**それとも**お酒にしますか。
(Would you like beer? Or would you prefer sake?)

(E) Conjunctions which mean 'TO CHANGE THE SUBJECT':

さて / change of subject <w> /

Note: *Sate* can be used not only in written Japanese but also in formal speech.

これで，スポーツ関係のニュースを終わります。**さて**次は天気予報です。
(This concludes sports-related news. Moving on, next we have the weather forecast.)

ところで / change of subject /

それはそうと / change of subject <s> /

話は変わります {**が** / **け(れ)ど**} / change of subject /

ときに / change of subject <s> /

このところやたらと忙しくてねえ。ゴルフをする時間もないんだよ。ゴルフをしないと，頭がすっきりしないねえ。{**ところで** / **それはそうと** / **話は変わるけど**} アメリカ行きどうなった？
(I've been awfully busy lately. I don't even have time for golf, you know. My mind isn't clear if I don't play golf. By the way, what happened to your trip to the U.S.?)

先週まで暖かかったのに，今週は寒いですねえ。{**ときに** / **それはそうと**}，お宅のお坊ちゃん，来年は大学受験ですね。
(It's been so warm up until last week, but it's cold this week, isn't it? By the way, your son is going to take a college entrance examination next year, right?)

話変わって / change of subject <w> /

シンデレラは片方の靴を脱ぎ落として，急いでお城を出ました。**話変わって**こちらシンデレラの家にはがっかりした姉達が帰ってきました。
(Cinderella left the castle in a hurry, losing one of her shoes on the way. Meanwhile back at Cinderella's house, her sisters had come home disappointed.)

(F) Conjunctions which indicate PARAPHRASING:

言い換えると / rephrasing /

言い換えれば / rephrasing /

日本人にとって戦後は実に長かった。{**言い換えると / 言い換えれば**}，戦争は1945年 8 月15日に本当に終わったのではなかったのだ。
(For the Japanese, the post-War period was truly long. In other words, the War didn't really end on August 15, 1945.)

つまり / rephrasing, conclusion / (538–42)

要するに / rephrasing, focus on a crucial point /

結局 / rephrasing, conclusion / (DBJG: 540)

大統領は税金を大幅に上げることを主張している。そのために，消費者の購買力が低下しても構わないという考えだ。{**つまり / 要するに / 結局**}，国民に犠牲を払え，と言っているのである。
(The President is insisting on raising taxes. His idea is that it does not matter if the consumers' purchasing power is lowered as a result. {In short / In a nutshell / After all}, he is saying that people have to make a sacrifice.)

(G) Conjunctions which mean 'FOR EXAMPLE':

例えば / exemplification /

例を挙げると / exemplification /

私は体の害になることはしません。{**例えば / 例を挙げると**}，たばこを吸うとか，カフェインを取り過ぎるとか，夜更かしをするとかはしません。
(I do not do things that are harmful to my body. {For example / To give examples}, I do not smoke, nor take in too much caffeine, nor sit up until late at night.)

(H) Conjunctions which mark A REASON FOR SOMETHING:

なぜなら(ば) / reason why /

なぜかと言うと / reason why /

なぜかと言えば / reason why /

なぜかって言うと / reason why <inf> /

と言うのは / reason /

と言いますのは / reason <fml> /

私はこのプロジェクトはやめた方がいいと思います。**なぜ {なら(ば) / かと言うと / かと言えば / かって言えば}** 同じようなプロジェクトをM社でもやっているからです。
(I feel that this project should be terminated. It is because a project similar to this one is being carried out at M. Company.)

出張旅行の時の領収書は全部取っておかなければなりません。**と {言う / 言います} のは**，税の申告の時に必要だからです。
(I have to keep all the receipts for my business trip. It is because they are needed at when you file your tax report.)

(I) Conjunctions that indicate CONTRAST:

一方 / contrast, <w / s> /

他方 / contrast, <w> /

それに対して / contrast /

私はどちらかと言うと人間嫌いだ。**一方**，弟は誰とでも友達のように話すタイプで，私と全然違う。
(I am a bit of a misanthrope. On the other hand, my younger

brother is a type of person who will talk with anybody like a friend; he is totally different from me.)

日本語を習う時，学生ははじめローマ字から入った方がいいと考える人がいる。{**他方 / それに対して**} はじめから，平仮名で習うべきだと考えている人もいる。
(There are people who believe that learners of Japanese should start with roman letters first. On the other hand, there are also people who believe that one should start with *hiragana*.)

Appendix 5 **Affixes: Prefixes and Suffixes**

Prefixes and suffixes are dependent, non-conjugational words attached to nouns or the stems of verbs and adjectives in order to form new independent words. There are many affixes in Japanese. The following list contains those which are commonly used.

The entries below are listed in *a-i-u-e-o* order.

1. Prefixes

お・御	[polite prefix]	お手紙 (letter); お上手 (skillful); お忙しい (busy) (⇨ ***o-*** (DBJG: 343–47))
可	-able; -ible	可燃物 (a flammable thing); 可溶性 (fusibility; solubility)
各	each; various	各国 (each country; various countries); 各部屋 (each room)
片	one	片手 (one hand); 片一方 (one of the two); 片時 (a moment)
逆	counter-; reverse	逆効果 (counterproductive); 逆コース (reverse course)
ご・御	[polite prefix]	ご家族 ((your) family); 御結婚 (marriage); ご丁寧 (polite) (⇨ ***o-*** (DBJG: 343–47))
準	semi-; quasi-; associate	準決勝 (semi-final); 準会員 (associate member)
諸	many; several; various	諸設備 (many / various facilities); 諸物価 (many / various prices)
素	bare	素足 (bare feet); 素焼き (unglazed (pottery))
前	former; last; ex-	前首相 (ex-prime minister); 前世紀 (last century)
全	whole; entire, full	全国民 (the whole nation); 全人口 (the

		entire population); 全ページ (full page)
総	entire; general; grand; full	総選挙 (general election); 総合計 (grand total); 総攻撃 (full-scale attack)
対	to; with; anti-	対米輸出 (export to America); 対日貿易 (trade with Japan); 対空ミサイル (antiaircraft missile)
耐	-proof; -resistant	耐火 (fireproof); 耐熱 (heat-resistant)
第	Number; -th	第二 (No. 2); 第四章 (the fourth chapter, Chapter Four)
超	super-; ultra-	超特急 (super-express); 超音波 (ultrasonic waves)
同	same	同世代 (the same generation); 同年配 (the same age)
初	first; maiden	初雪 (the first snowfall); 初航海 (maiden voyage)
半	half; semi-	半時間 (half hour); 半円 (semicircle); 半自動 (semiautomatic)
反	anti-; counter-	反社会的 (antisocial); 反作用 (counteraction)
非	non-; un-	非金属 (nonmetal); 非科学的 (unscientific)
被	-ed; -ee	被保険者 (the (person) insured); 被支払人 (payee); 被除数 (dividend)
不	un-; in-; dis-	不自然 (unnatural); 不正確 (inaccurate); 不満足 (discontent)
副	vice-; deputy; additional	副大統領 (vice-president); 副知事 (deputy governor); 副収入 (additional income)
真(っ)	right; due; pure	真上 (right above); 真北 (due north); 真っ白 (pure white)

毎	every; per	毎朝 (every morning); 毎分 (per minute) (⇨ ***mai-*** (DBJG: 233–36))
未	un-	未解決 (unsolved); 未開発 (undeveloped)
無	in-; un-; -less	無関心 (indifferent); 無条件 (unconditional); 無表情 (expressionless)

2. Suffixes

家	-er; -ian; -ist	音楽家 (musician); 専門家 (specialist); 資本家 (capitalist)
化	-ization; become	映画化 (cinematization); 複雑化する (become complicated)
限り	limited to; only	今週限り (limited to this week); 一度限り (only once) (⇨ ***-kagiri***[2])
方	how to; a way of	読み方 (how to read; a way of reading) (⇨ ***-kata*** (DBJG: 183–84))
方	[honorific plural marker]	あなた方 (you [pl.]); 先生方 (the teachers) (⇨ ***-tachi*** (DBJG: 440–41))
形	-shaped	卵形 (egg-shaped); 三日月形 (crescent)
型	type; model	箱型 (box type); A 型 (Type A); 1990 年型 (the 1990 model)
がち	tend to; often	忘れがち (tend to forget); 病気がち (often get ill) (⇨ ***-gachi***)
ぎみ	verging on	太りぎみ (verging on obesity); 風邪ぎみ (have a slight cold) (⇨ ***-gachi***)
君	Mr.; Ms.; Miss	山田君 (Mr. / Ms. / Miss Yamada); 太郎君 (Taro) (⇨ ***-kun*** (DBJG: 211))
頃	about; around	七時頃 (about 7 o'clock); 六月頃 (around June) (⇨ ***-goro*** (DBJG: 126–28))

さ	-ness	高さ (height); 静かさ (quietness) (⇨ ***-sa*** (DBJG: 381–84))
様	Mr.; Mrs.; Ms.; Miss	吉田弘様 (Mr. Hiroshi Yoshida); 上村真理様 (Mrs. / Ms. / Miss Mari Uemura); お客様 (guest) (⇨ ***-sama*** (DBJG: 384–87))
さん	Mr.; Mrs.; Ms.; Miss	高木さん (Ms. Takagi); 洋子さん (Yoko); おばさん (aunt); 課長さん (Section Chief); 酒屋さん (wine dealer) (⇨ ***-sama*** (DBJG: 384–87))
士	-er; -ant; -ist	弁護士 (lawyer); 会計士 (accountant); 栄養士 (nutritionist)
師	-er; -ian; -ist	美容師 (beautician); 薬剤師 (pharmacist); 庭師 (gardener); 宣教師 (missionary)
氏	Mr.; Mrs.; Ms.	小山進氏 (Mr. Susumu Koyama); 佐々木信子氏 (Mrs. / Ms. Nobuko Sasaki); キーン氏 (Mr. / Mrs. / Ms. Keen)
式	style; fashion; system	日本式 (Japanese style / fashion); ヘボン式 (the Hepburn System); 折りたたみ式 (collapsible)
者	-er; -ant; -ist	使用者 (user); 科学者 (scientist); 出席者 (attendant); 責任者 (person in charge)
手	-er; -or	運転手 (driver); 交換手 (switchboard operator)
所	place	事務所 (business office); 研究所 (research lab); 発電所 (power plant)
上	from the viewpoint of; for	教育上 (from the viewpoint of education) (⇨ ***-jō***)
状	-like; -shaped	ゼリー状 (jelly-like); 渦巻き状 (spiral)
場	place	駐車場 (parking lot); 野球場 (ball park);

		ゴルフ場 (golf course)
人	person; people	ドイツ人 (a German); 知識人 (an intellectual); 現代人 (modern people)
性	-ty; -ness	生産性 (productivity); 可能性 (possibility); 積極性 (positiveness)
製	made in / of / from	日本製 (made in Japan); ナイロン製 (made from nylon)
代[1]	generation; era	50代 ((in) one's fifties); 1990年代 ((in) the '90s)
代[2]	charge; rate; fare; rent; bill	コピー代 (copying charge); ホテル代 (hotel rates); バス代 (bus fare); 部屋代 (room rent); 電気代 (electricity bill)
たち・達	[plural marker]	私達 (we); 子供達 (children) (⇨ ***-tachi*** (DBJG: 440–41))
だらけ	full of; covered with	間違いだらけ (full of mistakes); ほこりだらけ (covered with dust) (⇨ ***-darake***)
ちゃん	[endearing suffix]	おじいちゃん (Grandpa); 花子ちゃん (Hanako) (⇨ ***-sama*** (DBJG: 384–87))
中	during; while; in; under	休暇中 (during the vacation); 授業中 (in class); 開発中 (under development)
手	-er	聞き手 (hearer); 送り手 (sender)
的	-ic; -ive; -al	現実的 (realistic); 客観的 (objective); 感情的 (emotional)
ども	[humble plural marker]	私ども (we) (⇨ ***-tachi*** (DBJG: 440–41))
人	-er; -or	差出人 (sender); 見物人 (spectator)
費	expense; cost; fee	生活費 (the cost of living); 住居費 (housing expenses); 会費 (membership fee)

風	style; looking like	日本風 (Japanese style); 学生風 (looking like a student)
分	worth; for	十ドル分 (ten dollars worth); 五人分 (for five people) (⇨ ***-bun***)
み	-ness	厚み (thickness); 悲しみ (sorrow) (⇨ ***-sa*** (DBJG: 381–84))
目	-th (one)	三つ目 (the third (one)); 四人目 (the fourth person)
面	(from) the aspect of; in terms of; regarding	運営面 ((from) the aspect of operation); 税金面 (in terms of tax) (⇨ ***-men***)
屋	store	本屋 (bookstore); パン屋 (bakery) (⇨ ***-ya*** (DBJG: 535–36))
よう	way	書きよう (a way to write) (⇨ ***-yō***)
用	for (the use of)	学生用 (for students); 練習用 (for practice use)
ら	[plural marker]	僕ら (we); 彼ら (they); これら (these) (⇨ ***-tachi*** (DBJG: 440–41))
来	for the past; since	二十年来 (for the past twenty years); 昨年来 (since last year) (⇨ ***-rai***)
料	fee; charge	入場料 (admission fee); 手数料 (handling charge)

Note 1: Affix characters function in a different way as elements of compounds which do not contain independent words. For example, in 反対 'opposite,' the prefix character 反 is used with 対, which is not an independent word. In this case, 反 is not a prefix.

Note 2: A sound change occurs with some prefixes. For example, 薄 + 氷 is 薄氷.

Appendix 6 **More Counters**

The following chart lists additional counters that are not listed in Appendix 6B of DBJG (604–07). (Although the counters given in parenthesis are the same as the ones given in DBJG, they are repeated here for your convenience.)

*For native Japanese numerals and Sino-Japanese numerals, see DBJG (602–03).

*Except in Item 59 (年生), "7" sounds more natural when it is pronounced [*nana*] rather than [*shichi*]

Type A: No phonetic change takes place either in the Sino-Japanese number or in the counter. (Exs. 枚, 倍, 番, 度, 畳, 部, 面)

Type A′: Exactly the same as Type A except than number 4 is pronounced *yo* not *yon*. (Exs. 時, 時間, 年)

Type A″: Exactly the same as Type A except that numbers 4, 7 and 9 are pronounced *shi*, *shichi* and *ku*, respectively. (Ex. 月 'name of the month')

Type A‴: Exactly the same as Type A except that the initial sound of the counter with number 3 changes from *wa* to *ba*. (Ex. 羽 'bird')

Type B: The counter starts with the sound of *h-* but changes to *p-* after 1, 3, 6, 8 and 10 as follows: 1 [*ipp-*], 3 [*sanb-*], 6 [*ropp-*], 8 [*happ-*], 10 [*jipp-*]. (Exs. 本, 杯, 匹)

Type B′: Exactly the same as Type B except that the initial sound of the counter with number 3 is not *b-* but *p-*. (Ex. 泊 'stay (overnight)')

Type C: When the counter starts with the sound of *k-* the last sound of the number changes for 1, 6, 8 and 10 as follows: 1 [*ikk-*], 6 [*rokk-*], 8 [*hakk- / hachik-*] and 10 [*jikk-*]. (Exs. 課, か月, 回, 巻, 個)

Type C′: Exactly the same as Type C except that the initial sound of the counter with number 3 can be either *k-* or *g-*. (Ex. 階)

Type D: When the counter starts with the sound of *s-* the last sound of the number changes for 1, 8 and 10 as follows: 1 [*iss-*], 8 [*hass-*] and 10 [*jiss-*]. (Exs. 冊, 歳, 隻)

Type D′: Exactly the same as Type D except that the initial sound of the counter with number 3 is *z-* not *s-*. (Exs. 足 'pair of footwear')

Type E: When the counter starts with the sound of *p-*, the last sound of the number changes for 1, 6, 8 and 10 as follows: 1 [*ipp-*], 6 [*ropp- / rokup-*], 8 [*happ- / hachi-*] and 10 [*jipp-*]. (Ex. ページ, ポンド)

Type F: When the counter starts with the sound of *t-*, the initial sound of the counter changes with regard to 1, 8 and 10 as follows: 1 [*itt-*], 8 [*hatt-*], 10 [*jitt-*]. (Exs. 頭, 等, 通, トン)

Irregular Types: The number is a mixture of Japanese numbers and Sino-Japanese numbers. (Exs. 晩, 日, 人)

Additional List of Counters

(In 'x' (y), 'x' indicates an item for which the counter is used and (y) indicates the type it belongs to.) The list is arranged in the *a-i-u-e-o* order. The irregular type, a new type introduced here, requires the use of native Japanese numerals 1 through a certain number depending on the counter (above which Sino-Japanese numerals are used).

あ行

1. **位** 'rank / place' (A)

   Ex. ジョンソンさんは日本語スピーチコンテストで三位になった。
   (Johnson was third place in the Japanese speech contest.)

2. **インチ** 'inch' (A)

   Ex. 昨日は雪が10インチも積もった。
   (Yesterday the snow piled up as much as 10 inches.)

3. **駅** 'station' (Irregular: 1 and 2 in the native Japanese numerals)

   Ex. 新宿は高田馬場から二駅です。

(Shinjuku is two stations away from Takadanobaba.)

4. **円** 'yen' (A′)

Ex. 1ドルは今百円ぐらいです。
(One dollar is now about 100 yen.)

5. **往復** 'return trip' (A)

Ex. 今日はうちと郵便局の間を三往復した。
(Today I made three trips between my house and the post office.)

6. **億** 'one hundred million' (A)

Ex. 日本の人口は一億以上で，アメリカの人口は二億以上だ。
(The population of Japan is more than one hundred million and the population of America is more than two hundred million.)

か行

7. **画** 'kanji stroke' (C)

Ex. 「聞(く)」という漢字は十四画の漢字です。
(The character 聞く has fourteen strokes.)

8. **家族** 'family' (C / Irregular: 1 and 2 in the native Japanese numerals)

Ex. この家には兄の家族と僕の家族の二家族が住んでいる。
(Two families are living in this house—my older brother's family and my family.)

9. **学期** 'semester' (A)

Ex. 僕はこの大学でまだ二学期しか教えていない。
(I have taught only two semesters at this college.)

10. **ガロン** 'gallon' (A)

Ex. この車は1ガロンで40マイル走る。
(This car gets 40 miles per gallon.)

11. **期** 'term' (C)

Ex. アメリカの大統領で三期務めた大統領はいますか。

(Is there an American President who served for three terms?)

12. 機 'machine / airplane' (C)

Ex. 空港にはジャンボジェットが十機ぐらい止まっていた。
(About ten jumbo jets were parked at the airport.)

13. 気筒 'cylinder' (C)

Ex. この車は八気筒だから，燃費が悪い。
(This car has eight cylinders, so gas consumption is bad.)

14. 行 'line' (A)

Ex. 先生，26ページの五行目の「これ」は何を指しているんですか。
(Professor, what does 'this' in the fifth line of page 26 refer to?)

15. 曲 'piece of music' (C)

Ex. 彼女はベートーベンのピアノ曲を三曲弾いた。
(She played three of Beethoven's piano pieces.)

16. キロ 'kilometer / kilogram' (C)

Ex. (a) 家から会社までは 8 キロあります。
(It is eight kilometers from home to work.)

(b) 私の体重は 56 キロです。
(I weigh 56 kilograms.)

Note: 1 キロ reads not [*ikkiro*] but [*ichikiro*]. For other numbers, キロ belongs to Type C.

17. 句 'haiku / waka' (C)

Ex. 僕は俳句を百句ぐらい作った。
(I have composed about one hundred haikus.)

18. グラム 'gram' (A)

Ex. 私は毎日繊維質を 20 グラムとっている。
(I take 20 grams of fiber every day.)

19. 桁 'digit' (C / Irregular: 1–4 in the native Japanese numerals.)

Ex. あの学生は二桁の数字の掛け算も出来ない。
(That student cannot do even multiplication of two-digit numbers.)

20. **軒** 'house' (C′)

Ex. この町には本屋が 八 軒もある。
(This city has eight bookstores.)

21. **間** 'distance' (= 1.9 yard) (C′)

Ex. あの店は間口二間の小さい店だ。
(That store is a small store with front measuring two *ken* (one *ken* = 5.695 ft.).)

22. **戸** 'house (fml)' (C)

Ex. この新しい住 宅地には家が 四十 戸ぐらい建っている。
(About forty houses stand in this new residential area.)

23. **語** 'word' (A)

Ex. 答えを百語以内の日本語で書きなさい。
(Write down your answer in Japanese using less than one hundred words.)

24. **校** 'school' (C)

Ex. 私は大学受験の時，三校に願書を出しました。
(During the college entrance examination period, I sent applications to three institutions.)

25. **号(車)** 'Number X (car)' (A)

Exs. (a) 私のアパートは 五号の 五階です。
(My apartment is on the 5th floor of building No. 5.)

(b) 食 堂車は 4 号車でございます。
(The dining car is car No. 4.)

さ行

26. **皿** 'plate' (D / Irregular: 1–4 in the native Japanese numerals)

Ex. これはフルコースでございますから，十皿以上出てまいります。
(This is a full course, so there will be more than ten dishes.)

27. **字** 'letter' (A)

Ex. ここの大学の日本語の一年生は漢字を三百字ぐらい勉強します。
(The first year Japanese students at this college study about three hundred kanjis.)

28. **社** 'company' (D)

Ex. 四社が同じ製品を作っているので，競争が激しい。
(Because four companies are making the same product, competition is fierce.)

29. **周** 'circling' (D)

Ex. 僕は毎日グラウンドを十周ぐらい走っている。
(I am run around the grounds about ten times every day.)

30. **週(間)** 'week' (D)

Ex. 夏の日本語の講座は九週間だ。
(The summer Japanese program is nine weeks long.)

31. **種(類)** 'kind' (D)

Ex. (a) 父は十種類ぐらい薬を飲んでいた。
(My father was taking about ten kinds of medicine.)

(b) 日本語には二種(類)の形容詞がある。
(There are two kinds of adjectives in Japanese.)

32. **章** 'chapter' (D)

Ex. 博士論文は全部で八章だが，まだ二章しか書いていない。
(The doctoral dissertation will be eight chapters in all, but I have written only two chapters so far.)

33. **升** 'amount of liquid / grains' (= 1.8 liter) (D)

Ex. 彼は酒を一升わけもなく飲んでしまう。
(He drinks one *shō* of sake quite easily.)

34. **食** 'meal' (D)

Ex. 私は忙しいので，一日三食食べる日は滅多にない。
(I am so busy that I seldom eat three meals a day.)

35. **色** 'color' (D)

Ex. (a) このクレヨンは十二色です。
(These crayons come in twelve colors.)

(b) 虹は七色です。
(The rainbow has seven colors.)

Note: In (b), 七色 reads not [*shichishoku*] but [*nanairo*].

36. **世紀** 'century' (D)

Ex. 二十一世紀の日米関係はどうなるだろうか。
(I wonder what will happen to the Japan-US relationship in the 21st century.)

37. **世帯** 'household' (D)

Ex. 日本には二世帯住宅や三世帯住宅が多い。
(There are many two-household and three-household residences in Japan.)

38. **世代** 'generation' (D)

Ex. わが家には三世代が同居している。
(Three generations live together in our house.)

39. **千** 'thousand' (D′)

Ex. 成田空港から東京まで電車で確か三千五百円ぐらいでした。
(If I remember correctly, the train fare from Narita Airport to Tokyo was ¥3,500.)

40. **銭** 'sen' (D)

Ex. 彼は一銭も無駄遣いをしない。
(He doesn't waste a penny.)

41. **センチ** 'centimeter' (D)

Ex. 私の身長は1メートル75センチです。
(I am 1 meter and 75 cms tall.)

42. **セント** 'cent' (D)

Ex. このセーターは99ドル99セントでした。
(This sweater was 99 dollars and 99 cents.)

た行

43. **ダース** 'dozen' (A)

Ex. すみませんが，赤鉛筆を1ダース買って来て下さいませんか。
(Could you kindly go and buy me a dozen red pencils?)

44. **題** 'problem' (A)

Ex. 数学のテストに問題が十題出た。
(In the math test there were ten problems.)

45. **台** 'machine' (A)

Ex. この部屋にはテレビが一台，ラジオが二台，CDプレーヤーが一台あります。
(There are one TV set, two radios and one CD player.)

46. **段** 'step' (A)

Ex. このお寺の階段は全部で三百段あります。
(The stairs of this temple total 300.)

47. **段落** 'paragraph' (A)

Ex. このエッセイは五段落から出来ている。
(This essay consists of five paragraphs.)

48. **着** 'suit' (F)

Ex. 彼は背広を三十着ぐらい持っている。
(He has about 30 suits.)

49. **丁** 'piece of tōfu / pistol / block' (F)

Ex. (a) このお豆腐，三丁下さい。
(Please give me three blocks of this tōfu.)

(b) 男はピストルを三丁も持っていた。
(The man possessed three pistols.)

50. **兆** 'one billion' (F)

Ex. この会社の資本金は約三兆円だ。
(The capital of this company is approximately 3 billion yen.)

51. **丁目** 'subdivison of a large city' (F)

Ex. 銀座四丁目の辺りはにぎやかですね。
(The No. 4 district of Ginza is bustling, isn't it?)

52. **月** 'duration of a month' (Irregular: only 1–4 in the native Japanese numerals and none of the Sino-Japanese numerals) cf. か月

Ex. 韓国語を三月韓国で勉強しました。
(I studied Korean for three months in Korea.)

53. **坪** 'area' (= 3.9 square yard) (F / Irregular: 1 and 2 in the native Japanese numerals)

Ex. 私の家は百坪ぐらいです。
(My house is about 100 *tsubo*.)

54. **滴** 'drop of liquid' (F)

Ex. 雨が一滴，二滴と，降り始めた。
(The rain started to fall, one drop, two drops . . . .)

55. **点** 'point' (F)

Ex. 日本語の期末試験は九十八点だった。
(I got 98 points in the final Japanese examination.)

56. **通り** 'way' (F / Irregular: 1 and 2 in the native Japanese numerals)

Ex. この問題の解き方は三通りある。
(There are three ways to solve this problem.)

57. **ドル** 'dollar' (A)

Ex. この車は2万5,000ドルぐらいでした。
(This car was about $25,000.)

な行

58. **人前** 'portion' (Irregular: 1 and 2 in the native and Sino-Japanese numerals)

Ex. すしを五人前お願いします。
(We'd like to order portions of sushi for five people.)

59. **年生** '~ year student' (A′)

Ex. カレンはスタンフォード大学の三年生です。
(Karen is a junior at Stanford University.)

は行

60. **パーセント** 'percent' (E)

Ex. 日本のキリスト教徒の数は人口の1パーセント以下である。
(The number of Japanese Christians is less than 1% of the population.)

61. **泊** 'overnight stay' (B′)

Ex. 北海道に一泊二日の旅行をします。
(I'll make a one night two day trip to Hokkaido.)

62. **箱** 'box' (B′ / Irregular: 1 and 2 in the native Japanese numerals)

Ex. たばこを毎日三箱吸っています。
(I am smoking three packs of cigarettes every day.)

63. **発** 'shot / round' (B′)

Ex. ピストルの弾は心臓に一発当たっていた。
(One shot of the pistol's bullet hit the heart.)

64. **番線** 'train track' (A)

Ex. 成田エクスプレスは3番線と4番線です。

(The Narita Express leaves from Track 3 and Track 4.)

65. **番地** 'a house number' (A)

Ex. 私の東京の住所は新宿区戸塚町3丁目25番地です。
(My address in Tokyo is 3–25 Totsuka-cho, Shinjuku-ku.)

66. **百** 'hundred' (B)

Ex. 百の発音では，三百，六百と八百に気を付けて下さい。
(In pronouncing '*hyaku*,' pay attention to '*sanbyaku*,' '*roppyaku*' and *happyaku*.')

Note: 百 is basically of Type B, but there are no *[*ippyaku*] or *[*jippyaku*].

67. **秒** 'second' (A)

Ex. 僕は100メートルを12秒で走ります。
(I run 100 meters in 12 seconds.)

68. **フィート** 'feet' (A)

Ex. 兄は背が6フィート10インチです。
(My older brother is 6 feet and 10 inches tall.)

69. **文** 'sentence' (A)

Ex. この論文の内容を十文でまとめなさい。
(Summarize the content of this paper using 10 sentences.)

70. **遍** 'frequency' (B)

Ex. 今日はメアリーに六遍電話をかけたが，いなかった。
(Today I called Mary six times, but she wasn't there.)

71. **歩** 'step' (B′)

Ex. 千里の道も一歩から。(Proverb)
(A journey of a thousand miles must begin with the first step.)

72. **ボルト** 'voltage' (A)

Ex. ここの電流は100ボルトです。

(The electric current of this place is 100 volts.)

ま行

73. **間** 'room' (Irregular: 1 and 2 in the native Japanese numerals, and beyond 3 the counter is seldom used.)

Ex. 私達の家には祖父母用に二間とってあります。
(In our house two rooms are reserved for our grandparents.)

74. **万** '10,000' (A)

Ex. 百万円もらったら何をしますか。
(What would you do if you were given ¥1,000,000?)

75. **名** 'person' (A)

Ex. この日本語のクラスには女子学生が三名，男子学生が五名います。
(This Japanese class has three female students and five male students.)

76. **メートル** 'meter' (A)

Ex. 富士山の高さは三千メートル以上です。
(Mt. Fuji is more than 3,000 meters high.)

77. **面** 'newspaper page' (A)

Ex. この新聞の三面と四面には国際関係の記事が出る。
(The third and fourth pages of this newspaper carry international articles.)

78. **問** 'problem' (A)

Ex. 数学の試験で五問中一問しか解けなかった。
(On the math test I was able to solve only one problem out of five.)

や行

79. **ヤード** 'yard' (A)

Ex. アメリカのプールはたいてい 25 ヤードだ。
(An American pool is usually 25 yards long.)

80. 山（やま） 'pile' (Irregular: only 1 and 2 in the native Japanese numerals and none of the Sino-Japanese numerals)

Ex. このりんごは一山500円（ひとやまごひゃく）です。
(These apples are ¥500 a pile.)

ら行

81. 里（り） 'distance' (= 2.5 miles) (A)

Ex. 子供（こども）の時（とき），小学校（しょうがっこう）まで毎日一里（まいにちいちり）歩（ある）かなければならなかった。
(When I was a child, I had to walk one *ri* everyday to my elementary school.)

82. リットル 'liter' (A)

Ex. 日本（にほん）のガソリンは1（いち）リットルいくらですか。
(How much is Japanese gasoline per liter?)

わ行

83. 割（わり） '10 percent' (A)

Ex. この靴（くつ）は三割引（さんわりび）きですよ。
(There is a 30% discount on these shoes, you know.)

84. ワット 'watt' (A)

Ex. 200（にひゃく）ワットの電球（でんきゅう）が欲（ほ）しいんですが。
(I need a 200 watt electric bulb.)

Appendix 7 **Cooccurrence**

Some adverbs, particles, and phrases commonly occur with certain kinds of sentence / clause endings, as listed below.

1. Adverbs, particles, and phrases which occur with negative sentence endings:

一概に(は)
漫画が教育上よくないとは，**一概には**言えない。
(We cannot make a generalization about comics being bad from an educational point of view.)

一(Counter) として
この会社には**一人として**尊敬できる上司がいない。
(There is not a single boss in this company whom I can respect.)

ここにあるコンピュータは**一台として**まともに動かない。
(Not a single computer here functions properly.)

一(Counter) も
先生は**一人も**パーティーに来なかった。
(Not a single teacher came to the party.)

この図書館には日本語の本は**一冊も**ない。
(This library houses no books in Japanese.)

(⇨ ***mo***² (DBJG: 250–53))

一向に
彼の言っていることは**一向に**要領を得ない。
(What he is saying doesn't make any sense.)

必ずしも
お金は**必ずしも**人を幸福にはしない。
(Money doesn't necessarily bring happiness to people.)

(⇨ ***kanarazushimo***)

からと言って
子供だ**からと言って**許すわけにはいかない。
(We cannot forgive him just because he is a child.)

(⇨ ***kara to itte***)

決して
彼は**決して**そんな人じゃない。

(He is not that kind of person at all.)

少しも 友達がたくさんいるので，**少しも**寂しくない。
(I have a lot of friends, so I don't feel lonely at all.)

全然 この辞書は**全然**役に立たない。
(This dictionary is totally useless.)

大して これくらいの翻訳なら**大して**時間はかからない。
(A translation like this wouldn't take much time.)

ちっとも 吉田先生の講義は**ちっとも**面白くない。
(Prof. Yoshida's lectures are not interesting at all.)

ちょっとやそっとで この問題は**ちょっとやそっとで**は解けない。
(This problem cannot be solved easily.)

とうてい この仕事は**とうてい**今日中には出来ない。
(We cannot possibly finish this job today.)

どうにも この故障は**どうにも**直しようがない。
(There's no way to fix this problem.)

二度と もう**二度と**こんな仕事はしたくない。
(I never want to take on such a job again.)

まさか **まさか**こんな所で君に会うとは思わなかった。
(I never dreamed I'd see you in a place like this.)

めったに 私は**めったに**うちで勉強しない。
(I seldom study at home.)

ろくに / ろくな 忙しくて**ろくに**新聞も読めない。
(I am so busy that I can hardly read the newspaper.)

ここ二，三日**ろくな**食事をしていない。
(I haven't eaten any decent meals these two or three days.)

(⇨ ***rokuni ~ nai***)

Vvol にも 新しい商売を**始めようにも**資金がない。
(I have no funds even if I want to begin a new business.)

(Wh-word) 一 (Counter)

私の友達には**誰一人**英語を話せる人がいない。
(Among my friends there's no one who can speak English.)

(Wh-word) も

今朝から**何も**食べていない。
(I haven't eaten anything since this morning.)

誰も手伝ってくれない。
(No one will help me.)

(⇨ ***mo***[2] (DBJG: 250–53))

The following adverbs and particles often appear with negative endings but can also occur with affirmative endings.

あまり

私は肉は**あまり**食べません。
(I don't eat much meat.)

cf. **あまり**暑かったので，パジャマを着ないで寝ました。
(It was so hot that I slept without pajamas.)

(⇨ ***amari*** (DBJG: 72–73))

さっぱり

彼の言っていることは，私には**さっぱり**分からない。
(I don't understand what he says at all.)

cf. 彼女との結婚は**さっぱり**あきらめた。
(I entirely gave up the idea of marrying her.)

なかなか

この問題は**なかなか**解けない。
(This problem cannot be solved easily.)

cf. このすしは**なかなか**おいしい。
(This sushi is pretty good.)

(⇨ ***nakanaka***)

別に

今日は**別に**予定はありません。
(I have no particular plan today.)

cf. これは**別に**送って下さい。
(Please send this separately.)

ほとんど

飛行機の中では**ほとんど**寝られませんでした。
(I could hardly sleep on the plane.)

cf. 日本語の映画でしたが**ほとんど**分かりました。
(Although it was a Japanese film, I understood almost all of it.)

まだ

会議は**まだ**始まっていません。
(The meeting hasn't begun yet.)

cf. ルームメートは**まだ**寝ています。
(My roommate is still asleep)

(⇨ ***mada*** (DBJG: 224–25))

まるで / まるっきり

川村は英語が**まるで**出来ない。
(Kawamura cannot speak English at all.)

cf. サリーは**まるで**日本人のように日本語を話す。
(Sally speaks Japanese just like a (native) Japanese.)

もう

もう遅刻はしません。
(I won't be late (for class) any more.)

cf. 朝ご飯は**もう**食べました。
(I've had my breakfast already.)

(⇨ ***mō*** (DBJG: 224–55))

N ほど

私は**田中さんほど**上手に話せない。
(I am not as good a speaker as Mr. Tanaka.)

cf. **今井さんほど**の実力があれば，どこへ行っても仕事には困らないだろう。
(With his capabilities, Mr. Imai should not have any trouble finding a job.)

(⇨ ***hodo*** (DBJG: 135–38))

2. Adverbs which occur with interrogative sentences:

一体

一体誰がそんなひどいことを言ったの?
(Who on earth said such a terrible thing?)

はたして

この計画は**はたして**うまくいくだろうか。
(I wonder if this plan will ever work out.)

cf. **はたして**彼はうちにいなかった。
(He wasn't home, as I expected.)

3. Adverbs which commonly occur with expressions of uncertainty:

恐らく

この仕事は**恐らく**彼には出来ないだろう。
(He probably cannot do this job.)

私が今日本に来ていることは，**恐らく**誰も知るまい。
(Probably no one knows that I am in Japan now.)

きっと

明日は**きっと**晴れるでしょう。
(It will surely be fine tomorrow.)

小林君は**きっと**そのことを知っているに違いない。
(Surely Mr. Kobayashi must know that.)

さぞ

母はこのことを話したら**さぞ**喜ぶことだろう。
(If I tell this to my mother, she will certainly be very happy.)

多分

森さんは**多分**そのことを知っているだろう。
(Mr. Mori probably knows about it.)

和田さんは**多分**来るまい。
(Ms. Wada probably won't come.)

ひょっとすると

ひょっとすると奨学金がもらえるかも知れない。
(I may possibly be able to get a scholarship.)

まさか

まさか私がアメリカ人と結婚するとは誰も思うまい。
(No one would ever dream that I am marrying an American.)

まさかこの秘密を人に漏らしたんじゃないだろうね。
(Don't tell me that you have told this secret to others.)

もしかすると

もしかすると私の勘違いかも知れない。
(It could possibly be my mistake.)

4. Adverbs which occur with expressions of appearance or resemblance:

いかにも

彼の話し方はとても論理的で**いかにも**科学者らしい。
(The way he talks is very logical, which is just like a (typical) scientist.)

幸男は**いかにも**気持ちよさそうに寝ている。
(Yukio is sleeping very comfortably (lit. looking very comfortable).)

清水氏は**いかにも**感心したように私の顔を見た。
(Mr. Shimizu looked at me, appearing to be truly impressed.)

今にも

今にも雨が降りそうだ。
(It looks like it will rain at any moment.)

さも

彼は**さも**満足そうにうなずいた。
(He nodded showing great satisfaction.)

田中は自分が**さも**その分野の専門家であるかのように話した。
(Tanaka talked as if he were a specialist in the field.)

まるで

木村さんは**まるで**酒を飲んだみたいだ。
(Mr. Kimura looks as if he has just drunk sake.)

サリーは**まるで**日本人のように日本語を話す。
(Sally speaks Japanese just like a (native) Japanese.)

5. Adverbs which occur with provisional or concession sentences:

一度

彼は**一度**約束したら，必ずそれを守る。
(Once he makes a promise, he never fails to keep it.)

核戦争は**一度**起きると，地球全体の破滅につながる。
(Once a nuclear war breaks out, it will lead to the destruction of the entire earth.)

仮に

仮に今度の失敗がなかったとしても，彼はやはり解雇されただろう。

(Even if he hadn't made this mistake, he would have been fired anyway.)

仮に今の二倍働いたところで，この借金は返せない。

(Even if I worked twice as much as I do now, I could not pay off this debt.)

たとえ

たとえ両親が反対しても，私は彼と結婚します。

(Even if my parents object, I will marry him.)

たとえ忠告してやったところで，彼は人の言うことなど聞きはしない。

(Even if you gave him advice, he would not listen to it (lit. others).)

万一

万一雨が降ったら，ピクニックは中止します。

(If it should rain, the picnic will be canceled.)

万一大地震が起きても，この建物は大丈夫です。

(Even if a big earthquake hits here, this building will be all right.)

万一彼が参加出来なかったところで，プロジェクトには支障はない。

(Even if he cannot participate in the project, it won't be affected.)

もし

もし村上さんから電話があったら，帰ったらすぐ電話すると言っておいて下さい。

(If Mr. Murakami calls me, please tell him that I will call him back soon after I return.)

もし来られないようなら，知らせて下さい。

(If it appears that you cannot come, please let me know.)

6. Other instances of cooccurence:

せっかく

Sekkaku typically occurs with the conjunction *noni*, (*no da*) *kara* and *temo*.

せっかく三年間も日本語を勉強したのに，あまり使う機会がない。
(I studied Japanese for (as many as) three years, but I do not have many chances to use it.)

せっかくニューヨークまで来たのだから，ついでにワシントンにも行ってみたい。
(Because I came as far as New York, I'd like to take the opportunity to visit Washington, D.C.)

先生が**せっかく**一生懸命教えても，学生が勉強しなければ何にもならない。
(Even if teachers work hard, it won't make any difference if students don't work.)

(⇨ ***sekkaku*** (DBJG: 392–94))

ぜひ

Zehi occurs with expression of desire, volition, request, and invitation.

ぜひ日本の大学に留学したいです。
(I'd really like to study at a Japanese university.)

アメリカにいるうちに，**ぜひ**一度グランドキャニオンを見ようと思っています。
(I'm seriously thinking about visiting the Grand Canyon (once) while I'm in the States.)

ぜひ私達のパーティーに来て下さい。
(Please do come to our party.)

もう {ちょっとで / 少しで}

Mō {*chotto de* / *sukoshi de*} often occurs with *tokoro datta*.

もう {ちょっとで / 少しで} 電車に乗り遅れるところだった。
(I almost missed my train.)

(⇨ ***tokoro da***[2] (DBJG: 496–501))

Appendix 8 **Functional Expressions and Grammatical Patterns**

Functional expressions, i.e., those expressions which are used to perform functions such as making requests, asking for permission, and giving suggestions, often involve certain grammatical patterns. The following is an inventory of functional expressions which involve such patterns.

Abbreviations:

<s>: Spoken Japanese only
<w>: Written Japanese only
inf.sit.: Informal situations only
m.: Used by male speakers only
(m.): Used mostly by male speakers
f.: Used by female speakers only
(f.): Used mostly by female speakers

1. Ordering someone to do something; giving instructions

a. Vcond (Gr. 1 verbs)

立て。
(Stand up!)

英語で**書け**。
(Write in English.)

Variation:
Vcond よ <s> inf.sit., m.

Note: Vcond is a strong command. Vcond よ is a milder expression and used only in spoken language.

(⇨ **Imperative**)

b. V*masu* ろ (Gr. 2 verbs) <s>

これを見**ろ**。
(Look at this!)

Variation:
V*masu* ろよ <s> inf.sit., m.

Note 1: V*masu* ろ is a strong command. V*masu* ろよ is a milder expression and used only in spoken language.

Note 2: The imperative forms of the irregular verbs 来る and する are 来い and しろ / せよ, respectively.

(⇨ **Imperative**)

c. V*masu* よ (Gr. 2 verbs) <w>

図 1 を見**よ**。
(Look at Fig. 1.)

(⇨ **Imperative**)

d. V*masu* なさい

漢字で書き**なさい**。
(Write in kanji.)

Variation:
お V*masu* なさい <s>

Note: V*masu* なさい is milder than the patterns in (a)–(c). お V*masu* なさい is even milder.

(⇨ ~ ***nasai*** (DBJG: 284–85))

e. Vinf·nonpast ように

今すぐ私の部屋に来る**ように**。
(Come to my office right away.)

f. V*te* 下さい

漢字で書いて**下さい**。
(Please write in kanji.)

Variations:
V*te* くれ <s> inf.sit., m.
V*te* ちょうだい <s> inf.sit., f.

(⇨ ***kudasai*** (DBJG: 209–10))

g. お V*masu* 下さい

お座り**下さい**。
(Please sit down.)
Note: お V*masu* 下さい is politer than V*te* 下さい.

(⇨ ***o ~ kudasai***)

h. お V*masu* 願います

お立ち**願います**。
(Please stand up.)

Note: お V*masu* 願います is politer than V*te* 下さい.

i. {Vinf·nonpast / N の} こと <w>

日本語で書く**こと**。
(Write in Japanese.)

5月1日までに提出の**こと**。
(Submit by May 1.)

(⇨ ***koto***)

j. Vinf·nonpast ことになっている

論文は英語で発表する**ことになっています**。
(You are supposed to present your paper in English.)

(⇨ ***koto ni naru*** (DBJG: 202–03))

k. V*masu* ます

まずお湯を沸騰させ**ます**。
(First, bring the water to a boil.)

Variation:
Vinf·nonpast <w>

Note: V*masu* ます and Vinf·nonpast are commonly used in giving directions.

l. Adj(*i* / *na*)inf or adverbial form

うるさい！
(Shut up! (lit. Noisy!))

邪魔だ！
(Get out of my way! (lit. Hindering!))

早く！
(Hurry! (lit. Hurriedly!))

静かに！
(Be quiet! (lit. Quietly!))

2. Ordering someone not to do something (prohibition)

a. Vinf·nonpast な <s>

動く**な**。
(Freeze! (lit. Don't move!))

(⇨ **Imperative**)

b. V*te* はいけない

辞書を見て**はいけません**。
(You must / may not consult dictionaries.)

Variations:
V*te* はだめだ
V*te* はならない

Note: ～ちゃだめ(だ), the contracted form of ～てはだめ(だ), is used in informal conversation.

(⇨ **~ *wa ikenai*** (DBJG:528))

c. Adj(*i* / *na*)*te* はいけない

コストが高くて**はいけない**。
(The cost should not be high.)

日常生活が不規則で**はいけない**。
(Your daily schedule (lit. life) should not be irregular.)

Variation:
Adj(*i* / *na*)*te* はだめだ

d. N はいけない

激しい運動**はいけません**。
(You should not do strenuous exercise.)

Variation:
N はだめだ

e. {Vinf·nonpast こと / N} はならない

この部屋を使うこと**はなりません**。
(You must / may not use this room.)

外泊**はなりません**。
(You may not stay out overnight.)

f. Vneg ないこと <w>

辞書は見**ないこと**。
(Do not consult dictionaries.)

(⇨ ***koto***)

g. Vneg ないように

夜は一人で外出し**ないように**。
(Do not go out alone after dark.)

Variation:
Vneg ないようにね <s> inf.sit.

h. Vinf·nonpast べからず <w>

無断で入る**べからず**。
(No entrance without permission.)

i. {Vinf·nonpast こと / N} を禁ず <w>

この付近で行商すること**を禁ず**。
(Peddling is prohibited around here.)

室内での飲食**を禁ず**。

(No food and drink in the room. (lit. Drinking and eating in the room is prohibited.))

Variation:

{Vinf·nonpast こと / N} を禁じます

j. N 禁止 <w>

芝生内立ち入り**禁止**。

(Keep off the grass. (lit. Entering the grass zone is prohibited.))

k. N 厳禁 <w>

張り紙**厳禁**。

(No posters. (lit. Posters strictly prohibited.))

l. N 無用 <w>

手かぎ**無用**

(No hooks.)

m. N お断り <w>

十八歳未満(の人の入場)**お断り**。

(No admission for minors. (lit. We refuse the admission of those under 18.))

n. Vneg ないで下さい

教科書を見**ないで下さい**。

(Please don't look at your textbook.)

Variations:

Vneg ないで <s> inf.sit., f.
Vneg ないでくれ <s> inf.sit., m.
Vneg ないでちょうだい <s> inf.sit., f.

(⇨ ***kudasai*** (DBJG: 209–10))

o. Vpot·neg ないことになっている

この建物内ではたばこは吸え**ないことになっています**。
(It is a rule that you cannot smoke in this building.)

(⇨ ***koto ni naru*** (DBJG: 202–03))

3. Making requests

a. {V*te* / Vneg ないで} 下さい

漢字で書いて**下さい**。
(Please write in kanji.)

教科書を見**ないで下さい**。
(Please don't look at your textbook.)

Variations:
{V*te* / Vneg ないで} 下さいますか
{V*te* / Vneg ないで} 下さいますでしょうか
V*te* / Vneg ないで <s> inf.sit., (f)
{V*te* / Vneg ないで} くれ <s> inf.sit., m.
{V*te* / Vneg ないで} ちょうだい <s> inf.sit., f.

Note: The question ending ますか (e.g., 書いて下さいますか) makes the request less direct and therefore more polite. The conjecture question ending でしょうか (e.g., 書いて下さいますでしょうか) makes the request even less direct and more polite. In general, the longer the ending is, the politer it is.

(⇨ ***kudasai*** (DBJG: 209–10))

b. お V*masu* 下さい

お座り**下さい**。
(Please sit down.)

Variations:
お V*masu* 下さいますか
お V*masu* 下さいますでしょうか

Note: お V*masu* 下さい is politer than V*te* 下さい. (Also, see Note in 3.a.)

(⇨ ***o ~ kudasai***)

c. お V*masu* 願います

お立ち**願います**。
(Please stand up.)

Variations:
お V*masu* 願えますか
お V*masu* 願えますでしょうか
お V*masu* 願えませんか
お V*masu* 願えませんでしょうか

Notes: 1. 願えます is the potential form of 願います.

2. The negative ending ませんか is less direct than the affirmative ending ますか; therefore, it makes the request politer than ますか. (Also, see Note in 3.a.)

3. The adverbial forms of some adjectives can also be used with this pattern. (e.g., お静かに願います。(Please be quiet.); お早く願います。(Please hurry.))

d. V*te* {くれませんか / 下さいませんか}

日本語を教えて**くれませんか**。
(Could you teach me Japanese?)

日本語を教えて**下さいませんか**。
(Could you please teach me Japanese?)

Variations:
V*te* くれません? <s> inf.sit., (f.)
V*te* 下さいません? <s> inf.sit., f.
V*te* くれない? <s> inf.sit.
V*te* 下さらない? <s> inf.sit., f.
V*te* 下さいませんでしょうか
(See Note in 3.a.)

Note: Affirmative versions of the above patterns with rising intonation can also be used to make requests, i.e.,
V*te* くれます? <s> inf.sit.

V*te* くれる？ <s> inf.sit., (m.)
V*te* 下さる？ <s> inf.sit., f.
V*te* 下さいます？ <s> inf.sit., f.
The difference is that the affirmative versions are more direct and therefore less polite than the corresponding negative versions.

e. V*te* {もらえませんか / いただけませんか}

ペンを貸して**もらえませんか**。
(Could I borrow your pen? (lit. Could I have you lend me your pen?))

ペンを貸して**いただけませんか**。
(Could I borrow your pen, please? (lit. Could I have you lend me your pen, please?))

Variations:
V*te* もらえません？ <s> inf.sit.
V*te* いただけません？ <s> inf.sit., (f.)
V*te* もらえない？ <s> inf.sit.
V*te* いただけない？ <s> inf.sit., f.
V*te* もらえませんでしょうか
V*te* いただけませんでしょうか
V*te* もらえる？ <s> inf.sit., (m.)
V*te* いただける？ <s> inf.sit., f.
V*te* もらえます？ <s> inf.sit.
V*te* いただけます？ <s> inf.sit.
(See Notes in 3.a and 3.d.)

f. Vneg ないで {くれませんか / もらえませんか}

邪魔をし**ないで {くれませんか / もらえませんか}**。
(Could you stop bothering me?)

Variations:
Vneg ないでくれません？ <s> inf.sit.
Vneg ないでもらえません？ <s> inf.sit.
Vneg ないでくれない？ <s> inf.sit.
Vneg ないでもらえない？ <s> inf.sit.
Vneg ないでくれないか <s> inf.sit., m.

Vneg ないでもらえないか <s> inf.sit., m.
Vneg ないでくれる? <s> inf.sit.
Vneg ないでもらえる? <s> inf.sit.
Vneg ないでくれます? <s>
Vneg ないでもらえます? <s>
(See Note in 3.d.)

Note: Vneg ないで下さいませんか and Vneg ないでいただけませんか are awkward because 下さいませんか and いただけませんか are very polite expressions but asking someone not to do something seems contradictory.

g. V*masu* たいんです(が)

これ，アメリカへ送り**たいんですが**。
(I'd like to send this to America. (Please tell me how I could do that?))
(⇨ ***tai*** (DBJG: 441–45))

h. {V*te* / Vneg ないで} {もらい / いただき} たいんです(が)

この報告書，今日中に書いて**もらいたいんですが**。
(I'd like to ask you to write this report today.)

ここに車を止め**ないでいただきたいんですが**。
(We'd like to ask you not to park here.)

i. {V*te* / Vneg ないで} ほしいんです(が)

今すぐ来て**ほしいんですが**。
(I'd like you to come right away.)

勝手にこの部屋に入ら**ないでほしいんですが**。
(I'd rather you wouldn't enter this room without permission.)

Note: The pattern in (i) is less polite than that in (h).

j. N (Prt.) お願いします

[To a taxi driver]

東京駅まで**お願いします**。
(To Tokyo Station, please.)

これ，航空便で**お願いします**。
((I'd like to send) this by airmail, please.)

Variations:
N (Prt.) お願い出来ますか
N (Prt.) お願いしたいんですが

4. Asking for help; seeking advice

Sinf んですが ((何か) いい N {はありませんか / を知りませんか})
(だ after Adj(*na*)stem and N changes to な.)

窓が開かない**んですが**。
(The window doesn't open. (Could you help?))

日本で仕事をしたい**んですが**，**何かいい**仕事**はありませんか**。
(I'd like to work in Japan. Are there any good jobs?)

(⇨ ***no da*** (DBJG: 325–28))

Note: In this pattern, S describes the situation with / for which the speaker wants help, advice, or suggestions.

5. Giving advice or making suggestions

a. Vinf·nonpast {べきだ / べきではない} (と思う)

専門家の意見を聞く**べきだ**(**と思う**)。
((I think) you/we should ask for a specialist's opinion.)

今すぐ結論を出す**べきではない**。
(You/We shouldn't reach a conclusion right now.)

Note: A suggestion with べきだ is quite strong. と思う can be used to soften the tone.

(⇨ ***bekida***)

b. Vinf ことだ

あまり心配しない**ことです**。
(You shouldn't worry too much.)

c. Vinf {ものだ / ものではない}

人の意見は聞く**ものだ**。
(You should listen to others' opinions.)

人の悪口を言う**もんじゃない**。
(You shouldn't speak ill of others.)

(⇨ ***mono*** **(*da*)** (DBJG: 257–61))

d. Vaff·inf·past 方がいい

病院へ行った**方がいい**ですよ。
(You'd better go see the doctor (lit. go to the hospital).)

Note: This pattern cannot be used with Vneg·inf·past.

(⇨ **~ *hō ga ii*** (DBJG: 138–40))

e. Vinf·nonpast 方がいい

先生に相談する**方がいい**です。
(It would be better to consult your teacher.)

このことは誰にも言わない**方がいい**ですよ。
(You'd better not tell anyone about this.)

(⇨ **~ *hō ga ii*** (DBJG: 138–40))

f. Vinf といい

タクシーで行く**といい**です。
(It would be a good idea to go by taxi.)

g. Vaff·inf·past らどうですか

アスピリンを飲んだ**らどうですか**。
(How about taking some aspirin? / Why don't you take some aspirin?)

(⇨ **~ *tara dō desu ka*** (DBJG: 457–58))

Variations:
Vaff·inf·past らいかがですか
Vaff·inf·past らいかがです? <s>
Vaff·inf·past らいかが? <s> inf.sit., f.

Vaff·inf·past らどうです?　<s> inf.sit., (m.)
Vaff·inf·past らどう?　<s> inf.sit.
Vaff·inf·past ら?　<s> inf.sit.

h. N はどうですか

日曜日**はどうですか**。
(How about Sunday?)

(⇨ ***dō*** (DBJG: 114–15))

Variations:
N はいかがですか
N はいかがです?　<s>
N はいかが?　<s> inf.sit., f.
N はどうです?　<s> inf.sit., (m.)
N はどう?　<s> inf.sit.

6. Asking for / granting permission

a. V*te*（も）いいです（か）

A: この辞書，ちょっと借りて**もいいですか**。
(May I borrow this dictionary for a moment?)

B: （ええ，）{いいですよ / どうぞ}。
(Sure.)

B′: あ，すみません。それはちょっと。
(I'm sorry, but I'd rather you didn't.)

Note: There are a variety of ways to respond to A's request negatively, but negative responses are usually expressed rather indirectly, as in B′. (i) is another example.

(i) あ，これからちょっと使うんですが。
(Oh, I'm going to use it now.)

Variations:
V*te* もよろしいでしょうか
V*te* もよろしいですか
V*te* もよろしい?　<s> inf.sit.

V*te* もかまいませんか
V*te* もかまいません?　<s> inf.sit., (f.)
V*te* もかまわない?　<s> inf.sit.
V*te* もいいでしょうか
V*te* もいいです?　<s> inf.sit.
V*te* もいい?　<s> inf.sit.

(⇨ ***~ te mo ii*** (DBJG: 471–73))

b. N,（ちょっと）いいですか

これ，**ちょっといいですか**。
(May I use / borrow / see / etc. this for a second?)

Variations:
N,（ちょっと）よろしいでしょうか
N,（ちょっと）よろしいですか
N,（ちょっと）よろしい?　<s> inf.sit.
N,（ちょっと）かまいませんか
N,（ちょっと）かまいません?　<s> inf.sit.
N,（ちょっと）かまわない?　<s> inf.sit.
N,（ちょっと）いいでしょうか
N,（ちょっと）いいです?　<s> inf.sit.
N,（ちょっと）いい?　<s> inf.sit.

c. V(causative *te*-form) いただけませんか

このワープロ，使(つか)わせて**いただけませんか**。
(Could you let me use this word processor?)

Variations:
V(causative *te*-form) もらえませんか
V(causative *te*-form) くれませんか
(See Variations in 3.e. and 3.f.)

d. V*masu* たいんですが，いいですか

ちょっと電話(でんわ)をかけ**たいんですが，いいですか**。
(I'd like to make a phone call. Is it all right?)

7. Extending invitations

a. V*masu* ませんか

A: 今晩，映画に行き**ませんか**。
(Would you like to go to a movie tonight?)

B: いいですね。行きましょう。
(Yes, let's.)

B′: すみませんが，今晩はちょっと予定があるんです。
(I'm sorry I have other plans tonight.)

Variations:
V*masu* ません? <s> inf.sit., (f.)
Vneg·inf? <s> inf.sit.

b. V*masu* ましょう（か / よ）

すしを食べ**ましょうか**。
(Shall we have sushi?)

すしを食べ**ましょう**(**よ**)。
(Let's have sushi.)

(⇨ ~ ***mashō*** (DBJG: 240–43))

Note: The sentence particle よ makes the invitation stronger.

c. Vvol（か / よ） <s> inf.sit., (m.)

すしを食べ**ようか**。
(Shall we have sushi?)

すしを食べ**よう**(**よ**)。 <s>
(Let's have sushi.)

(See Note in 7.b.)

d. N でもどうですか <s>

今晩 食事**でもどうですか**。
(How about dinner tonight?)

Variations:
N でもいかがですか <s>
N でもどう? <s> inf.sit.

8. Offering something; offering to do something

a. N {は / でも} {いかが / どう}ですか

コーヒー**はいかがですか**。
(Would you like coffee?)

b. N, どうぞ

このハンカチ, **どうぞ**。
(Please (use) this handkerchief.)

c. V*masu* ましょう

そのかばん, 持ち**ましょう**。
(Let me carry that bag.)

Variation:
お V*masu* しましょう

d. V*masu* ましょうか

そのかばん, 持ち**ましょうか**。
(Shall I carry that bag?)

Variation:
お V*masu* しましょうか

9. Expressing obligation / necessity

a. Vneg なければならない

明日井上さんに会わ**なければならない**。
(I have to meet Mr. Inoue tomorrow.)

Variations:
Vneg なければいけない
Vneg なくてはならない
Vneg なくてはいけない

Vneg ねばならない
Vneg ないといけない
Vneg なければ <s>
Vneg なくては <s>
Vneg なくちゃ(ならない / いけない) <s> inf.sit.
Vneg なきゃ(ならない / いけない) <s> inf.sit.

(⇨ ***~ nakereba naranai*** (DBJG: 274–76))

b. {Adj(*i*)stemく / Adj(*na*)*te* / N で} なければならない

学校(がっこう)の成績(せいせき)がよく**なければならない**。
(Your school grades must be good.)

体(からだ)が丈夫(じょうぶ)で**なければならない**。
(Your body must be strong.)

応募者(おうぼしゃ)は日本人(にほんじん)で**なければならない**。
(Applicants must be Japanese.)

Variations:
{Adj(*i*)stemく / Adj(*na*)*te* / N で} なければいけない
{Adj(*i*)stemく / Adj(*na*)*te* / N で} なくてはならない
{Adj(*i*)stemく / Adj(*na*)*te* / N で} なくてはいけない
{Adj(*i*)stemく / Adj(*na*)*te* / N で} ないといけない
{Adj(*i*)stemく / Adj(*na*)*te* / N で} なくちゃ(ならない / いけない) <s> inf.sit.
{Adj(*i*)stemく / Adj(*na*)*te* / N で} なきゃ(ならない / いけない) <s> inf.sit.

c. Vinf わけにはいかない

大切(たいせつ)な会議(かいぎ)なので休(やす)む**わけにはいかない**。
(Because it is an important meeting, I cannot excuse myself from it.)

(⇨ ***wake ni wa ikanai***)

d. Vneg ざるを得(え)ない

これは規則(きそく)だから従(したが)わ**ざるを得ない**。
(Since this is a regulation, we cannot help but obey it.)

(⇨ ***zaru o enai***)

e. Vinf·nonpast べきだ

この会議には君も出席す**べきだ**。
(You should attend this meeting, too.)

(⇨ ***bekida***)

f. Vinf·nonpast 必要がある

専門家に相談する**必要がある**。
(We need to consult a specialist.)

g. Vneg なくてもいい

この手紙は日本語で書か**なくてもいい**。
(This letter doesn't have to be written in Japanese.)

Variations:
Vneg なくてもかまわない
Vneg なくても大丈夫だ
Vneg ないでもいい
Vneg ないでもかまわない
Vneg ないでも大丈夫だ

(⇨ **~ *temo ii*** (DBJG: 471–73))

h. {Adj(*i*)stemく / Adj(*na*)*te* / N で} なくてもいい

背が高く**なくてもいい**。
(You don't have to be tall.)

日本語が上手で**なくてもいい**。
(You don't have to be good at Japanese.)

材料は金属で**なくてもいい**。
(The materials do not have to be metal.)

Variations:
{Adj(*i*)stemく / Adj(*na*)*te* / N で} なくてもかまわない
{Adj(*i*)stemく / Adj(*na*)*te* / N で} なくても大丈夫だ

i. Vinf·nonpast 必要はない

この書類は保存する**必要はない**。
(We do not have to keep this document.)

j. {Adj(*na*)stem / N} である必要はない

構造は柔軟**である必要はない**。
(The structure does not have to be flexible.)

場所は大都市**である必要はない**。
(The place does not have to be a big city.)

10. Expressing intentions / volition

a. V*masu* つもりだ

来年日本へ行く**つもりだ**。
(I'm planning to go to Japan next year.)

(⇨ ***tsumori*** (DBJG: 503–07))

b. Vvol と思う/思っている

家を買おう**と思っています**。
(I'm thinking of buying a house.)

(⇨ **~ *yō to omou*** (DBJG: 569–71))

c. Vinf·nonpast まい

もう彼とは会う**まい**と思った。
(I thought I would not see him any more.)

(⇨ ***mai***)

d. V*masu* ましょう

A: 誰か吉田さんに電話してくれませんか。
(Could someone call Mr. Yoshida?)

B: 私がし**ましょう**。
(I will.)

(⇨ **~ *mashō*** (DBJG: 240–43))

Variation:
Vvol <s> inf.sit., m.

11. Expressing decisions

a. Vinf·nonpast ことに{する / 決める}

日本の大学へ行く**ことにしました**。
(I've decided to go to a Japanese university.)

(⇨ ***koto ni suru*** (DBJG: 204–06))

b. N に{する / 決める}

私は天ぷら**にします**。
(I'll have tempura.)

c. Vinf·nonpast ことに{なる / 決まる}

その会議にはスミスさんが行く**ことになった**。
(It's been decided that Mr. Smith will attend the conference.)

(⇨ ***koto ni naru*** (DBJG: 202–03))

d. N に{なる / 決まる}

次期社長は上田氏**に決まった**。
(It's been decided that the next president will be Mr. Ueda.)

12. Expressing desires / wishes

a. N が欲しい

ピアノ**が欲しい**。
(I want a piano.)

(⇨ ***hoshii***[1] (DBJG: 144–46))

b. V*masu* たい

ヨーロッパを旅行し**たい**。
(I want to travel in Europe.)

(⇨ ***tai*** (DBJG: 441–45))

c. V*te* 欲しい

僕はメアリーに歌って**欲しい**。
(I'd like Mary to sing.)

(⇨ ***hoshii***[2] (DBJG: 146–47))

Variation:

V*te* もらいたい

d. Scond (いい) と思う

もっと時間が {あったら / あれば} **いいと思います。**
(I wish I had more time.)

Variations:

Scond いいんですが
Scond (いい) なあ <s> inf.sit., (m.)
Sinf·nonpast といいと思う
Sinf·nonpast といいんですが
Sinf·nonpast といいなあ <s> inf.sit., (m.)

13. Conveying information

a. Sinf そうだ

ブラウンさんが結婚する**そうだ。**
(I heard that Mr. Brown is getting married.)

(⇨ ***sōda***[1] (DBJG: 407–09))

b. Sinf らしい

河野さんがうちを買った**らしい。**
(I heard that Mr. Kono bought a house.)

(⇨ ***rashii*** (DBJG: 373–75))

c. Sinf と(か)いうことだ

パーティーは取り止めになった**と(か)いうことだ。**
(They say that the party has been canceled.)

d. Sinf とのことだ

永田さんは少し遅れる**とのことです。**
(I was told that Mr. Nagata is going to be a litte late.)

e. Sinf と言っている

スーザンは明日のパーティーには行かない**と言っている。**
(Susan says she will not go to tomorrow's party.)

Variation:

Sinf って <s> inf.sit.

(⇨ ***-tte***[2] (DBJG: 510–11))

f. Sinf と聞いている

吉田さんは神戸に転勤になった**と聞いています**。

(I hear that Mr. Yoshida has been transferred to Kobe.)

g. Sinf 由 <w>

(だ after Adj(*na*) and N changes to の.)

来週東京にいらっしゃる**由**，楽しみにしています。

(I hear that you are coming to Tokyo next week. I'm looking forward to seeing you.)

お元気の**由**，何よりです。

(I'm glad to hear that you are doing fine.)

h. N によると

テレビのニュース**によると**，昨日アラスカで大きな地震があったそうだ。

(According to a TV report, there was a big earthquake in Alaska yesterday.)

(⇨ ***sōda***[1] (DBJG: 407–09))

Variation:

N の話では

14. Expressing certainty

a. Sinf はずだ (だ after Adj(*na*) and N changes to な and の, respectively.)

ジョージとアリスも来る**はずだ**。

(I expect George and Alice will come, too.)

(⇨ ***hazu*** (DBJG: 133–35))

b. Sinf に違いない (だ after Adj(*na*) and N drops.)

好子がみんなにしゃべった**に違いない**。

(It must be Yoshiko who told everybody about that.)

(⇨ ***ni chigainai*** (DBJG: 304–06))

Variations:
Sinf に決まっている (だ after Adj(*na*) and N drops.)
Sinf に相違ない (だ after Adj(*na*) and N drops.)

c. Adverb of certainty + S

和男は**きっと**来る。
(I'm sure Kazuo will come.)

Note: Other adverbs of certainty include: 必ず (for sure); 間違いなく (without fail); 絶対 (absolutely)

15. Expressing uncertainty

a. Sinf {でしょう / だろう} (だ after Adj(*na*) and N drops.)

ジュディーはまだ帰っていない**でしょう**。
(Judy probably hasn't returned yet.)

(⇨ ***darō*** (DBJG: 100–02))

Variations:
Sinf であろう <w> (だ after Adj(*na*) and N drops.)
Sinf でありましょう <w> (だ after Adj(*na*) and N drops.)

(⇨ ***de arō***)

b. Vinf まい <w>

ジョンはこのことを知る**まい**。
(John probably doesn't know this.)

(⇨ ***mai***)

c. Vvol

この日本語なら一年生の学生でも**読めよう**。
(Even first-year students can probably read this Japanese.)

(⇨ ***yō***^{2})

d. Adj(*i*)stem かろう

このプロジェクトは難し**かろう**。
(This project will probably be difficult.)

(⇨ ***karō***)

e. {V*masu* / Adj(*i* / *na*)stem} そうだ

雨が降り**そうだ。**
(It looks like rain.)

この本は面白**そうだ。**
(This book looks interesting.)

(⇨ ***sōda***[2] (DBJG: 410–12))

f. Sinf らしい (だ after Adj(*na*) and N drops.)

松田さんはまだそのことを知らされていない**らしい。**
(Mr. Matsuda doesn't seem to have been informed of that yet.)

(⇨ ***rashii*** (DBJG: 373–75))

g. Sinf ようだ (だ after Adj(*na*) and N changes to な and の, respectively.)

この問題は学生には難しすぎる**ようだ。**
(This problem seems to be too difficult for the students.)

Variation:
Sinf みたいだ (だ after Adj(*na*) and N drops.)

(⇨ ***yōda*** (DBJG: 547–52))

16. Expressing possibility / impossibility

a. Sinf かも知れない (だ after Adj(*na*) and N drops.)

前田さんは来られない**かも知れない。**
(Mr. Maeda might not be able to come.)

Variation:
かも分からない

(⇨ ***kamoshirenai*** (DBJG: 173–75))

b. Vinf 得る

この報告が間違っていることもあり**得る。**
(It is possible that this report is wrong.)

そんなことは起こり**得ない。**
(Such a thing cannot happen.)

(⇨ ***uru/eru***)

c. Vinf·nonpast かねない

あの男ならそれぐらいのことはやり**かねない**。
(He may well do things like that.)

(⇨ ***-kaneru***)

d. Sinf とは限らない

体の弱い人が早く死ぬ**とは限らない**。
(It is not always true that frail people die young.)

(⇨ ***to wa kagiranai***)

e. {Vneg / Adj(*i*)stem く / Adj(*na*)*te* / N で} ないとも限らない

その証人の言っていることが間違ってい**ないとも限らない**。
(It is not impossible that what the witness is saying is wrong.)

f. Sinf わけがない
(だ after Adj(*na*) and N changes to な and である, respectively.)

彼にこの問題が解ける**わけがない**。
(It is impossible for him to solve this problem.)

(⇨ ***wake ga nai***)

17. Expressing ability / possibility

a. Vinf·nonpast ことが出来る

新幹線に乗れば東京から大阪まで三時間足らずで行く**ことが出来る**。
(By *Shinkansen* you can go from Tokyo to Osaka in less than three hours.)

(⇨ ***koto ga dekiru*** (DBJG: 200–01))

b. N が出来る

私はドイツ語**が出来ます**。
(I can speak German.)

c. Vpot

キャシーは中国語が**読める**。
(Kathy can read Chinese.)

(⇨ ***rareru***[2] (DBJG: 370–73))

d. V*masu* 得る

かなりの地震は予知し**得る**。

(Many earthquakes are predictable.)

(⇨ ***uru/eru***)

e. V*masu* かねる

それは私には答え**かねます**。

(I cannot answer that.)

(⇨ ***-kaneru***)

18. Expressing habits

a. Vinf·nonpast ことにしている

毎日一マイル泳ぐ**ことにしている**。

(I make it a habit to swim one mile every day.)

(⇨ ***koto ni suru*** (DBJG: 204–06))

b. Vinf·past ものだ

学生時代にはよく洋画を見た**ものです**。

(I used to see foreign films a lot when I was a student.)

(⇨ ***mono*** (***da***) (DBJG: 257–61))

19. Expressing experience

Vinf·past ことがある

私は中学校で英語を教えた**ことがある**。

(I have taught English at a junior high school.)

(⇨ ***koto ga aru***[1] (DBJG: 196–98))

20. Expressing resemblance

a. N のようだ

この湖はまるで海**のようだ**。

(This lake is just like the sea.)

Variation:

N みたいだ

(⇨ ***yōda*** (DBJG: 547–52))

b. N のように

マリリンは日本人**のように**日本語を話す。
(Marilyn speaks Japanese like a Japanese.)

(⇨ ***yōni***[2] (DBJG: 554–56))

21. Expressing comparison

a. A は B より

日本語**は**スペイン語**より**面白い。
(Japanese is more interesting than Spanish.)

(⇨ ***yori***[1] (DBJG: 564–67))

b. A と B とどちら(の方)が

日本語**と**ロシア語**とどちらが**難しいですか。
(Which is more difficult, Japanese or Russian?)

c. A の方が B より

日本語**の方が**ロシア語**より**難しいです。
(Japanese is more difficult than Russian.)

(⇨ ***yori***[1] (DBJG: 564–67))

d. A は B ほど ～ない

ロシア語**は**日本語**ほど**難しく**ない**。
(Russian is not as difficult as Japanese.)

(⇨ ***hodo*** (DBJG: 135–38))

22. Expressing happiness / relief

a. {V*te* / Adj(*i* / *na*)*te* / N + で} {よかった / 助かった / etc.}

日本語を勉強しておいて**よかった**。
(I'm glad that I studied Japanese.)

家賃が安くて**助かった**。
(I was lucky because the rent was cheap.)

b. {Vneg / Adj(*i*)stem く / Adj(*na*)*te* / N + で} なくて {よかった / 助かった / etc.}

あの飛行機に乗ら**なくて助かった**。
(I was lucky that I didn't take that plane.)

23. Expressing regret

a. Vcond よかった

カメラを持って来れば**よかった**。
(I wish I had brought a camera with me.)

(⇨ ***ba yokatta*** (DBJG: 87–89))

b. Vneg なければよかった

ジョンに会わ**なければよかった**。
(I wish I had not seen John.)

24. Expressing gratitude

a. N (を)ありがとう(ございます / ました)

お手紙，**ありがとうございました**。
(Thank you very much for your letter.)

b. V*te* {いただいて / 下さって / etc.} ありがとう(ございます / ました)

丁寧に教えて**下さってありがとうございました**。
(Thank you very much for showing me (the way) carefully.)

c. V*te* {いただいて / 下さって / etc.} すみません(でした)

長い間お借り**してすみませんでした**。
(Thank you for letting me borrow this for an extended period. (lit. I'm sorry that I borrowed this for an extended period.))

d. V*te* {いただいて / 下さって / etc.} 助かりました

送って**いただいて助かりました**。
(It was so helpful that you gave me a ride.)

25. Apologizing

V*te* すみません

A: 遅くなって**すみません**。
(I'm sorry I'm late.)

B: いいえ。
(That's all right.)

Variations:
すみません，V*te* <s>
V*te* ごめんなさい (f.)
ごめんなさい，V*te* <s> (f.)
V*te* ごめん <s> inf.sit.
ごめん，V*te* <s> inf.sit.
V*te* すまないね <s> inf.sit., m.
すまないね，V*te* <s> inf.sit., m.

ENGLISH INDEX

A

a *ni tsuki*
a way of -ing *-yō*[1]
a way to *-yō*[1]
à la *fū ni*
-able *uru/eru*
about *ni kanshite/kansuru, ni tsuite, no koto*
absolutely not *masaka*
according to *ni yotte/yori, no ue de wa*
accordingly *ni shitagatte/shitagai, shitagatte*
after ~ *kekka, (no) ue de*
after all *dōse, tōtō, tsumari*
after ~ style *fū ni*
against *ni hanshite/hansuru*
almost *-sō ni naru*
alone *nomi*
along with *to tomo ni*
also *mo, ~ mo ~ mo, sore to*
although *kuse ni, nagara(mo), ni mo kakawarazu, to iu noni, tsutsu*
although ~ say/said that *to itte mo*
am determined to *miseru*
amount equivalent to ~ *-bun*
and *-ku, sore to, -te,* V*masu*
and yet *kuse ni, shika mo*
anyway *dōse*
apparently *omowareru*
appear *omowareru*
apt to *-ppoi*
as *hodo, ni shitagatte/shitagai, ni tsurete/tsure, to dōji ni, tōri (ni), to tomo ni*
as a matter of fact *nanishiro, sore dokoroka*
as a result of *kekka*
as far as *kagiri*[1]
as far as ~ goes *no ue de wa*
as far as ~ is concerned *no ue de wa, ten (de)*
as few as *ni suginai*
as if to say/show (etc.) that *to iu fū ni*
as little as *ni suginai*
as long as *ijō (wa), kagiri*[1]*, sae*
as might be expected *sasuga*
as soon as *shidai, totan (ni)*
as well *sore to, ue (ni)*
as well as *igai, to dōji ni, to tomo ni*
as you know *wake da*
aspect *ten (de)*
assume that *to suru*[1]
at *ni atatte/atari, ni oite/okeru*
at ~ -est *tomo*
at all *dōse*
at all events *dōse*
at (long) last *tōtō, yatto*

cannot help -ing *naranai, wake ni wa ikanai, zaru o enai*
cause *koto de, koto ni naru*
certainly ~ but *tashikani ~ ga*
come to mean that *koto ni naru*
common *tada no*
compared with/to *ni kuraberu to/kurabete*
concerning *ni kanshite/kansuru, ni tsuite*
consequently *shitagatte*
considerably *nakanaka*
contrary to *ni hanshite/hansuru*
contrary to one's expectation/intention *-gatai*
conversely *-gatai*
covered with *-darake*

D

definitely *koso*
definitely ~ but *tashikani ~ ga*
depend on *shidai*
depending on *ni yotte/yori*
despite *ni mo kakawarazu*
difficult to *-gatai*
do *yaru*[1]
do/does/did V *wa*
do not have to *made mo nai*
do not need (to go as far as) to *made mo nai*
do s.t. in a ~ fashion / manner / way *-kata o suru*
don't tell me that *masaka*
Don't V Imperative, *koto*
drink *yaru*[1]
due to *ni yotte/yori, sei*
during *ni oite/okeru*

E

each *sorezore*
each time *tabi ni*
easily *sugu*
easy to *-ppoi*
eat *yaru*[1]
either ~ or ~ *mata wa*
end up (with) *koto ni naru*
even *dokoroka, sae*
even if *kara to itte, ta tokoro de, tomo*
even so *shikamo, sore demo, sō ka to itte*
even though *kara to itte, nagara (mo)*
even though ~ say/said that *to itte mo*
eventually *tōtō*
every time *tabi ni*
except (for) *igai*

F

fairly *nakanaka*
far from (that) *dokoroka, sore dokoroka*
feel ~ *to suru*[2]
filled with *-darake*
finally *tōtō, yatto*
following *ni shitagatte/shitagai*
for *-bun, de, ni totte, ni tsuki, ni wa, -rai*

for some reason *dōmo*
for some reason like ~ *toka de*
for the first time *te hajimete*
for the purpose of *ni wa*
for the reason *-jō*
for the sake of *-jō*
from ~ on *-kagiri*[2]
from the aspect of *-men*
from the standpoint/viewpoint of *-jō, -men, no ue de wa*
from ~ till/to ~ *~ kara ~ ni kakete, ~ kara ~ ni itaru made*
from ~ to *ni yotte/yori*
from what I gather *dōmo*
full of *-darake*
furthermore *shika mo, sono ue, sore ni, sore mo, ue (ni)*

G

give *yaru*[1]

H

hard *-kaneru*
hardly *rokuni ~ nai*
hardly possible *-kaneru*
have been -ing *-ppanashi*
have no (other) choice but to *wake ni wa ikanai, zaru o enai*
have to *-neba naranai, zaru o enai*
having done s.t. *te*
hesitate to do *-kaneru*
How ~ ! *donnani ~ (koto) ka, nā*
however *daga, tokoro ga*
however, it doesn't follow from this that *dakara to itte*

I

I admit that ~ but *tashikani ~ ga*
I cannot manage to *dōmo*
I don't know for sure, but *nan-demo*
I don't know why but *dōmo*
I don't mean that *wake de wa nai*
I gather that *dōmo*
I tell you *sa, zo*
I wish *nā*
I wonder (if ~) *kana, nā*
if *ni naru to, te wa*
if ~ as much/many as ~, it will be enough to *~ mo ~ ba*
if ~ at all *ijō (wa)*
if ~ at least *~ mo ~ ba*
if it is the case that *to naru to*
if it is true that *to naru to*
if it turns out that *to naru to*
if ~ just/only *sae*
if ~ say that *to iu to*
I'm telling you *zo*
immediately *sugu*
impossible *-gatai, masaka*
impressive *sasuga*
in *ni atatte/atari, ni oite/okeru, ni taishite/taishi, no moto de, -rai*
in accordance with *ni shitagatte/shitagai*
(and) in addition *sore ni, sore to, ue (ni)*
in any case *dōse*

J

K

L

less objectionable *mashida*
let *to suru*[1]
let alone *wa iu made mo naku*
-like *-ppoi*
like *fū ni, to*
(things) like ~ *nado to*
like ~ or ~ *~ nari ~ nari*
like this *kō shita*
likely *-yō*[2]
limited to *-kagiri*[2]
look ~ *to suru*[2]

M

may not *koto*
mean *to iu no wa ~ koto da*
mere *ni suginai*
merely *ni suginai*
might as well *mashida*
more ~ *yori*
more surprisingly *shika mo*
more ~ than ~ *to iu yori (wa)*
moreover *shika mo, sono ue, sore mo, sore ni, ue (ni)*
must *-neba naranai*
must be *-yō*[2]

N

namely *tsumari*
naturally *sasuga, -yō*[2]
(yes,) naturally *sore wa*
neither ~ nor ~ *~ mo ~ mo*
never dreamed *masaka*
never thought *masaka*
nevertheless *daga, nagara(mo), ni mo kakawarazu, shika mo, sore demo*
No -ing Imperative
no matter how *dōmo*
no matter ~ may be *tomo*
no matter what *nanishiro*
not *-nu*
not Adj. / N / V *wa*
not always *kanarazushimo, to wa kagiranai*
not ~ and / but *-naku*
not at all likely *masaka*
not easily *nakanaka*
not either *mo, ~ mo ~ mo*
not even *mo*
not just *dokoroka*
not limited to ~ (but also) *ni kagirazu*
not more than *ni suginai*
not necessarily *kanarazushimo, to wa kagiranai*
not necessary *koto wa nai*
not necessary (to bother) to *made mo nai*
not only ~ (but also) *~ bakari ka ~ (sae), ni kagirazu, o hajime (to shite), sono ue, ue (ni)*
not ought to *koto*
not properly *rokuni ~ nai*
not readily *nakanaka*
not satisfactorily *rokuni ~ nai*
not sufficiently *rokuni ~ nai*
not to mention *wa iu made mo naku*
not to speak of *wa iu made mo naku*

not to V Imperative
not until *te hajimete*
not well *rokuni ~ nai*
nothing more than *ni suginai*
notwithstanding *ni mo kakawarazu*
now that *ijō (wa)*

O

of *ni tsuite*
(yes,) of course *sore wa*
often *-gachi*
oh, surely *sore wa*
on *ni kanshite/kansuru, ni oite/okeru, ni tsuite, ni tsuki*
on behalf of *ni kawatte*
on every occasion *tabi ni*
on the basis of *ni yotte/yori*
on the contrary *kaette, sore dokoroka*
on the occasion of *ni atatte/atari, sai(ni)*
on the one hand ~, on the other hand *ippō de (wa) ~ tahō de (wa)*
on the side of *-men*
on top of that *shika mo, sono ue, sore mo, sore ni*
once *ijō (wa)*
only *-kagiri*[2], *ni kagitte, ni suginai, nomi, tada*
only (when, after, because, etc.) *koso*
only after *te hajimete*
only until *-kagiri*[2]
operate *yaru*[1]
or *~ ka ~ ka, mata wa*
~ or ~ (for example) *~ nari ~ nari*
~ or something like *nado to*
ordinary *tada no*
other than *igai*
ought *-yō*[2]
ought to *bekida*
owing to *ni yotte/yori*

P

per *de, ni taishite/taishi, ni tsuki*
plain *tada no*
play *yaru*[1]
please do s.t. *o ~ kudasai*
point *ten (de)*
portion *-bun*
possible *uru/eru*
precisely *koso*
preferable *mashida*
pretty *kekkō, nakanaka*
prior to *ni atatte/atari*
probably *de arō, karō, -yō*[2]

Q

quite *kekkō, nakanaka*

R

rank-and-file *tada no*
rather *kaette, kekkō*
rather than ~ *kurai, to iu yori (wa)*
readily *sugu*
really *ikanimo, sasuga*
regard *ten (de)*

S

T

X

(X) of all (X's) *ni kagitte*

Y

yet *daga, sō ka to itte, sore demo*
you know *sa, zo*
you may be surprised, but *nanishiro*
you would think that ~ but (that is not right) *ka to iu to*

JAPANESE INDEX

Note: Entries in non-bold type appear in DBJG, and entries in bold type are included in this book. X <Y> indicates that X is found under Y.

A

B

C

D

M

N

O

T

U

V

W

REFERENCES

Alfonso, Anthony (1966) *Japanese Language Patterns—a Structural Approach*, Volume I & II, Sophia University L.L. Center of Applied Linguistics, Tokyo.

Brown, Delmer M. (1987) *An Introduction to Advanced Spoken Japanese*, Inter-University Center for Japanese Language Studies, Yokohama.

Hinds, John and Irwin Howard (eds.) (1978) *Problems in Japanese Syntax and Semantics*, Kaitakusha, Tokyo.

Hirose, Masayoshi and Kakuko Shoji (eds.) (1994) *Effective Japanese Usage Guide—A Concise Explanation of Frequently Confused Words and Phrases*, Kodansha, Tokyo.

Japanese Language Promotion Center (ed.) (1981) *Intensive Course in Japanese—Intermediate*, Language Services, Tokyo.

Jorden, Eleanor H. and Mari Noda (1987) *Japanese: The Spoken Language* (Part 1), New Haven and London.

——(1988) *Japanese: The Spoken Language* (Part 2), New Haven and London.

Kamada, Osamu and Wesley M. Jacobsen (eds.) (1990) *On Japanese and How to Teach It—In Honor of Seiichi Makino*, The Japan Times, Tokyo.

Kuno, Susumu (1973) *The Structure of the Japanese Language*, MIT Press, Cambridge, Massachusetts.

Makino, Seiichi (1983) "Speaker / Listener-Orientation and Formality Marking in Japanese," *Gengo Kenkyū—the Journal of the Linguistic Society of Japan*, 84, 126–145, Taishukan, Tokyo.

Makino, Seiichi and Michio Tsutsui (1986) *A Dictionary of Basic Japanese Grammar*, The Japan Times, Tokyo.

Martin, Samuel (1975) *A Reference Grammar of Japanese*, Yale University Press, New Haven, Connecticut.

Masuda, Koh (ed.) (1974) *Kenkyusha's New Japanese-English Dictionary* (fourth ed.), Kenkyusha, Tokyo.

McClain, Yoko Matsuoka (1981) *Handbook of Modern Japanese Grammar*, Hokuseido, Tokyo.

McGloin, Naomi Hanaoka (1989) *A Students' Guide to Japanese Grammar*, Taishukan, Tokyo.

Miura, Akira and Naomi Hanaoka McGloin (1994) *An Integrated Approach to Intermediate Japanese*, The Japan Times, Tokyo.

Nagara, Susumu, et al. (1990) *Japanese for Everyone*, Gakken, Tokyo.

Sakuma, Katsuhiko and Frank T. Motofuji (1980) *Advanced Spoken Japanese: Tonari no*

Shibafu, Institute of East Asian Studies, University of California, Berkeley, California.

Shibatani, Masayoshi (ed.) (1976) *Syntax and Semantics 5: Japanese Generative Grammar*, Academic Press, New York and San Francisco.

Soga, Matsuo and Noriko Matsumoto (1978) *Foundations of Japanese Language*, Taishukan, Tokyo.

Soga, Matsuo (1983) *Tense and Aspect in Modern Colloquial Japanese*, University of British Columbia Press, Vancouver, Canada.

Soga, Matsuo, et al. (1987) *Standard Japanese*, Taishukan, Tokyo.

Suleski, Ronald and Hiroko Masada (1982) *Affective Expressions in Japanese*, Hokuseido, Tokyo.

Tatematsu, Kikuko, et al. (1991) *Formal Expressions for Japanese Interaction*, The Japan Times, Tokyo.

Tohsaku, Yasu-Hiko (1994) *Yookoso—An Invitation to Contemporary Japanese*, McGraw-Hill, New York.

Tsukuba Language Group (1991) *Situational Functional Japanese* (Vols. 1–3), Bonjinsha, Tokyo.

Tsutsui, Michio (1990) "A Study of Demonstrative Adjectives before Anaphoric Nouns in Japanese," in Kamada and Jacobsen (1990), 121–135.

浅野鶴子他編（1971）『外国人のための基本語用例辞典』（第二版）文化庁

大野晋・佐竹昭広・前田金五郎編（1974）『岩波古語辞典』岩波書店

大野晋・浜西正人編（1981）『角川類語新辞典』角川書店

加藤泰彦・福地務（1989）『テンス・アスペクト・ムード』（「外国人のための日本語例文・問題シリーズ」15），荒竹出版

茅野直子・秋元美晴・真田一司（1987）『副詞』（「外国人のための日本語例文・問題シリーズ」1），荒竹出版

北川千里・井口厚夫（1988）『助動詞』（「外国人のための日本語例文・問題シリーズ」8），荒竹出版

北川千里・鎌田修・井口厚夫（1988）『助詞』（「外国人のための日本語例文・問題シリーズ」7），荒竹出版

久野暲（1973）『日本文法研究』大修館書店

——— （1978）『談話の文法』大修館書店

——— （1983）『新日本文法研究』大修館書店

駒田聡他編（1990）『中・上級日本語教科書文型索引』くろしお出版

阪田雪子・倉持保男（1980）『教師用日本語教育ハンドブック　文法 II』国際交流基金

柴谷方良（1978）『日本語の分析』大修館書店

鈴木忍（1978）『教師用日本語教育ハンドブック　文法 I』国際交流基金

筑波大学日本語教育研究会編（1983）『日本語表現文型　中級 I』イセブ

——— （1983）『日本語表現文型　中級 II』イセブ

寺村秀夫（1982)『日本語のシンタクスと意味 I』くろしお出版
――― (1984)『日本語のシンタクスと意味 II』くろしお出版
――― (1991)『日本語のシンタクスと意味 III』くろしお出版
名柄迪・広田紀子・中西家栄子（1987)『形式名詞』(「外国人のための日本語例文・問題シリーズ」2)，荒竹出版
名古屋大学総合言語センター日本語学科編（1988)『現代日本語コース中級 I』名古屋大学出版会
――― (1989)『現代日本語コース中級 II』名古屋大学出版会
新美和昭・山浦洋一・宇津野登久子（1987)『複合動詞』(「外国人のための日本語例文・問題シリーズ」4)，荒竹出版
日本語教育学会編（1982)『日本語教育事典』大修館書店
日向茂男・日比谷潤子（1988)『談話の構造』(「外国人のための日本語例文・問題シリーズ」16)，荒竹出版
平林周祐・浜由美子（1988)『敬語』(「外国人のための日本語例文・問題シリーズ」10)，荒竹出版
牧野成一（1983)「物語の文章における時制の転換」『月刊言語』12:12, pp. 109–117, 大修館書店
牧野成一・畑佐由紀子（1989)『読解――拡大文節の認知』(「外国人のための日本語例文・問題シリーズ」18)，荒竹出版
益岡隆志・田窪行則（1989)『基礎日本語文法』くろしお出版
三浦昭・マグロイン花岡直美（1988)『語彙』(「外国人のための日本語例文・問題シリーズ」13)，荒竹出版
三上章（1970)『文法小論集』くろしお出版
――― (1972)『現代語法序説』くろしお出版
水谷信子（1987)『総合日本語中級』凡人社
――― (1989)『総合日本語中級前期』凡人社
宮地裕他編（1984)『日本語学』(複合辞特集）3:10，明治書院
――― (1986)『日本語学』(接辞特集）5:3，明治書院
メイナード泉子（1993)『会話分析』くろしお出版
森田良行（1977)『基礎日本語』角川書店
――― (1980)『基礎日本語 2』角川書店
――― (1984)『基礎日本語 3』角川書店
森田良行・松木正恵（1989)『日本語表現文型』アルク
横林宙世・下村彰子（1988)『接続の表現』(「外国人のための日本語例文・問題シリーズ」6)，荒竹出版

[**引用文献**]

志賀直哉（1968)『清兵衛と瓢簞・網走まで』(「新潮文庫」)，新潮社
島田潤一・土田英実（1986)『入門オプトエレクトロニクス』(「日経ハイテクシリーズ」)，日本経済新聞社